A PRACTICAL APPROACH TO
EFFECTIVE LITIGATION

A PRACTICAL APPROACH TO

EFFECTIVE LITIGATION

SIXTH EDITION

Susan Blake

OXFORD

UNIVERSITY PRESS

OXFORD
UNIVERSITY PRESS

Great Clarendon Street, Oxford OX2 6DP

Oxford University Press is a department of the University of Oxford.
It furthers the University's objective of excellence in research, scholarship,
and education by publishing worldwide in

Oxford New York

Auckland Cape Town Dar es Salaam Hong Kong Karachi
Kuala Lumpur Madrid Melbourne Mexico City Nairobi
New Delhi Shanghai Taipei Toronto

With offices in

Argentina Austria Brazil Chile Czech Republic France Greece
Guatemala Hungary Italy Japan South Korea Poland Portugal
Singapore Switzerland Thailand Turkey Ukraine Vietnam

Oxford is a registered trade mark of Oxford University Press
in the UK and in certain other countries

Published in the United States
by Oxford University Press Inc., New York

First edition published by Blackstone Press 1985
Second edition published by Blackstone Press 1987
Third edition published by Blackstone Press 1989
Fourth edition published by Blackstone Press 1993
Fifth edition published by Blackstone Press 1997

British Library Cataloguing in Publication Data

Data available

Library of Congress Cataloging in Publication Data

Blake, Susan H. (Susan Heather), 1953–
   A practical approach to effective litigation / Susan Blake.—6th ed.
   p. cm.
   ISBN 1–84174–010–1
   1. Attorney and client—Great Britain.   2. Civil procedure—Great Britain.
3. Trial practice—Great Britain.   4. Legal composition.   5. Briefs—Great
Britain. 6. Pleading—Great Britain.   I. Title.
   KD485.B558 2005
   347.41'0504—dc22

                                                                2005001375

ISBN 1–84174–010–1
EAN 9781841740102

1 3 5 7 9 10 8 6 4 2

Typeset by RefineCatch Limited, Bungay, Suffolk
Printed in Great Britain on acid-free paper by
Ashford Colour Press Limited, Gosport, Hampshire

DEDICATION

In memory of

Charles William Blake
1896–1934

and

Betty Ivy Loveday Blake
1928–2002

PREFACE

An effective litigation process is a basic requirement of a fair society, and this is recognised in Article 6 of the European Convention on Human Rights. The legal system in England and Wales is generally highly regarded, and indeed this is often the jurisdiction of choice for a case with international elements.

What defines an effective litigation process? The Civil Procedure Rules 1998 have taken significant steps towards streamlining and simplifying procedural rules, and have introduced an overriding objective which emphasises the importance of basic concepts such as effective use of time and not wasting costs. However it is not yet clear how far the Civil Procedure Rules are achieving their objectives, and there are still many issues relating to the complexity and cost of the litigation process. The significant shift to alternative dispute resolution may be welcome in controlling costs and giving litigants more control over the litigation process, but it may also suggest that people are moving away from the litigation process because they do not perceive it to be accessible and effective.

It can be difficult for lawyers starting out in practice to gain a realistic overview of the litigation process, or a practical understanding of how it works. It can therefore take some time for a lawyer to become an effective litigator. Training tends to separate out knowledge of procedure and evidence and skills such as drafting or advocacy, and in early practice a lawyer will tend to deal with just one stage in a case, or with individual applications to court on specific matters. It can be some years before a lawyer starts to see cases through from start to finish and gain an overall understanding of how to use all the elements of the litigation process comprehensively to best effect, and how to devise strategies for taking cases forward in the most effective way.

This book seeks to provide the kind of practical and integrated overview of the civil litigation process that is most likely to be helpful to the lawyer entering practice. It provides solid coverage of the rules of procedure and evidence, but the emphasis is on showing how rules and skills fit together and how they can best be used in a real case. The intention is to illustrate how legal professional techniques can be evolved and used.

In addition to being informative and practical, the book takes a critical approach where appropriate. While the Civil Procedure Rules 1998 undoubtedly provide a better and clearer basis for effective litigation than what went before there are still areas for improvement, and areas where change is not embedded.

Although the book takes a practical approach, it is not easy to provide simple checklists for each stage of litigation. Cases develop in different ways and rules often need to be complex to deal with a variety of situations. Bullet point lists are provided where possible, but within an adequate background of principle and guidance on general approach. It will always be necessary to check appropriate rules, and references to rules are provided for this purpose. There is also guidance on rules and forms at the end of relevant chapters and in Chapter 24.

In England and Wales there is a division between academic lawyers and practising lawyers that does not exist in other jurisdictions such as the United States of America. It is a theme of this book that this division is not helpful and that there are many benefits to be gained from academic and practising lawyers working much more closely together. More academic research into how different aspects of the litigation process work could be of great assistance in understanding the litigation process and helping to make it even more effective.

Susan Blake

Inns of Court School of Law

October 2004

CONTENTS—SUMMARY

Table of Cases		xix
1	What is 'Effective' Litigation?	1
2	The Roles of Legal Practitioners	33
3	The Professional Context—Ethos and Ethics	49
4	An Overview of the Litigation Process	73
5	Financing Litigation	107
6	Techniques for Meetings with Clients	127
7	Advising a Client and Taking Instructions	157
8	Establishing and Managing Facts	173
9	Managing and Using Legal Knowledge	189
10	Defining Issues to State a Case	207
11	Skills in Legal Writing	221
12	Drafting a Statement of Case	247
13	Deciding Who should Sue Whom	281
14	Pursuing Appropriate Remedies and Relief	299
15	The Vital Role of Evidence	317
16	Procedural Rules as Practical Tools	359
17	Defending an Action	397
18	The Contract Model	417
19	The Tort Model	459
20	Settling a Case	505
21	Preparing a Case for Trial	531
22	Presenting a Case in Court	551
23	Enforcing or Challenging a Judgment	581
24	Your Practice	599

CONTENTS

Table of Cases   xix

---

1 WHAT IS 'EFFECTIVE' LITIGATION?

  A INTRODUCTION   1.01
  B DIFFERING PERSPECTIVES   1.02
  C THE CHANGING LEGAL ENVIRONMENT   1.07
  D THE CLIMATE OF CHANGE   1.13
  E DEFINING EFFECTIVE LITIGATION AND THE EFFECTIVE LAWYER   1.32
  F THE OVERRIDING OBJECTIVE OF LITIGATION   1.42
  G THE ROLE OF THE WOOLF REFORMS   1.51
  H KEY KNOWLEDGE AND SKILLS FOR A LITIGATOR   1.55
  I REPRESENTING A CLIENT   1.68
  J LEGAL PRINCIPLES AS TOOLS   1.80
  K TAKING A PRACTICAL APPROACH   1.85
  L WORKING WITH OTHERS   1.89
  M THE TIME DIMENSION   1.97
  N THE COSTS DIMENSION   1.106
  O LAW AS A BUSINESS   1.118
  P THE PUBLIC IMAGE OF LAWYERS   1.123

---

2 THE ROLES OF LEGAL PRACTITIONERS

  A THE DIFFERENT TYPES OF LEGAL PRACTITIONER   2.01
  B THE ROLE OF A SOLICITOR   2.08
  C THE ROLE OF A BARRISTER   2.12
  D DIRECT ACCESS TO BARRISTERS   2.19
  E PARALEGALS   2.24
  F BRIEFING A BARRISTER   2.26
  G WRITING INSTRUCTIONS FOR A BARRISTER   2.41
  H THE CONTENTS OF A BRIEF   2.45
  I WORKING ON A BRIEF   2.52

---

3 THE PROFESSIONAL CONTEXT—ETHOS AND ETHICS

  A THE CONTEXT FOR PROFESSIONAL ETHICS   3.02
  B COMMERCIAL AWARENESS   3.12
  C GLOBALISATION   3.16
  D HUMAN RIGHTS   3.22
  E ACCESS TO LITIGATION FOR THOSE OF LIMITED MEANS   3.31
  F MONEY LAUNDERING   3.35

G   PROFESSIONAL CONDUCT   3.43
H   GENERAL ETHICS   3.55
I   CONFIDENTIALITY AND PROFESSIONAL PRIVILEGE   3.61
J   WHERE WORK FALLS SHORT OF PROFESSIONAL STANDARDS   3.77
K   PROFESSIONAL NEGLIGENCE   3.87

4   AN OVERVIEW OF THE LITIGATION PROCESS

A   THE LITIGATION PROCESS   4.02
B   THE ADVERSARIAL SYSTEM   4.11
C   JUDICIAL CASE MANAGEMENT   4.16
D   THE PRE-ACTION STAGE   4.18
E   STARTING AN ACTION IN TIME   4.33
F   CHOOSING A COURT   4.42
G   CLAIM FORMS   4.51
H   THE FRAMEWORK OF STATEMENTS OF CASE   4.75
I   TRACK ALLOCATION   4.81
J   THE MAIN ELEMENTS OF THE LITIGATION PROCESS   4.100
K   TIMETABLES, CASE MANAGEMENT, AND DIRECTIONS   4.110
L   OPTIONS FOR INTERRUPTING OR ENDING LITIGATION   4.117
M   FINAL PREPARATIONS FOR TRIAL   4.130
N   THE TRIAL AND JUDGMENT   4.135
O   COSTS ORDERS   4.139
P   AFTER JUDGMENT   4.143
Q   THE INTERNATIONAL PERSPECTIVE   4.144
    KEY DOCUMENTS

5   FINANCING LITIGATION

A   THE COSTS SIDE OF A CASE   5.01
B   HOW COSTS ACCUMULATE   5.10
C   DEALING WITH COSTS EFFECTIVELY   5.14
D   HOW PROBLEMS WITH COSTS ARISE   5.19
E   OPTIONS FOR THE FUNDING OF LITIGATION   5.21
F   CONDITIONAL FEE AGREEMENTS   5.26
G   PUBLIC FUNDING   5.38
H   ORDERS FOR COSTS   5.45
I   ORDERS FOR COSTS AT INTERIM HEARINGS   5.62
J   WASTED COSTS ORDERS   5.80
    KEY DOCUMENTS

6   TECHNIQUES FOR MEETINGS WITH CLIENTS

A   THE RELATIONSHIP WITH THE CLIENT   6.01
B   PROFESSIONAL RESPONSIBILITIES   6.10
C   THE ROLES OF THE CLIENT AND OF THE LAWYER   6.13

D	FIGHTING THE CLIENT'S CORNER	6.22
E	MANAGING CLIENT EXPECTATIONS	6.24
F	LITIGATION AS A PROCESS WITH TWO SIDES	6.29
G	PROFESSIONAL USE OF LANGUAGE	6.32
H	WHY A CLIENT COMES TO A LAWYER	6.37
I	MEETING AND CONTACTING A CLIENT	6.43
J	OBJECTIVES AND CHALLENGES IN MEETINGS	6.58
K	PREPARING FOR A MEETING	6.71
L	SETTING THE AGENDA	6.76
M	IDENTIFYING CLIENT OBJECTIVES	6.87
N	GATHERING INFORMATION	6.90
O	QUESTIONING TECHNIQUES	6.99
P	INFORMATION AND ADVICE	6.113
Q	CONCLUDING THE MEETING	6.116
R	DEALING WITH DIFFICULT CLIENTS	6.119

7 ADVISING A CLIENT AND TAKING INSTRUCTIONS

A	THE IMPORTANCE OF ADVICE AND INSTRUCTIONS	7.01
B	PROVIDING INFORMATION TO A CLIENT	7.05
C	CHOOSING HOW AND WHEN TO PROVIDE ADVICE	7.08
D	PROVIDING ADVICE TO A CLIENT	7.18
E	SETTING OUT OPTIONS	7.28
F	SETTING OUT STRENGTHS AND WEAKNESSES	7.32
G	RISK ASSESSMENT	7.36
H	ADVISING ON THE CHANCES OF SUCCESS	7.42
I	PROBLEM SOLVING	7.50
J	BREAKING BAD NEWS	7.54
K	ADVISING ON DIFFERENT ASPECTS OF THE CASE	7.59
L	TAKING INSTRUCTIONS	7.71

8 ESTABLISHING AND MANAGING FACTS

A	FOCUSSING ON FACTS	8.01
B	THE ELUSIVENESS OF TRUTH	8.11
C	SOURCES OF FACTS	8.30
D	THE STAGED AVAILABILITY OF FACTUAL INFORMATION	8.47
E	ANALYSING FACTS	8.50
F	INFORMATION MANAGEMENT	8.58
G	THEORIES, DEDUCTION, AND LOGIC	8.61
H	THE INTERACTION OF FACTS AND LAW	8.71
I	BUILDING A FACTUAL FRAMEWORK FOR A CASE	8.75

9   MANAGING AND USING LEGAL KNOWLEDGE

A	LAW IN PRACTICE	9.01
B	THE EVOLVING NATURE OF LAW	9.06
C	KNOWLEDGE MANAGEMENT	9.09
D	USING LEGAL PRINCIPLES	9.14
E	USING PRACTITIONER SOURCES	9.16
F	KEEPING UP TO DATE	9.40
G	STRATEGIC LEGAL RESEARCH	9.42
H	PLANNING RESEARCH	9.49
I	PRESENTING FINDINGS	9.69
J	USING LAW TO GET RESULTS	9.74

10   DEFINING ISSUES TO STATE A CASE

A	SEEING THE WOOD FOR THE TREES	10.02
B	TAKING A SYSTEMATIC APPROACH	10.07
C	FOCUSSING ON ISSUES	10.12
D	COMBINING LAW AND FACT TO DEFINE A CASE	10.19
E	SELECTING CAUSES OF ACTION	10.28
F	STATEMENTS OF CASE	10.33
G	STYLE IN STATEMENTS OF CASE	10.44
H	TACTICS IN STATING A CASE	10.48
I	THE STATEMENT OF TRUTH	10.55

11   SKILLS IN LEGAL WRITING

A	PROFESSIONAL LEGAL WRITING	11.03
B	PURPOSE AND AUDIENCE	11.07
C	CONTENT AND STRUCTURE	11.13
D	PROFESSIONAL USE OF LANGUAGE	11.16
E	NOTES	11.24
F	WRITING LETTERS	11.26
G	THE ROLE OF OPINIONS	11.33
H	PREPARING TO WRITE AN OPINION	11.54
I	THE FORMAT AND STRUCTURE OF AN OPINION	11.58
J	THE CONTENTS OF AN OPINION	11.63
K	THE IMPORTANCE OF CLEAR CONCLUSIONS AND ADVICE	11.88
	KEY DOCUMENTS	

12   DRAFTING A STATEMENT OF CASE

A	THE STATEMENT OF CASE	12.01
B	A BACKGROUND TO DRAFTING	12.06
C	THE PROCESS FOR PRODUCING A STATEMENT OF CASE	12.17
D	RULES FOR DRAFTING	12.31
E	PRINCIPLES FOR DRAFTING	12.39

F	HEADINGS FOR STATEMENTS OF CASE	12.76
G	THE CLAIM FORM	12.84
H	GENERAL FRAMEWORK FOR A PARTICULARS OF CLAIM	12.95
I	SPECIFYING REMEDIES AND RELIEF	12.99
J	OTHER DRAFTS FOR A CLAIMANT	12.112
K	REFINING A STATEMENT OF CASE	12.119
L	CHALLENGING A STATEMENT OF CASE	12.134
	KEY DOCUMENTS	

13 DECIDING WHO SHOULD SUE WHOM

A	INTRODUCTION	13.01
B	SELECTING THE CLAIMANT(S)	13.09
C	SELECTING THE DEFENDANT(S)	13.15
D	AGENCY AND VICARIOUS LIABILITY	13.25
E	A BUSINESS AS A PARTY	13.30
F	OTHER RULES FOR PARTIES	13.49
G	OTHER TYPES OF INVOLVEMENT IN A CASE	13.58
H	PART 20 CLAIMS	13.63
I	PART 20 PROCEDURE	13.78
J	DRAFTING THE PART 20 CLAIM	13.82
	KEY DOCUMENTS	

14 PURSUING APPROPRIATE REMEDIES AND RELIEF

A	THE IMPORTANCE OF IDENTIFYING POTENTIAL REMEDIES AND RELIEF	14.01
B	REMEDIES A COURT CAN ORDER	14.08
C	REMEDIES A COURT CANNOT ORDER	14.26
D	CLAIMS FOR DAMAGES	14.30
E	QUANTIFICATION OF DAMAGES	14.50
F	A PROACTIVE APPROACH TO DAMAGES	14.63
G	CLAIMS FOR INTEREST	14.68
H	DOING THE ARITHMETIC	14.78

15 THE VITAL ROLE OF EVIDENCE

A	THE IMPORTANCE OF EVIDENCE	15.01
B	IDENTIFYING WHAT NEEDS TO BE PROVED	15.07
C	TYPES OF EVIDENCE	15.16
D	COLLECTING EVIDENCE	15.48
E	THE KEY RULES OF ADMISSIBILITY	15.58
F	WHO HAS TO PROVE WHAT	15.92
G	FORMAL REQUIREMENTS FOR WRITTEN EVIDENCE	15.101
H	DRAFTING A WITNESS STATEMENT	15.109
I	DRAFTING AN AFFIDAVIT	15.136
J	EXPERT EVIDENCE	15.140

Contents

K	DISCLOSURE OF EVIDENCE	15.179
L	EXCHANGE OF WITNESS STATEMENTS	15.201
M	REVIEWING AND ADVISING ON EVIDENCE	15.206
	KEY DOCUMENTS	

16 PROCEDURAL RULES AS PRACTICAL TOOLS

A	USING PROCEDURAL RULES AS TOOLS	16.01
B	THE BASIC PROCEDURE FOR APPLICATIONS	16.15
C	THE SCALES OF JUSTICE	16.45
D	FAILURE TO ABIDE BY THE RULES	16.50
E	MAKING APPLICATIONS BEFORE A CASE STARTS	16.63
F	TIME STRATEGIES—CUTTING AN ACTION SHORT	16.79
G	TIME STRATEGIES—GETTING SOME ISSUES DECIDED QUICKLY	16.107
H	PEOPLE STRATEGIES	16.140
I	INFORMATION STRATEGIES	16.144
J	MONEY STRATEGIES	16.170
K	COSTS ORDERS FOR INTERIM APPLICATIONS	16.190
	KEY DOCUMENTS	

17 DEFENDING AN ACTION

A	INTRODUCTION	17.01
B	THE DEFENCE MINDSET	17.06
C	DEALING WITH A DIFFICULT CLAIMANT	17.10
D	BEFORE A CASE STARTS	17.16
E	WHEN A CASE STARTS	17.25
F	STRATEGY AND TACTICS IN PROGRESSING A CASE	17.28
G	THE MAIN TYPES OF DEFENCE TO AN ACTION	17.44
H	RULES FOR DRAFTING A DEFENCE	17.48
I	PRINCIPLES FOR DRAFTING A DEFENCE	17.70
J	DRAFTING A DEFENCE	17.78
K	MAKING A COUNTERCLAIM	17.86
L	CLAIMING A SET-OFF	17.93
M	GENERAL FRAMEWORK FOR A DEFENCE AND COUNTERCLAIM	17.101

18 THE CONTRACT MODEL

A	INTRODUCTION	18.01
B	POTENTIAL CAUSES OF ACTION IN A CONTRACT CASE	18.04
C	THE ELEMENTS OF A CONTRACTUAL CASE	18.07
D	CONTEXTUAL CONSIDERATIONS	18.13
E	ANALYSING CONTRACTUAL OBLIGATIONS	18.21
F	ANALYSING A CONTRACTUAL ACTION	18.33
G	SELECTING A CAUSE OF ACTION	18.54
H	SELECTING REMEDIES	18.61

I	PRINCIPLES FOR ASSESSING DAMAGES	18.78
J	DRAFTING A CONTRACT CLAIM	18.106
K	ADVISING A DEFENDANT	18.108
L	SAMPLE DRAFTS FOR A CONTRACT CASE	18.120

19 THE TORT MODEL

A	INTRODUCTION	19.01
B	POTENTIAL CAUSES OF ACTION IN TORT	19.06
C	THE ELEMENTS OF A NEGLIGENCE CASE	19.14
D	THE PRE-ACTION STAGE	19.27
E	ANALYSIS OF A TORT CASE	19.36
F	SELECTING A CAUSE OF ACTION	19.49
G	SELECTING REMEDIES	19.55
H	ASSESSING DAMAGES	19.59
I	ASSESSING PERSONAL INJURY DAMAGES	19.82
J	DRAFTING A TORT CLAIM	19.118
K	ADVISING A DEFENDANT	19.129
L	SAMPLE DRAFTS FOR A TORT CASE	19.137
	KEY DOCUMENTS	

20 SETTLING A CASE

A	THE IMPORTANCE OF NEGOTIATION AND ALTERNATIVE DISPUTE RESOLUTION	20.01
B	TYPES OF NEGOTIATION AND ALTERNATIVE DISPUTE RESOLUTION	20.07
C	DECIDING TO SETTLE AN ACTION	20.13
D	ACTING WITHIN INSTRUCTIONS	20.16
E	TIMING ATTEMPTS TO SETTLE	20.23
F	STRATEGIES AND TACTICS	20.36
G	OFFERS TO SETTLE	20.43
H	REACTING TO AN OFFER TO SETTLE	20.65
I	CONDUCTING A NEGOTIATION	20.69
J	DRAWING UP TERMS OF SETTLEMENT	20.84
K	AFTER A SETTLEMENT	20.103
	KEY DOCUMENTS	

21 PREPARING A CASE FOR TRIAL

A	COMPLETING THE PREPARATION STAGES	21.01
B	APPROACHING A CASE STRATEGICALLY	21.06
C	REVIEWING A CASE	21.25
D	COURT REVIEW OF A CASE	21.31
E	PREPARING A CASE FOR HEARING	21.42
F	PREPARING A SKELETON ARGUMENT	21.66
G	PREPARING TO GO TO COURT	21.78
	KEY DOCUMENTS	

22 PRESENTING A CASE IN COURT

A	HAVING A DAY IN COURT	22.01
B	THE FORMALITIES OF A TRIAL	22.04
C	THE STAGES OF A TRIAL	22.13
D	WINNING A CASE AT TRIAL	22.34
E	FINAL PREPARATIONS FOR ADVOCACY	22.41
F	ARGUMENT AND PERSUASION	22.55
G	THE PRESENTATION OF A CASE	22.65
H	OPENING A CASE	22.73
I	DEALING WITH WITNESSES	22.77
J	CONCLUDING A CASE	22.110
K	THE JUDGMENT	22.114
L	THE DRAWING UP OF ORDERS	22.125
M	GENERAL FRAMEWORKS FOR ORDERS	22.138
	KEY DOCUMENTS	

23 ENFORCING OR CHALLENGING A JUDGMENT

A	THE STEPS TO BE TAKEN AFTER TRIAL	23.01
B	ENFORCING A JUDGEMENT	23.04
C	DECIDING WHETHER TO APPEAL	23.26
D	GROUNDS FOR APPEAL	23.37
E	JURISDICTION FOR APPEALS	23.45
F	PROCEDURE FOR APPEALING	23.47
G	POWERS ON APPEAL	23.52
H	DRAFTING AN APPEAL	23.55
I	THE POSITION OF THE RESPONDENT TO AN APPEAL	23.65
J	PREPARING FOR AN APPEAL	23.71
K	PRESENTING AN APPEAL	23.82
L	THE APPEAL DECISION	23.88
M	COSTS ON APPEAL	23.96
	KEY DOCUMENTS	

24 YOUR PRACTICE

A	INTRODUCTION	24.01
B	CIVIL LITIGATION RULES, FORMS, AND PROCEDURAL GUIDES	24.04
C	LIBRARY AND RESEARCH MATERIAL	24.15
D	FURTHER PROFESSIONAL TRAINING	24.27

TABLE OF CASES

A v B plc (2002) 3 WLR 542 . . . . 16.120
AB Maritrans v Cornet Shipping Co Ltd [1985] 3 All ER 442 . . . . 18.105
Admiral Management Services Ltd v Para-Protect Europe Ltd (2003) 2 All ER 1017 . . . . 15.153
Agnew v Lansforsakringsbolagens AB (2001) 1 AC 223 HL 18.19
Ajami v Comptroller of Customs (1954) 1 WLR 1405 . . . . 15.146
Al-Kandari v JR Brown & Co [1987] 2 All ER 302 . . . . 3.96
Alcoa Minerals of Jamaica v Broderick (2000) 3 WLR 23 . . . . 18.103
Alfred Compton Amusement Machines Ltd v Commissioner for Customs and Excise
    [1974] AC 405 . . . . 3.72
Allen v Jumbo Holdings Ltd (1980) 1 WLR 1252 CA 16.129, 16.179
American Cyanamid Co v Ethicon Ltd (1975) AC 396 . . . . 16.114, 16.118
Anders Utkilens Rederei A/S v O/Y Lovisa Stevedoring Co A/B [1985] 2 All ER 669 . . . . 11.80
Anderton v Clwyd County Council (2002) 1 WLR 3174 . . . . 4.63
Andre et Cie v Ets Michel Blanc et Fils [1977] 2 Lloyds Rep 166 . . . . 18.88
Anglia TV v Reed [1972] 1 QB 60 . . . . 18.87
Anton Piller KG v Manufacturing Processes [1976] Ch 55 CA 16.08, 16.148
Antonelli v Wade Gery Farr [1994] 3 WLR 462 . . . . 5.86
Anufrijeva v Southwark London Borough Council (2004) 2 WLR 603 . . . . 14.24
Arab Monetary Fund v Hashim [1991] 1 All ER 871 . . . . 16.179
Arbuthnot Latham Bank Ltd v Trafalgar Holdings Ltd (1998) 1 WLR 1426 . . . . 16.106
Arsenal Football Club plc v Reed (2003) 1 All ER 137 . . . . 4.168
Arthur JS Hall & Co (a firm) v Simmons [2002] 2 WLR 543 . . . . 3.94
Ascherberg, Hopwood & Crew v Casa Musicale SNC [1971] 1 WLR 173 . . . . 12.57
Ashcroft v Curtin [1971] 3 All ER 1208 . . . . 12.106
Ashworth Health Authority v MGN Ltd (2002) 1 WLR 2033 . . . . 16.70
AT and T Istel Ltd v Tulley (1993) AC 45 HL 16.159, 22.97
Atlas Maritime Co SA v Avalon Maritime Ltd [1991] 4 All ER 769 . . . . 16.179
Attorney-General v Blake (2000) 4 All ER 385 . . . . 18.65
Auty v National Coal Board (1985) 1 All ER 930 . . . . 19.88
Axel Johnson Petroleum AB v MG Mineral Group [1992] 2 All ER 163 . . . . 17.95

B v B (Unmeritorious Applications) (1998) 3 FCR 650 . . . . 17.15
Bacon v Cooper Metals [1982] 1 All ER 397 . . . . 18.94
Balabel v Air India [1988] 2 All ER 246 . . . . 3.64
Bank America Finance Ltd v Nock (1988) AC 1002 HL 5.55
Banque Bruxelles Lambert SA v Eagle Star Insurance Co Ltd (1995) QB 375 . . . . 18.81
Banton v Banton, The Times, 4 April 1989 . . . . 21.62
Barclays Bank plc v Eustice (1995) 4 All ER 411 CA 3.72
Barclays Bank plc v Fairclough Building Ltd (1995) 1 All ER 289 . . . . 18.105
Barings plc, Re (1997) All ER (D) 1 . . . . 3.61
Barrett v Enfield LBC (1999) 3 All ER 193 . . . . 19.16
Barrister (Wasted Costs Order) (No 1 of 1991), Re (1993) QB 293 . . . . 3.84, 5.85
Barrister (Wasted Costs Order) (No 4 of 1993), Re (1993), The Times 21 April 1995 . . . . 5.87
Bartlett v Barclays Bank [1980] Ch 515 . . . . 14.74
Bates v Lord Hailsham of St Marylebone (1972) 1 WLR 137 . . . . 16.137
Beco Ltd v Alfa Laval Co Ltd (1995) QB 137 . . . . 5.51
Behbehani v Salem [1989] 2 All ER 143 . . . . 16.180

Bell Fruit Manufacturing Co v Twinfalcon (1995) FSR 144 . . . . 5.86
Bennett v Chemical Construction (GB) [1971] 1 WLR 1571 . . . . 19.121
Bermuda International Securities Ltd v KPMG (2001) CPLR 252 . . . . 16.74
Bessela v Stern (1877) 2 CPD 265 . . . . 15.65
Bestobell Paints Ltd v Bigg (1975) FSR 16.120
Biguzzi v Rank Leisure plc (1999) 1 WLR 1926 CA 1.42, 12.140, 16.59
Birkett v Hayes [1982] 2 All ER 70 . . . . 19.73, 19.100
Birkett v James (1978) AC 297 HL 16.104
Birse Construction Ltd v Haiste Ltd [1996] 2 All ER 1 . . . . 13.71
Black & Decker v Flymo Ltd [1991] 1 WLR 753 . . . . 3.72
Black v Sumitomo Corporation (2002) 1 WLR 1569 . . . . 16.73
Blue Town Investments Ltd v Higgs & Hill plc [1990] 2 All ER 89 . . . . 16.129
BP Exploration Co (Libya) v Hunt [1983] 2 AC 352 . . . . 14.74, 18.34
Brennan v Bolt Burden (a firm) and Others, The Times, 7 November 2003 . . . . 20.106
Brickfield Properties v Newton [1971] 1 WLR 862 . . . . 12.28, 12.132, 19.119
Brickman's Settlement, Re [1982] 1 All ER 336 . . . . 10.44
Brinks Ltd v Abu Saleh (No 1) (1995) 4 All ER 65 . . . . 15.84
Brinks Mat Ltd v Elcombe (1988) 1 WLR 1350 . . . . 16.180
British Anzani (Felixstowe) v International Maritime Management (UK) [1980] QB 137 . . . . 17.99
British Coal Corporation v Dennis Rye Ltd (No 2) (1988) 3 All ER 816 . . . . 3.70
British Steel Corporation v Cleveland Bridge Engineering [1984] 1 All ER 504 . . . . 18.92
British Steel Corporation v Granada Television [1981] 1 All ER 417, AC 1096 HL 15.90, 16.70
Broadley v Guy Clapham and Co (1994) 4 All ER CA 19.31
Broadmoor Special Hospital Authority v R (2000) QB 775 . . . . 13.54
Brown v Bennett, The Times, 13 June 2000 . . . . 21.71
Buckinghamshire County Council v Moran (1990) Ch 623 . . . . 20.44
Buckland v Farrar & Moody [1978] 3 All ER 229 . . . . 3.98
Bullock v London General Omnibus Co (1907) 1 KB 264 CA 5.55
Bumper Development Corporation v Commissioner of Police [1991] 4 All ER 638 . . . . 12.78, 13.57
Burgess v British Steel (2000) PIQR Q240 . . . . 20.61
Burgess v Burgess (1996) 2 FLR 34 . . . . 3.91
Burmah Oil Company v Bank of England (1980) AC 1090 . . . . 15.87, 15.200
Burns v Shuttlehurst (1999) 1 WLR 1449 . . . . 16.73
Bushwall Properties v Vortex Properties [1975] 2 All ER 214 . . . . 14.71
Business Computers International Ltd v Registrar of Companies [1987] 3 All ER 465 . . . . 21.12
Business Computers v Anglo African Leasing [1977] 2 All ER 741 . . . . 17.95
Buttes Gas & Oil Company v Hammer (No 3) (1981) 1 QB 223 . . . . 15.87
Byrne v Sefton Health Authority, The Times, 28 November 2001 . . . . 5.87

C & P Haulage v Middleton (1883) 1 WLR 1461 . . . . 18.84
C v C (wasted costs order) (1994) 2 FLR 34 . . . . 5.86
Calley v Gray (2002) 1 WLR 2000 . . . . 5.31
Cannock Chase District Council v Kelly [1978] 1 All ER 152 . . . . 12.54
Capital and Counties plc v Hampshire CC (1997) 2 All ER 865 . . . . 19.16
Carl Zeiss Stiftung v Herbert Smith & Co (No 2) (1969) 2 Ch 276 . . . . 14.23
Cassell & Co Ltd v Broome (1972) AC 1027 . . . . 19.65
Castle v Cross (1984) 1 WLR 1372 DC 15.70
Cave v Robinson Jarvis & Rolf (2003) 1 AC 384 HL 3.91, 4.39
Cayne v Global Natural Resources plc (1984) 1 All ER 225 CA 16.120
CBS UK Ltd v Lambert (1983) Ch 37 . . . . 16.176
CCC Films (London) Ltd v Impact Quadrant Films [1984] 3 All ER 298 . . . . 14.67, 18.87
Chan Wai Tong v Li Ping Sum [1985] AC 446 . . . . 12.101
Chanel v FW Woolworth [1981] 1 All ER 745 . . . . 20.105

Chaplin v Hicks [1911] 2 KB 786 . . . . 14.67
Chappell v Cooper [1980] 2 All ER 463 . . . . 3.91
Charlesworth v Relay Roads Ltd (2000) 1 WLR 230 . . . . 12.127
Chilton v Surrey County Council (1999) CPLR 525 . . . . 1.49
Chiron Corp v Murex Diagnostics Ltd (1995) All ER (EC) 88 . . . . 4.167
Clark (Inspector of Taxes) v Perks (2001) 1 WLR 17 . . . . 23.46
Clarke v Bruce Lane & Co [1988] 1 All ER 364 . . . . 3.98
Clarke v Marlborough Fine Art (London) Ltd, The Times, 4 December 2001 . . . . 12.128
Clef Acquitaine v Laporte Materials (Barrow) Ltd (2000) 3 All ER 493 . . . . 18.88
Co-operative Insurance Society Ltd v Argyll Stores (Holdings) Ltd (1997) 3 All ER 297 . . . . 18.76
Cohen v Nessdale [1981] 3 All ER 118 . . . . 18.76
Colledge v Bass Mitchells and Butlers Ltd (1988) 1 All ER 536 . . . . 19.101
Columbia Picture Industries v Robinson [1986] FSR 367, (1987) Ch 38 . . . . 16.152, 16.155
Conlon v Conlon's Ltd (1952) 2 All ER 462 . . . . 3.72
Conway v Rimmer (1968) AC 910 . . . . 15.86
Cooke v United Bristol Healthcare NHS Trust, The Times, 24 October 2003 . . . . 19.89
Cooper v Floor Cleaning Machines Ltd, The Times, 24 October 2004 . . . . 22.116
Copeland v Smith (2000) 1 WLR 1371 . . . . 19.31
Copeland v Smith and Another (2000) 1 All ER 457 . . . . 3.45
Costello v Chief Constable of Northumbria Police (1999) 1 All ER 55 . . . . 19.16
County Personnel v Alan R Pulber 3.96
Cox v Hockenhull (1999) 3 All ER 577 . . . . 19.113
Cranfield v Bridgegrove Ltd (2003) 3 All ER 129 . . . . 4.69
Cream Holdings Ltd v Banerjee (2003) 2 All ER 318 . . . . 16.120
Cream Holdings v Banerjee, The Times, 15 October 2004 . . . . 3.30
Crescent Farm (Sidcup) Sport Ltd v Sterling Offices Ltd (1972) Ch 553 . . . . 3.72
Cresswell v Eaton (1991) 1 All ER 484 . . . . 19.115
Crest Homes plc v Marks (1987) AC 829 HL 16.156
Croke v Wiseman (1981) 3 All ER 852 . . . . 19.97
Customs and Excise v Anchor Foods Ltd (1999) 1 WLR 1139 . . . . 16.176
Customs and Excise v Barclays Bank plc (2004) 1 WLR 2027 . . . . 16.182

D & C Builders v Rees [1966] 2 QB 107 . . . . 20.106
Dalgety Spillers Foods Ltd v Food Brokers Ltd (1994) FSR 504 . . . . 16.115
Daniels v Walker (2000) 1 WLR 1382 . . . . 15.169
Das v Ganju (1999) PIQR P260 . . . . 19.34
De Lasala v De Lasala (1980) AC 546 . . . . 20.100
Dennis v AJ White & Co (1916) 1 KB 1 . . . . 15.41
Denny v Yeldon (1995) 3 All ER 624 . . . . 9.39
Department of Transport v Chris Smaller (Transport) Ltd (1989) q All ER 897 HL 16.104
Derby v Weldon (No 2) (1989) 1 All ER 1002 CA 16.176
Derry v Peek (1889) 14 All Cas 337 . . . . 18.52
Designers Guild Ltd v Russell Williams (Textiles) Ltd (2000) 1 WLR 2416 . . . . 23.89
Despina R, The [1979] AC 685 . . . . 14.58
Detz v Lennig [1969] 1 AC 170 . . . . 20.106
Deutsche Ruchversicherung AG v Wallbrook Insurance Co Ltd (1995) 1 WLR 1017 . . . . . . 16.23
Dexter v Courtaulds Ltd [1984] 1 All ER 70 . . . . 19.100
Dickinson v Jones Alexander & Co [1990] FamLaw 137 . . . . 3.96
Dixon v Clement Jones Solicitors (a firm), The Times, 2 August 2004 . . . . 3.90
Dodd Properties (Kent) Ltd v Canterbury City Council (1980) 1 All ER 928 . . . . 19.62
Dolling-Baker v Merrett [1991] 2 All ER 890 . . . . 20.79
Dominion Mosaics & Tile Co Ltd v Trafalgar Trucking Co Ltd [1990] 2 All ER 246 . . . . . . 14.67
Domsalla v Barr [1969] 1 WLR 630 . . . . 12.106

Donoghue v Folkestone Properties Ltd (2003) All ER (D) 382 . . . . 19.12
Donovan v Gwentoys Ltd (1990) 1 WLR 472 HL 19.34
Douglas and Others v Hello! and Others (No 2), The Times, 30 January 2003 . . . . 12.141
Douglas v Hello! (2001) 2 WLR 992, (2001) QB 967 . . . . 3.30
Drane v Evangelou [1978] 2 All ER 437 . . . . 12.56
Dubai Aluminium Co Ltd v Al Alawi (1999) 1 WLR 1964 . . . . 3.72
Dubai Bank v Galadari (1989) 3 All ER 769 . . . . 3.72
Duncan v Cammell Laird & Co Ltd (1942) AC 1090 . . . . 15.86
Dunlop Pneumatic Tyre Co Ltd v New Garage and Motor Co Ltd (1915) AC 79 . . . . 18.116
Dunnett v Railtrack plc (2002) 2 All ER 850 . . . . 20.03
Dutfield v Gilbert H Stephens & Sons (1988) 18 Fam Law 473 . . . . 20.19

East v Maurer (1991) 2 All ER 733 . . . . 18.88
Easton v Ford Motor Co Ltd (1993) 4 All ER 257 . . . . 12.127
Edmeades v Thames Board Mills Ltd (1969) 2 QB 67 CA 15.158
Elgindata Ltd (No 2) (1992), Re 1 WLR 1207 . . . . 5.51
English v Emery, Reimbold and Strick Ltd (2002) 3 All ER 385, (2002) 1 WLR 2409 . . . 3.27, 5.51, 15.178
Ernst & Young v Butte Mining plc, The Times, 22 March 1996 . . . . 3.56
Esso Petroleum Co Ltd v Milton (1997) 1 WLR 938 CA 16.101, 17.100
Esso Petroleum Co Ltd v Southport Corporation [1956] AC 218 . . . . 12.15
Esso Petroleum Ltd v Mardon [1976] QB 801 . . . . 19.2
Evans v London Hospital Medical College [1981] 1 WLR 184 . . . . 15.22
Export Credit Guarantee Dept v Universal Oil Products Co [1983] 2 All ER 205 . . . . 18.116

Faccenda Chicken v Fowler (1986) 1 All ER 617 . . . . 16.120
Fairchild v Glenhaven Funeral Services Ltd (2002) 3 All ER 305 HL 15.178, 19.51
Family Housing Association (Manchester) Ltd v Michael Hyde and Partners (1993)
     1 WLR 354 CA 20.48
Fansa v American Express International Banking Corporation, The Times, 26 June 1985 . . . . 14.71
Farrell v Secretary of State for Defence [1980] 1 All ER 166 . . . . 12.16
Fawdry & Co v Murfitt (2003) QB 104 . . . . 16.52
Federal Commerce v Tradax Export SA [1977] QB 324 . . . . 14.58
Films Rover International Ltd v Cannon Film Sales Ltd [1986] 3 All ER 772 . . . . 18.67
Finelvet AG v Vinava Shipping Co [1983] 2 All ER 658 . . . . 18.74
Finers v Miro [1991] 1 All ER 182 . . . . 3.72
First Interstate Bank of California v Cohen Arnold & Co, The Times, 11 December 1995 . . . 18.86, 19.66
Fitzgerald v Lane [1988] 2 All ER 961, (1989) AC 328 . . . . 13.81, 19.77
Flynn v Scourgall (2004) 3 All ER 609 . . . . 20.57
Forbes v Wandsworth Health Authority (1997) QB 402 . . . . 19.31
Ford v GKR Constructions Ltd (2000) 1 WLR 1397 . . . . 20.61
Ford v Labrador, The Times, 5 June 2003 . . . . 16.38
Forsickringsaktiesalskapet Vesta v Burtcher (1989) AC 852 . . . . 18.105
Foss v Harbottle (1935) 2 KB 113 . . . . 13.43
Fowkes v Duthie [1991] 1 All ER 337 . . . . 3.86, 5.88
Fox v H Wood (Harrow) [1963] 2 QB 601 . . . . 12.54
Fuller v Strum (2002) 1 WLR 1097 . . . . 15.147

G v G (1985) 1 WLR 647 . . . . 23.89
Gale v Superdrug Stores plc (1996) 1 WLR 1089 CA 12.164
Garcin v Amerindo [1990] 4 All ER 655 . . . . 21.53
Garratt v Saxby (2004) 1 WLR 2152 . . . . 23.79
GE Capital Corporate Finance Group Ltd v Bankers Trust Co (1995) 1 WLR 172 CA 15.192
General Mediterranean Holdings SA v Patel (2000) 1 WLR 272 . . . . 4.09

George Doland Ltd v Blackburn Robson & Co [1972] 1 WLR 1338 . . . . 3.69
George Mitchell (Chesterhall) v Finney Lock Seeds [1983] 2 AC 803 . . . . 18.39
Ginty v Belmont Building Supplies Ltd (1959) 1 All ER 414 . . . . 19.10
GIO Personal Investment Services Ltd v Liverpool and London Steamship Protection and
    Indemnity Association Ltd (1999) 1 WLR 984 CA 22.85
Glandarroch, The (1894) P226 . . . . 15.94
Gleeson v J Whippell & Co [1977] 1 WLR 510 . . . . 15.102
Gnitrow Ltd v Cape plc (2000) 1 WLR 2327 . . . . 20.48
Godwin v Swindon Borough Council (2002) 1 WLR 997 . . . . 4.70, 16.92
Gonin, Re [1979] 1 Ch 16 . . . . 12.57
Goode v Martin (2002) 1 WLR 1828, The Times, 24 January 2002 . . . . 3.2, 12.132, 16.03
Gran Gelato Ltd v Richcliffe (Group) Ltd (1992) Ch 560 . . . . 18.91
Great Atlantic Insurance Co v Home Insurance Co (1981) 1 WLR 529 . . . . 3.70
Great Peace Shipping Ltd v Tsavliris Salvage (International) Ltd (2002) 4 All ER 689 . . . . 18.72
Grepe v Loam (1887) 37 ChD 168 . . . . 17.15
Grovit v Doctor (1997) 1 WLR 640 HL 16.106
Guinness Peat Properties Ltd v Fitzroy Robinson Partnership (1987) 2 All ER 716,
    1 WLR 1027 CA 3.68, 20.47

Hall v Avon Area Health Authority [1980] 1 All ER 516, (1980) 1 WLR 481 CA 19.47
Halsey v Milton Keynes NHS Trust [2004] EWCA (Civ) 576, The Times, 27 May 2004 . . . . . . 20.03, 20.06
Hamilton v Al Fayed (No 2) (2003) QB 1175 . . . . 3.27
Hanak v Green [1959] 2 QB 9 . . . . 17.90
Haq v Singh (2001) 1 WLR 1594 . . . . 12.133
Harley v McDonald Harley (a firm), The Times, 15 May 2001 . . . . 3.98
Harmony Shipping Co SA v Saudi Europe Line Ltd (1979) 1 WLR 1380 CA 15.19, 15.175
Harrison v Bloom Camillin, The Times, 12 November 1999 . . . . 3.90
Harrison v Michelin Tyre Co Ltd (1985) 1 All ER 918 . . . . 19.17
Harrison-Broadley v Smith [1964] 1 WLR 456 . . . . 14.15
Hashtroodi v Hancock (2004) 3 All ER 530 . . . . 4.65
Hatton and Others v UK (2002) 34 EHRR 1 . . . . 3.30
Hayes v James Charles Dodd [1990] 2 All ER 815 . . . . 18.102
Hayward v Pullinger & Partners [1950] 1 All ER 581 . . . . 12.106
Headley Byrne & Co v Heller & Partners Ltd (1964) AC 465 . . . . 18.51, 19.64
Heather v P-E Consulting Group Ltd (1973) Ch 189 . . . . 15.43
Hector v Lyons, The Times, 19 December 1988 . . . . 12.78
Heil v Rankin (2000) 3 All ER 138 . . . . 19.92
Henderson v Merrett Syndicates Ltd (1994) AC 145 . . . . 19.15, 19.64
Herbert v Vaughan [1972] 1 WLR 1128 . . . . 12.116
Hertfordshire Investments Ltd v Bubb (2000) 1 WLR 2318 . . . . 23.41
Hickman v Berens [1895] 2 Ch 638 . . . . 20.82, 22.82
Hicks v Chief Constable of South Yorkshire (1992) 1 All ER 690 . . . . 19.112
Hill v CA Parsons & Co Ltd (1972) Ch 305 . . . . 18.76
Hinde v Hinde [1953] 1 All ER 171 . . . . 20.96
Hodgson v Guardall Ltd [1991] 3 All ER 823 . . . . 5.55
Hoffman-La Roche (F) and Co AG v S of S for Trade and Industry (1975) A 295 HL 22.120
Hoicrest Ltd, Re (2000) 1 WLR 414 . . . . 1.49
Hollingham v Head (1858) 27 LJCP 241 . . . . 15.62
Holt v Payne Skillington, The Times, 22 December 1995 . . . . 19.53
Home and Overseas Insurance Co Ltd v Mentor Insurance Co (UK) Ltd (1990) 1 WLR 153 CA 16.98
Hong Kong and Shanghai Banking Corporation v Kloeckner & Co AG [1989] 3 All ER 513 . . . . 17.92
Horizon Technologies International Ltd v Lucky Wealth Consultants Ltd [1992] 1 All ER 469 . . . . 20.82
Horne-Roberts v SmithKline Beecham plc (2002) 1 WLR 1662 . . . . 12.133

Horsfall v Haywards (a firm) [1999] 1 FLR 1182 . . . . 3.90
Howard Marine and Dredging Co v Ogden [1978] QB 574 . . . . 19.52
Howglen Ltd, Re (2001) 1 All ER 376 . . . . 16.165
Hubbard v Pitt (1976) QB 142 CA 16.118
Huddersfield Banking Co Ltd v Henry Lister & Son Ltd [1895] 2 Ch 273 . . . . 20.106
Hughes v McKeown (1985) 1 WLR 963 . . . . 19.97
Hunt v East Dorset Health Authority [1992] 2 All ER 539 . . . . 2.36
Hunter v Butler, The Times, 28 December 1995 . . . . 19.97
Hurlingham Estates Ltd v Wilde & Partners (a firm), The Times, 3 January 1997 . . . . 3.96
Hurst v Evans (1917) 1 KB 352 . . . . 15.94
Hussey v Palmer (1972) 1 WLR 1286 . . . . 14.23

IBM United Kingdom Ltd v Prima Data International Ltd (1994) 4 All ER 748 . . . . 16.159
Ilkiw v Samuels [1963] 1 WLR 991 . . . . 12.106
Impex Transport Aktielskabet v AG Thames Holding [1982] 1 All ER 897 . . . . 17.91
India (President of) v La Pintada Cia Navegacion SA [1984] 2 All ER 773 . . . . 14.72, 20.85
International Business Machines Corporation v Phoenix International (Computers) Ltd (1995)
    1 All ER 413 . . . . 3.71
International Distillers and Vintners v JF Hillebrand (UK) Ltd, The Times, 25 January 2000 . . . . . . 13.62
Iraqi Ministry of Defence v Arcepy Shipping Co SA (1981) QB 65 . . . . 16.179
Iron Trade Mutual Insurance Co Ltd v JK Buckenham Ltd [1990] 1 All ER 808 . . . . 4.37
ITC Film Distributors v Video Exchange [1982] 2 All ER 246 . . . . 15.91

Jaggard v Sawyer (1995) 1 WLR 269 . . . . 19.57
James v Williams (2000) Ch 1 CA 14.23
Janov v Morris (1981) 1 WLR 1389 CA 16.61
Jefford v Gee [1970] 2 QB 130 . . . . 19.100
JJ Coughlan Ltd v Ruparella, The Times, 26 August 2003 . . . . 3.97
Johnson v Agnew (1980) AC 367 . . . . 18.83
Johnson v Gore Wood and Co (2002) 2 AC 1 HL 12.140
Jokai Tea Holdings Ltd, Re (1992) 1 WLR 1196 CA 12.127
Jones v University of Warwick (2003) 1 WLR 954 . . . . 15.33
Joseph Constantine Steamship Line Ltd v Imperial Smelting Corp Ltd (1942) AC 154 . . . . 15.94
Joyce v Yeomans [1981] 3 All ER 1031, (1981) 1 WLR 549 . . . . 19.97, 19.100
Junior Books Ltd v Veitchi & Co Ltd [1983] AC 520 . . . . 19.64

Kelly v Corsten (1998) 1 FLR 986 . . . . 3.93
Kelly v Dawes, The Times, 27 September 1990 . . . . 15.106
Kennaway v Thompson (1981) QB 88 . . . . 19.57
Kennet v Brown (1988) 1 WLR 582 . . . . 12.132
Kent v Griffiths (2000) 2 All ER 474 . . . . 19.16
Kershaw v Whelan, The Times, 20 December 1995 . . . . 3.69
Ketteman v Hansel Properties Ltd (1987) AC 189 HL 12.127
King v Telegraph Group Ltd, The Times, 21 May 2004 . . . . 5.20
Kingshott v Associated Kent Newspapers, The Times, 11 June 1990 . . . . 21.64
Kinnear v Falconfilms NV (1994) 3 All ER 42 . . . . 4.144
Kitchen v Royal Air Force Association [1958] 1 WLR 563 . . . . 4.39
Kleinwort Benson Ltd v Glasgow City Council (1999) 1 AC 153 HL 18.19
Kleinwort Benson Ltd v Lincoln City Council (1998) 4 All ER 513 . . . . 18.64
Kleinwort Benson Ltd v Lincoln City Council (No 2) (1998) 3 WLR 1095 HL 14.23

L (Police Investigation: Privilege), Re, The Times, 22 March 1996 . . . . 3.72
Ladd v Marshall (1954) 1 WLR 1489 . . . . 23.41

Lambert v Lewis (1982) AC 225 ....18.105
Lansing Linde Ltd v Kerr [1991] 1 All ER 418 ....16.121
Larner v British Steel plc (1993) 4 All ER 102 ....19.10
Lazenby Garages Ltd v Wright (1976) 1 WLR 459 ....18.86
Leach v Chief Constable of Gloucestershire Constabulary (1999) 1 All ER 215 ....19.16
Leaf v International Galleries [1950] 2 KB 86 ....12.15
Leigh & Sullivan Ltd v Aliakmon Shipping Co Ltd (1986) AC 785 ....19.64
Liddell v Middleton (1996) PIQR P326 CA 15.147
Liesbosch (Owners of Dredger) v Owners of Steamship Edison (1933) AC 449 ....19.63
Lillicrap v Nalder and Son (1993) 1 WLR 94 CA 3.69
Lilly Icos Ltd v Pfizer Ltd (2002) 1 WLR 2253 ....15.199
Lim Poh Choo v Camden and Islington Area Health Authority (1980) AC 174 ....19.96
Linotype-Hell Finance Ltd v Baker (1993) 1 WLR 321 ....23.51
Lipkin Gorman v Karpnale (1991) AC 548 ....18.65
Lister v Helsey Hall Ltd (2001) 2 All ER 769 ....19.17
Liverpool Roman Catholic Archdiocese Trustees Inc v Goldberg (No 2) (2001) 1 WLR 2337 .....15.153
Lloyde v West Midlands Gas Board (1971) 2 All ER 1240 ....19.48
Lloyds Bowmaker Ltd v Brittania Arrow Holdings plc [1988] 3 All ER 178 ....16.181
Lloyds v West Midlands Gas Board [1971] 1 WLR 749 ....23.44
Lock International plc v Bewick (1989) 1 WLR 1268 ....16.152
Lockheed-Arabia Corp v Owen (1993) QB 806 ....15.146
Longden v British Coal Corp (1998) 1 All ER 289 ....19.101
Lonhro plc v Tebbit [1992] 4 All ER 973 ....12.143
Loose v Williamson (1978) 1 WLR 639 ....16.69
Loveday v Renton (No 2) [1992] 3 All ER 184 ....2.31
Lownds v Home Office (2002) 1 WLR 2540 ....5.20

M v Home Office [1992] 4 All ER 97 ....3.56
McCann v Sheppard [1973] 1 WLR 540 ....23.42
McCauley v Vine (1999) 1 WLR 1977 CA 16.98
McFarlane v Wilkinson, The Times, 2 March 2004 ....3.98
McGoldrick & Co v CPS, The Times, 15 November 1989 ....5.87
Macmillan Inc v Bishopsgate Investment Trust (1993) 1 WLR 1372 CA 21.51
McNamara v Martin Motors & Co (1983) 127 SJ 69 ....20.20
McPhilemy v Times Newspapers Ltd (No 2) (2000) 1 WLR 1732, (2002) 1 WLR 934 ......15.204, 20.61
McQuaker v Goddard (1940) 1 KB 687 ....15.42
Maltez v Lewis, The Times, 4 May 1999 ....1.50
Marcic v Thames Water Utilities Ltd (2002) 2 WLR 932 ....3.30
Mareva Compania Naviera SA v International Bulk Carriers SA [1980] 1 All ER 213 ......16.08, 16.176
Masterman-Lister v Brutton & Co (2003) 3 All ER 162 ....13.51
Matrix Securities Ltd v Teodore Goddard (a firm) [1998] PNLR 3.87
Medcalf v Weatherill and another (2004) 3 WLR 172 ....8.04
Medway v Doublelock [1978] 1 All ER 1261 ....15.105
Meek v Fleming [1961] 2 QB 366 ....3.56
Megarity v DJ Ryan and Sons Ltd [1980] 2 All ER 832, (1980) 1 WLR 1237 CA 15.165
Mehmet v Perry (1977) 2 All ER 529 ....19.115
Melluish v BMI (No 3) Ltd (1996) 1 AC 454 ....9.39
Memory Corporation plc v Sidhu, The Times, 15 February 2000 ....3.47
Memory Corporation plc v Sidhu (No 2) (2000) 1 WLR 1443 CA 15.200, 16.20, 16.178
Meng Leong Developments Pte Ltd v Jip Hong Trading Co Pte Ltd [1985] 1 All ER 120 ....18.76
Mercedes-Benz AG v Leiduck (1996) 1 AC 284 ....16.111
Merchantile Group (Europe) AG v Aiyela (1994) QB 366 CA 16.70
Merret v Babb (2001) QB 1174 ....12.133

Metcalf v Mardell (2003) 1 AC 120 . . . . 5.83, 5.86
Midland Bank Ltd v Hett, Stubbs and Kemp (1979) 1 Ch 379 . . . . 15.147
Miliangos v George Frank (Textiles) Ltd [1975] 3 All ER 801, (1976) AC 3 . . . . 14.58, 18.97
Miliangos v George Frank (Textiles) Ltd (No 2) [1977] QB 489 . . . . 14.76
Miller v Minister of Pensions (1947) 2 All ER 372 . . . . 15.97
Millington v KSC & Sons, The Times, 22 July 1986 . . . . 22.72
Monk v Redwing Aircraft Co [1942] 1 KB 182 . . . . 12.106
Moore & Co v Ferrier [1988] 1 All ER 400 . . . . 4.38
Moore v Moore (1954) 1 WLR 927 . . . . 22.84
Morris v Bank of America National Trust (2000) 1 All ER 954, The Times, 25 January 2000 . . . . 1.20, 12.63
Morris v Murjani (1996) 2 All ER 384 . . . . 16.111
Morris v Murray (1991) 2 QB 6 . . . . 19.131
Morris v Stratford-on-Avon Rural District Council (1973) 1 WLR 1059 . . . . 15.77
Mortgage Express Ltd v Bowerman & Partners (a firm), The Times, 1 August 1995 . . . . 1.79, 3.97
Murphy v Brentwood District Council (1991) 1 AC 398 . . . . 19.32, 19.64
Murphy v Murphy (1999) 1 WLR 282 . . . . 16.70
Murphy v Young & Co Brewery Ltd (1997) 1 WLR 159 . . . . 5.56
Murrell v Healy (2001) 4 All ER 345 . . . . 19.26
Mutch v Allen (2001) CPLR 200 CA 15.174
Myers v DPP (1965) AC 1001 . . . . 15.60

N (a minor), Re (2000) 1 WLR 790 . . . . 15.147
Nadreph v Willmett & Co [1978] 1 All ER 746 . . . . 17.99
Nash v Eli Lilly and Co (1993) 1 WLR 782 . . . . 19.31
Nasser v United Bank of Kuwait (2002) 1 WLR 1868 . . . . 3.27
National Carriers v Panalpina (Northern) [1981] AC 675 . . . . 18.34
National Westminster Bank plc v Daniel (1993) 1 WLR 1 CA 16.99
Neste Chemicals SA v DK Line SA (1994) 3 All ER 180 . . . . 4.157
Ng v Lee, The Times, 25 May 1988 . . . . 19.48
Nordsten Allgemeine Versicherungs AG v Internay Ltd, The Times, 8 June 1999 . . . . 5.56
Norwich Pharmacal Co v Customs and Excise Commissioners (1974) AC 133 HL 16.68
Nurdin and Peacock plc v DB Ramsden & Co Ltd (1999) 1 All ER 941 . . . . 14.23
NWL Ltd v Woods (1979) 1 WLR 1294 HL 16.120

O (A minor) (wasted costs application), Re (1994) 2 (FLR) 842 . . . . 5.87
Oates v Harte Reade & Co (1999) PIQR P120 . . . . 4.40
OLL Ltd v Secretary of State for Transport (1997) 3 All ER 897 . . . . 19.16
Orchard v South Eastern Electricity Board [1987] 1 All ER 95 . . . . 5.87, 6.91
O'Sullivan v Management Agency and Music Ltd (1985) QB 428 . . . . 18.74
Oxy Electric Ltd v Zainuddin (1991) 1 WLR 115 . . . . 16.129

P v P (2004) FLR 1 . . . . 3.42
P v T Ltd (1997) 4 All ER 200 . . . . 16.70
Page One Records Ltd v Britton (1968) 1 WLR 157 . . . . 18.69
Palmer v Crone (1927) 1 KB 804 . . . . 15.41
Palmer v Dumford Ford [1992] 2 All ER 122 . . . . 15.22
Panayioutou v Sony Music Entertainment (UK) Ltd (1994) Ch 142 . . . . 21.51
Paragon Finance plc v Freshfields (1999) 1 WLR 1183 CA 3.69
Parker v CS Structured Credit Fund (2003) 1 WLR 1680 . . . . 16.75
Parsons v Uttley Ingham [1978] QB 791 . . . . 19.52, 19.54, 19.61
Paula Lee Ltd v (Robert) Zehil & Co [1983] 2 All ER 390 . . . . 14.67, 18.79
PCW (Underwriting Agencies) Ltd v Dixon (1983) 2 All ER 697 CA 16.179
Peacock v Peacock [1991] Fam Law 139 . . . . 20.106

Peco Arts Inc v Hazlitt Gallery Ltd (1983) 1 WLR 1315 . . . . 4.39
Peet v Mid-Kent Healthcare Trust (2002) 1 WLR 210 . . . . 15.173
Pepper v Hart (1993) AC 593 . . . . 9.39, 21.64
Perry v Sidney Phillips and Son (1982) 1 WLR 1297 . . . . 18.103
Pestrello E Companhia Limitada v United Paint Co [1969] 1 WLR 570 . . . . 12.15, 12.106
Peyman v Lanjani [1984] 3 All ER 703 . . . . 18.74
Philex plc v Golban (1994) 3 WLR 462 . . . . 5.86
Phipps v Orthodox Unit Trusts [1957] 3 All ER 305 . . . . 12.106
Pickersgill v Riley, The Times, 2 March 2004 . . . . 3.98
Porter v Magill (2002) 2 AC 357 . . . . 3.27
Posner v Scott-Lewis (1987) Ch 25 . . . . 18.76
Powell v Streatham Manor Nursing Home (1935) AC 243 HL 23.90
Prescott v Bulldog Tools Ltd (1981) 3 All ER 869 . . . . 15.158, 19.47
President of India v La Pintada Cia Navegacion SA [1984] 2 All ER 773 . . . . 14.72, 20.85
Price v Humphries (1958) 2 QB 353 DC 22.28
Price v UK 34 EHRR 1285 . . . . 3.30
Prince Abdul Rahman bin Turki al Sudairy v Abu-Taha [1980] 3 All ER 409 . . . . 16.176
Pritchard v JH Cobden Ltd [1987] 2 FLR 30, (1988) Fam 22 . . . . 14.67, 19.93
Pugh v Cantor Fitzgerald International (2001) CPLR 271 . . . . 16.90
Putty v Hopkinson [1990] 1 All ER 1057 . . . . 16.98

Quadrant Visual Communications Ltd v Hutchinson Telephone (UK) Ltd, The Times,
    4 December 1991 . . . . 17.92

R (Alconbury Developments Ltd) v Secretary of State for the Environment, Transport and the
    Regions (2003) AC 295 . . . . 3.29
R (Bernard and Another) v Enfield Borough Council, The Times, 8 November 2002 . . . . 3.23
R (Holding & Barnes plc and Others) v Secretary of State for the Environment (2001)
    2 WLR 1389 . . . . 3.23
R (KB) v Mental Health Review Tribunal (2003) 2 All ER 209 . . . . 3.23
R (Kehoe) v Secretary of State for Work and Pensions (2004) 2 WLR 1481 . . . . 3.29
R (Morgan Grenfell and Co Ltd) v Special Commissioner of Income Tax (2002) 3 All ER 1 . . . . 3.63
R (Morgan Grenfell and Co Ltd) v Special Commissioner of Income Tax (2003) 1 AC 563 . . . . 3.66
R (on the application of H) v Mental Health Review Tribunal and Secretary of State for Health
    (2001) 3 WLR 512 . . . . 3.23
R v Board of Inland Revenue, ex p Goldberg [1988] 3 All ER 248 . . . . 3.64
R v Bow County Court ex p Pelling (1999) 1 WLR 1870 . . . . 22.10
R v Cresswell (1873) 1 QBD 446 CCR 15.44
R v Derby Magistrates Court, ex p B, The Times, 25 October 1995 . . . . 3.64
R v Dillon (1982) AC 484 PC 15.44
R v Lord Chancellor ex p Witham (1998) QB 575 . . . . 17.15
R v McFadden, The Times, 10 December 1978 . . . . 3.86, 5.88
R v Marsham ex p Lawrence (1912) 2 KB 362 . . . . 22.82
R v Secretary of State for Transport ex p Factortame Ltd (No 7) (2001) 1 WLR 942 . . . . 12.132
R v Ward (1993) 1 WLR 619 . . . . 15.86
Rabin v Gerson Berger Association Ltd [1985] 1 All 1041 . . . . 11.34
Rahman bin Turki al Sudairy (Prince Abdul) v Abu-Taha [1980] 3 All ER 409 . . . . 16.176
Rank Film Distributors Ltd v Video Information centre (1982) AC 380 . . . . 22.97
Rasu Maritima SA v Perusahaan Pertambangan Minyak Dan Gas Bumi Negara (1978)
    QB 644 CA 16.176
Redland Bricks Ltd v Morris (1970) AC 652 . . . . 14.19, 16.110
Reed Executive plc v Reed Business Information Ltd (2004) EWCA Civ 887 . . . . 20.46
Reeves v Metropolitan Police Commissioner (1999) 3 All ER 897 . . . . 19.26, 19.131

Regan v Williamson (1976) 1 WLR 305 . . . . 19.115
Rentworth Ltd v Stephansen (1996) 2 All ER 244 . . . . 22.98
Rex Williams Leisure plc, Re (1994) Ch 350 CA 15.204
Ridehalgh v Horsefield [1994] 3 WLR 462 . . . . 3.85, 5.86
Rio Tinto Zinc Corporation v Westinghouse Electric Company (1978) AC 547 . . . . 22.97
Roberts, Re [1905] 1 Ch 704 . . . . 20.20
Roberts v Johnstone (1989) QB 878 . . . . 19.89
Robinson v Bird, The Times, 20 January 2004 . . . . 22.124
Rockwell Machine Tool Co Ltd v EP Barnes Ltd [1968] 1 WLR 693 . . . . 6.114
Roebuck v Mungovin (1994) 2 AC 224 . . . . 16.105
Rondel v Worsley (1967) 3 All ER 993 . . . . 3.92
Rose v Lynx Express Ltd, The Times, 22 April 2004 . . . . 16.75
Rowe and Davis v United Kingdom, The Times, 1 March 2000 . . . . 15.200
Royal Brompton Hospital NHS Trust v Hammond (2002) 1 WLR 1397 HL 13.71
Royscott Trust Ltd v Rogerson (1991) 2 QB 297 . . . . 18.88
Rush v Tompkins Ltd v Greater london Council (1989) AC 1280 . . . . 20.46
Ruxley Electronics and Construction Ltd v Forsyth (1996) 1 AC 344 HL 19.63

S v Gloucestershire CC (2000) 3 All ER 346 . . . . 19.16
Saif Ali v Sydney Mitchel & Co (a firm) (1980) AC 198 . . . . 3.93
Sanderson v Blyth Theatre Co (1903) 2 KB 533 CA 5.55
Sarwar v Alam (2002) 1 WLR 125 . . . . 5.31
Saunders v Edwards [1987] 2 All ER 651 . . . . 18.102
Sayers v Clarke Walker (2002) 1 WLR 3095 . . . . 23.48
Scammell v Dicker (2001) 1 WLR 631 . . . . 20.59
SCF Finance Co Ltd v Masri (1985) 1 WLR 876 . . . . 16.176
Science Research Council v Nasse (1980) AC 1028 . . . . 15.66
Seaconsar Far East Ltd v Bank Markazi Jomhouri Islami Iran (1994) 1 AC 438 . . . . 4.159
Selangor United Rubber Estates v Cradock [1965] 1 Ch 896 . . . . 12.54
Senior v Holdsworth, ex p Independent Television News [1976] QB 23 . . . . 8.44
Series 5 Software Ltd v Clarke (1996) 1 All ER 853 . . . . 16.115
Shanning International Ltd v George Wimpey International Ltd (1989) 1 WLR 981 CA 16.189
Shapland v Palmer (1999) 1 WLR 2068 . . . . 19.33
Shaw v Vauxhall Motors Ltd (1974) 1 WLR 1035 CA 16.73
Shearson Lehman Bros Inc v Maclaine Watson & Co Ltd (1987) 1 WLR 480 CA,
    [1989] 1 All ER 1056 . . . . 16.188, 20.79
Shearson Lehman Bros Inc v Maclaine Watson & Co Ltd (No 2) (1990) 3 All ER 723 . . . . 18.86
Sheldon v RHM Outhwaite (Underwrighting Agencies) Ltd (1996) AC 102 HL 4.39
Shepherd Homes Ltd v Sandham (1971) Ch 340 . . . . 18.67
Shocked v Goldschmidt (1998) 1 All ER 372 CA 22.11
Siebe Gorman and Co Ltd v Pneupac Ltd (1982) 1 All ER 377 . . . . 20.100
Sinclair Jones v Kay [1988] 2 All ER 611 . . . . 5.86
Siskina v Distos Compania Naviera SA (1979) AC 210 . . . . 16.111, 16.176
Sky Petroleum Ltd v VIP Petroleum Ltd (1974) 1 WLR 567 & 576 . . . . 18.69, 18.76
Smallman v Smallman [1971] 3 All ER 717 . . . . 20.82
Smith Kline Beecham plc v Generics (2004) 1 WLR 1479 . . . . 15.190
Smith New Court Securities Ltd v Scrimgeour Vickers (Asset Management) Ltd (1994)
    1 WLR 1271 . . . . 15.112
Smith New Court Securities Ltd v Scrimgeour Vickers (Asset Management) Ltd (1997)
    4 All ER 769 . . . . 18.88
Smith v Manchester Corporation (1974) 17 KIR 1 . . . . 19.98
Smoker v London Fire and Civil Defence Authority (1991) 2 AC 502 . . . . 19.101
Sol Industries UK Ltd v Canara Bank (2001) 1 WLR 1800 . . . . 17.100

Somatra Ltd v Sinclair Roche and Temperley (2000) 1 WLR 2453 . . . . 3.70
South Shropshire District Council v Amos (1986) 1 WLR 1271 . . . . 20.46
Spagro v North Essex District Health Authority (1997) PIQR P235 . . . . 19.31
Spaven v Milton Keynes Borough Council, The Times, 16 March 1990 . . . . 12.123
Spencer v Wood, The Times, 30 March 2004 . . . . 5.29
Spiliada Maritime Corp v Cansulex Ltd (1986) AC 460 . . . . 4.146, 4.161
Spittle v Bunney [1988] 3 All ER 1031 . . . . 19.100
Standard Chartered Bank v Pakistan National Shipping Corp (2003) 1 All ER 173 . . . . 18.91
Stanfield Properties v National Westminster Bank [1983] 2 All ER 244 . . . . 16.147
Stanley v Saddique (1992) QB 1 . . . . 19.115
Starr v National Coal Board (1977) 1 WLR 63 CA 15.158
Stephan v General Medical Council (1999) 1 WLR 1293 . . . . 3.27
Stephenson (SBJ) Ltd v Mandy, The Times, 21 July 1999 . . . . 1.50
Stevens v Gullis (2000) 1 All ER 527 CA 15.160
Stewart v Engel (2000) 1 WLR 2268 . . . . 16.98
Stringman v McArdle (1994) 1 WLR 1653 . . . . 16.189
Strover v Harrington [1988] 1 All ER 769 . . . . 3.96
Stubbings v Webb (1993) 2 AC 498 . . . . 19.35
Sudbrook Trading Estate v Eggleton [1982] 3 All ER 1 . . . . 18.76
Sun Valley Poultry Ltd v Micro-Biologicals Ltd, The Times, 14 May 1990 . . . . 14.57, 18.86
Swain v Hillman (2001) A ER 91 . . . . 16.97
Symphony Group plc v Hodgson (1994) QB 179 . . . . 5.56

Tanfern Ltd v Cameron-MacDonald (2000) 1 WLR 1311 . . . . 23.46
Tate & Lyle Foods and Distribution v Greater London Council [1981] 3 All ER 716,
    [1982] 1 WLR 149 . . . . 14.73, 14.76
Tate Access Floors Inc v Boswell (1991) Ch 512 . . . . 16.159
Taylor v Lawrence (2002) 2 All ER 353 . . . . 23.95
Taylor v Nugent Care Society, The Times, 28 January 2004 . . . . 13.13
Thatcher v Douglas, The Times, 8 January 1996 . . . . 22.72
Thomas v Bunn [1991] 1 All ER 193 . . . . 12.111
Thomas v Connell (1838) 4M&W 267 . . . . 15.72
Thomas Witter Ltd v TBP Industries Ltd (1996) 2 All ER 573 . . . . 18.52
Thompson v Commissioner of Police of the Metropolis (1997) 2 All ER 762 . . . . 19.65
Thorn plc v MacDonald (1999) CPLR 660 . . . . 16.93
Thorne v University of London [1966] 2 QB 237 . . . . 12.144
Thorpe v Alexander Fork Lift Trucks Ltd [1975] 1 WLR 1459 . . . . 16.105
Three Rivers District Council v Bank of England (No 2) (1996) 2 All ER 363 . . . . 9.39
Three Rivers District Council v Bank of England (No 3) (2001) 2 All ER 513 HL,
    (2003) 2 AC 1 . . . . 3.27, 12.143, 16.81
Three Rivers District Council v Bank of England (No 4) (2003) 1 WLR 210 . . . . 16.165
Three Rivers District Council v Bank of England (No 6), The Times, 12 November 2004 . . . . 3.76
Thwaite v Thwaite [1981] FLR 280 . . . . 20.106
Tingle Jacobs and Co v Kennedy (1964) 1 WLR 638 . . . . 15.44
Tito v Waddell (No 2) (1977) Ch 106 . . . . 18.76
Tolstoy-Miloslavsky v Aldington, The Times, 27 December 1995 . . . . 5.86
Tomlin v Standard Telephones and Cables Ltd (1969) 1 WLR 1378 . . . . 20.48
Tomlinson v Congleton BC All ER (D) 213 . . . . 19.12
Tower Hamlets London Borough Council v Begum (2003) 2 AC 430 . . . . 3.29
TSB Private Bank International SA v Chabra (1992) 1 WLR 231 . . . . 16.176

UCB Corporate Services Ltd v Halifax (SW) Ltd (1999) CPLR 691 . . . . 16.59
Unilever plc v Procter and Gamble Co (1999) 1 WLR 1630, (2000) 1 WLR 2436 . . . . 20.44, 20.50

Union Transport Group plc v Continental Lines SA (1992) 1 WLR 15 HL 18.19
United Bank of Kuwait v Hammond [1988] 3 All ER 418 . . . . 3.97
Universal City Studios Inc v Mukhtar & Sons [1976] 2 All ER 330 . . . . 16.149
Universal Cycles plc v Grangebriar Ltd (2000) CPLR 42 . . . . 5.54

Van Oudenhoven v Griffin Inns Ltd (2000) 1 WLR 1413 . . . . 19.96
Vandervell's Trusts (No 2) [1974] Ch 269 . . . . 12.56
Ventouris v Moutain (No 2) (1992) 1 WLR 817 . . . . 15.30
Vernon v Bosley, The Times, 19 December 1996 . . . . 3.45
Victoria Laundry (Windsor) v Newman Industries [1949] 2 KB 548 . . . . 18.82
Vinos v Marks & Spencer (2001) 3 All ER 784 . . . . 4.64

Wadsworth v Lydall [1981] 2 All ER 401 . . . . 14.73, 18.97
Waghorn v George Wimpey & Co [1969] 1 WLR 1764 . . . . 19.119
Wallersteiner v Moir (No 2) [1975] 1 QB 373 . . . . 14.74
Warner Bros Pictures Inc v Nelson (1937) 1 KB 209 . . . . 18.69
Warren v Mendy (1989) 3 All ER 103 . . . . 18.69
Warriner v Warriner (2002) All ER (D) 202 . . . . 19.96
Watson v British Board of Boxing Control (2001) 2 WLR 1256 . . . . 19.15
Watson v Willmott [1991] 1 All ER 473 . . . . 14.67
Waugh v British Railways Board (1980) AC 521 . . . . 3.67, 3.72
Waugh v MB Clifford & Sons [1982] 1 All ER 1095, [1982] Ch 374 . . . . 6.18, 20.21
WEA Records Ltd v Visions Channel 4 Ltd [1983] 2 All ER 589 . . . . 16.162
Wells v Wells (1997) 1 All ER 673 . . . . 19.96
Welsh Development Agency v Redpath Dorman Long Ltd (1994) 1 WLR 1409 CA 12.133
Western Web Offset Printers Ltd v Independent Media Ltd, The Times, 10 October 1995 . . . . 18.85
White Arrow Express Ltd v Lamey's Distribution Ltd, The Times, 21 July 1995 . . . . 18.97
Whitehouse v Jordan (1981) 1 WLR 246 . . . . 15.166
Wiedmann v Walpole (1891) 2 QB 534 . . . . 15.65
Wilkey v British Broadcasting Corporation (2003) 1 WLR 1 . . . . 4.69
Williams v Fanshaw Porter & Hazlehurst (a firm) [2004] EWCA 157 . . . . 3.91
Williams v Fanshaw Porter Williams (2004) 2 All ER 616 . . . . 4.39
Williams v Home Office (No 2) [1982] 2 All ER 564 . . . . 23.44
Williams v Natural Health Foods Ltd (1998) 2 All ER 577 . . . . 19.15
Willson v Ministry of Defence (1991) 1 All ER 638 . . . . 19.104
Wilson & Whitworth Ltd v Express Newspapers Ltd [1969] 1 WLR 197 . . . . 20.80
Wilson v First County Trust (2001) 3 WLR 42 . . . . 3.23
Wilson v First County Trust (No 2) (2003) 3 WLR 568 . . . . 3.26
Woodhouse v Consignia plc (2002) 2 All ER 737 . . . . 12.140, 16.61
Worldwide Corporation Ltd v Marconi Communications Ltd, The Times, 7 July 1999 . . . . 3.47
Wright v Lodge (1993) 4 All ER 299 . . . . 19.77
Wright v Morris (1997) FSR 218 CA 16.105
Wrotham Park Estate Co Ltd v Parkside Homes Ltd (1974) 1 WLR 798 . . . . 18.64

X Ltd v Morgan-Grampian (Publishers) Ltd (1991) 1 AC 1 HL 15.90, 16.68
X v Bedfordshire County Council (1995) 3 All ER 353 . . . . 19.16

Yell Ltd v Garton, The Times, 26 July 2004 . . . . 23.75
Youell v Bland Welch & Co Ltd [1991] 1 WLR 122 . . . . 3.72
Young v Purdy, The Times, 7 November 1995 . . . . 3.96
Yousif v Salama [1980] 3 All ER 405 . . . . 16.149

Zim Properties Ltd v IRC [1984] STI 741 . . . . 11.80
Zucker v Tyndall Holdings plc (1993) 1 All ER 124 CA 16.176

1

WHAT IS 'EFFECTIVE' LITIGATION?

A INTRODUCTION 1.01

B DIFFERING PERSPECTIVES 1.02
The process of litigation 1.03
The relevance of litigation for lawyers 1.04
The relevance of litigation for litigants 1.06

C THE CHANGING LEGAL ENVIRONMENT 1.07
Changes for lawyers. 1.08
Changes in the law 1.09
Changes in the litigation process 1.10
Changes in the commercial realities of litigation. 1.11
Changes in the training of lawyers 1.12

D THE CLIMATE OF CHANGE 1.13
Litigation v settlement 1.14
The compensation culture 1.16
The costs of litigation 1.18
The role of technology 1.19
The governance of the legal profession 1.21
The shape of the legal profession 1.22
Training lawyers. 1.24
Realism and idealism. 1.27
The role of research 1.29

E DEFINING EFFECTIVE LITIGATION AND THE EFFECTIVE LAWYER. . . . 1.32
Problems in making litigation effective 1.33
Working as an effective lawyer 1.35
The approach taken by this book 1.39

F THE OVERRIDING OBJECTIVE OF LITIGATION. 1.42
The Woolf reforms. 1.42
The Overriding Objective—CPR Part 1. . . . . 1.44
The use of the overriding objective. 1.47

G THE ROLE OF THE WOOLF REFORMS 1.51
The successes of the reforms 1.52
Ongoing issues about the reforms. 1.53

H KEY KNOWLEDGE AND SKILLS FOR A LITIGATOR.................. 1.55

The knowledge and skills a civil litigator requires 1.55
Using knowledge and skills at a professional level.............. 1.61
Entering the profession.................................... 1.64
Other lawyers as role models 1.66
Personal style 1.67

I   REPRESENTING A CLIENT................................... 1.68

The importance of the client in practice 1.68
Law as a service industry.................................. 1.69
Communicating with the client 1.72
The importance of acting on instructions 1.75

J   LEGAL PRINCIPLES AS TOOLS.............................. 1.80

Using legal principles 1.80
Remembering legal principles 1.83

K   TAKING A PRACTICAL APPROACH........................... 1.85

The importance of facts 1.86
Appreciation of real life situations 1.87
Getting the full facts of the case 1.88

L   WORKING WITH OTHERS 1.89

Others on the same side 1.91
Those on the other side.................................... 1.92
The judge.. 1.95

M THE TIME DIMENSION.................................... 1.97

Problems with time 1.99
What causes delay 1.100
Rules and powers relating to time.......................... 1.101
Dealing with a case expeditiously.......................... 1.103

N   THE COSTS DIMENSION 1.106

Problems with costs....................................... 1.107
The basic model for the costs of litigation................... 1.109
Rules and powers relating to costs 1.113
Dealing with costs effectively 1.115

O   LAW AS A BUSINESS..................................... 1.118

P   THE PUBLIC IMAGE OF LAWYERS 1.123

A INTRODUCTION

> The leading rule for the lawyer, as for the man of every other calling, is diligence. Leave nothing for tomorrow which can be done today
>
> Abraham Lincoln

This chapter considers the broad meaning and ingredients of effective litigation. The other **1.01** chapters of this book focus on different aspects of the litigation process, broadly following the progress of an action, and looking at how the litigation process can be carried out most effectively. The book focuses on how to analyse a case and on the practical techniques that practitioners use. Rules of litigation and evidence are described, but the emphasis is on how to make practical use of them.

B DIFFERING PERSPECTIVES

There are many different perspectives on the role and purpose of litigation. This can make it **1.02** difficult to form a coherent view of what the litigation process is about, of the role of lawyers within that process, and of how lawyers can best serve the needs of clients.

The process of litigation

There are many factors in the evolving role and purpose of litigation. **1.03**

- Adversarial litigation with cases prepared by each side and decided by an impartial judge remains an important process for settling a civil legal claim, but there are concerns about cost and complexity.
- Other ways of settling disputes, for example through arbitration and mediation are becoming more popular than litigation for some because they can be cheaper and offer more client control, but the lack of supervision of this process may lead to drawbacks.
- The process of civil litigation is changing substantially, for example with witness statements standing as evidence in chief, and with skeleton arguments increasingly being required before hearings. This may have implications for the skills required for advocating a civil case effectively.
- The process of litigation remains a key function of some lawyers, and particularly of barristers, but there has been a tendency for lawyers to move away from litigation work.
- There are claims that there is a growing 'compensation culture', but it is questionable whether this is true and whether the needs of litigants are taken sufficiently into account in the litigation process

The relevance of litigation for lawyers

People who become lawyers do so from many different perspectives and with many differ- **1.04** ent objectives. Many have no particular intention of becoming involved in or focussing on the litigation process, though the process has some relevance for all lawyers because of the extent to which case law resulting from litigation is used to interpret and develop the law.

1.05   To provide some perspectives on the litigation process from lawyers:

- For a solicitor, litigation may be something best avoided by ensuring that transactions are completed properly so that disagreements do not ensue, and also perhaps best avoided because of the work and risks associated with litigation.
- For a barrister, litigation may be a main focus of work through opinions, drafting and advocacy, though not all barristers appear regularly in court.
- For a judge, the litigation process requires the finding of fact and law from material presented by the two sides in a case, and the way in which material is presented is of prime importance.
- For an academic lawyer, interest in the litigation process may be limited save for the interpretation of the judgments that result from litigation.
- For a law student, becoming a litigation lawyer may appear a route to a prestigious career, but it may be difficult for a student to form a realistic understanding of how litigation operates in practice.

The relevance of litigation for litigants

1.06   It is arguable that the perspective of the litigant is most important in assessing the effectiveness of the litigation process. The main purpose of litigation might be said to be to achieve a fair outcome between litigants, but litigants may have a variety of standpoints that may affect the effectiveness of the process and the view of the litigant.

- Most litigants want a litigation system that is reasonably quick and reasonably inexpensive.
- Some litigants focus on realities and find the litigation process frustrating.
- Some litigants see the litigation process as a tool to further self interest.
- Some litigants are most concerned about a particular point of principle rather than the overall litigation process.
- Some litigants want difficult or even impossible outcomes that cannot be easily justified by existing law or available evidence.

C   THE CHANGING LEGAL ENVIRONMENT

1.07   The professional work of lawyers and the process for conducting litigation have changed massively over the last two or three decades. General public understanding of the role of lawyers and of litigation have inevitably not necessarily kept pace with change.

Changes for lawyers

1.08   As regards lawyers:

- The type of work lawyers do has changed. There has been a big shift from general high street practice to a much greater focus on commercial work. While much of this shift has related to transactions rather than litigation, there has been some change in the types of case and the types of issues that are being litigated.

- The role of lawyers has changed and distinctions have been blurred. While barristers still tend to focus more on litigation and court work, and to be used where specialist advice is required, solicitors are able to acquire fuller rights of audience in court. If advocacy in all levels of court and tribunal is considered, a significant proportion of advocacy is done by solicitors, and many barristers appear in court rarely. Direct access to barristers without the use of a solicitor is now possible in appropriate circumstances. Employed barristers and solicitors often do identical work. It is relatively easy to transfer from one branch of the profession to the other. In these circumstances this book refers to the role of a lawyer, save for where there is still a clear distinction between the role of a barrister and a solicitor.

Changes in the law

As regards the law: **1.09**

- The use of knowledge has changed. A wide and detailed retained knowledge of law was highly regarded. While this to some extent remains the case, the focus for legal practitioners is increasingly on knowledge management rather than knowledge retention. What is most important is to know and be able to use legal principles, and to be able to research detailed law effectively when necessary, see Chapter 9.
- The sources of law have changed. Traditionally lawyers dealt with the statute and case law of the jurisdiction. European Union law and human rights law have provided further layers of legal principle that can apply to a wide variety of civil cases. Communication and information technology (C&IT) has made many legal sources much more easily available and more likely to be used.

Changes in the litigation process

As regards the litigation process: **1.10**

- The ethos of civil litigation has undergone a radical change. The Civil Procedure Rules 1998 provide a full new code, written in plain English, and have modified the adversarial approach to litigation by introducing principles of achieving justice through managed cases where timetables are met and costs are not allowed to build up unnecessarily.
- The practice of civil litigation has undergone a massive change. While advocacy in the courtroom trial remains the ultimate focus for a civil case, there is a much greater emphasis on a 'cards on the table' approach that specifically encourages the use of negotiation and alternative dispute resolution (ADR) where possible to settle a case without the need to proceed to trial.
- Court work is now much more paper based with witness statements as evidence in chief and skeleton arguments supporting advocacy.
- There are increasing issues relating to confidentiality in litigation. The 'cards on the table' approach and the money laundering legislation are challenging and potentially limiting traditional views of confidentiality and legal professional privilege.

Changes in the commercial realities of litigation

1.11   As regards the commercial realities of litigation:

- The ways in which litigation is funded have changed. Very limited public funding is now available in civil cases, and a significant amount of litigation is now funded through conditional fee agreements, see 5.26–5.37.
- The expectations of clients have changed. There was a time when it might be said that clients tended to accept the expertise of a lawyer and costs were rarely mentioned. Clients now have much higher expectations of the professional standards of lawyers and are entitled to be informed of the progress of a case and of costs. Complaints about service levels are more common.
- There is a much greater acknowledgement of the role of risk analysis and insurance with regard to litigation. Clients insure against risks, and insurance providers play an important role in some areas of litigation. Lawyers are insured against negligence. Risk analysis in one form or another is fundamental to taking a case on a conditional fee basis, or to starting or continuing litigation.
- The pressures on solicitors and barristers in running their professional businesses have increased. The life of a professional lawyer arguably has less choice and flexibility than has been the case in the past. The need to provide an efficient service, meet reasonably high standards, and to compete with other lawyers has led to bigger firms and sets of chambers with more complex management structures.

Changes in the training of lawyers

1.12   As regards the training of lawyers to act in litigation:

- Legal professional training has changed. The introduction of the skills-based Bar Vocational Course for barristers and the Legal Practice Course for solicitors helps to ensure that students are more fully prepared for the professional work they will be doing. However many tensions remain. The legal profession has high expectations of those who enter it, and trainee lawyers have high expectations of the profession. On both sides expectations may not be entirely realistic.
- University law schools face a number of stresses. While law has become an increasingly popular subject, pressures on resourcing and staff have made it more difficult to provide students with a depth of understanding of law and with high quality legal research skills. Those who study law at an undergraduate level may go into a variety of careers, and in providing general education in law universities will not necessarily provide an ideal grounding for practice. There is a long standing debate in this area, but if law faculties provide a general liberal education in law they will inevitably not necessarily provide a tailored foundation for a practising lawyer or for a litigator.

D   THE CLIMATE OF CHANGE

There are many live concerns and issues that impact on the litigation process.   **1.13**

Litigation v settlement

There are significant questions about the role of litigation, such that the basis upon which   **1.14**
civil disputes are resolved might change within the next generation. The vast majority of
cases settle. Settlement is strongly encouraged by the overriding objective, pre-action protocols, and case management. Settlement gives the parties more control over the outcome of
the case and saves time and costs, see Chapter 20.

However settlement and alternative dispute resolution are not entirely good. The outcome   **1.15**
of disputes is less public, and procedural and evidential rules are less clearly followed. There
is little judicial overview of the outcome of negotiation unless a consent order is sought.
Currently parties normally prepare for litigations, albeit that the case may actually be settled.
It is questionable how far the pendulum should swing towards settlement if some of the
basic principles of litigation are less clearly followed.

The compensation culture

There are concerns about 'the compensation culture', with a perceived growth in litigation   **1.16**
to demand compensation for any problem that arises. In particular there are concerns about
claims against the NHS and other public bodies, which is seen to result in teachers having
concerns about taking children on school trips and so on. In public policy terms it is claimed
that money might be better spent on services rather than on litigation. However the truth
behind such concerns has been queried. Despite anecdotal claims concerns are not clearly
justified on the facts. For example the number of claims against the National Health Service
possibly reached a high in the late 1990s (when it ran to over 6,000 a year). More recently the
number of claims has been back below 5,000 a year. It is the cost of claims that is rising,
because of rises in damages for lost earnings, and because investing money to pay for future
care currently attracts relatively unfavourable returns.

Where actions for negligence are brought, the courts maintain the line that liability will only   **1.17**
arise where the actions of an individual or a body fall short of that which is supported by a
substantial body of fellow professionals. It is arguable that other countries have lower tests
for liability. There is also an extent to which the pooling of knowledge about claims governs
standards, in that, for example, a number of accident claims involve insurers, and public
authorities like hospitals pool knowledge through the NHS Litigation Authority.

The costs of litigation

Many ordinary people with legal problems find it difficult or impossible to afford legal   **1.18**
advice. Access to legal advice is changing with the government focussing public funding for
civil litigation on block contracts for the provision of advice. Conditional fee or 'no win no
fee' arrangements have not opened up the market as was anticipated, and middle-income

litigants can have real problems with affordable access. The government has expressed an intention to use the internet more fully to provide legal advice. There has been talk of 'supermarket law', with legal advice being a service offered outside traditional legal offices, but this depends on decisions about the future running of the profession. Lawyers rightly express concerns about lawyers in some way being 'owned' by a large corporation and shareholders, but some way of providing legal services on a walk-in-and-buy-it basis needs to be found if those with civil legal problems are to be properly served. For further discussion of funding litigation see Chapter 5.

The role of technology

1.19   Technology has already had many effects on the litigation process.

- Documents are now normally prepared electronically.
- Research increasingly uses electronic sources.
- Document management is increasingly electronic (though there tends to be duplication with large hard copy files).
- There are possibilities for filing documents electronically.
- Disclosure of documents and witness statements can take place electronically to effect simultaneous disclosure.
- The rules allow for interim hearings by telephone. It is becoming more acceptable for the telephone to be used rather than a court hearing, provided all the parties consent. The applicant will normally be responsible for making arrangements.
- Some draft interim orders need to be submitted to the court on disc.
- There have been experiments with 'high tech' courtrooms, for example at Kingston Crown Court, but they are not in regular use.
- Screens for simultaneous display of evidence are used at some big trials and enquiries but are not commonly available.
- Many judges use computers for various purposes, but not yet as part of a very coherent network.

1.20   This trend can only continue, though the use of technology in courts has still not developed to the level anticipated to support the Woolf reforms and the Civil Procedure Rules 1998. There have been experiments with the use of e-mail for communications with the court, PD 5B Pilot Scheme for communication, and filing of documents by e-mail, but the use of IT for litigation is still patchy and subject to available facilities and agreement between the parties rather than being the norm. There is a video conferencing protocol for the Royal Courts of Justice, but video conferencing and full IT facilities are not yet commonly available in courts. It is right that technology should only be used where it will save time and money and must not prejudice a party, *Morris v Bank of America National Trust* (2000) 1 All ER 954, but there is some way to go before modern technology can be fully used in court.

The governance of the legal profession

1.21   A specific driver for further change is likely to be the Review of the Regulatory Framework of the Legal Service being carried out by David Clementi, with a report due at the end of 2004.

This review is considering basic questions about the governance of the legal profession, and whether lawyers should be able to work in partnership with other professions such as accountants. The Clementi report will also cover matters such as whether non-lawyers should be able to invest in legal practices, which is relevant to the possible provision of 'supermarket law'. For further details see 3.02–3.05.

The shape of the legal profession

Whatever happens to the governance of barristers and solicitors, there are also wider questions about the future shape of the legal profession. Not only are the traditional roles of barristers and solicitors being broken down, but increasingly different parts of the role of the lawyer are being performed in different ways, for example through the use of paralegals. The government clearly has an ongoing agenda for change, with the Department for Constitutional Affairs replacing the Lord Chancellor's Department, and plans to create a Supreme Court. **1.22**

There are also questions about the ownership of legal practice, which are being considered as part of the Clementi review. Traditionally barristers have worked as individuals, albeit in groups jointly administered in a set of chambers, and solicitors have worked in partnerships, albeit sometimes distinguishing partners with a share from salaried partners. In recent years the size of chambers and firms has grown to provide better ranges of expertise and to finance a stronger infrastructure. This has arguably made chambers and firms more efficient, but it has also arguably caused lawyers to focus on commercial transaction work rather than on litigation. Already some firms are starting to form limited liability partnerships. **1.23**

Training lawyers

Continuing professional development training is now not only compulsory but also essential for practitioners to keep up to date, and to build new areas of expertise to meet changes in law and legal practice. **1.24**

There are many challenges in training new lawyers. The expertise required to go into practice inevitably involves an expensive training due to the range of the skills and knowledge required. The costs of training risks limiting access to the profession, but trying to cut down on training is likely to reduce the knowledge and flexibility of the individual and the potential service to the client. **1.25**

There is not a close and coherent fit between the legal training offered in universities and the professional training offered to graduates who choose to go into practice. Academic lawyers often quite rightly want to focus on problems in legal theory and interpretation, or to look at law in a social or philosophical context. The profession wants trainees with a clear grasp of principles of law in key areas such as contract and tort—which can be found in students who have taken a postgraduate diploma in law rather than in a law student who has focussed on such principles at the start of a law degree. There are no easy answers. More coherence might be achieved by having some law degrees focussing on practice and perhaps integrated with legal professional training while others provide a more general liberal training in law, but this might force students into making early choices. **1.26**

Realism and idealism

1.27   Despite the availability of a large amount of information on practice as a lawyer, public misconceptions about lawyers and litigation easily arise. This can arise because people gather views on lawyers and their role from the television world of 'Ally McBeal' or 'Kavanagh QC', from films, from John Grisham novels, or from newspaper headline cases. Inevitably these do not present the reality of the profession and the work it involves. Students training as lawyers can have unrealistic views of what their working life will involve. Clients can have unrealistic views of what lawyers can achieve and how they can achieve it.

1.28   There is also a question of the role of idealism in legal practice. Many law students start to study law with ideals about the power of law to achieve fairness in society, and get enthused by work in law clinics. In reality idealism is likely to be dented. Financing training may pull the trainee into areas of work that are not the first choice of the individual. The newly qualified barrister or solicitor may find that it is impossible to find work or make a living in a particular area of work—there has been a growth in human rights work and many firms and chambers do some *pro bono* work, but it is not easy to forge a career in areas like environmental law. Idealism can also be dented by the realities of work, if for example a client has unfair or unrealistic objectives. It can also be difficult working with the practical problems of facts and evidence. Despite these challenges some idealism continues to play a role for most lawyers.

The role of research

1.29   There is a lack of understanding of what makes some approaches to litigation more successful than others. How can one lawyer prepare a case more effectively than another? What can make a cross examination of an expert witness effective? What can make one closing speech more compelling than another? Without rational answers to such questions the litigation process is more of a lottery than it should be.

1.30   In some jurisdictions there is a close relationship between academic lawyers and legal practitioners. In the United States it is common for law faculties to have quite close relationships with local practitioners, and for individuals to combine successful practice with university teaching. It is unfortunate that in England and Wales there is a much greater divide between academic lawyers and practice. Some firms and chambers have academic lawyers as members, or form close links with them, but this is the exception rather than the rule. Some university law departments have active practitioner advisory groups, but again this is the exception rather than the rule.

1.31   It is difficult to see what purpose is served by this degree of separation. While academics need to focus on their specialist interests and practitioners need to focus on their profession and their clients, the separation means that relatively little research is done into areas like litigation and evidence. This is unfortunate—well conducted research could make litigation more effective to the benefit of lawyers and clients. Closer links could also foster imaginative thinking in developing law and assisting clients. Closer links could also assist law students who wish to enter practice. There is a need for legal research institutes and specialist lawyer associations involving both academics and practitioners that could be used as think tanks and as research centres.

E DEFINING EFFECTIVE LITIGATION AND THE EFFECTIVE LAWYER

With varied perspectives of litigation and the pressures of existing and ongoing change it is **1.32** not easy to define the objectives of effective litigation, what constitutes effective litigation, or what qualities the individual needs to work as an effective litigator.

Problems in making litigation effective

There are some quite profound tensions. **1.33**

- The litigation process can be vital for defending rights and liberties, but it can also be used as a tool by powerful litigants such as international corporations.
- Settling actions can been seen as desirable in terms of saving time and costs and providing more control to clients, but settlement can also indicate that parties do not like the litigation system, and settlements take cases out of judicial overview.
- More financial support for litigants can be seen as vital in enabling them to bring claims, but could also be seen as supporting a compensation culture.
- While 'fat cat lawyer' claims are much exaggerated, for each idealist who sees litigation as a route to achieve fairness for individuals there is a lawyer who is equally concerned with making a good living.
- The litigation process is not clearly conceptualised as a service for litigants. It is seen as having other purposes, such as clarifying legal principles, and indeed sometimes seems to have an importance as an historic system quite outside the needs of litigants.
- Many principles of evidence and procedure have evolved primarily through detailed academic analysis. While this provides strength, the principles are not necessarily tuned to the needs and understanding of many litigants.
- There is still a tendency to focus on law as a philosophical concept and to accept that justice can sometimes appear a bit of a lottery rather than to embrace more scientific concepts such as risk assessment that are very relevant to clients contemplating litigation.
- The feeling is often that it is lawyers who are in charge of the litigation process. Cases belong to and are often paid for by clients and they should be in charge of the process as far as possible.
- There is perhaps inevitably too great a tendency for lawyers to accept high costs in litigation rather than to focus on providing a service that clients can afford.
- Problems of access to civil justice for people of moderate means are not being sufficiently grasped and addressed. The problems tend rather to be passed around because the government already pays a very large figure for legal support for individuals, and lawyers find it difficult to work more cheaply.
- Despite efforts and initiatives, funding and costs issues have arguably got worse rather than better. It is not easy for clients to get really reliable information about the likely costs of an action on which to base decisions. The decline in public funding for civil actions has not really been filled by conditional fee funding, as lawyers inevitably tend to take the cases that are likely to succeed.

Without a reasonably clear and coherent concept of the relevance and importance of litiga- **1.34** tion in modern society it is not easy to identify what will make litigation most effective. In broad terms, effective litigation is probably that which is based on a clear system, and which fairly meets the needs of a litigant in reasonable time and at reasonable cost. The overriding objective of the Civil Procedure Rules probably does quite well in identifying the key ingredients in effective litigation at a fairly high level. Questions relate to how far the overriding objective can be achieved.

Working as an effective lawyer

1.35 Whatever the principles of the litigation system, it can only function effectively if lawyers work effectively. Many things can make it difficult for a lawyer to work effectively.

- It is difficult to keep on top of a significant number of cases that are all progressing at different speeds.
- Clients often fail to give full information or clear instructions.
- It can be difficult or impossible to gather full information about a case so that one has to work with gaps.
- The system for gathering and then exchanging documents and witness statements is probably inevitable, but getting information in stages can make it difficult to form an overview of a case, see 15.55.
- However efficiently lawyers on one side work, the lawyers on the other side can make progress in litigation difficult.
- It is difficult to keep costs down if one is to make best use of the litigation process.
- The level of pure hard work in preparing a case and taking it forward can be high. In a film a lawyer often achieves success with apparent ease through a key question in cross examination or the sudden discovery of a late piece of evidence. Needless to say real life is rarely like that.

1.36 Working as effectively as possible is, however, most likely to be successful, not only in achieving goals for the client, but also in building the practice of the lawyer. The key elements to working effectively are probably:

- being able to identify the key issues in a case clearly, 'seeing the wood for the trees', see Chapter 10;
- taking a systematic and analytical approach to facts and evidence;
- knowing and being able to apply key principles of law, especially in basic areas such as contract and tort;
- having good research skills, especially in ensuring law is up to date, and being able to deal with areas of law that are unfamiliar;
- being able to use the rules of evidence and procedure properly and tactically;
- being able to take an overview of a case, to identify the goals to be achieved and how to achieve them;
- being aware of the financial and other realities that surround the client and the litigation;
- having a sufficiently clear and realistic understanding of the environment within which lawyers work and litigation is conducted.

1.37 Perhaps an over-arching quality of an effective lawyer is flexibility. The law changes, each case is different, fact patterns change as more information comes in and a case develops.

Steering a consistent course through all of this is most likely to produce results. It is also useful to take a flexible approach to the use of law. Traditionally the study of law has tended to focus on studying and memorising detailed law, but query how far memorising detailed law is a good investment with the growth of legal sources and the speed of legal change. A thorough working knowledge of principles of law and very good research skills are more important.

There can of course be no single approach that will guarantee success, but this book seeks to **1.38** provide a framework within which the individual lawyer can develop, and continue to develop, his or her skills. It will probably take some time for a lawyer to accumulate the experience and skills to work really effectively, but taking the right approach from the earliest possible stage and building consistently on good foundations should work well.

The approach taken by this book

To provide a structured and manageable framework, this book focusses on the legal profes- **1.39** sional knowledge and skills required to work effectively in the context of civil litigation in England and Wales. The chapters broadly follow a civil case through the stages that may be involved in preparing and presenting a case. Much of the guidance given should be equally relevant to a barrister or a solicitor, or to a paralegal dealing with a particular type of case, but the roles of different types of professional lawyers are distinguished where relevant. The book seeks to provide a model on which a pupil or trainee can build with observation and experience of practice. It also seeks to provide the sort of model upon which an individual can build his or her own style.

The book seeks to bridge the gap between knowledge of law (the primary focus of most law **1.40** degrees) and the use of professional skills (the primary focus of vocational training), integrating both as fully as possible. Relevant rules of procedure, evidence, and, where relevant, substantive law are dealt with in some detail. However it is not the purpose of this book to deal comprehensively with substantive law—the full detail of relevant rules and cases MUST always be checked using practitioner sources.

It is also a recurrent theme of this book that litigation and litigation lawyers will become **1.41** more effective if more substantial and systematic research is undertaken into the litigation process. England and Wales have a well respected litigation process that has been refined over many centuries, but the needs of those using the process are going to be best met only if we focus on current and future needs.

F THE OVERRIDING OBJECTIVE OF LITIGATION

The Woolf reforms

In April 1999 a whole new code for civil litigation was introduced following a full review **1.42** led by Lord Woolf. The intention was not only to review and update previous procedural rules in a coherent way, but also to support a new approach to civil litigation. The break with the past is underlined by the resistance of the courts to having old cases cited to aid interpretation, *Biguzzi v Rank Leisure plc* (1999) 1 WLR 1926.

1.43 Key elements in the overall approach taken by the new rules include:

- introducing much more court control of the litigation process;
- an approach of openness rather than secrecy between parties to litigation;
- an emphasis on trying to settle actions rather than to litigate where possible;
- more focus on the pre-action stage;
- an attempt to control costs, and to keep clients more informed about the costs of litigation.

The Overriding Objective—CPR Part 1

1.44 The principle that litigation should be conducted as effectively as possible is very well supported by the Civil Procedure Rules 1998, and is enshrined in the overriding objective of those Rules, CPR r 1.1.

(1) These Rules are a new procedural code with the overriding objective of enabling the court to deal with cases justly.

(2) Dealing with a case justly includes, so far as is practicable—

    (a) ensuring that the parties are on an even footing;

    (b) saving expense;

    (c) dealing with the case in ways which are proportionate—

        (i)   to the amount of money involved;

        (ii)   to the importance of the case;

        (iii) to the complexity of the issues; and

        (iv)   to the financial position of each party;

    (d) ensuring that it is dealt with expeditiously and fairly; and

    (e) allotting to it an appropriate share of the court's resources, while taking into account the need to allot resources to other cases.

The court must further the overriding objective by actively managing cases. It remains the case that the approach to litigation in England and Wales is essentially adversarial, with each party preparing and presenting its own case for judgment, but the court will be proactive in progressing a case.

1.45 By CPR r 1.4 active case management includes:

(a) encouraging the parties to cooperate with each other in the conduct of proceedings;

(b) identifying the issues at an early stage;

(c) deciding promptly which issues need full investigation and trial and accordingly disposing summarily of others;

(d) deciding the order in which issues are to be resolved;

(e) encouraging the parties to use an alternative dispute resolution procedure if the court considers that appropriate, and facilitating the use of such procedure;

(f) helping the parties to settle the whole or part of the case;

(g) fixing timetables or otherwise controlling the progress of the case;

(h) considering whether the likely benefits of taking a particular step justify the cost of taking it;

(i) dealing with as many aspects of the case as it can on the same occasion;

(j)   dealing with the case without the parties needing to attend at court;

(k)   making use of technology; and

(l)   giving directions to ensure that the trial of a case proceeds quickly and efficiently.

In practical terms this means that the court can ensure that a case proceeds in an effective **1.46** way even if the lawyers do not. In particular the court can fix a timetable, make orders on its own initiative, dispose of issues that should not proceed to trial, make 'unless' orders with sanctions if the parties do not proceed with a case in a proper way, and disallow costs which are disproportionate.

The use of the overriding objective

The word 'effective' may not appear specifically in the overriding objective, but the clear **1.47** intention is to make litigation more effective. The words of the overriding objective, and of the approach to be taken by the courts, can on one level be read as being very general— perhaps a 'wish list'—but they are given effect because the court has to give effect to the overriding objective when making decisions, CPR r 1.2. The parties are expected to help the court to further the overriding objective, CPR r 1.3.

This means that the elements in the overriding objective can and should be raised wherever **1.48** appropriate in a letter to the other side, in a negotiation, or in addressing a judge in support of a particular course of action. They can be used strategically to support a particular course of action.

Lawyers litigating cases should be fully familiar with the words of the overriding objective so **1.49** that they can make full use of them in writing and in advocacy. The fact that the primary concern of the court is to do justice can be used as the basis for a submission. It can also be used as a simple persuasive argument for a single step. For example, in a case where a schedule of loss apparently claimed only a few thousand pounds it was found that dealing with a claim justly involved dealing with the real claim, so that the statement could be amended to claim damages of about £400,000, *Chilton v Surrey County Council* (1999) CPLR 525. Equally a claim started inappropriately may be allowed to continue as a different type of action instead of being struck out and putting the claimant to the expense of starting another action, *Re Hoicrest Ltd* (2000) 1 WLR 414.

On the other hand the general concept of justice cannot be called in aid in all circumstances. **1.50** It has been held that a party who cannot afford an expensive lawyer cannot prevent the other side from having the lawyer of their choice for reasons of justice, *Maltez v Lewis* The Times, 4 May 1999. Equally it may not be appropriate for the court to be asked to hear an appeal against an interim order if the full trial of the matter is due in a couple of weeks, *Stephenson (SBJ) Ltd v Mandy* The Times, 21 July 1999.

G   THE ROLE OF THE WOOLF REFORMS

The Civil Litigation Rules 1998 are based on the full review of the civil litigation rules **1.51** conducted by Lord Woolf. The new rules were intended to make some fundamental changes in the conduct of litigation. Are the rules having that effect? It is difficult to take a clear view. There has been research on the effect of some changes in the rules but not others. There are a number of forces for change that overlap with the rules themselves.

The successes of the reforms

1.52 In broad terms it can probably be said that the Civil Litigation Rules have made litigation more effective in that:

- the thoroughness of the review undertaken by Lord Woolf, the principles made explicit in the overriding objective, and the presentation of the rules in clear English have provided a massive step forwards in providing effective litigation;
- the training for lawyers linked to the new rules has led many lawyers to review the way in which they practice;
- Law Society research has shown that a significant majority of solicitors think that litigation is overall quicker and more efficient;
- active case management by judges has had some success, with cases moving forward more steadily and with hopeless cases being weeded out. However it seems that judges are not entirely consistent in enforcing rules and imposing sanctions;
- alternative dispute resolution and mediation are more widespread, and pre-action protocols appear to be leading to more pre-action negotiation. The number of High Court Queens Bench actions has fallen from about 120,000 in 1998 to about 17,000 in 2002, though there may be arguments as to whether an increase in settling actions is necessarily a sign of a more effective litigation process.

Ongoing issues about the reforms

1.53 The rules cannot be said to be entirely successful for the following reasons.

- Relatively few solicitors think that litigation is cheaper. It has not proved possible to control costs as was hoped with the framing of the rules. The costs of litigation remain high and arguing about costs has become a fringe industry with costs assessors, so that the cost of resolving cost issues can sometimes exceed the costs in dispute. Significant amounts of damages were delayed in reaching claimants while some principles for the costs regime were clarified. Summary assessment of costs for interim hearings has also created problems in that a judge can't easily tell if costs claims are justified, so decisions can appear to be inconsistent.
- The increased use of pre-action protocols has front-loaded costs, because of the amount of information to be collected and exchanged before starting an action. The result can be that costs for a case that settles might be higher rather than lower.
- The technological advances needed to support the procedural reforms are coming into place slowly, with some problems with resourcing. The use of technology is still patchy (see 1.19). Some areas are moving in a 'paperless' direction, such as Inland Revenue cases, but this is not yet the routine approach. Systematic electronic document management is still some way off, and it is difficult to tell when coherent and systematic use of electronic and video facilities will be available in courts.

1.54 While the principles in the overriding objective now make consideration of the time and cost involved in litigation much more important, delays and costs remain significant issues for many litigants, though the Woolf reforms alone could not solve such matters.

H KEY KNOWLEDGE AND SKILLS FOR A LITIGATOR

The knowledge and skills a civil litigator requires

Underlying all these principles and problems, effective legal practice is founded on key areas **1.55** of knowledge and skills. Various research projects and articles have sought to identify the essential knowledge and skills required from analysing the work lawyers do, and asking lawyers about what they do. The results of such research are now reflected in professional legal training requirements, and in particular the content of the Bar Vocational Course and the Legal Practice Course.

Civil lawyers need knowledge of: **1.56**

- the main principles of contract and tort law;
- the main principles of land law and trust law;
- the specialist areas of law in which they practice;
- sufficient background in general areas of law such as remedies and legal personality;
- the rules of procedure and evidence;
- the Code of Conduct relevant to their professional practice.

The key skills of a civil lawyer are: **1.57**

- case analysis—an ability to analyse facts comprehensively so as to define issues;
- legal research—an ability to carry out strategic and focussed legal research;
- legal writing and drafting—an ability to express a case clearly and precisely in writing;
- people skills—an ability to interact effectively with different types of clients, with different types of witnesses including experts, and with other lawyers;
- advocacy/presentation—an ability to explain a case clearly, concisely, and persuasively.

Underlying these skills, and common to many of them, there are other skills and qualities **1.58** that are important to success and effectiveness:

- general analytical skills
- organisational skills
- financial and business awareness
- time management skills
- clarity and conciseness in any mode of expression
- thoroughness and an eye for detail
- problem solving skills.

It is often thought that lawyers deal primarily in words, but in practice skills in numeracy are **1.59** also very important. Matters of costs need to be covered with a client and with the court. Complex arithmetic may be required in a commercial case or to deal with damages. It may be necessary to read or explain a set of accounts or a balance sheet. Even if there is an accountant or an actuary to deal with figures, the lawyer will need to understand them sufficiently to grasp a case thoroughly, to take an expert through evidence, and perhaps to challenge figures in cross examination.

1.60   Increasingly high level IT skills are important for the effective lawyer. Firms, chambers, and courts use electronic systems to store, access, and transfer documents. Many firms and chambers will keep their own pro formas and precedent documents in electronic formats. Communication and information technology and video systems are increasingly used where appropriate to present evidence. Electronic sources are increasingly used for legal research. Larger firms have complex electronic knowledge management systems. Skills in all these areas are increasingly prerequisites for effective legal practice.

Using knowledge and skills at a professional level

1.61   Each of the above knowledge and skills areas may seem reasonably straightforward in isolation. The challenges in practice are that:

- the skills and knowledge must be used in combination in complex scenarios;
- the skills and knowledge must be used at a professional level—the levels required for legal writing and for advocacy are much greater than for general writing and speaking skills;
- it is rarely possible to sit down and just apply relevant knowledge and skills to a case. The facts emerge gradually, and the view of the client and of the other side may change;
- cases in specialist practice may have some degree of similarity, but every case has individual characteristics that need to be spotted and that can make a crucial difference;
- the lawyer often has to use knowledge and skills in areas in which she or he has limited personal knowledge—a contract involving a pig farm one day and an accident in a cement factory the next;
- using legal knowledge is not what one might expect. Many large commercial cases involve points about jurisdiction and comparative law rather than commercial law, and if the case does go to trial it may be on a basic contractual principle rather than on a complex specialist legal point;
- it is very challenging not only to juggle law, facts, evidence, and procedure, but also to orchestrate them into a coherent and convincing case.

1.62   Analysis, writing, and speaking at legal professional level requires high standards. The work must merit the fee. The standard of the work must be that which it is reasonable to expect from a professional barrister or solicitor. This is further considered in the next chapter.

1.63   There is also the pure hard work. Television can make it appear that cases are won on clever points and stylish advocacy, but in fact most cases are won by thorough, time-consuming preparation. You can only explain a case to a client, an opponent, or a judge if you understand it fully yourself, and the confidence to persuade someone else of the strength of your case is most likely to come from proper preparation rather than sudden inspiration.

Entering the profession

1.64   Every law student who decides to go into practice will have most of the skills and knowledge required at some level. A number of the skills required in practice are inherent in degree-level work. However a keen desire to enter legal professional practice can result in an underestimation of the leap that is required to reach professional practice standards. It can be too easy to assume that because one broadly understands a task one is capable of doing it. But an enthusiastic trainee or pupil will often find that although a draft statement of case or a cross examination looks relatively straightforward it is in fact far from easy to achieve. In fact an experienced lawyer will often make something appear simple because of the experience they have where a lot of work has gone into refining their instinct. A medical student may have passed examinations in anatomy, diagnosis, and anaesthesia but you would not necessarily want that student to perform an operation on you without proper assessment of their competence. The new lawyer should not be over-confident and cavalier in using clients as guinea pigs.

A degree of humility and willingness to learn is important for the trainee or the pupil. **1.65** Surveys of firms and chambers have shown that those joining the profession often lack some of the knowledge and skills required for success. The divide between legal practice and academic law can again be a problem here. Students who have spent three years studying legal principles and have got good degrees tend to feel that they are already good lawyers and have little to learn. A greater integration of skills within legal study could provide a more coherent training, and a proper valuation of skills as well as knowledge. The greater integration of practice and academic law to provide more research into litigation processes and practice skills and knowledge as proposed in 1.29–1.31 could be of assistance.

Other lawyers as role models

Working with other lawyers is an important aspect of learning and developing legal profes- **1.66** sional skills. More experienced lawyers can provide useful role models even after the formal training contract or pupillage period. It is best to have a structured approach. Role models should be chosen carefully, and each draft or advocacy performance should be analysed, judged for its effectiveness, and considered reflectively to identify good practice to be followed and to avoid perpetuating bad practice.

Personal style

There is not one single way of conducting litigation that is effective. A significant role is **1.67** played by personal style, provided that style is based on sound practice.

I REPRESENTING A CLIENT

The importance of the client in practice

The transition to be made in becoming an effective legal practitioner is most clearly illus- **1.68** trated in the need for a practitioner to represent a client. For the academic lawyer, and for many law students, the detail and the theory of the law is the priority, and a legal problem is at the centre of most activities. For the lawyer seeking to conduct an efficient practice, the priorities in a case are the client, the client's objectives, and the client's practical position. The practising lawyer is there to identify and address the client's problem, which may turn more on points of evidence than on points of law.

Law as a service industry

1.69 Knowledge and expertise can make a lawyer appear to be the most important person in a case, but the lawyer is only there because the client needs representing. The lawyer is an agent or mouthpiece for a client. From the first interview to the end of the case it is the client's situation and the client's objectives that should dictate how a case progresses.

1.70 An understanding that legal practice is essentially a service industry is fundamental to effective litigation. The purpose of litigation is to meet a client's needs—the lawyer should not take over and the case should not develop a life of its own.

1.71 This can be a significant shift of viewpoint for someone who has spent some years enjoying the academic study of law. The point is not to fit a client into the pages of a legal textbook, but to see whether small sections of law can be of practical assistance to a real person. The shift from focussing on books and law to focussing on people and facts can be exhilarating, but it can also be unsettling.

Communicating with the client

1.72 Because the client is so important, the ability to communicate with a wide range of clients quickly and with relative ease is important to becoming an effective lawyer. The lawyer is essentially a mouthpiece for structuring and putting forward the client's arguments. All too often clients complain that their lawyer did not really understand what they said, or did not fully explain what was going on. It can be all to easy to create a negative impression on a client without meaning to do so, and confidence is easily undermined unless a proactive approach is taken to building a constructive relationship with the client. The outcome of litigation is at risk if the lawyer does not fully understand the client's case, and does not properly explain to a client how a case is progressing. For techniques in communicating with a client, see Chapter 6.

1.73 Communication needs to run right through the case. At the first meeting the solicitor must take care to discuss the facts fully rather than jumping to conclusions. A barrister meeting a client in conference must make sure the client is not intimidated and can talk freely. If the case comes to trial it may be just another day in the lives of the lawyers, but it will be a crucial day for the client, and the lawyers should talk to the client before and afterwards to explain the procedure and outcomes.

1.74 There is a great skill in explaining legal concepts to a lay client, and adapting terminology to different types of client. Some will understand legal terminology, others will not. The lawyer also needs a quick and imaginative mind to see situations from many possible angles, and to grasp new concepts quickly. There is also skill in bringing out relevant information from a client—the lawyer can rarely work only with what the client volunteers.

The importance of acting on instructions

1.75 There are some basic professional duties linked to representing a client properly, in particular acting on the client's instructions, protecting client confidentiality, and maintaining a proper professional relationship with the client. It is not for the lawyer to tell the client what to do. It is for the lawyer to provide advice, and the client then tells the lawyer what to do. The lawyer must not take decisions or act on assumptions.

The client's objectives are central to the whole case. What the client wants to achieve dic-   **1.76**
tates how the case is taken forward and what remedies are sought. If it is difficult or impossible to achieve what the client wants this must be explained with care. Every course that
might realistically help the client must be explored, but false optimism is not ultimately
useful to a client and may prove expensive if a case is lost. Options and alternatives must be
explained to the client and the client should make choices. This is further explored in
Chapter 7.

The lawyer may too easily assume that the cause of action and the remedies that are legally   **1.77**
strongest should be pursued, but this may not match with what the client really wants.
There may be complex discussions to be had and decisions to be made matching the relative
strengths of legal options with their relative importance to the client.

The lawyer who fails to obtain and act on client instructions is open to a complaint involv-   **1.78**
ing breach of professional duty. There are some particular areas where the lawyer must take
especial care in advising a client properly. In negotiating a settlement of a case the lawyer
must ensure that a proper outcome is being achieved for the client, and that the client
accepts the settlement offered. Once a settlement is reached it will be difficult or impossible
to undo it, and if a lawyer accepts a settlement that is not in the client's best interests then an
action for negligence may be possible. The difficulties of incomplete and vague settlements
in contract and divorce cases have been seen in several cases, and the courts have been
critical of lawyers who have not acted properly for their clients. It is also vital that any
settlement be based on express instructions from the client. While a lawyer has a power as
agent to negotiate for the client, there is no right to take over and tell the client what to
accept.

If the lawyer represents more than one client in a single case, equal duties are owed to all.   **1.79**
This may put the lawyer in a difficult position requiring scrupulous care, *Mortgage Express Ltd
v Bowerman and Partners* The Times, 1 August 1995.

J LEGAL PRINCIPLES AS TOOLS

Using legal principles

In a House of Lords case that is reviewing the law in a particular area, a lawyer in professional   **1.80**
practice and a professor of law may analyse and interpret law in similar ways. However the
majority of cases turn on facts and evidence as much as on law, so that a lawyer conducting
litigation is often using law as an element in litigation, rather than as a centrepiece. Chapter 9
considers the use of law by a practising lawyer.

Law students normally initially experience law as a large body of knowledge to be studied in a   **1.81**
coherent way for its own sake. This is the approach taken by most law degrees and by conversion courses for those with a first degree in a subject other than law. Legal principle can be
studied from many perspectives, including philosophical, sociological, and historical ones.
The evolution and interrelation of legal principles for a particular area may be studied, and
some details may be examined in particular depth. A course may focus on the reasons behind
and the links between legal principles. An analytical or critical perspective may be taken.

1.82   For the legal practitioner, coherent knowledge of a whole area of law remains important for specialist practice, but for the individual case law is used in a very different way. A large commercial dispute involving millions of pounds and many lawyers can easily turn on quite simple points as to what the terms of a contract were and whether they were breached.

- Only a few individual legal principles may be relevant.
- It is generally only the law as it is now that matters, not the law as it might be.
- There may be no legal issues at all—it may be necessary only to decide how the law applies to a particular set of facts.
- Legal principles are used as tools to achieve desired ends, and not as areas of interest in themselves.

Remembering legal principles

1.83   In learning law, remembering legal principles may be important and relevant to assessment. In practice, a substantial retained knowledge of legal detail is less important. In most circumstances a particular area of law can be researched for a particular case. Indeed it is important to rely on research rather than memory to ensure that one uses law that is up to date. The lawyer can check law before writing an opinion or before going to court, or with the client in the room.

1.84   In practice, retained knowledge of law is important in specific ways.

- It is important to have a general, up to date, working knowledge of the main principles of law in all the areas in which the lawyer practises so as to be able to identify legal issues quickly in an interview or conference with a client.
- It is necessary to have a thorough grasp of basic legal principles, so as to be able to identify what areas of law may be important in a case.
- It is necessary to be able to assess the relative legal strengths of different potential causes of action so as to be able to advise a client.
- Retained detailed knowledge of procedural and evidential rules is important as such knowledge may be required quickly during a trial or hearing in court.

K   TAKING A PRACTICAL APPROACH

1.85   In becoming a practising lawyer and undertaking litigation, one is choosing to offer a practical service to people with real, often serious, problems. For effective litigation it is important to have the confidence to find out what the real problems are and to wrestle with the facts of the case rather than to move too quickly to legal principle. It is the function of litigation to find a solution, and that will not always be a legal solution. It should go without saying that being practical should also involve trying to ensure that a case is dealt with in a reasonable time and at a reasonable cost.

The importance of facts

One aspect of being practical is appreciating the crucial importance of facts, together with **1.86**
the difficulties of establishing the truth of facts. In academic study the student may be
developing theoretical legal arguments on the basis of scenarios where the facts are not open
to question. In practice facts can present far more difficulties than law, with gaps and contradictions. There may be no witness, or a witness may have a poor memory, or may not be
motivated to tell the full truth. It is almost inevitably the case that the lawyers on the other
side will have been given a very different or significantly different version of the facts.
Techniques for dealing with facts as a practising lawyer are considered in Chapter 8.

Appreciation of real life situations

Another aspect of being practical is to appreciate the position that the client is in as fully as **1.87**
possible. This can be a particular problem where a client has a very different life experience
from that of the lawyer. The lack of commercial awareness amongst those entering the legal
profession has been identified as a particular problem. A new lawyer may find this a particular problem—someone who does not have a mortgage or own shares can find it difficult to
comprehend commercial financial realities. The growth of *pro bono* work linked with undergraduate law courses and legal professional training can be of great assistance in building a
practical approach, as can work experience with firms of solicitors and barristers' chambers.

Getting the full facts of the case

A further aspect of being practical is trying to get as full an understanding as possible of the **1.88**
circumstances in dispute. If a client goes to a lawyer having suffered a serious accident in a
factory then the lawyer needs to know about the geography of the factory, the manufacturing processes, what the client did and what workmates were present at the time of the
accident. Usually it will only be with that degree of factual knowledge that a legal textbook
may be relevant, though there will inevitably be some cross fertilisation between facts and law.
If the lawyer moves on to law too quickly there is a serious risk of unconsciously moulding
the facts to suit the law rather than getting to grips with the real facts.

L   WORKING WITH OTHERS

Although a lawyer may sometimes feel rather alone in conducting litigation and promoting **1.89**
and defending a client's case, even the best litigation lawyer will rarely win a case alone. An
important part of conducting litigation effectively is working productively with others.

In conducting litigation a lawyer will need to deal with the material in the case to suit **1.90**
different situations and different audiences. Being able to get points across to a range of
people may be more important than making fine legal distinctions. Very different ways of
communicating and working may be needed in dealing with a client, in dealing with an
expert witness, in dealing with the lawyers on the other side, and in dealing with a judge.
A judge may want detailed legal points. A client will often prefer reasonably clear advice to

fine distinctions. Careful judgment may be required to know what to say to each person involved in a case, and how and when to say it.

Others on the same side

1.91   It is possible for litigation to be entirely conducted by a litigant in person or by a solicitor with appropriate rights of audience. However most litigation is conducted in a team that will include a solicitor and barrister. Both are likely to have some support staff. The solicitor may have a trainee and the barrister may have a pupil. On a large case there will often be a team of staff at the solicitor's office. The lawyers will need to form an effective working relationship, in the client's interests and their own. This may happen most easily where the lawyers are used to working with each other, otherwise it may need positive attention. Divisions of work must be clearly agreed between all involved so that nothing is left out and repetition is avoided. Overall responsibility must also be clear, and may pass from the solicitor to the barrister when the barrister is briefed, and then back to the solicitor when the barrister has completed work on the brief. If the lawyers get on well they should make sure that this does not make the client feel cut out when there are conferences, or when they meet outside court.

Those on the other side

1.92   Effective litigation requires a constructive working relationship between the sides in the case. This is perhaps even more important than in the past with the 'cards on the table' approach of the Civil Procedural Rules 1998. The relationship with the lawyers on the other side should be objective and professional—the lawyers are there to assist in resolving conflict rather than to exacerbate it.

1.93   There is little point in having an antagonistic relationship with the other side, though a relationship may become strained if the other side do not conduct the litigation in a reasonably cooperative way. In most cases it will be counter-productive to be difficult or unreasonable as it is likely to cause them to be equally difficult. On the other hand, lawyers on opposing sides should not be obviously too friendly or accommodating, or the client may feel he or she is not being properly represented. This is especially important for barristers, who may well know each other in a relatively small profession—a client may resent seeing his or her barrister leaving court joking with the barrister on the other side, especially if the case has been lost!

1.94   The Civil Procedure Rules specifically support maintaining an open and constructive relationship with the other side. Pre-action protocols encourage early contact and exchange of information well before an action is commenced. In any event it is worth contacting the other side at a very early stage—exchanges before formal action can put a client's version of events in a rather different light, or may encourage settlement of the action.

The judge

1.95   If a case goes to court, the relationship between the lawyers and the judge becomes crucial. The increased use of judicial case management has made this relationship perhaps more important than it was. A well prepared and clearly presented case is always most likely to appeal to a judge. It is important to remember what the judge does and does not know about the case in advance, though the extent to which skeleton arguments etc are now available for the judge to read before a hearing or trial make this easier. The importance of using the documents that the judge is likely to read before the case to set out the key points in the case cannot be overstated.

During a trial or hearing it is important to help the judge to understand the case, with plans **1.96** and photographs if necessary, and with specific references to important parts of the evidence and to legal authorities.

M   THE TIME DIMENSION

> Sir Leicester has no objection to an interminable Chancery suit. It is a slow, expensive, British, constitutional kind of thing.
>
> Charles Dickens, *Bleak House*

The law's delays are apocryphal. Justice will rarely be achieved if it takes too long, whatever **1.97** the final judgment. Effective litigation must be timely litigation, and a client is not well served by a lawyer who is too slow and inefficient.

There is no inherent reason why a case should take a long time, as is shown by the relatively **1.98** tight timetable laid down for a fast track case. If a case that is not particularly complex is prepared properly and conducted properly it should normally be possible to complete it within months rather than years.

Problems with time

Time factors can be confusing for someone relatively new to the litigation process. There are **1.99** now quite tight timetables for cases of lower value that are allocated to the small claims or fast track route. However in the larger cases time can have an 'Alice in Wonderland' feel.

- It may be some time before a potential litigant approaches a lawyer.
- It may take a few years for a case to be formally started because the parties are collecting and exchanging information and possibly seeking to settle the action.
- The significant exchange of information now often made before an action starts under pre-action protocols, and possibilities for making pre-action applications to court, can give the impression of a case going a long way before it is formally started.
- It can seem strange that some time limits are mandatory whereas others can be changed by the agreement of the parties.
- The number of interim applications that may be made can greatly extend the length and complexity of a case.
- There may be problems in setting and keeping to trial dates if the courts are very busy or if key people fall ill.
- Progress in an action may falter while attempts at settlement are made.
- It can take time for damages to be paid and costs to be assessed after the action.

What causes delays

1.100 Some delays will occur in almost any case. It takes time to prepare a case properly, and a case should be properly prepared before it goes to trial as an appeal cannot normally be brought on the basis of information that could reasonably have been found and used in the original trial. It may quite properly take time:

- to collect evidence from witnesses, and in particular to get an expert evidence;
- to research a difficult point of law that is important to the case;
- to see how serious damage or an injury is, so that damages can be properly assessed;
- to make best use of opportunities to make pre-action and interim applications to the court;
- to try to reach a settlement.

Rules and powers relating to time

1.101 The overriding objective now provides for cases to be dealt with expeditiously, and this is backed up with the case management powers of the courts and the ability to set a timetable. There are particular stages in a case when timing is important.

- An action must be started within the limitation period, see 4.33–4.61.
- Once an action is started, the time limits for serving proceedings and for getting statements of case in place are important.
- Compliance with time frames is important for small claims and fast track cases.
- If a party fails to meet appropriate or reasonable deadlines then the court can make an 'unless' order, providing that a statement of case will be struck out if prescribed steps are not taken by a prescribed time.

1.102 Generally speaking there is rather more flexibility about the completion of the other stages in an action. While the court will set a timetable, deadlines can be extended by agreement of the parties (which should be recorded in writing) or with the consent of the court. The parties cannot interfere with dates that involve the court as well as the parties:

- the date for a case management conference;
- the date for a pre-trial review;
- the date for filing pre-trial checklists;
- the date set for a trial.

Dealing with a case expeditiously

1.103 The effective approach to dealing with time in a legal action is therefore broadly:

- to ensure that the case always moves forward as fast as is reasonably possible;
- to ensure that key dates such as the expiry of the limitation period are complied with;
- not to seek to modify any date that will affect the court without applying to the court for a change of date;
- to review a case that arrives quickly to check what stage the case has reached and what dates need to be met for certain actions;
- if an action is going to take some time it is important to consider interim measures, such as seeking an interim payment or an interim injunction.

It is not easy to give general guidance as to how long a case should take. Much will depend **1.104** on how long it takes a client to go to a lawyer in the first place and how difficult it is to gather information and evidence. Much will also depend on whether there are a large number of interim applications while the case is prepared for trial, and whether there are significant delays for attempts to settle. In very broad terms, a case that is not very valuable or complex can be determined through fast track procedure in less than a year from the time that the claim form is issued. Unless there is a settlement a multi track case will often take longer than this, though if both parties are proceeding in an efficient way there is no inherent need for it to take substantially longer than this. For a time frame for a fast track case see 4.90.

Only the most complex case should take several years to reach resolution. If there is a serious **1.105** accident with difficulties assessing the seriousness of injuries and collecting evidence the claim form may only be issued just before the limitation period expires (three years from the accident). Interim applications and attempts to settle can mean that the case is not determined for another two to three years. A complex and high value contract case that is hotly contested and where financial loss is difficult to assess would have to be started within the limitation period of six years, and could then again take at least two years to reach final resolution.

N   THE COSTS DIMENSION

> The lawyers have twisted it into such a state of bedevilment that the original merits of the case have long disappeared from the face of the earth. It's about a Will, and the trusts under a Will—or it was once. It's about nothing but Costs now.
>
> Charles Dickens, *Bleak House*

The cost of litigation is equally apocryphal. Those entering the legal profession may not be **1.106** strongly motivated to learn about costs—the whole area can seem complex and uninteresting. Having said that, the lawyer will be interested in ensuring that she or he gets paid, and achieving the client's objectives at a reasonable cost is a basic element of effective litigation. This area is dealt with more fully in Chapter 5.

Problems with costs

There are many reasons why problems arise with regard to costs. **1.107**

- Litigation is inevitably expensive with the costs of lawyers, experts, witnesses etc.
- It can be very difficult to forecast the likely cost of a case accurately, making it difficult for a client to take a sensible decision about whether a case should be brought.
- In some jurisdictions such as North America each side in litigation bears their own costs. In England and Wales the loser is normally ordered to pay the winner's costs. This can be a fair way of ensuring that a claimant is properly compensated, but on the other hand an unsuccessful litigant faces paying the costs of both sides.
- The lawyer can easily see costs as a subsidiary issue, but accumulating costs can become as important as the progress of the litigation for the client who is having to bear costs as they arise.

- Conversely, a lawyer may be concerned about accumulating costs where the lawyer may not be reimbursed if he or she is working under a conditional fee agreement.
- The assessment of costs has become an industry in its own right.
- If one is not entirely confident about the case it can be embarrassing to talk about costs to the client.

1.108 It can be very difficult for people of moderate means to litigate. The government funds legal aid and the Community Legal Service at a cost of about £2 billion a year, which is generous compared to many countries. However over recent years fewer people have qualified for assistance, and rates of pay for lawyers have become so low that some have ceased to provide such work. This is partly because more of the budget is required to fund assistance in criminal cases, especially some high cost ones. Money has become focussed on Citizen's Advice Bureaux and law centres, and contracts for particular areas. Some advice work is done by non-lawyers, and there has been a growth in online advice through www.clsdirect.org.uk run by the Community Legal Service.

The basic model for the costs of litigation

1.109 The basic model for litigation is that the client initially retains a solicitor. The solicitor retained must provide the client with written information about how costs will be charged, and there must be an agreement as to how costs will be paid. The solicitor may charge a flat fee for the case or may charge an hourly rate for time spent (the rate depending on the experience of the lawyer). As litigation may take some time, the solicitor may not wish to wait to the end of the case to be paid, and may ask for staged payments as the action progresses. See 5.10–5.13 for more detail.

1.110 If the case requires specialist legal advice then the solicitor and client may agree that a barrister be briefed. Normally the barrister will work on the basis of a separate fee for each brief, charging a separate fee for writing an opinion, drafting a statement of case, making an interim application to court or appearing at trial. The fees will be higher for more experienced barristers. Brief fees are normally negotiated between the solicitor and the barrister's clerk or chambers manager. They will need to be paid once the work on the brief has been completed.

1.111 There are a number of alternatives to costs being paid personally by the client.

- If the client has insurance to cover legal fees the insurer may pay.
- If the client is a member of a relevant body such as a trade union, that body may cover costs, but again this must be specifically checked
- A conditional fee agreement may be put in place. Such an agreement will provide for the costs to be met from damages, but in the meantime the lawyer will bear out of pocket costs and will not be paid (see 5.26–5.37).
- If the client has limited resources the Community Legal Service may meet the costs, but only with advance authorisation.

1.112 It is very difficult to give general guidance about the likely cost of litigation. Even cases that on their facts are broadly similar can lead to very different cost bills with a few differences in how they are conducted. Once lawyers are involved in a case the costs even for a small claim are likely to be at least a few hundred pounds. The costs in a fast track case can easily run into thousands, and the costs in a multi-track case can run into tens of thousands of pounds. In the most serious cases costs can be hundreds of thousands of pounds.

Rules and powers relating to costs

The importance of costs is reflected in some of the provisions in the Civil Procedure Rules **1.113** 1998. The overriding objective includes the need to save expense. The need for lawyers to deal with costs responsibly is also reflected in some of the provisions of the legal professional Codes of Conduct. The Solicitors' Practice Rules require solicitors to provide clients with client care letters which provide information about costs. This is supported by the Solicitors' Costs Information and Client Care Code, which requires solicitors to consider funding options suited to client needs.

The party who incurs costs will be liable to pay them unless and until there is an order to any **1.114** other effect. The main options are:

- an order as to costs may be made at the end of interim hearings as the case progresses. Such an order may provide for immediate payment or may set out provisions to be taken into account when an overall order is made at the end of the case (see 5.62–5.78);
- At the end of the case the court can make an order for costs. Normally the loser will be ordered to pay the winner's costs (though there is a discretion depending on the circumstances of the case and the order will not necessarily cover everything that has been spent) (see 5.45–5.61).

Dealing with costs effectively

The costs of an action may be a crucial factor for a client. A client who is paying costs **1.115** personally will be concerned as costs accumulate, and may have concerns about being able to pay the costs. The possibility of reimbursement if the case is won may seem very distant. The accumulation of costs may be a key factor in deciding to negotiate.

The good lawyer will not only be aware of this but will be open with information, and **1.116** proactive in raising and addressing costs issues. Costs issues will arise constantly throughout litigation. A particular piece of evidence might be useful, but does its potential value justify its likely cost? The lawyer must be broadly familiar with the main elements in costs bills, the main ways in which litigation can be funded, and the sorts of orders that a court can make with regard to costs.

The ways in which costs may accumulate, and the ways in which costs may be kept down, **1.117** are dealt with more fully at 5.10–5.18. As part of monitoring the effect of costs, the likely damages will need to be assessed at an early stage and regularly balanced against the likely costs. The options for making an offer to settle should also be regularly reviewed (see 20.13–20.15 and 20.23–20.35).

O   LAW AS A BUSINESS

1.118   Those choosing to enter the legal profession may well be interested in the law itself. In practice law will not always be the prime concern. Those who offer legal advice professionally will have to ensure in one way or another that they can offer advice on a basis that is commercially viable. Business needs have led, for example, to an increase in the size of chambers and firms, and to changes in the way that litigation is supported. Costs issues can be as important to the lawyer as to the client. The client who comes to a lawyer for assistance in conducting litigation is effectively buying a service—a basic commercial transaction.

1.119   In a firm of solicitors, litigation is likely to be organised as a separate department. There is likely to be a firm-wide system for the use of document pro formas, and a firm-wide system for supporting legal research. In a large firm a team of lawyers may be assigned to a case and tasks will be assigned to different members of the team. Only a few members of the team may be involved in meeting the client or going to court. This has implications for how litigation will be conducted.

1.120   In barristers' chambers each barrister will work individually on a case (unless, for example, a silk and a junior are retained). The barrister is also likely to be briefed to deal with only one stage of a case at a time. Increasingly there will be chambers-wide systems for dealing with pro formas, but barristers are more likely to be working alone. Each barrister is running a one-person business, as well as forming a part of the business of running the chambers.

1.121   Business implications are beyond the scope of this book, but cannot be ignored because of the potential impact on litigation work.

- Ensuring how the costs of a case will be met is important, as if costs are not paid there will be a significant loss.
- Where work is taken on a conditional fee basis there will always be a risk of loss if the case is not won, so the risks of conditional fee cases must be carefully assessed.
- It must be possible to justify the fees charged to clients, so, for example, solicitors will need to keep careful records of time spent on working for a client through a system for 'billable hours'. As litigation work may be done in small sections over a long time, keeping such records can be burdensome. Barristers should keep similar records of time spent and tasks performed in order to be able to justify fees.
- It may be important to consider the possibility of future work—a barrister may wish to be briefed again by a solicitor and a solicitor may wish to be used to conduct future litigation.
- There will be various pressures within firms or chambers relating to negotiating and collecting fees.
- Steps taken in a case may not be governed solely by legal principles but need to be seen in terms of a cost/benefit analysis.
- There are some senses in which the client needs to be seen as 'the customer', who should know what service they are buying and how much it is likely to cost.

1.122   There is no escape from the business context. The big city firm may feel pressures of competition from other firms that might take work. The High Street law firm working in the context of community legal service funding and conditional fee arrangements can find it difficult to maintain income and to deal with clients who cannot easily afford legal fees. The Law Centre can find it difficult to attract and maintain sources of funding.

P   THE PUBLIC IMAGE OF LAWYERS

> What have you got if you have a lawyer buried up to his neck in sand?
> Not enough sand!
>
> How many lawyers does it take to stop a moving bus?
> Never enough!
>
> What do you call 100 lawyers at the bottom of the ocean?
> A good start.
>
> Why have scientists started using lawyers for laboratory experiments?
> They get too attached to the rats.
>
> The first thing we do, let's kill all the lawyers.
> Shakespeare, *Henry V Part 2*

Jokes about lawyers have become very widespread, particularly in the United States, where a **1.123** number of firms of lawyers and law schools have their own web pages devoted to jokes. Doing an internet search for lawyer jokes can easily distract one from doing anything effective for a whole morning.

That many of these jokes were actually created by lawyers shows healthy self-awareness. The **1.124** fact that many of the jokes are quite savagely negative about the value of lawyers, and the fact that the negative image goes right back through Dickens to Shakespeare should be worrying. Lawyers may have a better image in this jurisdiction than they do in the United States, but there is still the tendency for the press to be negative with stories of 'fat cat' incomes. This should be a matter of concern to those entering the profession.

There is no doubt research to be done into why lawyers tend to be unpopular, and into how **1.125** unpopular they really are, but basic reasons are not difficult to find. Most people only go to see a lawyer if something unpleasant has happened in their lives—such as a death, a serious accident, or the breakdown of their marriage—and it is not surprising that negative feelings about events may attach to the lawyer. Some clients have unrealistic expectations for what any lawyer could achieve in a certain situation and they are inevitably disappointed. There are concerns about the costs and delays of the law. Even where a lawyer wins a case for a client, the client would probably rather not have had to litigate the matter in the first place.

An awareness of the views that a client may hold of lawyers and the possible reasons for **1.126** those views may assist a lawyer in dealing constructively with a client. This is not only important with individual relationships—addressing negative perceptions about lawyers can also assist the profession as a whole, not least at a time when much change is in the air.

Lawyers are unlikely to become popular—it is difficult, but possibly amusing, to consider **1.127** what campaign a marketing or PR firm might run. However there is a positive image to be conveyed. Many lawyers are very committed to doing their best for a client, and many lawyers work very hard for relatively modest rewards.

1.128   Perhaps the realistic targets relate to convincing clients and the public that lawyers do provide a good service. Sometimes litigation is inevitable, and the client should ideally feel that their experience of going to a lawyer has been as fair and reasonable as was realistically possible. Efficiency and reasonable cost are important factors. Some delays are inevitable but they should be kept to a minimum; legal advice and litigation are not cheap but openness about costs and the chances that an action may not succeed should enable the client to make informed decisions. The client should also be convinced that the lawyer understands the case, and that the case is being properly promoted through the collection of evidence and applications to court.

1.129   There are some purposes for which humour is a positive force in legal practice—where humour encapsulates a key point, focusses on the real rather than the pompous, or shows spirit in the face of adversity. Some humour used for some of these purposes is included in this book.

2

THE ROLES OF LEGAL PRACTITIONERS

A THE DIFFERENT TYPES OF LEGAL PRACTITIONER 2.01

B THE ROLE OF A SOLICITOR 2.08

C THE ROLE OF A BARRISTER 2.12
    Reasons for briefing a barrister 2.13
    Effective working relations between barristers and solicitors 2.15

D DIRECT ACCESS TO BARRISTERS 2.19
    BarDIRECT 2.20
    Public direct access 2.21

E PARALEGALS 2.24

F BRIEFING A BARRISTER 2.26
    The nature of a brief 2.26
    Acceptance of a brief 2.32
    Briefing more than one barrister 2.36
    The contents of a brief 2.39

G WRITING INSTRUCTIONS FOR A BARRISTER 2.41
    Prescribing the work to be done 2.41
    The contents of instructions 2.43

H THE CONTENTS OF A BRIEF 2.45
    Documents to include in a brief 2.45
    The backsheet 2.50

I WORKING ON A BRIEF 2.52
    On receipt of a brief 2.53
    Reading a brief strategically 2.56
    Dealing with missing information 2.59
    Next steps 2.61

Equity sends questions to Law. Law sends questions back to Equity; Law finds it can't do this, Equity finds it can't do that; neither can so much as say it can't do anything, without this solicitor instructing and this counsel appearing for A, and that solicitor instructing and that counsel appearing for B.

Charles Dickens, *Bleak House*

A   THE DIFFERENT TYPES OF LEGAL PRACTITIONER

2.01   While it is possible for litigation to be conducted by a litigant in person without a lawyer, litigation is normally conducted with appropriate assistance from those with legal professional qualifications.

2.02   In some jurisdictions the same lawyer can perform all functions in the litigation process, though in practice sometimes specialising in particular parts of the process. In England and Wales specialisation is built into professional structures with separate professional regulation for solicitors (who have traditionally focussed primarily on non-contentious transactions and on advice leading up to and supporting litigation) and for barristers (who have traditionally performed the role of specialists in advocacy and referral work). This division is enshrined in separate professional bodies, with the Bar Council for England and Wales governing the work of barristers and the Law Society of England and Wales governing the work of solicitors. This professional regulation is partly within a statutory framework set by the Courts and Legal Services Act 1990.

2.03   The distinctions between the different branches of the profession have been somewhat eroded over recent years. It has become possible for solicitors to obtain higher rights of audience so as to be able to act as advocates in a fuller range of cases, through legislation and amendments to the Code of Conduct. Direct access to barristers has been opened up in appropriate circumstances where a professional client does not necessarily need a solicitor as an intermediary. It has become more common for barristers to re-qualify as solicitors, and some firms of solicitors employ former barristers to perform litigation work.

2.04   There are a number of key remaining differences between barristers and solicitors.

- Only a solicitor or a litigant in person is authorised to commence and conduct litigation under the Courts and Legal Services Act 1990. This means that a solicitor can file documents at court, issue proceedings, acknowledge service, issue applications, and carry on correspondence with the other side in litigation, but a barrister cannot.
- Under code of conduct rules, only a solicitor should normally carry out functions associated directly with the preparation of the case for court, such as taking proofs of evidence from witnesses. The barrister should not normally see witnesses other than the client or an expert witness.
- A solicitor can hold client funds in a client account but a barrister cannot.
- A barrister has wider rights of audience on qualification, relatively few solicitors having taken up higher rights of audience.

2.05   There is a separate professional structure for Legal Executives. There has also been a significant growth in training for paralegals (who support particular legal processes), and for advisers in specialist legal areas such as immigration.

2.06   Professional regulation and the distinctions between different types of legal practitioners continue to be the subject of review and change. In particular the Clementi Review of the regulation of the legal profession is reviewing the governance of the legal profession.

2.07   This chapter takes an overview of the distinctions between the roles of different types of legal practitioner in the litigation process. As the distinctions between different types of legal practitioner have been eroded the book generally refers to 'the lawyer', but it remains the norm in England and Wales that a client will initially approach a solicitor, who may then brief a barrister to seek specialist advice, or to carry out key functions such as drafting statements of case or appearing in court if litigation proceeds.

B   THE ROLE OF A SOLICITOR

The client will normally initially make contact with a solicitor, and the solicitor will remain   **2.08** the lawyer who has direct contact with the client. The solicitor will gather information and instructions from the client and will deal with the client on a day to day basis. The solicitor will keep files on the progress of the case, and will keep track of the costs. It is the solicitor who collects evidence to support the case and deals with potential witnesses. If an action is started it is the solicitor who files the claim form and the statements of case, and who deals directly with the court.

A solicitor may deal with applications at an interim stage, or may deal with the whole case in   **2.09** a county court. If the decision is taken to instruct a barrister (see below) then it is the role of the solicitor to write the brief and to provide relevant supporting papers. If a barrister has been briefed then the barrister may give directions to the solicitor as regards the conduct of the case, though normally the lawyers will work as a team.

Unless the client is acting as a litigant in person, the name of the solicitors acting in the case   **2.10** should appear on the court papers. A client may choose to change his or her solicitors, in which case there are requirements relevant to the payment of fees and the handing over of papers, and see CPR Part 42 Change of solicitor and PD 42 Change of solicitor.

For more material on the role of a solicitor in a case see www.lawsociety.org.uk and Law   **2.11** Society, *Guide to the Professional Conduct of Solicitors* (8th edn, 1999 as amended)

C   THE ROLE OF A BARRISTER

A barrister will normally become involved in a case on the basis of being instructed by a   **2.12** solicitor to carry out a particular task in a case. The instructions from the solicitor to the barrister will be provided in the form of a written brief. Normally a barrister is only briefed to deal with a particular stage of a case at a time, such as to provide an opinion or to appear at a hearing, though the same barrister may be briefed to do more than one thing at the same time.

Reasons for briefing a barrister

The main reasons why a solicitor may choose to instruct a barrister in a case are: **2.13**

- the solicitor may want specialist advice because the case involves legal complexities in a specialist area of law;

- the size and complexity of the case might mean that specialist consultant advice is appropriate;
- the case is to go for trial in a court where the solicitor has no right of audience;
- if the solicitor feels that a case is quite likely to result in High Court litigation, the solicitor may well want to involve the barrister who is eventually likely to act as an advocate in the case at an early stage to ensure the coherent development of the case;
- the solicitor may want an opinion on a particular point if the case is outside the normal work done by the solicitor, or if the point is a difficult one and the solicitor feels that counsel's opinion should be sought to provide support for a particular course of action;
- many firms specialise in non-contentious work, and brief barristers for contentious work as a matter of normal practice;
- if the client wishes to instruct a barrister to get a specialist opinion;
- as the overheads of a solicitor's office tend to be higher than those for a set of chambers, in costs terms it can be cheaper to brief a barrister than to send a solicitor to deal with a particular matter in court;
- briefing a barrister may be partly a tactical move in showing how seriously the case is being taken;
- someone who is not actually a party to a court case may still have an interest in what is said and the outcome, and a barrister may be given a noting or watching brief to sit in court to take a note of the legal arguments and evidence. Since the client is not a party to the action the barrister will not take a part in the proceedings but just note their implications.

2.14   For more material on the role of a barrister in a case see www.barcouncil.org.uk and Bar Council, *Code of Conduct of the Bar of England and Wales* (7th edn, 2000 as amended)

Effective working relations between barristers and solicitors

2.15   A barrister who has been briefed to deal with a matter must act within the instructions of the solicitor (the professional client) and the client (the lay client). The brief should be prepared with care to make the barrister's task clear.

2.16   Where a barrister has been briefed, the solicitor will continue to deal with other aspects of the case such as communicating with the client and filing papers with the court. It is important that the relationship between the barrister and the solicitor works effectively, and this is best maintained through good communication.

2.17   The barrister should keep the solicitor fully informed as to when an opinion or draft is likely to be available. When the barrister has completed a piece of work as instructed the outcome should be marked on the backsheet and the whole brief returned to the solicitor.

2.18   While continuity in dealing with a case is important, and the same barrister may be briefed to carry out different stages in a case, it is also possible that different barristers will be briefed to deal with different parts of a case. For example one barrister may be briefed to deal with an interim application, and another barrister may be briefed when the case goes to trial.

D DIRECT ACCESS TO BARRISTERS

Until only a few years ago a barrister could only act in a case when briefed by a solicitor. **2.19**
There are now two exceptions that are both governed by professional conduct rules. Outside
these exceptions it remains the case that a barrister must be briefed by a solicitor.

BarDIRECT

It is now possible for a barrister to act for clients without a solicitor under the BarDIRECT **2.20**
Rules and Recognition Regulations (see Annex F of the Bar Code of Conduct). This exception
is designed primarily to provide for members of professional bodies who might appropriately seek an opinion from a barrister without a practical need for a solicitor. The bodies that
have been approved for direct access include accountants and taxation advisers, architects,
surveyors, engineers, valuers, actuaries, chartered secretaries, and insurers. BarDIRECT Terms
of Engagement and Information Packs for barristers and clients are provided by the Bar
Council.

Public direct access

New rules for direct access to barristers came into force on 6 July 2004. The change is **2.21**
intended to provide a wider service for clients rather than make changes in the work of the
barrister. Details can be found on the Bar Council website, but in summary a barrister who
has been in practice for at least three years after pupillage can now undertake work on the
direct instructions of a lay client without the need for a solicitor, provided he or she has
attended a designated training course, and notified the Bar Council and the professional
insurer of the intention to undertake such work.

It remains the case that a barrister cannot conduct litigation by issuing proceedings or **2.22**
writing to the other side, so a solicitor will normally be required to conduct litigation unless
the client acts as a litigant in person. The result in general terms is that a barrister could take
direct access work that, for example, sought an opinion, but not direct access work relating
to advocacy and active litigation. If a barrister accepts direct access work the position
should be kept under review in case direct access should become inappropriate, or the
appointment of a solicitor is advisable. Some areas of criminal, family, and immigration
work are prohibited for direct access.

Direct access is backed up with detailed professional conduct rules and guidance with which **2.23**
the barrister must be fully familiar, and which should be appropriately explained to the
client. In direct access cases the relationship with the client will be different from a case
where a solicitor is involved and the position needs to be clearly explained and understood.
The terms of the agreement with the client must be clear. The Bar Council provides a draft
client care letter. Individual arrangements will need to be made for fee collection. The relationship with the client should be properly and fully documented so that any complaints
can be addressed

E   PARALEGALS

2.24   There are a variety of ways in which the traditional professions of solicitor and barrister are now supported or partly paralleled by paralegals. A paralegal working for a law firm may carry out a specific support role, for example carrying out research or collecting evidence. In such a case the paralegal is subject to the supervision of the employer

2.25   Alternatively a paralegal may offer advice to a client in a specific area such as immigration law, though the paralegal would not be able to conduct litigation and would need to advise the client to instruct a solicitor or to conduct litigation in person if litigation became necessary. There is much blurring of distinctions in law centres and advice centres, but it remains the case that only a barrister or solicitor properly instructed can act as a solicitor or barrister in litigation.

F   BRIEFING A BARRISTER

The nature of a brief

2.26   A barrister can only act in relation to a case if he or she has a brief. The brief is not a formal contract or agreement between the solicitor and the barrister—the solicitor does not employ the barrister—but the contents of the brief are the basis of the work to be done and the barrister should only act on those contents and within the instructions given. Note however, that it is possible for a barrister to enter a contract to provide services, Courts and Legal Services Act 1990, s 61. A barrister can represent more than one client in a case, so long as there is no conflict of interest or substantial difference in the case of each.

2.27   It is not possible for a barrister to act under any general agreement to give advice to a particular solicitor or client whenever necessary—there should be a separate brief for each case as and when it arises, though there may be a retainer to act for a client provided there are separate briefs for each case.

2.28   A decision to brief a barrister should be carefully timed. It should be sufficiently early for the barrister to give proper consideration to the case, but the brief should not be sent until sufficient information is available for the barrister to take a properly informed view. If the brief is sent off without the right documents there will still be a delay while the barrister asks for them. On the other hand if there is real urgency, the solicitor may telephone the barrister for advice, and send the brief on later.

2.29   Selection of the barrister should be a decision of the client and solicitor, normally based on the advice of the solicitor. An established firm of solicitors will regularly brief the same barristers or the same set of chambers, which is advantageous to all in building up a working relationship. Numerous guides to lawyers specialising in particular areas of work are available in hardcopy and electronically, and many chambers provide brochures or information on their websites.

2.30   A barrister will normally be paid an agreed lump sum as a fee for each brief. The fee will depend on the nature of the brief and the experience of the barrister, and will normally be negotiated by the barrister's clerk or practice manager. There must be a separate fee for each brief, not a fixed fee for several briefs. If a barrister often does work for the same client or solicitors there must still be a separate fee for each brief. The fee should be marked on the brief, though it is possible for the barrister to waive all or part of the fee.

The fee agreed covers all the work to be done under the brief, that is reading it and drafting any **2.31** documents necessary as a result of instructions (*Loveday v Renton (No 2)* [1992] 3 All ER 184). The fee may only be altered by specific agreement between the clerk and the solicitors, for example if the brief turns out to need much more work than was expected. If the brief is for the conduct of a trial that may go on for some days it is normal for there to be daily 'refreshers' with an additional sum paid for each day of the hearing. The fee agreed will normally be payable even if the case settles. If the solicitor is working on a conditional fee agreement then a further conditional fee agreement will need to be negotiated for the barrister.

Acceptance of a brief

There are some specific provisions in the Code of Conduct for the Bar of England and Wales **2.32** relating to the circumstances in which a barrister should accept a brief. The 'taxi rank' principle is intended to ensure that there should be equal access to justice, with no one seeking legal representation unable to get it. The principle is that a barrister, like a taxi driver, should accept any customer who reasonably requires his or her services, and should not pick and choose clients on the basis of personal preference. A barrister should normally accept any brief in the courts in which he or she normally practises that concerns any type of work he or she normally does, and for which he or she is offered a fair fee, as provided by rules 209 and 501 of the Code of Conduct of the Bar. The taxi rank principle has been undermined in recent years by problems with public funding for legal cases in areas such as family work, and by conditional fee agreements that are based on an assessment of the case.

A barrister should not undertake any task which he or she does not have adequate time and **2.33** opportunity to prepare for or perform. If a barrister receives a brief or instructions which he or she believes to be beyond his or her competence the brief should be declined. Annex H of the Code of Conduct provides more generally that a barrister should not accept a brief in any matter if he or she would be embarrassed in the discharge of his or her duties as a barrister by doing so, and that a barrister should not appear in a case in which he or she has a personal interest. A barrister is justified in refusing a brief if there is a conflict of interest. A barrister is not obliged to accept a brief if he or she has already advised another person in connection with the same matter. If it becomes clear that there will be a problem after the brief has been accepted the solicitor should be informed immediately.

There may be a change of barrister at the request of the client, but a barrister who has **2.34** accepted a brief is bound as a matter of professional duty to do the work requested. There are only limited circumstances in which the brief may be returned. If the barrister gives strong advice to the client on the way that the case should be conducted which the client refuses to accept, then the barrister can tell the client that in those circumstances he or she does not feel it is possible to go on representing him, though this should only be done as a last resort in an extreme case. In a criminal case, if the client admits guilt to the barrister then the barrister cannot go on defending him on a plea of not guilty but must return the brief if the client does not choose to plead guilty. The analogy in a civil case is that the lawyer should not be personally involved in misleading the court, and therefore should not present the case on a basis she or he knows to be false.

2.35   The move to fixed dates for trials has made it less likely that a barrister will need to return a brief due to not being available for a court hearing. Any return of a brief at a late stage should be avoided as client confidence may be undermined. The Bar has made it clear that a barrister has a duty to do everything possible to avoid having to return a brief at a late stage—if it becomes clear this may be necessary the situation should be explained to the solicitor, and all efforts should be made to find a suitable replacement barrister. If the replacement comes from the same chambers it should be possible to discuss the case with the person who has had to return the brief. A barrister should especially try to avoid return-ing a brief in a case where he or she has already met and advised the client in conference, and should of course never return a brief for social reasons. For all these rules, see rule 506 of the Code of Conduct of the Bar.

Briefing more than one barrister

2.36   A Queen's Counsel or silk should only be briefed in addition to a junior barrister in appropriate circumstances, when the complexity or value of the case merits it. The cost of employing a silk in the magistrates' court will need to be justified (*Hunt v East Dorset Health Authority* [1992] 2 All ER 539). In a complex high value case a silk may be assisted by more than one junior.

2.37   Each barrister in a case must have a separate brief. There must be a separate fee for every barrister instructed in the case, but each fee is agreed separately, and there is no longer a rule that a junior should necessarily be paid two-thirds of the fee paid to the leader; it will depend on the amount of work done by each.

2.38   Sometimes a pupil will do 'devilling' work on a brief sent to a more senior member of chambers. In such a case the senior member of chambers will be responsible for the work done.

The contents of a brief

2.39   A brief normally consists of the following, though instructions can be sent without other papers if appropriate if, for example, the solicitor is asking for advice on a specific legal point.

- Instructions, which set out what the barrister is asked to do, see 2.43.
- Copies of statements of case, if a claim form has been issued.
- Documents relevant to the case that the solicitor has collected, see 2.45.
- Written statements of evidence. Early in the case these will be informal proofs taken from the client or witness by the solicitor. Later in the case these will be replaced by copies of the formal witness statements.

2.40   There are distinctions to be made between the papers enclosed in a brief. Any statements of case and formal witness statements are likely to have been revealed to the other side through normal procedural steps, depending on the stage the case has reached. The instructions and informal statements from witnesses will only be known to the client and his or her lawyers. Such distinctions must be taken into account in offering advice.

G WRITING INSTRUCTIONS FOR A BARRISTER

Prescribing the work to be done

The main tasks that a barrister may be instructed to carry out are: **2.41**

- To write an opinion on a case. An opinion may be sought at any stage in a case, and may be a general opinion on all the aspects of the case or may be limited to a specific issue, see Chapter 11.
- To write an opinion on a specific matter, such as the evidence in a case or the quantum of damages.
- To draft a statement of case. A solicitor may draft statements of case, but counsel may be instructed. If it is likely that a barrister will be instructed to conduct the case in court or to try to settle it, it is preferable for the barrister to draft the statements of case as they frame the case, see Chapter 12.
- To hold a conference with the client. The solicitor will meet the client in the first instance and take an informal statement of facts or proof of evidence from the client. It is normal for this to be sent to the barrister as part of a brief. However the barrister may meet the client in conference if the client wants such a meeting, or if the barrister wants to meet the client to get more information about the case, and about what the client hopes to achieve, see Chapter 6.
- To appear at an interim hearing. A solicitor can deal with interim stages, but a barrister may be briefed to appear for an important or contentious hearing, such as an application for an interim injunction. The barrister who will conduct the case at trial will be expected to appear for a pre-trial review, see Chapter 16.
- To try to negotiate a settlement. A solicitor may handle all negotiations on a case, or may brief a barrister to carry out a negotiation, especially if the negotiation is particularly likely to require skills akin to advocacy, or if there is merit in the negotiation being handled by someone other than the solicitor with normal conduct of the case. A barrister may be briefed to seek a negotiated settlement immediately prior to appearing in court on a matter, see Chapter 20.
- To advocate a case at trial. If a case goes to trial in the High Court it remains the norm that a barrister will be briefed to advocate the case, see Chapter 21.
- To advise on the possibility of an appeal. If a client wishes to appeal the barrister who had conduct of the case at trial will often be retained, though the client may choose a different barrister.

Some of these tasks fall to be performed at a particular stage in the case, but others will vary **2.42** depending on the stage the case has reached. For example an opinion on the merits of a case may be sought at a very early stage, or to review evidence and possibilities for settlement shortly before trial. A barrister may be asked to try to settle a case before a claim form has been issued, or shortly before trial. The material available and the task involved will vary significantly with the stage the case has reached.

The contents of instructions

2.43   The writing of the instructions from the solicitor to the barrister is an important art. The work the barrister is asked to do for the solicitor and the client is defined by the instructions. In a very simple case it may be sufficient to give brief instructions along the lines of 'Counsel is requested to advise our client Mrs X in this case', but normally the instructions will need to be more detailed. There are no binding rules for the writing of instructions, and in practice they vary considerably in length, content, and style. If a solicitor has any concerns about the course to take where professional negligence might be claimed if something is not done properly then the solicitor may want advice from counsel to assist in defending such an action—if so the point on which counsel's advice is sought should be set out clearly.

2.44   The main contents of a good set of instructions will normally be:

- A brief summary of the context in which advice is sought so that the barrister can immediately see what the case is about. This might include a brief summary of key facts.
- A clear statement of precisely what the barrister is asked to do with regard to the case, for example 'Counsel is asked to advise on liability, and who should be joined as defendant should an action prove necessary. Counsel is also asked to give general advice on damages, including whether the client's loss of earnings will be recoverable. Counsel is not asked to draft particulars of claim at this stage'.
- Any specific queries that the solicitor or client has should be set out clearly, for example 'Counsel is asked to advise whether an interim injunction should be sought'.
- A summary of any provisional views that the solicitor has formed with regard to the case may be included, together with any particular steps or arguments that the solicitor thinks appropriate. If the solicitor has given provisional advice to the client it is useful to summarise this so that the barrister can agree, or give reasons for any disagreement.
- Any special points about the case should be clearly brought to the attention of the barrister, if, for example, the limitation period will expire soon or there is some other need for special urgency.
- A list of the contents of the brief, normally put at the beginning or end of the instructions and beginning with 'Counsel has herewith . . .'. This helps the solicitor in checking that the appropriate documents have been included, and is a useful guide for the barrister starting to read the brief.
- It may be useful to make references to the documents contained in the brief to show their relevance.

H   THE CONTENTS OF A BRIEF

Documents to include in a brief

2.45   The barrister will need relevant documents to be able to provide sound advice. For effective litigation the preparation of a brief is not just a matter of collecting together all the papers that are available. The brief should only include relevant documents, and as many relevant documents as can reasonably be collected at that stage in the case. If care is not given to the inclusion and order of documents, the barrister will inevitably have to spend a lot longer sorting out what is in the brief, and perhaps waiting while further documents are obtained.

The documents needed in a brief will vary with every case, but as a general guide, the **2.46** following types of information may be included:

- Any existing statements of case.
- Any other document which is central to the case, such as a contract, deed, or will. A solicitor may just write out the relevant clauses of the document in the instructions, but although this may be sufficient, it is better to send the whole document so that the barrister can check if there are any other relevant clauses.
- A statement of facts or proof of evidence from the client, especially where there is an important issue of fact, such as how an accident occurred. The solicitor may summarise what the client says in the instructions, but it is normally better to send a document setting out what the client says that has been prepared by the client or as a result of a meeting between the solicitor and the client.
- A map or plan should be included if relevant, for example in a road traffic accident or a boundary dispute.
- Photographs of a location or a physical object may be included if directly relevant.
- A proof of evidence from any relevant witness that is available when the brief is prepared.
- Any existing correspondence with the other side which is directly relevant to the task the barrister is asked to perform (though not normally a full file of correspondence—the view of the other side may be summarised in the instructions).

Careful judgment is required to send what is most relevant and to send sufficient material **2.47** while not sending too much. If there are piles of documents or correspondence of limited relevance then the solicitor should consider carefully what really needs to be sent. If an important document is not immediately available then the reason why this is the case and the steps that have been made to find it should be set out in the instructions.

The papers sent in a brief are normally subject to privilege see 3.61–3.76. The contents **2.48** should not be revealed to anyone unless this is necessary for the proper discharge of the duties of the barrister and with the prior consent of the client.

However important information is, it will not necessarily be possible to include it in a brief: **2.49**

- In purely practical terms it may be difficult to gather together all the relevant documents at an early stage in a case.
- Some information may not be available because it is held by the other side and will only be available on disclosure.
- It may take time for a document to be found, so it may be best to send the brief with that document to follow.
- Some information may only be available at a significant cost, and the expense may not be justified in terms of the value of the case.
- Some information may be relevant but not available from any source, for example because no witnesses have been found.
- The solicitor may take the view that it is more efficient for the barrister to say what information is required for the barrister to give an opinion than for the solicitor to collect information that may or may not be relevant.

The backsheet

2.50 To complete a brief, the documents are collected together, with the instructions at the front, and a backsheet is either folded round them or placed on top, with the papers all being tied together with pink tape. The backsheet for the brief should as a matter of practice have certain information recorded on it:

- The name of the case. If the case has not yet begun this will just be a simple 'In the matter of Mrs Jones' or 'Re Mr Smith', that is the name of the client. If the case has begun the full title should be given, the court the case is in, the number of the case, and the names of the parties set out as on the claim form.
- The name of the barrister briefed and the address of chambers.
- The type of Instructions to Counsel. The instructions should specify basically what counsel is being asked to do, for example 'Instructions to counsel to advise'.
- The name and address of instructing solicitors.
- The brief fee must be agreed and written on the brief before the barrister goes into court, to show that the fee does not depend on the outcome of the case.

2.51 The backsheet should be used as appropriate for certain formal purposes:

- Once the case is finished, or the piece of work requested in the instructions is done, the barrister will endorse the brief to this effect and return it to the solicitor. The brief is endorsed by making a mark through the title and writing the date when the work was completed, with counsel's signature.
- A short summary of the outcome of the case may also be noted on the backsheet.
- The backsheet can also be used to record in writing any special instructions given by the client. It is useful to do this and to get the client to sign the instruction if the client gives instructions against counsel's advice.
- The backsheet can be used to record simple terms of an agreement made by the parties, with the terms of the agreement endorsed on the brief and signed by the parties.

I   WORKING ON A BRIEF

2.52 A brief may instruct a barrister to meet a client in conference, to write an opinion, to draft a statement of case, to negotiate a settlement, or to appear at trial. The detailed work to be done will depend on the task(s) requested. This section covers general principles.

On receipt of a brief

2.53 On receipt of a brief, the barrister should give it a preliminary consideration at the earliest reasonable opportunity, to check whether there is any particular urgency in the case, and how long it may take to complete the work on the brief, if for example it may require lengthy legal research. The preliminary review may show that something is missing from the brief which will be needed to give full advice, in which case the solicitor should be contacted to provide the missing information.

2.54 If there is any need for quick action, for example because the limitation period is running out or because an injunction should be sought quickly, the barrister should work on the brief as soon as possible. Otherwise work should be completed within a reasonable time, depending on the needs and complexity of the case. The solicitor should be given a reasonable estimate of when work on the brief is likely to be completed if an opinion or a draft has been sought.

Much of the conduct of a case stems from the impressions formed on the first reading of a **2.55** brief, so careful and structured reading is important. If the brief has been properly prepared by the solicitor it should be easy to read, but sometimes preparatory work may be required in sorting out tasks and documents before a full reading.

Reading a brief strategically

It is important to assimilate the information in a brief methodically in a structured and **2.56** critical way. Ideally a brief should be read when no form of distraction is present. It is vital not to miss or misread a point that may alter the advice given, and to read with a mind that is receptive to detail. The first step will of course be to read the instructions. The tasks to be completed and any special questions asked need to be noted. Work on the brief will need to focus on these matters.

The next step will be to read the other papers in the brief. The papers should be read in a **2.57** useful order, and some sorting may be required prior to reading to ensure that the understanding of the case gained is focussed, limiting the risk of being distracted by detail of limited relevance. Any statements of case should normally be read before other documents as they should provide an outline of the main issues in the case. The next stage will normally be to read any statement by the client, which should provide an overview of the facts from the client's point of view, and insights into what the client hopes to achieve. After this any other crucial document should be read, for example any contract. The next step will be to read any statements or reports by experts or other witnesses, and finally anything else that has been put in the brief, such as correspondence between the solicitors. It is usually best to read letters in chronological order, the earliest first, to understand how the case has developed.

It is useful to have a strategy when reading a brief, so as to make best use of the information **2.58** provided. It may be best to read the brief once underlining nothing and making no notes simply to get a clear grasp of the case. Plans can then be made for a second reading, which might include a systematic use of highlighters for information relevant to different issues in the case. Strategic reading might also include systematic note taking. In particular there may be merit in noting all the dates in the case, all the people involved and the relevant information about each person, and all the figures in the case. It is also useful to make notes grouping together facts related to each issue in the case. Reasonably neat copies of such notes may be useful for later work on the case:

- When writing an opinion it is useful to have summaries of the facts rather than continually searching through the brief for details.
- When advising in conference it can be useful to have summaries of facts for quick reference while talking to the client about the details of events.
- If the barrister is briefed again later in the case, summary notes can help to remind the barrister of the key facts of the case quickly.

- Summaries of facts can be very helpful when preparing a skeleton argument or preparing a case for court.

Dealing with missing information

2.59 No brief will ever include everything the barrister might want to know. For all the reasons set out in 2.49, some information will simply not be available. It is important to consider the information that is not in the brief as well as the information that is there. If missing information is ignored or assumptions are made this could lead to potentially serious weaknesses in the actions taken and advice given in relation to the brief. Consideration should be given in particular to the following.

- Is it clear what the barrister is asked to do and what the client hopes to achieve? If not these matters need to be clarified.
- Is any key information missing on something the barrister is instructed to deal with, such as a cause of action? If the information directly affects the advice to be given, the matter needs to be checked.
- Might it be significantly easier to understand or to visualise key matters with the help of a plan or photographs that could be provided reasonably easily?
- Is it only going to be possible to understand a matter properly with expert advice, so that the solicitor and client should be consulted about seeking an expert report?

2.60 If these items of missing information are crucial to the advice the barrister is giving now then they need to be taken up immediately with the solicitor. If the matters are not immediately crucial but will be relevant to the future conduct of the case then the barrister should make a list of further documents required, photographs and diagrams that may be useful, questions to be put to witnesses etc. It is normal to include in an opinion a list of the further information and evidence the solicitor is asked to obtain.

Next steps

2.61 If the brief relates to a conference with a client, see Chapter 6 and 7; if to writing an opinion see Chapter 11; if to drafting a statement of case see Chapter 12; if to making an interim application, see Chapter 16; if to trying to settle the case see Chapter 20; or if to advocating a case at trial see Chapters 21 and 22.

2.62 There are a few general points that may apply when a barrister is deciding what to do.

- If the barrister needs extra information before completing the work as instructed then the solicitor should be contacted as soon as possible with clear guidance as to what is required. In requesting further information the barrister will need to be reasonable as to what is realistically likely to be available and the possible cost. If the information may be needed for a later stage in the case rather than for immediate decisions this can be pointed out in the opinion or on returning the brief.
- The barrister may feel a need to see the client before giving advice. It may be important to hear what the client has to say personally, if for example the client has been involved in a personal accident, or if it is important to weigh up how the client might appear as a witness, or to clarify the objectives that the client wishes to achieve. In such circumstances

the barrister should discuss with the solicitor the possibility of arranging a conference before writing an opinion or before appearing in court as relevant.

- If significant legal research is required before an opinion can be produced the solicitor should be informed and given a time estimate. Consideration should be given as to whether the limitation period might expire, or whether steps in the case need to be completed by a certain time.
- If there is any difficulty in fulfilling the tasks in the instructions the solicitor should be told.

3

THE PROFESSIONAL CONTEXT—
ETHOS AND ETHICS

A THE CONTEXT FOR PROFESSIONAL ETHICS 3.02
    The changing context 3.02
    Basic principles 3.06

B COMMERCIAL AWARENESS 3.12
    The importance of commercial awareness 3.12
    The elements of commercial awareness 3.13

C GLOBALISATION 3.16
    The relevance of different systems of law to a case 3.16
    The relevance of international considerations for practice 3.19

D HUMAN RIGHTS 3.22
    The Human Rights Act 1998 . . . . 3.22
    Human rights and the CPR 3.24
    Article 6 and the right to a fair trial 3.25

E ACCESS TO LITIGATION FOR THOSE OF LIMITED MEANS 3.31

F MONEY LAUNDERING 3.35
    The money laundering legislation 3.35
    The relevance to litigation 3.40

G PROFESSIONAL CONDUCT 3.43
    Professional duties to the court 3.45
    Professional duties to the client 3.46
    The Code of Conduct for the Bar of England and Wales 3.48
    The Code of Conduct for Solicitors 3.50
    Breaches of professional conduct 3.53

H GENERAL ETHICS 3.55

I CONFIDENTIALITY AND PROFESSIONAL PRIVILEGE 3.61
    Privileged communications 3.62
    The basis for privilege 3.67
    The waiver of privilege 3.69
    The limits of legal professional privilege 3.72

Privilege and disclosure. 3.73

J   WHERE WORK FALLS SHORT OF PROFESSIONAL STANDARDS 3.77
Complaints about the standard of work 3.78
Wasted costs orders 3.83
Disallowance of costs 3.86

K   PROFESSIONAL NEGLIGENCE. 3.87
The test for professional negligence 3.87
Immunity from action 3.92
Examples of professional negligence 3.96

Why don't sharks attack lawyers?
Professional courtesy.

3.01   Maintaining a professional and ethical approach is fundamental to the working life of a lawyer. A tough approach may be appropriate in representing a client in litigation, but this must be carefully judged to stay within proper professional and ethical boundaries. The context within which lawyers work is changing, with implications for how they work. For sources on professional conduct and ethics see 24.21.

A   THE CONTEXT FOR PROFESSIONAL ETHICS

The changing context

3.02   The fairness of the litigation process depends on lawyers maintaining professional standards and taking an ethical approach to their work. This requires a strong commitment on the part of the professional bodies responsible for setting and maintaining standards, and also on the part of individual lawyers. Ethics, standards, and professional rules are the threads that bind the legal profession in its current form, and are fundamental to the modes of delivering legal advice and litigation services. Over recent years there have been many initiatives to support standards, including the further development of existing complaints procedures.

3.03   The context within which professional ethics operate is undergoing rapid change. Key developments include problems of financing litigation and the use of conditional fee agreements, the shift of focus from private client work to commercial work especially in large firms, and the growth of globalisation and competition in legal practice. There has also been a significant growth of work related to human rights, and in work performed on a *pro bono* basis.

3.04   Review and change are ongoing. A specific driver for further change is the Review of the Regulatory Framework of the Legal Service carried out by David Clementi, with a report made at the end of 2004. The terms of reference for this review include identifying what regulatory framework will best promote competition, innovation, and public and consumer interests in an efficient, effective and independent legal sector, and also identifying a framework that will be independent in representing public and consumer interest, comprehensive, accountable, consistent, flexible and transparent, and no more restrictive or burdensome than is clearly justified. The coverage so wide that it may bring significant further change in how lawyers work and how legal services are delivered.

A basis of the Clementi Review is that the present framework for the legal profession is seen   **3.05** as outdated, inflexible, and overcomplex. Objectives for the future include providing access to justice, protection of consumer interests, maintenance of a strong legal services industry and fair competition between the parts of that industry. The final Report proposes that the regulatory functions for the profession would be overseen by a super regulator, a Legal Services Board, chaired by a lawyer but with a majority of lay members, though the professional bodies would keep the majority of their regulatory functions. In addition a significant issue being considered by Clementi is the extent to which lawyers should be able to work jointly with other professions. It appears that joint legal disciplinary practices with barristers and solicitors in partnership may be permitted (as already happens to some extent in law centres), but that there are still too many ethical problems about partnerships between different professions, such as solicitors and accountants.

Basic principles

Litigation will only function effectively and fairly if professional standards of conduct and of   **3.06** work remain reasonably high. Standards are maintained in a variety of ways:

- There are detailed professional conduct codes for both barristers and solicitors, see 5.38–5.44.
- There are professional disciplinary processes for solicitors and barristers who are alleged to be in breach of professional conduct codes.
- Many ethical principles are built into statutes and rules for evidence and procedure.
- Both the Bar Council and the Law Society have complaints and compensation procedures for clients who feel they have not been properly represented.
- If a barrister or solicitor has behaved in such a way that costs are unnecessarily incurred a wasted costs order can be made against the lawyer personally.
- A solicitor or barrister who has clearly fallen short of the professional standards to be expected with the result that a client has suffered loss can be sued by the client for professional negligence.

The basic professional duties that a lawyer owes are given below.

Ethical responsibilities to clients

The lawyer's knowledge of law and legal procedure provides great power to influence the   **3.07** client, but the lawyer must work under the instructions of the client. The lawyer has a duty of confidentiality to each client. A lawyer has general duties to see that each case is pursued to the best of his or her abilities, and that it is completed within a reasonable time period and at reasonable cost.

Ethical responsibilities to the court

3.08 The lawyer is an officer of the court and has a general duty to the court to see that justice is fairly administered and the court is not misled. The court needs high standards in the presentation of cases to be able to reach fair decisions.

Ethical responsibilities in dealing with other lawyers

3.09 Lawyers need to be able to place reasonable trust in each other when dealing with cases. There should be fairness in dealing with opponents to ensure that cases can be prepared properly, and can be settled fairly if a case does not proceed to trial.

Ethical responsibilities with regard to money

3.10 Solicitors often hold large amounts of client money and have duties with regard to how that money is held and dealt with. Barristers cannot hold client funds, but much litigation is to do with money in terms of damages and costs. There are general professional duties to ensure that financial matters are dealt with properly.

General ethical responsibilities

3.11 There are general ethical responsibilities as in the exercise of any profession, so as, for example, not to be used as an instrument by an unethical client.

B   COMMERCIAL AWARENESS

The importance of commercial awareness

3.12 There is now a strong demand for those entering practice as lawyers to have 'commercial awareness', to the extent that training for some solicitors has become increasingly focussed on a commercial model. Although the litigation lawyer is not often concerned with mergers and acquisitions or corporate finance, general commercial and financial awareness is important.

- Significant awareness of how a business is run and of accounts may be relevant to assessing damages in a contract case.
- Financial awareness and skills in arithmetic are often required to assess damages in a serious personal injury case.
- The personal injury lawyer will need financial and commercial awareness to negotiate a structured settlement.
- The environmental lawyer will need commercial and financial awareness to be able to deal effectively with the potential cost of environmental control.
- The exploitation of intellectual property is essentially about business opportunities and potential profits.
- Skills in maths and risk assessment are vital to assess offers to settle in any case.

The elements of commercial awareness

3.13 It is not easy to define what is meant by commercial and financial awareness. The examples given above show the wide range of commercial and financial understanding to be expected of a lawyer. Those who stress the importance of commercial awareness tend to relate it to the needs of their own practice. Some of the key areas and concepts that are important are:

- A general ability to deal with figures. Law is not just about words, but all too often involves arithmetic. Any lawyer should be able to deal with basic financial concepts such as capital, income, and different types of interest.
- A general understanding of how financial products such as mortgages and insurance work.
- A general understanding of how commercial finance works, including an ability to read accounts.
- A general understanding of how corporate finance works, including a basic understanding of how share capital is based and operates.
- A general understanding of the ways in which a business can be run, as a sole trader, through a company, through a partnership, or through a limited liability partnership.
- A practical approach to a financial situation.
- Having a sense of 'business' concepts—the need to market to customers and to make an income.

3.14 It is unrealistic to expect the typical entrant to the legal profession to have an adequate depth and breadth of understanding in all these areas, not least because a practical understanding can only be built with experience. Students entering the legal profession straight out of university will generally not have had a mortgage, and will have limited experience of insurance and share ownership, albeit that they may well have experience of debt management! Perhaps the realistic expectation is that those entering the profession should understand the importance and relevance of commercial and financial awareness for effective practice. The lawyer will not always need a detailed personal knowledge—an accountant or an actuary may assist—but the lawyer will need to be able to appreciate and address issues.

3.15 There is no simple source of commercial awareness. Some books might be of assistance, such as W M Clarke, *How the City of London Works* (5th edn, 2004, Sweet & Maxwell) or C Proctor, *Mann on the Legal Aspect of Money* (2005, Oxford University Press). Websites might also provide assistance such as www.companylawclub.co.uk, a company law gateway.

C   GLOBALISATION

The relevance of different systems of law to a case

3.16 The work in significant sections of legal practice is influenced by international as well as national factors. There has been a massive growth of transnational elements in the law to the extent that few lawyers can entirely ignore international or transnational factors.

3.17 The main ways in which international factors can impinge on legal practice and litigation are:

- International law can be relevant to a case, for example regulations and cases in European Community law.
- The principles of law shared by different nations can affect a case, for example through human rights law.

- Where the law of another country can be applicable in a case, either through the terms of an agreement or through the facts of a case.
- Where the facts of a case may involve the law of a number of countries, if for example a national of country A is badly injured in country B by a national of country C.

3.18 A case that on the face of it is a commercial case or a tort action may in fact turn on points of comparative law. This is considered further at 4.114–4.168.

The relevance of international considerations for practice

3.19 In additional to international considerations affecting a case, international considerations can also have a direct effect on the work of lawyers. Firms and chambers, especially those working in London, increasingly face international competition. Where a business is conducted through a group of companies or linked companies in different jurisdictions, or where the facts of the case mean that a case could be brought in more than one jurisdiction, then the client will have a choice not only as to firm but also as to the country in which lawyers are instructed. This can make it important for a firm to have branches in different countries, to build relationships with firms in other countries, and to build expertise in dealing with cases in different jurisdictions.

3.20 Legal practitioners normally qualify to work in one jurisdiction, though it is becoming increasingly common for lawyers to qualify to work in more than one jurisdiction. It is also likely that rules for practising as a lawyer will be increasingly harmonised throughout the EC. Where this happens there are issues not only of basic qualification requirements, but also about ethics where different ethical systems may apply. For example other jurisdictions do not make a distinction between barristers and solicitors.

3.21 International considerations are also relevant to the whole process of litigation. If there is a choice of jurisdiction then the client will consider matters such as the cost and speed of litigation. Maintaining an effective litigations system is important for England and Wales in remaining a forum of choice.

D   HUMAN RIGHTS

The Human Rights Act 1998

3.22 The Human Rights Act 1998 incorporated the European Convention on Human Rights into English law, making most (though not all) of the Convention rights directly enforceable in English courts. The effects of this are not retrospective. The European Convention on Human Rights is an international treaty that was adopted in 1950. The rights affect relations between individuals, and between individuals and public authorities. Some rights are absolute, but some are qualified (allowing the general public interest to be taken into account) and others are limited (allowing a government to enter a derogation, which must be in pursuit of a legitimate aim and proportionate). There is some flexibility, with countries allowed a 'margin of appreciation', and the convention being seen as a 'living instrument'. For sources of law on human rights see 24.19.

The main results of the human rights legislation are: **3.23**

- Primary and subordinate English legislation must be read and given effect in a way that is compatible with Convention rights, Human Rights Act 1998, s 3.
- The High Court or any court superior to it can make a declaration of incompatibility declaring that an English legal provision is incompatible with a Convention right, Human Rights Act 1998 s 4, *R (Holding & Barnes plc and Others) v Secretary of State for the Environment* (2001) 2 WLR 1389. A declaration of incompatibility has been made as regards the Mental Health Act 1983, ss 72–3, *R (on the application of H) v Mental Health Review Tribunal and Secretary of State for Health* (2001) 3 WLR 512. A declaration of incompatibility has also been made as regards s 127 of the Consumer Credit Act 1974, *Wilson v First County Trust* (2001) 3 WLR 42. If a direction of incompatibility is sought the relevant Minister must be given notice and can take part in the action.
- Any court or tribunal determining a question which has arisen in connection with a convention right must take into account the jurisprudence of human rights bodies in Strasbourg, Human Rights Act 1998, s 2.
- It is unlawful for a public authority to act in a way which is incompatible with a Convention right. The definition of 'public authority' seems to be quite wide. If it does a victim may make a claim, and the court may grant such relief or remedy as is just and appropriate, Human Rights Act 1998, ss 6–8. Damages are available where this is necessary to satisfy the claims of the victim, and they should be assessed in line with comparable torts, *R (KB) v Mental Health Review Tribunal* (2003) 2 All ER 209, and *R (Bernard and Another) v Enfield Borough Council* The Times, 8 November 2002. Claims can go to the European Court of Human Rights, which has judges from each contracting state. A three-judge committee sifts out unfounded cases.

Human rights and the CPR

In principle the Human Rights Act should fit easily with the Civil Procedure Rules 1998 as it   **3.24** is an overriding principle of the CPR that cases should be dealt with justly. In addition, the Human Rights Act 1998, s 3 requires that the provisions of the CPR be given effect in a manner which is compatible with Convention rights so far as possible. It has been said that the human rights legislation provides the court with an extra tool in interpreting procedural rules, *Goode v Martin* The Times, 24 January 2002.

Article 6 and the right to a fair trial

Article 6 is directly relevant to litigation as it provides for the right to a fair trial.   **3.25** Article 6(1) provides:

> In the determination of his civil rights and obligations . . . everyone is entitled to a fair and public hearing within a reasonable time by an independent and impartial tribunal established by law. Judgment shall be pronounced publicly, but the press and public may be excluded from all or part of the trial in the interest of morals, public order or national security in a democratic society, where the interests of juveniles or the protection of the private life of the parties so require, or to the extent strictly necessary in the opinion of the court in special circumstances where publicity would prejudice the interests of justice.

3.26 The Article relates to the process of trial and the need for a case to be brought and tried on its merits. Article 6 does not create a right of action where no right exists, *Wilson v First County Trust (No 2)* (2003) 3 WLR 568.

3.27 Much of the litigation relating to Article 6 is founded in criminal litigation. In civil litigation, Article 6 has been interpreted in the following way:

- There is a right to a public hearing, though there can be a hearing in private, for example in child custody proceedings. It is not essential that the party is present for the whole hearing.
- There is a right to access to a court to litigate a dispute, *Hamilton v Al Fayed (No 2)* (2003) QB 1175.
- There is a right to an unbiased judge, so that a judge who may have any conflict of interest should stand down, *Porter v Magill* (2002) 2 AC 357.
- There should be an adversarial procedure that allows each party the right to present evidence and to see and comment on other evidence submitted to the judge.
- There should be equality of arms between the parties as regards time and facilities. However there cannot be complete equality, and one side cannot be prevented from having a QC simply because the other side cannot afford one, *Maltez v Lewis* The Times, 4 May 1999.
- Limitation periods must not be unduly unduly restrictive.
- A requirement for security for costs is acceptable provided a party's means and the right of access to a court are taken into account, *Nasser v United Bank of Kuwait* (2002) 1 WLR 1868.
- Striking out is acceptable so long as it does not rule out whole categories of cases.
- Summary judgment is acceptable, *Three Rivers District Council v Bank of England (No 3)* (2003) 2 AC 1.
- There should be a hearing within a reasonable time, though this depends on the complexity and importance of the case.
- Reasons should be given for decisions, *English v Emery Reimbold and Strick Ltd* (2002) 1 WLR 2409 and *Stefan v General Medical Council* (1999) 1 WLR 1293.

3.28 An example of the use being made of human rights law can be seen in the case being brought at the European Court of Human Rights by the two individuals sued by the McDonalds Corporation for libel for distributing leaflets criticising McDonalds food. They are claiming that there was inequality before the court in that they had to represent themselves and have now been ordered to pay costs of £40,000, as against the resources available to a multinational corporation.

3.29 The approach to be taken when it is alleged that a right to litigate has been improperly replaced by an administrative system was set out in *R (Kehoe) v Secretary of State for Work and Pensions* (2004) 2 WLR 1481. The test involves considering whether civil rights and obligations are concerned, whether there is court control of the administrative process, and whether restrictions on access to court are proportionate. See also *R (Alconbury Developments Ltd) v Secretary of State for the Environment, Transport and the Regions* (2003) AC 295 and *Tower Hamlets London Borough Council v Begum* (2003) 2 AC 430.

3.30 Other Articles may be used in ways relevant to civil litigation.

- In *Price v UK* 34 EHRR 1285 a severely disabled woman was committed in custody for a judgment debt. She was held in a cell that had no special adaptation and male officers had to assist her on and off the toilet, which was held to be degrading treatment contrary to Article 3.
- Article 8 provides for a right to respect for a private and family life, home, and correspondence. This has been used to found nuisance type cases where there is alleged to be an interference with private life, *Marcic v Thames Water Utilities Ltd* (2002) 2 WLR 932 and *Hatton and Others v UK* (2002) 34 EHRR 1. This Article has also been used to support rights of confidentiality, *Douglas v Hello!* (2001) 2 WLR 992. Orders for disclosure need to provide for a fair trial but balance that with respect for the private life of parties and those who are not parties to the litigation. Interim orders need to respect private life and peaceful enjoyment of possessions.
- Article 10 provides for freedom of speech. This means that an interim injunction will not easily be granted to prevent publication unless the claimant has a strong case, *Cream Holdings v Banerjee* The Times, 15 October 2004, though potentially grave results of disclosure are also relevant.
- Other Articles might also be so used to protect confidentiality, for example Article 1 of the First Protocol provides for the peaceful enjoyment of property.

E   ACCESS TO LITIGATION FOR THOSE OF LIMITED MEANS

It is difficult, though not impossible, for a litigation process to avoid being expensive. For **3.31** those of limited means the potential options are:

- advice from a Law Centre or Citizens Advice Bureau;
- support from the community legal service support;
- use of the small claims court;
- *pro bono* support;
- entering a conditional fee agreement.

These sources overlap. Only the Community Legal Service or a conditional fee agreement **3.32** will potentially pay the cost of a lawyer, though a lawyer may act for free on a *pro bono* basis. The other options may provide advice and support for an individual who would then need to bring the case as a litigant in person. A spokesperson may appear for a party in a tribunal hearing in areas like employment or immigration. A qualified solicitor or barrister may only represent a client within the terms of the relevant Code of Conduct. Sources of funding are considered further in Chapter 5.

There has also been a significant growth in *pro bono* work, fuelled partly by a sense of **3.33** responsibility in individuals and firms that earn high fees. A national *Pro Bono* week is sponsored each year by Bar Council, Law Society, Legal Executives, and the Department of Constitutional Affairs. About half of all solicitors report having done some *pro bono* work, and a significant number of barristers work with the Bar Pro Bono Unit.

There has also been a significant growth of advice clinics and *pro bono* work linked to Law **3.34** Departments in universities and to legal professional training providers. There are various different models, some of which provide advice to clients, some of which represent clients, some of which work closely with practising lawyers or with charities, and some of which write proposals for law reform.

F MONEY LAUNDERING

The money laundering legislation

3.35 There has been international concern about the extent to which professionals have become unknowingly involved in dealing with money that has been improperly obtained. This is by no means restricted to lawyers who specialise in criminal cases—a wide range of business organisations may be used directly or indirectly to try to legitimise the proceeds of criminal activity. This sort of concern is more likely to relate to transactional work rather than litigation, but the litigation lawyer needs to be aware of the requirements of the 'money laundering' legislation because of the obligations imposed and the potentially serious consequences of not complying.

3.36 Money laundering has been described as the third largest global industry (after oil and prostitution!). The European Community has sought to address this through the Second Money Laundering Directive (2001/97/EC), which has been brought into effect in England and Wales through the Proceeds of Crime Act 2002 and the Money Laundering Regulations 2003. The Bar Council and the Law Society provide guidance, and the National Crime Intelligence Service website is useful (www.ncis.co.uk). There is concern that the proposed Third Directive on money laundering may go further in undermining traditional professional privilege.

3.37 Parts of the legislation apply to professionals such as lawyers, bankers, and accountants. The implications of the legislation are wide because any kind of transaction can be relevant, and the legislation covers money tainted by any form of illegality and not just money produced from serious crime such as drug trafficking. There are no distinctions between degrees of criminal property, so that, for example, lawyers may be obliged to report income tax or VAT avoidance.

3.38 Very briefly, key requirements of which the civil litigator should be aware are:

- It is an offence to conceal criminal property, s 327.
- Suspicious transactions should to be reported to the NCIS if the professional knows or suspects or should reasonably know or suspect that a client is engaged in money laundering. About 1,000 reports a month are being made by solicitors.
- If the professional comes across something suspicious while working on a client's business then the lawyer must not become involved in the arrangement. If having taken instructions from a client a solicitor or barrister knows or suspects will become involved in an arrangement that might involve the acquisition, retention, use, or control of criminal property, then an authorised disclosure should be made and the appropriate consent sought, s 328. Consent must be sought from the NCIS before continuing with the transaction, using approved forms from the NCIS website. There will then be a defence of authorised disclosure under s 338 if the transaction is completed and any possible charge

arises. This is important as without clearance a lawyer may be subject to a penalty of up to 14 years in prison. Solicitors are responsible for 82 per cent of requests for clearance, currently making up to 1,500 a month. Once the report is made, if nothing is heard from the NCIS within seven days then the lawyer can proceed with the transaction, and this will be the norm. If the NCIS wishes to consider the case further then a 31-day moratorium will be imposed.

• If the client is aware of the notification to the NCIS then the client might take steps to avoid detection. It is therefore an offence to 'tip off' the client, s 333. The lawyer should make the report to the NCIS but not tell the client. If this creates significant problems because of the need to take further steps in a case or a transaction then the NCIS may agree what can be said to the client. If necessary direction from the court should be sought if a hearing is imminent.

Most of the other provisions of the legislation are primarily relevant to lawyers dealing with criminal rather than civil cases, but other provisions may be relevant. For example disclosure orders can be made by the Crown Court to order the production of documents relating to assets that are the proceeds of crime. Civil proceedings can be taken to recover property that is or is derived from the proceeds of crime. The lawyer with any suspicion that funds tainted with illegality are involved in a case should check the position. It is important for legal offices to have procedures to capture and check information adequately at a sufficiently early stage, and records should be kept of information provided. **3.39**

The relevance to litigation

This legislation is very wide ranging and relatively recent. It has given rise to many concerns about relations between lawyers and clients, confidentiality, and civil liberties. There are also concerns about the workload and costs imposed on lawyers to train staff and to make reports. The fact that trivial as well as serious proceeds of crime are captured has arguably undermined respect for the legislation—the practical effect appears to be that family lawyers report tax avoidance rather than that major sources of illegal money are identified. How should clashes with legal professional privilege be addressed? What if a chain of transactions is involved? Many of these problems are still being worked through with support from Law Society guidelines. The Joint Money Laundering Steering group website may also be useful (www.jmlsg.org.uk). On professional privilege see 3.61–3.76. **3.40**

An example of how the legislation might apply to a litigation lawyer is that a client might claim that he or she wished to bring a large commercial claim, causing the solicitor to ask for a significant payment on account that the client provided. The client might then say that the claim was not to be pursued so the money would need to be returned. On the face of it this money would then appear to come from the perfectly legitimate source of the client account. As a further example, an apparent settlement of a possibly spurious claim could be used to provide an apparently legitimate cloak for a transfer of money. **3.41**

The duties of lawyers under these provisions were considered in *P v P* (2004) FLR 1, a family law case with more general application. If there is suspicion then an authorised disclosure should be made and the appropriate consent sought. The client should not be told or this may amount to a 'tip off'. If the lawyer is acting normally in professional duties then **3.42** protection should follow, provided the client did not reveal the information to further a criminal purpose. The lawyer should then be able to communicate with the client and opponent as necessary.

G   PROFESSIONAL CONDUCT

3.43   There is no single source of professional standards and ethical considerations for lawyers in England and Wales. The Bar Council provides a Code of Conduct for barristers, and the Law Society provides a Code of Conduct for solicitors. There are a number of provisions in the Codes that are similar as regards basic duties to the court and to the client, and the need to avoid conflicts of interest.

3.44   Over recent years the distinctions between barristers and solicitors have been eroded. The main current distinctions between the professions are:

- a solicitor can conduct litigation (file statements of case with the court etc), but a barrister cannot;
- clients have direct access to a solicitor, but normally have access to a barrister through instructions sent by their solicitor. It has become possible to have direct access to a barrister, but subject to detailed rules (see 2.19–2.23);
- solicitors can hold client funds but barristers cannot;
- barristers have full rights of audience in the courts; solicitors have more limited rights of audience on qualification, but can extend their rights.

Professional duties to the court

3.45   In general terms the main legal professional duties owed to the court are as follows.

- Lawyers are officers of the court, and they have a duty not to deceive or knowingly or recklessly mislead the court, Courts and Legal Services Act 1990, ss 27–28 as amended by Access to Justice Act 1999, s 42. See also para 302 of the Code of Conduct for the Bar.
- Although a lawyer has a duty to act fearlessly to help a client's case, there is an overriding duty to assist the court in the administration of justice. If for example a client refuses to disclose all relevant documents, a lawyer who is aware of this should withdraw from the case.
- There is a duty to bring to the attention of the court all relevant legal provisions and cases, whether or not they are favourable to the case, *Copeland v Smith and Another* (2000) 1 All ER 457.
- There is a duty to bring procedural irregularities to the attention of the court.
- There is a duty to dress and behave appropriately and politely in court, and not to assert personal views that are not justified by the facts and laws of the case.
- There is a duty not to make statements about or ask questions of a witness in a way that is merely scandalous or calculated to insult or annoy the witness.
- There is a duty not to coach or rehearse witnesses, see para 705 of the Code of Conduct for the Bar.
- There is a duty to bring to the attention of the court a material change in circumstances,

such as an improvement in a disability for which damages are claimed, *Vernon v Bosley*
The Times, 19 December 1996.
- Lawyers of course have a duty to comply with court orders and to try to ensure that clients comply with court orders. An undertaking given to the court on behalf of a client will be binding, see para 18.01 of the Code of Conduct for Solicitors.

Professional duties to the client

In general terms the main legal professional duties owed to a client are as follows. **3.46**

- An advocate has a duty to argue a case fearlessly and by all proper and lawful means.
- There is a general duty to ensure that the client's interests are protected.
- There is a duty to take and act on the instructions of the client, and not to put undue pressure on the client to accept any particular course.
- There is a duty to avoid any conflict of interest.
- There is a duty to keep the client's confidence, see para 702 of the Code of Conduct for the Bar, and para 16.01 of the Code of Conduct for Solicitors.
- A lawyer is under a duty only to accept a case that he or she is competent to conduct. For a barrister there is also the cab-rank rule, which requires the barrister to accept any instructions from a client for a proper professional fee in an area in which the barrister practises, irrespective of the nature of the case or any view which the barrister has of the case, see paras 603–610 of the Code of Conduct for the Bar. There are some exceptions to this rule.
- There is a general duty to provide reasonably accurate and reliable advice, in terms that the client can understand, and to ensure that the client understands the possible consequences of any judgment or decision.
- A solicitor has a duty to set out the terms on which the client is being represented in a client care letter, and a barrister working on direct access has a similar duty.
- If the lawyer has breached his or her duties to the client in a way that may be actionable, the lawyer has a duty to advise the client that there is a possibility of a claim and that the advice of another lawyer should be sought.

There may occasionally be overlaps and conflicts between a lawyer's duties to the court and **3.47**
to the client. A client is bound by a lawyer's assurances to a court even if the lawyer may be subject to a negligence claim, *Worldwide Corporation Ltd v Marconi Communications Ltd* The Times, 7 July 1999. If there is a conflict of duties, the court must look at the background, *Memory Corporation v Sidhu* The Times, 15 February 2000, where on a interim application there were problems with what the lawyers told the court as regards the terms of an order, and as regards the evidence supplied by the client.

The Code of Conduct for the Bar of England and Wales

A barrister in practice must hold a practising certificate, carry insurance under the Bar **3.48**
Mutual Indemnity Fund, and comply with the requirements of the Code of Conduct for the Bar of England and Wales provided by the Bar Council. The Code includes general provisions, for example para 301 provides that a barrister must not engage in conduct which is dishonest or discreditable to a barrister, which is prejudicial to the administration of justice,

which is likely to diminish public confidence in the legal profession, or which is otherwise likely to bring the legal profession into disrepute.

3.49   Specific provisions in the Code cover how various elements of the work of the barrister should be approached. There are a series of Annexes to the Code covering different areas. Where there is no specific provision in the relevant Code, the barrister should abide by the spirit of the Code. The Code of Conduct of the Bar of England and Wales (7th edn, 2000, as amended) can be found on www.barcouncil.org.uk.

The Code of Conduct for Solicitors

3.50   A solicitor in practice must hold a practising certificate under the Practising Certificate Regulations 1995, and carry insurance with the Solicitors' Indemnity Fund. Solicitors also have to abide by a code of conduct for solicitors which is contained in the Guide to the Professional Conduct of Solicitors (8th edn, 1999, as amended) which can be found on www.lawsociety.org.uk. These rules come from the Solicitors Act 1974 and the Solicitors' Practice Rules 1990. There are also supporting Codes, including the Law Society's Code for Advocacy (and the Guide to Professional Conduct in Litigation and Advocacy), and the Solicitors' Costs Information and Client Care Code.

3.51   As regards basic principles, para 1.01 of the Rules and Principles of Professional Conduct provides that a solicitor shall not do anything in the course of practising as a solicitor, or permit another person to do anything on his or her behalf, which compromises or impairs or is likely to compromise or impair any of the following:

- the solicitor's independence or integrity;
- a person's freedom to instruct the solicitor of his or her choice;
- the solicitor's duty to act in the best interests of the client;
- the good repute of the solicitor or of the solicitors' profession;
- the solicitor's proper standard of work;
- the solicitor's duty to the court.

3.52   Solicitors often hold client money in relation to particular transactions or steps in a case. There are strict rules for holding such money in client accounts and producing annual reports under the Solicitors' Accounts Rules 1998. There are also duties as regards supervising and running an office, including policies on ownership, storage, and destruction of documents. Solicitors, where relevant, are also subject to special requirements relating to the provision of financial services under the Financial Services Act 1986. The Financial Services Authority website, www.fsa.gov.uk may be useful.

Breaches of professional conduct

3.53   If professional conduct does fall short of that which is to be expected, both the Law Society and the Bar Council have disciplinary procedures that can lead to a variety of penalties, including, in an extreme case, the lawyer being struck off or disbarred.

3.54   The Bar Council has a Professional Conduct and Complaints Committee and acts under the Complaints Rules and Disciplinary Tribunals Regulations. The Committee can deal with a wide variety of issues from allegations of incompetence to criminal convictions. The Law Society acts through the Solicitors Disciplinary Tribunal.

H   GENERAL ETHICS

Professional Codes of Conduct cannot specifically cover all situations. Beyond the professional codes of conduct, there are general ethical principles for how a lawyer should behave. Some general points may arise from the spirit of a code of conduct, or be effectively an extension of one of the principles in the code. **3.55**

To provide some examples of general ethical points not specifically covered by a code of conduct: **3.56**

- If a lawyer gives the impression that he or she is providing an undertaking on some matter, that will be treated as binding, *M v Home Office* [1992] 4 All ER 97.
- A lawyer cannot take advantage of a mistake made by an opponent to which the lawyer has contributed, even in hostile litigation, *Ernst & Young v Butte Mining plc* The Times, 22 March 1996.
- The lawyer has a duty to reveal to the court information that may have a direct bearing on the outcome of a case, *Meek v Fleming* [1961] 2 QB 366, but while this duty is clear for prosecutors in a criminal case it is much less clear how it might apply in a contested civil case.

Breach of general ethical principles might be taken into consideration by a judge in charge of a case, for example, in making orders at an interim stage, exercising a discretion in a hearing or at trial, or in making orders as to costs. **3.57**

The limits of ethical behaviour are not easy to define, and there can be a conflict with the duty of the lawyer to act fearlessly for the client. There tends to be an assumption that a lawyer will recognise and practice ethical behaviour through general experience of the traditions, practices, and customs of the profession. However the idea that professional ethics can be acquired by some sort of osmosis is perhaps breaking down under the pressures of modern practice. From time to time concerns surface about how ethically lawyers behave, and there has been an increased emphasis on ethical conduct in training and in professional regulation. **3.58**

In other jurisdictions, such as the USA, there is significant academic study of legal professional ethics. This is less the case in England and Wales, though academic study of this area has been increasing in recent years, and hopefully this move will grow. There could usefully be more research into and study of professional ethics; and more emphasis on ethics in undergraduate training might help to lay stronger foundations. **3.59**

Although there are some common concepts of legal professional ethics in different countries, there are also significant differences. For example, in the English courts, unlike courts in some other jurisdictions, the lawyer's duty is to argue on the basis of the existing law and never to argue that the law should be different. **3.60**

I   CONFIDENTIALITY AND PROFESSIONAL PRIVILEGE

3.61   The client who comes to a lawyer for advice will probably assume that anything he or she tells the lawyer will be treated as confidential. In principal this is the case, and it has long been held that a client should be able to communicate fully with a lawyer when seeking legal advice without the fear that anything said to or shown to the lawyer will be disclosable, see for example *Re Barings plc* (1997) All ER (D) 1. Client confidentiality is protected by the doctrine of legal professional privilege, though this is perhaps a misleading title as it is the client's confidentiality that is protected.

Privileged communications

3.62   The lawyer has a professional duty to protect client confidentiality. A lawyer should not reveal to anyone else something that a client has said in confidence. It may be very tempting to discuss an interesting case but the temptation must be resisted. It is acceptable to discuss a case with another lawyer to seek advice, but on the basis that the lawyer does not mention names and only outlines the details relevant to the advice sought from the lawyer colleague.

3.63   Legal professional privilege is a more formal concept. In order to be able to prepare a client's case properly a lawyer must be able to communicate freely with the client, so any communication that takes place between the client and the lawyer in the course of preparing a case is privileged from disclosure for possible use in evidence. This is designed to ensure that any individual can get informed legal advice without any concern that what is said might later be used against them in some way. The client's right to confidentiality was a common law right, now reflected by Article 8 of the European Convention on Human Rights, see *R (Morgan Grenfell and Co Ltd) v Special Commissioner of Income Tax* (2002) 3 All ER 1.

3.64   Privilege can arise where anyone is offering legal advice, and is not limited to barristers and solicitors (Courts and Legal Services Act 1990, s 63), including in-house lawyers. Privilege can cover the following.

- Written and oral communications between a lawyer and a client.
- Written and oral communications between lawyers acting in the same case for the same client, including instructions to counsel and the opinion sent in reply. The drafts and notes of a lawyer would also normally be privileged, though not if they have a wider purpose than consisting of advice, for example recording the outcome of a hearing on the backsheet of a brief.
- Notes and records relating to witnesses, *R v Derby Magistrates Court, ex p B* The Times, 25 October 1995, save for witness statements that are served as evidence.
- Written and oral communications between an expert and a client and the client's lawyers. This includes material provided to the expert and any draft report, save for a report which is served for use in evidence.
- Notes and working papers prepared for meetings at which possible legal action is discussed, *Balabel v Air India* [1988] 2 All ER 246.
- Notes and photocopies prepared for seeking legal advice, *R v Board of Inland Revenue, ex p Goldberg* [1988] 3 All ER 248.

It is the communication that is privileged, not the material in it. A witness can still be called **3.65** to give evidence about a matter mentioned in a privileged communication, provided that witness is properly called and the evidence is admissible. Privilege will not attach to other documents simply because they are in some way linked with a privileged document—sending a collection of privileged and non-privileged documents with the same covering letter will not give privilege to those that are not privileged.

There is no general power to override legal professional privilege, even for public interest **3.66** reasons. A statute can override legal professional privilege, but only with a clear provision, so this will be rare, *R (Morgan Grenfell & Co Ltd) v Special Commissioner of Income Tax* (2003) 1 AC 563.

The basis for privilege

To be privileged the purpose of the communication must be the provision of legal advice for **3.67** the client, and the advice must be about the appropriate course of action in a particular legal context and not just general advice on the law. A document will be privileged if litigation was already pending or contemplated when the document was created, and if the dominant purpose for which the document was prepared was to send it to the legal adviser as part of getting advice on the litigation, *Waugh v British Railways Board* (1980) AC 521.

It is not crucial whether or not lawyers have been formally instructed as long as the test is **3.68** otherwise met, *Guinness Peat Properties Ltd v Fitzroy Robinson partnership* (1987) 1 WLR 1027 CA. If a document is created for more than one purpose, such as an accident report, the test is which purpose was the dominant one. The court will look not at the purpose of the person writing the report but at the purpose of the person for whom it is being prepared, and will focus on the time the document was created without looking at how the document was later used.

The waiver of privilege

The privilege is that of the client rather than the lawyer and it can be waived by the client, as **3.69** in *George Doland Ltd v Blackburn Robson & Co* [1972] 1 WLR 1338, where the claimant called his lawyer to give evidence as to what was said in a telephone conversation between them. If a client sues a solicitor for professional negligence there is an implied waiver of privilege to allow the court to judge the case fairly, *Lillicrap v Nalder and Son* (1993) 1 WLR 94 CA, but only as regards work done for that client in that capacity, *Paragon Finance plc v Freshfields* (1999) 1 WLR 1183 CA. A client waives privilege for documents held by one solicitor if they are relevant to an action the client later brings against another solicitor, *Kershaw v Whelan* The Times, 20 December 1995.

The court will look carefully to see how much privilege has been waived, *Great Atlantic* **3.70** *Insurance Co v Home Insurance Co* (1981) 1 WLR 529. A waiver for one purpose in a case may be taken as a complete waiver, *Somatra Ltd v Sinclair Roche and Temperley* (2000) 1 WLR 2453. However privilege will not be waived merely by referring to the document, and waiver of privilege on one document will not automatically waive privilege on another. It may be possible to separate parts of a large document, *British Coal Corporation v Dennis Rye Ltd (No 2)* (1988) 3 ALL ER 816.

3.71   If a party inadvertently discloses a privileged document, the party who has inspected the document may use the document or its contents only with the leave of the court (CPR r 31.20). The court may not give permission if, for example, the documents were got by fraud or an obvious error. The court will look at the nature of the case, what claim has been made for privilege etc in taking a decision, *International Business Machines Corporation v Phoenix International (Computers) Ltd* (1995) 1 All ER 413.

The limits of legal professional privilege

3.72   There are various circumstances in which legal professional privilege will not apply or will be lost. It is the party making a claim for privilege who must justify it. The court will consider individual communications, rather than the broad purpose of the client in consulting the lawyer, or some general apprehension of possible future litigation.

- Privileged material does not include documents produced before litigation is contemplated, *Alfred Compton Amusement Machines Ltd v Commissioners for Customs and Excise* [1974] AC 405.
- Privilege does not extend to records of accidents prepared by an employer as a routine matter, *Waugh v British Railways Board* [1980] AC 521.
- A communication that is intended to be passed on to other parties will not be privileged, *Conlon v Conlon's Ltd* (1952) 2 All ER 462.
- A document is not privileged merely because it is in the possession of a party's lawyer, *Dubai Bank v Galadari* (1989) 3 ALL ER 769.
- Legal professional privilege does not extend to communications made in pursuance of a crime or fraud, including wider forms of dishonesty such as a fraudulent breach of contract, *Crescent Farm (Sidcup) Sport Ltd v Sterling Offices Ltd* (1972) Ch 553, and see *Finers v Miro* [1991] 1 All ER 182.There is a distinction between legal advice on the effects of a transaction and advice on how to carry out a fraudulent transaction, *Barclays Bank plc v Eustice* (1995) 4 All ER 411 CA. Illegality can stem from a breach of provisions such as the Data Protection Act 1984, *Dubai Aluminium Co Ltd v Al Alawi* (1999) 1 WLR 1964.
- There is no privilege for information in a witness statement or report once it has been served, *Youell v Bland Welch & Co Ltd* [1991] 1 WLR 122 and *Black & Decker v Flymo Ltd* [1991] 1 WLR 753.
- Privilege does not extend to child care cases where the role of the court is essentially investigative, *In re L (Police Investigation: Privilege)* The Times, 22 March 1996.
- Privilege may be overridden for specific purposes, for example under the Proceeds of Crime Act 2002, see 3.35–3.42 above.

Privilege and disclosure

3.73   There is inevitably a tension between a possible claim for privilege and the duty of disclosure, and this tension has perhaps become more acute with the 'cards on the table' approach to litigation. In principle all documents relevant to a case are disclosable. One party may claim privilege for a document, but if it is relevant the other side may be keen to see it, not least if it is thought that a claim for privilege might be based on a concern the document could harm the case.

A relevant document will be disclosable unless a claim for privilege is justified by the person **3.74** claiming it. This may need careful explanation to a client. Recent cases have shown how fiercely a claim for privilege may be contested, as there may be big questions relating to commercially sensitive information. There is currently some uncertainty for lawyers and clients as to where the balance lies, and there are problems for document creation management and storage policies for solicitors and clients if privileged information needs to be dealt with in a distinct way. There are also problems about different policies on disclosure in different jurisdictions for an international case. The role of in-house lawyers is also far from clear. The situation is not an easy one—openness is important for effective litigation, but openness could be abused or could add to the length and cost of litigation.

In a John Grisham-like example, the government of the United States of America has filed a **3.75** potentially massive law suit against some of the world's leading tobacco companies. One of these is British American Tobacco (BAT), which sought advice from Lovell's litigation department. BAT has a controversial policy on document retention/destruction (under which a large database was systematically destroyed in 1998), and it has argued that this policy is covered by legal professional privilege. The Court of Appeal has expressed the view that while parts of their policy may be covered by privilege others are not, and that the doctrine of legal professional privilege has roots in the nineteenth century and merits a full review.

In *Three Rivers District Council v Governors and Company Bank of England (No 6)* The Times, **3.76** 12 November 2004 (relating to the collapse of BCCI) the Bank of England sought to protect sensitive correspondence between itself and Freshfields Bruckhaus Deringer, including material relating to a private in-house enquiry carried out by a judge. The Court of Appeal held that the material should be disclosed because legal advice privilege should be distinguished from litigation privilege, and legal advice privilege should only apply where a person is seeking or obtaining legal advice concerning rights and/or obligations, and only as regards documents passing between the client and the lawyer, and not therefore advice on the presentation of evidence. On appeal the House of Lords reversed this approach holding that legal advice privilege could apply to advice as to the presentation of material to an enquiry. While this maintains a more traditional approach, it is clear that courts will now look into circumstances rather than accept general assertions of legal advice privilege, and that privilege will not necessarily extend far beyond documents specifically created for litigation.

J WHERE WORK FALLS SHORT OF PROFESSIONAL STANDARDS

A client may be dissatisfied with the outcome of a case, even if the litigation is conducted **3.77** effectively. Few cases have a 100 per cent chance of success, and for each party that wins a case another may lose. There may be a possibility for appeal, see 23.26–23.44. Alternatively the client may be prepared to accept a negative outcome because he or she has been fully advised about the chances of success and has chosen to accept the possibility of not winning.

Complaints about the standard of work

3.78 If a client is dissatisfied with the standard of work done by a lawyer then various options are available:

- Firms of solicitors will normally have a procedure for dealing with complaints about the conduct of a case, and each client should be provided with information about this. Some barristers' chambers also have complaints procedures.
- A complaint may be made to the Bar Council or the Law Society, as appropriate. Compensation may be provided, albeit at relatively modest levels.
- Concerns can be raised with the Legal Services Ombudsman.
- The concerns may be dealt with in relation to costs.
- In an extreme and appropriate case, an action may be brought for professional negligence.

3.79 In each case it will be for the client to show that there is a proper basis for complaint, and that the concern relates to the conduct of the lawyer, and not to a complaint about something else, such as the relevant law.

3.80 The Law Society has a process for dealing with complaints. They are considered by the Office for the Supervision of Solicitors, see Chapter 30 of the *Guide to Professional Conduct of Solicitors*. Details of the procedure are accessible from the home page www.lawsociety.org.

3.81 The Bar Council has a complaints procedure introduced in 1997. A Complaints Commissioner sifts complaints, and where there is a *prima facie* case complaints go to an adjudication panel. Possible penalties include requiring the barrister to apologise, requiring the barrister to repay or reduce fees, and requiring the barrister to pay compensation up to £5,000 for poor service. In a serious case a disciplinary tribunal may order that the barrister be disbarred or fined, as well as the above remedies. Details of the procedure are accessible from the home page www.barcouncil.org.

3.82 The Legal Services Ombudsman oversees the handling of complaints by the professional bodies, Courts and Legal Services Act 1990. A complainant who is dissatisfied can ask for the case to be reviewed and the Ombudsman can require further action. For details see www.olso.org.

Wasted costs orders

3.83 Solicitors and barristers need to work efficiently to support efficient litigation. With greater case management powers, a court should be able to ensure that time and costs are rarely wasted. However, if a court feels that a solicitor or barrister conducts a case in such a way that costs are incurred improperly or without reasonable cause, or if there is any undue delay or other misconduct in bringing the case, then the court may make an order as regards costs under the Supreme Court Act 1981, s 51. The result of an order may be that the costs are simply disallowed (so that the barrister or solicitor does not get paid), or that the lawyer is ordered to pay costs incurred personally.

3.84 Costs can be wasted if they result from an improper, unreasonable, or negligent act or omission on the part of the lawyer, including costs incurred before such an act or omission if the court thinks it unreasonable they be paid in the light of the act or omission. The judge will consider whether in all the circumstances just to order the lawyer to compensate the applicant for all or part of the wasted costs, *Re a Barrister (Wasted Costs Order) (No 1 of 1991)* (1993) QB 293.

The procedure for making an order is dealt with at 5.80–5.88. A court should be slow to make **3.85** a wasted costs enquiry unless there is a clear case, but the possibility of an application should be a matter of concern for a lawyer. The defects of the lawyer in the conduct of the case must be clearly formulated, and there must be a causal link between the poor conduct and the costs wasted, *Ridehalgh v Horsefield* [1994] 3 WLR 462.

Disallowance of costs

As a less serious alternative, certain costs may be disallowed. A judge may make remarks in **3.86** giving judgment as to what costs should be allowed by the taxing master if the judge feels that the lawyer has not conducted the case properly, *R v McFadden* The Times, 10 December 1978. As a matter of general policy costs may be disallowed if there is a late application to adjourn, or if lawyers are not properly prepared, *Fowkes v Duthie* [1991] 1 All ER 337.

K PROFESSIONAL NEGLIGENCE

The test for professional negligence

A lawyer owes a professional duty of care to the client to deal with the case as a reasonably **3.87** competent lawyer. This duty will be owed in tort by a solicitor or barrister to a client, and will be an implied term of a contract between a lawyer and client. If a barrister or solicitor practises in a specialist field, the standard to be expected is that of such care and skill as would be exercised by a reasonably competent practitioner in that field, *Matrix Securities Ltd v Theodore Goddard (a firm)* [1998] PNLR 290. An action for professional negligence may be brought where a lawyer fails to satisfy the standard of care owed to the client. Although barristers and solicitors must take out professional indemnity insurance to cover such claims, all lawyers will wish to avoid a claim being made.

In case there might be an action for professional negligence a lawyer should give advice in **3.88** writing and keep a written record of key points discussed. Those records need to be retained while an action remains possible. If there is a possibility of a claim being made, for example because a claim form has not been issued before the expiry of the limitation period, then the lawyer against whom the claim might lie has a duty to advise the client to consult another lawyer, so that the new lawyer can advise the client on the claim.

The client will have to show specifically how the barrister or solicitor in question has fallen **3.89** short of the standard normally to be expected of a competent lawyer. This may be done if the lawyer has made a clear error of law, has failed to take a procedural step that should clearly have been taken, has clearly failed to use important evidence properly, or has failed to achieve a remedy that should have been achieved. It may be difficult to show negligence where there could be genuine debate about the relevant law, procedure, and use of evidence. The test is not that a cross examination could have been done differently or a statement of case better drafted, but the normal negligence test of whether the lawyer has clearly fallen short of generally accepted professional standards.

3.90   The client suing a lawyer for professional negligence will also have to show the causation of loss. If a case would probably have been lost even if something had been done differently then little or no loss may arise. The burden is on the claimant to show there would have been a different outcome but for the alleged negligence. This may be difficult as, for example, the judge cannot be compelled to give evidence. If the claimant has lost a chance to litigate then damages will be assessed as a loss of a chance, see *Dixon v Clement Jones Solicitors (a firm)* The Times, 2 August 2004, where an action was struck out for failure to serve a statement of case and it was held the chance of success of the case would have been 30 per cent. In making an assessment the court can take into account that the case may have settled rather than proceeded to court, *Harrison v Bloom Camillin* The Times, 12 November 1999. The claimant will need to take steps to mitigate loss, *Horsfall v Haywards (a firm)* [1999] 1 FLR 1182.

3.91   The fact that an action fails does not mean the client can sue his lawyer forthwith. It may be possible to issue another claim form within the limitation period, or get an existing claim form extended, *Chappell v Cooper* [1980] 2 All ER 463. It is not a defence to claim for negligence that a judge has approved an order, *Burgess v Burgess* (1996) 2 FLR 34. There may be limitation issues in suing a lawyer as it may take the client some time to find out that advice is flawed, or that a step in the case has been concealed from the client, see *Cave v Robinson Jarvis & Rolf* (2003) 1 AC 384 and *Williams v Fanshaw Porter & Hazelhurst (a firm)* [2004] EWCA 157.

Immunity from action

3.92   It was held in the past that a barrister or advocate should be immune from an action for negligence based on anything done in court. The leading case on immunity is *Rondel v Worsley* (1967) 3 All ER 993, in which the House of Lords held that immunity was justified by public policy, particularly in protecting the decisions of courts from being relitigated, to allow advocates freedom to fight a case as they thought best, and to support the primary duty of the lawyer to the court.

3.93   The basis for this immunity has been reviewed and gradually restricted. In *Saif Ali v Sydney Mitchel & Co (a firm)* (1980) AC 198 it was held that there was not immunity for every piece of work connected with litigation, and that protection should not be any wider than was absolutely necessary to protect the interests of justice. In *Kelly v Corsten* (1998) 1 FLR 986 it was said that any blanket immunity from action was out of date and that immunity only applied to the conduct and management of a case in court by an advocate, and there were comments on the problems of suing a lawyer where this would involve attacking a decision of the court.

3.94   There was an overall review in *Arthur JS Hall & Co (a firm) v Simmons* [2002] 3 WLR 543, where the House of Lords heard appeals in three cases involving claims of negligence against solicitors. In each case the defence was that advocates conducting a case were immune from negligence claims. The House of Lords held that there should no longer be a general immunity in respect of the conduct of a case, and indeed a blanket immunity might be a breach of Article 6 of the Convention on Human Rights. The overriding duty of the advocate to the court was supported, but various other anomalies caused concern and the judges reviewed the position in other jurisdictions. The House of Lords felt that public confidence in the legal profession might be undermined if lawyers could not be sued for negligent work.

The decision in the case gave rise to concerns that floodgates of actions against lawyers **3.95** would open and that insurance premiums would rocket. In fact there have only been a few cases, and relatively few that have succeeded. Unmeritorious claims are struck out at an early stage, and it is not easy to satisfy the tests for the action to succeed.

Examples of professional negligence

Examples of actions for professional negligence that have succeeded include: **3.96**

- If the solicitor fails to investigate the facts of a case properly so that the client recovers less than he or she should, the solicitor can be liable, *Dickinson v Jones Alexander & Co* [1990] Fam Law 137.
- Where a solicitor practising in the areas of conveyancing and commercial law appeared to be unaware of relevant tax provisions, *Hurlingham Estates Ltd v Wilde & Partners (a firm)* The Times, 3 January 1997.
- Where solicitors accepted a specific obligation to retain the passport of a father who regained it by making false representations and then used it to remove children from the jurisdiction, solicitors had a professional liability to the children's mother, *Al-Kandari v JR Brown & Co* [1987] 2 All ER 302.
- Where the solicitors fail to pass on important information to their clients, *Strover v Harrington* [1988] 1 All ER 769.
- Where solicitors who had negotiated a business lease failed to notify the client of an unusual clause with regard to rent that was used to raise the rent dramatically, *County Personnel v Alan R Pulber* [1987] 1 All ER 289.
- Where a solicitor improperly terminated a client retainer in a case, *Young v Purdy* The Times, 7 November 1995, though it was held that the solicitor was not liable for loss following from the fact that the former client then represented herself personally, filed defective documents, and settled before relief was determined.

If a solicitor has more than one client in a transaction there is a duty to explain matters fully **3.97** to each, *Mortgage Express Ltd v Bowerman & Partners (a firm)* The Times, 1 August 1995. Where a solicitor acts within his or her ostensible authority, and does work which was within the normal business of a solicitor then liability can attach to the firm as a whole, *United Bank of Kuwait v Hammoud* [1988] 3 All ER 418. There may be an issue as to how far one partner in a firm of solicitors binds others where it could be argued that the partner was acting outside the normal course of business, *JJ Coughlan Ltd v Ruparella* The Times, 26 August 2003. Advice or an opinion which prevents a case from coming to court might be the basis for a negligence action.

Examples of where an action for negligence has not succeeded include: **3.98**

- The mere fact that advice given by a lawyer is not ultimately successful cannot found an action, or no lawyer would risk giving advice where the law was not clear, see *Buckland v Farrar & Moody* [1978] 3 All ER 229.
- A lawyer only has to act within the scope of instructions received. If for example the client is an experienced businessman the lawyer has no obligation to investigate matters

outside her or his instructions, or to provide warnings about the commercial risks of a transaction, *Pickersgill v Riley* The Times, 2 March 2004.

- In *McFarlane v Wilkinson* The Times, 13 February 1997 a barrister sued in negligence only and the claim failed on appeal. The client sued the barrister saying that breach of statutory duty should also have been used, but this failed as it was held that on the facts it would not have added anything to the case.
- A lawyer is not necessarily in breach of duties of competence and care by pursuing a very weak case, though this will depend on the circumstances, *Harley v McDonald Harley (a firm)* The Times, 15 May 2001.
- The lawyer's duty is limited to acting with proper professional care for the client, and is not a blanket duty to protect anyone who may be affected by a case or transaction, *Clarke v Bruce Lane & Co* [1988] 1 All ER 364.

4

AN OVERVIEW OF THE LITIGATION PROCESS

A THE LITIGATION PROCESS 4.02
Why cases do not all proceed in the same way 4.02
Background to the litigation process 4.06

B THE ADVERSARIAL SYSTEM 4.11
Strengths and weaknesses of the adversarial approach 4.12
Implications of the adversarial approach for litigation 4.14

C JUDICIAL CASE MANAGEMENT 4.16

D THE PRE-ACTION STAGE 4.18
The first stages in a case 4.18
Contact with the potential defendant 4.23
Pre-action protocols 4.25
Steps prior to issuing a claim form 4.28

E STARTING AN ACTION IN TIME 4.33
Limitation periods 4.33
Issues relating to limitation periods 4.36

F CHOOSING A COURT 4.42

G CLAIM FORMS 4.51
Timing the issue of the claim form 4.53
Completing a claim form 4.57
Issuing a claim form 4.59
The service of a claim form 4.60
Problems in serving a claim form 4.67
The acknowledgement of service 4.72

H THE FRAMEWORK OF STATEMENTS OF CASE 4.75
Types of statement of case 4.76
The particulars of claim 4.78
The defence 4.80

I TRACK ALLOCATION 4.81
Principles for allocation 4.81
Small claims 4.85

Fast track 4.89
Multi-track 4.96
Changes of track 4.98

J   THE MAIN ELEMENTS OF THE LITIGATION PROCESS 4.100
Reasons why the stages are not always clear cut 4.100
Development of the statements of case 4.102
Applications for interim orders 4.104
Disclosure of evidence 4.106

K   TIMETABLES, CASE MANAGEMENT, AND DIRECTIONS 4.110
Overall 4.110
Key stages for case management 4.113

L   OPTIONS FOR INTERRUPTING OR ENDING LITIGATION 4.117

M   FINAL PREPARATIONS FOR TRIAL 4.130

N   THE TRIAL AND JUDGMENT 4.135

O   COSTS ORDERS 4.139

P   AFTER JUDGMENT 4.143

Q   THE INTERNATIONAL PERSPECTIVE 4.144
International issues 4.144
Identifying relevant substantive law 4.149
Deciding on jurisdiction 4.151
Within EC countries 4.153
For other countries 4.159
Forum non conveniens 4.161
Enforcement of judgments 4.162
References to EC courts 4.165

KEY DOCUMENTS

The one great principle of English law is to make business for itself. There is no other principle distinctly, certainly, and consistently maintained throughout all its narrow turnings.

Charles Dickens, *Bleak House*

4.01   Despite the relative clarity of the Civil Procedure Rules 1998, it can be difficult to gain a clear overall picture of the civil litigation process. This chapter seeks to provide such an overview. This is only an overview and appropriate practitioner sources must be used to check detail and to ensure that information is up to date. There is a guide to practitioner sources for the Civil Procedure Rules 1998 and related sources at 24.04–24.14.

A THE LITIGATION PROCESS

Why cases do not all proceed in the same way

Although in principle the stages of a civil action are fairly clearly defined and the stages are **4.02** governed by time limits or by overall court control, there are many reasons why cases vary substantially in the way they progress.

- There may or may not be significant activity before an action is formally started.
- There can be huge variations in the time it takes to gather and evaluate evidence.
- Important factors in the case may change significantly as further information comes to light.
- There may be significant pauses while the parties negotiate.
- There can be great variations in the number and complexity of interim applications to court before the case goes to trial.
- Cases can stop at different stages in the process, not only through settlement but also through the failure of a party to take a key step such as file a defence.

In addition cases can appear to take rather a long time to come to trial because the parties try **4.03** to settle, or because of the time it takes to collect and evaluate evidence. This is not necessarily a bad thing, and some cases of their nature take some time to reach decision, for example because it is necessary to see the medium to long term effects of injuries to assess damages properly.

It can be particularly difficult for a lawyer training for practice to get a clear overview of the **4.04** litigation process. Some of the rules of procedure are quite complex, and in a training contract or pupillage one will often only see a part of the process. A trainee lawyer can often be involved in a small part of a case, such as an interim application, and may be in practice for some time before seeing a case move from first contact with the client to a court decision.

When studying the rules for the different stages of litigation, the detail on procedures that **4.05** are not used often and the exceptions to cover unusual cases can make it difficult to get a clear grasp of the framework through which most cases progress. To try to counteract this, the following overview concentrates on the basic framework, giving practical explanations of each stage, and the things that each procedure can be used to achieve. These summaries should not be relied on alone in dealing with a case.

Background to the litigation process

It is important to have an overview of the litigation process in order to understand what **4.06** should happen at different stages, to make proper use of each stage, and to take an overview of the strategy in a case. One of the main keys to effective litigation is to make coherent and strategic use of procedural stages and options.

The practical purpose of the civil litigation process is to provide a sufficiently flexible **4.07** structure within which parties to a dispute can:

- define the issues in dispute in a way that is clear to both sides and to the court;

- obtain and exchange relevant documentary information;
- obtain and exchange relevant and properly admissible evidence from witnesses;
- apply to court for orders to help them to prepare for their case;
- apply to court for interim decisions before a final decision can be reached if justice so requires;
- enable steps to be taken before the case is ready for trial where this is necessary to ensure fairness;
- ensure that appropriate information comes before an independent judge so as to allow the case to be fairly decided;
- achieve the above within reasonable time and at a reasonable cost.

4.08 Procedure in the High Court is governed by the Supreme Court Act 1981 and procedure in the County Court is governed by the County Courts Act 1984, though proceedings in both levels of court are now streamlined. Detail is contained in the Civil Procedure Rules 1998 drawn up by the Civil Procedure Rules Committee, Civil Procedure Act 1997, ss 1–2. The Civil Procedure Rules are supplemented by Practice Directions. The Rules and Practice Directions have been supplemented, amended, and updated quite significantly over the last few years because of the need to clarify the fully revised rules introduced in 1999.

4.09 There are special procedural provisions for some specialist courts, such as the Commercial Court Guide and the Mercantile Courts Guide. The High Court has a historical inherent jurisdiction to deal with areas not covered by the Rules. The Rules Committee can be challenged if it exceeds its statutory powers, *General Mediterranean Holdings SA v Patel* (2000) 1 WLR 272.

4.10 This chapter outlines the main stages that any litigation will normally go through before trial. More detailed comment on the potential use of stages in litigation is made in other chapters, such as Chapter 16.

B   THE ADVERSARIAL SYSTEM

4.11 Despite a change of emphasis in the Civil Procedure Rules 1998, the litigation process in England and Wales remains essentially adversarial. The judge does not have the inquisitorial role of seeking evidence with a view to establishing truth. The judge's role is rather to decide between the cases presented by each side, and in a civil case to do that on the balance of probabilities. The onus is on the lawyers for each side to prepare and present their case in the best way they can.

Strengths and weaknesses of the adversarial approach

4.12 The adversarial principle has various strengths and weaknesses. One strength is that each side is strongly motivated to present their case fully and well. Another is that a client will often feel strong support from lawyers presenting his or her case.

4.13 On the other hand, it is a particular weakness of the adversarial system that it can be difficult for a lawyer to form a balanced view of the strengths and weaknesses of a case in its early stages. Most clients will pitch their case at its very best, possibly even embellishing it, in early meetings with a lawyer, and they may be slow to reveal potential weaknesses in the case. The lawyer may not be able to form an informed overview of the case until the case for the other side is revealed, which may not really happen until litigation is well under way and the stage of disclosure of evidence is reached. The lawyer may be led into giving over-optimistic advice, and costs may build up before the more balanced view of the case emerges. This weakness has been partly addressed through pre-action protocols which require the exchange of basic information about a case before any action commences, see 4.25–4.27. It is nonetheless wise during the early stages of a case for the lawyer to bear in mind the potential gap between what your client says and what the other client is likely to be telling his or her lawyer!

Implications of the adversarial approach for litigation

The importance of the lawyer in framing the case and taking it forward means that much can **4.14** depend on the efficacy of the lawyer as well as on the inherent strength of the case. The adversarial approach has several consequences for the effectiveness of litigation.

- It can make the way that a case is conceptualised by a lawyer particularly important. It is the lawyer who takes primary responsibility for identifying causes of action and defendants.
- It can make the way that the lawyer frames the action in a statement of case particularly important as statements of case largely govern what the issues in the case will be.
- The choices taken by the lawyer in framing the case in the statement of case largely dictate the issues that will be decided at trial and the evidence that will be relevant.
- It makes the presentation of a case through persuasive advocacy particularly important.

The adversarial principle is also at the root of a number of rules of procedure and evidence. **4.15** For example the fact that a court hearing is adversarial makes it necessary to have rules on the burden and standard of proof, and the fact that a case is prepared on an adversarial basis makes it necessary to have rules on disclosure.

C JUDICIAL CASE MANAGEMENT

Although the adversarial principle remains fundamental to the approach to litigation in **4.16** England and Wales, the Civil Procedure Rules now provide for a judge to have a much clearer and stronger role in overseeing the progress of a case than was previously the case, CPR Part 3, The Court's Case Management Powers. Although the decisions in a case remain largely in the control of the parties, the court has significant powers of intervention to ensure that a case progresses properly.

- A judge provides for the progress of a case through giving directions.
- A judge can maintain an overview of the progress of a case through case management conferences and other hearings.
- The parties cannot vary key dates in the progress of a case without the approval of the court.
- There are a number of instances where a court has the power to make an order even if one of the parties has not applied for it.

4.17   The combination of the adversarial system and judicial case management mean that most formal documents in the litigation process must be both lodged with the court and served on the other side.

D   THE PRE-ACTION STAGE

The first stages in a case

4.18   The earliest stage of litigation is when a client first approaches a lawyer to ascertain whether there is a legal case and what chance of success it has. This stage is important as many impressions about the type and strength of the case will be formed very quickly.

Client objectives

4.19   The most important objective at this stage is to get as clear a picture as possible from the client as to the circumstances that give rise to the potential litigation, and what the client wants to achieve.

Information gathering

4.20   It will be necessary to consider how much information gathering and decision taking should take place before any contact is made with the other side. How much evidence can and should be gathered to assess the strength of the case? The lawyer has to balance the need to be able to form as sound a view as possible with the drawback of building up costs before any decision has been taken as to whether litigation is realistic and likely to succeed. It may be appropriate to seek the views of counsel as to the strength of a potential claim before taking any action. The collection of evidence is covered in Chapter 15.

Getting instructions

4.21   Before any contact is made with the potential defendant, basic and provisional decisions should be taken as to the probable cause of action and the remedies sought. The client needs to be fully informed about potential causes of action and potential defendants, the likelihood of success and the potential time taken by and cost of litigation. The client should give instructions for the case to be brought. Taking client instructions is covered in Chapter 7.

Clarifying how litigation will be funded

4.22   The client should be informed as clearly as possible about the possible cost of bringing an action, and about the possible impact of costs orders (such as having to pay the defendant's costs if the action is lost). It should be decided whether the costs of the action are to be met from the client's own pocket, from some other source, or from a contingency fee agreement, see 5.21–5.25.

Contact with the potential defendant

4.23   Though there might be some tactical advantage in issuing a claim form to surprise a defendant, there are many reasons for contacting a potential defendant before starting any formal action. In most circumstances the defendant will in any event be aware that litigation is possible because he or she knows that an accident has been caused or a contract breached.

- It is important to test the strength of the case by getting an indication of the defendant's view. This is often done in a letter before action, which sets out the type of case contemplated and the remedy sought. Sometimes the response to a letter before action will provide a rather different view of the potential case and the position may need to be reviewed and perhaps more evidence sought before any action is taken.
- The response of the potential defendant may be relatively helpful—liability may be accepted fairly quickly so that the only issue will be damages.
- Even if the response is very negative—a case may be hotly defended on all issues—that will give an indication of the approach the potential defendant will take. There may be a number of informal contacts with the potential defendant, such as telephone calls, as well as formal letters. It will be important to keep a note of these.
- It may be possible to avoid litigation or to limit the issues to be litigated.

The importance of contact with the potential defendant is emphasised by Pre-action Protocols. Even where a Pre-action Protocol does not apply, the spirit of the protocol should be followed. Offers to settle are possible, see 20.58 and 20.85. **4.24**

Pre-action protocols

The Civil Procedure Rules encourage openness and cooperation before an action is started. While a lawyer may have concerns about losing tactical advantages through openness at this stage, there are potential advantages in clarifying the possible strengths and weaknesses of the case or in achieving a settlement before costs start to escalate. **4.25**

Pre-action protocols have been drawn up for particular types of action setting out what should normally happen at a pre-action stage. There are specific pre-action protocols for many types of cases, including personal injury, medical negligence, professional negligence, building disputes, defamation claims, and judicial review. Where no specific protocol applies the court will expect the spirit of the pre-action protocol approach and the overriding objective to be followed, see PD Protocols 4.1–4.10. **4.26**

- At the pre-action stage a key obligation for a potential claimant is to send a letter setting out the claim and what is sought, enclosing copies of essential documents, and seeking an acknowledgement within a period of 21 days. This letter of claim should follow a standard format.
- A potential defendant's response should make it clear whether the claim is accepted or wholly or partly denied. If the claim is not accepted then reasons should be given, supported with essential documents. Details of insurers should be given if sought. If there is no reply the claimant can immediately commence an action. The defendant will have a reasonable period to investigate the claim.
- There should be an early exchange of a standard list of documents.
- Expert evidence should be agreed if possible, with joint selection of an expert.
- The possibility of alternative dispute resolution should be considered.

If a failure to comply with a pre-action protocol can be justified, or is minor, no adverse consequences will ensue. If the failure to comply is deliberate or not justified and as a result **4.27** an action is started unnecessarily then the court can take this into account in making orders as regards costs or interest on damages, to try to ensure that the innocent party is in no worse position than would have been the case had the protocol been complied with (PD Protocols, para 2.3).

Steps prior to issuing a claim form

4.28   Unless a limitation period is about to expire, various steps should be taken before issuing a claim form. Even if no specific pre-action protocol applies, the general approach of the pre-action protocol should be followed, by contacting the defendant and attempting to settle the case without formal litigation if possible. Other steps to be taken are detailed below.

Taking decisions about how the case will be framed and pursued

4.29   Decisions about causes of action, remedies sought, and who should be sued will need to be taken prior to the issue of the claim form, and/or the issue of the particulars of claim.

Gathering sufficient evidence

4.30   The time and money spent on gathering evidence before starting the case must be considered. On the one hand it is important to have sufficient evidence to be able to assess adequately the type of case involved and its chances of success. If damages are claimed there will need to be a provisional assessment of the sum to enable the claimant to take an informed decision about whether it is worth suing. On the other hand there is little point is gathering too much evidence before it is reasonably clear how much of the case the defendant is likely to dispute. It is likely to be most important to get statements from key witnesses, to get key documents such as accident reports, and to get appropriate expert evidence on matters like the cause of an accident and the extent of injuries. The expert to be used should be agreed if possible to save costs.

Complying with formalities

4.31   In some cases notices in proper form must be sent before commencing an action, for example in some consumer credit and landlord and tenant cases.

Seeking court orders before action

4.32   Sometimes it may be necessary to seek a court order before commencing proceedings. Possible examples of this include seeking information about the identity of a potential defendant and seeking pre-action disclosure. These are dealt with more fully at 16.63–16.78.

E   STARTING AN ACTION IN TIME

Limitation periods

4.33   It is fair and practical that an action be started within a reasonable time of the cause of action arising. If too much time passes then evidence may be difficult to collect or of limited value, law may have changed, and there may be significant unfairness to a defendant. For that purpose limitation periods for different types of action have been established by law. A reasonable limitation period will not infringe a potential claimant's human rights.

The fact that an action is not started within a limitation period is not a total bar to it **4.34** continuing, but it can and normally will be raised as a defence. If it is successfully raised the claimant will not be able to proceed with his or her action however well founded it is. Because of the potentially serious penalty of a claimant not being able to pursue an action there are statutory rules to ensure as much fairness as possible, and a body of case law has grown up.

Limitation periods are governed by the Limitation Act 1980, and the periods for the most **4.35** common types of litigation are:

Type of action	Limitation period
Personal injuries claims in negligence, nuisance, or breach of duty (including contract or statute)	3 years
Fatal Accident Act claims on behalf of dependents of the deceased	3 years
All other tort actions	6 years
Contract claims (other than personal injury)	6 years
Contributions under the Civil Liability (Contributions) Act 1978	2 years
Recovery of land	12 years
Breach of trust	6 years

A human rights claim should be brought within one year of the act complained of, or such longer period as the court considers equitable in the circumstances.

Issues relating to limitation periods

In general terms time starts to run from the time when all the elements of the cause of action **4.36** are in place and there is a potential claimant and defendant. Therefore time will not run against someone under a disability, such as a child. Time is normally calculated up to the day the claim form is issued. However a set off or counterclaim is deemed to have been started at the same time as the original action, which may save a claim that is otherwise time-barred. Part 20 claims are deemed to start when the Part 20 claim form is issued.

There are special rules as to when time starts to run in tort cases where there is personal injury **4.37** or latent damage and these are dealt with in Chapter 19. The fact that one cause of action is time-barred does not mean that another will be—an action barred in contract may not be barred in tort, *Iron Trade Mutual Insurance Co Ltd v JK Buckenham Ltd* [1990] 1 All ER 808.

The problems that can follow if a case of action is not picked up quickly enough can be seen **4.38** in *Moore & Co v Ferrier* [1988] 1 All ER 400, where a firm of solicitors was instructed to draft contracts in 1971. It was not appreciated that some of the terms did not have the intended effect, and no action was brought on the inadequate drafting until 1985. It was held that time started to run when the terms were negligently drafted, and therefore the action was brought out of time.

If a defendant has deliberately concealed a fact relevant to the claimant's cause of action **4.39** then time will only run once the claimant discovers or could with reasonable diligence have discovered the concealment. This can include a case where the concealment has happened after time has started to run, *Sheldon v RHM Outhwaite (Underwriting Agencies) Ltd* (1996) AC 102 HL. Time will not run if a defendant is deliberately concealing information as in *Williams v Fanshaw Porter Williams* (2004) 2 All ER 616, where a solicitor failed to inform a client that an action had been settled, and *Kitchen v Royal Air Force Association* [1958] 1 WLR 563, where a solicitor failed to advise a client of a potential cause of action, or that an offer to settle had been made. However the concealment must involve active steps and deliberate wrongdoing and not just a failure to take proper care, *Cave v Robinson Jarvis and Rolf* (2003) 1 AC 384 HL. Equally time does not run if the claimant's action arises from the consequences of a mistake, until the mistake is or could with reasonable diligence have been discovered, see *Peco Arts Inc v Hazlitt Gallery Ltd* (1983) 1 WLR 1315.

4.40 It can be difficult categorising a claim to decide which limitation period applies. In *Oates v Harte Reade and Co* (1999) PIQR P120 a former client sued a solicitor for professional negligence in the handling of a divorce action (a claim in tort and contract). The claim included damages for anxiety and distress, and it was held it was therefore a personal injuries claim with a three-year limitation period.

4.41 Although there are limited powers to extend a limitation period, the risk of starting an action outside a limitation period should never knowingly be taken. If a client approaches a lawyer at a late stage or if negotiations are continuing, the claim form should still be issued within the limitation period. Should a claim form not be issued within the limitation period due to the failure of a lawyer to inform the client of the importance of starting an action before the limitation period expires and/or failing to ensure that the action is started in time then the claimant may be able to sue the lawyer for professional negligence, with the measure of damages related to the loss of the chance to win the original action.

F   CHOOSING A COURT

4.42 There is a broad overlap of jurisdiction and procedure between the High Court and the county court. Cases of more limited value and importance will be heard by a county court, but in many cases the claimant will have a choice.

4.43 The High Court has three Divisions, the Chancery Division, the Queen's Bench Division, and the Family Division. There are also some specialist courts within these Divisions. The most important of these for general litigation purposes are the Commercial Court which is part of the Queen's Bench Division, and the Companies Court which is part of the Chancery Division. There are also Mercantile Courts which provide specialist judges at District Registries and county courts. The High Court has 133 District Registries. There are over 200 county courts.

The High Court and the county court have concurrent jurisdiction for many types of proceedings. The most important distinctions are as follows.

4.44 Claims that must be brought in the country court:

- Personal injury claims with a value not exceeding £50,000 must be brought in the county court.

- Consumer credit cases with an upper credit limit not exceeding £25,000 must be brought in the county court.
- Other money claims with a value not exceeding £15,000 must be brought in the county court.
- Claims for possession of land should normally be brought in the country court where the land is situated.

Claims that must be brought in the High Court: **4.45**

- Equity proceedings, proceedings under the Law of Property Act 1925, and contentious probate proceedings must be brought in the High Court if their value exceeds £30,000.
- Judicial review and defamation proceedings must be brought in the High Court.
- Claims under the Human Rights Act 1998, s 7(1)(a) in respect of a judicial act must be brought in the High Court.
- Proceedings can be brought in the High Court where they are appropriate for a special list, such as the Company Court.

Essentially the county court can grant the same remedies as the High Court, CCA 1984 **4.46** s 38(1), save for applications for judicial review. A county court cannot grant a search order and has limited power to grant a freezing order (though a case can be transferred to the High Court for the making of such an order and then be transferred back!).

In the cases where there is a choice between the High Court and the county court the most **4.47** relevant factors for taking a decision are:

- the importance of the case;
- whether the case involves difficult questions of law or fact;
- whether the higher costs of bringing the case in the High Court are justified, not least in that there may be penalties in costs in using the High Court when it is not really appropriate, even if the claimant is successful;
- the convenience of the location of the court for the parties, and possibly for key witnesses.

These factors show that a variety of practical and tactical matters may need to be considered **4.48** in deciding which court should be used. If there is a choice to be made, the options and the pros and cons of each should be explained to the client for a choice to be made. Even if a case is technically capable of proceeding in the High Court, the county court will often be used for convenience and to keep costs down. Damages claimed will often be at least twice as high as the technical limit before a High Court action is seriously considered.

It is possible for a case to be transferred to another court, the court having a discretion to be **4.49** exercised on specific criteria such as the value of the claim and the convenience of the court, CPR r 30.3. For example in the case of a money claim against an individual that is defended the case is transferred to the defendant's home court, CPR r 26.2. A case may be transferred to the High Court if there is a real prospect of the court making an order of incompatibility under the Human Rights Act 1998.

Within the High Court, the Chancery Division is generally more appropriate where the case **4.50** will be a matter of reading or interpreting documents and of legal argument rather than one of disputed fact and the examination of witnesses. It will be appropriate for any matter connected with a trust, and for some contract actions.

G   CLAIM FORMS

4.51   Formal litigation is started with the issue and service of a claim form. See CPR Part 7 How to start proceedings—the claim form, and PD 7 How to start proceedings—the claim form. The Civil Litigation Rules 1998 make it clear that litigation should be seen as a matter of last resort if a case cannot be settled.

4.52   The early stages of a case are governed by quite strict rules designed to ensure that:

- the claimant formally notifies the court that a claim is being brought by 'issuing' the claim form;
- the defendant receives notification of the claim through 'service' of a copy of the claim form;
- the claimant provides sufficient detail of the claim in particulars of claim.

Timing the issue of the claim form

4.53   Once the claim form has been issued it must be served on the defendant within four months, and the particulars of claim setting out the details of case must be served with the claim form or very soon thereafter. Other steps like track allocation will follow quite quickly, forcing the pace of the litigation and causing costs to build. Unless limitation is about to expire, the issuing of the claim form should only take place when the case is properly prepared.

4.54   The claimant should choose the timing of the issue of the claim form carefully.

- It is important to have sufficient overall information about the case to take clear and justifiable decisions about the appropriate cause(s) of action and the appropriate defendant(s).
- It is important to have gathered sufficient evidence on key issues (including expert evidence if appropriate) to be able to judge the strength of the case.
- It is desirable to have sufficient information on injuries and/or losses to make appropriate decisions about the remedies to be sought.
- Any relevant pre-action protocol should have been complied with if possible.
- It should be reasonably clear that there is no purpose to be served in waiting any longer before starting the action, for example that no early settlement seems likely.
- The client should have been fully advised and have given instructions to start the action.

4.55   Having said this:

- It can be difficult to judge when there is sufficient evidence to take sound decisions about the case.
- There may be particular difficulties when assessment of the strength of the case partly depends on evidence which is only held by the defendant. Save for the extent to which this has been revealed under a pre-action protocol or voluntarily it will not be revealed until the disclosure stage. It may be necessary to start an action and then to review it after disclosure.
- Pre-action contact with the defence may lead to attempts to negotiate, and it can be difficult to decide when these are getting nowhere and an action needs to be started.

If the formal action is started too early it is likely to be more difficult to define the issues in   **4.56**
the case properly, which is likely to waste time and costs. It can be even more serious to
commence an action too late—if the action is not started within the relevant limitation
period it will be time-barred. There may be tactical reasons for selecting the time to issue
the claim form. The issue of the claim form can show the defendant that the claimant is
serious about seeking redress, which may help to focus minds and attempts to settle may
follow.

Completing a claim form

A claim form must be in a prescribed form, Form N1. This requires setting out the court in   **4.57**
which the action will be brought, the names and addresses of the parties, and a concise
statement of the nature of the claim and the remedy sought. The claim form must also
include a statement of truth signed by the claimant or the claimant's representative, which
means that the contents can be used as evidence.

The claim form must also include statements to assist with allocation of the case. If a claim is   **4.58**
for money the amount sought must be specified, or there must be a statement whether the
sum claimed is no more than £5,000, between £5,000 and £15,000 or over £15,000. For a
personal injuries claim there should be a statement whether the amount expected for pain,
injury, and loss of amenity is above or below £1,000. If the case is to be issued in the High
Court, this must be justified by a statement that the claimant expects to recover more than
£15,000 (or £50,000 in a personal injury case), or by reference to an Act specifying that the
case must be brought in the High Court. If the case is to go to a specialist court list, that
should also be justified.

Issuing a claim form

The formal litigation process is commenced with the issue of a claim form. 'Issuing' is the   **4.59**
process of informing the court of the action. The claim form is issued by being sent to the
relevant court office. This is normally done by the solicitor, who should produce enough
copies of the claim form for the court and for each defendant, and a covering letter saying
the claim is to be issued. If time is short, the claim form can be taken to the court office. The
court office will issue the claim form by stamping it, giving it a number, and entering the
details of the action on the court records.

The service of a claim form

Not only must the court be informed of the intended action through issue of the claim form,   **4.60**
a defendant must be informed of the action by service of a copy of the claim form on him or
her. Provided the defendant is within England and Wales, service on the defendant should
be by an appropriate method within four months of issue, CPR r 7.5. This is a vital step—the
defendant must be properly informed of an action in order to be able to properly defend it.
There are therefore a number of rules to ensure that service is properly carried out, see CPR
Part 6, Service of documents and PD 6, Service. The rules are largely common sense, but it is
vital that they be properly complied with or the action may not be properly commenced,
and it may be expensive or impossible to start a further action.

4.61   Service on the defendant is normally effected by the court using ordinary first class post, though the rules provide for alternatives. A response pack is included for the convenience of the defendant. Service must be by an appropriate method and to an appropriate place, CPR r 6.2 and 6.5, to try to ensure that the claim form comes to the attention of the defendant. An individual is usually served at his usual or last known residence. A business is normally served at the current or last known place of business. A company is served at its principal place of business or registered office, CPR r 6.5.

4.62   The full list of permissible methods of service is:

- First class post to the appropriate address as above.
- Personal service on the defendant.
- Leaving a document at the appropriate address as above.
- Service by document exchange, fax, or other electronic means is also possible if a party has indicated willingness to be served in this way and has supplied the number or address to be used, PD 6 para 3.
- By service on the parties' solicitor at the solicitor's office, if this has been agreed.

4.63   If the claim form is served by post there are binding rules for when it will be deemed to be received, CPR r 6.7. Note that service is deemed to take place on the second day after first class posting even if this is a Saturday or Sunday, and that this presumption is irrebuttable, *Anderton v Clwyd County Council* (2002) 1 WLR 3174. Since 30 June 2004 a certificate of service must be verified by a statement of truth.

4.64   There are many options for effecting service to allow plenty of choice for the claimant, not least if the defendant seeks to avoid service. On the other hand the rules are applied quite strictly to protect a defendant from a claim that may not come to his or her attention. The need to comply with the rules for service cannot be over emphasised, and failure to do so may not be easy to address, see for example *Vinos v Marks & Spencer* (2001) 3 All ER 784.

4.65   Most claim forms are served soon after they are issued. However the claimant may choose not to serve the claim form immediately, for example because negotiations are continuing or because he or she wants a little more time to collect evidence. The period of validity of the claim form may be extended by the court, but only in specific circumstances. The period may be extended if the court has been unable to serve the defendant, or the claimant has taken all reasonable steps to serve the claim form but has been unable to do so. The application should be made promptly, supported by written evidence, and should normally be made before the claim form expires. The case will be decided according to the principles in the overriding objective. In broad terms an extension may be granted if the defendant is evading service or if the parties had agreed there be no service while they negotiated. General problems with getting evidence or a general wish not to upset a negotiation are less likely to be successful. The claimant needs to show what period of extension is justified. For the principles to be applied see *Hashtroodi v Hancock* (2004) 3 All ER 530.

4.66   If a claim form expires a new claim form may be issued if the limitation period is not over.

Problems in serving a claim form

Although the intention of the rules is very straightforward, there can be significant problems **4.67** in effecting service:

- It may be difficult to locate the defendant.
- The defendant may seek to avoid service so as to avoid the action.
- There may turn out to be an error relating to the identity or legal personality of the defendant.
- Documents may get lost in the post or after an unsuccessful attempt has been made to deliver them.
- If service is left to the last minute things can easily go wrong.
- A defendant may easily be motivated to contest service, especially if it may then be argued that limitation has expired so no action is possible.

The only sensible approach is to take care to identify the defendant accurately and to take **4.68** care to issue and serve the claim form by a proper means in plenty of time. If in any doubt, check the detail of the rules, and the case law illustrating the difficulties that can arise and the attitude of the court. This is not simply boring bureaucracy but a vital step.

As regards addressing any problems that do arise: **4.69**

- It may be necessary to consider which form of service for the claim form is most likely to succeed, and if necessary try more than one method.
- It may be possible to get an order for service by an alternative method under CPR r 6.8, if there may be some way of making contact with the defendant beyond the prescribed methods for service.
- If it proves impossible to serve the claim form within four months an application can be made to extend its validity as set out at 4.65, but such an application should be made before the claim form expires and the validity will only be extended in limited circumstances.
- It may be possible for there to be an order dispensing with service in an exceptional case, *Wilkey v British Broadcasting Corporation* (2003) 1 WLR 1, or where there is a minor problem with service, *Cranfield v Bridgegrove Ltd* (2003) 3 All ER 129.
- If the limitation period has not expired a further claim form can be issued, but costs will have been spent needlessly

If it has not proved possible to serve the claim form, and if the limitation period has expired, **4.70** it may be impossible to proceed with the action, *Godwin v Swindon Borough Council* (2002) 1 WLR 997. It may be possible to sue the lawyer for negligence if it can be shown that this is the fault of the lawyer.

If it comes to the attention of the claimant that the claim form or particulars of claim have **4.71** not reached the defendant then the claimant must act properly. If, for example, particulars of claim have been served by post but are returned undelivered the claimant should take no further steps, CPR r 13.5, but may apply to the court for directions. Depending on the circumstances, it may be possible to get an order for service by an alternative method, or to treat the particulars of claim as having been served if there is evidence to show that the defendant got them but has sent them back to avoid the action.

The acknowledgement of service

4.72   To check that the claim has come to the attention of the defendant, an acknowledgement of service must be filed with the court by the defendant within 14 days of the service of the claim form. If the particulars of claim is served separately from the claim form, then the time for acknowledgment is extended to 14 days from service of the particulars, see CPR Part 10 Acknowledgment of Service and PD 10 Acknowledgement of service.

4.73   A defendant may choose to ignore a claim form and/or the particulars of claim in an attempt to avoid the claim. Provided these documents have been properly issued and served the court will not normally allow a defendant to escape justice in this way, and if the defendant fails to acknowledge service or to file a defence, a judgment in default is likely to be granted to the claimant, see Chapter 16.

4.74   A party to litigation must have an address for service to be used by the court and by other parties. Normally this will be the business address of the solicitor of the party. This is the solicitor 'on the record'. Any change of solicitor must be recorded following the proper procedure, CPR r 42.2.

H   THE FRAMEWORK OF STATEMENTS OF CASE

4.75   Once the claimant has notified the court and the defendant of the claim, the rules focus on clarifying the issues between the parties through the exchange of statements of case.

Types of statement of case

4.76   The types of statement of case that may be used as necessary to define the issues to be litigated are:

Particulars of claim:	The claimant sets out the factual allegations that comprise the alleged cause of action
Defence:	The defendant responds to the allegations (within 14 days)
Reply:	The claimant can respond to points made in the defence (within 14 days)

If the defendant wishes to bring a cause of action against the claimant this is done by:

Counterclaim:	The defendant sets out the claim (often added to the defence)
Defence to counterclaim:	The claimant responds to those allegations (this can be added to a reply)
Reply to defence to counterclaim:	The defendant can respond to points in the defence to counterclaim

If a further claim is to be made joining an additional party, this is normally done through Part 20 proceedings:

Part 20 claim:	The party sets out the factual allegations that comprise the alleged additional claim
Defence to Part 20 claim:	The party to whom the Part 20 claim is addressed responds to those allegations

Each statement of case must be filed at the court and served on other parties. For defining **4.77** issues for expression in a statement of case see Chapter 10, for drafting a statement of case see Chapter 12, and for taking decisions on parties and remedies see Chapters 13 and 14.

The particulars of claim

The particulars of claim is a very important document. It sets out the claimant's cause(s) of **4.78** action, and is the basis for deciding the issues in the case, and thus what evidence is relevant and admissible.

The particulars of claim may be entered on the reverse of the claim form, or served as a **4.79** separate document within 14 days of the service of the claim form, CPR r 7.4. This period can be extended by agreement or by an order of court. In cases of any complexity the particulars of claim will normally be set out in a separate document, which counsel may be asked to draft.

The defence

Once the defendant has the particulars of claim, he or she must send a sufficiently detailed **4.80** response to the claimant, essentially summarizing how much of the case is accepted or disputed. To do this a defence should be served within 14 days of the service of the claim form, or service of the particulars of claim if that is served later, Rule 9.2, see CPR Part 15, Defence and Reply and PD 15 Defence and Reply. If the defendant has a claim against the claimant, this may be added as a counterclaim, CPR Part 9 Responding to particulars of claim—general.

I TRACK ALLOCATION

Principles for allocation

Subject to jurisdictional rules, the claimant will select the court in which the claim is **4.81** brought. The court, in consultation with the parties, will allocate the case to a particular 'track'. The division of cases into three tracks fits with the ethos of the overriding objective, in particular as regards dealing with cases fairly and expeditiously and proportionately. Cases of lower value and simpler cases get a simpler approach. Track allocation, through the answers to the questionnaires Form N150, can provide a fairly comprehensive review of how well the preparation of the case is progressing. See CPR Part 26 Case management—preliminary stage and PD 26 Case management—preliminary stage: allocation and reallocation.

Soon after the defence is filed, allocation questionnaires will be sent to the parties by the **4.82** court. There is a power to dispense with formal questionnaires, but only if for example there has already been an application to court that has been treated as an allocation hearing. The parties will have at least 14 days to complete these questionnaires, and cannot vary the date by agreement as the information is required by the court. The questionnaires are only a few pages long, and they ask about what needs to be done to get the case ready for trial.

Questions cover areas such as the parties' views on the appropriate track, about witnesses and any intended applications to court, whether a pre-action protocol has been complied with, and whether the case should be transferred or should be stayed pending an attempt to settle. The parties are encouraged to cooperate in completing the questionnaires, including agreeing directions for the future conduct of the case. Each party must enclose an itemised statement of costs to date. Further information can be supplied to the court if it is agreed. There are various possible penalties for failing to file an allocation questionnaire, CPR r 26.5, including the payment of costs, other sanctions, and in an extreme case the striking out of a statement of case.

4.83   When the allocation questionnaires are returned, or the time for filing them is expired, they will be considered by a District Judge, who can seek further information or hold an allocation hearing. The court then issues an allocation notice. The decision is based primarily on the financial value of the case, though the complexity and importance of the case, the remedy sought, the number of parties, the views of the parties, and the amount of oral evidence are also relevant, CPR r 26.8. Case management directions can be made at the same time as track allocation.

4.84   In outline the three tracks are as follows. Many of the points on strategy and tactics in this book are likely to be most relevant to a multi-track case, but similar principles apply to litigation in a fast track case, subject to the simplified procedural framework and the need to keep costs down. Fast track procedure provides a good simple summary of the main stages in litigation. Specialist courts have their own procedures for allocating cases and for managing their progress.

Small claims

4.85   This is a very streamlined procedure for relatively straightforward cases, such as smaller breaches of contract. It deals with claims for no more than £5,000, though a personal injuries claim will not normally be allocated to this track unless the damages claimed for pain, injury, and loss of amenity are less than £1,000. The parties can agree that the case be allocated to this track, but the ultimate decision is with the court. The track is not appropriate for the case where the hearing is likely to last more than a few hours, or for a claim that is not essentially seeking money as the remedy.

4.86   This procedure allows for limited pre-trial preparation. Expert evidence is not allowed without permission. The case is normally progressed on the basis of standard directions from the court. The steps in the case will be very simple, such as all documents relied on in the case being exchanged between the parties and filed at court at least 14 days before the hearing. A preliminary hearing is possible if issues relating to the trial make this appropriate. Interim remedies are generally not available.

4.87   By agreement the case can be decided by a judge without a hearing. If there is a hearing it may be held in the judge's room rather than a court room (though it will still be an open court). The court will not follow the rules of evidence strictly—the judge may ask questions or take all the evidence in chief first. Judgment will normally be given immediately and will be in a simple form, possibly with the terms of the decision being discussed by the parties.

Cost orders will normally only cover fixed fees, court fees, and witness expenses, unless one **4.88** party has acted unreasonably or a fast track case has been dealt with as a small claim by agreement. See CPR Part 27 The small claims track, and PD 27 Small claims track

Fast track

The fast track is for cases that merit more preparation than a small claim but not the detail of **4.89** the full multi track procedure. It is appropriate where the financial value of the claim is not more than £15,000. This track is not appropriate for a case where the hearing is expected to last more than a day. See CPR Part 28 The fast track and PD 28 The fast track

If a case is allocated to the fast track, the court will immediately or within a short time give **4.90** directions for the management of the case, normally setting a timetable that goes right up to trial. The time between these directions and trial will normally be no more than 30 weeks. This means that the whole procedure from issue of proceedings to judgment should be less than a year. A typical timetable up to allocation might be:

Issue of proceedings	
Service of proceedings	2 weeks (must be within 4 months)
Acknowledgement of service	4 weeks
Service of defence and service of allocation	
questionnaires	6 weeks
Return of allocation questionnaires	8 weeks
Allocation to fast track	10 weeks

A typical timetable from the allocation notice to trial might be:

Allocation questionnaire	
Disclosure of documents	4 weeks
Exchange of witness statements	10 weeks
Exchange of expert reports	14 weeks
Pre-trial checklist sent out	20 weeks
Pre-trial checklist returned to court	22 weeks
Trial bundle agreed	28 weeks
Trial bundle lodged with the court	29 weeks
Statement of costs filed and served	day before trial
Hearing	30 weeks

The parties may agree modifications to the timetable, but only the court can alter the date **4.91** for returning the pre-trial checklist or the date for the trial itself, CPR r 28.4. The court will only change a trial date as a matter of last resort, putting emphasis on the need for the overall timetable to be met.

Standard directions are used, though they can be tailored to meet the needs of the case. They **4.92** are designed to identify the issues quickly, and to ensure that evidence is prepared and disclosed. The full range of interim orders may be sought if required, but applications should be made promptly so as not to delay the timetable. The parties will normally be expected to instruct a single expert unless there is good reason for another approach, PD 28 para 3.9.

Complexity may be reduced by other means such as allowing each side to instruct an expert but relying solely on their written reports at trial.

4.93 There may be a pre-trial hearing, or the court may simply confirm the trial date and perhaps give some further directions for trial. The parties should have at least three weeks notice of the trial.

To allow the judge to read the papers before the trial a trial bundle of documents must be agreed and the claimant should ensure that a copy is lodged with the court. This should include a short case summary.

4.94 The trial will normally take place in a county court, and the judge will normally have read the papers in advance. At trial procedures are simplified, perhaps dispensing with opening statements, and having the witness statements stand as examination in chief. A timetable for the trial may be set in advance with a direction setting out how much time should be spent on each section of the trial.

4.95 With this relative simplicity there can be significant savings in costs. Costs will normally be dealt with by the trial judge at the end of the trial. There are set fees for counsel up to £750 and for a solicitor in attendance, if necessary, of £250, CPR r 46.2–4. If a case settles, a proportion of the fee will be allowed for preparation.

Multi-track

4.96 This will be the normal track for all cases that are not properly allocated to the small claims or fast track, thus covering most cases of any size. The broad stages of a multi-track case are set out below. See CPR Part 29 The multi-track and PD 29 The multi-track.

4.97 Multi-track cases are normally dealt with at Civil Trial Centres, the larger courts, but only the most important cases justify the use of the resources of the Royal Courts of Justice. Cases worth less than £50,000 will normally be transferred (PD 29 para 2.2), unless they have to be tried in the High Court, or are relatively complex cases, for example involving a fatal accident.

Changes of track

4.98 It is possible for a case to be reallocated to a different track. A party who is dissatisfied with a track allocation can apply for a hearing with the judge who made the allocation if there was not a hearing in the first place, or if there has been a material change of circumstances. If there was a hearing and the party was present or represented then the only option is to appeal.

4.99 The allocation of a case may need to be reviewed if there are significant changes such as Part 20 proceedings bringing in another party, or an amendment to a statement of case that substantially increases the value of a claim. However an amendment may not be allowed in such circumstances if the case is already well advanced, *Maguire v Molin* (2003) 1WLR 644.

J THE MAIN ELEMENTS OF THE LITIGATION PROCESS

Reasons why the stages are not always clear cut

The main elements and stages in a civil action after the defence has been served can appear   **4.100**
confusing for a number of reasons.

- The rules vary for the different tracks.
- Once the defence has been served there is flexibility in stages and timeframes, especially in a multi-track case.
- A wide variety of interim applications can be made and interim orders sought, making significant differences in how individual cases progress.
- Rules for different procedural and evidential matters do not necessarily mesh together very coherently.
- The parties may agree some variations in procedure and timetables.
- The nature of the case and the way it needs to move forward may change significantly as more information becomes available and the case is reviewed.

In fact the essential litigation process is relatively straightforward. Many of the procedures   **4.101**
and stages are broadly what one might put in if one were designing a litigation system from
scratch—especially since the full review that produced the Civil Procedure Rules. The multi-
track procedure essentially follows the relatively simple stages of the fast track. There has to
be provision for defining the issues to be decided, for the exchange of information, and for
some decisions to be taken before the whole case is decided. Complexity comes because
there are so many different procedures that might be relevant, because things can happen in
different orders, and because no two cases are the same.

Development of the statements of case

The causes of action, the remedies sought, and the issues in the case should be defined in the   **4.102**
statements of case, see 4.76. A case may be defined in the particulars of claim and the
defence, but many cases become more complex than this because:

- the statement of case may need to be further refined as more evidence comes to light through investigation or on disclosure;
- the statement of case may need to be adjusted to take into account the way that the other side are putting their case in their statements of case;
- there may be more than one cause of action, made by more than one party;
- more parties may be joined, requiring more claims to be set out and responded to (see Chapter 13).

Although the rules provide for statements of case to be filed and served to a fairly tight   **4.103**
timetable, in practice the parties can agree to longer timeframes if needed, subject to case
management by the court. In principle it is possible to continue to refine the statements of
case right up to and sometimes even during the trial, if this is thought necessary to achieve
justice, and subject to the party who wishes to amend paying appropriate costs.

Applications for interim orders

4.104 It may well take many months to define the issues in the case and to collect all the relevant evidence. Inevitably a number of matters may need to be addressed before the case finally comes to trial, and this can be done by applying to the court for an interim order. This is dealt with in Chapter 16.

4.105 To provide just a few examples:

- A claimant may want to stop the defendant from doing something pending a decision in the case, and can do this through seeking an interim injunction.
- A severely injured claimant may need money before a negligence case is finally decided, and can seek an interim payment.

Disclosure of evidence

4.106 To enable each party to prepare for court, and to review the case with a view to assessing its strength and possibly proposing terms for settlement, it is important that each side should be able to see the evidence that the other side proposes to rely on. In the past the approach was often to 'keep the cards close to one's chest' and delay revealing evidence for tactical reasons. A number of films set in a litigation context turn on evidence dramatically revealed only at trial. However the predominant approach in civil litigation is now for openness, and 'putting one's cards on the table' to save costs and encourage settlement.

4.107 It may take a significant amount of time for information on all the issues in the case to be gathered, and for the information that has been collected to be reviewed and assembled as the evidence to be used in the case. The informal statements that clients and witnesses have given to lawyers need to be turned into formal witness statements. Expert reports may need to be reviewed and developed. All the evidence must be checked for gaps and ambiguities.

4.108 The disclosure of evidence should normally be orchestrated to happen at a time when both sides have been able to gather their evidence, and should happen simultaneously as a matter of fairness. Two processes should be distinguished:

- Disclosure of evidence. Once the parties have assembled the documents that they intend to rely on they need to exchange lists of documents. The parties are then able to inspect each other's documents seven days later, normally by sending copies through the post, see 15.179–15.200.
- Exchange of witness statements. Each party must decide which potential witnesses to rely on, and to prepare the evidence of each witness as a formal witness statement or affidavit. This written evidence must be exchanged, see 15.201–15.211.

4.109 Inevitably parties may not be keen to make full disclosure, and various procedures are available for clarification and further exchange of evidence. These include making requests for further information, see 16.144–16.169.

K TIMETABLES, CASE MANAGEMENT, AND DIRECTIONS

Overall

Theoretically even a multi-track case could pass through all its stages and come on for   **4.110**
hearing in only a few months if the parties were fully prepared and everything were done as
quickly as possible. However, in practice, most High Court actions will take many months to
reach trial. Effective litigation should avoid unnecessary delay, but some delays are
necessary.

- In a complex case it may take time for the issues in dispute to be fully defined through
  the statements of case. Amendments may be needed as more information emerges and as
  a result of amendments to the cases of other parties.
- In a complex case all parties may wish to make a number of interim applications to the
  court.
- In a complex case the initial disclosure of evidence may make it clear that the parties
  need to collect more evidence to deal with matters that are emerging.
- If a case has multiple parties and/or multiple causes of action then defining issues,
  making interim applications, and dealing with evidence are all inevitably more complex.
- The making and consideration of offers to settle can be made more time consuming by
  all the above.

To allow for all these matters to be dealt with justly there has to be flexibility in the timetable   **4.111**
for progressing a multi-track action. The time for filing or serving any document can be
extended with the written consent of the parties, or by the court on such terms as are just.

In the past the progress of the case was primarily in the hands of the parties, which could   **4.112**
easily result in significant delays. The Civil Procedure Rules now provide for the court to
oversee and to review the progress of a case. Much still remains in the hands of the parties,
and if the case is progressing efficiently and with a reasonable level of agreement between
the parties the court will have a light touch. If there are difficulties the court can intervene to
give directions, and if necessary to impose penalties.

Key stages for case management

Directions on track allocation

On track allocation the court will usually give directions about the future conduct of the   **4.113**
case. This is often done by the court on its own initiative without a hearing, but in a more
complex multi-track case the court may convene a case management conference to involve
the parties in agreeing directions as far as possible. The directions will provide for matters
like the exchange of information, and will probably provide for a broad timetable up to the
date for the return of pre-trial checklists

Directions at a hearing

If and when the case comes back to court for any interim hearing or for a decision on any   **4.114**
application the progress of the case can be reviewed and the directions can be amended or
further directions given as necessary.

A case management conference

4.115 If a case is particularly complex there may be a specially convened case management conference for the progress of the case to be fully reviewed. The review can cover whether issues have been clearly defined in the statements of case. Matters of evidence can also be reviewed, including disclosure and expert evidence, and requests for further information can be considered. The court may seek to encourage agreement where possible. Directions may be amended or further directions given for the future management of the case. A case management conference can be fixed at any time after allocation, Rule 29.3 and PD 29.5. As the title suggests, the intention is that the process involves discussion rather than simply directions.

4.116 The making of directions for the conduct of the litigation can be initiated by agreement, by one of the parties or by the court.

L   OPTIONS FOR INTERRUPTING OR ENDING LITIGATION

4.117 The timetable for making progress in a case may be modified or interrupted for various reasons. The parties may agree extensions of time between themselves so long as the date for returning pre-trial checklists and the date of the case itself are not affected. A judge may agree to a change in the timetable through directions at a hearing or a pre-trial review.

4.118 There are a variety of formal ways in which a case can become dormant or be ended. It is important to be aware of the differences between the options, and to select the appropriate option if a case ceases to follow the normal litigation process. If a claim form has not been issued then a claim can be informally dropped at any time.

4.119 The most common way for an action to end is with a settlement, but this of itself does not end an action. If a settlement is reached after the claim form has been issued then the action must be dealt with in one of the following ways (see also 20.84–20.102).

Early judgment

4.120 A case may be ended through summary judgment, or through a judgment in default, see Chapter 16. Such a judgment will depend on the inaction of a party.

Adjournment

4.121 A judge may agree to adjourn a hearing or a case if persuaded that this is the right thing to do. A case may be adjourned for a set period, or it may be adjourned indefinitely. A case may be adjourned on terms agreed by the parties that are recorded.

Consent orders

4.122 A judge may be prepared to make a consent order, but this can only be done once a claim form is issued and when a judge is in a position to make an order in relation to the case.

Staying an action

4.123 The High Court has an inherent power to stay an action on the application of a party or on its own initiative, SCA 1981, s 49, and the county court has a similar power, County Courts

Act 1984, s 38. While an action is stayed no steps can be taken (though time can continue to run as regards the validity of a claim form, *Aldridge v Edwards* (2000) CLPR 349). An application for a stay can be made by application notice, supported by evidence if appropriate. A stay may be appropriate for a substantive reason, for example to allow arbitration or mediation to take place, to allow expert evidence to be gathered, or while some other legal issue is decided such as whether proceedings should be allowed to proceed in another jurisdiction.

A stay may also be appropriate for procedural reasons, for example if a payment into court is accepted or an order for security of costs is not met. The stay can be removed by the court when good reason is shown.   **4.124**

The court has a positive duty to encourage the parties to settle the case or to use alternative dispute resolution, and may order a stay in the proceedings to assist this. This may be done on the request of the parties or at the court's initiative. A stay will initially be for a month, but can be extended as the court thinks appropriate without having to have a further hearing, though an extension of more than four weeks would need to be justified. If there is a stay for this purpose the claimant is under a duty to tell the court if the case is settled. If the case is not settled the court will give directions of the continuance of the case. A claim may be automatically stayed if nothing is done for six months. Such a stay may be lifted on a reasoned application by a party.   **4.125**

Discontinuance

All or part of an action can be discontinued if a party voluntarily gives up all or part of their claim, which should be formally recorded by filing Form N279 and serving it on the parties, see CPR Part 38 Discontinuance. Normally this can be done voluntarily, but consent may be required if another party might otherwise be prejudiced, for example if an interim injunction has been granted or an interim payment made, CPR r 38.2.   **4.126**

A discontinuance counts as the formal determination of the action, so that costs will be assessed, CPR r 38.6. If the discontinuance is after the defence then the claimant will not be able to start a further action on the same facts without the consent of the court, CPR r 38.7. A defendant may apply within 28 days to have the discontinuance set aside if for example the claimant has done it for tactical purposes. In the case *Castanho v Brown & Root (UK)* [1981] 1 All ER 143, the claimant was a Portuguese sailor injured on a Panamanian ship in an English port, who sued here and got an interim payment, but was then persuaded to bring his action in the United States to get higher damages. It was held that he could not be prevented from discontinuing his action here.   **4.127**

Abandonment

A claimant may decide to abandon a claim. In such a case a court might well not allow the claimant to bring a later case on the same facts.   **4.128**

Sanctions

In extreme circumstances a case may be stayed or dismissed by a judge as a penalty, if for example a party is in serious breach of directions on the conduct of the case without good reason. This would normally be done following an 'unless' order—that the action would be dismissed unless the party took a specified step by a specified time.   **4.129**

M   FINAL PREPARATIONS FOR TRIAL

4.130   The main elements in preparing for trial are:

- ensuring that the issues in the case are defined as clearly as possible in the statements of case;
- ensuring that the evidence in the case has been fully prepared;
- ensuring that there has been disclosure of evidence to the other side;
- ensuring that any and all appropriate interim applications have been made;
- exploring the possibilities of settlement as far as is reasonably possible.

4.131   Completing all of these functions and doing so within a reasonable time frame will be governed by the directions of the court. Once these functions have been completed the case should be ready for trial. To ensure that this is the case the parties will be asked to complete and return to the court a pre-trial checklist covering compliance with directions and the evidence to be used at trial. Once these are filed with the court a trial date or window will be set.

4.132   In a multi-track case the date for return of pre-trial checklists is likely to be set at the allocation stage and the period within which the trial should take place may also be proposed at that stage. These dates may be reviewed and if necessary changed by directions, for example at a case management conference.

4.133   To ensure that everything is ready for the trial to take place efficiently in a complex case a pre-trial review may be held, with discussions between the court and the parties. Matters to be covered could include:

- How will the trial be conducted? (For example, will there be opening speeches as well as closing speeches?)
- How will evidence be used? (Will witness statements and reports stand as evidence in chief? Who will be called for cross examination? Will special facilities such as computers or video screens be needed?)

4.134   Final preparations for trial may include briefing the barrister who will argue the case in court, serving witnesses with witness summonses, preparing trial bundles of documents, and drafting a skeleton argument to be filed with the court and served on the defendant. These matters are dealt with more fully in Chapter 21.

N   THE TRIAL AND JUDGMENT

4.135   Sometimes a case will settle at the door of the court. If this happens the judge may be asked to deal with relevant matters such as the making of a consent order.

4.136   Provided the case does not settle, the trial will proceed on the basis of any relevant pre-trial directions and any pre-trial review. It is not considered to be in the interests of justice for a party to be taken by surprise at this stage. It is not impossible to amend a statement of case or to introduce new evidence at the trial itself, but the permission of the judge will be required.

The basic format for procedure at trial is as follows. The presentation of a case in court is **4.137**
dealt with in Chapter 22.

- Opening speech by the claimant.
- Presentation of the claimant's witnesses and other evidence, including cross examination of each witness by the defence.
- Opening speech by the defendant.
- Presentation of the defendant's witnesses and other evidence, including cross examination of each witness by the claimant.
- Closing speech by the claimant.
- Closing speech by the defendant.

A case may settle during the trial. If it does not, at the end of the hearing the judge will give **4.138**
judgment, or may reserve judgment to be delivered at a later date if time for reflection is
required.

O   COSTS ORDERS

At the end of the case, and perhaps also at the end of interim hearings, the judge may make **4.139**
an order as regards costs. The parties may agree who should pay costs, especially if the case is
settled, otherwise the court has a discretion to make a costs order, Supreme Court Act 1981,
s 51 and CPR r 44.3. Costs are considered more fully in Chapter 5.

Costs are initially borne by the party who incurs them. This will remain the case unless the **4.140**
court makes an order as to costs. It is part of the overriding objective that courts should deal
with cases in ways that will save expense and are proportionate to the nature of the case. At
the end of the trial the court may make an order relating to who should bear the costs
bearing in mind the final outcome. The general rule is that the unsuccessful party will be
ordered to pay the costs of the successful party, CPR r 44.3. There are exceptions, if for
example it is a technical victory and only nominal damages are awarded, or if the successful
party has acted unreasonably.

In exercising its discretion the court is required to have regard to all the circumstances of the **4.141**
case, including the extent to which it was reasonable for the parties to raise, pursue, or
contest each of the allegations or issues, the manner in which the parties have acted,
whether the successful party exaggerated the claim, whether a party was only partly successful, and whether there was a payment into court or offer to settle. There may also be orders as
to costs made at an interim stage to be taken into account.

If an order for costs is made, it may still take some time to assess the actual amount that **4.142**
should be paid. A detailed assessment of costs can only be made by a costs officer.

P   AFTER JUDGMENT

4.143   Judgment will often not be the end of the case.

- It may take time for the details of orders to be determined, see 22.114–22.140.
- It may take months for costs issues to be finally resolved, see 5.45–5.61.
- It may take time to enforce the judgment given, and separate applications may have to be made as regards enforcement, see 23.04–23.25.
- One or both parties may wish to appeal against the judgment, see 23.26–23.44.

Q   THE INTERNATIONAL PERSPECTIVE

International issues

4.144   It is increasingly common for litigation to have an international dimension. Businesses work on an international basis, firms have international links, people travel on business, work abroad, or have accidents while they are on holiday. A wide range of different legal jurisdictions may potentially be involved even where the facts are relatively simple. For example an English actor working on a film being made by an American film company with financial backers from various countries may suffer a serious accident while filming in Spain and then die in a private hospital run by a French company (facts based on but not identical to *Kinnear v Falconfilms NV* (1994) 3 All ER 42). This has risen to the level where a commercial law practitioner can easily spend as much time dealing with jurisdictional issues as with substantive commercial law.

4.145   It is not feasible to cover all the complex issues that can arise in detail here, but the main areas to be considered and researched are summarised. Essentially an international issue must be settled either by reference to an international agreement, or by reference to the separate legal systems of each jurisdiction potentially involved in the case. This can give rise to significant complexities and require detailed research. For sources of law on international issues see 24.20.

4.146   There may be a number of strategic and practical problems where a case has international elements. A claimant will often want a case brought in the courts of his or her own country, but this may not be fair to the defendant, or very practical. If an accident takes place in Spain then the evidence and the witnesses are likely to be in Spain and it is more practical for the claimant to bring the case there, with the assistance of Spanish lawyers, rather than trying to bring all the witnesses to England. In terms of strategy, one jurisdiction may offer a longer limitation period than another, so the choice of jurisdiction may be basic to whether the case can proceed, *Spiliada Maritime Corp v Cansulex Ltd* (1986) AC 460.

4.147   While a client may have particular fears where litigation has international elements, some potential problems can be dealt with relatively easily. In a contractual situation it is possible to provide in the contract itself which law should govern the contract and where any dispute should be settled, and this should normally be done to avoid later difficulties as far as possible. Where a case does need to be litigated in another jurisdiction, major English firms of solicitors have branches overseas or have international contacts to assist in the choice of local lawyers.

If a question about the law of another country arises during a court hearing, it will normally **4.148** be dealt with by getting expert evidence from a suitably qualified lawyer from the jurisdiction concerned.

Identifying relevant substantive law

One issue in a case with international elements may be which legal system should provide **4.149** the substantive law to govern the case. The basic scenario outlined above could give rise to actions in contract and tort, but would it be English, American, Spanish, or French law that would apply? This would require research into questions of conflict of laws.

To set out only the most basic principles, a contract may itself make provision for the law **4.150** that will apply to any breach, and is likely to do so in a situation that has an international perspective. If the contract makes no provision, then the law of the place where the contract is to be performed might be most appropriate. For a tort action, the relevant law is likely to be that of the place where the tort occurred.

Deciding on jurisdiction

A quite separate question will relate to which legal system has jurisdiction to try the case. **4.151** The case does not have to be brought in the courts of the country whose substantive law applies to the cause of action. This might not be convenient or desirable for the parties and it may not be feasible. In the scenario above English law might apply to a contract claim and Spanish law to a tort claim but it would probably be desirable to have only one legal action. The main questions therefore are: Where should legal proceedings be commenced? Can those proceedings be served in another jurisdiction if the defendant lives in another jurisdiction? If more than one country might have jurisdiction to hear the case, which might take precedence?

Rules in this area are quite complex and the following broad principles are only designed to **4.152** provide a starting point for research. Overall the provisions generally provide that a defendant be sued where he resides, that a case is tried in the most appropriate place, and that only one action should proceed. The question of where a case is to be tried is most simply answered if the defendant submits to jurisdiction by agreement with the claimant, or does not dispute jurisdiction after acknowledging service.

Within EC countries

The situation is relatively straightforward for a claimant in England if the intended defendant **4.153** is within a state that is a member of the European Union (other than Denmark), as Council Regulation (EC) No 44/2001, which came into force on 1 March 2002, provides for service of legal proceedings without the need for special court approval. This was given effect in England and Wales by the Civil Jurisdiction and Judgments Order 2001 SI 2001/3929, amending the Civil Jurisdiction and Judgments Acts 1982 and 1991. It must be remembered that Scotland and Northern Ireland are separate jurisdictions, essentially within this category.

4.154 In broad terms, other western European jurisdictions are also covered by the Civil Jurisdiction and Judgments Acts 1982 and 1991 though through different links. Denmark is covered by the Brussels Convention (which formerly covered all EU countries). European Free Trade Association countries such as Norway, Switzerland, and Poland are covered by the Lugano Convention.

4.155 The principle behind these agreements is that someone domiciled in a Member State should be sued in the courts of that Member State, whatever their nationality. In broad terms a person is domiciled where he is resident and has a substantial connection. A corporation is domiciled where it is registered or incorporated.

4.156 There are exceptions where someone domiciled in one Member State can be sued in another. A contractual claim can be brought in the courts of a country where the obligation in question was to be performed, a tort claim can be brought where the harmful event occurred or may occur, and a trust claim can be brought where the trust is domiciled. The principle is extended so that if there is more than one defendant they can all be sued in the country where one is domiciled (provided the claims are so closely connected it is expedient to hear them together). Counterclaims and third party claims can in broad terms be added to a case that is already proceeding. If a party is domiciled in a member state, jurisdiction can be conferred on the courts of England and Wales by agreement.

4.157 It is important to save expense and the possibility of conflicting judgments by having only one set of proceedings. Once proceedings have been started, courts in another state must decline jurisdiction—they cannot hear a challenge to the jurisdiction of the first court. If proceedings are linked rather than dealing with exactly the same subject matter, the later proceedings can be stayed. These rules are not necessarily easy to apply, *Neste Chemicals SA v DK Line SA* (1994) 3 All ER 180.

4.158 The claim form must include statements that the court has power under the relevant regulations to hear the case, and that there are no other proceedings pending. Service should be in accordance with the rules of the country where the defendant is being served. There is an extended period to acknowledge service and the claim form will be valid for six months rather than four. If the defendant wishes to dispute jurisdiction he or she must first acknowledge service. Where a defendant has been served outside the jurisdiction without the need for permission a judgment in default can only be obtained with permission.

For other countries

4.159 For other countries, essentially those outside western Europe, it is necessary to get court permission to serve proceedings abroad for an action being brought here. Permission is sought on an application that must be supported by evidence, but that is made without notice and decided by a judge alone, CPR r 6.21. The relevant principles are largely set out in *Seaconsar Far East Ltd v Bank Markazi Jomhouri Islami Iran* (1994) 1 AC 438 and CPR r 6.20. Essentially there must be a good arguable case that the court has jurisdiction within one of the grounds set out in CPR r 6.20, and that it has a reasonable prospect of success on the merits. The main types of case covered are:

- where the claim is for a breach of contract within the jurisdiction;

- where the claim is in respect of a contract made in the jurisdiction, subject to English law or where it is agreed it be subject to English law (or where this would be the case if the contract were valid);
- where a tort or the damage arising from it occurred within the jurisdiction;
- where there is already a real claim and it is necessary or proper to join the person outside the jurisdiction as a party.

The court must also be satisfied that England and Wales is the proper place in which to bring **4.160** the claim, CPR r 6.21—this means where the case can most suitably be tried here in the interests of all the parties and of justice (this includes factors such as where they do business, where witnesses live, which law is relevant law). See CPR Part 6 Service of documents, and PD 6B Service out of the jurisdiction

Forum non conveniens

Inevitably there may be practical and/or tactical reasons for seeking to bring an action in one **4.161** jurisdiction rather than another. To prevent inappropriate proceedings continuing a court can stay English proceedings on the basis that England and Wales is not the appropriate place for the case to be heard (*forum non conveniens*). The court will consider which jurisdiction is appropriate, matters of justice, and whether there is a proper personal or legal reason for using this jurisdiction, *Spiliada Maratime Corporation v Cansulex* (1987) AC 460

Enforcement of judgments

Related to questions of jurisdiction, there may be questions about whether a judgment **4.162** obtained in one jurisdiction will be enforceable in another, see CPR Part 74 Enforcement of judgments in different jurisdictions and PD 74 Enforcement of judgments in different jurisdictions; see also 23.19–23.25.

A judgment obtained in one jurisdiction will be enforceable within that jurisdiction in the **4.163** normal way. If a case proceeds in England enforceability will be a matter of the normal English rules for enforceability, supplemented where there are international agreements. Inevitably it may be difficult to enforce a judgment where assets are held or moved overseas, and this may be addressed by seeking a freezing order at an early stage in the case to prevent a defendant from disposing of assets that may be needed to satisfy a judgment. Such an order can be worldwide if appropriate. The details of freezing orders are at 16.175–16.182. If a judgment is obtained abroad the assistance of lawyers in that jurisdiction will be needed as to the options for enforcement. See also 23.19–23.25.

There is a further linked question of whether the costs of the action will be recoverable. **4.164** Essentially the relevant rules will be those of the jurisdiction in which the case is heard. A party may be particularly concerned about the costs of bringing an action where there are international elements and it may be difficult to recover costs even if an order for costs is made. A claimant can seek a freezing order to cover costs as well as damages. A defendant may seek an order for security for costs, and this is also dealt with at 16.172–16.174.

References to EC courts

4.165 In certain circumstances, through international treaty, it may be possible for a reference to be made from a court in one jurisdiction to a court outside that jurisdiction. For England and Wales the main possibility is that European Community law provides possibilities for private individuals and others with legal personality to obtain remedies from the European Court of Justice or the European Court of First Instance. The details of such actions are beyond the scope of this book, but the options are summarised here as they may be important in addressing potential litigation effectively, see CPR Part 68 References to the European Court and PD 68 References to the European Court.

4.166 The main options are:

- Seeking a preliminary ruling on the interpretation or validity of EC law. Such a reference is made by a national court before which a case is proceeding and in which a point of EC law has arisen. The proceedings are suspended while the point is decided. The European Court cannot deal with matters of national law or with findings of fact. There is an obligation to make a reference where a question arises and there is no possibility of appeal from the court decision, otherwise a point may be referred if it is necessary to enable the court to give judgment. There is no point in a reference being made before issues are clear or before facts are decided. Some actions can only be brought by Member States, but the following can be open to individuals.
- It is possible to seek annulment of an act of a community institution under Article 230. There are clear limits on the types of actions that may be annulled and who can seek an annulment. There must be a ground for annulment, such as a lack of competence to effect the act, infringement of procedural requirements, or misuse of power. The effect of a successful application will be that the act must be undone.
- It is possible to claim that a regulation is illegal under Article 241, though this can only be used in the course of a case and does not provide a separate right of action.
- It is possible to complain about a failure to act under Article 232. There are again limitations on who can make such a claim, and the institution must be informed of the claim and given an opportunity to act before a case can be brought.
- Under Article 288 there can be an action where damage has been caused by an institution of the EC or its servants, which broadly allows for an action for tort. There must be a sufficiently strong and clear case, and it is difficult to establish liability for legislative acts.

4.167 Even if an action is proceeding within the jurisdiction, there are circumstances in which a reference can be made to a court outside the jurisdiction. Where there are questions relating to the Treaties establishing the EC, or the interpretation or validity of any act of the institutions of the EC, Article 234 of the European Community Treaty provides that the European Court of Justice shall have jurisdiction to give preliminary rulings. It is only mandatory for such a reference to be made where there is no further possible judicial remedy under national law, usually because the highest court of appeal has been reached, see *Chiron Corp v Murex Diagnostics Ltd* (1995) All ER (EC) 88. However even then a reference does not have to be made if the point has already been decided by the European Court or the application of community law is obvious. A reference should also be made if a national court intends to question the validity of an act of a community institution, Practice Direction (ECJ) (1997) All ER (EC) 1.

A reference can be made where a court considers a decision on a point necessary to enable **4.168** it to give judgment. This means reasonably necessary rather than unavoidable, and the European Court cannot interpret national law or challenge findings of fact, *Arsenal Football Club plc v Reed* (2003) 1 All ER 137. Only a judge can order a reference. The reference will normally be made before the trial and proceedings will be stayed. The question referred should be drafted with care. The reference may be expensive, and the costs will be decided at trial.

KEY DOCUMENTS

The Civil Procedure Rules 1998

Court guides

Queen's Bench Guide
Chancery Guide
Admiralty and Commercial Courts Guide
Mercantile Courts Guide
Patents Court Guide
Technology and Construction Court Guide

Pre-action Protocols

Pre-action Protocol for Personal Injury Claims
Pre-action Protocol for the Resolution of Clinical Disputes
Pre-action Protocol for Construction and Engineering Disputes
Pre-action Protocol for Defamation
Professional Negligence Pre-action Protocol
Pre-action Protocol for Judicial Review
Pre-action Protocol for Disease and Illness Claims
Pre-action Protocol for Housing Disrepair Cases

Court forms

The forms most commonly in general use for civil litigation are as follows:

N1 Claim Form
N1A Notes for claimant
N1C Notes for Defendant
N9 Defence Response Pack
N9A Admission (specified amount)
N9B Defence and Counterclaim (specified amount)
N9C Admission (unspecified amount and non money claim)
N9D Defence and Counterclaim (unspecified amount and non money claim)
N11 Defence Form

N211 Part 20 Claim Form

N213 Part 20 Acknowledgement of service

N215 Certificate of service

N150 Allocation Questionnaire

N153 Notice of Allocation or listing hearing

N154 Notice of allocation to the fast track

N155 Notice of allocation to the multi-track

N157 Notice of allocation to the small claims track

PF 52 Order for Case Management Directions (CPR Part 29)

N244 Application notice

N16A General form of application for an injunction

N117 General form of undertaking

N260 Statement of costs

N265 List of documents for standard disclosure

N266 Notice to admit facts

N268 Notice to prove documents at trial

N285 General form of Affidavit

N242A Notice of Payment into Court (Part 36)

N242 Notice of Payment into Court (Part 37)

N243A/Form 201 Notice of acceptance (Part 36)

N170 Pre-trial checklist

N20 Witness Summons

N163 Skeleton argument

N24 General form of judgment or order

Practice Form 45 Judgment after trial by a judge without a jury

Practice Form 109 Order for reference to the European Court

N259 Notice of Appeal

All these are easily available in hard copy and electronically, see Chapter 24.

5

FINANCING LITIGATION

A THE COSTS SIDE OF A CASE 5.01

B HOW COSTS ACCUMULATE 5.10
Paying the solicitor and the barrister 5.10
The heads of cost in a case 5.13

C DEALING WITH COSTS EFFECTIVELY 5.14
How costs escalate 5.16
How costs can be kept down 5.17

D HOW PROBLEMS WITH COSTS ARISE 5.19

E OPTIONS FOR THE FUNDING OF LITIGATION 5.21

F CONDITIONAL FEE AGREEMENTS 5.26
Rules for conditional fee agreements 5.27
Issues surrounding conditional fee agreements 5.32

G PUBLIC FUNDING 5.38

H ORDERS FOR COSTS 5.45
Principles for costs orders 5.45
Rules and powers relating to costs 5.49
The assessment of costs 5.57

I ORDERS FOR COSTS AT INTERIM HEARINGS 5.62
Sample schedule of costs (Form N260) 5.76

J WASTED COSTS ORDERS 5.80
The procedure 5.81
The test 5.85

KEY DOCUMENTS

What is the difference between a lawyer and a herd of buffalo?
The lawyer charges most.

A   THE COSTS SIDE OF A CASE

5.01   The cost of litigation is quite a fundamental issue. There is an inevitable tension between providing a service that is of good quality and examines issues properly, and providing a service at reasonable cost. Costs are likely to be a major issue for most clients. For sources of law on costs and funding litigation see 24.17.

5.02   The overriding objective includes the need to save expense. The need for lawyers to deal with costs responsibly is also reflected in some of the provisions of the legal professional Codes of Conduct. The Solicitors' Practice Rules require solicitors to provide clients with client care letters which provide information about costs. This is supported by the Solicitors' Costs Information and Client Care Code, which requires solicitors to consider funding options suited to client needs.

5.03   The aim of providing affordable justice is supported by a principle of 'proportionality', which means that expense should be balanced against the value of what is to be achieved. There have been deep concerns about the level of public funding for civil litigation through legal aid, and now through the community legal service, and it must be a matter of great concern that many people of modest and moderate means would probably feel that they could not afford to litigate a civil claim. Litigation cannot be effective if people do not have access to the litigation system.

5.04   In practical terms there are inevitably limits on how much financial support can be provided from the public purse, and other ways to provide access to the legal system are to make the system less expensive, or to provide options that are less expensive. Initiatives in these areas include:

- the approach taken in the overriding objective to keeping costs down;
- providing the small claims track and the fast track, where stages of the litigation process are streamlined;
- providing that the monitoring of costs be a regular part of case management;
- the professional obligation on a solicitor to inform a client about the basis for charging for work.

5.05   The basics for effective litigation are that:

- it must be decided at an early stage how litigation will be financed;
- the lawyer should always deal with costs with the client in a transparent way, outlining in advance how costs will build up, as well as keeping the client informed of the current bill;
- when procedural steps are discussed, the potential cost should always be part of the decision as to whether the step be taken.

5.06   There is a strong element of risk assessment and management, and even perhaps of assessing odds and gambling, in conducting litigation. This tends to be acknowledged in commercial litigation, or where insurers are effectively funding the case, but not in all areas of litigation. To make informed decisions about a case a client needs to know the following, each updated as the case progresses:

- the damages are likely to be £A;
- the chances of winning and getting that figure are B per cent;
- the costs will be in the region of £C, and that of this the client might have to pay £D even if the case is won and the defendant is ordered to pay costs;
- that if the case is lost the combined costs of the claimant and the defendant that the client will have to meet will be about £E;
- if there is a conditional fee agreement, then the sum payable will be £F.

The position can become very complex because of other considerations, like the repayment **5.07** of benefits in a tort case, or if there is more than one claim or a counterclaim, but this is no reason for not being as specific about costs as possible.

There is much research to be done into the effects of cost on deterring people from bringing **5.08** an action at all, and on the way in which people conduct litigation. It is possible to take out 'after the event' insurance under which one side can take out insurance to cover costs that might be payable to the other side. Inevitably this is expensive and it is normally tied in with a conditional fee agreement.

The Solicitors' Costs Information and Client Care Code sets out the information and advice **5.09** that a solicitor must provide for a client as regards funding and complaints. The basis for charging must be transparent, and the client must be updated as to costs at each stage of the proceedings. A failure to comply may lead to disciplinary proceedings, or to a solicitor not being able to recover all or part of the fees due.

B   HOW COSTS ACCUMULATE

Paying the solicitor and the barrister

The basic model for litigation is that the client initially retains a solicitor. The solicitor **5.10** retained must provide the client with written information about how costs will be charged, and there must be an agreement as to how costs will be paid, see client case letter at 11.30. The solicitor may charge a flat fee for the case or may charge an hourly rate for time spent (the rate depending on the experience of the lawyer).

As litigation may take some time, the solicitor will normally not wish to wait to the end of **5.11** the case to be paid, and will ask for staged payments as the action progresses. The client will also be asked to pay court fees and the costs of getting reports etc as they arise, though this may be incorporated into the staged payments. If the action succeeds then it is likely that the defendant will be ordered to reimburse the claimant for the costs at the end of the day. However the client will be concerned about meeting these bills as they arise as a costs order may be a long way in the future. Even if the case is won, the costs awarded by the court will not necessarily cover all the costs incurred by the client, if for example some costs are thought to have been incurred unreasonably or are too high. If there is a costs order the defendant may not pay it. The client may also be extremely worried that if the case is lost, he or she will be at risk of being ordered to pay the other side's costs in addition to his or her own. Insurance against having to pay the other side's costs can be taken out, but it is very expensive unless linked to a conditional fee arrangement.

5.12 If the case requires specialist legal advice then the solicitor and client may agree that a barrister be briefed. Normally the barrister will work on the basis of a separate fee for each brief, charging a separate fee for writing an opinion, drafting a statement of case, making an interim application to court, or appearing at trial. The fees will be higher for more experienced barristers. Brief fees are normally negotiated between the solicitor and the barrister's clerk or chambers manager. They will need to be paid once the work on the brief has been completed.

The heads of cost in a case

5.13 The main elements of costs in an action are (though some of these may overlap):

- the cost of the solicitor's work, whether as a flat fee or based on the number of hours the solicitor has worked;
- the out of pocket expenses or disbursements incurred by the solicitor (postage, phone calls etc);
- the costs of getting evidence, eg paying for expert reports;
- administrative costs, eg preparing and copying papers to send to other parties and to the court;
- court fees (set amounts are payable when a claim form is issued etc);
- a barrister's brief fee or fees;
- the costs of trial, eg paying travel expenses for witnesses.

For an example of how costs may be summarised see 5.78.

C   DEALING WITH COSTS EFFECTIVELY

5.14 The costs of an action may be a crucial factor for a client. A client who is paying costs personally will be concerned as costs accumulate. The possibility of reimbursement if the case is won may seem very distant. The accumulation of costs may be a key factor in deciding to negotiate.

5.15 A client will most appreciate a lawyer who shows sufficient awareness of client concerns, is open with information, and proactive in raising and addressing costs issues. Costs issues will arise constantly throughout litigation. A particular piece of evidence might be useful, but does its potential value justify its likely cost? The lawyer must be broadly familiar with the main elements in costs bills, the main ways in which litigation can be funded, and the sorts of orders that a court can make with regard to costs.

How costs escalate

5.16 In the broadest terms costs are likely to be increased if:

- the lawyers on each side do not cooperate, leading to delays, extra applications to court to ensure compliance etc;
- if issues are not clarified at a reasonably early stage, or if the issues in dispute change significantly at a relatively late stage;

- the litigation becomes more complex than it needs to be, for example with the addition of causes of action and parties who have limited real relevance;
- the parties are not reasonably open in disclosing evidence and making admissions, as costs of getting information and evidence will escalate;
- the case of its nature involves complex evidence such as disputes between experts;
- there is a failure to meet case management requirements and a tendency to make numerous applications to court for orders;
- offers to settle are not taken seriously.

How costs can be kept down

Costs are likely to be kept down if: **5.17**

- the lawyers on each side act with as much cooperation as possible;
- the detail or spirit of pre-action protocols is followed;
- the issues are clarified at a reasonably early stage and issues of little merit are dropped;
- only some issues are litigated, for example liability for an accident is admitted but the amount of damages is in dispute;
- requirements for evidence can be kept to a reasonable minimum;
- parties follow case management requirements and there are as few interim applications as possible;
- the case can be settled before costs build up too much.

As part of monitoring the effect of costs, the likely damages will need to be assessed at an early   **5.18**
stage and regularly balanced against the likely costs. The options for making an offer to settle should also be regularly reviewed, see 20.13–20.15 and 20.23–20.35.

D   HOW PROBLEMS WITH COSTS ARISE

There are many reasons why problems arise with regard to costs.   **5.19**

- Litigation is inevitably expensive with the costs of lawyers, experts, witnesses etc.
- It can be very difficult to forecast the likely cost of a case accurately, making it difficult for a client to take a sensible decision about whether a case should sensibly be brought.
- In some jurisdictions such as North America each side in litigation bears their own costs. In England and Wales the loser is normally ordered to pay the winner's costs. This can be a fair way of ensuring that a claimant is properly compensated, but on the other hand an unsuccessful litigant faces paying the costs of both sides.
- The lawyer can easily see costs as a subsidiary issue, but accumulating costs can become as important as the progress of the litigation for the client who is having to bear costs as they arise.
- Conversely, a lawyer may be concerned about accumulating costs where the lawyer may not be reimbursed if he or she is working under a conditional fee agreement.
- The assessment of costs has become an industry in its own right.
- If one is not entirely confident about the case it can be embarrassing to talk about costs to the client.

5.20 The position where there is concern that the other side is building up costs in a extravagant way was commented on in *King v Telegraph Group Ltd* The Times, 21 May 2004. The options include seeking a cost capping order or a wasted costs order from the judge, or seeking a retrospective assessment of costs under *Lownds v Home Office* (2002) 1 WLR 2450.

E   OPTIONS FOR THE FUNDING OF LITIGATION

5.21 At an early meeting it will be vital to identify how any litigation might be funded. Sometimes the answer will be obvious, if for example an insurer immediately accepts potential responsibility for the costs. Sometimes there may be significant difficulties about costs and the various options will need to be discussed and agreed with the client. This will not necessarily be done in a meeting to discuss the case if a firm has a system in place for dealing with costs options.

5.22 The main options for funding litigation are:

- the client may be paying personally, in which case some money may be sought in advance and staged payments agreed;
- there may be another source of funds, such as an insurance policy or a trade union;
- the Community Legal Service may fund the action, though the requirements are quite strict and this source cannot fund some types of litigation, such as personal injury claims;
- a conditional fee agreement may be entered into.

5.23 The aspects of costs that should be adequately explained to a client are:

- the solicitor is professionally obliged to tell the client the basis for charges, which is likely to involve hourly rates rather than a set fee for all but quite basic litigation;
- the elements of costs in a case—court fees, the costs of gathering evidence, making applications etc;
- the types of orders that a court can make with regard to costs;
- as far as possible, the rough overall potential cost of the action;
- the risk of having to pay the costs for the other side if the case is lost—the greater the chance that the case may not succeed, the more important it is to ensure that the client is aware of the risk of having to pay the costs of the other side as well as his own costs in the event of losing;
- how the costs of the case are developing as the case progresses.

5.24 The main alternatives to costs being paid personally by the client are as follows.

- If the client has insurance to cover legal fees the insurer may pay. The client should be asked if he or she is insured—such insurance may be part of car or house insurance for an individual. The terms of any relevant insurance policy should be checked and the insurer should be contacted as soon as possible to check cover.
- If the client is a member of a relevant body such as a trade union, that body may cover costs, but again this must be specifically checked.
- A conditional fee agreement may be put in place. Such an agreement will provide for the

costs to be met from damages, but in the meantime the lawyer will bear out of pocket costs and will not be paid.
- If the client has limited resources the Community Legal Service may meet the costs, but only with advance authorisation.

It is very difficult to give general guidance about the likely cost of litigation. Even cases that on their facts are broadly similar can lead to very different cost bills with a few differences in how they are conducted. Once lawyers are involved in a case the costs even for a small claim are likely to be at least a few hundred pounds. The costs in a fast track case can easily run into thousands, and the costs in a multi-track case can run into tens of thousands. In the most serious cases costs can be hundreds of thousands of pounds. **5.25**

F   CONDITIONAL FEE AGREEMENTS

It was not legally acceptable for a lawyer to have a financial interest in a case prior to the Courts and Legal Services Act 1990. That Act made conditional fee agreements (CFAs) legal in defined circumstances. The rules for CFAs are now in the Conditional Fee Agreements Regulations 2000, SI 2000/692. **5.26**

Rules for conditional fee agreements

In some jurisdictions, including the United States of America, it is quite acceptable for litigation to be funded by the client agreeing that the lawyer will be paid a certain amount from the damages when the action is won—for example 10 per cent of the sum recovered. This is known as a contingency fee, as payment is contingent on the action being won. Agreements linking fees to the success of an action were illegal and unenforceable in England and Wales, and remain so save for conditional fee agreements as described below. There are various objections to contingency fees—they give a lawyer too great a degree of interest in the success of the action and may threaten objectivity, they can cut into damages that have been carefully calculated to meet the claimant's needs so that the claimant is under-compensated, and a poor client may feel compelled to accept too high a fee for the lawyer. **5.27**

Since 1998 conditional fee agreements (CFAs) have been permitted for funding all civil cases save for matrimonial cases. A conditional fee agreement is not linked directly to the damages recoverable but rather to the fee the lawyer would normally be paid for doing the work. If the action is successful then the lawyer is paid normal fees, and also if agreed a 'success fee' of up to 100 per cent of the normal fee (which can effectively double the normal fee). It may be appropriate for the success fee to be 100 per cent where a case has a 50 per cent chance of success, the logic being that if a lawyer has two such cases she or he should be appropriately remunerated overall. However, where cases have a 90 per cent likelihood of success a much lower success fee, say 20 per cent, is likely to be appropriate, *Callery v Gray* (2002) 1 WLR 2000. In road traffic cases a success fee of 12.5 per cent is the norm as such cases tend to settle, though the success fee can be higher if the case goes to trial. **5.28**

To be effective, a CFA must be in writing and must comply with the Conditional Fee Agreements Regulations 2000, SI 2000/692, which are drawn up to ensure that the interests of **5.29** clients and of justice are met. Model agreements have been agreed by the Law Society and the Bar Council. If counsel is instructed there must be separate agreements between the client and the solicitor, and between the solicitor and the barrister. Agreements that provide for a success fee must state the percentage, which must be within prescribed maxima and related to the chance of losing and the disadvantage of having to wait to be paid. Note that the agreement cannot, if the case is lost, prevent an order that the claimant pays the defendant's costs, but insurance can be taken out to cover this at cost to the claimant. It is also common for the lawyer to ask the client to pay disbursements such as court fees so that the lawyer is not actually out of pocket. Any failure to comply with the details of the Regulations can make the agreement unenforceable, *Spencer v Wood* The Times, 30 March 2004.

5.30   If a CFA is an option there should be a meeting with the client to explain clearly the meaning and possible effects of it. The client must be clear about the effect on damages of the CFA, and insurance for costs in case the case is lost. The details of the CFA may need to be negotiated rather than laid down, as there is an extent to which this is a commercial transaction. In a big case independent advice for the client about the CFA may be justified. Everything should be set out in writing for the client to avoid any misunderstanding, see 11.26–11.32.

5.31   If there is a CFA, a notice in prescribed form must be provided for the other side with the claim form. If the client wins, the damages should reimburse him or her for the disbursements and the insurance fee and potentially the success fee. Costs can include any additional liability under a conditional fee funding agreement, CPR r 43.2, including the success fee and the insurance premium. The details of this rule are complex, *Calley v Gray* (2002) 1 WLR 2000, and *Sarwar v Alam* (2002) 1 WLR 125. It is possible for the client to challenge the level of the costs and the success fee, CPR r 48.8.

Issues surrounding conditional fee agreements

5.32   The attraction of a CFA for a client is that fees do not have to be paid up front, which may make it possible for the client to bring an action that could not otherwise be brought. The possible attraction to the lawyer is the additional fee, and the possibility of a client who might not otherwise feel able to bring an action, the drawback being the risk that the lawyer will not be paid if the case is lost.

5.33   The detailed working of CFAs was a matter of uncertainty for some time, and issues have only gradually been worked out. There are various reasons why the agreements have not proved as popular as had been anticipated. They have not led to an explosion of 'ambulance chasing' litigation as was at one time feared.

5.34   For the lawyer, risk assessment is key to undertaking conditional fee agreements and deciding which cases to accept. The lawyer will not be paid at all if the case is lost, and may suffer a cash flow problem in the gap of time between doing work and being paid, as the usual staged payments as the case progresses will not be there. The resources that will need to be committed to doing the case, the chances that the case will succeed, and the potential reward including the success fee will need to be weighed up. There is the problem that significant investigation may have to be done before the strength of the case can be assessed and refined risk assessment can be difficult. The lawyer cannot afford to lose too many cases taken on a conditional fee basis, and will therefore tend only to take those most likely to succeed. But there is a paradox here—if the client has a strong case then should a CFA really be necessary?

There can be problems in advising a client identically if the client is paying personally or if **5.35** there is a CFA. As the lawyer has an interest in winning, albeit not directly in the amount of damages, this can affect how advice is given, how the lawyer reacts to instructions, and how negotiations are carried out.

There are some issues about pressure on lawyers to act under CFAs where the chances of **5.36** success are not good. There is an art to assessing the chance of success of an action which is not easy for someone new to practice.

No win no fee deals have produced problems and have not taken off as expected. There has not **5.37** been an explosion in claims as fears of a compensation culture might anticipate. The extent to which CFAs are used depends on the extent to which lawyers are prepared to accept risk, and the detailed regulation surrounding the agreements. If the no win no fee approach is to widely help those who cannot otherwise afford to litigate the position may need to be revisited.

G PUBLIC FUNDING

It can be very difficult for people of moderate means to litigate. The government funds legal **5.38** aid and the Community Legal Service at a cost of about £2 billion a year, which is generous compared to many countries. However over recent years fewer people have qualified for assistance, and rates of pay for lawyers have become so low that some have ceased to provide such work. This is partly because more of the budget is required to fund assistance in criminal cases, especially some high cost ones. Money has become focussed on contracts to provide advice for particular areas, Citizen's Advice Bureaux, and law centres. Some advice work is done by non-lawyers, and there has been a growth in online advice through www.clsdirect. org.uk run by the Community Legal Service.

State-funded assistance is available to individuals in certain circumstances. This was for- **5.39** merly through legal aid (which continues to operate where a legal aid certificate was granted). Since 1 April 2000 the system is for funding through the Community Legal Service Fund run by the Legal Services Commission, as provided by the Administration of Justice Act 1999. The systems have a number of common features. The focus is on providing support for those most in need of help and is based on cost-benefit analyses. Some types of case are excluded, such as matters related to the carrying on of a business or partnership law, conveyancing, and wills. Claims for personal injury, death, or damage to property are also excluded (save for clinical disputes), these being envisaged as particular areas for CFAs. The rules for financial eligibility mean that in effect only the poorest are helped. There are also detailed criteria for funding, which take into account alternative ways of seeking a remedy or funding the action and the prospect of success.

Lawyers may be asked to advise on whether a case merits public funding, see 11.45. The **5.40** lawyer has a duty to the fund as well as to the client in providing a view on funding. There are professional rules on how this be done, in Annex E of the Code of Conduct for the Bar. In money claims there are clear categories of cost-benefit.

- The prospects of success are very good (80 per cent or more) and the value of the claim exceeds the likely costs.
- The prospects are good (60–80 per cent) and the value of the claim is at least twice the likely level of costs.
- The prospects of success are moderate (50–60 per cent) and the value of the claim is at least four times the likely level of costs.

5.41   These categories underline the importance of assessing damages, chances of success, and costs before starting an action. They may provide useful general analogies for assessing the likelihood of success in advising a client.

5.42   The service provides for the following levels of service:

- Legal help is designed to offer basic advice on how the law applies to a case without taking the case forward. Such advice is normally provided through franchise holders, which include not only solicitors but also Citizens Advice Bureaux, law centres, and independent advice agencies.
- Help at court pays for legal representation at a particular hearing without the lawyer becoming the legal representative for the whole case.
- Legal representation potentially covers all the stages of an action but is divided into two levels. Investigative help is aimed at the work necessary to gather information to see whether a claim is worth pursuing. Full representation can cover bringing or defending an action, but the certificate will define what is covered for a particular case.
- Support funding can provide assistance with the costs of a high cost case that a lawyer may not be prepared to take on a CFA basis. Again there are two levels, investigative support and litigation support. There are detailed definitions—high costs for litigation support are solicitors' fees exceeding £20,000 or disbursements exceeding £5,000.

5.43   The money spent to fund litigation under the Community Legal Service is potentially recoverable under the Access to Justice Act 1999. The sum spent becomes a first charge on property recovered or preserved in the funded action. This means for example that damages are payable to the Community Services Commission and costs are deducted before they go to the claimant. If a house is part of the dispute, a charge of the costs will attach to the house. There are exceptions, and a charge can be postponed.

5.44   If the action is lost, there is a risk that a funded party might be ordered to pay costs. There is protection against this kind of order under the Administration of Justice Act 1999, s 11. Any costs order will not exceed what it is reasonable for the assisted litigant to pay, and this will include considering what order would have been made in a normal case and looking at the resources of the funded and the non-funded parties. Orders made tend to be modest. This may of course not be fair to the defendant who won, so there is provision for an order to be made against the Legal Services Commission where it is just and equitable that costs be paid from public funds and the non-funded party may suffer financial hardship. Detailed requirements are in the Community Legal Service (Cost Protection) Regulations 2000, SI 2000/824. An application must be made in three months with full details of costs and resources.

H   ORDERS FOR COSTS

Principles for costs orders

Each litigant is primarily liable to pay his or her own costs, including court fees and fees due **5.45** to lawyers. Payments due in respect of contracts made by and the obligations of the litigant must be paid by the litigant. In some jurisdictions this is the end of the matter. For example in the United States of America each litigant pays his or her own lawyer whether the case is won or lost. Such an approach means that the litigant selects and pays for the level of legal support he or she wants. Weak cases can be thrown out at an early stage so that a defendant does not have to spend too much in defending a weak claim. Some forms of insurance can be taken out to meet legal expenses.

It can be argued that such an approach is inherently unfair. One party can choose to make **5.46** many applications and refuse to settle thus forcing up the costs, forcing the other party to incur expense to defend his or her position. If a court cannot make orders to address the costs position then a wealthy litigant can have an unfair advantage over a poor one. If a successful party cannot recover his or her costs then the damages that the party receives will effectively be reduced by the costs so that the party is out of pocket.

In England and Wales judges have powers to make orders with regard to costs. The normal **5.47** approach is that an unsuccessful party is ordered to pay the costs of the successful party, though to ensure fairness costs have to be taxed and a successful party will not recover anything that is not thought to have been spent reasonably. Over recent years the exercise of powers with regards to costs have been significantly extended so as to allow the court to take an overview of costs as the case progresses, and so as to allow wasted costs orders to be made where it is thought that the conduct of a lawyer has allowed costs to be incurred without good reason.

While costs orders can help to ensure fairness, and it is useful for the court to take an **5.48** overview of the costs in a case, there are problems. The assessment of costs following a case has become a fringe industry with much time and effort spent on costs issues alone. The risk of having to pay the costs of both sides if the case is lost can be a significant disincentive for a potential litigant.

Rules and powers relating to costs

The Civil Procedure Rules 1998 make detailed provisions for costs orders, see CPR Part 43 **5.49** Scope of cost rules and definitions, CPR Part 44 General Rules about costs and PD 43–48 Practice Direction about costs. There are special rules for fixed costs, CPR Part 45, for fast track trial costs, CPR Part 46, and for Costs—special cases, CPR Part 48.

The party who incurs costs will be liable to pay them unless and until there is an order to any **5.50** other effect. The main options are:

- An order as to costs may be made at the end of interim hearings as the case progresses. Such an order may provide for immediate payment or may set out provisions to be taken into account when an overall order is made at the end of the case (see 5.62–5.79).

- At the end of the case the court can make an order for costs. Normally the loser will be ordered to pay the winner's costs (though there is a discretion depending on the circumstances of the case and the order will not necessarily cover everything that has been spent).

5.51   At the end of any case the position on costs will need to be reviewed. The parties may agree who should pay costs, especially if the case is settled, otherwise the court has a discretion to make a costs order, Supreme Court Act 1981, s 51 and CPR r 44.3. At the end of the trial the court may make an order relating to who should bear the costs bearing in mind the final outcome. The general rule is that the unsuccessful party will be ordered to pay the costs of the successful party, CPR r 44.3. There are exceptions, if for example it is a technical victory and only nominal damages are awarded, if the successful party has acted unreasonably, or if the success has resulted from a late amendment to the case, *Re Elgindata Ltd (No 2)* (1992) 1 WLR 1207 and *Beco Ltd v Alfa Laval Co Ltd* (1995) QB 137. If a party is partly successful there should be an overall award of costs rather than an attempt to make different orders for costs on different issues, *English v Emery, Reimbold and Strick Ltd* (2002) 1 WLR 2409.

5.52   In exercising its discretion the court is required to have regard to all the circumstances of the case, including the extent to which it was reasonable for the parties to raise, pursue, or contest each of the allegations or issues, the manner in which the parties have acted, whether the successful party exaggerated the claim, whether a party was only partly successful, and whether there was a payment into court or offer to settle.

5.53   There are seven possible variations of the main rule that the unsuccessful party should pay the successful party's costs, CPR r 44.3.

- that a party pay only a proportion of the other party's costs;
- that a party pays a specified amount in respect of the other party's costs;
- that a party pays costs from or to a certain day only;
- that a party pays costs incurred before the proceedings began;
- that a party pay costs only as regards to certain steps in the proceedings;
- that a party pay costs only for a distinct part of the proceedings;
- that a party pay interest on the costs from or to a certain date.

5.54   There may be separate orders for costs if there is a claim and a counterclaim, though not normally if there is simply a set off, see *Universal Cycles plc v Grangebriar Ltd* (2000) CPLR 42. A costs order may include an order for the payment of pre-action costs if for example there has been pre-action disclosure. It should be noted that a claimant who brings more than one cause of action in respect of the same damage is not entitled to the costs of any more than the first claim, Civil Liability (Contribution) Act 1978, s 4.

5.55   The order for costs is inevitably likely to be more complex where there are more than two parties, *Hodgson v Guardall Ltd* [1991] 3 All ER 823. If for example a claimant sues two defendants and wins against A but not B, the natural result might well be that the claimant would have to pay the costs of B but could recover costs from A. But this is not necessarily as straightforward as it may seem. One option is that the claimant should pay B's costs but could then recover them from A, *Bullock v London General Omnibus Co* (1907) 1 KB 264 CA. A second option is that A should be ordered to pay B's costs direct to B, *Sanderson v Blyth Theatre Co* (1903) 2 KB 533 CA. The court will look at all the circumstances of the case to decide what is fair, *Bank America Finance Ltd v Nock* (1988) AC 1002 HL. If there are Part 20 proceedings the court has the power to make such order as it thinks just, based on who has won against whom and the reasonableness of how the parties have behaved.

In exceptional cases it is possible for a non-party to be ordered to pay costs, CPR r 48.2, **5.56** provided they have a sufficient opportunity to make representations. The third party must be involved in the action in some way, for example providing funds for a party, see *Symphony Group plc v Hodgson* (1994) QB 179, *Murphy v Young & Co Brewery Ltd* (1997) 1 WLR 159, and *Nordstern Allgemeine Versicherungs AG v Internav Ltd* The Times, 8 June 1999.

The assessment of costs

In addition to there being an order for costs, the actual costs to be paid need to be assessed, **5.57** CPR Part 47 Procedure for detailed assessment of costs and default provisions. There may be questions as to whether costs were reasonably incurred, and whether the amount of each cost item is reasonable. The quickest and cheapest way of achieving this is by agreement between the parties, but this may not be possible. An assessment is normally made on a standard basis, which includes only costs that are proportionate to the matters in issue, and which resolves any dispute on the reasonableness and proportionality of costs in favour of the paying party, CPR r 44.4. An indemnity basis is used for a client paying his own solicitor or as a penalty—then the proportionality rule does not apply and any doubts are resolved in favour of the receiving party, CPR r 44.4. A summary assessment can be made by a judge at the end of a hearing, see 5.62–5.79.

A detailed assessment of costs can only be made by a costs officer. This can be a District Judge **5.58** in the County Court or the Supreme Court Costs Office for a High Court case. This will take time as parties will have to produce detailed summaries of their costs, and written summaries of points in dispute. The procedure is almost a mini trial procedure, with the person claiming costs commencing assessment proceedings within three months of the order giving the right to costs, CPR r 47.7, supporting the application with a bill of costs. The paying party should serve written points of dispute within 21 days, and the claiming party may reply. The hearing is relatively informal and is based on submissions on these documents. A detailed assessment must normally be made of costs payable to or for a child or patient.

In order to be able to make a case for costs at the detailed assessment, solicitors and barristers **5.59** need to keep clear and consistent records of the work done on each case, including the task done and the time taken. The Bar Council provides Guidance on Counsel's Fee Notes requiring barristers to keep notes of the time spent on each item of work and its complexity.

There is also the question of what should happen as regards the costs of the interim applica- **5.60** tions to court that are likely to have been made in the case. These may have happened months or even years before the trial, and if the whole question were simply left to the end there could be significant arguments about relatively stale events. A simple approach might be to say that the loser would pay the costs of all these applications, but there are many circumstances in which this would not be fair. For example the party who eventually won the action could have made a great number of interim applications with little or no merit whereas the party who lost at the end of the day might have been careful to avoid making any unnecessary interim applications.

5.61   The fairest approach is therefore for the judge to consider the matter of costs at the end of each interim application so that as few decisions as possible remain to be made at the end of the trial.

I   ORDERS FOR COSTS AT INTERIM HEARINGS

5.62   The matter of costs is so important that the Civil Procedure Rules provide that when a case goes to court for an interim hearing or a case management hearing the court should normally be informed of the current costs situation with an updated statement of costs, so that the accumulation of costs can be monitored.

5.63   It is normally at the discretion of the court to make a summary assessment of costs at the end of a hearing. The costs of interim hearings lasting less than a day are likely to be decided by an immediate summary assessment. This will be based on the statements of costs that the parties have to produce, but the court can also take into account other evidence (such as counsel's brief fee) and argument as to the work involved in the case. An assessment is unlikely to be overgenerous in these circumstances. Some courts evolve norms for awards in different types of cases, and this approach may become standardized in the future. There are some concerns about the lack of consistency in summary assessment awards.

5.64   There is a variety of orders that may be made by a judge as regards the costs of an interim hearing. The lawyer should consider the options and decide which should be sought as being most favourable to the client in the circumstances, with a fall back should the judge not accept that as appropriate. The specific orders that can be made for costs are detailed below.

5.65   Costs or costs in the event. The party who gets this order is entitled to have their costs for this application paid by the other side whatever later orders say. This would be the normal order where one party has effectively won on the particular interim hearing.

5.66   Costs in the case or costs in the application. The party who gets an order for costs at the end of the proceedings will be entitled to the costs of this application. This is appropriate where the hearing is just part of the case with no winner, for example a case management conference.

5.67   Costs reserved. The costs order is reserved for decision at trial. If no further order is made this will be the same as costs in the case, but a costs reserved order suggests that the matter be reviewed after trial. This is an appropriate order for an application made without notice.

5.68   Claimant's or defendant's costs in the case or in the application. Provided the named party wins the action they will get the costs of this hearing. If that does not happen, each party will bear their own costs. This may be appropriate where a case is adversarial and is effectively won by the argument put forward at the hearing.

5.69   No order as to costs/ parties pay own costs. Each party will bear his or her costs of the hearing in any event, whoever wins the case at the end of the day.

5.70   Costs thrown away. If a party gets a default judgment or sanction set aside they may be ordered to pay the costs thrown away by the other side in getting it. This is appropriate where the other side was justified in seeking the order in the first place. The order will include the costs of the original hearing and of the hearing at which the order or sanction was set aside.

Costs of and caused by/ costs of and arising from. Where there is an order for a specific thing **5.71** such as an amendment to a statement of case, it may be appropriate that the party who gets the order should be responsible for paying knock-on costs, such as the costs of other parties having to amend their statements of case as a result.

The costs order will be incorporated into the order made by the court. If one party is ordered **5.72** to pay the costs of the hearing they will be payable within 14 days. Unless the order specifies the sum to be paid a detailed assessment of costs will be required. The judge should be asked to state whether the application merited the appearance of counsel to justify the brief fee as part of the costs.

If there is no clearly appropriate order for the costs of the interim application then a decision **5.73** on costs may be reserved until the case is finally decided. If no order is made as to costs, each party will be left to bear their own.

In general terms the facts that the court will consider as regards an interim costs order are as **5.74** follows.

- Did one party effectively 'win' a contested application by getting the order they sought, in which case that person should normally get their costs.
- Was one party at fault in necessitating the costs of an application that could have been avoided, in which case that party should normally pay the costs.
- Was the application made by one party and assisted only that party, in which case that party should probably pay for it.
- Was the hearing of equal benefit to both parties, in which case both should probably pay for it.
- Is there a clear case for costs to be paid straightaway as it is quite clear which party should pay the costs and the other party should not be left out of pocket? Or would it be fairer for the costs to be paid when the costs for the whole action have been decided?
- If neither party can really be said to have won the interim application then there is likely to be an order that whichever party wins the case at trial will get costs to include the costs of the interim application.

In considering the amount of costs that is appropriately payable in a summary assessment at **5.75** the end of an interim hearing the court will consider what is reasonable, though the court may have limited evidence and practice round the country varies.

Sample schedule of costs (Form N260)

The information provided must include: **5.76**

- the number of hours of work claimed for each solicitor, the hourly rate claimed, and the grade of the fee earner;
- the amount and nature of disbursements;
- solicitor's costs for attending or appearing at the hearing;
- counsel's fees (if any);
- VAT where appropriate.

5.77   The grades for fee earners are essentially:

- A: Solicitors with at least eight years' post-qualification experience, including eight years' experience of litigation;
- B: Solicitors and Fellows of the Institute of Legal Executives with at least four years' experience of litigation;
- C: Other solicitors and FILEx qualified with at least six years' experience of litigation;
- D: Trainees and paralegals.

5.78   Sample schedule for costs

IN THE HIGH COURT OF JUSTICE   Claim No 2005 HC 1234
QUEEN'S BENCH DIVISION
BETWEEN

A. B.	Claimant
and	
C. D.	Defendant

CLAIMANT'S STATEMENT OF COSTS
TO 1 APRIL 2005

Claimant's statement of costs for the interim application hearing on 1 April 2005

Fee earners advising on case
Jane Brown—£120 per hour Grade B (JB)
John Smith—£80 per hour Grade D (JS)

Attendance on client JB: 3½ hours at £120 per hour	£420
Attendance on opponents JS: 1½ hours at £80 per hour	£120
Work done on papers JB: 1 hour at £120 per hour JS: 2 hours at £80 per hour	£120 £160
Counsel's fees Emma Curtis: fee for hearing	£250
Court fees	£200
VAT on solicitors' and counsel's fees at 17.5%	£187.25
Total	£1,457.25

The costs set out above do not exceed the costs which the claimant is liable to pay in respect of the work which this statement covers.

Dated 1 April 2005

Signed: (Solicitors)

If a summary assessment of costs is to be made, the judge will ask the advocates to address **5.79** her or him on the statement of costs filed by the party who is to receive costs. Counsel should if appropriate be briefed to do this, as the reasons for money being spent will not appear on the schedule. The matters that may be disputed might include the level of the fee earner, the hours spent on the work or Counsel's fee. The judge will take proportionality into account. Although the schedule of costs of the person paying costs will not be examined, it may not be very logical for one party to object to a fee if that party has incurred similar costs.

J WASTED COSTS ORDERS

There is a general professional duty under which barristers and solicitors should not allow **5.80** a client's assets to be dissipated by allowing costs to build to the level where they cease to be proportionate to the amount that is in dispute. Costs must never be allowed to build up without good reason, and this is relevant to each decision made in the case. If costs are incurred without good reason a wasted costs order may be made against a lawyer, see 3.83–3.85.

The procedure

Solicitors and barristers need to work efficiently to support efficient litigation. With greater **5.81** case management powers, a court should be able to ensure that time and costs are rarely wasted. However, if a court feels that a solicitor or barrister conducts a case in such a way that costs are incurred improperly or without reasonable cause, or if there is any undue delay or other misconduct in bringing the case, then the court may make an order as regards costs under the Supreme Court Act 1981, s 51. The result of an order may be that the costs are simply disallowed (so that the barrister or solicitor does not get paid), or that the lawyer is ordered to pay costs incurred personally.

Costs can be wasted if they result from an improper, unreasonable, or negligent act or **5.82** omission on the part of the lawyer, including costs incurred before such an act or omission if the court thinks it unreasonable they be paid in the light of the act or omission.

The procedure is governed by CPR r 48.7, and PD 48. An order will normally only be con- **5.83** sidered once a case has ended. An application can be made against the legal representatives of either side, *Metcalf v Mardell* (2003) 1 AC 120, and can relate to advice and drafting as well as court advocacy. A court should be slow to make a wasted costs enquiry unless there is a clear case.

The first stage is for the complainant to satisfy the court that there are grounds for a wasted **5.84** costs order, such that a legal representative should be invited to show cause why a wasted costs order should not be made. The court should take into account the likely costs of an enquiry as against the costs claimed. If there is an enquiry the lawyer should be informed fully and clearly of the complaint, but complex statements and disclosure should be avoided, though the lawyer is likely to fight the case strongly. There should then be a hearing for the lawyer to show cause why the order should not be made. The primary point is not so much to punish the lawyer as to protect the client and provide an indemnity. A lawyer can be asked about non-privileged documents relevant to an application for a wasted costs order, *Brown v Bennett (No 3)* The Times, 4 January 2002.

The test

5.85 The test for whether a wasted costs order should be made has three stages, *Re a Barrister (Wasted Costs Order) (No 1 of 1991)* (1993) QB 293:

- Has the lawyer acted improperly, unreasonably, or negligently?
- If so, did that lead the applicant to incur unnecessary costs?
- If so, is it in all the circumstances just to order the lawyer to compensate the applicant for all or part of the wasted costs?

5.86 This means that the defects of the lawyer in the conduct of the case should be clearly formulated, and that there must be a causal link between the poor conduct and the costs wasted, *Ridehalgh v Horsefield* [1994] 3 WLR 462.

- It is not necessary to establish gross misconduct, *Sinclair Jones v Kay* [1988] 2 All ER 611. 'Improper' covers not only conduct that might normally lead to disbarment or striking off, but also any significant breach of a duty imposed by a relevant code of professional conduct, and conduct which would be regarded as improper by the consensus of professional opinion.
- Conduct is 'unreasonable' if it is designed to harass the other side rather than to advance the resolution of the case.
- Conduct is 'negligent' if there is a failure to act with the competence to be expected of an ordinary member of the profession, though it does not have to amount to professional negligence.
- The conduct does not have to amount to a breach of the rules of professional conduct, though acting contrary to the Bar Code of Conduct as in pleading a case in fraud without a proper basis may be improper conduct, *Metcalf v Mardell* (2003) 1 AC 120.
- An order may be made where an advocate appears to be unclear about the issues involved and makes a rambling submission with embarrassing pauses, *Antonelli v Wade Gery Farr* [1994] 3 WLR 462.
- A solicitor may be ordered to pay costs if he or she acts without the authority of the client, *Bell Fruit Manufacturing Co v Twinfalcon* (1995) FSR 144.
- An order may be justified where a solicitor gives fanciful and unreasonable advice that gives a client unreasonable expectations, *C v C (wasted costs order)* (1994) 2 FLR 34.
- An order may be made where a solicitor has assisted with a case that is hopeless or which is an abuse of process, *Tolstoy-Miloslavky v Aldington* The Times, 27 December 1995.
- An order may be made if an offer to settle is unreasonably refused.
- An order may be made if steps in the case are not properly pursued, or if a lawyer proceeds with an application that is inappropriate, or after new evidence shows it is unlikely to succeed, *Philex plc v Golban* (1994) 3 WLR 462.

5.87 Liability may be avoided in certain circumstances:

- It seems that allowances should be made for real practical difficulties, *Re a Barrister (Wasted Costs Order No 4 of 1993)* The Times 21 April 1995.

- A barrister pursuing a hopeless case will not necessarily be penalised if acting under client instructions, having taken the case due to the cab rank principle.
- Making an application that has little chance of success will not necessarily merit a wasted costs order if there is a reasonable explanation of the action, *Re O (A minor) (wasted costs application)* (1994) 2 FLR 842.
- A solicitor is likely to avoid liability if acting on counsel's advice, but can not necessarily avoid all liability for independent professional judgment simply by briefing counsel.
- There must be good cause for an order, *Orchard v South Eastern Electricity Board* [1987] 1 All ER 95, not iust a mistake, *McGoldrick & Co v CPS* The Times, 15 November 1989.
- An order cannot be made against a lawyer who did not conduct the litigation where the client went on to use a different solicitor, *Byrne v Sefton Health Authority* The Times, 28 November 2001.

As a less serious alternative, certain costs may be disallowed. A judge may make remarks in **5.88** giving judgment as to what costs should be allowed by the taxing master if the judge feels that the lawyer has not conducted the case properly, *R v McFadden* The Times, 10 December 1978. As a matter of general policy costs may be disallowed if there is a late application to adjourn, or if lawyers are not properly prepared, *Fowkes v Duthie* [1991] 1 All ER 337.

KEY DOCUMENTS

County Court Fees Order 1999 (list of fees)
Supreme Court Fees Order 1999
Supreme Court Costs Office Guide
Conditional Fee Agreements Regulations 2000
Community Legal Service (Costs) Regulations 2000

Costs Precedents (Schedule to PD 43–48)
Includes model forms of bills of costs etc
N260 Statement of costs
N258 Request for detailed assessment hearing

These are easily available in hard copy and electronically, see Chapter 24.

6

TECHNIQUES FOR MEETINGS WITH CLIENTS

A THE RELATIONSHIP WITH THE CLIENT. 6.01

The importance of the relationship with the client 6.01
The ingredients of a good working relationship 6.04
Problems in building a working relationship 6.06

B PROFESSIONAL RESPONSIBILITIES. 6.10

C THE ROLES OF THE CLIENT AND OF THE LAWYER 6.13

Defining roles 6.13
Balancing roles 6.17

D FIGHTING THE CLIENT'S CORNER 6.22

E MANAGING CLIENT EXPECTATIONS 6.24

The importance of managing expectations 6.24
Active management of expectations. 6.28

F LITIGATION AS A PROCESS WITH TWO SIDES. 6.29

G PROFESSIONAL USE OF LANGUAGE 6.32

H WHY A CLIENT COMES TO A LAWYER. 6.37

I MEETING AND CONTACTING A CLIENT. 6.43

Patterns for contact and meetings. 6.43
Where to meet a client 6.47
Who should be at a meeting 6.52
Virtual meetings. 6.55
The use of the telephone 6.56

J OBJECTIVES AND CHALLENGES IN MEETINGS 6.58

Clarifying the purpose of a meeting 6.58
Possible problems 6.61

K PREPARING FOR A MEETING 6.71

A checklist for preparation 6.71
Preparing for a meeting to gather information 6.74
Preparing for a meeting to offer advice 6.75

L SETTING THE AGENDA 6.76
Key ingredients for an agenda 6.76
Starting a meeting 6.81
Setting the context and involving the client. 6.86

M IDENTIFYING CLIENT OBJECTIVES. 6.87

N GATHERING INFORMATION 6.90
The importance of gathering information. 6.90
Techniques for information gathering 6.92
Problems in gathering information 6.95
Techniques for dealing with problems 6.96

O QUESTIONING TECHNIQUES. 6.99
Types of questions 6.100
Forming questions. 6.106

P INFORMATION AND ADVICE 6.113

Q CONCLUDING THE MEETING 6.116

R DEALING WITH DIFFICULT CLIENTS. 6.119
The client may fail to provide relevant information 6.121
The client may fail to provide clear instructions or may change
    instructions. 6.123
The client who seeks to play too strong a role 6.125
The stressed or emotional client 6.127
The client may provide false information 6.130
Failure to build a working relationship with the client. 6.135

How many lawyers does it take to change a light bulb?
Lawyers don't change light bulbs—they prefer to keep clients in the dark.

A   THE RELATIONSHIP WITH THE CLIENT

The importance of the relationship with the client

6.01 The purpose of litigation is to achieve the best possible outcome for the client. It could be said that effective litigation is that which gets closest to achieving the client's aims, at a proportionate cost and within a reasonable time.

6.02 The client and the client's objectives must therefore be at the centre of the case, and it is essential for the lawyer to have an effective working relationship with the client. Many lawyers are now fully aware of the importance of the relationship with the client, and the old fashioned style of lawyer who could seem very remote from the client and at times patronising or condescending is now hopefully a thing of the past. For books relevant to building a working relationship with a client see 24.23.

No assumptions should be made about the seriousness of a case to a client, or about what the client wants to achieve. A neighbour cutting down a hedge can be more important to one person than a £1,000,000 contract is to another. It is all too easy for a busy lawyer to be tempted into over managing a case, and it can be important to allow the client sufficient input at all stages of the case. The importance of managing relationships with clients is such that it will often be done by senior rather than junior lawyers. **6.03**

The ingredients of a good working relationship

Each lawyer will relate to different clients in different ways, but the key ingredients of a good working relationship are probably: **6.04**

- ensuring that the client has sufficient confidence to provide all relevant information about the case;
- ensuring that the lawyer understands clearly what the client wants to achieve;
- checking general understanding—to be sure that lawyer and client are not using words in very different ways;
- ensuring that the lawyer appreciates the realities of the situation that the client is in, which may require thought and imagination;
- ensuring that the client really understands advice that is given;
- seeing where there are gaps in what the client is saying, trying to appreciate why there are gaps (for example embarrassment), and finding appropriate ways to fill those gaps;
- showing a reasonable degree of sympathy for the client—this does not mean emotional support, but giving the client the feeling that you are on his side; the client should not get the feeling that his own lawyer is judging him rather than assisting him, or is doing more for the other side than for his own client;
- keeping the client fully informed of how the case is progressing, including explaining procedural steps.

There are good practical reasons for building such a relationship. **6.05**

- The lawyer will generally want to have the fullest and most accurate information available about the case from an early stage to avoid being taken by surprise by new information at a late stage.
- The lawyer will not want to be embarrassed in front of a judge and colleagues in court by a client suddenly providing information that the lawyer should have elicited at a much earlier stage.
- The lawyer will want the client to feel reasonably positive about the service he is getting to avoid quibbles about paying the lawyer's fees, and hopefully to ensure that the client will recommend the lawyer to other potential clients.

Problems in building a working relationship

It can be reasonably easy for a lawyer to establish a good working relationship with a client from a similar background to his or her own. There are greater challenges where the lawyer **6.06** has a very different background, or where there is an impediment to the relationship such as embarrassment or a reluctance to tell the truth.

6.07   It is clear that a number of people who consult a lawyer find it at least partly a negative experience. Research into this area, including how well clients feel that their lawyer has understood their case, would be very helpful in helping to address such perceptions.

6.08   There are a number of reasons why a client may have negative feelings about a meeting with a lawyer. While one can understand these situations, they explain rather than justify allowing a poor relationship to develop with the client.

- A client may have unrealistic expectations of what the law can achieve in a particular case.
- The client may well have made contact with the lawyer only because of a serious problem, and it may be very difficult for anyone to make the resolution of the problem a positive experience.
- A client may find it difficult to fully comprehend matters of procedure and evidence.
- The lawyer may find it difficult to communicate easily with a client from a very different background.
- The lawyer may find it difficult to explain legal principles in a clear way.
- Conducting litigation can be pressurised and stressful, and sometimes a lawyer may share a joke with the lawyer for the other side, failing to remember that a nervous client is watching.
- Conducting litigation can be complex, and the lawyer may not always have communication with the client as a high priority, even if it should be.
- A lawyer may well feel more interested in the legal content of the case than the personal position of the client.

6.09   Techniques for building a relationship with a client must of course be adapted to different types of practice, and to the case in hand. Generalisations are difficult—businessmen vary significantly in their approach to legal problems, and an accident victim may be easy to empathise with or may be embittered and wary. Some clients will be able to follow quite a complex legal argument and others will need to have basic legal terminology explained. The important thing is to be able to adjust—'people skills' are something that firms and chambers look for in recruiting.

B   PROFESSIONAL RESPONSIBILITIES

6.10   The importance of maintaining the correct relationship with the client is a matter of proper professional conduct. The Codes of Conduct for the Bar and for Solicitors specifically include a number of points, see 3.46. The good working relationship must be a professional one with sufficient objectivity and distance. The point is not to become a friend of the client, which could in itself be a problem for the professional relationship; what is necessary is to ensure good communication and inspire confidence.

6.11   In maintaining a professional relationship it is of course irrelevant whether or not the lawyer agrees with the client's views. It is not for the lawyer to 'judge' the client, but only to assess objectively the chances of success of potential causes of action, and whether particular remedies are achievable. The lawyer must keep personal views private. If the personal views are so strong as to make it difficult to represent the client properly, suggest that the client might be better represented by another lawyer

A duty to the court may outweigh a duty to the client in terms of how a case is presented and **6.12** how witnesses are treated. The lawyer should not become involved in anything improper or unlawful on the part of the client. Professional duties with regard to clients have been made much more complex by the Proceeds of Crime Act, which requires a report to be made if the lawyer has reason to suspect that money or assets involved in the case have originated from criminal activity. The relevant provisions are dealt with in 3.35–3.42.

C   THE ROLES OF THE CLIENT AND OF THE LAWYER

Defining roles

It can be all too easy for a lawyer to take too great a role in a case, leaving too small a role for **6.13** the client. The lawyer will normally have much or all of the expertise on law and evidential and procedural rules, and may be more articulate than the client. The lawyer will have more familiarity with meetings in solicitors' offices or chambers, and with the court room.

On the other hand the client brings to the relationship not only the finance but also the facts **6.14** of the case and the objectives to be achieved. Litigation is going to be most effective when the skills and resources of clients and lawyers are properly mixed.

The lawyer should be a manager rather than a decision taker. The lawyer is an agent or **6.15** mouthpiece for the client, and is not personally a party to the case. The role of the lawyer is primarily to:

- elicit information relevant to the case from the client;
- oversee the gathering of evidence from other sources;
- research the law;
- analyse the issues, the law, and the evidence;
- advise the client on the strengths and weaknesses of the options available for progressing the case;
- ensure the correct procedure is followed in taking the case forward;
- follow the client's instructions.

The role of the client is primarily to: **6.16**

- provide factual information about the situation that the client wishes to have addressed;
- set the objectives for the case;
- decide which of the options set out by the lawyer to pursue and to give instructions on that basis.

Balancing roles

The relationship between the lawyer and client needs to be properly balanced and integrated **6.17** in each case. The client may only know what factual information is relevant through the guidance of the lawyer. The client may want to know what remedies are available before deciding what he wants to achieve. The client may find it difficult to decide between options and may ask what the lawyer recommends, which will need a carefully worded response to ensure decisions stay with the client.

6.18   The lawyer has no right to impose solutions on a client. It is the client's case, not least when negotiating a settlement. For example, in *Waugh v MB Clifford & Sons* [1982] Ch 374 the solicitors negotiated a settlement for a claim arising from defects in houses without the clients' consent. It was held that the clients were still bound by the settlement as the solicitors had actual or ostensible authority to act on behalf of the clients, and full agreement had been reached, and the clients would have been very concerned at this result. However, it may be possible for the agreement to be set aside if the lawyer did not have authority and the agreement has not been perfected or put into effect.

6.19   Balancing roles is not easy. It may be difficult to balance what needs to be done to win the case with the instructions given by the client. It may be difficult to get clear instructions. The client may change the instructions. Problems may be wholly or partly avoided by explaining the roles of the client and the lawyer at the first meeting.

6.20   There will be differences in how different lawyers and clients work. Despite the growth of direct access to barristers, it is normally the solicitor who will have consistent contact with the client throughout the case. The barrister is likely to be briefed for specific purposes, and may only see a client in conference at key points in the case and at trial.

6.21   The role of a barrister is slightly different when a case comes to trial, as the barrister is in charge of a case in court, and it is for the barrister to decide what witnesses to call and what questions to ask, though he or she should follow the client's wishes unless there is good reason to do otherwise. In more than one of the 'Rumpole' stories by John Mortimer the barrister wins the case by calling a witness or asking a question directly contrary to his client's wishes, but winning by doing so. It is not easy to align the Rumpole approach with appropriate professional conduct!

D   FIGHTING THE CLIENT'S CORNER

6.22   The lawyer's role is to represent the client to the best of his or her ability. In an adversarial system the lawyer is there to take a side and to fight the client's corner. The lawyer is there to find out how the case can legally and evidentially be put in the best possible light, to advise on how the case can be put in its best light, and to conduct the case in the strongest possible way. No purpose is served by being over-optimistic, but the best case possible should be made.

6.23   The lawyer should not take on the role of judge. Any advice or opinion should focus on assessing strengths and weaknesses, looking at how to promote the former and address the latter. Possible outcomes for the case may be suggested, but the lawyer should not offer 'judgment'.

E MANAGING CLIENT EXPECTATIONS

The importance of managing expectations

Clients often come to lawyers with very high expectations. They are likely to have given **6.24**
significant thought to a problem before approaching a lawyer. The outcome of a contract
claim may be vital for saving a business or for having enough money to keep paying the
mortgage on the family home. The outcome of a personal injury claim may be central to the
life not only of the person injured but to his or her family. A client may see a lawyer as a
person who can transform a very difficult situation. Such expectations are not always
expressed, but that does not mean they are not there.

One possible response is to encourage client expectations. This is initially an easy way to **6.25**
maintain a good relationship, and it can be very hard to give bad news to someone to whom
a particular outcome to litigation is really important. However, allowing a client to remain
unrealistically optimistic through overgenerous advice on the chances of success or the likely
measure of damages is likely to lead to disappointment at trial or problems in negotiating a
settlement.

One possible response is to ignore client expectations. It is quite justifiable for a lawyer to **6.26**
ignore a client's personal views so long as the lawyer is providing realistic advice. The
difficulty with such an approach is that it leads to a divergence. If the client proceeds with
high expectations and the lawyer works with reasonable expectations that again can store up
difficulties for trial or dealing with settlement offers, and the client may lose confidence in
the lawyer.

A third response is to meet unreasonable client expectations head on. If a client expects too **6.27**
much it is quite justifiable to make that clear to them, but if this is done without constructive
management the client's trust in the lawyer may be undermined.

Active management of expectations

Active management of client expectations should help the client to take realistic decisions **6.28**
and avoid disappointment that may take the form of complaints about the lawyer. Active
management is best achieved through:

- open communication;
- asking a client about expectations at an early meeting—what does the client hope for
  from the case and why;
- gauging how realistic these expectations are and addressing anything that is unrealistic—
  this may need to be done carefully over time to retain the client's confidence;
- emphasising strengths and weaknesses and the reasons for them in providing advice;
- reviewing client expectations against likely outcome as the case progresses.

F   LITIGATION AS A PROCESS WITH TWO SIDES

6.29   In completing a legal transaction, such as drawing up a contract, a lawyer will essentially identify client objectives, outline the legal options, and complete the transaction. There may be two sides to consider, such as a landlord and a tenant if the lawyer is drawing up a lease, but points at issue can normally be resolved by negotiation as there will be a shared interest in making the agreement work.

6.30   The dynamic in litigation is rather different. A case will be based on a contractual or tort relationship that has gone seriously wrong, or on an accident or damage to property. There are likely to be negative feelings and deep concerns. There are inevitably two sides. This has various consequences.

- The lawyers retained by each side must and should focus primarily on preparing the case for their own side in the strongest way, and it is important to the adversarial process that they do so.
- In most serious cases both sides will have legal advice. It is important to try to predict what the lawyers on the other side will be advising their client.
- Each side will have their own objectives. It is useful to try to predict what the objectives of the other side may be if you hope to reach a settlement.
- The client may be tempted to embellish the truth in recounting relevant events.
- The client may be very defensive to any suggestion that he was partly to blame.
- The client may be over-enthusiastic in presenting the faults of the other side.

6.31   The whole litigation process is adversarial—it is predicated on there being two sides. Not only does this provide an important content, but it lies behind many rules for exchanging information etc.

G   PROFESSIONAL USE OF LANGUAGE

6.32   For good communication the lawyer and the client need to be able to understand each other. This may be easy if the lawyer and client have similar backgrounds and a similar understanding of the context of the litigation, but there may be many challenges in the client understanding legal terminology and in the lawyer understanding a context a client is explaining. There is no merit in oversimplification. Most clients are quite capable of understanding legal terminology and the point is to explain, not to patronise.

6.33   Techniques for ensuring understanding include:

- identifying terminology of any kind that may not be commonly understood and ensuring that it is explained;
- adjusting the level of legal terminology and explanation to suit each client;
- asking for guidance where necessary—if an accident happens in a factory the lawyer may need to get to grips with an industrial process, or if a contract case involves misrepresentations about a work of art the lawyer may need to understand the finer points of how works of art are valued;

- checking understanding—if the client may not have understood advice, the lawyer can say to the client 'I may not have put that very clearly—would you mind telling me what you think I said?' To check his or her own understanding the lawyer can summarise in the form 'Now, as I understand it the situation is this, but do tell me if I am wrong . . .'.

Effective communication has other ingredients. An important test of a useful meeting is whether the right person is doing most of the talking. If a lawyer is explaining law then the lawyer should be doing most of the talking. If a client is answering questions or giving instructions then the client should be doing most of the talking. Some lawyers seem to find it difficult to ensure that the client does enough of the talking! **6.34**

The use of pauses should not be forgotten. A pause can be very useful to help those involved to collect their thoughts and review what has happened. Silence can be useful in getting someone to keep talking and to provide information. **6.33**

An understanding of body language can also be useful in a professional context. The way that a person sits and reacts during a meeting can reveal something of a client's attitude. Posture can also tell the client something about the lawyer. The lawyer who sits in a way that is open and attentive expresses much more interest to the client and is easier for the client to talk to. **6.36**

H WHY A CLIENT COMES TO A LAWYER

Why does a particular client end up seeing a particular lawyer? This may sound like a question for a marketing manager or a sociologist, but it has a basic relevance to whether the litigation process will progress effectively. A client will get best service from a lawyer with appropriate expertise for their case. Systems must provide routes by which the client can reach an appropriate lawyer, and lawyers need to provide adequate assistance to the process. **6.37**

Relaxations in professional rules about the extent to which lawyers can advertise has vastly increased the amount of information available to clients about firms, chambers, and individual lawyers. Professional guides, both hard copy and web-based, make it increasingly likely that a client will be able to identify a lawyer with appropriate expertise. The tendency for lawyers to specialise in particular areas of practice is also likely to have made it easier for a client to make an appropriate choice. **6.38**

However the system has weaknesses. A personal recommendation may not be well informed. Advertising may be more designed to attract clients than to give information about a firm. A client may not be able to formulate the type of case he or she has very clearly, and may not be able to make best use of available information about lawyers. **6.39**

These considerations provide an important context for the first meeting between a client and a lawyer. If the client has not necessarily identified a lawyer with appropriate expertise, this has implications for the preparations required before a meeting, for client expectations, for what needs to be covered in the first meeting, and for how an action might progress. **6.40**

6.41 Perhaps the best way forward is to try to identify the type of case involved reasonably quickly. A new client who wants to make an appointment should be asked:

- what type of case the client thinks is involved;
- how urgent the case is in general terms, and whether any letters or other documents have given key dates by which things must be done;
- to bring all relevant documents;
- if possible, to write and bring a written summary of all the main dates and facts.

6.42 If any questions arise as to the appropriateness of the expertise of the lawyer they should be addressed. Most firms of any size may be able to provide a referral to a colleague. As a base line, professional conduct rules provide that a lawyer should not take a case outside his or her expertise.

I MEETING AND CONTACTING A CLIENT

Patterns for contact and meetings

6.43 Regular contact must be maintained with a client. This is not simply to exchange information but also to build mutual confidence and a shared understanding of how the case is being conducted. The client should always know what will happen next and when it will happen. Having said this, contact and meetings must be strategically organised. Each communication will add to costs, and meetings may not be easy to organise.

6.44 Most contact can be made easily and at reasonable cost by telephone, through a letter, or by electronic means. If the purpose of communication is to provide information or updating then the complexity and expense of a face to face meeting is best avoided. The only question will be which form of communication is appropriate, and ensuring that a record gets to the case file, especially in the case of a telephone conversation.

6.45 A face to face meeting will need to be organised where a more complicated discussion is required, or where several people need to be involved. Meetings between a solicitor and client, or a conference with a barrister, solicitor and client need to be held at appropriate points in the development of the case. A meeting or conference may be called in the following circumstances.

- When a client first contacts a solicitor and there is a need to ascertain the nature of the case, the key facts, and what might happen.
- When, following initial contact, further information has been gathered by the solicitor and/or the client.
- When an important communication has come from the other side and it is important to respond to it.
- When it is necessary to take a decision about a key procedural or evidential step.
- A conference may be arranged with a barrister if it is decided to brief a barrister because of the complexity of the case, if the barrister needs to meet the client to understand the case fully, and/or if the barrister needs to meet the client to see how he or she may appear as a witness in court.

- A client may wish to have a conference with a solicitor, and a barrister, at any stage of the case.
- A conference may be called to discuss terms if an offer to settle the case is made or is contemplated.
- If the case does go to trial it may well be necessary to have a conference shortly before the trial to review the arguments and evidence and strategy and to ensure that everything is ready.

Meetings need to be timed to fit with the needs of the case. It can be expensive to hold **6.46** meetings and difficult to find an ideal time. The timing of some meetings may be obvious, if for example counsel has sent an opinion and solicitor and client need to discuss it, but it may be difficult to identify ideal times to meet to review the progress of a case, especially in a complex case where a number of matters regarding seeking evidence and making applications to court are proceeding at the same time.

Where to meet a client

A solicitor will normally see a client at the solicitor's office and a barrister will normally hold **6.47** a conference in chambers. The location of a meeting can have various implications for how effective the meeting will be.

If the meeting takes place in the lawyer's office, the lawyer has control over the location. The **6.48** size of the room, the types of chairs used, and the spaces between them can have an effect on the dynamics of the meeting and how comfortable those present feel. The traditional large desk covered with papers, that could form a rather intimidating barrier, has gone in favour of conference tables where lawyers and clients can spread their papers. Different room layouts may be useful for different purposes—comfortable chairs and a small table might be appropriate for talking to personal injury clients, with a big table and chairs for a contract case with a lot of documents. The tidiness of the room can give an impression, whether or not accurate, of how efficiently the case might be run.

There are other locations over which the lawyer has less control. For example lawyers and **6.49** clients often need to talk to each other outside a court before a case, during or after a case. One has to find the best ways to deal with the difficulties of the location. It is important to become familiar with courts to discover if there are more private places for speaking to a client. If the court is unfamiliar, ask a court official. There may be very real difficulties in talking right outside court, for example if witnesses for the other side are waiting in the same place.

A further problem of trying to conduct an interview outside court is that the lawyer has less **6.50** control over who is present. In the office or in chambers the lawyer can propose who should attend, but outside court well-meaning relatives and friends may be present and may well wish to talk to the lawyer themselves. It may be important for the lawyer to take control and make it clear whom he or she needs to talk to, and if necessary whom he or she should not talk to.

There are practical points relating to dealing with locations away from the office. It may be **6.51** necessary to organise papers so that they are easy to look at even if a table is not available, and to carry a notepad to take notes where there is no table to lean on.

Who should be at a meeting

6.52   If a meeting is to serve its purpose, the right people will need to be present. Most meetings will be between the lawyer(s) and the client, but there are a number of circumstances in which further decisions need to be taken. The cost of a meeting could be wasted, or weak decisions may be taken, if a relevant person is not there.

- If the client is a business, which people should be at a meeting to discuss the case? Should it always be the same people?
- If the client is a company or partnership, so that different legal personalities are involved, who should properly be dealing with the contemplated litigation?
- If several people want to come to a meeting, is there a risk that a lawyer might see someone who should not be at that meeting, such as a potential witness in the case?
- If the client is a child the parents will probably want to come too. Should both parents be allowed to come or only the parent (or other person) who is acting as the child's Next Friend for litigation purposes?

6.53   Even the basic option of the client and the lawyer has a number of variations. A solicitor might see a client alone, or with a trainee or administrator to take a note. A complex case might require more than one solicitor to deal with different aspects of the case. If a barrister is briefed and there is a conference, normally held at the barrister's chambers, then the solicitor will normally attend as the professional client of the barrister, with the client as the lay client. A pupil may sit in on the conference. In a very complex case there may be more than one barrister, often a Queen's Counsel and a junior.

6.54   There are professional rules as to when a lawyer should meet a witness in a case. A solicitor may meet a witness to take a proof of evidence. A barrister may have contact with a witness prior to trial, subject to the limitations laid down in Annex H of the Code of Conduct. In no circumstances should the barrister rehearse or coach the witness (a practice common in the USA), or put any pressure on a witness to say anything other than the truth. However, the barrister may properly explain court procedure to put the witness at ease, answer questions, and talk objectively to witnesses about the evidence they will give. To avoid any misunderstandings, the barrister should avoid meeting the witness alone, or meeting more than one witness at the same time.

Virtual meetings

6.55   Technology can now provide for virtual meetings. A virtual meeting may save costs or be more convenient for the client, and there is no reason why such a meeting should not be conducted following normal rules. The particular considerations that might arise are as follows.

- The capabilities of the facilities being used—will it be possible for all participants to see the faces of all other participants all the time?
- Are there any documents to be shared? Arrangements will have to be made in advance as documents cannot be physically tabled.
- Presentations of advice can be more difficult through electronic conference facilities unless properly thought through and prepared in advance.

The use of the telephone

A telephone meeting can offer many potential advantages: **6.56**

- A telephone conversation can ensure that information is available much more quickly.
- Use of the telephone can be much cheaper and much more convenient.

The use of the telephone also has potential disadvantages: **6.57**

- It may be necessary to set up a call at a certain time to ensure that the lawyer is focussed on the case and has the case file available.
- Unless a conference call is set up, only two parties can be involved in the call.
- The lack of visual contact can make it more difficult to assess the reliability of what is being said.
- It is all too easy to misunderstand something said quickly on the telephone, or to fail to take a proper note.

J   OBJECTIVES AND CHALLENGES IN MEETINGS

Clarifying the purpose of a meeting

It is crucial to be clear when arranging a meeting what the meeting will be about. Meetings at   **6.58**
different stages in the case will have different focusses. A first interview with a solicitor is
likely to be largely fact gathering, whereas a conference with a barrister when an action
is under way may well consist largely of advice on law, procedure, and evidence.

In general terms the objectives for an effective interview might be: **6.59**

- to elicit all relevant facts;
- to clarify and understand the client's objectives;
- to weigh up the client as a potential witness;
- to explain law and procedure to the client;
- to advise the client on options;
- to take instructions from the client;
- to agree what will happen next.

Identifying the purpose of a meeting should assist in identifying who should be present and   **6.60**
what documents etc are required. It may be useful to decide an outline agenda for a meeting
in advance and to identify what decisions need to be taken.

Possible problems

There are a number of problems that may arise in meetings. A failure to ask a key question, or   **6.61**
to explain an important matter in terms the client can understand can undermine the whole
purpose of a meeting. A lax approach can cause a case to fall apart at a later stage, increase
costs, and lead to significant client dissatisfaction. A meeting which goes wrong can have a
very negative impact on the relationship between lawyer and client, and on the progress of
the case. It is worth identifying in advance of any meeting what might go wrong and having
techniques in mind to address the potential difficulties.

Time management

6.62 Effective time management is very important. Many interviews and conferences will be scheduled for a set time, such as an hour, and there will be knock-on effects for other clients if the meeting overruns. Sometimes there will only be a limited period of time for a meeting, for example collecting last minute facts and instructions before going into court. In any event meetings should not be longer than they need to be or costs will build up. Time should be managed by identifying the key areas to be covered and ensuring appropriate time is allocated to each.

Keeping a focus

6.63 It can be very difficult to keep a meeting focussed on the matters the lawyer wishes to cover. Clients often have particular concerns that they wish to voice, and they may fail to understand what is really most important for the legal case. It can be quite difficult to keep a meeting on track, especially if a client is angry or emotional, but each lawyer needs to build techniques to do this.

Lack of information

6.64 Even if the timing of the meeting has been carefully considered, lack of particular pieces of information can make it difficult for a meeting to achieve its purpose. It is important to try to foresee what information is likely to be required.

Problems in communication

6.65 The lawyer may have drawn up a list of questions to which answers are required, but clients do not always produce clear and concise answers. The client may not understand a question, may ramble, or may not remember. A good lawyer will use techniques to tie the client down.

Getting the atmosphere right

6.66 Especially in an early meeting it can be quite difficult to get an appropriate atmosphere of objectivity and empathy. Appearing too cold and businesslike can be off-putting. Expressions of sympathy may need to be carefully judged. A busy lawyer can too easily carry feelings from one meeting to another and should take care adopt an appropriate tone.

Getting the detail right

6.67 Most clients want and can understand a reasonable level of detail about their case. If the lawyer deals with the case in too superficial a way it can undermine client confidence and understanding.

Giving bad news

6.68 It is easy to deliver bad news too bluntly, or to be too vague about advice that will not be welcome to the client. It is worthwhile thinking through in advance how to break bad news to a client.

Tying up the ends

6.69 It can be quite difficult to pull a meeting to a reasonably comprehensive conclusion, especially if discussion has been wide ranging, if some things have had to be covered very quickly, or if the client is unhappy with some of the advice given. There can be particular problems if a meeting runs out of time and has to be ended abruptly. To ensure all the advice and instructions and next steps are tied together it is worthwhile leaving some time to tie things together at the end, and having a checklist of key points to cover.

It is easy for a meeting to be much less effective than it could be. Everyone will have memor- **6.70** ies of the negative effects of poorly run meetings—the important job interview where there were odd questions and no chance to make important points, or the visit to the doctor that left one feeling just as worried and unclear as before because of problems in explaining symptoms and understanding advice given.

K PREPARING FOR A MEETING

A checklist for preparation

Preparation is an important way to make a meeting effective. The lawyer who is properly **6.71** prepared will get most from the meeting and give the best impression. If the client needs to do something in preparation for the meeting, this should be clearly conveyed to the client.

Appropriate preparations will vary with the type of case involved, the stage the case has **6.72** reached, and the current key issues in the case. Good preparation should ensure that everyone gets what they need from the meeting, that decisions can be taken, and that no loose ends are left hanging at the end of the conference.

Some preparation will need to be done well in advance of the meeting and some preparation **6.73** may take considerable time. As a basic checklist for preparation:

- the lawyer and the client should be reasonably clear about the purpose of the meeting;
- the lawyer should be clear about what needs to be covered in this meeting at this stage of the case;
- the solicitor and/or barrister should ensure that all the relevant documents are to hand;
- so far as possible, the purpose of the meeting should be made clear to the client, and the client should be asked whether he/she wants any particular matters covered;
- the client should be asked to bring any relevant material;
- the lawyer should have read or reread relevant material so as to be clear about the case;
- the lawyer should have identified what decisions need to be taken by the end of the meeting.

Preparing for a meeting to gather information

If the meeting is primarily about gathering information then the lawyer's preparation may **6.74** need to include:

- becoming fully familiar with the documents and information that is already available so as to identify the issues in the case;
- having a list of key dates/people/documents for ease of reference;
- having a list of the areas in which further information is needed;
- having a list of the key points that need to be clarified;

- noting key areas for questioning, and perhaps thinking about specific questions where an area needs particular care or detail;
- identifying areas where expert advice may be required so this can be raised with the client;
- considering whether maps/plans/photos etc might help in understanding the facts of the case;
- having sketched out advice on options that might be given depending on what information emerges.

Preparing for a meeting to offer advice

6.75 If the meeting is primarily about giving advice then preparation needs to include:

- having worked out clearly what the options are in the case;
- having carried out relevant legal research, possibly having some cases and statutes to hand to show to the client;
- having decided how to present the advice to the client—in a commercial case charts etc may assist;
- ensuring that any books that might be required for reference during the interview are to hand, for example to refer to a case or statute of key relevance;
- listing the matters on which you need to take client instructions.

L   SETTING THE AGENDA

Key ingredients for an agenda

6.76 A meeting is most likely to be effective if it has some sort of agenda, however informal. A basic agenda will help with time management, with ensuring that everything gets covered, and in managing a difficult case or a difficult client.

6.77 Basic ingredients for an agenda might include the following.

- Starting the meeting. What preliminary matters need to be covered?
- Content of the meeting. What are the key areas that must be covered?
- Structure for the meeting. Is there a good order to cover matters in?
- Advice. What main areas of advice need to be covered?
- Outcomes. What needs to be agreed by the end of the meeting?
- Procedure. Are there procedural matters to be discussed?
- It may be useful to see if the client has anything to suggest as regards the agenda for the meeting.

6.78 It can also be useful to allocate a rough division of time to each aspect of the meeting. This will help to ensure all areas are given appropriate attention. The allocation should be followed with a degree of fluidity, and not follow an agenda too tightly or a client will be discouraged from raising points.

6.79 There may be logical or even strategic issues relating to the order in which it is best to deal with topics. In an accident case the topics to cover might be: accident, contributory negligence, injuries, loss of earnings, general damages. There might be an argument for showing empathy with the client and dealing with the injuries first, and maybe coming to contributory negligence last, when the client may feel more confident in dealing with it. All questions relating to an area must be asked before advice on that area is given, or there may be a professional conduct problem in appearing to suggest to a client that particular answers might help the case. If advice on a particular topic of concern to the client can be given without asking any questions then that might be done at the start.

Unforeseen matters may emerge, or important areas make take longer to discuss than had been envisaged, but an eye should be kept on the overall agenda. At the end of each part of the meeting there can usefully be a summary of key points before moving on. This can assist in taking notes, and in pulling the meeting together at the end. **6.80**

Starting a meeting

The start of the meeting will often set the tone for the meeting. It should lay the foundation for the client to be open and to trust the lawyer's advice. The lawyer who shows confidence, a business-like approach, and clarity at the start of a meeting is likely to find it easier to progress the meeting. **6.81**

The aim at the very start of the meeting is to make the client feel comfortable. Basics can help, such as ensuring the client knows what to do with his coat, knows where to sit, has space for papers, and is offered a drink. Introductions may be needed, and the involvement of each person in the case clarified. If a trainee solicitor or pupil barrister is present that person should be introduced and it should be ascertained that there are no objections to that person being present. If someone is attending to take a note or if the meeting is being taped for later reference that should be made clear. **6.82**

The lawyer, or senior lawyer, present will normally take overall control of the conduct and pace of the meeting, even if it is the client who has asked for the meeting. There are many ways to start and run the meeting, but it is useful to introduce the agenda proposed. The merits of this are: **6.83**

- if everyone present has the framework for the meeting in mind it can assist in running the meeting efficiently;
- refreshing everyone's memory as to the proposed agenda can help to ensure that everything that everyone wants to cover is included—this can help to give the client confidence;
- the pace of the meeting can be kept up by reference back to the agenda, for example 'Well, we have probably spent enough time on this and we probably need to move on to . . .';
- setting an agenda can help to make it clear where the client's concerns will be dealt with so that the client does not keep interrupting with a particular concern, for example 'I realise you will have a number if worries. I hope we will deal with these as we go along, but we will deal with anything that still worries you at the end';
- it is useful to make it clear whether questions will be dealt with as they arise, or will be covered at the end—if the latter the client should be encouraged to note questions so they are not forgotten;
- listing the areas that will be covered in gathering information and questioning can help the client in providing information coherently;

- it may be appropriate to tell the client that if he or she does not understand something they should make that clear;
- it can be very useful in controlling a difficult client, for example 'I do understand your concerns on this issue, but we said we would deal with it later'.

6.84 An overall example of how to start a meeting might be 'I think it's best if we start by running through the areas that we need to cover at this meeting. I need a lot of information to be able to advise you. I will ask you about the contract, then about what went wrong. I'll also need to make a list of the losses you have suffered. It's only once I have that information that I can advise you on the options. Is there anything else you want to cover at the meeting, or any particular concerns you want to raise now? If not there will be time at the end of the meeting for any further questions you have'.

6.85 It should be established at the start of a meeting who will take a note of what as it will be too late to do this later on. It will be necessary to have an adequate record of information disclosed and decisions taken. The lawyer should keep a record of the advice given to the client to avoid any misunderstanding. It may be desirable for a formal note or recording to be taken and shared by all those present. The lawyer may take a note personally, though taking substantial notes can add to the time taken in the conference, and can be difficult to do if the lawyer is focussing on framing questions and considering what advice to give. At a conference with a barrister it may be agreed that the solicitor will take the note. In a consultation with a silk, the junior barrister in the case will normally take the note. If a trainee solicitor or pupil barrister is asked to take a note they need to be clear what aspects of the meeting need to be recorded.

Setting the context and involving the client

6.86 The context for the meeting may need to be established. In addition to the lawyer taking charge, it is important to provide a context for the role of the client. It may be important to get the client talking, especially if the client is a little apprehensive, so that the client takes a full part in the meeting. Relevant factors may include:

- Checking basic relevant information such as address, phone numbers, place of work, and relevant family and financial details can be a starting place for a first meeting, but will not be necessary for a later meeting unless there is reason to think they are not up to date. However it is much better to have such information put on a form on file before the meeting and not to use the time of the lawyer to deal with such details.
- A way of starting a meeting early in a case is to review what the client wants to achieve and why. This can provide a useful focus for the meeting.
- It may be useful to review what has triggered the meeting. This is an obvious starting point for a new case, if a client has received a document such as a claim form, or if an important stage in the case is due to happen.
- In the later stages of a case it will be likely that the meeting has a specific purpose such as considering an offer for settlement, and the meeting can move straight to that.
- If one issue in the case is particularly serious it may be appropriate to start a meeting by moving straight to that. If, for example, there is a question as to whether a limitation period has expired it may be best to deal with that first before having any more general discussion.

- If there has not been a meeting for some time, or if the case is complex, it may be appropriate to start a meeting by briefly summarising the stage the case has reached, establishing and clarifying any points that are in doubt.

M   IDENTIFYING CLIENT OBJECTIVES

Part of the definition of effective litigation is that it gets as close as possible to achieving what **6.87** the client wants. This makes identifying and checking the client's objectives a matter of key importance. It is all too easy to make assumptions or to generalise—but this same line must be avoided. A claimant may not want what the lawyer would want were the lawyer in similar circumstances. A defendant may want to maintain an ongoing relationship with a claimant rather than simply disputing the case.

Client objectives should be addressed in a reasonably explicit and detailed way. **6.88**

- A client will not necessarily want the highest possible damages. Something else might be more important, such as getting an agreement to stop a particular activity.
- The highest possible damages might not be the best remedy for a businessman. An ongoing commercial relationship in which more money might be gained in profits might be more valuable.
- The client and the lawyer may have very different priorities. Sometimes getting a public apology can mean as much to an individual as getting damages.
- Most cases settle rather than go to trial. It is important to have possible terms for settlement in mind from the early stages of litigation, and those terms should be based on what the client wants to achieve.
- A failure to deal specifically with what a client wants to achieve may mean that a lawyer fails to identify that specific interim applications need to be made, such as an application for an interim injunction or an interim payment.

Identifying client objectives is closely tied in with the professional duty to act within client **6.89** instructions. There are various elements to keeping a focus on client objectives.

- When first meeting a client, what the client wants to achieve should be specifically discussed.
- When reviewing the case at various stages, a check should be made that the objectives remain the same.
- Wherever relevant options should be explained to the client so that the client makes choices.

N   GATHERING INFORMATION

The importance of gathering information

The importance of getting factual information from a client cannot be over-stressed. Those **6.90** entering the profession tend to focus on giving advice, but advice may be flawed if it is not based on clear and full information. Information gathering is an ongoing process. A basic informal first proof of evidence will normally be provided when a client first goes to a solicitor, but that is only a starting point. As the case is prepared for litigation the solicitor may need to ask questions to fill in gaps, a barrister may need to ask questions to check all the elements of potential causes of action, and details must be checked again when the information is put into a formal witness statement.

6.91 Information gathering will be a normal part of most meetings between a client and a lawyer. In the early stages of a case this may be a major purpose of the meeting. The problems of failing to get sufficient information from a client are illustrated by *Orchard v South Eastern Electricity Board* [1987] 1 All ER 95. The claimant instructed his solicitors to sue the electricity board for negligence causing water damage in his house. The Board made it clear to the solicitors that they thought the action was misconceived and that they would apply for the solicitors to pay the costs personally. The claimant lost, it being found that his son had caused the damage, and the Board sought an order that the solicitor pay costs personally. The wasted costs order was avoided only because there was some evidence to support the claimant's case.

Techniques for information gathering

6.92 There are various techniques that can assist in gathering information effectively.

- It may be useful for the lawyer to start by summarising what areas of information are needed and why they are needed.
- It may be useful for the lawyer to start by summarising the situation as he or she sees it, and then asking the client to comment on the key points.
- It can be useful to ask the client to outline the problem in his or her own words, but this is probably best done with a client who has some knowledge of what information is most relevant.
- It is important to help the client to provide information by progressing through areas of questions in a logical way rather than darting from one topic to another. This can be signposted for the client, for example 'Right, I think I have what I need on the collision, lets move on to the injuries you suffered'.
- It is necessary to use techniques for moving the client on, for example 'I have got a full note on that point now, let's consider . . .'.
- It is vital to ask sufficient questions in areas of key importance, for example 'I'm afraid I need to know a lot more about this conversation in which the terms of the contract were agreed'.
- Save for the most experienced practitioner, there is merit in preparing a list of key areas for questions and putting those areas into a suitable order.

6.93 There are various views on the merits of preparing detailed lists of questions in advance. A detailed list can be useful if the lawyer is dealing with an unfamiliar area of law, or if an issue in a case is particularly complex. It can also be useful to consider in advance the best wording for a question the client may not find it easy to answer. On the other hand a long list of detailed questions has drawbacks if followed too closely. It can give the lawyer a false sense of security that everything has been covered when it may not have been. Also the lawyer may be too busy checking the next question to listen to an answer that is being given—and the answer is more important than the question!

It is probably more useful to use a general checklist of areas for questions. For example it can **6.94** be useful to have a reminder that in a case involving an accident at work questions should normally cover the employer, the place of work, working practice, workmates, injuries, and losses. Questions should cover all matters relevant to cause of action, defences, and remedies. Such a checklist can jog the memory, and help make good use of time.

Problems in gathering information

There are a number of reasons why gathering information can be challenging. **6.95**

- The lawyer can only gather information if the client is doing the majority of the talking, but this can make it difficult to keep adequate control of the meeting and to keep up pace.
- The client and the lawyer may not share views in what information is most important.
- The client may not understand what information the lawyer is seeking.
- The client may not know or be able to find out the information that the lawyer is seeking.
- The client may not wish to reveal the information that the lawyer is seeking.
- The lawyer may not be able to find the right question to get the information that is required.
- The lawyer may take too superficial an approach that fails to get all the relevant information out.
- A lawyer may place too much reliance on an initial client statement (which will almost certainly have many gaps) rather than amplifying and testing what is in that statement.
- A quiet client may need to be brought out, and a voluble client may need to be controlled.
- A client who is tense may fail to provide very clear information.

Techniques for dealing with problems

Ensuring information comes out

The client should be given sufficient opportunity and encouragement to raise anything that **6.96** is relevant. While the client should not be allowed to ramble, it is important in assessing the case properly that all matters that should be investigated, or that matters which put a different complexion on the case be raised. Effective information gathering is not achieved by focussing on papers and bombarding the client with questions, but by being sufficiently familiar with the papers to focus on the client, with regular eye contact, and listening carefully to answers. If there are gaps or contradictions in what the client says they should be clarified with the client, perhaps by summarising and running through what the client has said to check details.

Dealing with points that don't support the case

The client should be directly questioned about possible weaknesses in his case—he or she **6.97** may hesitate to volunteer unfavourable information. Cross-examination should be avoided or the client's confidence in the lawyer may be undermined. However it is necessary to test the main points in the case so as to be able to form a reliable overview. The client should be specifically asked if any points that may be argued against the case are known. This must be done tactfully by reminding the client that the lawyer can only give reliable advice if he or she is aware of all relevant matters. It is better to get a negative point from the client and plan how to deal with it than for it to come as a surprise in the middle of a negotiation.

Assessing the client as a witness

6.98 The lawyer may need to form a view of how good a witness a client might be should the case come to court. The lawyer has to take what the client says as *prima facie* truthful, but inevitably some clients may lie to strengthen a case, and this is dealt with below. Even if providing broadly credible evidence, some clients are rather more convincing than others. What the client says should be probed with further questions, conflicting evidence should be put to the client for comment, and the client may be reminded that he or she will be liable to be cross examined in court, and should be aware of the sort of questions that may be asked. Weighing up the client as a witness is particularly important where the case turns on disputed fact and there is little corroborative evidence, especially if effectively a key point turns on one person's word against another's.

O   QUESTIONING TECHNIQUES

6.99 Factual information is as important to a case as the law. Some factual information comes from documents, but much factual information comes from people. To ensure that the information that comes from witnesses is as accurate and complete as possible effective questioning techniques should be used. It is not difficult to understand the different types of questioning techniques and their uses, but it can be very difficult to put this knowledge to use while talking to a client.

Types of question

Open questions

6.100 These give the widest possible scope for answer, for example, 'What can you tell me about the accident?' This allows the person replying to tell a story as he or she sees fit. This is the best possible type of question for getting the client to reveal information in his or her own words at an early meeting. Open questions are important for understanding a situation fully as the open question imposes no judgments or limitations. However, the open question does have some disadvantages—a very open question gives no guidance at all to the client of what the lawyer needs to know, and thus gives scope for irrelevancies and rambling.

Semi-open questions

6.101 The semi-open question gives some indication of the area in which a response is required, for example, 'What did the man in the red car do?' or 'What sort of damage did the lorry suffer?' Such questions give some guidance on what information is important, without restricting what the answer can cover too much. Such questions can help significantly in structuring an interview and in focussing on the potential elements of a cause of action. A possible disadvantage is that a busy lawyer might start to use semi-open questions too early in an interview, channelling responses too narrowly before there has been time for the client to tell the whole story in general terms, and thus shutting out potentially important information.

Closed questions

There are various types of closed question, but all basically limit substantially the range **6.102** within which the answer can be given. For example, 'Was the car in the side road silver or green?' or 'Was the damage to the passenger door serious?' In its strictest form, the closed question limits the possible reply to 'yes' or 'no', for example, 'Did the silver car stop at the junction?' Such questions are invaluable in getting specific information, and to clarify particular points. However, such questions may prevent a very accurate or full answer being given, which may be an advantage in a cross examination, but which may be very undesirable in getting information from one's own client!

Leading questions

Leading questions are a well known category. A leading question leads to a particular answer, **6.103** for example, 'So the car was a foot from the kerb?' or 'It would be right to say that the silver car was being driven very dangerously, wouldn't it?' The limits on response are tight because words are being put into the mouth of the person being questioned, rather than allowing freedom for that person to choose their own words. The use of leading questions in court is limited because words are coming primarily from the person asking the question rather than the person responding. On occasion a lawyer may use leading questions in a private interview with a client, possibly with the good intention of trying to stop the client rambling. This may be useful if the client has already provided detailed information and the lawyer is checking it, but it can be very dangerous if the lawyer starts to make assumptions and just gets odd comments from the client, rather than getting full and accurate information from the client.

Rhetorical questions

The rhetorical question does not expect an answer, and therefore has little place in an **6.104** interview, although it may have some place in making a point in court.

The normal pattern will be that each area of information will be opened with one or two open **6.105** questions, followed up by semi-open questions to focus in on what is most important, and then closed questions to clarify detail. It is important to get sufficient detail on important areas and not be satisfied with general answers.

Forming questions

In order to get the information sought individual questions need to be well formed. This **6.106** requires attention to the length of the question, the language used and so on. The tone of voice may also be relevant, if for example a client may need encouragement to answer.

Concise questions

Short and concise questions stated as clearly as possible are normally to be preferred. They **6.107** are easiest for the person being questioned to understand and to formulate a reply to. They can also be used to focus on precise points. There are however possible disadvantages—the person questioned may feel that the replies should also be brief and therefore may not include wider relevant information. It can also be difficult to deal with a long series of short questions unless they follow clear lines rather than moving about over a range of material.

Longer questions

6.108 Longer questions may be useful to outline material that the lawyer wishes to be dealt with in the response. A longer question may be used to check understanding. Longer questions may be unavoidable in a complicated case or to get at precise details. A long question may give the client more time to consider the answer. However, if a question is overlong there is the danger that the person being questioned may lose the thread, or may be encouraged to give a rambling reply. The risks of multiple questions must be avoided. A multiple question asks about more than one thing at the same time. For example, 'Was he angry, shouting, violent ... did he threaten you?' The person responding may find it difficult to answer at all if several questions are rolled together, or may only deal with one question, leaving the rest unanswered.

Ordering questions

6.109 The lawyer may feel that he or she only needs to focus on a few points of weakness in the case, and may be tempted just to jump from one point to the next. While this may meet the lawyer's needs it can be very confusing for the client, who will not know where the conversation will go next. To help the client to answer it is best to deal with topics in a logical order, and normally to tell the client in advance what the order will be.

Active listening

6.110 During a question and answer session responses may be made that are not specific questions, for example: 'Yes', 'Um', 'I see'. Such a response can serve many purposes. It may indicate support, may indicate that the lawyer is listening, or may encourage the response to go on. This can keep an interview actively moving without pushing it in any particular direction by introducing a new question.

6.111 An alternative to the short, encouraging, or non-committal response is silence, which can itself play a positive role in a question and answer session. A simple silence may encourage the client to go on and fill it by saying more. Or it may challenge what has been said, so the client feels that he or she should modify or explain it. The lawyer should never feel embarrassed by a silence—it may simply give both lawyer and client time to collect their thoughts. But silence should have a purpose and not signify a lack of preparation or control.

Helping with the answer

6.112 If the client appears to have difficulty answering a question, the lawyer should try to work out why this is and try to find an appropriate solution. If the client does not understand the question it may need to be rephrased. If the client does not understand the point of the question, that may need to be explained. If the client does not have the knowledge to answer the question that may have to be accepted—the client should not be pressed to try to invent an answer. If the client does not know how to express the answer the lawyer may have to assist, but needs to be careful not to put words into the client's mouth. If the client is embarrassed or is finding it difficult to talk about a particular topic the lawyer may need to be supportive. The questions should not simply be dropped if the answers are important.

P   INFORMATION AND ADVICE

It is often part of a meeting for a lawyer to provide information. This may relate to informa-   **6.113** tion about the law, procedure, or evidence. Providing information can be distinguished from giving advice because it involves outlining what the law is on a particular topic, or what will happen at a hearing in court in a descriptive way.

The extent to which a client needs information will depend on how familiar the client is   **6.114** with law and legal processes and what is required for the case in hand. The client may ask for information, but there are many circumstances where a lawyer should volunteer informa- tion. For example the lawyer should ensure that a client sufficiently understands what will happen when there is to be a hearing at court, what a procedural step that is to be taken will involve, and what the costs implications are for particular options. It is important, for example, to explain to a client the extent to which disclosure of documents needs to be made under a pre-action protocol or if an action is started, see *Rockwell Machine Tool Co Ltd v EP Barnes Ltd* [1968] 1 WLR 693.

The lawyer is also likely to need to provide advice. This is dealt with further in Chapter 7.   **6.115**

Q   CONCLUDING THE MEETING

An effective interview or conference needs a clear conclusion. Failure to clarify decisions at   **6.116** the end of a meeting and confusion about matters that are left open can be major causes of uncertainty and delay in litigation.

Appropriate ways of concluding a meeting might include: **6.117**

- Checking that everything that the lawyer and the client wished to raise has been covered. There may be merit in specifically asking the client if he or she has anything else to say if the client has not played a very strong part in the meeting.
- Summarising important points that have been covered.
- Summarising the decisions reached. If any important decisions are outstanding, clarify what the decision depends on and when the decision will be taken.
- Summarising the action points, including who is responsible for each. If further evidence is required it should be clear who will get what to satisfy the need.
- Summarising what will happen next in the case and when it will be done by, especially if a matter is urgent.
- Checking client instructions. If instructions are not yet clear, for example because the client wants to think something over, it should be clear when and how instructions will be given.
- Checking that the client has adequately understood information and advice given. A test for whether a client has really understood what a lawyer has said is whether the client

will be able to repeat key points to business associates, relatives, or friends who have not been at the meeting. Research with doctors and patients has shown that patients understand and retain relatively little of what a doctor has told them—similar research in law might produce interesting and possibly worrying results!

- If further information or evidence is needed, clarifying as precisely as possible what information or evidence will be sought, by whom, and from what source. This needs to be considered in the context of whether the information is realistically available and how much it might cost to get it. It may also need to be decided what will happen once the information is available.
- Agreeing whether there should be a further meeting, or whether there will be further communication by telephone etc.
- Identifying any points of law that may need to be researched, together with how those results will be dealt with, for example in a letter to the client, or an opinion if a barrister is involved.
- Agreeing other follow-up action such as instructing a barrister.

6.118 If the meeting has been a conference with a barrister, the barrister may be instructed to take further action such as writing an opinion or drafting Particulars of Claim, in which case the barrister will retain the brief for that purpose. If the brief was only to advise in conference then the brief will be returned to the solicitor who will proceed with the case, though the barrister may be briefed again for a later stage of the case. A proper record of all these matters should be kept. Memory will fade quickly in a busy working life and it is important to have a reminder.

R   DEALING WITH DIFFICULT CLIENTS

6.119 Sometimes the client can prevent litigation being as effective as it might be. Most clients are rational and cooperative, provide information reasonably willingly, accept advice, and provide reasonably clear instructions. However all lawyers will encounter clients who make it difficult for the lawyer to represent the client well. It can be worrying or embarrassing to encounter a difficult client, especially if the problem arises suddenly. An advance awareness of the types of problems that can arise and strategies for dealing with them is very useful.

6.120 In an extreme case a lawyer can be pulled into acting badly and possibly into professional misconduct. To avoid this a problem might usefully be raised directly with the client, 'I'm afraid I can't do my best for you in this case unless . . .'. Maintaining a detached and professional approach is important in avoiding and addressing problems. It may be necessary to halt a meeting temporarily to reflect on how to address a difficulty. The advice of a senior colleague or even a professional body may also be very helpful in a serious case. The following paragraphs illustrate some of the problems that clients may present, and how those problems may be addressed.

The client may fail to provide relevant information

6.121 It can be difficult to elicit relevant facts from a client. This is potentially a significant problem, as lack of information may make it difficult to assess or conduct the case. The problem may arise because the client genuinely does not know or cannot remember the information. It may happen because the lawyer is taking a strong role and the client is intimidated, inarticulate, or worried. It may happen because the client is giving information that is not true and the client wishes to avoid saying too much.

Although it takes time and can be laborious, the quiet client must be drawn out and given **6.122** time to answer. Showing irritation at slow progress will rarely help. A clear statement that the lawyer needs certain information to be able to progress the case will hopefully assist. It is particularly important to ask a full range of questions, and to be particularly careful to use a range of wide and specific questions to cover everything, giving the client every chance to answer. It may be possible to fill gaps with information from other sources. Gaps should not be filled by assumptions.

The client may fail to provide clear instructions or may change instructions

Some clients are slow to provide clear instructions. On the face of it the docile client is not a **6.123** great problem, but the situation is potentially serious, as the lawyer who does not have clear instructions may be at risk of a charge of breach of professional conduct or a negligence action. The client who appears to be happy to leave the lawyer in charge may suddenly decide that he or she does not like the way the case is going and may claim that the lawyer is not acting on instructions given. The problem may arise because the client is indecisive, or is too heavily dependent on the lawyer. It is important to check that a client approves of a particular course, and it may be prudent to get this in writing to avoid later problems.

It can also be a problem if a client keeps vacillating and changing instructions. It must be **6.124** made clear to such a client that such an approach will undermine the chances of success. Again the best approach is probably to get the client to sign written instructions.

The client who seeks to play too strong a role

Some clients are difficult to control. The client may talk too much in meetings, make fre- **6.125** quent demands on the lawyer, and/or seek to take decisions about the case that do not follow advice given. This is not unnatural if a client is very worried about a situation, but it is a problem if the lawyer cannot conduct the case in a way that fits with his or her professional judgment.

This may be addressed by the lawyer taking clear and calm control of meetings and other **6.126** communications. It may help to allow the client to let off steam, but arguments must be avoided, perhaps by making explicit the need for the lawyer to exercise professional judgment in running the case. If the client does not easily follow advice then it may be best to set the advice out in writing. If the client fails to accept that advice and tries to give instructions that the lawyer does not feel are realistic then the lawyer may need to make it clear that the client should seek another lawyer.

The stressed or emotional client

However well managed the litigation process is, it is quite possible that a client will suffer **6.127** stress at some time. A client who has suffered serious injuries or who faces a massive loss may understandably become emotional. Client emotion can stand in the way of the lawyer doing the job, and can be embarrassing or, very rarely, dangerous. A client who is upset or angry may not provide reliable information or good instructions.

6.128 Lawyers will have different personalities and reactions, but a calm and constructive reaction is likely to be most productive and unembarrassing. If a client becomes distressed and/or starts to cry, one option is simply to stay quiet and wait until the crying stops, so long as this is done in a controlled way rather than for lack of any alternative. Another option is to continue to talk in a quiet way until the client recovers, or to offer a symbol of empathy such as a tissue. A third option is to ask the client if he or she would like a few moments alone. Someone might be asked to assist—a male solicitor might feel uncomfortable about dealing with a distressed female client and might invite a female secretary or trainee to help to provide support, so long as this can be done quickly and efficiently and without embarrassment to anyone involved. If the client remains distressed a temporary halt in the interview may be necessary.

6.129 The client may become argumentative or angry, especially on receiving negative advice about the prospects for a case. The anger may be understandable, but needs to be defused. One option is simply to continue the meeting, taking a firm and authoritative tone that will help the client to realise that anger is not an appropriate reaction. Another option is to express understanding for why the client is angry but to say that anger will not help and that the client needs to calm down to listen to the rest of the advice. It is rarely productive to get into an argument with the client, and if the client is losing control it may be necessary simply to end the meeting for a time, either by asking the client to go, or by the lawyer walking away.

The client may provide false information

6.130 The client who lies, or who is extremely economical with the truth, can cause great problems in litigation. There will be motives to lie where a lot of money is a stake. If the client chooses to conduct litigation on the basis of providing false information it is likely that the other side will attack and quite possibly expose the lie, and the penalty will then be that the client is at risk of losing the case in whole or in part, and at risk as to costs.

6.131 If a lawyer is unsure about the completeness and veracity of information, he or she should warn the client in appropriate terms of the risk of losing and of being liable for costs. The client should also be warned that statements of case and witness statements include statements of truth and that lying in them is potentially a matter of contempt of court.

6.132 The lawyer has a professional duty not to mislead the court, and cannot become a party to presenting information that is known to be false to the court. The lawyer should not include information known to be false in drafting a statement of case or a witness statement. If the client persists in wishing to put forward a lie the lawyer may have to refuse to act further in the case.

6.133 If the lawyers suspects a client is lying, or at least not telling the whole truth, the lawyer should not normally express disbelief, but should probe what the client says with further questions or point out inconsistencies with other evidence. If this does not work, the lawyer can explain the risks when the case is tested in court by cross examination. The client may not intend to mislead, but may simply have gone over relevant events so many times in his or her own mind or in conversations with friends that the truth has been embroidered and gaps in real knowledge filled by supposition.

It may not be easy to detect if a client is lying, but a significant motive to lie and/or an **6.134** apparent conflict between what the client says and other evidence that appears to be reliable should cause the lawyer to consider the position carefully.

Failure to build a working relationship with the client

The solicitor or barrister will inevitably sometimes find that however detached and profes- **6.135** sional they are it proves very difficult to build a working relationship with the client. The lawyer may have little sympathy with a client. Some clients may appear to be authors of their own difficulties, others may not be very attractive because of personal attributes or their attitude to what they wish to achieve through litigation. It goes without saying that personal views are irrelevant to the professional conduct of a case and should not be allowed to show or to get in the way of the conduct of the case.

The lawyer must try to overcome problems that may arise. As in any relationship, problems **6.136** are probably better identified and aired to see if anything can be done to remedy the situation. Both barristers and solicitors have professional duties not to abandon a client, especially if, for example, a trial is near, but a lawyer may have to say that he or she cannot represent a client properly and the client is best advised to seek another lawyer.

7

ADVISING A CLIENT AND
TAKING INSTRUCTIONS

A THE IMPORTANCE OF ADVICE AND INSTRUCTIONS 7.01

B PROVIDING INFORMATION TO A CLIENT 7.05

C CHOOSING HOW AND WHEN TO PROVIDE ADVICE 7.08
    Factors in choosing the best way to provide advice 7.08
    Other factors 7.13

D PROVIDING ADVICE TO A CLIENT 7.18
    The ingredients of good advice 7.18
    Structuring advice 7.20
    Expressing advice clearly 7.24

E SETTING OUT OPTIONS 7.28

F SETTING OUT STRENGTHS AND WEAKNESSES 7.32

G RISK ASSESSMENT 7.36

H ADVISING ON THE CHANCES OF SUCCESS 7.42
    Assessing chances of success 7.42
    Expressing chances of success 7.46

I PROBLEM SOLVING 7.50

J BREAKING BAD NEWS 7.54

K ADVISING ON DIFFERENT ASPECTS OF THE CASE 7.59
    Advice on causes of action 7.60
    Advice on parties 7.62
    Advice on remedies 7.64
    Advice on damages 7.65
    Advice on evidence 7.67
    Advice on procedure 7.68
    Chances of success 7.69
    Costs 7.70

L TAKING INSTRUCTIONS 7.71

Decisions to be taken by the client 7.71
Problems in taking instructions. 7.73

What is the difference between a cat and a lawyer?
One is an arrogant creature who ignores you and treats you with contempt unless it thinks it can get something out of you. The other is a house pet.

A   THE IMPORTANCE OF ADVICE AND INSTRUCTIONS

7.01   Providing advice to a client is a key function of a professional lawyer. For litigation to be as effective as possible it is crucial that the advice given by a lawyer is as full and clear as possible, and that the client is fully informed about options for taking the case forward, and the strengths and weaknesses of each. It is the professional duty of the lawyer to act on and within client instructions. Good information and advice is necessary for a client to be able to give informed instructions.

7.02   Clients appear not always to be impressed by the quality of legal advice, and the extent to which a lawyer understands and acts on instructions given. Research into how advice can best be provided would be valuable. Client criticism may result from the fact that they do not like the advice given (albeit that it is entirely sound advice) rather than that there is a problem with the way in which the advice is given. On anecdotal evidence it would seem:

- that advice is too often incomplete or superficial;
- that all too often a lawyer can appear to be taking decisions for a client rather than offering options to a client, and explaining the strengths and weaknesses of each;
- that a lawyer can fail to separate giving advice and taking instructions sufficiently clearly;
- that advice can too easily be delivered by giving a client a legal lecture rather than engaging in a two-way process with the client.

7.03   Advice can be provided orally on the telephone or at a meeting, or in writing in a letter or opinion. Important advice that is given orally should normally be put into writing, especially if it is advice that the client may not have understood fully or advice that the client may not be very happy with. This should help client understanding and will provide a record on file should the client later contest the advice given.

7.04   The importance of focussing on client objectives is also addressed at 1.68–1.79, 3.46, and in Chapter 6. For books relevant to building a working relationship with a client see 24.23.

B   PROVIDING INFORMATION TO A CLIENT

7.05   A client needs to understand the litigation process sufficiently in order to be able to play a proper part in it. Sometimes a lawyer will need to provide a client with information about law and the legal process. Many clients will have limited familiarity with the law and the litigation process, but others will not. The amount of information needed will vary from one client to another, as a client who has never previously been involved in litigation will need more information than one who has.

A client may need information before advice can make sense. A client may, as appropriate, **7.06** need information on:

- the elements of an area of law;
- a procedural step, such as seeking an interim injunction;
- an evidential matter, such as the disclosure process;
- how decisions about costs are taken.

Some clients will ask for information on particular topics, but will not always know what to **7.07** ask, or may feel inhibited about asking. It may be for the lawyer to identify areas where the client may need information to understand a situation properly so as to be able to play a full role in the litigation. The lawyer can offer to provide information that may be useful to a client at a particular point without being patronising, for example 'Would you like me to run through what will happen when we get to court?' Providing information should be a simple matter, but it can be quite a skill to explain a legal concept or process in a way that is clear to a client.

C   CHOOSING HOW AND WHEN TO PROVIDE ADVICE

Factors in choosing the best way to provide advice

There are options as to how and when to give advice. Sometimes one alternative may be **7.08** better than another to meet the circumstances of the case. Advice can be given orally or in writing. If orally, it can be given over the telephone or at a meeting. Advice can be summarised or provided in detail. Advice can be given on a number of topics at a time or focussed on different topics. Advice can be reinforced and updated. These all have different implications for how much a client understands and retains.

Factors in providing oral advice by telephone include: **7.09**

- advice by telephone can be provided quickly and cheaply;
- it is important to ensure that all papers are to hand and that advice is not rushed;
- it is important to keep a record of the advice given as misunderstandings or inaccurate memory can affect telephone advice.

Factors in providing oral advice at a meeting include: **7.10**

- a meeting can include an appropriate balance of fact gathering, information giving, and advice;
- the client will have the best opportunities to ask questions and follow points up;
- the lawyer will be able to use questions to check that the client understands the advice;
- a meeting is useful if it would be helpful to have fairly free discussion about options;
- face to face communication can best support a full exchange of views.

Factors in providing written advice in a letter or opinion are: **7.11**

- it may be easier to set out the advice and options more fully and coherently in writing;
- it is possible to check the written document before it is sent to ensure accuracy whereas it can be difficult to control the content and coverage of a meeting;
- complex advice or advice that needs time to reflect on may most usefully be delivered in writing;
- providing advice in writing may be preferable where the case or the client are difficult.

7.12 Options can be combined. Complex written advice can be followed up by a meeting once the client has digested what has been said. If advice is given orally the key points in the advice still need to be put in writing for the file. As always, cost must be considered. A meeting may be quite expensive to arrange, depending on who is to attend and distances of travel. Equally the time spent in writing a significant piece of written advice may make that quite expensive.

Other factors

7.13 However keen a client is to get advice from a lawyer, sound advice can only be based on adequate information. Advice will be of limited value, and may even be misleading, if given without a sufficiently full understanding of the facts. A client is most likely to understand information and advice if it is delivered at the right point in the development of the case.

7.14 There can also be professional conduct points on the timing of giving advice. The lawyer has a duty to the court and should try to avoid becoming an instrument for providing information to the court that is not entirely truthful. To this end the lawyer should ask the client what the facts are before providing advice, and should not advise generally or on theoretical possibilities. If the lawyer provides advice before gathering sufficient facts there is a risk that the lawyer will give a client clues as to where providing inaccurate information might assist the case. In addition to the professional duty, a case can be undermined where a lawyer works on information that is later revealed as untrue.

7.15 Normally the provision of information and advice will need to be staged as the case progresses, and the stages need to be clearly separated in the mind of the lawyer and the client.

Stage 1. This will focus on information gathering. The client may need some information about legal processes, but such information is likely to be fairly general. The client will also want some provisional advice as quickly as possible, but at this stage the lawyer can probably at most give general guidance, with warnings that proper advice cannot be given yet.

Stage 2. The time will come when the lawyer has sufficient information to provide reasonably reliable advice. The point when this stage is reached needs to be carefully judged. It comes when sufficient evidence is available to make a proper assessment, and this may, for example, include an expert report. At this stage full advice should be given to the client and decisions about the case taken.

Stage 3. In most cases the advice given will need to be fully reviewed, for example because the case for the other side has been revealed, and/or a settlement is contemplated.

7.16 The provision of written and oral advice and the timing of meetings need to be fitted carefully into these stages. Too few meetings and letters may leave the client anxious and ill-informed. Too many meetings and letters can lead to weak decision-taking and too many shifts in the way the case is being conducted.

In any individual telephone conversation, meeting, or letter the lawyer will need to balance **7.17** appropriately the time spent on gathering information, on providing information, and on giving advice. It is all too easy to get the balance wrong so that there is too little time for a client to understand advice fully, ask questions about the advice, and then be able digest everything before giving instructions.

D   PROVIDING ADVICE TO A CLIENT

Good counsellors lack no clients.

Shakespeare, *Measure for Measure*

The ingredients of good advice

In whatever form and at whatever length it is given, advice is advice. It is not for the **7.18** lawyer to take decisions and instruct the client—it is for the client to take decisions and give instructions to the lawyer.

Advising a client in relation to litigation overall includes: **7.19**

- ensuring that the client is aware that he/she is the person responsible for taking decisions on the conduct of the case and giving instructions to the lawyer;
- ensuring that the client understands the legal context of the case as fully as is reasonably possible;
- advising the client on the need to prove allegations on the evidence that is available and the evidence that needs to be collected;
- advising the client on what may be obtained through whatever procedural possibilities are available;
- advising the client on potential remedies and figures;
- advising the client on the options for taking the case forward;
- advising the client on the overall strengths and weaknesses of the case;
- advising the client on how long the main steps in the case might take;
- advising the client on how to take the case forward;
- advising the client on costs.

Structuring advice

The provision of advice can usefully have some sort of introduction, to make it clear that the **7.20** lawyer is moving on from previous discussion and is providing advice. It may also be relevant to remind the client that it will be for the client to decide how to proceed following the advice, that the client should ask questions if anything is not fully understood, and to point out any information that is still not available and that may affect the advice the lawyer is giving.

In a difficult case the lawyer may also make it clear that he or she is assisting the client as far **7.21** as possible, but that the lawyer needs to give objective advice and some points may not be as favourable as the client might like. It can be useful to tell the client that questions will be dealt with at the end so that the client does not interrupt while the advice is being given. Interruptions can result in advice being less coherent than it should be, or in relatively unimportant matters getting undue coverage.

7.22 It will be important to structure the giving of information or advice so that the client can follow what is being said reasonably easily. In a complex case this may need advance planning.

- There may be merit in outlining to the client what the structure will be so that the client does not try to move too early to areas the lawyer plans to cover later.
- It may be useful to provide information before outlining options.
- It may be useful to divide the advice into sections, not least if there is quite a lot of advice, so that the client can digest each area of advice more easily.
- If a significant amount of advice is given orally, there will need to be pauses to check that the client understands and to see if there are any questions.
- Rather than having a slab of advice at the end of a meeting, there may be merit in dividing the meeting into topics, gathering information, and giving advice on one topic before moving on to another. For example it is often useful in an accident case to get facts relevant to liability and advise on that, and then separately to gather facts relevant to quantum and advise on that.

7.23 The advice on each area of the case may also usefully be structured to provide reasons as well as conclusions. Each piece of advice might include as relevant:

- a very short summary of the relevant facts as the lawyer understands them;
- a very short summary of relevant legal principles;
- the legal strengths and weaknesses on the legal element or the issue;
- the evidential strengths and weaknesses on the legal element or the issue;
- any information that is not yet available that might affect the advice given;
- any procedural points that might be of use;
- the options available;
- the key reasons for the advice the lawyer is giving.

Expressing advice clearly

7.24 Advice is only effective as advice if the client understands it. An acid test of whether a client understands advice is whether he or she will be able to report the key points in the advice when relating it to a friend or colleague later in the day. If a client cannot answer the question 'So what did the lawyer say?' reasonably accurately then the advice has not been given as well as it should have been.

7.25 A key point in expressing advice clearly is to adapt terminology to the individual client, and to explain any concepts the client does not understand. It also helps if advice is based on an understanding of what the client hopes to achieve, and shows a practical understanding of the position the client is in. There may be limited business purpose in advising at length on fighting a case if ongoing commercial relations would be better served by a settlement.

7.26 Advice also needs to be focussed on taking the case forward. Too much information on an interesting legal point the lawyer has researched which is unlikely to help the case, or on an option that there is unlikely to be evidence to support will only be helpful if the case is a difficult one such that every avenue has to be explored.

If the law and/or the evidence available do not provide a clear answer or a clear remedy, the **7.27** lack of clarity and the reasons for it need to be explained to the client. Clients can find it difficult to accept that the law does not provide clear answers, but little purpose is served by giving the client a certainty that is not justified. Breaking bad news is dealt with below.

E   SETTING OUT OPTIONS

Sometimes the only advice that can be given will be fairly straightforward. The lawyer may **7.28** be unable to find a viable cause of action and/or remedy for a potential claimant. There may be a single potential cause of action, such as breach of contract, so that advice will simply take the client through the appropriate term to found the action and the alleged breach.

However most cases will involve at least some choices. Even a relatively straightforward **7.29** contract case can involve choices as to the terms to be relied on and the breach(es) to be alleged. Where there are options they should normally be put to the client, even if the lawyer will give clear advice as to which choice should be preferred and why.

Just to give some examples of where there may be a choice to be put to the client: **7.30**

- Should an action be framed as breach of implied terms and/or as misrepresentation if both are arguable on the facts?
- If there is more than one potential cause of action and the cost of getting the evidence to support one is likely to be significantly more than the cost of proving another, which cause(es) of action should be used?
- Should a piece of evidence be sought immediately if it might have a bearing on the case but will be very expensive to obtain?
- Should the claim form be issued quickly or should there be an attempt at settlement?

Wherever such choices are to be made, the choice is ultimately for the client giving instruc- **7.31** tions rather than for the lawyer. The lawyer should not make a choice and simply present that to the client. In providing advice the lawyer should:

- make explicit the fact that there is a choice to be made;
- set out clearly what the options are;
- set out the potential benefits and drawbacks and the possible costs of each;
- give the professional view of the lawyer as to which option is to be preferred and why;
- if the lawyer has a very strong view on the course that should be taken that view can be expressed, but not so as to take from the client a choice that should be for the client.

F   SETTING OUT STRENGTHS AND WEAKNESSES

7.32   For the client to be in a position to take sound decisions and to give informed instructions, it is essential that the client is as fully aware as possible of the strengths and weaknesses of a case, and of each element in a case.

7.33   It is not always easy to set out strengths and weaknesses clearly, and to ensure that a client understands them.

- Time in a meeting may be limited.
- The client may feel that the lawyer is not pursuing the case strongly if there is too much emphasis on possible weaknesses.
- It can be difficult to express a problem relating to an unclear point of law or a difficulty regarding the admissibility of evidence in a way that a client can understand.

7.34   The effective lawyer should build up techniques for identifying and communicating strengths and weaknesses. The strengths and weaknesses of a particular course of action are likely to relate primarily to:

- whether the legal principles relevant to the elements of a cause or action are clear or not;
- whether there is clear, persuasive, and admissible evidence relating to all the elements of a cause of action;
- how strongly contested the case is.

7.35   To provide some examples:

- In a contract case, there may be strengths in that the legal principles are clear, and that it is easy to show a breach of an alleged term and some losses arising from that breach, but there may be weaknesses in that the client seeks to rely on an oral contract the terms of which are disputed, and in that it is disputed that some losses the client alleges were caused by the breach.
- In a negligence case, there may be strengths in that it is possible to show serious injury to the client suffered on the defendant's premises, but there may be weaknesses in that the law on whether there is duty of care in the circumstances of the case is open to debate, and in that there is an allegation of contributor negligence.

G   RISK ASSESSMENT

7.36   The phrase 'risk assessment' is not very common in legal text books or legal training. It may be controversial to suggest that risk assessment is fundamental to conducting the litigation process effectively, but whether or not the phrase 'risk assessment' is used, that is what properly occurs in deciding how best to progress a case.

7.37   Risk assessment is common in many areas of modern life. Most businesses and public authorities carry out risk assessment exercises. What are the main risks that might cause the business to fail or to suffer serious loss or expense? How likely is it that each risk will actually arise? What plans should therefore reasonably be made to address each risk in a proportionate way? Potential problems are balanced with the possible cost of addressing them.

This is arguably what lawyers and clients actually do in planning how to take a case forward. **7.38** What is the risk of losing the case? How reasonable is it to take that risk in the light of potential costs, time taken, and so on? If assistance from the Community Legal Service is sought then the potential chances of the case succeeding must be weighed fairly precisely. Similar calculations are appropriate for the private client.

It may be even more controversial to suggest that the language of gambling might be used **7.39** with regard to litigation, but an analogy can be made. The lawyer and the client can hopefully weigh up the legal and evidential strengths and weaknesses of the case more accurately than the form of the horse and the going on a racecourse, but at the end of the day the case will be won or lost. The litigant who fails is likely to lose not only the costs he or she has already staked but also pay the opponent's costs.

The professional training of lawyers perhaps carries the impression that there is an art in **7.40** judging whether a case is likely to be successful or not. For the client who needs to make an informed and potentially expensive decision it is important that the judgment and advice on the chances of winning the action be as accurate and reliable as possible. It is arguable that the assessment of the likelihood of success of an action should be as scientific as possible. With the number of unknowns and variables in an action, it is difficult to see that a mathematical formula could predict the outcome of a case, but a structured approach can assist a client in taking a justifiable decision.

Risk assessment is likely to form a background for litigation where insurers and large **7.41** businesses are involved

---

H   ADVISING ON THE CHANCES OF SUCCESS

Assessing chances of success

Essential questions often posed by a client contemplating litigation are: **7.42**

- What are the chances of winning the case?
- What is likely to be recovered if the case is won?
- What are the costs likely to be if the case is won?
- What are the costs likely to be if the case is lost?

A client deserves the best possible answers to these questions. The second question is about **7.43** remedies and damages, the third question is about civil litigation, and the last question is about costs. The first question relates to law and evidence, and it can be the most difficult to answer.

Advice on chances of success pulls together all the above areas, and is perhaps the most **7.44** important single piece of advice. Having said this, advice on chances of success is not easy to give. Causes of action, evidence, and procedure may interrelate in complex ways. Two cases may have relatively similar facts, but the chances of success may be radically different because one has a particular piece of evidence that the other does not. Two claimants who suffer a similar type of accident may get different damages because the loss of earnings is very different in each case.

7.45 Perhaps a real 'feel' for how likely a case is to succeed can only come with experience, but the lawyer new to practice will need to build a 'feel' through accurate analysis and proper consideration of all the elements of the case. It is also relevant to remember that a claimant has to prove his or her case, but that the test is the balance of probabilities rather than a higher degree of certainty.

Expressing chances of success

7.46 The chances of success need to be assessed as accurately as possible, and conveyed to the client as clearly as possible. Perhaps surprisingly there is no agreed method or terminology for conveying chances of success. As chances of success are absolutely key to the decisions that lawyers and clients have to take, research into what lawyers say and how that is understood would be very helpful in moving to greater clarity.

7.47 Chances of success can be expressed in words. A lawyer may say 'This case has a good chance of success'. However it is very difficult to establish what the words mean. If a room full of lawyers is asked what 'a good chance of success' is, answers tend to vary from 'more likely than not to succeed' or 'a 60 per cent chance of winning' to 'very unlikely to lose' or 'an 85 per cent chance of success'. If chances of success are expressed in words it should be clear to the lawyer and the client what those words mean.

7.48 Chances of success can be expressed arithmetically, for example using percentages. This is the approach required for assessing whether the community legal fund should support an action, see 5.40. A client can probably understand the difference between a 60 per cent chance of success and a 90 per cent chance of success, though the shading between 65 per cent and 70 per cent may be more difficult. The use of percentages is probably to be preferred. To pass the balance of probabilities test a case needs to have a better than 50 per cent chance of success. The closer the case gets to 100 per cent the more likely it is to be won, but the extent to which likely success falls short of 100 per cent can help to focus the mind on the reasons why the case might not succeed. Contributory negligence is normally assessed as a percentage. An arithmetical approach can assist in the taking of decisions relating to numbers such as damages and building up cost. A cost that is acceptable with an 80 per cent chance of success may not be acceptable with a 60 per cent chance of success.

7.49 If a client is making a decision that may involve tens of thousands of pounds, vagueness is not professionally acceptable. The lawyer should not be vague due to inadequate work on the case, or through the misguided view that being vague is a good way to break bad news to a client. Words may not have clear meanings and may need to be explained. Arithmetic may seem stark and will need to be explained and put in context.

I PROBLEM SOLVING

For a number of clients the context of a case will be wider than the arithmetic of damages   **7.50**
and costs. Some clients will want to win with money not being the prime factor, some clients
will be primarily concerned to establish a matter of principle, and many clients will want to
solve a problem. Quite a lot of litigation takes place in the context of a wider problem that
goes well beyond the issues in the case—the client may need to keep a business going to
protect the livelihoods of a number of people, or the client and his or her family may all be
trying to live with the consequences of severe injury. At the end of the day many clients will
want the best available solution in all the circumstances.

In getting information from a client and offering advice it can be helpful to pay some   **7.51**
attention to what underlies the problem. What are the client's real practical problems? What
is the range of possible solutions, whether or not they are all things that a judge can order? If
effective litigation is about achieving the best outcome for a client, then a problem-solving
approach can provide useful insights and can assist in identifying remedies.

A 'problem-solving' approach centres on defining the problem clearly, defining the objec-   **7.52**
tives accurately, and looking at the full range of ways of reaching a solution. This involves
the consideration of non-legal factors and potential non-legal answers. It can be a matter of
using imagination constructively, and a matter of seeing the client's position as a living
problem to be saved rather than just a legal case.

A problem-solving approach may mean that the best approach is not to litigate but to   **7.53**
settle—not only can time and costs be solved in this way, but some remedies can be agreed
in a settlement that cannot be ordered by a court.

J BREAKING BAD NEWS

> Advice is seldom welcome; and those who want it the most always like it the least.
>
> The Earl of Chesterfield

Sometimes it is necessary to give a client advice that the client does not want to hear—for   **7.54**
example that there is no viable cause of action, the remedy the client wants is unlikely to be
available, or the damages may not be as much as the client hopes.

The lawyer should not be unduly pessimistic about a case. The lawyer is there to fight the   **7.55**
client's corner, and should look for every reasonable option for achieving what the client
wants. If there is a possible cause of action, albeit with a limited chance of success (say no
more than 55 per cent), then that option should be outlined to the client. It is not for the
lawyer to judge whether the case should go forward, but to outline the options for the client
to choose. Some clients will be quite prepared to take a 50 per cent chance of success in
certain circumstances.

On the other hand, the lawyer should not provide false optimism. If a case has a limited   **7.56**
chance of success then the client needs that information to make a sensible choice. If a case

has legal weaknesses or is unlikely to meet the 'on the balance of probabilities' test for evidence then the client has the right to know that.

7.57   Bad news is probably best broken clearly, with reasons, and as part of explaining the strengths and weaknesses of the case to a client. A client who sees that there are more weaknesses than strengths in the case is most likely to understand and accept the advice being given. The full consequences of the risk of losing must be clear to the client, including possible orders for costs. Judicial powers of case management over a weak case may also usefully be covered.

7.58   The strength of a case should not be judged prematurely—the test is not whether there is evidence to hand but whether evidence can be obtained. A client may be warned that a case is weak as it stands, and then possibilities of getting more evidence might be discussed.

K   ADVISING ON DIFFERENT ASPECTS OF THE CASE

7.59   Advice on a case will normally need to cover the following seven areas overall. These areas do not all need to be covered every time any advice is given, but all should be covered, and advice on each area should be kept up to date if there is any significant change.

Advice on causes of action

7.60   The claimant should be advised on all the causes of action that may be available. Advice should cover all the elements that will need to be shown for an action to succeed on that basis, and this is covered more fully in 10.19–10.32.

7.61   The claimant can use a single claim form to start all the claims which can conveniently be disposed of in the same proceedings. There are a variety of reasons for advising that more than one cause of action be joined in the same case, and these are considered in 10.19–10.32.

Advice on parties

7.62   It is important to choose the right parties to an action not only for legal reasons but also for practical reasons. It is those with direct legal rights and obligations who should be made parties. Sometimes there is no choice as to defendant and the question is simply whether the person who should be sued is worth suing. This area is covered more fully at 13.15–13.57.

7.63   Sometimes there is a choice, and it is necessary to advise on whether to sue all or just some of the potential defendants. The choice of potential defendants is dealt with at 13.15–13.57.

Advice on remedies

7.64   Advice from a lawyer should cover potential remedies as fully as potential causes of action and parties. The client will want to know what he or she is likely to get out of the case at the end of the day. A victory in the case is of limited value if the court will not put the client in the position that the client wishes to be put in as a result of the action. The lawyer should check at an early stage what the client really hopes to get from the case. Remedies that can be ordered by the court are covered at 14.08–14.24. If the client seeks a remedy that the court cannot order, such as an apology, then a negotiation may be an effective alternative to litigation.

Advice on damages

In many cases the most important remedy that the client will seek will be damages. The **7.65** lawyer will need to advise specifically on what items may be recoverable, should give as precise a figure as possible on what is likely to be recovered for each item, and should try to provide a reasonably accurate overall figure. Only then can the client weigh up the chances of success, what may be recovered, and the likely costs. In a particularly complex case, for example a personal injury case with high loss of earnings, nursing costs etc, the opinion of a barrister may be sought dealing wholly or largely with the quantification of damages. For advice on damages in a contract case see 18.78–18.105, and for damages in a tort case see 19.59–19.117.

A lawyer will probably give general advice about damages initially, and then when sufficient **7.66** information is available provide reasonably comprehensive advice about the recoverable heads of damage and the likely figure for each. If a client raises concerns about the recoverability of specific heads of damage or specific figures of loss, that matter will need to be dealt with.

Advice on evidence

Evidence is not just a matter for the lawyer to consider. The client should be advised on the **7.67** main relevant issues relating to the evidence in a case, see Chapter 15.

Advice on procedure

The client who is not familiar with the litigation process should be given information about **7.68** procedure. In addition the client should be advised about relevant procedural issues, see Chapter 16.

Chances of success

All the above advice should be weighed up and pulled together to provide overall advice on **7.69** the chances of success as set out at 7.42–7.49.

Costs

Giving advice on costs is dealt with in Chapter 5.   **7.70**

L   TAKING INSTRUCTIONS

> How many lawyers does it take to screw in a lightbulb?
> Only one—he just holds it and waits for the world to revolve around him.

Decisions to be taken by the client

7.71   It is a professional duty for the lawyer to act on the instructions of the client, see 3.46. However strongly the lawyer feels about the right course in the case, the lawyer should not seek to impose a decision on the client. Almost all meetings will involve taking instructions from the client as to what should happen next in the case, and this may be achieved most clearly by having a discrete section of a meeting where instructions are taken, normally near the end. The taking of instructions should not be rushed—the client may need to ask questions about the advice that has been given and may need some time to reflect. If necessary it can be agreed that the client will take a decision and let the lawyer know within a fixed period after the meeting.

7.72   The client should be involved in taking as many decisions as possible, not just as regards whether litigation should take place at all, but also as regards the cause of action, who to sue, whether optional procedural steps should be taken, and whether relatively expensive items of evidence should be sought. These are all related to whether the action will succeed and the costs of the action so the client should be involved. The language and tone in which advice is given should make it clear that decisions are for the client. This is yet another area where research could inform litigation—how far do clients feel they are in charge of a case, and what issues do they feel they are in charge of?

Problems in taking instructions

7.73   If the advice given is clear, reasonably comprehensive, and supported by points about the strengths and weaknesses of the case then there should be no difficulty—the client will see the sense of what the lawyer says and is likely to agree with it.

7.74   It can be difficult to take instructions from a client in certain circumstances.

- A client may seem not to understand the advice given by the lawyer. This is normally best addressed by a further attempt to explain the position and the reasons why the lawyer suggests a particular course.
- A client may find it difficult to take a decision. This may be because the strengths and weaknesses of a case are balanced, or because the advice and the reasons for it have not been clearly explained. This may be manifested by the client asking the lawyer to take the decision. The lawyer should give a careful answer—the best way forward and the reasons for it can be given but the client should take the decisions.
- A client may be unwilling to accept the advice given by a lawyer, and may insist on giving instructions that do not fit with the advice given by the lawyer. This may relate to a relatively small matter such as seeking an interim order, in which case the lawyer can only repeat the reasons for the advice given and try to get the client to give reasons for the client not wishing to follow the advice of the lawyer. The disagreement may relate to

a major matter such as whether an action be brought on a particular basis, in which case the lawyer may have to explain very clearly the possible problems of the course the client wishes to take.

These situations should not be taken lightly. There is a risk that the lawyer may be in breach 7.75 of rules of professional conduct if the lawyer rather than the client takes decisions about the conduct of the case. There may also be a risk that the client may sue the lawyer for professional negligence if the case is later lost and the client feels the lawyer is to blame for following a particular approach that the client did not agree with.

Sometimes a lawyer may need to give quite strong advice, if for example law and/or evidence 7.76 do not support steps a client wishes to take, but decisions must still be for the client. If it is necessary to give strong advice it is best that the strong advice be recorded in writing, whether or not originally given orally.

If there may be any problem about instructions given by the client, the lawyer should put 7.77 the apparent instructions in writing and get the client to sign them.

It may sometimes be necessary, though it should be rare, for the lawyer to tell the client that 7.78 it is not possible for the lawyer to continue to act on the basis of the instructions given by the client. The lawyer should try to avoid having to take such a step at a key point in the case as the client might be disadvantaged by changing lawyers at such a point.

8

ESTABLISHING AND
MANAGING FACTS

A FOCUSSING ON FACTS 8.01

The importance of facts 8.01

The need to deal with facts proactively 8.05

Data protection and access to data 8.08

B THE ELUSIVENESS OF TRUTH 8.11

The problems of establishing the truth 8.11

Practical problems with facts 8.16

Ways of addressing problems with facts. 8.17

C SOURCES OF FACTS. 8.30

The client 8.32

Documents 8.36

People 8.38

Physical objects—inspection 8.42

Physical objects—plans and photographs 8.43

Facts and figures. 8.45

D THE STAGED AVAILABILITY OF FACTUAL INFORMATION. 8.47

E ANALYSING FACTS. 8.50

Ingredients in analysis 8.51

F INFORMATION MANAGEMENT. 8.58

G THEORIES, DEDUCTION, AND LOGIC. 8.61

H THE INTERACTION OF FACTS AND LAW 8.71

I BUILDING A FACTUAL FRAMEWORK FOR A CASE 8.75

The overall factual structure of a case. 8.75

Chains of facts 8.78

You can only form the minds of reasoning animals upon facts: nothing else will ever be of any service to them. Stick to facts, sir!

Charles Dickens, *Hard Times*

A   FOCUSSING ON FACTS

The importance of facts

8.01   It is a natural perception that legal cases will normally turn on questions of law. In practice only a minority of cases will turn primarily on questions of law. The law provides a vital framework for each case in setting the elements that need to be proved to establish a cause of action, but most cases turn on whether the facts required to meet each legal element can be established. Cases involving points of law are more commonly found in the Court of Appeal, where the law may be clarified but decisions on fact are not normally taken.

8.02   For the litigation lawyer a case will often be concerned with the sorts of questions of fact a journalist asks—who, what, where, when, and how? Who is the appropriate defendant on the facts? Do the facts show a breach of contract or a breach of duty? What are the facts relevant to the quantification of damages? Effective litigation requires sufficient attention to establishing and analysing the facts relevant to a case.

8.03   This can be quite unsettling and challenging at the start of legal practice. The lawyer will have built up a significant knowledge of law, often over several years of study, and will wish to use it; but even a large and complex commercial case can turn on the problems in establishing facts relating to relatively simple legal matters such as offer and acceptance. It is easy to dismiss factual analysis as a straightforward matter—but really being able to see the wood for the trees in a complex factual scenario is one of the key skills in preparing a case and conducting it effectively. For books relevant to developing skills in fact analysis, see 24.25.

8.04   There is a professional duty to deal with the facts that are provided. For example a barrister should not invent facts to assist the client's case in statements of case, evidence, or advocacy, para 704 Code of Conduct for the Bar, and see *Medcalf v Weatherill and another* (2004) 3 WLR 172.

The need to deal with facts proactively

8.05   The concept of investigating a case may seem somewhat alien to the normal working life of a solicitor or barrister. Hercule Poirot belongs at an aristocratic house party and Miss Marple in a village with an abnormally high murder rate. Television may suggest that modern investigators work only on criminal cases. The No 1 Ladies Detective Agency tends to deal with criminal cases. But while the modern civil lawyer is not a private investigator, a spirit of investigation is fundamental to getting to grips with a case.

8.06   The system of civil justice in England and Wales is adversarial rather than inquisitorial, in contrast with a number of other systems. This means that it is not the function of the judge to seek the truth of the situation. It is for the lawyers to present their cases and for the judge to decide between them. It is therefore a function of the lawyers to gather and present the facts. This needs a proactive approach. The facts do not just arrive on the desk with the post. It can be difficult to find them, or to be sure they are reliable once found. They can be difficult to interpret, and there are normally gaps.

8.07   In addition to gathering sufficient facts, there is the chicken-and-egg problem of interrelating facts and law—the lawyer can only apply the law once he or she has enough facts, and it is only possible to know what facts are most relevant by looking at legal principles. This quandary is best addressed through a structured analytical approach, and through flexibility. It is all too easy to try to 'label' a case as quickly as possible after the client arrives at a meeting or a barrister starts to read a brief. The danger is that from then on all information will be seen in the context of this label, with the result that important facts may be twisted to fit or ignored. Some provisional legal label has to be used to enable case analysis to proceed, but it is an important point not to attach a legal label earlier than is necessary, and to keep it constantly under review to see if it does still fit as the collection of factual information proceeds.

Data protection and access to data

The management and use of factual information has become an important matter in the modern world. On the one hand the right of individuals to keep private information about themselves is protected by legislation. On the other hand, the right of individuals to have access to information, especially personal information, or information relating to public bodies and to government, is promoted by legislation. These rights exist quite independently of litigation processes and can be used as part of initial fact gathering. **8.08**

It is beyond the scope of this book to deal with these areas in detail, save to say that the Data Protection Act 1998 enables individuals to have access to information of which they are the subject, for example a person's own education or medical records, credit reference file etc. On making a request an individual is entitled to have in an intelligible form any data relating to the individual, whether held as an electronic record or within a filing system, on payment of appropriate costs. There are some exceptions, and the interests of other individuals who may be identified may need to be balanced against the needs of the individual. A court order can be sought if the information requested is not provided. **8.09**

In future the Freedom of Information Act 2000 (which comes into force on 1 January 2005) will give people the right to request information from public authorities, for example as regards policies and decisions. There are also other possibilities, for example the Environmental Information Regulations 2004 provide people with access to environmental information. **8.10**

B   THE ELUSIVENESS OF TRUTH

Facts are such horrid things!

Jane Austen, *Lady Susan*

The problems of establishing truth

A law student will often consider how the law applies to a fact pattern—a set of facts are given and discussion considers how the law applies. In real life, facts are much more difficult to capture. **8.11**

- A witness who saw an accident may not have had a good view of what happened, or may have been distracted by something so as not to see the whole accident.

- An oral agreement may be difficult to establish if only two parties were present and they give very different evidence of what was said.
- Some 'facts' are very difficult to pin down at all because they are really opinions.
- People can have different understandings of what they read and see.

8.12 Events that happened in the past are notoriously difficult to recreate accurately. Various research projects have been done in this area. A quite well known example is staging a short incident in a full lecture hall, such as a person rushing in, shouting something, waving something, and disappearing. Asking questions a few minutes later about what the person was wearing, what they shouted, and what they waved will normally produce a wide range of answers. It is virtually impossible to establish the whole truth from witnesses, even though they are a strongly respected source of evidence.

8.13 Equally the events surrounding an accident or the making of a contract can be very difficult to reconstruct so as to identify the truth with any great degree of certainty. The events may have happened some time ago or very quickly, and those involved in the events may not have been paying great attention or may not have noticed details. Even with a full set of documents in a contract case or a video of an accident in a tort case you do not know everything about the events. What was said before the documents were drawn up? Was a driver distracted by something not in the camera's view? Many cases can go to trial solely because of this sort of problem in identifying what really happened. Effective litigation requires skills in recreating events as well as in applying the law.

8.14 The nature of truth, and of recreating events truthfully cannot be considered at great length here. Suffice it to say that some understanding of the nature of truth is useful in dealing with facts and evidence in a case. Most academic disciplines have issues concerned with the nature of truth. Many scientific disciplines are strongly founded in the importance of discovering and analysing true facts. In history the 'truth' of historical events can vary radically as new evidence is discovered, or depending on the viewpoint of the person. This sort of insight can be useful to the lawyer.

8.15 To go a stage further, truth about a past event can be actively manipulated by someone with a motive. While parties to civil litigation will not seek to manipulate memory and written evidence at the level imagined in *1984* by George Orwell, some appreciation of the nature of facts and truth can help a lawyer to approach a case in a sound way, with strategies for addressing potential problems.

Practical problems with facts

8.16 Collecting together all the facts relevant to a case can be like herding cats.

- It can be difficult to get the initial facts of a case because the client has lost documents, does not have a good memory, or does not find it easy to talk fully and objectively about the problem.
- It will rarely be possible to get all the facts of a case from a client—some facts may only be known to others and will have to be gradually collected together.
- It may be quite impossible to establish some facts at all because no source of evidence on particular points is available.

- The cost of gathering some facts may be too expensive compared to their relevance, so the lawyer may have to make a judgment without them.
- Apparent 'facts' from different sources will often be to some extent contradictory.
- Some facts are matters of impression or interpretation rather than 'hard' facts.
- Some facts may be difficult to understand without, or sometimes even with, the assistance of an expert.
- The litigation process means that facts accumulate gradually over time—there is rarely the luxury of having all the facts together at one time, and facts will need to be re-evaluated as more material becomes available.
- The meaning and relevance of facts may seem to change as more facts are known.

Ways of addressing problems with facts

To try to address practical difficulties it is useful to identify ways of dealing with particular types of problem. **8.17**

Focussing on the most relevant information

There is an almost unlimited amount of information that may have some factual connection with a case. While the lawyer will want sufficient factual information to provide a basis for sound decisions, collecting facts will take time and cost money. Strategic decisions will be required to focus on the information that is really necessary to allow decisions to be taken. There is a careful professional judgment to be made in balancing fact-gathering with the importance of what the fact relates to. **8.18**

In considering formal evidence the test for admissibility is whether something relates to a fact in issue in the case. For informal fact-gathering at an earlier stage the lawyer must collect and assess a wider range of information to be able to decide what the issues are. Perhaps a useful test at an early stage is to collect information that is most likely to show what causes of action and remedies may be available. This requires judgment—it is not always immediately apparent which facts are most important. The client's view of what is most important is not necessarily the same as what is legally most important. **8.19**

The lack of factual resources

In most cases there will be gaps in the information the lawyer has. This is quite natural—it is impossible to know everything about a situation, and expensive and unnecessary to find out almost everything. The lawyer does not need to know everything. The point is not that a fact is not known, but rather how important it is that it be known. **8.20**

If unknown information is important then creative thinking may be required to identify how the required information may be found. Sometimes a witness can be found or a research process can reveal the information. As always the cost must be considered. A barrister should not ask a solicitor to provide information without considering how and at what cost the information will be found. **8.21**

Some information is simply not available through any realistic method or at realistic cost. If this information is crucial it may prevent a case being brought, but gaps can be filled in various ways through analysis as outlined at 8.61–8.70, and through advocacy as outlined at 22.55–22.64. **8.22**

The unreliability and inaccuracy of factual sources

8.23 Unreliability and inaccuracy can affect even the most fundamental factual sources—the witnesses and the documents. Even when a witness is trying very hard to tell the truth details may be inaccurate. A written document is not always totally reliable—mistakes and misunderstandings can easily creep in. Every source should be approached with the awareness that there may be some inaccuracies. If there are contradictory versions of an event then one version is probably inaccurate, so it should be checked, and evidence to corroborate the client's version found if possible.

Avoiding assumptions

8.24 It is all to easy to assume something to be a fact because it seems obvious. If an assumption remains unquestioned until trial then a case may crumble if the assumption turns out to be untrue. It is the basis for many good detective stories that an assumption made by the reader or a character suddenly turns out to be false. The remedy is clearly to avoid making assumptions and to seek objective factual support for all the ingredients of the case.

Interpreting facts accurately

8.25 Something that is said or done may mean one thing to one person and something quite different to someone else. There are many instances in oral contracts where one party understands one thing to have been agreed and the other party understands the term to be very different. This is also fertile ground for detective stories—Hercule Poirot often interprets a set of facts that appeared to mean one thing to mean something very different. The lawyer should query whether one interpretation of a set of facts is the only possible interpretation.

Dealing with ambiguities and contradictions

8.26 Facts can often be ambiguous or even contradictory. Indeed some cases turn on an ambiguity or a contradiction. The mere fact that there is an ambiguity or a contradiction is not necessarily a problem—what matters is to identify the ambiguity or contradiction and to try to find more facts to support the version proposed by the client.

Separating facts from interpretations

8.27 Many elements of the factual background to a case are not necessarily 'facts' in their own right. It may be necessary to decide whether a machine is fit for purpose, or whether someone operating a machine is performing his or her job properly. These are not individual matters of fact, but are matters of putting together various matters of fact that may have been observed and interpreting them to reach conclusions.

Sifting out bias

8.28 All clients and witnesses will speak from a particular viewpoint. There is normally rather less motivation for a client or a witness to lie in a civil case than in a criminal case. Nonetheless clients will be motivated to win and may over-egg the pudding or be economical with the truth. A witness may be an employee or a friend who does not want to let the side down. Witnesses who do not have a direct personal interest in the outcome of a case may still have a variety of motivations, such as not wishing to divulge personal information, or not wishing to be involved. The strength of a case can be misjudged if facts are taken at face value. The safest approach is to keep in mind the possibility of bias when reading client and witness statements, and to try to tactfully probe anything that may be overstated. It may be possible to cross check something in a statement with another source.

Proving facts

At the end of the day a fact is only going to be really useful in litigation if it can be proved **8.29** through admissible evidence, though some facts that are suspected and cannot be proved may be useful in dealing with witnesses and in advocacy. It is important not to move too quickly to the formal rules of evidence—it is best to consider facts generally before narrowing the scope of inquiry—but in due course admissibility will become an issue and this is considered further at 15.58–15.91.

C SOURCES OF FACTS

There is perhaps a natural tendency for a lawyer to think of written documents as the **8.30** primary source of facts. This is justified to some extent—written documents are of particular importance in areas like contract law and land law, much of a case is recorded in writing, and increasingly written documents play an important role in trials. However it is advisable to think widely, practically, and imaginatively about potential sources of facts in order to get a full picture of the factual scenario behind a case, and be in a position to gather the best evidence. The more widely the lawyer considers potential sources of factual information, the more the lawyer will know and the more fully the case can be prepared.

It is necessary to find appropriate sources for factual information to support all parts of the **8.31** case. Facts on remedies and to support interim applications can be just as important as facts establishing a cause of action. The solicitor will be primarily responsible for collecting factual information even if a barrister is briefed, albeit that if a barrister is briefed he or she is likely to set out what further information and evidence is required to enable sound advice to be given. The cost of getting information and the time it will take is a consideration with regard to any potential source of facts.

The client

The client will be a major source of factual information in most cases. The client may not be **8.32** able to give admissible evidence on all areas at trial (for example because the client will not be accepted by the court as an expert) but the client can assist in initial information gathering.

- The client's initial informal proof of evidence is likely to be extended by questioning from the solicitor and barrister.
- The client is likely to have key documents and will be able to gather some types of information that may be relevant such as accounts or bank statements.
- The client may be able to suggest potential witnesses.
- The client may be able to provide photographs or sketch plans to assist the lawyer.
- The client may be able to help to explain a process or situation to the lawyer as part of weighing up whether expert evidence is required.

8.33   The first step in gathering information from the client is normally to get him or her to provide an informal 'proof'. This is simply for use between the lawyer and client and it is a privileged document. This may be achieved in various ways. The client may be asked to bring a written summary of relevant facts, a junior member of staff may be asked to meet the client and collect background facts before the meeting with the lawyer, or the client may be asked to tape record the facts for the lawyer to listen to before a meeting. This first factual summary is unlikely to include all the relevant matters the client is aware of—the client may forget things and may not know what is legally relevant.

8.34   The lawyer will need to use meetings and other forms of communication to elaborate on the informal proof, ensuring that all the relevant factual information that the client can provide has come out, that the summary is reasonably accurate, and that the lawyer understands it. More information may emerge through letters and telephone calls, and this may need to be kept with the original proof for later integration.

8.35   It is only if litigation proceeds that the informal privileged statement will be put into the form of a witness statement or affidavit for formal use and for exchange with the other side and with the court. This is dealt with at 15.109–15.135.

Documents

8.36   Written documents will often be an important source of facts. The lawyer will always need to see a key document such as a contract, a lease, or a will before giving any advice. See also 15.24–15.29.

8.37   It is nonetheless important not to rely too heavily on a limited range of key documents without considering a wider context. Other documents may be relevant, such as accident reports or business records. Some documents record specific information that may be useful, such as credit card statements or receipts. There may be a written record that might support other evidence, such as notes of telephone calls or minutes of meetings. Sometimes it may be useful to be imaginative about the types of written records that may be available. It may be useful simply to jog the client's memory 'Is there anything else in writing that might help us with this?'

People

8.38   People will often be the most important source of facts. Even where there are documents, people may have much to say about how they came into existence and what they mean. For many centuries the evidence of witnesses has been the preferred source of evidence in court. For all witnesses there will be the same process as with the client of starting with an informal proof that may later become a formal witness statement or affidavit. This is covered at 15.17–15.22. The barrister should not normally see potential witnesses other than the client and expert witnesses.

8.39   There will usually be a variety of people who know facts relevant to a case. Some will be obvious sources because, for example, they know about how a contract was breached, or they witnessed an accident. Sometimes it will be less obvious who it might be useful to gather information from—the best approach is probably to think quite widely about who may have seen something relevant or may otherwise have relevant knowledge. It is not always easy to contact potential witnesses, but this may be done by one person being aware of another, or by using publicity such as a local newspaper. Some possible witnesses may not be easily available, for example because they are overseas, and ways of getting evidence from them may need to be identified.

There may be problems in getting information from people even if they have it. A person **8.40** who may know something relevant will not necessarily be ready to disclose it. A person may not wish to become involved, or may have a reason for not wanting to give information, for example an employee may not wish to disclose information against his or her employer. There are limited ways in which an unwilling person can be forced to provide factual information, and only a few of these operate before a case has been commenced (see 16.63–16.78). In the early stages of a case factual information will primarily come from those who are willing to provide it.

There is no property in a witness, so that in a broad sense a party can approach anyone to **8.41** gather factual information, but each party will normally want to use as witnesses those who will voluntarily support his or her case, not those who are unwilling to talk or unsupportive. Witnesses who are unhelpful are best called for the other side and then cross examined.

Physical objects—inspection

There are many circumstances in which physical objects or physical locations will be rele- **8.42** vant to a case. To give just a few examples, property that is damaged or not fit for purpose may need to be examined, the condition of land may be relevant, or the working of a machine that has caused an accident may need to be examined. If the client owns or has access to the object or location then inspection can be arranged. If the client does not have access then an order may need to be sought, see 15.30–15.31 and 16.144–16.169.

Physical objects—plans and photographs

It is often only possible to understand something properly if one can see it. This is normally **8.43** best addressed with the help of plans and photographs, for example as regards the location of an accident. Photographs may also be of assistance in understanding physical damage to something. A video may be helpful for the lawyer in understanding the case—the question whether it might be admissible and useful in court can be decided later. The client may be able to provide some photos and/or a sketch map, or the solicitor may need to arrange for photographs to be taken or for a map to be drawn up. See 15.32–15.34.

Sources of physical information may be very wide-ranging. For example, a useful photo- **8.44** graph need not be taken by the parties. In *Senior v Holdsworth, ex p Independent Television News* [1976] QB 23 the claimant sued a policeman for assault at a pop concert, and he was granted an order that ITN should produce film that they took of the event, though only the part that was relevant. However, it should be noted that this type of application has raised questions about the position of the press, where photographs and films are sought for an event with a political element. If the relevance of the information and the costs justify it, a visit to the site may be arranged.

Facts and figures

8.45   Numerical information is often required, whether in the form of financial information, or perhaps measurements and distances linked to photographs and plans.

8.46   As regards existing financial information, business accounts may be relevant, as may details of profits, income, or living expenses. Hopefully financial records will have been methodically kept, but sometimes this will not be the case and it may be necessary to try to get copies of records such as bank statements or bills. It may also be necessary to deal with financial issues such as tax implications, mortgages, loans etc. Even more challenging, it may be necessary to try to estimate potential future loss of income or earnings as projections from existing figures. Such matters are covered in 14.50–14.65.

D   THE STAGED AVAILABILITY OF FACTUAL INFORMATION

8.47   A lawyer rarely has the luxury of being able to sit down and consider all the relevant factual information at one time. As a matter of logistics, and as a result of the adversarial system, information normally becomes available in stages. There are usually some facts known only to the other side, which may only be available on disclosure and/or exchange of witness statements.

8.48   In very general terms, the main stages at which factual information is likely to become available are as follows. These stages are likely to take place over several months.

  • The first meeting between the lawyer and the client, which should produce a written summary of what the client says, and key documents relevant to the case.
  • Further meetings between the lawyer and the client, as the client produces further information that the lawyer has requested, and further information that is easily available is collected.
  • The production of any expert report requested, which will take time to produce.
  • The first contact with the other side. A letter before action to the other side is likely to produce at least some information as to what matters are really in contention. If a pre-action protocol applies, a rather more significant exchange of information should follow.
  • The statements of case. As these are essentially summaries of factual allegations they will often provide factual information.
  • Disclosure and inspection of documents. Subject to a pre-action protocol or voluntary exchange, this is the stage at which key documents in the possession of the other side will be seen. See 15.179–15.200.
  • The exchange of witness statements. This may be the first time a party becomes aware of the detailed factual evidence another party is relying on. See 15.201–15.205.

8.49   One therefore has to accept that factual analysis is normally provisional and ongoing—it has to be reviewed as further information emerges. Advice is provisional because sufficient information is not yet available, and this needs to be made clear to the client. Advice may be provisional because:

  • it is based on the facts as they are currently known;

- it is conditional on being able to prove something that cannot yet be proved;
- it is based on certain facts being provable;
- it is based on evidence that may not be entirely reliable, if for example a witness modifies the factual information he or she has given;
- some facts may be difficult or impossible to prove and arguments may need to be based on carefully linking facts that are provable in advocacy.

E   ANALYSING FACTS

Once sufficient facts have been gathered they will need to be analysed and assessed as **8.50** systematically as possible. This is not an easy task, not least because analysis can rarely occur as a comprehensive activity because of the staged way in which information becomes available. This section considers the initial analysis of facts. More refined analysis of the overall case is considered at 10.07–10.27, and analysis of evidence is considered at 15.01–15.15 and 15.92–15.100.

Ingredients in analysis

The analysis of facts is a complex professional skill. Many cases involve a lot of factual **8.51** material, and if all possible sources of further information were followed up there would be even more material. Finding a clear and useful path through a mass of material is central to working effectively. Different lawyers will have different techniques, but useful ingredients in analysis are given below.

Deciding which facts are probably most important

This may not be easy. What the client sees as most important is not necessarily most impor- **8.52** tant in legal terms. What seems important one day may not seem as important a few weeks later. The client may offer a lot of information that is of concern to the client, but which is unlikely to be relevant to litigation.

Inevitably the lawyer will want to start to try to put 'legal' labels on facts, but this is best not **8.53** done too quickly or the investigation of facts can be narrowed. General questions about what really concerns the client and what the client really wants to address are best asked before law plays too great a part in the analysis. Focussing too quickly or narrowly on potential contractual terms may mean that information that might show a possible collateral contract or misrepresentation is not uncovered. Moving too quickly to identify one possible breach of duty in tort may mean that other possible breaches of duty are not identified.

Deciding how reliable the facts currently known are likely to be

Some facts are inherently more reliable than others and consideration of levels of reliability **8.54** can inform analysis. In a contract case some facts may be completely clear cut—for example the contract may be in writing. Some facts may be fairly reliable—for example it may appear to be reasonably easy to show that the goods were defective and that there is ongoing loss. Other facts might be quite difficult to show—for example it may be alleged that oral misrepresentations were made but with no independent support for the client's version of what was said.

8.55 Facts that appear to relate to the same matter are not necessarily equally reliable. One person may have heard something clearly whereas another might be further away and distracted by background noise. Two people who see an accident may be different distances away, have different obstructions to their view of events, or have different levels of eyesight.

Considering what the other side might know

8.56 The case for the other side will only be revealed later, but an analysis should be able to predict what view the other side is likely to take of the facts, and thus to identify potential weaknesses in the factual scenario. The client is likely to have presented facts in a light that favours his or her case, so it is important to consider what is known of the facts that may support the other side, and how the other side might view the facts known.

Deciding how much importance to attach to facts that are not known

8.57 When carrying out an overall analysis, it is useful to identify the most important facts that are not known. If very important facts are not known the lawyer will have to identify precisely how and when relevant information can be gained, and the information should probably be obtained before advice is given to the client. If the facts not yet known are not crucial the lawyer can give provisional advice on options, setting out what needs to be known, and what effect the information may have.

F   INFORMATION MANAGEMENT

8.58 Even a relatively straightforward case can involve a mass of factual information. That information needs to be collected, recorded, and stored methodically, in a structured and accessible way. Firms and chambers increasingly employ sophisticated information management systems that are largely or partly electronically based. In addition to storing information, such systems can assist in the analysis of information if sufficiently well organised. Individual lawyers need not only to use such systems efficiently, but also to run mini information management systems for each case they work on.

8.59 An effective information management system needs to ensure that effort is not duplicated by having to repeat analysis that has already been done, and that information can be retrieved easily. A good information management system might include the following.

- The preparation and storage of a chronological list of events. In a complex case there may be separate chronologies for separate parts of the case. Decisions should be taken as to how much detail is useful.
- A list of the people involved in the case, with basic information about each. There may be a separate list of witnesses. Decisions should be taken as to what key details about each can usefully be included.
- Notes of meetings and telephone calls need to be made and stored with the information they relate to. The date and the source of an item of information should normally be recorded.

- In a complex case more sophisticated work can usefully be done cross referencing factual information on charts or spreadsheets. No single approach will work for all lawyers and for all cases, but using a suitable way for organising facts is important.
- Important documents may need to be copied and marked up in different ways for different purposes. Alternatively a coherent system for the use of highlighters etc is likely to make working with documents much more efficient. Post-it notes that might fall off or pencil annotations that may be illegible should be avoided.
- Notes made in analysing facts should normally be stored in a reasonably neat form. Odd notes on bits of paper are easily lost or may be difficult to reread so that analysis has to be done all over again.

Good structured fact analysis that is properly stored will have many potential uses—it will **8.60** lay the foundations for advising the client and for drafting a statement of case. It will also be helpful for reference during a negotiation, or for preparing a skeleton argument prior to going to court.

G   THEORIES, DEDUCTION, AND LOGIC

> Sherlock Holmes and Dr Watson went camping. They both woke up in the middle of the night. 'How bright the stars are!' said Dr Watson. 'Indeed, and what do you deduce from that my dear Watson?' said Holmes. 'That it is a particularly beautiful night?' Watson suggested. 'Possibly,' Holmes replied 'but I deduce that someone has stolen our tent!'

An ability to get fully to grips with the facts of a case, to focus on what really matters and to **8.61** see the truth behind the obvious is one thing that distinguishes a really effective lawyer from a competent one. A full appreciation of the importance of factual analysis lies behind drafting statements of case, making submissions and cross examination.

Even after analysis some gaps in the facts of the case will remain. Sometimes a gap is one of **8.62** inference rather than hard fact, for example where there is a question as to whether a particular breach can be shown to have led to a particular loss. Such gaps in facts can and should be addressed in a constructive way.

The first stage is to identify gaps in facts that are relevant to the outcome of the case as **8.63** precisely as possible. Can it be shown that a misrepresentation induced a contract? Can it be shown that a particular loss was caused by a particular breach? A gap in facts will not necessarily be a problem if the fact is admitted.

The second stage is to assess whether the gap is really a problem. If a gap in facts means that **8.64** an element of a cause of action cannot be shown then the case cannot go ahead so it is very serious. If the gap in facts means that it may be difficult to recover a particular head of loss then the gap is not fatal to the case, but its potential effect needs to be made clear to the client. A gap is not necessarily a problem at all if it relates to a matter that is admitted or not in issue.

The third stage is to identify how the gap might be filled.   **8.65**

- A gap might still be filled by further questions to a witness or an expert.

- A gap might be filled by information from the other side, either through normal disclosure or through a special application to court.
- A gap in facts might be addressed through cross examination of a witness in trial, but such an approach comes very late in the day and cannot be guaranteed to work.

8.66   An alternative route is to fill the gap not with further facts but with argument and advocacy based on facts that are known. There must be no confusion—a lawyer cannot give evidence and therefore cannot personally make facts known to the court. What a lawyer can do is to use advocacy to show how the facts that are available should be interpreted. The basic options are as follows, and they are explored further in 22.55–22.64.

A theory of the case

8.67   Much advocacy at a trial or for an interim hearing relies on the advocate using a theory for a case. The lawyer uses the facts that can be shown to suggest the most likely overall pattern of events. Things that can be proved may suggest that an accident probably happened in a particular way, even if all the details of how the accident happened cannot be proved. A theory of the case draws together what is known to create a coherent and therefore persuasive whole.

Deductions and inferences

8.68   Equally one fact may be deduced or inferred from others. This is often done through an argument based on logic, or through presenting a chain of interdependent propositions— because this happened and this happened it is likely that this happened. Deductions may be built up from a series of inferences, with each inference fitting in with all known facts and with other inferences, to put together a coherent theory. The causation of an accident or the causation of damage following a breach of contract or duty may need to be argued in such a way.

8.69   As an example the overall relationship between two parties, previous business dealings and interactions between them that can be proved may make it more likely than not that particular representations were made or that particular terms should be implied into a contract. As a further example an expert may not be able to say how an accident happened, but an expert report may suggest that from the facts known it is most likely that the accident happened in a particular way.

8.70   A problem with gaps in facts may make it advisable to settle a case rather than take it to trial (though the lawyer should not advise that the case be brought at all if there is a fundamental gap in the facts). The options for filling the gaps should be fully considered before the case is settled for less than it might really be worth.

H   THE INTERACTION OF FACTS AND LAW

8.71   The professional lawyer faces something of a chicken-and-egg quandary—the lawyer can only apply the law once he or she knows sufficient facts, but equally it is only possible to know what facts are most relevant by looking at legal principles.

8.72   There is no solution to this dilemma—it is best addressed by taking care to avoid trying to get too close to any decisions on relevant law until the factual scenario is reasonably clear. It is all too easy to try to give a legal 'label' to a case as quickly as possible after the client arrives at a meeting or a barrister starts to read a brief. The danger is that the moment a case has a legal label, for example as a breach of contract case, the tendency is to try to see everything as fitting that label rather than gathering enough factual information to see if a rather different legal label, such as misrepresentation or mistake might apply.

Probably the best approach is one of the greatest possible flexibility. The lawyer will natur- **8.73** ally think of legal labels, but the emphasis must remain on the facts in the early stages of the case while potentially important facts are still emerging. A suitable approach is:

- to focus on building up a full factual understanding of the facts that are probably most important in the case;
- to identify what key factual information is missing, and give priority to collecting that information;
- to keep possible legal labels for the case at the back of the mind (breach of implied term?) but actively seek wider factual information, looking for other possible legal labels, and seeing if the legal label provisionally identified still applies as further information emerges.

It is only at a later stage, after facts have been fully and openly considered, that law should **8.74** start to play a more prominent part in analysis. This is considered further at 10.19–10.32.

I BUILDING A FACTUAL FRAMEWORK FOR A CASE

The overall factual structure of a case

The objectives of establishing and managing the facts in a case are: **8.75**

- to provide a sound basis for advising a client on the type of case that may be brought (see 7.18–7.27 and 11.58–11.87);
- to provide a sound basis for drafting a statement of case (see 12.95–12.111);
- to provide a basis for taking decisions about the evidence required to progress the case (see 15.07–15.15 and 15.92–15.99);
- to provide a basis for preparing a case for hearing (see 21.42–21.77);
- to provide a basis for dealing with witnesses (see 22.41–22.55 and 22.77–22.109).

All these require the clearest strongest possible overall factual framework for the case. It is **8.76** arguable that more cases are lost due to inadequate fact analysis than due to weaknesses in the legal arguments used in a case, as many of the strengths and weaknesses of a case are based in its facts rather than in the law.

A strong factual framework is likely to include: **8.77**

- working within an overall factual knowledge of the case that takes into account as far as possible all the known facts;
- possessing a range of factual knowledge that covers potential causes of action, potential defences, and damages and other remedies;

- have sufficient understanding of which facts are most important, and the factual strengths and weaknesses of the case;
- using a clear system for information management so that information that comes in is taken into account and not lost;
- maintaining a flexible view of the facts, and reviewing that factual framework of the case when significant amounts of new material have been gathered.

Chains of facts

8.78 An analogy for a factual structure for a case might be building a 'wall' for the case made of factual 'bricks'. This is perhaps useful when it comes to building a case with pieces of admissible evidence. In terms of general factual analysis the analogy of a web may be more useful. Many facts are linked into chains by deductions and inferences, especially as regards showing that a breach of a term or of a duty caused particular items of loss and damage.

8.79 As some examples of chains of fact:

- It was an implied term of the contract that John would repair Jane's plumbing by 5.00 pm. John did not repair the plumbing in time and forgot to tell Jane. Jane turned the water on and it flooded her flat. Because Jane's flat was flooded water seeped into the flat below and ruined antique furniture.
- It was dark and the weather was very cold. Ruth should have known there was likely to be ice on the road. There was ice on the road but Ruth drove her car too fast. The car slid on the road and badly damaged the front of Raj's shop. Because he had to deal with the damage Raj could not go on a holiday he had booked.

8.80 Chains of facts may be particularly important in deciding the content and structure of a statement of case or an advocacy submission. They provide links of foreseeability and causation that are crucial to building a case.

9

MANAGING AND USING LEGAL KNOWLEDGE

A LAW IN PRACTICE 9.01

B THE EVOLVING NATURE OF LAW 9.06

C KNOWLEDGE MANAGEMENT 9.09
The firm and chambers level 9.09
The individual level 9.12

D USING LEGAL PRINCIPLES 9.14

E USING PRACTITIONER SOURCES 9.16
Statutes and statutory instruments 9.16
Case law 9.21
Books and journals 9.28
European Union law 9.31
Electronic sources 9.33
Other lawyers 9.37
The meaning of words 9.39

F KEEPING UP TO DATE 9.40

G STRATEGIC LEGAL RESEARCH 9.42
The importance of strategic legal research 9.42
Working in a strategic way 9.47

H PLANNING RESEARCH 9.49
Drawing up a plan 9.49
Legal analysis 9.55
The areas for research 9.58
The questions for research 9.59
Key words and phrases 9.61
Selecting sources 9.62
Using sources 9.65
Keeping focussed 9.67

I PRESENTING FINDINGS 9.69
Personal records of legal research 9.70
Preparing a formal note of legal research 9.71

J   USING LAW TO GET RESULTS 9.74

Advising a client. 9.75

Advising in writing 9.77

Skeleton arguments. 9.78

Constructing legal arguments for court 9.79

A lawyer without books would be like a workman without tools.

Thomas Jefferson

A LAW IN PRACTICE

9.01 The extent to which different people use legal knowledge for different purposes is not acknowledged as fully and explicitly as it might be. A House of Lords judge may be most concerned with the precise meaning of a section of a statute or a case—his or her decision must be soundly based on precedent and he or she cannot review a decision as to fact. An academic lawyer may be most interested in the theory behind an area of law—looking for a coherent structure and philosophy for the law and how individual cases fit within it. A campaigning lawyer may be as interested in what the law should be as in what it is.

9.02 An appreciation of perspective and purpose is important in using law effectively. The lawyer in practice will hopefully appreciate how the superior court judge, the academic lawyer, and the campaigning lawyer use the law, but will use the law in a different strategic way in approaching cases. The majority of lawyers initially study law at university, and while a wide range of approaches to law is reflected in different university courses, it is perhaps fair to say that the different ways in which law may be used after the university course is not made very transparent or explicit. This can make the transition from learning law to using law in practice more difficult than it might be.

9.03 This is not to suggest that all lawyers in practice use law in the same way. The silk may be using legal argument frequently in the Court of Appeal and the House of Lords, while the more junior lawyer is likely to be using legal points less in cases at first instance, though specialist areas of practice may make more use of law in particular areas. However there are some common threads in how litigation lawyers are most likely to use the law to assist in meeting the needs of a client.

9.04 The main ingredients of using law as a tool to serve the client are:

- having a very sound knowledge of basic legal principle, especially in key areas such as contract and tort;
- having a sufficient knowledge of general legal principles that can apply across a range of cases, such as legal personality and agency;
- having a sound understanding of the operation of the principles linking legal liability and legal remedy, including principles such as causation and mitigation;
- being able to identify the specific legal principles relevant to a particular factual scenario, and to apply those principles;

- being able to apply legal principles to meet practical objectives;
- having good skills in legal research;
- having the ability to ensure that law used is up to date, and the flexibility to take significant changes of law on board.

While many of these ingredients are inherent in studying law, they are not necessarily **9.05** explicit or fully developed when the student starts professional study. Work done in law clinics and *pro bono* work can assist significantly in understanding how law is used in practice, but there can still be a distinct transition from studying law to using law as a means to an end. For books relevant to developing skills in legal analysis see 24.25.

B THE EVOLVING NATURE OF LAW

> What is the argument on the other side? Only this, that no case has ever been found in which it has been done before. That argument does not appeal to me in the least. If we never do anything which has not been done before, we shall never get anywhere. The law will stand whilst the rest of the world goes on, and that will be bad for both.
>
> Lord Denning

There is an understandable tendency to feel that one learns 'the law'—a relatively fixed body **9.06** of information that once understood and known will be a resource for life, and emphasising the importance of committing law to memory. This has a strong foundation in truth—many basic principles of civil law and liability have changed relatively little for decades or even centuries. However the law is also a living body of information with constant changes and additions, and the pace of change in law has quickened. Recent changes have also seen a massive rise in the size of the body of law that it is relevant for a practitioner in England and Wales to know.

These points suggest a strategic approach to learning and using law for the practitioner. **9.07**

- It is important to invest in understanding and memorising the main principles of law in key areas like contract and tort, as these areas form the basis of the majority of civil actions.
- It is best to focus on the framework of an area of law and the elements of causes of actions rather than fine points of detail that may change.
- For a practitioner it is as important to know about potential remedies as about potential causes of action.
- High quality legal research skills that encompass using a range of hard copy and electronic practitioner sources are key to dealing with the detail of an individual case.
- There is merit in looking at difficult issues and cases to understand an area of law, but these are not of regular use to the practitioner.
- It is important not to compartmentalise legal knowledge—one case can easily involve contract, tort and legal personality.
- It is necessary to be aware of the principles of law in areas that can affect any case, like human rights law.
- It is vital to be proactive and systematic in keeping up to date with legal developments.

This list may sound challenging, and indeed it is as it is describing a professional level of **9.08** skill. The key points are the importance of principle rather than detail as this is what will help in case analysis, and the investment in building research skills.

C KNOWLEDGE MANAGEMENT

The firm and chambers level

9.09 The concept of knowledge management is important in modern professions and businesses. It is not possible to know and remember everything in a complex and fast-moving computer age, but to be effective it is important to be able to find, store, and retrieve knowledge efficiently. The importance of information management with regard to factual information was considered at 8.58–8.60. This section deals with the parallel need to manage legal knowledge.

9.10 The main firms of solicitors and the main barristers' chambers have centralised knowledge management systems in place. This will often include structured access to hard copy and electronic legal research, support for legal research, updating services, and banks of precedents and pro formas. It is now common for any organisation large enough to have a Head of Knowledge Management rather than a librarian. The role of professional support lawyers has been developed to provide legal research services within firms. Knowledge networking may be shared across branches or through a particular organisation. Increasingly lawyers provide access to legal knowledge to clients in addition to providing advice and other legal services.

9.11 The range and scope of knowledge management systems is beyond the scope of this book, save to say that the effective lawyer should be fully familiar with and competent in using the knowledge management systems and support that are in place in a particular firm or set of chambers. It is easy to be embarrassed about asking questions about using databases for fear of showing ignorance, but the question is always best asked if the answer may assist in preparing a case.

The individual level

9.12 The principles of knowledge management can be reflected at a personal level. It is all too easy to be random in dealing with legal knowledge, using whatever book or resource comes to hand, or otherwise being conservative and using a source because one is familiar with it, whether or not it remains the best source or is fully up to date.

9.13 Personal knowledge management techniques can involve:

- regularly reviewing the sources one uses for research to ensure that they remain the best available sources;
- making sure that time is made available for updating and training;
- making use of professional groups and journals to follow developing trends in law;
- systematically retaining records of research undertaken that may be useful for a later case;
- building a personal database of statements of case etc for later reference.

D USING LEGAL PRINCIPLES

The importance of a good working knowledge of legal principle for effective legal practice **9.14** cannot be overemphasised. The legal specialist will build a much more detailed knowledge of a particular area of law, and any lawyer may need to research and check detail for a particular case, but there are many areas of legal practice where it is a wide knowledge of principle that is useful.

Knowledge of legal principle will be useful: **9.15**

- when identifying potential causes of action and remedies in a set of facts;
- as a key tool in analysing a case (see 10.19–10.27);
- in defining the elements of a cause of action for use in a statement of case (see 12.95– 12.111, 18.21–18.52, and 19.06–19.26);
- to be able to give broad legal advice immediately on the telephone or in a meeting with a client (see 7.18–7.35);
- to be able to identify which points require research (see 9.42–9.48);
- to be able to carry out effective research, for example in knowing what words may be useful in using an index or a search engine (see 9.49–9.68).

E USING PRACTITIONER SOURCES

Statutes and statutory instruments

Statutes are a primary source of law, and statutory instruments have the same force as stat- **9.16** utes. Statute law may be completely irrelevant to a case, if for example it is based entirely on principles of common law. Sometimes a statute may have limited relevance, for example allowing a particular remedy in a particular situation, such as the Misrepresentation Act 1967. The statute may be the authority for a point, but the precise wording of the statute will have little relevance and is unlikely to be a matter for argument.

Sometimes a case will turn largely or entirely on the precise wording of a statute—there may **9.17** for example be an argument as to whether a particular statutory section applies in a particu- lar situation, or about what a particular statutory section means. If a statute or statutory regulation is relevant it may be necessary to check:

- the precise words of the statute;
- whether it is in force (for example using the *Is it in force?* volume of Halsbury's Statutes or Legislation Direct on the web);
- whether it has been amended (check whether the version of the statute that you are looking at includes amendments);
- how the wording of the statute has been interpreted in case law (using something like the Current Law Legislation Citator);
- whether it has not been repealed (and if an Act has been passed repealing all or part of a statute, whether that statute has come into force).

9.18 Research may be assisted by using an annotated version of the statute, such as Current Law Statutes Annotated, or through using electronic search resources. If quoting a statute in court the Queen's Printer's copy with no annotations should be used. Printed forms of statutes can be obtained from www.tso.co.uk/bookshop/. The original forms of statutes are also available electronically on www.hmso.gov.uk, and on www.legislation.hmso.gov.uk. The text of bills before parliament can be obtained from www.publications.parliament.uk.

9.19 Statutory Instruments are used to provide detail within a framework provided by a statute, and to deal with detailed regulations in areas of industry, employment etc. They are also used to put European Union Directives and Regulations into effect in England. Statutory instruments can be found in Halsbury's Statutory Instruments. Case law relevant to statutory instruments can be found in the Current Law Statutory Instrument Citator. New statutory instruments can be viewed at www.legislation.hmso.gov.uk/stat.htm.

9.20 A relevant statutory section or statutory instrument should be referred to in advising a client orally or in writing, and in addressing the court. In a case of breach of statutory duty (common where for example there has been an accident at work) the precise wording of relevant regulations will be important in case analysis and in drafting the statement of case, see 19.08–19.10 and 19.141.

Case law

9.21 Cases relevant to a particular legal topic may be found through reading the relevant section of a textbook, through the use of an annotated statute, or through a web search. The reference for a case may be found using the Current Law Cases Citator (which covers every case considered since 1947), or the Digest (an encyclopaedia of case law under subject headings).

9.22 A search for case law can be very time consuming and wide ranging, raising as many questions as it answers, so the purpose of the search should be defined.

- Is it necessary to search for case law at all?
- If case law might be helpful, which issues might case law assist with?
- How much research into case law is justified by the importance of the issue?
- How detailed should the research on each case be? Will it be sufficient to read the headnote and only read more if the case is very close to the issues?
- What record should be kept of the cases that are most legally relevant, closest on the facts, or most up to date? Should specific references and quotes be noted?

9.23 If a case is to be cited in court, the most authoritative source should be found and used. The official Law Reports are to be preferred as they are checked by the judges and usually include a summary of counsels' arguments. Otherwise the Weekly Law Reports should be used, or the All England Law Reports. Authoritative specialist series or an official transcript of an unreported case may be used if there is not a more authoritative report. Neutral citation is used as many cases appear on the web before they appear in hard copy, see Practice Note (2001) 1 All ER 293 and Practice Direction (2002) Practice Direction 1 WLR 346.

9.24 It is not essential to quote case law to conduct litigation. Many cases turn on their facts rather than on the law, especially in the early years of practice. Reported cases normally deal primarily with points of law, with findings of fact made by the tribunal simply being set out. Quoting cases that offer a vague analogy with no more precise purpose can confuse rather than assist.

Cases may be useful in illustrating the advice being given by the lawyer to a client where: **9.25**

- the case is a clear authority for the law on a particular point;
- the case is close on the facts;
- the case is up to date and illustrates the current approach of the courts.

Cases should be chosen with care for use in court. A case will often not be useful if it turns on **9.26** its own facts or if there is only a general similarity with the case currently being considered. A case may be of assistance to a judge if there is a legal issue in the case and if:

- the case shows the modern interpretation of a point of common law;
- the case shows how a relevant statutory section has been interpreted;
- the case shows the judge how another court has recently dealt with similar facts or a similar legal issue.

As electronic resources have made access to legal resources easier, and with the growth of the use of skeleton arguments, it has perhaps become tempting to quote more legal authorities. Judges have specifically discouraged the excessive quotation of cases in trials. For example, Lord Diplock has said:

> The citation of a plethora of illustrative authorities, apart from being time and cost consuming, presents the danger of so blinding the court with case law that it has difficulty in seeing the wood of legal principle from the trees of paraphrase (*Lambert v Lewis* [1981] 1 All ER 1185).

Similarly, Lord Roskill said:

> I hope I shall not be thought discourteous or unappreciative of the industry involved in the preparation of counsel's arguments if I say that today massive citation of authority in cases where the relevant legal principles have been clearly and authoritatively determined is of little or no assistance and should be discouraged (*Pioneer Shipping Ltd v BTP Tioxide Ltd* [1981] 2 All ER 1030).

This is summarised in the Practice Direction (Citation of Authorities) (2001) 1 WLR 1001. **9.27** The lawyer should:

- in a list of authorities or a skeleton argument state the proposition of law which each case demonstrates;
- cite a case only if that case clearly establishes a new principle or extends the law, or if the inclusion of the case can otherwise be specifically justified;
- cite more than one authority for each proposition only if that can be justified;
- cite authorities only from England, the European Court of Justice, and the European Court of Human Rights, unless the inclusion of the authority is justified.

Books and journals

Text books and other academic works are not primary sources of law and are not normally **9.28** accepted as authorities in court. Having said this, a text book will often be a starting point for research into an area of law. The temptation to read long sections of a book should be resisted or research can become very time consuming. Strategic use of textbooks might include:

- using a specialist practitioner textbook;
- selecting where possible a textbook that is kept reasonably up to date through a loose leaf format, supplements, or website support;
- using Halsbury's Laws, a general legal encyclopaedia, or an electronic search, where an area of law is unfamiliar.

9.29   Legal journals, even specialist practitioner journals, are also not normally used in court. They can however be of significant use to the practitioner in keeping up to date, and for providing ideas for developing an argument in a case. The practitioner will probably regularly read specialist journals relevant to his or her practice. Articles in an unfamiliar area of law may perhaps most easily be found through an internet search using for example Lawtel or the Legal Journals Index. Books and journals can be used in a meeting with a client and referred to in an opinion or letter.

9.30   A practitioner textbook should only be referred to in court if a particular passage provides a particularly helpful summary or argument that can take a specific point in the case forward. Normally the lawyer should simply adopt the argument from the book as part of her or his advocacy, but a leading practitioner work may be accepted as persuasive in an area like procedure or evidence.

European Union law

9.31   The European Union provides a variety of regulations, directives, and decisions. This is published in the Official Journal of the European Union. As with English legislation, it is important to check that it is in force and whether it has been amended or interpreted. It may not be easy to find how and when Directives have been implemented within the jurisdiction.

9.32   Decisions of the European Court of Justice are officially reported in the European Court Reports. The Common Market Law Reports provide key cases from Member States as well as from the European Court of Justice.

Electronic sources

9.33   Electronic legal research databases can be very convenient. In some ways they can be deceptively easy to use, particularly because of the range of material available and the power of search engines. In other ways they can be difficult or frustrating to use, depending on the design of the CD or website and the ease of navigation.

9.34   To make best use of electronic research it is important:

- to undertake training to use the database to best effect—the ability to conduct a search effectively feeds directly to the quality of the results;
- to check what each database does and does not include, so as to use the best available database for research, and so as to undertake other research in areas not covered by the database;
- to check the form in which the website stores information—for example some hold the full text of cases etc and others hold summaries;

- to be aware of the different ways to use search engines, including especially careful choice of keywords to search;
- to be aware of what display screens do and do not include;
- to check that the information is up to date—it is a great advantage that information accessed via the web can be more up to date than hard copy, but this is not always the case and the researcher should check the basis on which information on a site is updated; CD Roms can be very convenient, but they are not necessarily more up to date than hard copy.

Some of the main legal electronic databases are: **9.35**

- www.butterworths.com. Full text for cases and legislation, including Halsbury's laws and legislation with amendments. This includes the All England and Times Law Reports.
- www.justis.com. Full text for cases and legislation, including European law. This includes the Weekly Law Reports.
- www.lawtel.co.uk. This does not include full text for cases, but has advantages in including cases quickly and including unreported cases. Also summaries of journal articles.
- www.lexisnexis.co.uk. Full text statutes and cases including amendments and including European law and summaries of journal articles.
- www.westlaw.co.uk. Westlaw UK. Full text statutes and cases as amended and access to journal articles, but to some extent a different range from LexisNexis.

Some legal gateways provide good general access to legal research resources, including **9.36**

- www.venables.co.uk
- www.sosig.ac.uk/law
- www.law.cam.ac.uk/jurist/index.htm
- www.hmso.gov.uk
- www.dca.gov.uk
- www.parliament.uk
- www.courtservice.gov.uk
- www.bailii.org
- www.barcouncil.org.uk
- www.lawsociety.org.uk

Other lawyers

Other lawyers can be used in a structured way to assist in providing legal information about a **9.37** case. A solicitor may seek a barrister's opinion where the legal aspects of a case are complex. Solicitors may work in teams on a complex case. Professional support lawyers, trainee solicitors, and pupil barristers may be used to assist with legal research.

Another lawyer may be helpful less formally. Most lawyers work in chambers or firms. **9.38** Within that organisation they will normally have access to other lawyers who can provide expertise in a variety of areas of law. This is an important resource—colleagues can be used informally to provide information if they have a particular speciality or have recently done a case that is similar to the one under consideration. Equally colleagues can be used as a sounding board for a particular approach to a case, or they may have ideas that can provide a fresh perspective. When consulting a colleague informally about a case it is important to act ethically, not mentioning the name of the client but taking the 'I represent someone who . . .' approach, see 3.46.

The meaning of words

9.39 The meaning of words is an important ingredient of much legal research. The meaning of a statute or case that has been found may need to be carefully interpreted. The sources of legal meanings of words are:

- a definitions section in a contract or similar document;
- the definitions sections of statutes and regulations, and the Interpretation Act 1978;
- using Hansard to interpret what Parliament intended in passing a statute, if legislation is ambiguous, obscure or leads to an absurdity, *Pepper v Hart* (1993) AC 593, or to establish the purpose of a statute, *Three Rivers District Council v Bank of England (No 2)* (1996) 2 All ER 363. The same applies in construing statutory instruments, *Denny v Yeldon* (1995) 3 All ER 624. However Hansard is not admissible for more general purposes, *Melluish v BMI (No 3) Ltd* (1996) 1 AC 454. The procedure for using Hansard is set out in Practice Direction (Hansard:Citation) (1995) 1 WLR 192;
- cases that have considered the meanings of words;
- legal dictionaries, see 24.25.

F KEEPING UP TO DATE

9.40 Keeping up to date is a constant element of effective legal practice, to the extent that change rather than stability is the norm. Each individual should have strategies for keeping up to date. Obvious threads for this are membership of a specialist professional organisation, regular attendance at good quality updating conferences, and subscriptions to appropriate specialist legal journals. Beyond this the plethora of sources for keeping up to date can be confusing and a structured approach is important.

9.41 Useful elements in keeping up to date include the following. Keeping up to date is hard work, but using fully up to date law and recent cases can be of strategic assistance in court or in a negotiation. The practitioner should:

- select and make regular use of an appropriate legal updating service. Occasional or 'binge' updating can be dangerous. Some firms and chambers offer good updating services. Alternatively all major internet-based research sources offer updating services, including Lawtel, Westlaw, and Law Direct. For those who prefer or can more easily use hard copy there is Current Law;
- make a practice of using the sources that are most up to date in conducting research;
- check as a matter of course that statutes are researched in their current form, and that up to date cases commenting on relevant points have been found.

G STRATEGIC LEGAL RESEARCH

> 'If the law supposes that', said Mr Bumble, 'the law is a ass—a idiot.'
>
> Charles Dickens, *Oliver Twist*

The importance of strategic legal research

There is no single successful approach to legal research. People work in different ways and **9.42** need to carry out research for different purposes. However it is important to appreciate that legal research for a legal practitioner is a highly focussed process—it is designed to find the best answer to a specific legal question related to a practical problem. This contrasts quite strongly with other forms of legal research—for example the research required for a dissertation is likely to be much more comprehensive and to provide more scope for following up interesting tangents.

It is necessary to be realistic about what research can achieve. Legal research can assist in **9.43** uncovering and elucidating legal principles and seeing how relevant legal principles have been interpreted and applied by the courts. Legal research will not always produce certainty—the law on many points is not entirely clear and a number of cases are litigated purely because the law is not clear. Legal research is only going to be of very limited help where a case turns on its facts rather than the law—it is analysis rather than research that will assist with facts.

While there is no perfect way to carry out research, there are suitable strategies for particular **9.44** types of research. The professional lawyer needs to be able to carry out research that:

- accurately identifies the legal questions in the case (see 10.19–10.27);
- is tightly focussed on those legal questions;
- covers those legal questions reasonably comprehensively;
- provides a reasonably accurate and reliable answer to those legal questions;
- is conducted reasonably quickly and at reasonable cost.

In practice there can be many problems in carrying out legal research. It can be difficult: **9.45**

- to identify and access the most appropriate sources for research;
- to identify the legal questions in a case that require research, and to identify all the legal questions;
- to know where to start with research, and to structure research carefully;
- to know what material found is most relevant, and whether that material is reliable and up to date;
- to focus legal research on what is important in a case without going off on tangents of little or no relevance;
- to know when enough research has been done, and that more is likely to confuse rather than assist;
- to conduct research within a reasonable time and at a reasonable cost;
- to record research findings in such way that they are useful, that sources can be found again quickly, and that research does not need to be repeated.

9.46 Unfortunately many lawyers do not go into practice with an ability to identify and use efficient research strategies. This may be because there is an assumption that law students will acquire legal research skills without this skill being specifically taught and assessed at degree level, or it may be that the sort of source books that tend to be available to support law degrees tend to give a false impression of what is involved in carrying out legal research.

Working in a strategic way

9.47 Strategic legal research is based on:

- combining a planned scientific approach and the art of professional judgment;
- identifying all the legal areas relevant to the case, including questions relating to defences and remedies as well as to possible causes of action;
- identifying the precise legal questions that need to be answered in the case in hand;
- deciding the relative importance of the legal questions, so as to be able to focus on those of most importance to the case and/or which are most likely to be in dispute;
- judging as realistically as possible what depth and width of research is needed for each question, so as to avoid going off on tangents;
- identifying the best source for research for each question—a plain copy of a statute will provide the wording of a section, but an annotated statute may be more useful in identifying other relevant material;
- following research through logically from one source to another;
- working flexibly to identify areas requiring further work, but seeking to avoid red herrings;
- being able to make careful selections of what material is really relevant, and being able to put to one side excess material;
- appreciating that there will often not be a clear legal answer, but that principles and analogies may need to be brought together to construct an argument on the law;
- being able to present the results clearly.

9.48 In carrying out research it is important to work with an open mind. Clearly the lawyer will wish to look for the law that supports the client's case, but it is equally important to identify points that may give rise to problems—the other side may well find this law and it will need to be possible to respond to it. Research should not simply justify a preconceived view of the case, but should be used to review the law on key issues.

H   PLANNING RESEARCH

Drawing up a plan

9.49 With the amount of legal information that is now available, the complex ways in which that information overlaps and changes, the number of ways in which the legal information can be accessed, and the number of ways in which legal information may be used, it can be very difficult to get started on research, and very easy to get lost and disheartened.

9.50 A professional approach is not based on reading a legal text with the general hope of finding something relevant, or to put together a mass of notes and photocopies that do little to take the case forward coherently. This is more likely to add to confusion rather than resolution. Such an approach may undermine rather than support progress in a case, and will tend to lead to tiredness, poor decision making, and time wasting.

It is best to be realistic about what research can achieve. It can find the right or the best **9.51** possible argument on a legal point, but it will be of limited assistance in dealing with the facts of the case. Research into substantive law will give limited clues about steps in litigating a case, it is research into procedural law that will assist here. Most research will leave some loose ends that one does not have time to follow up, and there can be a nagging doubt (often not founded!) that one has not found a key legal source.

Research is most likely to be effective if it is planned and systematic. In time practical **9.52** research techniques will become natural, the lawyer will become increasingly familiar with the sources available, and less new research is likely to be required for each case. However for the lawyer entering practice or researching an area of law he or she knows little about, a plan for research is vital. Making a focussed plan helps to control the process of research and keep it on track, see 10.19–10.27.

Sometimes planning will be very easy. There may be only one or two legal issues in a case, **9.53** they may be reasonably easy to define, and there may be an obvious starting point. If your client is injured while visiting a building you are likely to want to check the terms of the Occupiers Liability Act 1957 and recent cases on it. An annotated version of the statute or Clerk & Lindsell on Tort will be obvious starting points.

Sometimes planning will be much more difficult. The facts provided to the lawyer might be **9.54** that a man buys tickets to a wildlife park on the internet for himself and his two children. While they are at the park one child is chased by a dog and is injured when he falls over scaffolding poles beside a new enclosure that is being built. The other child is allowed to hold a monkey that is newly arrived at the park, but two weeks later suffers a rare illness that the family doctor feels may have been caught from the monkey. Where do you start?

Legal analysis

The first stage for planning research is to analyse the case without going anywhere near a **9.55** research source. First reactions might include research on the law relating to wildlife parks, but limited material is available on this as a discrete topic. Searching an index in Halsbury's or doing a general electronic search is likely to open up rather than focus research, revealing material about the law for importing and keeping wild animals, much of which is likely to be irrelevant.

More systematic analysis would hopefully be more structured, and related to identifying **9.56** legal elements in the case.

- Contract: There appears to be a contractual relationship through the purchase of tickets. Does purchase through the internet make any difference?
- Wildlife park: Is there any special law relating to running a wildlife park?
- Children: Might there be special duties of care relating to the children?
- Chased by a dog: What duty of care is owed by the owner of the dog? What duty of care is owed by the owners of the park? Occupiers liability?

- Falls over scaffolding: Left by park owners or sub contractors? Do any special regulations apply to work carried out where the public have access?
- Child allowed to hold newly arrived monkey: Are there any regulations attached to contact between a child and a wild animal? Anything special about it being newly arrived?
- Child becomes ill: Can causation of the illness by the animal be shown?

9.57 Legal points may relate to matters other than the cause of action, for example:

- Remedies: Could the father get an apology from the wildlife park? Could he get them to accept that there should have been barriers and warning notices round the scaffolding?
- Procedure: Can the father claim damages on behalf of the children or do they need to be joined as claimants?
- Evidence: Does there need to be a specialist report on the child's illness and how it was caused?
- EU law: Are there EU regulations about importing wild animals and running wildlife parks?

The areas for research

9.58 The analysis of the case may initially indicate the possible relevance of a number of areas of law. Many of the areas identified may not in fact require research, or may only require limited research on defined or specific points.

- Contract: Questions relating to who the contract is between and what the express and implied terms of that contract are will probably be matters of evidence and factual analysis rather than legal research.
- Wildlife park: The facts do not require a thorough knowledge of the law relating to wildlife parks. The relevant matters are whether special duties attach to owning and running such a park.
- Children: A lawyer may well have a general knowledge of the law relating to duties to children.
- Chased by a dog: Again the lawyer may have sufficient general working knowledge of the general duties of care owed by dog owners and by occupiers. If not this area may require some research.
- Falls over scaffolding: Statutory regulations apply to many situations where work or industrial processes are carried on, so this needs to be checked.
- Child allowed to hold monkey: Do special duties attach to allowing access to wild animals? Any rules relating to importing wild animals?
- Child becomes ill: Causation of the illness would be a matter of medical evidence rather than law.
- Remedies: Damages is probably the only remedy, unless regulations require barriers and notices in such circumstances.
- Procedure: The lawyer will probably be aware that the children need to be joined as co claimants and to act through their litigation friend.
- Evidence: The lawyer is probably aware that there will have to be sufficient evidence of causation.
- EU law: Probably would not add anything to the above points but could be checked.

The questions for research

Areas where analysis shows that law might be relevant are thus narrowed to areas where **9.59** research is actually required. Before starting research, the next stage is to identify what specific questions need to be answered, as in most circumstances it will not be necessary to generally study a whole area of law. From the above the questions of research might be identified as:

- Wildlife parks: What are the duties of the owner of a wildlife park as regards the safety of visitors and the access of visitors to animals?
- Dog owners: Is the duty of care of dog owners to the general public and to children legally defined?
- Occupiers liability: Are occupiers liable for animals brought onto their property by third parties, and for materials brought onto their land by contractors? Are there any regulations relating to barriers and notices that should be put up?
- Importation of animals. Is there any obligation to put a monkey into quarantine or to restrict access to it when it is imported?

Having identified the questions, it may be useful to put them into order of importance as **9.60** regards the action. For example here the main action is likely to be against the park owner, so query if it will also be worth suing the dog owner and whether research into that question is worthwhile. It may also be useful to decide whether all the research needs to be done at the same time. Here it may be adequate to do sufficient research to be able to form a general view on the strength of the case against the park owner and then research further details later.

Key words and phrases

Once the questions for research are identified it will be necessary to decide how to look them **9.61** up. Most research is done using indexes or electronic searches, so there is skill in deciding what 'key' words or phrases should be looked up. A key word or phrase should ideally combine key facts in the case with potential legal relevance. Key words should emerge reasonably easily from the sort of analysis outlined above—here they might be 'Wildlife park—visitors', 'wildlife park—access to animals', 'Dog owners—duty of care', 'Occupiers liability—animals', 'Occupiers liability—contractors', and 'importation of animals—quarantine'.

Selecting sources

All the above stages are usefully completed, at least mentally, before going to the library **9.62** bookshelf or opening the search engine on the computer. A list of the legal questions that actually need answering and the potential key words and phrases to be used should be decided, and this might usefully be noted down. The final stage before starting research is to select the best source to use.

There will be a range of potential sources to answer any legal question. Sometimes a range of **9.63** sources should be considered in relation to a single question, if that question is particularly important to the case or particularly esoteric. Often the best approach will be to try to use the most appropriate source to answer each question, only going on to another source if the answer found is not adequate.

9.64   For the questions identified above, the index of a general work such as Halsbury's Law would probably be a good place to go to look for answers. Annotated statutes might be best used to check the Occupiers Liability points as they might direct the researcher on to relevant case law.

Using sources

9.65   It should only be necessary to read a whole chapter of a book if the researcher is totally unfamiliar with an area or has a lot of questions to answer. It should only be necessary to read a whole case if it is of significant importance to the action. Normally it is possible to speed-read to find relevant sections, or to check a summary or head note of a case to see whether it has relevant points.

9.66   A short note is best kept of each source used. Even if the source is not helpful a note that it has been checked may prevent one from wasting time going back to it later. If a source is relevant the precise relevance is usefully encapsulated. When you read something relevant it is easy to imagine that you will retain a clear memory of it. In fact that memory is likely to fade or be lost in a busy life, and much time (and possibly client money) can be wasted trying to trace something that you are sure you read somewhere. If in doubt as to whether something is relevant keep a note.

Keeping focussed

9.67   One of the most difficult things in research can be to keep focussed. Extra potential areas of research can emerge while reading, and it may be tempting to find out more general information about an area of law than is really needed. As the researcher becomes a little tired, and perhaps frustrated if a clear answer is not emerging, it can be all too easy to allow the research to become fuzzy.

9.68   It is important to return to the questions to be answered and to review progress on them. The legal questions to be answered may change as the research and the case develop, but this should be a matter of positive decision rather then drift. When the current questions are adequately answered the research is probably complete. It may be necessary to be strong minded to avoid being side tracked. It is normally more important to get sufficient depth of search round the particular questions in the case than to research widely.

I   PRESENTING FINDINGS

9.69   The goal of legal research is not to find relevant legal material but to answer the questions that analysis has shown to be directly relevant to the case. An adequate record needs to be kept of the questions and the answers so that they can be used as the case progresses.

Personal records of legal research

The record of research may be primarily for the personal use of the lawyer. In these circum-   **9.70**
stances the format of the record of the research will be individual, and may be limited to the
key sources used and notes of the relevant material found. The basics are that the material be
filed and be sufficiently clear for future use, with references that are sufficiently specific to
avoid any risk that the research will need to be repeated. The elements outlined below may
usefully be included even where the research is for personal purposes. Time spent on
research must also be adequately documented for costs purposes.

Preparing a formal note of legal research

One lawyer may carry out legal research for the use of another lawyer. In particular a trainee   **9.71**
solicitor or a pupil barrister may be asked to carry out research on a case for a senior lawyer.
In such a case the findings of the research will need to be more fully and clearly presented.
There is no single format to be used. Some firms may ask for a pro forma to be completed or
the individual may devise and use one. In any event there will need to be a clearly legible
and structured note that goes on file.

The key ingredients in summarising the findings of legal research are: **9.72**

- The name of the case should be clearly stated, and which party the lawyer acts for.
- The note should be clearly structured so that it is easy to read, with use of subheadings,
  bullet points etc where this may assist clarity.
- The legal questions that the research seeks to answer should be set out.
- The answer or most likely answer to each legal question should also be set out. Each
  answer should be as clear and concise as possible. If the answer is not clear then the main
  reservations should also be set out.
- All the statutes, cases, and books consulted and found to be relevant should be specific-
  ally referred to, with full references so that each can easily be found again.
- Only relevant authorities should be given, not everything looked up.
- Cite primary sources in preference to secondary sources if possible.
- Key points and references from each source should be set out, with specific references to
  paragraphs, and precise quotes where they may be helpful.
- If it is worth adding a photocopy or printout of a key source that could be done.
- Notes showing checks made to ensure that the law is up to date should be added.
- The date on which the research was carried out should appear, in case the research needs
  to be updated at a much later time.
- The name of the person who has carried out the research should appear.

Law that does not support the client's case needs to be recorded as well as law that supports   **9.73**
the client so that the case can be properly evaluated, and arguments to address the case for
the other side prepared if possible.

J   USING LAW TO GET RESULTS

9.74   Legal research is a means to an end for the practising lawyer and not an end in itself. The answers to legal research need to be fully and properly used in taking litigation forward.

Advising a client

9.75   The extent to which legal research is presented to the client in a meeting will vary from case to case. Some clients, especially business clients, may well wish to have details of relevant legal sources, with details and possibly with copies. The lawyer may need to present the outcome of research in a meeting, see 7.18–7.35.

9.76   Other clients may be more interested in advice than in the law itself. They will want to know what can be achieved and are not particularly concerned with the names of statutes and cases, save in that hearing key sources referred to may provide confidence that the lawyer is doing a thorough job.

Advising in writing

9.77   When writing a letter or opinion to a client there is again a need to adjust to meet different needs for different clients, see 11.26–11.32 and 11.58–11.87. However there is more justification for including references to statutes, cases, and textbooks in writing, so that the references are formally on file. It is the norm for a barrister to include legal sources in an opinion so that the solicitor can look them up. Key authorities may be quoted in writing to the other side where this may help to persuade them of the strength of your case.

Skeleton arguments

9.78   Skeleton arguments should include specific references to all authorities on which the party intends to rely as regards the matter in question. This will require a careful selection from the sources researched, see 21.66–21.77.

Constructing legal arguments for court

9.79   In court the judge and the lawyer representing the other side will understand the law, so no purpose is served in dealing with basic legal principles in detail. There is also rarely a point in setting out a trail of legal research, unless perhaps the Court of Appeal or the House of Lords is reviewing the law in an area. It is where an issue in the case turns on a point of law that the law should be fully argued, see 21.61–21.65 and 22.41–22.54.

10

DEFINING ISSUES TO STATE A CASE

A SEEING THE WOOD FOR THE TREES 10.02

B TAKING A SYSTEMATIC APPROACH........................... 10.07
  Facts... 10.08
  Law.. 10.09
  Procedure 10.10
  Evidence 10.11

C FOCUSSING ON ISSUES.................................... 10.12
  Matters that are not in dispute 10.13
  Identifying what is in dispute 10.16

D COMBINING LAW AND FACT TO DEFINE A CASE................ 10.19
  The legal elements of a cause of action 10.20
  The factual elements of a cause of action 10.25

E SELECTING CAUSES OF ACTION 10.28
  Assessing a cause of action............................... 10.28
  Using more than one cause of action....................... 10.30

F STATEMENTS OF CASE 10.33
  The role of statements of case 10.33
  General contents for a statement of case................... 10.36
  Checking a statement of case.............................. 10.41

G STYLE IN STATEMENTS OF CASE 10.44

H TACTICS IN STATING A CASE.............................. 10.48
  The burden of proof 10.49
  Pitching the case 10.50
  Matters of detail... 10.51
  Problems with information 10.52
  Dealing with an issue that does not have to be addressed 10.53
  Making positive statements................................ 10.54

I THE STATEMENT OF TRUTH 10.55

The definition of issues is at the heart of litigation. The purpose of the statements of case is to   **10.01** define the issues, and the issues as defined in the statements of case govern the admissibility of evidence and what is argued and decided at trial. Effective litigation depends on the accurate definition of issues.

A   SEEING THE WOOD FOR THE TREES

10.02 It is arguable that the key skill for the effective litigator is an ability to see the wood for the trees—that is the ability to identify what is most important in a case. This relates not just to identifying relevant legal areas, but to identifying the precise points that the case will turn on. In most cases only a few issues are really in serious dispute.

10.03 The reasons why it can be so difficult to identify and focus on what is most important and what is really at issue in a case include the following.

- It can be very difficult to tie together what the client wants to achieve with the information and instructions given by the client and with what is possible in legal terms.
- The amount of factual data that is available and potentially available, and the way that data accumulates over time rather than being available at one time can be confusing.
- It is not always easy to understand the circumstances behind a case, such as a business transaction or an accident, even with assistance from an expert.
- While it is not necessarily difficult to identify potential causes of action, it can be rather more difficult to identify accurately all the legal elements that need to be proved for each cause of action, and to see whether each can be made out on the information available.
- Although the basic stages in civil litigation are relatively straightforward, the number and variety of potential interim applications can be confusing.

10.04 For the lawyer with limited experience of practice, dealing with all the above at the same time can be very challenging and easily confusing. Not only is it difficult to see the wood for the trees, but with several areas of the case all moving forward together it may also be a question of trying to be a juggler keeping several balls in the air at the same time.

10.05 For the lawyer with limited experience, facts, law, potential causes of action, and procedural and evidential issues may seem to multiply outwards rather than move into focus. Legal research can appear to increase rather than decrease issues. Problems in tying down facts and evidence can make it seem difficult to reach any conclusions at all. There is a risk this will result in client meetings, advice and statements of case that are too vague and do not properly advance the client's case.

10.06 To work effectively the lawyer needs a disciplined and systematic approach to each case. Professional techniques should assist in identifying and keeping a focus on what really matters in a case. For books relevant to developing skills in legal analysis see 24.25.

B TAKING A SYSTEMATIC APPROACH

The main ingredients of bringing a case overlap significantly. They are best approached **10.07** separately initially to ensure a full deconstruction of the case, and the best possible under-standing of how the different elements of a case can best fit together.

Facts

Facts are most likely to be confusing if the case papers are read in an undiscriminating way **10.08** and the lawyer then either seeks far too much further information or fails to ask for the further information that is really necessary. The problems of dealing with facts are outlined and addressed in Chapter 8.

Law

The legal position is most likely to be confusing if the lawyer does not have a good working **10.09** knowledge of general principles of law (and so cannot take sensible decisions about possible cause of action), or if research is carried out by indiscriminate reading round the area rather than through a structured plan for research. A systematic approach to dealing with legal issues is outlined in 9.42–9.68.

Procedure

Procedure can appear confusing because of the many different ways in which a case can **10.10** progress, and the different types of application that can be made to forward each case. Chapter 4 provides an outline of the overall framework of civil litigation, and Chapter 16 identifies how interim procedures can be used appropriately.

Evidence

The requirements for evidence can seem complex because a number of the rules have signi- **10.11** ficant historical background, and there has not been a thorough review of evidence as there has been of civil procedure. However in practice the rules for evidence in a civil case are relatively straightforward compared to the rules for a criminal case, and it should not be difficult to select and present relevant evidence once there has been clear analysis of what actually needs to be proved, see 15.07–15.15 and 15.92–15.100.

C FOCUSSING ON ISSUES

The main threads through all the aspects of each case are the issues. If the issues are **10.12** adequately defined and progress in all areas focusses on the issues then the case should proceed properly.

Matters that are not in dispute

10.13   In all cases there are a number of things that are not actually in dispute between the parties. Indeed in many cases the major part of the factual framework for the case will at some stage or another be agreed. However fiercely fought a case is, it is likely that only a few matters will actually be the subject of the fierce dispute. For example, it may be agreed that a contract has been made, that it has particular terms, and that particular events happened—the only point in contention may be as to whether the events actually constituted a breach of the contract. Sometimes it may even be agreed that there has been a breach of contract, and the point at issue may be the causation of loss and damage claimed by the claimant. As a separate example, it is often agreed that an accident has happened—the dispute may centre on whether it was caused by the defendant. Sometimes liability for an accident is accepted in full and dispute relates only to the quantum of damages.

10.14   Matters that are not in dispute need to be identified and put on one side so that they do not cause unnecessary work or cloud the picture. If a matter is not in dispute it does not normally require evidence, legal research, or argument.

10.15   The fact that a major part of many cases may not be in dispute should not however give a false sense of security.

- Whether matters are in dispute may only emerge slowly. A defendant may well wish to defend a position initially rather than rush to make an admission or concession (see Chapter 17).
- There are great risks in accepting at too early a stage that a matter is not in dispute. Facts and law must be sufficiently examined to determine whether there is a dispute or not. The lawyer who does not dispute a point that should be disputed is at risk of a complaint or professional negligence claim.
- Many tactical considerations may need to be considered before it is accepted that a matter is not in dispute.

Identifying what is in dispute

10.16   The core of any case is what is actually in dispute. The real issues will not necessarily be immediately apparent, and may not be what a party initially says they are. A client may say that his or her main concern is getting full compensation for loss of profit to a business, and on analysis it may emerge that the key issue in the case is whether a particular term can be established as part of an oral contract. A client may say that his or her main concern is stopping a neighbour from keeping a noisy dog, but the key issues may relate to the interpretation of a single clause in an old contract and the interpretation of three negligence cases.

10.17   Key issues in dispute can be issues of law or of fact or of both. There may be one key issue in a case or several. The key issues in a case will not necessarily be the same for all the parties. The key issues may change as the case develops. All these points can lead to problems in identifying them.

10.18   It is suggested that a good system for identifying key issues is as follows.

- Keep a completely open mind about a case on first reading the documents and first meeting the client as the key issues may take some time to emerge.

- Gather as much factual information as is realistically possible that is relevant to the case and can be gathered at reasonable cost and within reasonable time.
- Take a provisional decision about the cause(s) of action that are most likely to be relevant and to identify as precisely as possible the elements that need to be shown to justify each cause of action.
- Take a provisional decision as to the remedies sought and the elements that will need to be shown to obtain each remedy.
- Check whether each of the elements for the cause(s) of action and the remedies can be shown from the existing factual information (and that there is likely to be admissible evidence to prove them should the need arise).
- Put the cause(s) of action and the remedies sought to the potential defendant and get the defendant's reaction.
- The key issues in dispute will be the legal and factual elements needed to show the cause(s) of action and the remedy, save for those elements that the defendant admits.
- If it proves necessary to start a formal litigation process with a claim form then the issues in dispute will be formally defined by the statements of case, see 10.34–10.44.

D   COMBINING LAW AND FACT TO DEFINE A CASE

Having been analysed separately, law and fact must be integrated to define potential causes   **10.19** of action. The elements of a cause of action are defined by law, but showing that those elements exist in a particular case is a matter of fact and evidence.

The legal elements of a cause of action

The elements that are required to justify a specific cause of action are derived from the basic   **10.20** principles of common law or statute. A short list of relevant elements can be compiled for any cause of action. A few simple examples are given below.

- In a breach of contract case the main elements are:
  — the making of a valid contract
  — consideration
  — express terms of contract
  — implied terms of contract
  — performance of contract
  — breaches of contract.
- In a misrepresentation case the main elements are:
  — the representations made
  — that they were false
  — that they induced the contract
  — that they were intended to induce the contract
  — losses arising from the misrepresentation.
- In a basic tort case the main elements are:
  — the existence of duty of care
  — nature of duty of care

— breach of duty of care
— led to loss and damage.

10.21 The analysis of the facts of a case should indicate which causes of action may be relevant. To ensure that a cause of action can be used it is necessary to check that all the elements of the cause of action can be shown from the facts.

10.22 In creating a full case other legal elements may need to be added, such as the elements required to lead to a remedy, such as causation, and elements that show vital legal links such as agency or vicarious liability. If these are added to the examples above the relevant legal elements for a whole case might be:

- Elements for a breach of contract action:
  — the making of a valid contract
  — agency
  — express terms of contract
  — implied terms of contract
  — performance of contract
  — breaches of contract
  — losses arising from the breach
  — causation of loss
  — foreseeability of loss.
- Elements for a misrepresentation action:
  — the representations made
  — that they were false
  — that they induced the contract
  — that they were intended to induce the contract
  — losses arising from the misrepresentation
  — causation of loss
  — foreseeability of loss.
- Elements for a negligence action:
  — existence of duty of care
  — nature of duty of care
  — vicarious liability
  — breach of duty of care
  — general damages for pain and suffering
  — special damages for losses to date
  — ongoing future loss.

10.23 It is important for a lawyer to have a clear idea of the elements of the potential causes of action that are likely to arise in the area in which the lawyer practices. This is not to underestimate the importance of the more detailed knowledge of law that will be required to develop arguments about legal points that are in issue, but for basic analysis of issues it is knowledge of basic elements of causes of action that matters.

10.24 It is a complaint of firms and chambers that those joining them tend to lack the facility to apply law to identify the key elements for a cause of action. There are many possible reasons for this—study of tort and contract tends to come relatively early in a law degree and may not be well remembered some years later, and the study of academic law will move far beyond basic principle so that the student may recall specific issues rather than basic principle. Those who have studied law as a one year postgraduate course rather than as a first degree may find it easier to identify the key elements in a cause of action. In any event, it is important to be able to spot key elements as outlined in 10.20–10.22.

The factual elements of a cause of action

The structured approach, that will become automatic with experience, is as follows. **10.25**

- Review the facts of the case to identify what causes of action may exist and what remedies may be sought.
- Identify the elements of each cause of action that may arise, as illustrated in 10.20.
- Identify the elements of each remedy sought, including causation and foreseeability.
- Identify other elements that may be relevant to putting a full case together, including legal personality, agency etc, as illustrated in 10.22.
- Systematically analyse the facts and the evidence relating to each element identified.
- Consider whether further evidence might be sought to fill any gaps.
- Consider where the other side are most likely to contest the facts and the evidence.
- If any elements of a cause of action or of a remedy cannot be shown in the facts then that cause of action cannot be brought. If all the elements of a cause of action can be shown in the facts then that cause of action can potentially be brought.
- The statement of case is a statement of the facts that show the elements of a cause of action and the remedies sought. This is dealt with more fully below and in Chapter 12.

The sort of analysis proposed in 10.25 can be carried out using a chart. For example (based **10.26** on 10.22)

Legal elements identified	Facts in this case	Evidence to support client	Evidence for other side or not yet available	Definition of any issue between the parties
Making of contract				
Agency				
Express terms				
Implied terms				
Performance				
Breaches				
Loss/damage				
Causation of loss				
Foreseeability of loss				

10.27 It may be helpful to remember that the judge will effectively carry out a similar analysis when judging a case. A party will succeed with a cause of action if that party can prove to the judge that all the elements for that cause of action exist. A party will be granted a remedy if all the elements leading to that remedy can be proved.

E   SELECTING CAUSES OF ACTION

Assessing a cause of action

10.28 Systematic analysis should lead to decisions as to what cause(s) of action might be available in a case.

- Analysis of fact should suggest what causes of action may be relevant.
- Analysis of the legal elements of each potential cause of action should be matched against the facts to see if all the relevant elements can be shown.

10.29 If the facts and the legal elements show that there is a potential cause of action then the strength of the cause of action should be tested before it is actually decided to bring the case.

- The strength of the case will partly depend on the strength of that evidence, including how much evidence there is and how credible it is.
- The strength of the case will also depend on what is known of how much evidence the other side has and how credible that evidence is.
- The strength of the case will also depend on how clear the law is relating to the legal elements.
- The likelihood of recovering a particular remedy will depend on the strength of the law and evidence to support the elements of that remedy.
- The existence and strength of any defence will also be part of assessing the strength of the cause of action, see Chapter 17.

Using more than one cause of action

10.30 Sometimes there will be only one possible cause of action and the lawyer will advise on the chances of success of that. Sometimes there may be a choice of causes of action, for example because duties in contract and tort overlap. In principle causes of action can be joined and commenced with the issue of one claim form so long as they arise from the same or similar facts and can conveniently be tried together.

10.31 In deciding whether to use more than one possible cause of action the following principles may be of assistance:

- If one potential cause of action has a good chance of success there is probably little to be gained in adding a weaker cause of action if it will just make statements of case more complex and add to costs.
- If two potential causes of action turn on very similar facts and neither is significantly stronger than the other, it is probably worth bringing both causes of action. Drafting will not be made much more complex, and if there is any difficulty with one cause of action the other might succeed.

- There may be tactical advantages in bringing more than one cause of action if both are properly sustainable.
- If the facts of the case are complex, so that there would be significant problems in trying to draft statements of case and provide evidence for more than one cause of action there may be merit in relying only on the strongest cause of action.
- Different causes of action may provide different remedies.
- There will rarely be a case where more than three causes of action can usefully be joined.
- If the relative strengths of causes of action may be resolved with more information, it is probably best to get that information before starting an action.
- If a limitation period is about to expire, it may be best to include a cause of action about which there is any doubt, and then discontinue the action if it does turn out to be weak.

In identifying causes of action decisions will also have to be taken as to who should sue **10.32** whom. There may be only one potential claimant and one potential defendant, but legal personality must be correctly identified. If there is a choice of potential parties then a careful selection must be made. This area is dealt with at 13.15–13.48.

F STATEMENTS OF CASE

The role of statements of case

A statement of case is a summary of facts of the case, insofar as they show the legal elements **10.33** required for a case to succeed. Clear and complete statements of case are central to effective litigation. They demonstrate that a party has prepared a case properly, assist other parties in preparing their case, and should be of great assistance to the judge in understanding the case. The pattern of statements of case used to define the issues in the case is set out at 4.75–4.77.

The statement of case involves encapsulating a case for the other side and for the court. A **10.34** legal opinion or a client meeting are privileged consultations regarding the case where all options need to be fully explored and discussed; a general investigation of fact and law is a private matter for the lawyer and client. The statement of case is exchanged with other parties and with the court and it sets out only the results of decisions as to who should be sued and for what. The statement of case is a very refined document that should set out only the key elements of the case being alleged, and nothing that is general background.

In the past, court documents have been characterised by complexity of structure and lan- **10.35** guage. It is one of the great reforms in litigation in recent years, as underlined by the CPR (CPR Part 16 Statements of Case and PD 16 Statements of Case), that statements of case now focus on:

- a clear and concise summary of a case;
- a content that consists largely or entirely of factual allegations, based on the legal elements of the party's case;
- factual allegations structured to show that all the legal elements for a particular cause of action are fulfilled;
- a document written in plain English;

- providing information to the other side of the case against them;
- ensuring that time and costs are not wasted;
- ensuring that surprise at trial is avoided.

The drafting of a particulars of claim is dealt with at 12.77–12.112. The drafting of a defence is dealt with at 17.47–17.100.

General contents for a statement of case

10.36   There is no single right correct way to state any case—a good statement of case will be drafted with a clear understanding of the case and of the role and purpose of the document.

10.37   A statement of case should normally include:

- a clear identification of parties and cause(s) of action;
- a summary of the facts that provide the legal elements of the cause of action in the case;
- sufficient particulars for parts of the case that might otherwise be vague, such as an allegation of negligence;
- a clear identification of the remedies sought;
- facts supporting each remedy, including the heads of loss and damage suffered, facts showing how the loss and damage arose from the cause of action alleged, and facts to assist in the calculation of damages payable.

10.38   A statement of case should not normally include:

- immaterial facts;
- evidence that is not necessarily involved in setting out the key facts of the case;
- law and matters presumed by law, save where the law has a special relevance, such as a statutory defence;
- legal argument.

10.39   Good style for a statement of case will normally involve:

- a clear structure, so that the elements of the case are set out in a logical order that is easy to follow and understand;
- reasonably short numbered paragraphs, with each paragraph focussing on a separate issue;
- a clear sentence structure within paragraphs, with sentences that are normally short rather than long, and with each sentence making a separate point;
- the use of clear, plain English;
- accurate and precise use of vocabulary, including appropriate use of specialist and technical words or phrases with an accepted meaning where appropriate;
- the use of schedules and appendices to deal with long or detailed material.

10.40   The lawyer settling a statement of case has responsibilities to the court as well as to the client. He or she may not make any allegation unsupported by the client. A barrister may not make any allegation unsupported by instructions (Code of Conduct, rule 606). In particular, there is a special rule for fraud, which, as a quasi-criminal allegation, should never be pleaded in a civil case unless the barrister has clear instructions to plead fraud, and has reasonably credible material which as it stands establishes a *prima facie* case of fraud. There may be a penalty in costs if an allegation of fraud is made but does not succeed.

Checking a statement of case

A statement of case needs to be based on clear and justifiable decisions, and should be **10.41** checked carefully before it is sent out. Complete accuracy in a statement of case is important because:

- the statement of case sets out the case to the other parties and to the court;
- the relevance and admissibility of evidence will be judged by reference to the statement of case;
- the more clearly the issues are set out the best chance there is of saving costs;
- although amendment may be possible later, it may only be allowed if the party amending pays all resulting costs;
- some errors can be fatal, if for example a limitation period expires and amendment to a cause of action or a party is no longer possible.

Having drafted a statement of case there is merit in leaving it for a little while, and then **10.42** going back to it when the mind is fresh to check that it makes sense and says all the things that it should say. This is a good test to see whether points have been set out well and clearly.

A second test is to read the statement of case from the viewpoint of the other side. The side **10.43** receiving the statement of case will not have background information to go with it, so the statement of case must make sense as it stands without omission and without additional information that should not be included. This test should also provide tactical insight into how the other side may react to the document when they receive it.

G STYLE IN STATEMENTS OF CASE

It was once thought that legal documents with long words and complex sentence construc- **10.44** tions were more impressive, and that antiquated phrases had merit because long use had given them particular meanings. The days of obscure legal documents are now past, and one can only agree with Megarry VC in the case of *Re Brickman's Settlement* [1982] 1 All ER 336 in saying 'brevity, clarity and simplicity are the hallmarks of the skilled pleader'.

The emphasis following the Woolf reforms is on clarity and plain English in statements of **10.45** case, though not all precedent sources have yet been fully revised, and some need to be approached with some care. The emphasis on clarity and plain English does not mean that drafting statements of case has become easier. More specific guidance on style in statements of case is provided at 12.06–12.76. More guidance on legal writing is provided at 11.03–11.23.

In building skill in drafting statements of case it can be useful to read a number of different **10.46** examples from a critical point of view. This will build familiarity with appropriate language, and the variations in structure and content that may suit different cases. It is useful to consider what elements there are in each statement of case and why they are there. It may also be possible to identify better or clearer ways of drafting specific points.

10.47 It is now common for statements of case to be stored electronically, both as pro formas and as samples. These may be used as a resource for a firm, a set of chambers, or an individual lawyer. This can be very useful, but it should go without saying that each statement of case should be drafted with great care to fit the facts of the individual case.

H TACTICS IN STATING A CASE

10.48 In the past stating a case involved tactical considerations. A lawyer taking a combative approach might choose for example to set out a case vaguely until forced to provide more detail. Personal style and tactics have become less important with the emphasis on clarity and on placing one's cards on the table in litigation. There are however still some areas where there are choices for personal style and for the conduct of the case.

The burden of proof

10.49 The party which alleges something in a statement of case carries the burden of proving it. This may have tactical consequences if there is any choice as to which side might raise an issue, or the detail in which an issue might be dealt with.

Pitching the case

10.50 Factual allegations can be put in a variety of ways. The lawyer should normally choose phraseology that is as favourable as possible for the client, while being justified by the facts and evidence available. There is a careful line to be drawn between stating a case as highly as possible without being open to attack at trial for not being able to prove what is stated. Overstatements, or particular uses of words, may sometimes antagonise an opponent making settlement more unlikely.

Matters of detail

10.51 Some areas of a case must be set out in detail, such as particulars of breach or negligence. Having said this, there is often a choice as to quite how much detail to give. Giving limited particulars may be appropriate where the case and the evidence is strong. There may, however, be advantages in giving fuller particulars, where this may make the case appear widely based.

Problems with information

10.52 If there is insufficient factual information or evidence on a key element of the case then normally the case should not proceed at all, but sometimes it is possible to draft a little widely. If for example the exact date when a contract was made is not known it is possible to say it happened 'on or about' a certain date, or between one date and another. If the exact location or cause of an accident is not known then one can only be as precise as possible, provided sufficient information is given to found a cause of action.

Dealing with an issue that does not have to be addressed

Each statement of case only needs to deal with facts the party needs to allege, or anything **10.53** raised in response to a statement of case of the other side. There are only minor exceptions to this, where, for example, it is clear on the face of the pleading that the limitation period should have expired and the statement of case needs to include reasons why the action should go ahead. It may be tempting to anticipate the case for the other side and to try to deal with it in advance. It will rarely be good policy to put something into a statement of case in anticipation of what the other side will argue, as it may alert the other side to an argument they had not thought of, or may become confusing if they do not run their case as anticipated.

Making positive statements

Some allegations can be made in a positive or negative way (for example 'the defendant did X' **10.54** might be an alternative to 'the defendant did not do Z'). Positive allegations are normally to be preferred as negative allegations can be difficult to prove, and negative pleading can become ambiguous, especially if a double negative arises from the sentence construction used.

I THE STATEMENT OF TRUTH

The purpose of a statement of case is to set out factual allegations. Prior to the CPR it was the **10.55** normal rule that evidence should not be included. This was quite logical on the basis that the purpose of the statement of case was to set out allegations—proof was a matter for trial and the statement of case was at risk of becoming too long and complex if evidence was included.

The Civil Procedure Rules 1998 have relaxed the rule so that detail which is technically **10.56** evidence can be included. This can be an advantage, particularly in simpler cases, but it is not an excuse for inaccurate or verbose drafting.

The Civil Procedure Rules 1998 also brought in a new provision that every case must be **10.57** verified by a statement of truth, CPR r 22.1. This statement is normally added at the end of the statement of case and, as relevant, the wording is 'I believe/the claimant believes/the defendant believes that the facts stated in this claim form/particulars of claim/defence are true'. This should be signed by the party whose statement it is, or by the party's legal representative, see CPR Part 22 Statements of truth and PD 22 Statements of truth.

If the statement of truth is signed by the client, the lawyer must explain to the client that the **10.58** client must read the statement of case and must only sign it if the client believes all the allegations made to be true. If a statement of case is drafted by a barrister, that barrister must take care that only allegations that are set out in the papers in the brief are included, and that any other allegations are checked with the client by the solicitor, so that the statement of truth can be properly signed.

If a person makes or causes to be made a false allegation verified by a statement of **10.59** truth without honest belief in its truth, the Attorney General (or a party with the permission of the court) may bring proceedings for contempt of court. This could result in a fine or imprisonment. In *Kabushiki Kaisha Computer Entertainment v Ball* (2004) EWHA 1984 there was held to be contempt of court where a defendant signed a statement of truth on a witness statement saying that he had ceased trading in a type of computer chip—this was not true but he had convinced himself the statement was a legitimate way to defend the action!

10.60 As a statement of case is essentially a summary of allegations of fact, the effect of the statement of truth is to turn the document into a form of evidence. This can be used for example in support of an interim application. The statement of truth emphasises that the statement of case should be a clear summary of provable factual allegations.

11

SKILLS IN LEGAL WRITING

A PROFESSIONAL LEGAL WRITING 11.03

B PURPOSE AND AUDIENCE 11.07
A document written to the client 11.08
A document sent by one lawyer to another when both are on
the same side 11.09
A document sent from lawyers on one side to lawyers on the
other side. 11.10
A document sent to the court 11.11
Communications with experts and other potential witnesses. . . 11.12

C CONTENT AND STRUCTURE 11.13

D PROFESSIONAL USE OF LANGUAGE 11.16
The best possible English 11.17
Terminology 11.18
Figures 11.21
References to legal sources 11.22
The role of language other than English 11.23

E NOTES. 11.24

F WRITING LETTERS 11.26
Sample letters 11.30

G THE ROLE OF OPINIONS 11.33
The nature of an opinion 11.33
Types of opinion related to litigation. 11.39

H PREPARING TO WRITE AN OPINION 11.54

I THE FORMAT AND STRUCTURE OF AN OPINION 11.58
Conventions for writing an opinion 11.58
General framework for an opinion in a civil case. 11.60

J THE CONTENTS OF AN OPINION 11.63
Summarising the facts of the case. 11.65
Summarising the advice sought 11.67
The summary of advice. 11.68

Cause(s) of action 11.71
Defences 11.77
Remedies... 11.79
Facts and evidence... 11.81
Procedural matters... 11.83
Practical points... 11.87

K THE IMPORTANCE OF CLEAR CONCLUSIONS AND ADVICE 11.88

KEY DOCUMENTS

> Lawyers: people who write a 10,000 word document and call it a brief.
>
> Franz Kafka

11.01 Writing is an increasingly important key skill for the effective litigator. While there is still a focus on oral advocacy at trial, written advocacy has become increasingly important with the focus on defining issues in the statements of case, and the increasing use of skeleton arguments.

11.02 In addition to the need for effective writing in documents to be used in court, there is the need to write clearly in opinions and letters that communicate clearly with the client, or as appropriate with the other side or with the court and other lawyers.

A PROFESSIONAL LEGAL WRITING

11.03 Anyone who qualifies as a lawyer should be able to write to a reasonably good standard. However the skills and style that are appropriate for a university essay or a dissertation are not necessarily appropriate for writing to a client or to a court. The individual seeking to become an effective litigator will need to review his or her personal writing style. Although there is no need to write in a closely prescribed 'lawyer' style, there is a need to write legal documents at a professional standard to meet professional objectives.

11.04 The criteria for professional legal writing, which all need to be fulfilled to a high standard, are generally that the document:

- is written for a specific purpose;
- is appropriately written for the intended audience;
- has the necessary content to serve its purpose;
- is well structured;
- is clear and concise;
- is as easy as possible for the person to whom it is sent to understand;
- is accurate;
- has correct grammar, punctuation, and spelling to assist clarity;
- is written in good quality plain English and is easily comprehensible;
- is relevant, has clear objectives, and reaches clear conclusions.

Most lawyers will develop an individual style in legal writing. Some prefer a very formal style **11.05** while others are more comfortable with something a little less formal. This is as natural as having slightly different styles in advocacy. There is no 'right' style for a letter or an opinion, provided the contents are right and the writing meets the criteria in 11.04.

While building a personal style as a lawyer there is merit in reading critically other docu- **11.06** ments produced by lawyers to identify good practice. All documents that come from another lawyer or from an opponent can be used for this purpose. Each document read should be considered in the light of whether it satisfies the criteria in 11.04. There is also merit in re-reading one's own documents with a critical eye, both to assess them objectively, and to assess them from the point of view of the client or the court. For books relevant to developing skills in legal writing see 24.24

B PURPOSE AND AUDIENCE

Each piece of legal writing is written for a specific purpose and has a specific audience. For **11.07** any legal writing the first question is to be clear about the purpose and the objectives of what is to be written. The second question is to determine the audience to whom the document is written and the implications of writing to that audience. Sometimes a document will be written to more than one audience.

A document written to the client

This might be a letter from a solicitor or an opinion from the barrister. Communications **11.08** with the client are likely to be privileged if litigation is contemplated and can therefore be reasonably open. Any document written to the client needs to be sensitive to the client's position and objectives. It should be written in a way the individual client can understand, and it should contain clear information and advice. For a sample letter to a client see 11.30.

A document sent by one lawyer to another when both are on the same side

The writing of instructions from a solicitor to a barrister is dealt with at 2.41–2.44. The **11.09** writing of an opinion is dealt with below. Again such communications are likely to be privileged if litigation is contemplated, but it must be remembered that the client might see the document.

A document sent from lawyers on one side to lawyers on the other side

This might be in the form of a letter dealing with the case before action or dealing with a **11.10** procedural step (see 11.31) or it might take the form of a formal statement of case served on one party by the other (see Chapter 12). Any communication with the other side needs to have clear objectives and to be carefully judged and expressed. Communications between parties are not privileged from use in court unless they are expressed to be and are in fact 'without prejudice', see 20.44–20.50.

A document sent to the court

11.11   The statements of case will be issued at court. There will need to be other communications with the court relating to the completion of questionnaires. There may be communications about the progress of the case, for example to arrange interim hearings, and these must be carefully handled so that each side maintains a proper relationship with the court. The parties should keep the court properly informed of progress in the case. The parties cannot alter dates such as trial or pre-trial reviews without the permission of the court.

Communications with experts and other potential witnesses

11.12   An expert may need to be instructed, see 15.140–15.178, and for a sample letter of instruction see 11.32. Other communications with witnesses are likely to relate to getting an informal proof, turning it into a formal witness statement or affidavit, or arrangements for trial. In the past one might have said that such communications made when litigation was contemplated would be privileged, but the situation is now not so clear, see 3.61–3.76. Communications with witnesses should be objective so as not to breach rules of professional conduct.

C   CONTENT AND STRUCTURE

> How do you know a wordprocessor belongs to a lawyer?
> Whatever font you choose, everything comes out in fine print.

11.13   The legal and factual content of any piece of legal writing need to be carefully selected. Much will depend on the objectives of the written document and the audience for it, see 11.07–11.12.

11.14   As regards content, appropriate criteria are as follows.

- Is the content carefully chosen to meet the objectives of the document?
- Is the content carefully chosen for the person to whom the document is sent?
- Is all the relevant material included?
- Has all irrelevant material been left out?

11.15   The structure of a document is crucial to clarity, understanding, and ease of use. Appropriate criteria are as follows.

- Is the structure of the document clear so that it is easy to find material on different topics?
- Is the document reasonable easy to read?
- Is the document well laid out on the page?
- Is the document as clear as it could be?
- Does the document offer advice or reach conclusions that are easy to find?
- Have sub-headings been used to make the document easier to read and understand?
- Are all paragraphs reasonably short?
- Is the material divided into paragraphs that each clearly deal with a separate matter?

D   PROFESSIONAL USE OF LANGUAGE

There has been a long tradition of legal documents being written in language that is impos-   **11.16**
ing rather than easily comprehensible. When the Common Law was first being formed,
Latin and Norman French were used for legal documents as the language of the rulers rather
than of the people. In Victorian times there was a preference for long words and complex
constructions. The move to the use of plain English in litigation has only really taken place
over the last few decades.

The best possible English

The main purpose of this move is to assist comprehensibility and clarity. The standard of the   **11.17**
English that is used should be very high. As regards the vocabulary to be used, there is no
magic in long words. As far as possible everything should be expressed so that the client as
well as the lawyers can understand it. Colloquial expressions and abbreviations should be
avoided.

Terminology

Terminology must be carefully chosen to be as accurate as possible. It should also be used   **11.18**
consistently, even if this makes the document appear repetitive. For example if a document
is once referred to as 'the contract' it should always be referred to as 'the contract'.

It is normal to refer to the solicitors as 'instructing solicitors'. The person that the lawyer is   **11.19**
representing is referred to as 'the client' or perhaps by name as 'Mr X' or 'Mrs X', and when
referring to the case against the client it is normal to say 'the other side', or again to use the
name 'Mr Y' or 'Mrs Y'. Once the action has begun it is acceptable to refer to the parties as
'the claimant' and 'the defendant' as appropriate, though in an interim application it is less
confusing to refer to 'the applicant' and 'the respondent'.

Technical, medical, and other expert terminology that is relevant to a case must be used   **11.20**
where relevant and used accurately. The lawyer may at the start of the case know little about
a particular technical procedure, but it is a necessary part of preparing the case to become
familiar with and use appropriate terminology. Accurate terminology has to be used in
statements of case, in witness statements, and in oral evidence, and it should equally be used
in letters and opinions. There are various ways of becoming familiar with appropriate
terminology. Lawyers doing personal injury cases will use medical dictionaries. Where an
expert is providing evidence in a case the lawyer can seek help from the expert through a
meeting or suggestions for helpful reading. The client may be able to help if the client has
knowledge of the area of expertise in question.

Figures

Figures are as important as words. Figures for damages and costs permeate most litigation   **11.21**
and they must be dealt with using the same thoroughness and accuracy used when dealing
with words. Figures should be dealt with where relevant in any communication. Dates,

sums, and other numbers should be expressed in figures and not in words, for example, a sum of money should be '£10,000' and a date should be '10 June 2005'.

References to legal sources

11.22 References to legal authorities should always be made accurately so that the court or a lawyer can check them. The actual wording of a statute, case, or legal document should be referred to and quoted where it is directly relevant to the issues in the case.

The role of language other than English

11.23 In stressing the use of plain English, there is a wider question. Increasingly lawyers practicing in England are dealing with clients and with other lawyers for whom English is not the first language. The growing international dimension means that a lawyer will often deal with lawyers and clients for whom English is not the first language. Proper provision must always be made for the use of interpreters and translations. The fact that a language other than English is used by a client or lawyer should not be a reason for less clarity or information in communication.

E   NOTES

11.24 In effective legal practice, good note taking ranks alongside the writing of other legal documents. The taking and storing of good notes can be an important part of the records of the case, not only for progressing the case itself, but also for documenting the progress of the case should there be queries about the costs or the conduct of the lawyer. In a busy working life detail can easily be forgotten or recalled inaccurately, so a good note is of value. It is easy to take an inadequate note and then to have to check information again, which is a waste of time and costs.

11.25 The occasions when it is important to take good notes include:

- During a meeting with the client—so that the instructions given by the client and the evidence that the client may be able to give are recorded.
- During a telephone conversation with the client or with another lawyer—so that the contents of the conversation are properly recorded in the file.
- When reading a brief—to avoid having to read the brief repeatedly to check information.
- While listening to a witness in court—so as to be able to quote what the witness said when cross examining the witness or when making a closing speech.
- While listening to a judgment—so as to be able to advise the client immediately whether there is a basis for appeal, and so as to be able to draft grounds of appeal quickly if instructed to appeal.

F WRITING LETTERS

The writing of letters will normally be a matter for the solicitor. It is beyond the scope of this **11.26** book to deal with letter writing in detail, but some key points may usefully be made. A number of the points about the characteristics of a good opinion will also apply to effective letters. A letter may usefully be used to record the content of an important telephone conversation.

Letters to the client. **11.27**

- Letters to the client must incorporate appropriate matters of client care, including information about the progress of the case and costs.
- Letters to the client will normally be privileged from disclosure if litigation is contemplated and can therefore be reasonably open, see 3.61–3.76.
- Thought should be given to ensuring that each letter to a client makes coherent sense in terms of what the client knows of the case. The client will not necessarily know all that the lawyer knows.
- Any letter written to the client should be clear about the context in which the letter is written, what information is being given to the client, and any actions that the client is expected to take.

Letters to the other side. **11.28**

- Letters to the other side will normally be disclosable and can be used at trial, unless they are headed 'Without prejudice as to costs' and include a genuine offer to settle the case. On the importance of wording in such a case, see 20.44–20.50.
- A letter to the other side may be used to seek information or admissions.
- The content of any letter to the other side should be carefully considered. It should only include information and admissions where this is required, for example under a pre-action protocol, or where this is strategically useful and it is not a difficulty that the letter is used in court.
- Even if there is no full admission, an acknowledgement of a state of affairs may have implications, for example an acknowledgment of a debt can be relevant to the limitation period for recovery of the debt.
- Any letter to the other side should be judged in terms of its overall effect in advancing the case. Communications with the other side should in broad terms follow the principles in the overriding objective, but there may also be tactical considerations.
- Particular care must be taken where it is hoped that there will be a settlement of the case, but where such an outcome is not guaranteed.

Letters to the court. **11.29**

- Communications with the court will tend to be formal letters related to the progress of the case, for example relating to the completion of questionnaires.
- There may be communications about special steps in the case, for example to arrange interim hearings, and these must be carefully handled so that each side maintains a proper relationship with the court.

- The parties cannot alter dates such as trial or pre-trial reviews without the permission of the court.
- The court should be kept properly informed if for example a case is settled.

Sample letters

11.30   Client care letter (appropriate for an accident case)

Hemmings & Condell, Solicitors
Globe House, New Place, Stratford Upon Avon

Mr K. Lear,
1, The Heath,
Stratford Upon Avon

1 April 2005

Dear Mr Lear,

Your accident claim

You have instructed this firm to pursue your claim for damages in relation to the accident you suffered on 24 December 2004. I am writing to confirm the basis on which the firm will act. I am Tom Foole an assistant solicitor in this firm and I will be dealing with your case.

At this stage I can only provide a general estimate of what it will cost for us to act for you. It is too early for me to be able to assess the strength of your case clearly, and we do not yet know how strongly your claim will be resisted by the defendant. The majority of claims are settled without going as far as a trial, and it may be that we can settle the case without even starting formal proceedings.

The hourly rate for my work on your case will be £120 per hour. This will be the rate charged for time spent meeting you and witnesses, preparing documents, or going to court. Short matters such as dealing with telephone calls are charged on the basis of 6 minute units (1/10 of an hour). I would estimate that your case will take about 30 hours of work, but it may be more if the case is strongly defended or there are difficulties in gathering evidence. I will let you know if it is necessary for me to re-estimate the time the case will take.

The following steps may be necessary to pursue your claim:

Preparation of a written statement from you; a detailed letter of claim to the defendant; correspondence with the defendant's solicitors and insurers; obtaining a medical report; obtaining details of your financial losses; issuing court proceedings; preparing a schedule of your financial losses; completing documents for the court; considering documents served by the defendant's solicitors; disclosing relevant documents; taking statements from other witnesses; dealing with any request for a medical examination of you; possible attendance at a case management conference; preparing papers for trial; arranging for a barrister to represent you at trial; attending trial with you; dealing with the recovery of damages and costs.

In addition to my charges there will be other disbursements. These are likely to include the barrister's fee, court fees, the cost of a medical report, and the cost of a medical consultant attending trial.

I would expect that you will recover compensation and a contribution to your costs from the defendant. You will be liable to pay this firm's costs and the disbursements whatever the outcome of the case is. If you get a contribution to your costs from the defendant that should cover most of these costs, but I have to warn you that there may be a shortfall between the costs you incur and the costs the defendant has to pay.

I must advise you that if you bring proceedings and the claim does not succeed the court is likely to order you to pay the defendant's costs. As I explained to you, it is possible to take out insurance to cover costs, but you did not wish to do this. We also discussed the possibility of a conditional fee arrangement. You were going to consider this, and you might particularly wish to consider it if the case is not settled at an early stage and it is necessary to issue proceedings. I advised you that support from the Community Legal Service is not available for this case.

We will try to deal with your case efficiently and reasonably quickly. Please raise any concerns about the case with me. If you are not satisfied with my response the firm has a complaints procedure. You can get a copy of this from our receptionist, or see it on the firm's website.

When you have read this letter please sign one copy and return it to me to show that you have read and understood it. If you have queries about this letter or about your claim please telephone me or make an appointment to see me.

Yours sincerely

Letter of claim (based on the guidance of pre-action protocols) **11.31**

Hemmings & Condell, Solicitors
Globe House, New Place, Stratford Upon Avon

1 April 2005

Dear Mr Edmund,

Our client: Mr King Lear
Our Client's address: 1, The Heath, Stratford upon Avon
Our client's employer: Britannia Horticulture, Back Lane, Stratford upon Avon

We are instructed by Mr Lear to claim damages in connection with a road traffic accident on 24 December 2004 on the A20 near Dover, Kent.

Please confirm the identity of your insurers. Please note that the insurers will need to see this letter as soon as possible, and it may affect your insurance cover and/or the conduct of any subsequent legal proceedings if you do not send this letter to them.

The circumstances of the accident were that our client was travelling east along the A20 on his motorcycle. You were driving west along the road in a car the registration number of which was X FEM 111. In overtaking a lorry you drove onto our client's side of the road and forced him off the road, with the result that he ran into a ditch and hit a tree.

The reason why we are alleging you were at fault is that you were driving fast, were overtaking another vehicle when it was unsafe to do so, that you failed to see or to make proper allowance for the safety of our client, and that you failed to pull back onto your side of the road so as to allow our client to drive safely on his side of the road.

A description of our client's injuries is as follows:

Fractured left leg

Fractured left arm

Cuts abrasions and bruises

Our client received treatment for his injuries at Dover General Hospital.

Mr Lear is employed as a gardener and has had to take 3 months off work following the accident. His approximate net weekly income is £180.

We are obtaining a police accident report and will let you have a copy of this upon your undertaking to pay half the fee.

At this stage of our enquiries we would expect the documents contained in Section A (*insert relevant parts of standard disclosure list*) to be relevant to this action.

A copy of this letter is enclosed for you to send to your insurers. We expect an acknowledgement of this letter within 21 days by yourself or you insurers.

Yours faithfully,

11.32 Letter to instruct an expert (based on the guidance of pre-action protocols)

Hemmings & Condell, Solicitors
Globe House, New Place, Stratford Upon Avon

Dr Katherina Baptista
Padua Row
Stratford upon Avon

1 April 2005

Dear Dr Baptista,

Our client:	Mr King Lear
Our client's address:	1, The Heath, Stratford upon Avon
Date of birth:	1 January 1940
Telephone number:	01234 567890
Date of accident:	24 December 2004

We are acting for the above named in connection with injuries he received in an accident which occurred on the above date. The main injuries appear to have been a fractured left leg, a fractured left arm, cuts, abrasions, and bruises.

We should be obliged if you would examine our client and let us have a full and detailed report dealing with any relevant pre-action medical history, the injuries sustained, treatment received and present condition, dealing in particular with his capacity for work, and giving a prognosis.

It is central to our assessment of the extent of our client's injuries to establish the extent and duration of any continuing disability. Accordingly, in the prognosis section we would ask you to comment specifically on any areas of continuing complaint or disability or impact on daily living. If there is such continuing disability you should comment on the level of suffering or inconvenience caused and, if you are able, give your view as to when or if the complaint or disability is likely to resolve.

Please send our client an appointment for this purpose. We confirm that we will be responsible for reasonable fees. Please can you request the client's general practitioner and Dover General Hospital to send notes and records relating to the client's treatment, and advise them that any invoice for the provision of the records should be sent to us.

In order to comply with Court Rules we would be grateful if you could address your report to the Court. The report should refer to this letter and any other instructions given, and it should give details of your qualifications. At the end of the report you should include a statement that you understand your duty to the Court and have complied with it. Please insert before your signature at the end of your report a statement that the contents are true to the best of your knowledge and belief.

In order to avoid further correspondence we can confirm that on the evidence we have there is no reason to suspect that we will be pursuing a claim against the hospital or its staff.

We look forward to receiving your report within 4 weeks. If you are not able to prepare your report within this period, please telephone us upon receipt of these instructions.

When acknowledging these instructions it would assist us if you could give an estimate of the likely timescale for the provision of your report and also an indication as to your fee.

Yours faithfully,

G   THE ROLE OF OPINIONS

The nature of an opinion

An opinion consists of formal written legal advice provided by a barrister and it is provided **11.33** in response to a brief, see 2.26–2.51. It is effectively a particular type of formal legal letter. An opinion is normally written for a solicitor and a client, but an opinion from a barrister can also serve other purposes, for example to advise on the strength of a case and whether the case merits public financial support, or where a court is asked to give approval to a settlement on behalf of a child or someone of unsound mind.

As an opinion is normally a document passing from barrister to client, it will normally be **11.34** privileged from disclosure. In *Rabin v Gerson Berger Association Ltd* [1985] 1 All ER 1041 it was held that counsel's opinion was not admissible to prove the meaning of a deed, even though the meaning was at issue in the case. The barrister will normally produce the opinion personally with the assistance of word processing, and it will then be sent back to the solicitor with the brief. The solicitor will then call the client into the office and explain the points made in the opinion. Alternatively the opinion may be sent to the client at the same time as it is sent to the solicitor.

11.35 An opinion must focus on providing advice. It is not a document in which the barrister should write generally about the case, nor is it a document in which the barrister should appear to give judgment on the case.

11.36 For some purposes, such as commenting on whether a case should receive public funding, an opinion should be very balanced and objective. However most opinions are written to support one side of a case, so while it is important to consider points from both sides, all arguments that might favour the client's case should be fully explored. It is not for the barrister to say 'I have decided that this client has no case', but to put forward the ways in which the case could be most favourably put for the person represented, developing whatever arguments are possible to achieve what the client wants within existing legal principles. It is for the client to decide what course to take, and this should be clear in the wording of the opinion.

11.37 The normal audience for an opinion is the solicitor and the client, and this should be taken into account in phrasing points made. The opinion can be used to suggest that instructing solicitors take certain steps with regard to procedure and evidence to advance the case, and such suggestions should be put politely. They should also be put clearly so that the solicitor understands exactly what he or she is being asked to do, and such requests should be realistic. If the solicitors have taken steps or given provisional advice that the barrister does not agree with this should be dealt with tactfully. The way that the barrister writes should maintain a good working relationship with the solicitor.

11.38 The client is an important audience because the opinion is being paid for by the client or on his behalf. The opinion should try to address the problems the client has from the client's point of view. It should show appreciation of the client's objectives and seek to pursue them as far as is reasonably possible. There should be adequate empathy for the client, especially if it is necessary to give advice that there is unlikely to be a case. A good opinion should also be of use to the barrister if the case comes back for further advice or to prepare for trial, if the summary of the facts and of the issues is of sufficiently good quality.

Types of opinion related to litigation

11.39 There are few formal requirements about what an opinion should contain or how it should be written, but a number of conventions have grown up. Opinions in different types of case may well be very different. An opinion in a case where litigation is contemplated will normally relate primarily to potential causes of action, remedies, and associated matters of procedure and evidence, though an opinion may be sought at many different stages in a case, and this can have a fundamental effect on the content and the kind of advice that can be given.

11.40 The main types of opinion that may be sought in relation to litigation are as follows, though in a complex case an opinion may be sought at other stages. An opinion may be sought to fulfil more than one of the following purposes at the same time.

An opinion providing general advice at an early stage

An opinion may be sought at a very early stage, where a client has simply brought a problem **11.41** to a solicitor and the question is whether there might be a legal action. At this stage only limited factual information is likely to be available, especially as regards the case for the other side. An opinion at this stage is likely to focus on legal options and possible remedies, but it may well be difficult to give clear advice and the opinion is most likely to summarise options and suggest what further information might most usefully be sought. If appropriate advice might be included on orders that can be sought before an action is commenced.

An opinion at this stage might also usefully cover as appropriate: **11.42**

- a relevant pre-action protocol, see 4.18–4.32 and 19.27–19.35;
- seeking pre-action orders, see 16.63–16.78;
- emergency injunctions, see 16.66–16.67 and 16.108–16.137;
- the collection of evidence, see 15.01–15.57.

An opinion advising whether an action should be brought

An opinion may be sought when a decision is to be taken as to whether a claim form should **11.43** be issued. At this stage there should be much more information, especially if the case is one to which a pre-action protocol applies. An opinion at this stage should focus specifically on what causes of action should be used, who should be sued, and what remedies might be claimed. The opinion should consider whether there is evidence to support each element of each proposed cause of action. If there are options these should be clearly outlined so that the client can take an informed decision. The chances of success should be estimated as clearly as possible. If appropriate the opinion may also include advice on whether an offer of settlement should be made before the claim form is issued, and/or on procedural steps that might be taken soon after the issue of the claim form.

An opinion at this stage might also usefully cover as appropriate: **11.44**

- the timing of bringing an action, see 4.33–4.41 and 4.51–4.74;
- the choice of parties, see 13.01–13.61;
- the choice of causes of action, see 10.19–10.44 (for contract actions see 18.04–18.12 and 18.21–18.60; for tort actions see 19.06–1926 and 19.36–19.58);
- the choice of remedies, see 14.01–14.29;
- matters relating to the claim form and the particulars of claim, see 12.85–12.112;
- matters regarding the early conduct of the case, see 4.75–4.109.

An opinion advising on public funding

For a case to get such funding an opinion will normally be required assessing the chances **11.45** of success of the case. In such a case opinions must comply with The Funding Code, see 5.38–5.44. The opinion must state the level of service sought and the case category into which the case falls. It must set out factual and legal disputes clearly and any problems of lack of evidence. The chances of success must be assessed as very good (greater than 80 per cent), good (60–80 per cent), moderate (50–60 per cent), borderline, or less than 50 per cent.

The opinion must also set out what the client is likely to get and the benefit for the client. The opinion should also set out investigative work required, and any limitations that should be imposed on public funding. The Bar Council provides Guidelines on Opinions under the Funding Code. These guidelines might also be taken into account in writing other opinions, for example as regards assessing chances of success.

An opinion advising on the progress of litigation

11.46 Once a claim form has been issued and litigation is progressing an opinion may be sought to advise on the progress of the case. This is most likely to happen in a bigger or more complex case. The contents of such an opinion will depend entirely on how the case is progressing, but it might relate to interim applications or the possibility of settling the case.

11.47 An opinion at this stage might also usefully cover as appropriate:

- the possibility of making interim applications, see 16.15–16.49—this could include review strategy as regards the use of time, see 16.79–16.141, review of strategy as regards information, see 16.142–16.167, and review of strategy as regards money, see 16.168–16.187;
- a review of the evidence in the case, see 15.100 and 15.205–15.210;
- a review of options for settlement, see 20.13–20.35 and 20.43–20.68;
- comments on case strategy, see 21.06–21.24;
- comments on how the case for the other side is progressing, and the possibility of seeking sanctions if there are problems, see 16.50–16.62;
- a review of the progress of the case within the time frame set for the case, including possible references to the use to be made of a case management conference or a pre-trial review, see 21.25–21.41.

An opinion advising on remedies

11.48 It may be difficult or impossible for a barrister to advise in detail on remedies, and especially on the measure of damages, when the case is first received. At that stage the main question will be whether there is a cause of action, and there may well be insufficient evidence to give detailed advice on damages. In particular in a personal injuries case it may take time for the effect of the injuries and details of loss of earnings and other losses to become available. That said, even at an early stage the barrister should try to give general advice on remedies and to give a 'ball park' figure for damages as this is likely to be important for the client. In a contract or tort case where substantial damages are claimed the barrister may be specifically asked to advise on damages at a later stage. An opinion on damages should consider all the heads of damage and all the figures relevant to each, including how such figures might be proved. The opinion should also consider arguments of causation, mitigation, contributory negligence etc as relevant, see 14.37–14.44. The assessment of damages in a personal injuries claim is considered at 19.82–19.117. An advice on damages is likely to be used as a basis for seeking a settlement to the action, so advice should normally be included about offers to settle, see 20.43–20.68.

11.49 An opinion at this stage might also usefully cover as appropriate:

- consideration of the range of remedies available, see 14.01–14.29;
- consideration of contract remedies, see 18.61–18.105; and
- consideration of tort remedies, see 19.55–19.117.

An opinion advising on evidence

In a complex case an opinion may be sought specifically with regard to the evidence in the **11.50**
case. This might in particular happen after the disclosure of documents and the exchange of
witness statements when the evidence to be used by both sides should be clear. Such an
opinion should identify the matters in issue in the case, and should systematically review
what admissible evidence each side has on each point. It is also likely to be relevant to
consider what arguments on the evidence might be used by each side in court as part of
assessing the strengths and weaknesses of the case for each side. The opinion should include
advice on any procedural steps that should be taken with regard to evidence, for example
seeking admissions, see Chapter 15. An advice on evidence may also result in attempts to
settle the case because of the degree to which the opinion is likely to clarify the chances of
success of the action.

An opinion at this stage might also usefully cover as appropriate: **11.51**

- identifying the issues in the case, see 15.92–15.98;
- identifying what needs to be proved, see 15.07–15.15;
- identifying what further evidence should be sought, see 15.48–15.57;
- consideration of the admissibility of evidence, see 15.58–15.91;
- drafting witness statements, see 15.108–15.134;
- obtaining expert evidence, see 15.134–15.177;
- the exchange of evidence and of witness statements, see 15.179–15.205;
- the desirability of amending a statement of case, see 12.120–12.134;
- the desirability of challenging a statement of case, see 12.135–12.143;
- the desirability of seeking further information, see 12.146–12.158;
- the desirability of seeking admissions, see 12.159–12.165;
- the options for obtaining particular types of evidence relating to documents and property, see 16.144–16.167.

An opinion advising on settlement

From the above it will be clear that advice on settlement may be part of an opinion at many **11.52**
stages. An opinion may be sought specifically to advise on settlement, and perhaps instructing
the barrister to act in a negotiation. Advice on settlement will need to focus on summarising
the strengths and weaknesses of the case in terms of law and of evidence, and should look at
the terms that might be offered or accepted in a negotiation, see Chapter 20. Advice may
usefully be given on practical and strategic considerations.

An opinion at this stage might also usefully cover as appropriate: **11.53**

- if the case has not yet started, the relevance of pre-action protocols, see 4.18–4.32;
- the timing of attempting to settle, see 20.23–20.35;
- the making of offers to settle, see 20.43–20.50;
- Part 36 offers and payments, see 20.51–20.64, or responding to such offers, see 20.65–20.68.

H   PREPARING TO WRITE AN OPINION

11.54   A good opinion will result from thorough preparation.

- The brief should be read thoroughly to ensure the fullest possible understanding of the case (see 2.52–2.62).
- The legal, factual and evidential information in the brief should be fully analysed (see Chapter 8 and 10.01–10.32).
- Any additional information that might reasonably be available at this stage should be sought from the solicitor.
- Any necessary legal research should be completed (see 9.42–9.79)

11.55   The amount of information available will depend on the stage that the case has reached. Often the barrister will not have every piece of information she or he would like before writing an opinion, but this is a function of the way in which litigation progresses, of practical reality, and of costs. There is professional skill in identifying what information is not yet available and taking an appropriate decision. If the information is crucial to the opinion that the barrister is asked to write and is realistically obtainable then the barrister should ask the solicitor to obtain it. If the information is not crucial yet but will be important in taking the case forward then the opinion should specifically identify what information is required so that the solicitor can seek it. It may be possible to give provisional advice on the basis that if the information shows A then the result in the case will be X, whereas if the information shows B then the result in the case will be Y.

11.56   Legal research for an opinion will normally need to be carefully focussed. A barrister will normally be writing an opinion in an area in which he or she is a specialist, or an area in which he or she normally practices, which may mean that only limited research is required. If a barrister is writing an opinion in an unfamiliar area then background reading may be required. In any event, research should primarily relate to the key legal issues in the case, and ensuring that the law used is fully up to date. Research may well need to cover potential remedies, such as quantum, as well as the cause of action.

11.57   Some barristers, especially experienced ones, may do much of their preparation mentally, but notes made in preparation for writing an opinion can be a useful resource while writing, and can be kept to provide assistance if the barrister is briefed again later in the case. A good set of notes might include the following.

- A list of the objectives, the client's concerns and objectives, and any specific questions asked by the solicitor, as all must be specifically covered in the opinion.
- Factual summaries, including a chronological list of facts, a list of people involved and key points about each, a list of facts that can be proved and facts that still need to be proved.
- Notes of the potential causes of action identified by the barrister and the legal elements of each, together with notes on legal and evidential issues with regard to each issue.
- Notes of the legal research carried out, with the sources used, with specific references to key points, and perhaps with quotations from statutes or cases.

I   THE FORMAT AND STRUCTURE OF AN OPINION

Conventions for writing an opinion

Although there are no formal rules, there is a strong convention governing the way in which **11.58** a legal opinion should be written.

- Normally the document will have a cover sheet that sets out the name of the case (with details of the court it is proceeding in etc), and the word OPINION in tramlines. The name of the barrister and the address of chambers will normally appear in the bottom left hand corner.
- The opinion itself will normally simply be headed OPINION.
- An opinion is normally printed on A4 paper with an easily legible size of type.
- At the end of the opinion will be the address of the barrister's chambers, the date, and the barrister's name and signature.
- For ease of reference it is conventional to divide the opinion up into different sections with sub-headings and numbered paragraphs. An effective opinion will make good use of sub-headings and will ensure that each paragraph deals with a different point so that it is easy to read the opinion, and then to find a specific point in it quickly.
- A summary of advice should be included for the convenience of solicitors and clients. Many barristers put a summary of their advice at the beginning of the opinion, then going on to elaborate each point in more detail. Others find it more natural to put a summary of their advice at the end of the opinion.
- A basic summary of the main facts of the case as understood on the basis of the material available to the barrister should be included. This may simply provide a quick guide to refresh the memory about the case at a later date, but it may also be important to show what the barrister's advice related to if there is any later question of possible professional negligence.
- It is good practice to list in one place further evidence that is required so that this can be used as a checklist.
- It is good practice to list in one place things that instructing solicitors are asked to do.
- It may be useful to have a 'Next Steps' section which summarises what should happen next in the action, including procedural points.

Appropriate legal terminology should be used in an opinion. The solicitor can explain **11.59** this to the client if necessary. Appropriate technical terminology should also be used wherever appropriate. As a matter of style, the barrister should avoid too much use of 'I' and 'In my opinion'; it is assumed that the opinion is the personal professional view of the barrister, and it is not suitable for him or her to project apparently personal views. Equally it should be made clear what is undisputed law and what is a personal view of how the case should be argued—it is important not to mislead the solicitor and client by confusing the two.

General framework for an opinion in a civil case

An opinion is probably most likely to have a clear structure and be comprehensive if it **11.60** evolves from a skeleton of key points. This is quite easily done with a word processor, not least if basic outlines for opinions in different types of case are stored, and if the notes made in preparing to write an opinion are word processed so that material can be cut and pasted.

11.61   A skeleton for an opinion should not be seen as a rigid format, but only as a guide to content and order. The importance of different parts of an opinion will vary substantially with different cases. Sometimes liability may not be in dispute and the opinion will need to focus almost entirely on remedies. Sometimes there will be few evidential issues in a case and sometimes success will turn on the evidence. Coverage must be adapted to meet the needs of the individual case.

OPINION

1. Introduction

The main facts of the case should be summarised briefly.
The main matters on which the barrister is asked to advise should be identified, together with any specific questions put by the solicitor, and any specific objectives that the client hopes to achieve.

2. Summary of advice

The main elements of the advice given by the barrister should be clearly and specifically summarised so that they may be easily and quickly understood.
The summary of advice should cover all the main points relating to, as relevant, cause(s) of action, remedies, key points of procedure, and evidence.
Clear advice should be included on the chances of success of the action, and the best possible estimate of damages.
Answers should be given to any specific questions put by the solicitors.

3. Cause(s) of action

Each possible cause of action in the case should be set out and analysed, using sub-headings and paragraphs to separate different possible causes of action/defendants.
With regard to each potential cause of action there should be discussion of whether all the necessary legal elements are present, and whether there are any legal, factual, or evidential difficulties with any necessary element.
If there is more than one possible cause of action the barrister should advise which one or more it would be best to follow.
All the possible arguments in the client's favour should be examined.

4. Defences

Each potential defence to the client's claim should be examined. The defences may be linked to each cause of action, or be dealt with in a separate section.
Any defence suggested in the instructions should be covered, together with any other defence that the barrister feels may arise. Both partial and full defences should be covered.
The barrister should weigh up as far as possible the legal and evidential value of any defence, and the chances of it succeeding.

5.   Remedies

All the possible remedies that may be available to the client if the action succeeds should be dealt with.

If damages are sought, the barrister should identify separate heads of damage, and deal with legal and evidential issues relevant to recoverability.

6.   Other points

Various other matters should be dealt with in the course of the opinion, or at the end:

- Any matter which instructing solicitors have specifically asked the barrister to advise on.
- Evidence, that is what evidence there already is and also what more will be needed. The solicitor should be given clear instructions on the evidence to be sought, see Chapter 15.
- Procedural points. The barrister should bear in mind and mention any procedural step that may be valuable, see Chapter 16.

7.   Next steps

It is useful to conclude with any appropriate comments about the next steps to be taken in the case.

Address of barrister's chambers

Signed by barrister

Dated

This pro forma might usefully be used as a skeleton for noting points from a brief for a real **11.62** opinion. Preparing such a skeleton can help to ensure that nothing is missed, that structure can be planned, and that the relative importance of different parts of the opinion can be assessed. The skeleton can then be used to produce a full opinion, with the author free to concentrate on detail and style.

J   THE CONTENTS OF AN OPINION

The content of an opinion should be fully decided before the opinion is written. It is only if **11.63** analysis and research is complete that the opinion can be properly structured and written in a concise and clear way. The barrister should know what advice he or she intends to give before starting to write. The opinion should not contain preparatory work or general discussion but should encapsulate conclusions.

There are several ways in which the overall content of an opinion should be consistent and **11.64** coherent.

- In terms of overall advice, the material in the body of the opinion should support and explain the conclusions and the summary of advice so that there is no confusion about the advice being given. The body of the opinion should weigh up strengths and weaknesses, but should form a coherent whole with the overall advice given.

- The whole of the opinion should be focussed on achieving the client's objectives, approaching issues from the client's point of view. The facts and the law need to be weighed objectively, but wherever possible arguments should be found to support what the client seeks to achieve.

- The whole of the opinion should focus on giving advice rather than pronouncing judgment. Options should be outlined, and the chances of success of each option estimated as closely as possible, but it must be clear that choices are for the client, and that ultimately the barrister works within the instructions of the client.

- The whole of the opinion should reflect a practical understanding of the stage the case has reached.

Summarising the facts of the case

11.65   The reason for beginning the opinion with a summary of the key facts is to put the opinion in context. It is also valuable to anyone reading the opinion, including the solicitor with a busy work schedule, or the barrister doing further work on the case some time later. The summary may also be of assistance to the barrister if there is later any question as to what the barrister was advising on and what the barrister took into account.

11.66   Summarising complex facts briefly and clearly is a skill. Sections of the instructions or of documents in the brief, should not be copied out as they will go back to instructing solicitors with the opinion. To provide some simple examples:

> I am asked to advise in a case involving a breach of a contract of employment. The client, Mr A was employed by B Ltd for a fixed term of five years, but has been dismissed after two years without a clear reason being given. Mr A has been unable to find alternative employment and has suffered significant loss. Instructing solicitors have supplied me with a copy of the contract of employment and the letter dismissing Mr A.

> Instructing solicitors have asked me to advise in a case involving a running down accident. It appears that in January 2005 the client Mrs C was knocked down by a car driven by Mr D while she was crossing a zebra crossing. She suffered a broken arm and some head injuries, the full effects of which are not yet clear. Although Mrs C has been able to return to work, she has been unable to resume all the housework and gardening that she previously did, and has had to employ a nanny to assist with the care of her two children.

Summarising the advice sought

11.67   It is useful to list the points on which advice is sought to provide a focus for what follows, and as a checklist for the points to be covered. To provide simple examples:

> Mr A seeks advice on whether he can sue his former employers and whether all his damages will be recoverable. He also wishes to know whether his damages will be reduced if he does take another job. Instructing solicitors ask for advice on terms for a possible settlement.

> Instructing solicitors indicate that the defendant may be prepared to accept liability in this case, so that the primary issue will be quantification of damages. However it appears that Mrs C has

indicated that she was preoccupied on the morning in question and did not look properly before crossing the road. I am asked to advise whether this may affect liability and/or quantum.

The summary of advice

It is good practice to provide a concise and clear summary of the advice given on all the   **11.68** questions raised in the case. This is effectively an executive summary to enable the client to grasp the advice being given quickly, or to assist the solicitor in passing on advice quickly to the client once the opinion has been received. Neither the solicitor nor the client should have to hunt through the document to find advice on a key point. Arguably the summary of advice is the most important part of the opinion as the rest of the opinion simply supports and explains that advice.

The summary should include: **11.69**

- what cause or causes of action may be open to the client;
- any main defence or difficulty as regards each cause of action;
- an indication of the likely chances of success of each cause of action;
- what remedies the client is likely to achieve, and any key problems as regards remedies;
- the amount of damages that might be recovered, expressed as closely as possible at the stage the case has reached;
- a summary of any key evidential points;
- a summary of any key procedural points;
- specific answers to any questions that the solicitor has raised.

For example: **11.70**

It would appear that Mr A has a clear case of breach of contract of employment against his former employers. On the facts before me success seems virtually certain as there appears to be no defence as the employers accept that Mr A performed his duties in a totally satisfactory way. However it would appear that Mr A has failed to mitigate his loss by taking alternative employment, and I do not think the court will accept his argument that he did not wish to take employment that was slightly further away from his home. Mr A should accept reasonable alternative employment, and the effect will be to reduce the damages he can claim. On the figures before me it appears that he has lost a salary of £40,000 a year but that he could get a job for £35,000 a year. It would therefore appear that a settlement for £15,000 would be reasonable, though such a settlement should only be finalised once Mr A has taken another job.

It appears from these papers that those representing Mr D are likely to accept liability in this case. However the evidence shows that there may be contributory negligence on the part of Mrs C and damages might be reduced by up to 25 per cent for that reason. I cannot give full advice on quantum until an up to date medical report is supplied, though I would advise that a minimum of £10,000 should be recoverable for the injuries sustained. Mrs C should be able to recover for her other losses, save that I do not think it can be successfully argued that the employment of the nanny was a consequence of the accident.

Cause(s) of action

The barrister should examine in appropriate detail each cause of action that the client may   **11.71** have. Even if the barrister is going to recommend a particular cause of action, it is valuable to mention any alternatives to see if they may provide any benefit, and to show the instructing solicitor that every possibility has been considered. Even in a fairly straightforward case there may be a variety of causes of action, such as negligence/occupier's liability/breach of statutory duty and it is important to consider which will be best in terms of the likelihood of establishing the cause of action, and the remedies that may follow from a particular cause of action.

11.72 For each potential cause of action the barrister should consider:

- what the legal elements of the cause of action are;
- whether those elements are likely to be established on the facts;
- whether those elements can be proved on the evidence available;
- whether the remedies available for the cause of action will meet the client's objectives;
- what case the other side is likely to present as regards that particular cause of action.

11.73 If there is only one viable cause of action then the barrister should advise on that. If there is more than one potential cause of action, the barrister should advise which cause(s) of action should actually be pursued. Areas where one would commonly pursue more than one cause of action include professional negligence, where liability in tort and contract overlap. If there is any real doubt it is probably better in most circumstances to put the cause of action in and then cease to pursue it at the earliest point possible, rather than to try to add it later.

11.74 The barrister may need to advise not only on the potential causes of action but also on the potential defendants. If there is a choice then the opinion should present the options, see Chapter 13. For example, if someone is injured by a machine in a building it may well be possible to sue the person using the machine which inflicted the injury, the person who made the machine which inflicted the injury, the occupier of the building and/or a contractor responsible for the use of the machine in the building. It may also be relevant to consider vicarious liability, agency, and other types of indirect involvement. It is possible to sue everyone against whom there is a potential cause of action, but the result may be to build costs without any benefit, as at the end of the day it will only be possible to recover once for the losses suffered. The factors for choosing which defendant to sue would normally include deciding against whom the case is legally and evidentially strongest, and also deciding who is most likely to be able to pay damages, or to meet any other remedy sought. If there is clearly a preferred defendant then that defendant should be sued. It will be open to that defendant to add other parties under Part 20 proceedings. If there is doubt as to who is the preferred defendant it is probably better to add all the most likely defendants, with the option of dropping the case against one or more of them if emerging evidence shows a strong case against one defendant only.

11.75 It may not be easy to find an appropriate cause of action. If there is an obvious cause of action then the solicitor may deal with the case without briefing a barrister. It is inevitable that barristers are more likely to be briefed in cases where there is not an easy answer. It is the job of the barrister to develop every possible argument in the client's favour, and any cause of action against any defendant that is arguable should be set out in the opinion. It is not for the barrister to be falsely optimistic or unduly pessimistic—the realistic chances of success should also be made clear, and the decision whether or not to proceed should be left to the client. There are some cases that simply cannot be brought however strongly the client feels—if there is no arguable cause of action against any potential defendant then this must be the advice given.

Having said that the barrister should develop legal arguments where possible; disputed **11.76** evidence and complicated and clever legal arguments that are primarily of academic interest must be treated with care. Costs can build up quickly if there are complex legal or evidential points in a case, and the chances of success and the possible costs must be made clear to the client.

Defences

It is a part of advising a client to try to anticipate what the case for the other side may be and **11.77** how strong it is. Whatever loss or harm a client has suffered an action should not be brought against a potential defendant who has a complete defence. Anticipating defences may require imagination—the defence may not be set out in the instructions but may be envisaged from working out how the other side is likely to view the case, see 17.27–17.46.

One should try to contemplate every possible line of defence. There may be a defence on the **11.78** law, a defence on the facts, or a defence on the evidence available. There may be a defence to the cause of action and/or to the remedies claimed. There may be a complete defence or a partial defence. The barrister should try to assess the possible strength of each line of defence, and advise on whether the potential defence means that the action should not be pursued, or that damages will be reduced.

Remedies

If the client is advised that a cause of action is available, the client will also wish to know **11.79** what remedies may result from a successful action. Indeed in practical terms the potential remedies may be of more importance to the client than the cause of action, so potential remedies may need to be covered in some detail. If the other side has admitted or is likely to admit liability, the entire opinion may need to centre on remedies and the measure of damages. Each remedy that may be available should be considered to see what will best achieve the client's aims. Potential remedies are dealt with at 14.01–14.29.

All figures that are available should be dealt with in the opinion, including appropriate **11.80** calculations relevant to the measure of damages. It may also be necessary to cover other financial issues—for example the possible impact of taxation on damages. While tax is not payable on damages for personal injuries, tax may be payable on damages for loss of income, or for damage to a capital asset. It has been held that capital gains tax is potentially payable on damages related to a contract for sale of land, *Zim Properties Ltd v IRC* [1984] STI 741, or related to negligent damage to property, *Anders Utkilens Rederi A/S v O/Y Lovisa Stevedoring Co A/B* [1985] 2 All ER 669.

Facts and evidence

The extent to which an opinion deals with evidence will vary substantially from case to case. **11.81** Sometimes the main purpose of the opinion will be to deal with evidence. Sometimes only key points of evidence relating to potential causes of action or remedies may need to be included. Almost any opinion will need to deal with evidence to some extent. The most ingenious legal argument is worth little if the facts of the case cannot be proved.

11.82   Facts and evidence will be of particular importance where there is a dispute about facts, see 10.12–10.18. The opinion may need to consider specific problems with evidence, such as the making of an oral contract or how an accident happened. Analysis will need to include what evidence is available, what evidence may become available (for example in disclosure), and what evidence may need to be sought. The opinion may also need to consider the admissibility of evidence. A full analysis of all available evidence may only be possible at a relatively late stage in the case.

Procedural matters

11.83   It is often appropriate for an opinion to include advice on procedural points that might assist the client. Usually the solicitor will be responsible for taking procedural steps, but a barrister who has been briefed in the case may give advice on appropriate procedure. The matters that might usefully be covered will depend on the stage that the case has reached.

11.84   Before an action has been started advice on procedural matters might include:

- fulfilling the requirements of a pre-action protocol;
- which court the case should be brought in;
- any applications to court that can be made before the action has started.

11.85   At the time an action is launched the matters to be covered might include:

- track allocation;
- interim applications.

11.86   Shortly before trial matters to cover might include:

- preparations for trial;
- trial procedure.

Practical points

11.87   It is important for the barrister to show an awareness of the practical reality of the position that the client is in. An effective opinion is one that most clearly provides a real person with useful advice on a real problem—this will give the client most confidence and will probably bring the most satisfactory end to the case. To give just a few examples of giving practical advice:

- A practical option may meet the client's objectives better than legal action.
- It is important to keep a clear focus on what the client desires as an outcome.
- Within the context of a legal action, practical action may be more effective that a legal step. If for example the claimant is troubled by noise there may be a practical way to decrease the noise rather than seeking an interim injunction.
- Litigation is likely to have a negative effect on the relationship between the parties. If there is a lasting relationship between them then mediation or negotiation should be considered.

- The remedies that a court has the power to order are somewhat restricted. A settlement or consent order may be able to cover many details that an order by a judge could not.
- The desirability of any step should always be weighed against potential cost, and what the plaintiff in question can afford.

K   THE IMPORTANCE OF CLEAR CONCLUSIONS AND ADVICE

It is worth repeating that any legal writing, and in particular an opinion, should wherever **11.88** possible reach clear conclusions and provide clear and justified advice. Effective litigation cannot be conducted through a vague or rambling approach. Providing a clear summary of advice is arguably the most important part of an opinion.

It is just as important to give clear advice on the problems of a case as on its strengths. If it is **11.89** difficult or impossible to put forward a case that will meet the client's objectives then this must be handled with care. If the client has a strong desire to sue but no cause of action can be identified, or if the client seeks high damages but little or nothing is recoverable in the circumstances then that must be made clear. Although a barrister acts on the instructions of the client, the barrister should not advise that an unfounded action be brought simply to satisfy the client. The costs implications and the likelihood of the action being struck out should be clearly explained, and if necessary the barrister may have to refuse to act further for the client if the client will not accept the advice given.

It is important to assess the chances of success of a case in advising a client in writing as at a **11.90** meeting, see 7.28–7.49. A written assessment of the chances of success is if anything even more important than an oral assessment, as it is something the client can keep and refer back to. A written assessment of the chances of success is probably most helpfully done as a percentage, for example 'something like a 60 per cent chance of success'. It is difficult to provide general guidance on the assessment of chances of success. Much depends on the details of the individual case. An accurate assessment depends primarily on the assessment of strengths and weaknesses.

KEY DOCUMENTS

Pro forma letters can be found in the Pre-action Protocols:

Pre-action Protocol for Personal Injury Claims
Pre-action Protocol for the Resolution of Clinical Disputes
Pre-action Protocol for Construction and Engineering Disputes
Pre-action Protocol for Defamation
Professional Negligence Pre-action Protocol
Pre-action Protocol for Judicial Review
Pre-action Protocol for Disease and Illness Claims
Pre-action Protocol for Housing Disrepair Cases

These are easily available in hard copy or electronically, see Chapter 24.

12

DRAFTING A STATEMENT OF CASE

A THE STATEMENT OF CASE 12.01

B BACKGROUND TO DRAFTING............................... 12.06
   The history of drafting 12.06
   The modern approach 12.11

C THE PROCESS FOR PRODUCING A STATEMENT OF CASE 12.17
   The steps to be taken.................................... 12.17
   The use of precedents 12.25

D RULES FOR DRAFTING 12.31
   The general approach of the CPR 12.31
   Specific rules in the CPR................................. 12.34
   Rules for particulars of claim 12.36
   Rules for a defence...................................... 12.37
   Other rules 12.38

E PRINCIPLES FOR DRAFTING............................... 12.39
   Including only material facts.............................. 12.41
   Including sufficient material facts 12.49
   Providing particulars where needed to clarify a case 12.52
   Including facts rather than law 12.55
   Including facts rather than evidence 12.59
   Including facts rather than arguments...................... 12.64
   Appropriate terminology and wording 12.67

F HEADINGS FOR STATEMENTS OF CASE...................... 12.76
   The rules for headings................................... 12.76
   Sample headings 12.82

G THE CLAIM FORM 12.84

H GENERAL FRAMEWORK FOR A PARTICULARS OF CLAIM 12.95
   General principles 12.95
   Outline for a particulars of claim 12.98

I SPECIFYING REMEDIES AND RELIEF 12.99
   Allegations supporting a remedy 12.99
   Listing remedies and relief sought 12.103

Claims for damages 12.105
Claims for interest 12.108

J OTHER DRAFTS FOR A CLAIMANT 12.112
The reply (and defence to counterclaim) 12.112
Outline for a reply and defence to counterclaim 12.118

K REFINING A STATEMENT OF CASE 12.119
The need to refine a statement of case 12.119
The process for amending a statement of case 12.123
Principles for major amendments 12.130

L CHALLENGING A STATEMENT OF CASE 12.134
Reasons for challenging a statement of case 12.134
Striking out a statement of case 12.138
Requesting further information 12.145
Responding to a request 12.151
Seeking admissions 12.158

KEY DOCUMENTS

A THE STATEMENT OF CASE

12.01 Litigation is a process for deciding a fair outcome where a dispute has arisen. Central to the litigation process is the definition of precisely what the issues in the case are and which are in dispute.

12.02 Defining what is in dispute must be done through a process of analysis of law and fact, as set out at 10.19–10.33. The result of that analysis is the statement of case. In summary the key points regarding the role and purpose of a statement of case are given below.

- A key audience for the statement of case is the court—a good draft will assist the judge in defining the issues in dispute.
- The other key audience is the opponent—the statement of case is the key document setting out the case for the other side.
- The statement of case should identify the case to be met by the opponent.
- The statement of case embodies key decisions about the case—who is being sued, for what cause of action, and what remedies are sought.
- The case is normally defined through a series of factual allegations that show how the legal ingredients of a cause of action are alleged to be made out.
- The statement of case does not need to include law—legal arguments may be set out in a skeleton argument later and will be argued at trial.
- The statement of case must be based on evidence but does not need to include evidence—evidence on each point alleged and in dispute will be needed at trial.

12.03 Because the litigation process is adversarial, statements of case need to be drawn up and exchanged by both sides in a structured process, see 4.75–4.80. A statement of case is a formal document that is filed with the court and served on other parties in the case. The main types of statement of case are (CPR r 2.3):

- Particulars of Claim (Claimant)
- Defence (and Counterclaim) (Defendant)
- Reply (and Defence to Counterclaim) (Claimant)
- Part 20 Claim Form (Part 20 Claimant)
- Particulars of Part 20 Claim
- Part 20 Defence
- Further information (CPR Part 18)

General matters of style for statements of case and broad matters of tactics are covered at **12.04** 10.33–10.54. A statement of case, being a summary of facts, should have a statement of truth, and thus forms part of the evidence in the case.

This chapter deals with the detailed rules for stating a case, and also with how statements of **12.05** case can be refined. It is necessary to distinguish litigation commenced by a claim form under Part 7 of the CPR from cases appropriately brought as Part 8 claims, which are not covered by this book. For books relevant to developing legal drafting skills see 24.24.

B   A BACKGROUND TO DRAFTING

The history of drafting

The Civil Procedure Rules 1998 brought about significant changes in focussing on plain **12.06** English statements of case. It is useful to have some understanding of the background to current drafting as many concepts of drafting are based on the traditional approach, and many precedents and practitioners are still heavily influenced by what went before.

The concept of legal pleadings began in the reign of Henry II, when each party to an action **12.07** gave a brief oral statement of his or her case which was written onto parchment rolls (hence the title of Master of the Rolls). The idea was simple and logical—each party needed to state clearly what the basis of the dispute was. However the simple statements soon became hedged about with a number of strict rules and formalities which had to be observed. A correct formula of words had to be used for each case and the right form of action had to be chosen or the case would fail, whatever the facts and the justice of the case. Common law and equity actions had to be brought separately, and a defendant could only record one defence, even if a variety of defences might be open on the facts.

Changes were made over the centuries, but complex rules for pleading remained the norm. **12.08** In the early Victorian period it was necessary to plead in detail every element of the case and to exclude all possible exceptions, so that lengthy pleadings with many sub-clauses were inevitable, even though much of what was included was not strictly relevant to the case. In response the defendant had to deal with every possible argument in the case and every possible defence. Anything not in the pleadings could not be argued in court, however relevant it was, so pleading was not only complex but vital, and cases could easily be won or lost on the pleading alone.

12.09 Fundamental reform came with the Common Law Procedure Acts 1852–60 and the Judicature Act 1873, which form part of the basis for the modern system of drafting. The rules had become so complicated that pleading tended to obscure rather than clarify a case, and the effect of the legislation was to remove the old rules so that it was no longer necessary to plead on a wide number of matters that were not directly relevant to the case itself, but only to plead on the central facts and arguments in the case. It also became much easier to amend a pleading, so that a defect in pleading is now rarely fatal to a case. The CPR has gone further in supporting clear statements of case.

12.10 This history is of interest because of the return to the basic concept that litigation should be based on a clear and simple statement of the case of each party. The Victorian approach with complex terminology and many sub-clauses has died hard, having to some extent passed from one generation of lawyers to another as they learn drafting techniques, and still being seen in some precedent books.

The modern approach

12.11 Effective drafting is that which sets out a simple and accurate case. It should consist of those factual allegations which show the legal elements of a cause of action and of the remedies claimed. Although drafting has returned to the simple need to set out a case, the content of that case remains important. If a factual element is missing then the cause of action will fail or the remedy will not be granted. It may be possible to address this by amendment, but that is at the discretion of the court and may attract a costs penalty.

12.12 The purpose of the exchange of statements of case is to define issues in dispute. This will as a result define what evidence is admissible at trial and what issues need to be argued before the judge.

12.13 A statement of case is best drafted from scratch for each case to ensure that it fits the needs of the case as closely as possible. It may be useful to evolve a statement of case from a skeleton of key points, just as it was suggested at 11.60–11.62 that an opinion is best evolved from a skeleton of key points.

12.14 Good drafting is important for a number of reasons.

- A good statement of case will demonstrate a clear analysis of the legal and factual elements of the case. A vague or inaccurate draft shows weak preparation and is easily attacked.
- A strong and clear statement of case can be used strategically to persuade an opponent to accept a weakness in his or her case, or to negotiate.
- The statements of case are normally the first thing that a judge will read in a case. A good statement of case has much potential for creating a strong impression, whereas a weak one will create a poor impression.
- A good statement of case provides a strong basis for the conduct of a case at trial.
- Matters that are improperly pleaded can result in a costs penalty if the result is that the costs of preparing the case are unnecessarily increased.

12.15 To illustrate where weak drafting may cause a problem, in the well-known case of *Leaf v International Galleries* [1950] 2 KB 86 the claimant bought a painting for £85 having been told that it was a Constable, and when he found out that it was not he sued claiming rescission. The judge held that the remedy of rescission was not available due to lapse of time, and the claimant could not get damages because they were not claimed. In *Esso Petroleum Co v Southport Corporation* [1956] AC 218, a ship was stranded and a beach polluted by it. The case went to the House of Lords, and it was held there had been no negligence but the accident was due to a defect in the ship. As unseaworthiness had not been pleaded, the defendant did not have to deal with it and the claimant failed. In *Perestrello E Companhia Limitada v United Paint Co* [1969] 1 WLR 570 there was an action for breach of contract which the claimant won, but the pleading claimed only some wasted expenditure and not general loss of profit, and it was held that only what was pleaded could be recovered. Although such problems might today be remedied at an earlier stage through active case management or through amendment that should be no excuse for failing to draft accurately.

Many judges still stress the importance of good pleadings, as in the remarks made by Lord **12.16**
Edmund Davies in *Farrell v Secretary of State for Defence* [1980] 1 All ER 166 where he said:

> It has become fashionable in these days to attach decreasing importance to pleadings, and it is beyond doubt that there have been times where insistence on complete compliance with their technicalities puts justice at risk, and indeed may on occasion have led to its being defeated. But pleadings continue to play an essential part in civil actions.

C THE PROCESS FOR PRODUCING A STATEMENT OF CASE

The steps to be taken

There is not one 'right' statement of case for a particular action. Producing an effective **12.17**
statement of case requires a focus on:

- the particular statement of case required;
- the role of that statement of case in the action;
- the importance of using the statements of case to clarify factual allegations.

The stages in creating an effective statement of case are probably: **12.18**

- analysis of facts and law to identify the relevant elements of potential causes of action and whether they fit the facts of the case, so as to identify causes of action, see 10.19–10.27;
- the identification of the parties, see 13.01–13.62;
- the identification of remedies, see 14.01–14.29;
- the drawing up of a skeleton outline draft to check overall content and logical order;
- checking the division into paragraphs and the proposed content of each paragraph;
- drafting each paragraph in full;
- re-reading and checking.

The key elements of a statement of case for a claimant are: **12.19**

- alleging a specific cause(s) of action;
- showing all the elements of the cause(s) of action alleged by summarising the facts which amount to that cause(s) of action;
- alleging facts that show what damage and loss have arisen;

- alleging facts that show how that loss and damage arise from the alleged cause of action;
- providing a summary of the remedies sought.

12.20 The key elements of a statement of case for a defendant are:

- alleging a specific defence(s), or other reasons why a cause of action cannot be sustained;
- alleging where relevant that loss or damage has not arisen;
- alleging where relevant that the loss or damage was not caused by the alleged cause of action.

12.21 It should be possible to read through a statement of case quickly and easily and at the end to have a clear understanding of what a case is about. An effective statement of case is one which is written in this way. To achieve this:

- a logical structure for the statement of case is needed;
- each paragraph should deal with a single issue or element of the cause of action;
- each sentence should deal with a separate relevant point;
- if there is more than one cause of action, either cumulatively or in the alternative, then each should normally be covered separately, unless there is a very strong overlap in the details of what is alleged.

12.22 Usually the most logical approach will be chronological, setting out what happened in the order in which it happened, but there may be reasons for not following a strict time sequence, for example where something relevant to the measure of damage may have happened at an early stage, but may be most logically covered in the latter part of the statement of case where loss and damage is covered.

12.23 Every sentence and every word in a statement of case should be there because it needs to be. There should be no sentences or words that do not contribute directly to the statement of case. Each word should be carefully chosen.

12.24 Sometimes a form is used, but the principle for completing the form will be the same as for drafting a separate statement of case. In an important or complex case the statement of case will be drafted separately rather than inserted on a form.

The use of precedents

12.25 It can be attractive to seek to use a precedent to assist in drafting a statement of case. Precedents can help, but all precedents must be used with great care if they are to have real value. Precedents may be consulted for ideas, but a statement of case should not merely be word processed from a statement drawn up for another case. The facts of all cases are different, and a statement of case is a summary of facts.

12.26 The potential advantages of using precedents are that:

- they can provide a useful starting point in an area with which the lawyer is not very familiar;
- they can provide useful guides to the elements to be pleaded for a case in a particular area, including guidance on the right level of detail;
- they may suggest particularly useful words and phrases;
- they may provide ideas for overall structure.

The potential drawbacks of using precedents are that: **12.27**

- a false sense of security that a draft is good can be provided because the draft looks like a precedent, when in fact the draft is weak because the individual case has not been sufficiently analysed;
- a precedent that is not sufficiently adapted to the individual case can have fatal weaknesses, for example in leaving out important material;
- irrelevancies may be left in through poor copying or word processing, which will give a poor impression to the other side and to the court;
- a precedent can fall out of date quite quickly. Precedents drafted before the CPR should only be used with great care.

To illustrate the possible problems, in *Brickfield Properties v Newton* [1971] 1 WLR 862 a   **12.28** statement of claim for negligence and breach of statutory duty was copied from *Atkin's Court Forms*, but it was held that it should have been pleaded differently as a failure to supervise was involved. The claimant was allowed to amend the draft, but there was a potentially significant weakness in the case.

With the massive storage capacity and ease of retrieval that technology now offers it has   **12.29** become the norm for individuals to build up a store of their own drafts, and for firms and chambers to build up banks of precedents in areas in which they regularly work, which may include an element of house style. There are also generally available sources of precedents, the main one being *Atkin's Court Forms* (Butterworths), which comes in 42 volumes with indexes, and is regularly updated. *Atkin* contains notes and examples in general areas of pleading, such as county court actions and appeals, in general areas of law, such as contract or negligence, and also in specific areas of law, from charities to plant breeders rights! Each area has an explanatory text, as well as precedents with notes.

When seeking precedents to use, the following stages may assist in getting the advantages of   **12.30** the precedent without suffering the drawbacks.

- Before looking for a precedent it is important to identify the type of precedent required as clearly as possible, for example 'Particulars of claim. Tort, Negligence or breach of statutory duty. Damages', or 'Defence, Contract, Misrepresentation. Damages or rescission'.
- The best available source of precedents should be used, and if possible two or three precedents should be found so that they can be compared and the most useful parts taken from each.
- There is merit in seeking a separate precedent for each element of the case rather than a single precedent for the whole case. The appropriate parts of each precedent can then be pulled together to form a draft. For example the outline structure of the particulars of claim may come from one precedent, the way to plead particulars from a second, and the remedies sought from a third.
- Having found precedents, each should be analysed carefully to see what is really directly relevant to the individual case taking different elements from each. Particularly good expressions should be noted and used.
- Having found precedents, it is best to draft the new draft from scratch rather then simply try to adapt an existing precedent. This is most likely to make each word as appropriate as possible.
- Always remember that the current case is important, not the precedent.

D   RULES FOR DRAFTING

The general approach of the CPR

12.31   There are relatively few formal Civil Procedure Rules relating to the drafting of statements of case. There are some rules for specific types of statement of case, and some of these should probably be seen as being of general application. There are also Court Guides that can provide assistance in drafting, especially the Queen's Bench Guide, the Chancery Guide, and the Commercial Court Guide. These Guides incorporate some material previously in the rules of court. A number of principles that flow from the rules are outlined in the following paragraphs.

12.32   Only a fundamental failure to comply with the CPR might be fatal to a case. If at any stage in the proceedings something is done or left undone so that there is a failure to comply with the rules, that failure will be treated as an irregularity and will not nullify the proceedings, any step in them, or any document. If there is a failure to comply with the rules, then the court can set aside all or part of the proceedings or any step in them or any document on such terms as to costs or otherwise as the court thinks just, or the court may allow amendments or make an order dealing with the proceedings generally as it thinks fit.

12.33   However this flexibility should not be seen as supporting weak drafting. The penalties for weak drafting may be:

- an order to pay costs, where for example failure to clarify issues has put the other side to extra expense—this could be quite a large penalty if unnecessary applications to court have to be made because of the weak drafting;
- a failure to achieve the best possible outcome for the client if the causes of action or the remedies are drafted weakly;
- losing the case if for example a significant defect in drafting is not discovered until after the end of the limitation period.

Specific rules in the CPR

12.34   The form of a statement of case, PD 5.

- Every document prepared for use in court must be divided into numbered paragraphs and have all numbers, including dates, expressed as figures.
- Statements of case and other documents drafted by a legal representative should be signed by that representative.

12.35   Details relating to statements of case:

- If exceptionally a statement of case exceeds 25 pages (excluding schedules) an appropriate short summary must also be filed and served, PD 16 para 1.
- A party may:
  - refer in his statement of case to a point of law;
  - give in his statement of case the name of any witness he intends to call;
  - attach to his statement of case a copy of any document which he considers necessary to his case (including especially any expert's report), PD16 para 13.

Rules for particulars of claim

12.36

- Particulars of claim must include a concise statement of the facts on which the claimant relies, CPR r 16.4.
- A claimant must specifically set out the following matters if he wishes to rely on them, PD 16 para 8:
  — Any allegation of fraud
  — The fact of any illegality
  — Details of any misrepresentation
  — Details of all breaches of trust
  — Notice or knowledge of a fact
  — Details of unsoundness of mind or undue influence
  — Details of wilful default
  — Any facts relating to mitigation of loss or damage

Rules for a defence

12.37

- Where a defendant denies an allegation he must state his reasons for doing so, and if he intends to put forward a different version of events from that given by the claimant he must state his own version, CPR r 16.5.

Other rules

There are some specific details that must be pleaded by statute or by rules of court. For **12.38** example:

- A claimant who wishes to rely on evidence that someone has been convicted of an offence must state that he intends to do so and give details of the conviction, namely the offence, the date of conviction, the court, and the issue in the claim to which the conviction is relevant (PD 16 para 8).
- When pleading a claim under the Fatal Accidents Act 1976 it is necessary to plead appropriate details of the dependants, and this is dealt with at 19.111–19.117.
- A claim for exemplary or provisional damages must also be specifically pleaded, see 19.104–19.105, as must any claim of illegality.
- In proceedings against the Crown it is necessary to plead why the Crown is alleged to be liable, and the government department and officers involved.

E PRINCIPLES FOR DRAFTING

In addition to the rules for drafting statements of case, there are a number of principles that **12.39** are invariably followed in practice. Many of these principles have their origins in the rules, and while it is not strictly necessary to comply with them, the practice of lawyers over the years is strongly influential. This can be a difficult area for an inexperienced lawyer—imitating more experienced lawyers is a good way to learn, but weak practice may be copied as well as good practice. Perhaps the best test when looking at a sample draft is to consider whether there seems to be a good reason for doing something in a particular way.

12.40 A statement of case should not be internally inconsistent or contradictory, and one statement of case of a party should not be inconsistent or contradictory as regards another. A statement of truth cannot logically say that contradictory things are true. However alternatives can be included where the party does not know how the precise truth and where the alternatives are specifically set out as such. This should not be used as an excuse for vague drafting—pleading alternatives can show a weakness in a case. Pleading in the alternative should only be used where the evidence justifies alternatives.

Including only material facts

12.41 This principle is really just an interpretation of the rule that a statement of case should include a statement in summary form of the material facts. The point is to set out the story that includes the elements of the cause of action as clearly and concisely as possible. Clear allegations are required rather than full narrative style. Essentially the other side should have a clear picture of the case being made without having basic questions about it.

12.42 The test for whether a fact is 'material' is whether it needs to be shown for the case to succeed. A fact is material if it forms part of the causes of action alleged or the remedies sought. A point that is directly part of the case is 'material', and this should be distinguished from general background information.

12.43 It is normally material to include matters like:

- the parties to the contract, as a contract must be made between parties who reach agreement;
- the consideration for the contract, or it will not be enforceable;
- matters relating to parties and liability, such as that one person was the agent of another in a contractual action, or that someone was acting in the course of their employment if they were suing their employer for injuries in a tort action;
- facts showing causation or foreseeability of loss.

12.44 It is not normally material to include matters like:

- terms of the contract that were not in dispute;
- descriptions of parts of the factory with no relationship to the accident.

12.45 To provide an example, if the basic facts of a claim are:

- the claimant bought a car from the defendant for £2,000;
- it broke down one week later;
- it broke down because of a defect of which the defendant should have been aware;
- it cost £600 to have it repaired,

it would also be material to include:

- the date the contract was made, to avoid any confusion;

- why the car broke down;
- what it is alleged that the defendant should have been aware of and why;
- any other losses the claimant suffered, such as having to hire another car while the car was repaired.

It might also be material to include: **12.46**

- any terms that might be directly relevant, if for example the claimant had the car on approval for a month and was allowed to return it;
- any representations that were made about the roadworthiness of the car;
- the nature of the journey being taken when the car broke down (if this is relevant to damages).

It would not be material to include: **12.47**

- the colour of the car;
- other journeys taken in the car (unless they are directly relevant);
- arrangements for insuring the car (even if the breakdown is covered by insurance, the person who is responsible for the problem is the person who should pay).

A statement of case can include any facts which have arisen at any time, though the cause of **12.48** action itself must have arisen before the claim form is issued.

Including sufficient material facts

Having decided that a particular area of fact is material, it can be difficult to decide how **12.49** much detail is required. Essentially the test is that there must be sufficient detail for the other side to know the case that they have to meet. The sort of area where detail is normally required includes:

- precise legal relationships, for example where it is alleged that there is vicarious liability or agency;
- facts that give rise to a legal relationship, for example why it is alleged that a tort duty of care exists in particular circumstances, and what that duty is;
- facts that are part of defining legal obligations, for example what implied terms are alleged to form part of a contract and why they are alleged to be implied eg from a previous course of dealing;
- a condition to be fulfilled before something else happens should be included;
- there should be sufficient detail to show how it is alleged that an accident happened.

The balance between what facts are material and must be pleaded and what can and should **12.50** be left out is quite fine. Sometimes there is not a clear answer, and different lawyers could have a different approach.

There may be tactical decisions to make as regards level of detail. If a court would be likely to **12.51** order that further information be provided on a particular point then it should normally be included from the start. However putting in too much detail can be a problem in that the party will normally be bound at trial to the version of events set out in the statement of case. Where there is uncertainty a careful path must be trodden to supply adequate detail but to leave some flexibility to adapt arguments to emerging evidence at trial. If a fact is in the statement of case it will have to be proved if necessary. If an allegation is not made then evidence on it will only be admissible with the leave of the judge. Material allegations should not be kept secret—if something comes as a surprise at trial it will only be allowed in with the leave of the judge. If an issue is known about and evidence is available for trial but the issue is not raised then the point cannot normally be made on appeal.

Providing particulars where needed to clarify a case

12.52　There is a tension between the requirements that material facts should be set out concisely and that the opposing party should know the case that is to be met. This tension is resolved by the requirement that particulars should be given of material allegations that might otherwise be vague. Areas where particulars are normally required include allegations of breach, negligence, misrepresentation, and damages. Particulars should also be given of fraud, breach of trust, wilful default, or undue influence on which a party relies. Where a party alleges any condition of the mind of any person, whether any disorder or disability of mind or any malice, fraudulent intention, or other condition of mind except knowledge, particulars should be given of the alleged state of mind and how it is said to have come about. The requirement for particulars is part of indicating how much detail should be provided on a particular point.

12.53　If particulars should be provided they can be included as part of a paragraph, though common practice is to give a sub-heading of 'Particulars', or 'Particulars of Negligence' or 'Particulars of Loss and Damage' and list the details.

12.54　The rules for when particulars are required are not hard and fast. In *Selangor United Rubber Estates v Cradock* [1965] 1 Ch 896 it was said that if there was an allegation of a breach of a duty arising from a confidential or trust relationship, particulars of that relationship should be given. In *Cannock Chase District Council v Kelly* [1978] 1 All ER 152 there was an allegation that the Council had acted in bad faith, and it was held that particulars of the breach of faith or abuse of power should be given. As a further example, in *Fox v H Wood (Harrow)* [1963] 2 QB 601 the claimant was injured at work in putting his foot through the floorboards, but his employers denied liability. It was held that where it was alleged that a party ought to have known something, particulars of the circumstances from which that knowledge was said to have arisen should be given.

Including facts rather than law

12.55　It was formerly the case that law should not normally be included in a statement of case. This was quite logical. A statement of case is normally written by a lawyer for other lawyers and for the judge, and as these are people who also know the law, it is not necessary to include law. The statement of case should focus on facts and allegations. Legal argument should take place at trial, and would properly be set out in a skeleton argument rather than a statement of case.

12.56　The focus on facts is an advantage in that a party can raise any legal argument that is based in his or her statement of case, *Re Vandervell's Trusts (No 2)* [1974] Ch 269, and provided a statement of case contains all the facts necessary to establish a cause of action that cause of action can succeed although it is not the main cause of action pleaded, *Drane v Evangelou*

[1978] 2 All ER 437 (a case of trespass). Nonetheless, the legal arguments should be raised in the skeleton argument, and there might be a costs penalty if the line of argument raised at a late stage increased costs.

There have always been some exceptions—where law should be included. When asking the **12.57** court to act under a power that it has only because of a specific statutory section, the statute should be referred to, *Re Gonin* [1979] 1 Ch 16. But note that if a statute merely modifies, extends, or clarifies an existing legal principle, remedy, or defence, it is not necessary to mention the statute itself, but rather to plead all the elements required by the statute should be pleaded. For example, it is not necessary to refer to the Misrepresentation Act 1967 in a statement of case, but it is necessary to set out all the elements required to establish a case of misrepresentation. Another small exception is that it is necessary to plead private Acts of Parliament where relevant, or to plead any appropriate point of foreign law. In *Ascherberg, Hopwood & Crew v Casa Musicale SNC* [1971] 1 WLR 173 there was an action regarding the copyright to two Italian operas, and it was held that the relevant Italian law should be pleaded.

The position now is that points of law may be referred to, PD 16 para 13. Law should still **12.58** generally be omitted, but the inclusion of law may be justified where that helps to elucidate the case to be met, where there is a statutory defence or exception to be dealt with, or there is a particularly unusual point of law.

Including facts rather than evidence

The statement of case sets out the factual elements of the case. The case will need to be **12.59** proved as and when it comes to court, but the evidential proof does not need to be in the statement. Indeed it is better that evidence is not included or the statement of allegations will not be so clear and concise. Strategically a lawyer might choose to keep evidence private in the early stages of a case.

However, the relationship between the facts and the evidence that proves those facts is of **12.60** necessity quite close. The facts are the story of what happened, whereas the evidence is how you show the story was true. For example, 'the claimant was injured when his hand was caught in the machine' is an allegation of fact, whereas the evidence to prove the allegation will be provided by the claimant or other witnesses to the accident. Sometimes facts and evidence overlap, so that evidence is inevitably pleaded as part of pleading the case. For example 'a written contract was made' is an allegation of fact, but the evidence of the contract is the written document itself.

There is also the link that an allegation should only be included in a statement of case if **12.61** there is evidence that it is true. This does not need to be compelling evidence as the strength of the evidence is a matter for trial, but there must be some evidence that an allegation is true. The evidence of the client can be sufficient for this purpose.

The CPR has brought a change of emphasis. It remains the case that a statement of case **12.62** should focus on factual allegations and that evidence should not be included if it will make the statement long or unfocussed, but it is now acceptable for evidence to be included, and there may be merit in this where the evidence is strong or where the case is relatively straightforward. It can also be useful to include evidence in a statement of case where it might assist at an interim hearing.

12.63 Documents can be quoted in a statement of case where that is necessary to identify facts and issues, *Morris v Bank of America National Trust* The Times, 25 January 2000. In a contractual case a copy of the contract should be attached to the statement of case.

Including facts rather than arguments

12.64 A good statement of case is a series of statements of facts. These statements are best not cluttered with arguments, explanations, or theories. The place for argument is the skeleton argument and submissions in court.

12.65 The facts that may lay the foundation for an argument should be in the statement of case—if there is an argument that a head of loss was foreseeable because one party gave information about it to the other then the facts of the giving of the information need to be pleaded. The point is that the argument linking the facts should not be set out in the statement of case.

12.66 In tactical terms there is in any event little to gain from putting an argument into a statement of case—it can limit the arguments that can be raised at trial, it can alert the other side to arguments so that they can prepare a response, and it is likely to make the statement of case less focussed. If there is thought to be merit in using an argument to persuade the other side of the strength of the case before trial then the argument can be put in a letter or a negotiation.

Appropriate terminology and wording

12.67 There are some phrases that are particularly useful in a statement of case, having an accepted meaning that fulfils a particular purpose and giving a professional tone where they are used appropriately.

Parties

12.68 The claimant should be referred to throughout as 'the claimant' and the defendant should always be referred to as 'the defendant'. A person referred to in the pleading who is not a party should normally be called by their full name, eg 'John Smith'.

Short form references

12.69 To avoid having to repeat a long title, a short form reference can be given the first time the title is used, and then only the short form used later. For example after setting out fully 'Longstanding Construction (London) PLC ("the company")', later references can simply be to 'the company'. This can normally be used as an alternative to the more traditional 'the said company'.

At all material times

12.70 This phrase briefly alleges that a particular relationship or state of facts continued throughout the period covered by the pleading.

Further or in the alternative

This is a useful phrase where there are alternatives in a case, be it alternative causes of action, **12.71**
alternative breaches, alternative types of negligence, etc. The phrase means that the allegation following it is either in addition to or an alternative to the allegation already made,
giving the option of succeeding with one or the other or both. Alternatives can be alleged if
it is not known how something happened.

As alleged or at all

This phrase is useful to deny how or why something happened, in that it can be used to deny **12.72**
specific allegations and any other allegations that have not been set out specifically.

If, which is denied

This will effectively allow two alternative lines of argument to be put. The first is that the **12.73**
allegation is denied, and the second is that, if the allegation is found to be true, a further
argument on the facts or the law is advanced.

In the premises

Although a little antiquated, this expression is useful to pull together a number of factual **12.74**
allegations to suggest a particular factual conclusion.

The precise words of a document or conversation should be summarised, unless the words **12.75**
are directly relevant.

- Any document which is an essential element of a case must be referred to specifically,
  including when it was made, by whom, and if appropriate, where.
- If any clause of a written document is of particular importance it should be set out
  verbatim, otherwise the meaning of a relevant term can be summarised.
- Any oral statement that is of particular importance must be identified clearly, setting out
  who made the statement, when, and where.
- If an oral statement is of particular importance, for example as an oral term or a
  misrepresentation, it should be set out verbatim or summarised, for example 'the
  defendant orally represented to the claimant that the car was in perfect condition'.

F   HEADINGS FOR STATEMENTS OF CASE

The rules for headings

The heading of a statement of case must follow a prescribed form, PD 7 para 4. The title **12.76**
should state:

- the claim number;
- the court or division in which the claim is proceeding;
- the full name of each party;
- the status of each party in the proceedings (claimant etc).

The claim number is assigned by the court when the claim form is filed. A space should be **12.77**
left for the claim number if the number has not yet been assigned, or it should be copied

from an earlier statement of case. A High Court number normally consists of the year the claim form is filed, followed by HC and a number. In the county court the number normally consists of letters identifying the court, with a single number identifying the year and then the court number. The choice of court and division are referred to at 4.42–4.50.

12.78 The names used in an action need to identify the party clearly, and a party must have independent legal personality. Choice of parties is covered at 13.01–13.62. It is vital to name the parties accurately—if the right person is not joined then the action may fail, though this will not necessarily be the case if a mis-description of a party does not actually lead to any mistake as to who is intended. The involvement of different parties needs careful consideration. For example, if one person negotiates a contract on behalf of another it should be the principal, not the agent, who is joined, *Hector v Lyons* The Times, 19 December 1988.

- The full name of an individual should be given if known, without abbreviations, and without 'Mr' or 'Mrs'. A further description may be added in brackets if there might be any confusion as to identity of the party, for example as regards the sex of a party, though this is now rarely done.
- A company is a separate legal entity, and the correct full name of the company should be used, including Limited or PLC.
- Where a person is using a trade name, the real name of the person should be given with the addition of 'trading as . . .'.
- Partners can sue or be sued in their own names or in the name of the partnership, adding the words 'a firm' in brackets, as in 'Easiphix Plumbers (a firm)'.
- A limited liability partnership should use the name of the partnership with the addition of LLP.
- An unincorporated association may also be involved in an action, the normal method being to join an officer of the body, such as the Treasurer or Secretary, to represent it.
- A government department, local authority, or health authority can sue or be sued as such.
- A body recognised by foreign law, such as an Indian temple can be accepted as a party, *Bumper Development Corporation v Commissioner of Police* [1991] 4 All ER 638.
- If a person has died, his executors or personal representatives may sue or be sued in his place, with the added words 'executors of the will of ZZ deceased' or as appropriate.
- A person who is bankrupt can only bring an action or be sued by the trustee in bankruptcy, who would be described as 'The trustee of YY a bankrupt'.
- A person under the age of 18 should be identified as a child. A child must be represented by a litigation friend, whose name should also be given. The heading should read 'Alexander Allen, a minor, by Alexis Allen his litigation friend'.
- A person under a disability must be represented by a litigation friend, whose name should also be given. The heading should read 'Colin Coutts, by Darren Drake his litigation friend'.

12.79 If the patient or minor is the claimant then the litigation friend should be named in the claim form. However, if the patient or minor is the defendant then only the name of the patient or minor need be given by the claimant in the claim form, as the litigation friend will be decided on by the other side.

12.80 Clear decisions as to parties should be given before the claim form is issued. The misjoinder or non-joinder of a party should not of itself prove fatal to an action so long as there is no real mistake as to identity and no one has been seriously prejudiced or misled. The test is whether there has been a genuine mistake in the name but there is no real doubt about the identity of the party. The court can allow an amendment, save that a party cannot normally be joined after the end of the limitation period, it may be difficult to amend in the later stages of an action, and there may be a penalty in costs.

The reason why each party is joined must be clearly set out in the body of the statement of case, if for example it is alleged that there is agency or vicarious liability. **12.81**

Sample headings

IN THE CAMBRIDGE COUNTY COURT   Claim No CA5/1234   **12.82**

BETWEEN

ADRIAN ADNAM   Claimant

and

BRIAN BEST   Defendant
(trading as Best Builders)

_____

PARTICULARS OF CLAIM
_____

IN THE HIGH COURT OF JUSTICE   Claim No 2005 HC 1234   **12.83**
QUEEN'S BENCH DIVISION
(Winchester District Registry)

BETWEEN

(1) CUMFY CARS LIMITED
(2) DD   _____   Claimant

and

(1) EE
(2) FF (a firm)_____   Defendants

_____

DEFENCE
_____

G   THE CLAIM FORM

The claim form is the formal document which must be used to commence the action. It must state the parties and the nature of the claim. The form for a claim form is set by Civil Procedure Rules 1998. Proper care should be taken in completing it, to adapt it to the case in hand, filling in blanks and striking out any parts which are not appropriate. **12.84**

12.85   A claim form must (CPR r 16.2):

- contain a concise statement of the nature of the claim;
- specify the remedy which the claimant seeks;
- contain a statement of value if the claim is for money;
- contain such other matters as may be set out in a Practice Direction.

12.86   There should be a statement of value (CPR r 16.3). This is relevant to court jurisdiction and track allocation. The amount stated should ignore any counterclaim or set off and also interest and costs. The claimant should state:

- the specific amount claimed;
- that the claimant expects to recover not more than £5,000;
- that the claimant expects to recover more than £5,000 but not more than £15,000;
- that the claimant expects to recover more than £15,000, or the claim can only be commenced in the High Court under a specific enactment; or
- that the claimant cannot specify what he/she expects to recover.

12.87   For a personal injury claim the claimant must state whether he/she expects to recover not more than or more than £1,000 for pain, suffering, and loss of amenity. For the action to be started in the High Court there must be a statement that the claimant expects to recover £50,000 or more.

12.88   In addition PD 16 provides that

- if practicable the particulars of claim should be set out in the claim form;
- it must contain the claimant's address;
- it must contain the defendant's address, if the claimant knows it.

12.89   The nature of the claim and the remedy sought should be put in the box on the form even if the particulars of claim are attached. This should specify causes of action and remedies sought, though a court can grant a remedy even if it is not specified in the claim form, CPR r 16.2.

12.90   It will only be practicable for the particulars of claim to be set out on the claim form where they are very short, or where an abbreviated form of claim can be made, for example for payment for goods sold and delivered, or for work done and materials supplied. There are no set words to be used, the rule being only that there must be a concise statement of the nature of the claim or the relief or remedy required. This will generally consist of just a few sentences that give basic details of the type of action and what is claimed. If the claim is for a debt or liquidated demand, there must be a statement of the amount claimed (and that the proceedings will be stayed if that amount is paid to the plaintiff or his solicitor or agent within the time limited for appearing). If the action is for the possession of land there must be a statement of whether the claim relates to a dwelling house and, if it does, its rateable value. If the action is to recover possession of goods there should be a statement of the value of the goods.

12.91   A few simple examples of concise statements are:

> The claim is for damages for breach of a contract made in writing on 1st January 2005 for the sale of a painting, and for interest.

The claimant's claim is for:

(i)   Damages for personal injury and loss caused to the claimant by the negligence of the defendant on 3rd January 2004 at 4, Grays Inn Place, London.

(ii)   Interest pursuant to s 35A Supreme Court Act 1981.

Although the summary is brief, it is part of the statements of case in the action, and is **12.92** binding. The particulars of claim cannot contain a claim or cause of action which is not mentioned in the claim form or does not arise from the facts in it, though the particulars of claim may alter, modify, or extend any claim made in the claim form.

The full particulars of claim do not have to be indorsed on the claim form, but can be a **12.93** separate document. Whether the particulars of claim are issued at the same time as the claim form is a matter for the claimant. If the work of drafting is done it is cheaper and more convenient to deal with both together. However, in practice a claim form may be issued before the particulars of claim is drafted, if for example the limitation period is about to expire. There may also be tactical reasons for issuing a claim form, for example to show the other side that you do intend to pursue the case seriously, especially if negotiations have gone on for some time and it is hoped that this will encourage settlement.

A claim form is issued by being sealed by an officer of the Central Office in the High Court in **12.94** London or at a District Registry. It is necessary to take copies for the defendant(s) as well as the original and also a form of acknowledgment of service for each defendant.

H   GENERAL FRAMEWORK FOR A PARTICULARS OF CLAIM

General principles

Some particulars of claim have a prescribed form, for example for the possession of residential **12.95** property (PD4). In general terms the particulars of claim should set out the following.

- The material facts that comprise all the essential elements that must be shown as a matter of law to justify a cause of action.
- The remedies being claimed, including any claim for exemplary, exaggerated, or provisional damages.
- The particulars must also include interest claimed with the authority for claiming it, the rate, and the period.
- Costs need not be specifically claimed.
- The particulars of claim must include a statement of truth (CPR r 22.1).

If a party seeks to raise a human rights point, precise details of the Convention right relied **12.96** on must be set out, together with details of the alleged infringement and the relief sought (PD 16, para 16.1).

This is based on decisions as to: **12.97**

- causes of action;
- defendants, see Chapter 13;
- the remedies sought, see Chapter 14;
- the quantification of the damages sought, see Chapter 14.

Outline for a particulars of claim

12.98   IN THE HIGH COURT OF JUSTICE   Claim No 2005 HC 1234
QUEEN'S BENCH DIVISION
BETWEEN

A.B.	Claimant
and	
C.D.	Defendant

PARTICULARS OF CLAIM

1. (Establish as far as is relevant to the action who the parties are and what they do.)
2. (Set out any relevant facts prior to the cause of action arising.)
3. (Set out the basic relationship from which the cause of action arises, eg, the contract, duty of care, trust. Give all appropriate details, such as dates.)
4. (Set out relevant details of the duty, eg, relevant terms of the contract.)
5. (Set out the cause of action, eg, breach of contract, negligence.)

PARTICULARS OF BREACH/NEGLIGENCE

(Set out all appropriate details of the breach, negligence etc.)

6. As a result of these matters aforesaid the Claimant has suffered loss and damage.

PARTICULARS OF DAMAGE

(Set out the details of special damage with figures, that is any loss which is already quantifiable.)

7. (Set out the basic facts of any type of loss or damage which you wish to claim for, but which is not an obvious result of the facts already pleaded. Include facts relevant to causation and forseeability.)
8. (Set out a claim for interest if appropriate.)

AND the Claimant claims:

1. (List in separate paragraphs all remedies sought, including a claim for interest if that is sought)
2. . . . .

Statement of Truth   (Signed)

Dated etc.

For samples of particulars of claim in contract see 18.121, 18.122, 18.123, 18.124, 18.125, 18.129, and 18.132. For examples of particulars of claim in tort see 19.138, 19.142, 19.145, 19.146, 19.147, 19.148, and 19.150.

I   SPECIFYING REMEDIES AND RELIEF

Allegations supporting a remedy

The remedies and relief that may be available, including measures of damage and the quan- **12.99** tification of damage, are covered at 14.01–14.29, 18.04–18.60, and 19.06–19.58. It is quite possible to ask for different types of remedy and relief in the alternative if it would not be possible to claim both.

The particulars of claim should include factual allegations relevant to all remedies and relief **12.100** sought. The allegations should be properly integrated into the body of the statement of case, with facts that set out:

• each head of loss and damage;
• facts showing that the loss or damage was caused by or arose from the cause of action;
• any facts showing the foreseeability of the loss or damage, or that it was within the reasonable contemplation of the parties.

In recent years there has been some growth in the amount of detail supplied in pleading **12.101** damages. It has become increasingly common to plead loss in detail, to strengthen the claim, and probably to give a better basis to the other side for deciding what they might offer in settlement or might pay into court. In *Chan Wai Tong v Li Ping Sum* [1985] AC 446 it was said to be good practice in an action for damages for personal injuries to plead loss of future earning capacity in detail, to give fair notice to the defendant. In a personal injuries claim there must now be a schedule of past and future expenses and losses, PD16 para 4.2.

If in any doubt, provided there is some evidence to justify the claim, it is generally advisable **12.102** to include all potential remedies and relief that meet the client's needs, and to pitch each claim as high as is reasonably possible, on the basis that the remedy or relief will not be granted if it is not sought. Once the remedies sought are specified it is then for the other side to argue in their statement of case, a negotiation or in court whether what has been sought should in fact be granted.

Listing remedies and relief sought

The remedies sought are normally listed at the end of the statement of case, in the part **12.103** referred to as the prayer, beginning 'AND the Claimant claims' followed by a list of the remedies sought, with each one stated briefly and numbered separately. It is quite possible to ask for any number of remedies or relief cumulatively or in the alternative provided each is available on the facts, and the judge in the case will have power to grant it.

If there is more than one defendant, it should be made clear whether all remedies are sought **12.104** against both or whether some remedies are sought against one and some against another, which can be done either by having a separate numbered list against each defendant, or by making it clear in each numbered point against whom the remedy is sought.

Claims for damages

12.105 In pleading a claim for damages it is vital to think comprehensively about what has been lost. Issues of measure of damages, quantification of damages, and heads of damage are covered in Chapter 14. There has been a growth in the amount of detail to be provided regarding a claim for damages, not least to make it easier for an appropriate payment into court to be assessed.

12.106 There are a number of cases in which a claimant has failed to recover something lost because it was not pleaded, or if pleaded was not proved. Although amendment might now be allowed in these cases, they illustrate the need for specific claims and detail.

- In *Pestrello E Companhia Limitada v United Paint Co* [1969] 1 WLR 570 there was an action for breach of contract in which the claimant claimed wasted expenditure, but not loss of profit. It was held that he could recover nothing under the second head—he should have raised the point with precise figures if appropriate and it was too late to amend his pleading at trial.
- In *Ilkiw v Samuels* [1963] 1 WLR 991 the claimant was injured at work and the statement of claim alleged a specific loss of £77, but said nothing about a continuing loss of £200 pa. It was held that therefore nothing was recoverable for this continuing loss.
- In *Domsalla v Barr* [1969] 1 WLR 630 the claimant fell off a steel erection at work and suffered continuing dizziness. He claimed that as a result he had had to turn down a job he had hoped to get in Nigeria, and was no longer fit enough to set up his own business eventually as he had hoped. It was held that he could not recover damages for these things because they were not pleaded, and because he could not provide sufficient evidence that these things would have happened.
- In *Ashcroft v Curtin* [1971] 3 All ER 1208, a man was injured in a car accident and alleged that as a result he was no longer lively and dynamic enough to carry on his one man business. It was held that he could not get damages for this because there was insufficient evidence to show it was true.
- In *Hayward v Pullinger & Partners* [1950] 1 All ER 581 there was an action for wrongful dismissal, and it was held that figures for lost salary and commission lost due to the dismissal were special damages and details should be pleaded.
- In *Monk v Redwing Aircraft Co* [1942] 1 KB 182 again in an action for wrongful dismissal, it was held that the defendant was entitled to know whether the claimant had found a new job and, if so how long it was for and what the salary was, as this was all directly relevant to the quantification of damage.
- In *Phipps v Orthodox Unit Trusts* [1957] 3 All ER 305 it was held that the defendant was entitled to know something of the claimant's tax position where this was relevant to the quantification of damage, although it would not normally be suitable to put this type of detail in the statement of claim.

12.107 It will be for a defendant to plead facts challenging a claim for damages, arguing for example lack of foreseeability or causation, or failure to mitigate loss. This is dealt with at 17.46.

Claims for interest

12.108 Where there is a claim for the payment of a sum of money or damages, the claimant may wish to claim interest in addition. In times of relatively high rates of interest and inflation this can be important. A claim for interest should be set out in the particulars of claim, CPR r 16.4. It is necessary to state the basis on which interest is claimed. The bases on which interest may be claimed are covered at 14.68–14.77.

For a claim for an unspecified amount it is sufficient to claim interest under the Supreme **12.109** Court Act 1981, s 35A or under the County Courts Act 1984, s 69. The amount of money or damages on which interest is payable will need to be specified.

For a claim for interest on a specified amount it is necessary to state the basis on which **12.110** interest is claimed, the rate of interest claimed, the date from which interest runs, the date to which interest has been calculated (eg on filing the claim form), the amount of interest claimed to date, and the equivalent daily rate thereafter. This is to enable the defendant to be able to calculate how much interest is payable at any particular time.

Note that different elements of a damages claim may require separate arguments and calcu- **12.111** lations as to the relevant interest entitlement. Note that if there is a split trial and quantum is decided after liability, it has been held that interest runs from the date quantum is decided in a personal injury case, *Thomas v Bunn* [1991] 1 All ER 193.

J   OTHER DRAFTS FOR A CLAIMANT

The reply (and defence to counterclaim)

The defendant may well file a defence, which is dealt with at 17.47–17.84. The defence is **12.112** often the last statement of case in an action, as the claimant is not taken to admit any matters raised in the defence, so it is not necessary to file a reply simply to take issue with the defence. Even if a claimant files a reply but fails to deal with a matter in the defence, then the claimant is still taken to require the matter to be proved, CPR r 16.7. In a relatively straight-forward case where the statement of case has been well drafted, there should normally be no need for a reply. The defence may have a counterclaim added, see 17.85–17.91.

The reasons why a claimant may wish to file a reply are: **12.113**

- to admit facts raised in the defence to save costs;
- to make it clear that a particular matter raised in the defence is denied and is actively contested;
- to reply to new allegations in the defence;
- where there is value in the claimant setting out the claimant's version of events raised in the defence to assist in clarifying the issues in dispute in the case;
- in any event to assist in defining issues, for example by responding to allegations in the defence such as contributory negligence or failure to mitigate loss, or to help to clarify matters if the defence is quite long or complicated;
- that a reply may be used if the defendant appears to have misunderstood the claimant's case, but there is no purpose in using a reply to restate matters that are in the particulars of claim.

If it is decided that there is a purpose to be served in filing a reply, the content must be **12.114** chosen with care. The key objectives to be achieved in the reply should be defined with care.

It is not necessary to deal with every allegation in the defence, but each separate allegation in the defence should be considered to decide whether there is merit in commenting on it. If nothing is said then it will be assumed that the defendant is required to prove the allegation, so allegations should be admitted or denied where relevant.

12.115 Principles for drafting a reply include the following.

- A reply will normally only refer to specific paragraphs and allegations in the defence. Careful consideration should be given to whether to deny what is said or to make positive assertions.
- The reply will be set out in separate numbered paragraphs, and it is often useful, though not necessary, that it should follow the order of the defence.
- There is a limitation in that a party shall not in any statement of case make an allegation of fact, or raise any new ground or claim which is inconsistent with a previous pleading of his.

12.116 The reply should not normally be used for material that should be in the particulars of claim. The particulars of claim should be amended instead. Amendment may be required to avoid inconsistency. A reply cannot be used to allege a totally new cause of action—this should be done by amending the statement of claim if appropriate, or by commencing a new action. In *Herbert v Vaughan* [1972] 1 WLR 1128 the claimant alleged undue influence by one person, but then in his reply tried to allege undue influence by a totally different person, and it was held that this was a new cause of action which should not be raised in a reply.

12.117 If there is a counterclaim with the defence then a defence to counterclaim can and normally should be added to the reply. The same rules apply as for drafting a normal defence.

Outline for a reply and defence to counterclaim

12.118   IN THE HIGH COURT OF JUSTICE   Claim No 2005 HC 1234
QUEEN'S BENCH DIVISION
BETWEEN

A.B.	Claimant
and	
C.D.	Defendant

REPLY

(Plead to any allegations in the defence that you wish to deal with, in separate numbered paragraphs.)

1. As to paragraph   of the defence, the Claimant denies that. . . . .
2. As to paragraph   of the defence, the Claimant admits that. . . . .
3. The Defendant is required to prove that. . . . .
4. (Add any additional facts that are relevant because of what is in the Defence.)

<u>DEFENCE TO COUNTERCLAIM</u>

(Plead to all the allegations in the counterclaim in separate numbered paragraphs in the same way as pleading a Defence.)

4.

5.

6.

Statement of Truth   (Signed)

Dated etc.

K   REFINING A STATEMENT OF CASE

The need to refine a statement of case

Ideally a well crafted statement of case will not need to be altered. It should not need to be   **12.119** altered simply because it was not sufficiently well drafted in the first place. However, the litigation process may make it inevitable that a statement of case be revised, and the statements of case should be reviewed from time to time.

- The statements of case from the other side may reveal some misunderstandings about the nature of the case that needs to be addressed.
- Evidence that was previously unavailable may show the desirability of modifying the way the case is cast, such as refining the particulars of negligence.
- Evidence from the other side on disclosure or exchange of witness statements may show the need to refine the case.
- The case is very complex and/or takes a long time to come to trial and the overall character of the case needs to be reviewed.
- The statement of case had to be drafted before full information was available because a limitation period was about to expire and it needs to be polished up.
- One lawyer takes over a case from another and feels that it is difficult to argue the case as currently framed.
- The statements of case are reviewed shortly before trial and need to be polished up, because the case can only be argued on the basis set out in the statements of case.

A change in a statement of case may be relatively small, such as correcting an error or   **12.120** refining particulars of breach, or it may be quite significant in terms of changing a cause of action or a party.

Refining a statement of case is desirable to the extent that it helps to define and reduce the   **12.121** issues and may save costs. It should be avoided where it may increase the costs of the litigation, and there may be penalties in costs (including having to pay the costs of the other side if they have to refine their statements of case in response). It may be expensive if the amendment shows that the costs of some preparations already made have been wasted because something that was an issue is no longer an issue. It may be difficult because the consent of the court is likely to be required, and it may be impossible if the limitation period has passed and the change seeks to add a party or a cause of action.

12.122 A party's own statement of case may be refined by discontinuing some part of the action, by making an admission on a particular issue, or by amending the statement of case.

The process for amending a statement of case

12.123 Amendment should be carried out to assist in defining the issues, but it should not be undertaken lightly. As much analysis and care should go into an amendment as into the original drafting of the statement of case. There may need to be an amendment to reflect a decision as to a change in the way the case is conducted, and the new wording should be selected with great care, see *Spaven v Milton Keynes Borough Council* The Times, 16 March 1990. See generally CPR Part 17 Amendments to statements of case and PD 17 Amendments to statements of case.

12.124 Amendment is allowed without permission at any time before a statement of case has been served on any party, CPR r 17.1. A party served with a statement of case amended without permission can seek an order disallowing the amendment.

12.125 An amendment may be allowed with the written consent of all the parties, CPR r 17.1.

12.126 An amendment may be made with the permission of the court, CPR r 17.1. Application is by application notice accompanied by a draft of the proposed amendment, PD 17 para 1.The test will be the application of the overriding objective, so arguments will need to be put forward, for example showing that the case will be better defined or costs saved. If permission is granted, the party given permission will normally have to pay costs of and caused by the amendment.

12.127 An amendment to correct an error will be allowed relatively easily. Normally justice will require that a party be allowed to put his or her case accurately, so an amendment to this end is likely to be granted, particularly where a new allegation or cause of action lies wholly or largely within what is already pleaded. However a significant amendment will not necessarily be allowed at a late stage in the case, *Ketteman v Hansel Properties Ltd* (1987) AC 189 HL, *Charlesworth v Relay Roads Ltd* (2000) 1 WLR 230 and *Easton v Ford Motor Co Ltd* (1993) 4 All ER 257. Also it will not be possible to amend a statement of case that has arisen since the case was started—a new action must be commenced. The judge may propose an amendment to encapsulate the points being argued more clearly. An amendment may be refused if it will serve no useful purpose, *Re Jokai Tea Holdings Ltd* (1992) 1 WLR 1196 CA.

12.128 An amendment cannot be made to a statement of case if the result would be contradictory statements of case for the same party, both supported by a statement of truth, *Clarke v Marlborough Fine Art (London) Ltd* The Times, 4 December 2001.

12.129 If amendment is allowed it may be acceptable to retype the document in its new version, or with amendments simply indicated with insertions and striking through in black ink. However the court may direct that a method of showing the original and the amended version be used, PD 17 para 2, such as the traditional approach of showing all amendments in red on original black type (with subsequent amendments in green, violet, and yellow). Text that has been deleted should be crossed out in the relevant colour with new text put in or underlined in the same colour. The amended document must be endorsed as being amended, quoting the relevant order. Substantial changes may require a further statement of truth.

Principles for major amendments

If the amendment involves the removal, addition, or substitution of a party, any alteration **12.130** after the service of the claim form will require court approval. The main test is whether the amendment is desirable, CPR Part 19. To add a new party the test is also whether adding the party will enable the court to resolve all matters in dispute in the proceedings, or there is an issue involving the new party and an existing party which is connected to the matters in dispute and it is desirable to add the new party so that the court can resolve that issue, CPR r 19.2. The test for substituting a party is that the existing party's interest or liability has passed to the new party and it is desirable to substitute the party so that the court can resolve all matters in dispute in the proceedings.

Application can be made by an existing party or by someone who wants to be a party, **12.131** CPR r 19.4. There will normally need to be notice to other parties and there will usually be evidence in support. If the order is made it will grant permission to amend and may include other consequential directions for the proper involvement of the new party in the proceedings. It should be served on the parties and anyone else affected. A party can only be added as a claimant if they consent in writing, CPR r 19.4.

Amendment after the end of the limitation period is very difficult. Essentially neither the **12.132** High Court nor the County Court can allow any new claim other than an original set-off or counterclaim in the course of any action after the expiry of the limitation period, Limitation Act 1980, s 35. There can be no addition or substitution of either a new cause of action or a party. A new cause of action can be added only if it is an original set-off or counterclaim by a party who has not previously made any claim in the action, or if the court disapplies the personal injury limitation period, or if it arises out of the same or substantially the same facts as are already in issue. It seems that an original set-off or counterclaim is one between the original claimant and defendant, *Kennet v Brown* (1988) 1 WLR 582. Negligent design and negligent supervision can arise from the same set of facts, *Brickfield Properties Ltd v Newton* (1971) 1 WLR 863, but adding further boats to an existing compensation claim has been held to involve adding separate facts, *R v Secretary of State for Transport ex p Factortame Ltd (No 7)* (2001) 1 WLR 942. A claimant may be permitted to plead a further claim based on facts raised in the defence, *Goode v Martin* (2002) 1 WLR 1828.

A new party may be added if the claim cannot properly be carried on unless the new party is **12.133** added or substituted, CPR r 19.5. It seems that this provision will be construed quite narrowly, *Merrett v Babb* (2001) QB 1174. A new party may be added as an amendment of the capacity of a party, provided the capacity is one the party had at or since the start of the proceedings, CPR r 17.4. Again this has a fairly narrow construction, *Haq v Singh* (2001) 1 WLR 1594. A new party can be added if there was a mistake, CPR r 19.5, see *Horne-Roberts v SmithKline Beecham plc* (2002) 1 WLR 1662. A new party can also be added if the court disapplies the personal injury limitation period. Note that timing is crucial, and amendment and service should be affected before the expiry of the limitation period if these restrictive rules are not to apply, *Welsh Development Agency v Redpath Dorman Long Ltd* (1994) 1 WLR 1409 CA.

L   CHALLENGING A STATEMENT OF CASE

Reasons for challenging a statement of case

12.134   There are many reasons for wishing to challenge the statements of case of an opponent. In the past challenges might be made for a variety of tactical reasons, but with the modern approach to litigation, challenges should be aimed primarily at defining issues and saving costs.

12.135   The main reasons for challenging an opponent's statement of case might be:

- if fundamental problems can be shown in a statement of case, indicating that the statement of case is unlikely to succeed, the opponent may drop the action;
- if significant problems can be shown, indicating real weaknesses in the case, the opponent may be more inclined to make an offer in settlement;
- smaller points may be unlikely to affect the outcome of the case, but might persuade an opponent to make a concession on a particular issue.

12.136   On the other hand, there may be little to be gained in challenging relatively small points, not least if the point is likely to be contested and costs built up. Indeed a challenge may be counter-productive in prompting the opponent to amend the statement of claim to strengthen it. The options may need to be considered carefully in terms of the desired outcome and the potential costs. Challenging a statement of case may be necessary if the case for the other side is so poorly stated that it is difficult for the lawyer to prepare his or her own case. Challenging a statement of case may be of limited use if the result is that the other side are prompted into improving their analysis and preparation—in such a case it may be better to wait until trial and point out the weaknesses then.

12.137   There is a variety of ways in which a party can challenge a statement of case of an opponent:

- If no statement of case is filed and served. In this event there should be an application for a default judgment. This is dealt with at 16.84–16.94.
- If the statement of case is fundamentally flawed. In this event there may be an application to strike out the statement of case. Note that in tactical terms the result may be that the opponent amends the statement of case so that it is not struck out. It may be better to apply for summary judgment if that is a realistic alternative.
- If the statement of case is so weak it is unlikely to succeed. In this event an application for summary judgment should normally be made. This is dealt with at 16.95–16.102.
- If the statement of case has weaknesses. If the statement of case is vague, inconsistent, or superficial, a request for further information may be made.
- If the statement of case includes allegations that should probably not be contested at trial it may be appropriate to seek admissions.

Striking out a statement of case

12.138   This is clearly the most radical way of attacking a statement of case, as it is broadly alleging that the whole case, or at least the statement of case, is unfounded or misconceived. A party has a right to seek legal redress, not least under Article 6, so a court will be slow to strike out a statement of case. An application should normally only be made if there is a reasonably good chance of success, or the risk is that the application will fail and the applicant will have to pay costs. If the case may be saved by amendment the court is likely to allow that rather than to strike the case out entirely, and a party may be given the opportunity to save a statement of case by providing more information or documents. It is a matter of professional courtesy to warn the other side informally before applying to have their pleading struck out, normally by the lawyer who will make the application telephoning the lawyer who drafted the statement of case. See generally PD3 Striking out a statement of case.

Under CPR r 3.4, a court can strike out a statement of case, or part of the statement of case, if   **12.139**
it appears to the court:

- that the statement of case discloses no reasonable ground for bringing or defending the claim;
- that the statement of case is an abuse of the court's process, or is otherwise likely to obstruct the just disposal of the proceedings; or
- if there has been a failure to comply with a rule, practice direction, or court order.

A claim can be struck out: **12.140**

- if it does not disclose a legally recognisable claim, or for example it is a basic allegation without sufficient background facts, or if there are allegations of breach without pleading a contract;
- if it is unfounded, for example because evidence in support has not been produced;
- if it is incoherent or does not make sense;
- if it is an abuse of process as being vexatious or otherwise unfounded, if for example a limitation period has expired. A case may be vexatious if the case has effectively already been adjudicated, *Johnson v Gore Wood and Co* (2002) 2 AC 1 HL. A case can be struck out for wholesale disregard of court rules, *Biguzzi v Rank Leisure plc* (1999) 1 WLR 1926 CA;
- for behaviour that destroys the chance of a fair trial, such as destruction of evidence.

A defence may be struck out: **12.141**

- if it is a bare denial, rather than a reasonably detailed defence to the allegations made;
- if it otherwise fails to set out a coherent statement of facts;
- if the facts set out do not amount to a defence in law;
- if the defendant has destroyed evidence prior to the start of the action in a way that amounts to an attempt to pervert the course of justice, *Douglas and Others v Hello! Ltd and Others (No 2)* The Times, 30 January 2003.

An application to strike out should specify exactly what is alleged to be wrong with the   **12.142**
pleading, not just show general dissatisfaction. Examples of where there may be no reasonable cause of action or defence are set out in PD 3. Striking out can be initiated by an application, or by the court of its own initiative. There may not need to be evidence in support if the point can be argued on the statement of case itself. The application to strike out should be made as soon as possible after the statement of case is served. On striking out the court may give such judgment as the other party is entitled to, PD 3 para 4.2. If particulars of claim are struck out the claim will be stayed or dismissed. If defence is struck out then judgment will be entered for the claimant.

12.143 Striking out will only be ordered in a clear case—if the point requires significant argument then the implication is that the case needs to continue, *Three Rivers District Council v Bank of England (No 3)* (2001) 2 All ER 513 HL and *Lonrho plc v Tebbit* [1992] 4 All ER 973. If the case is capable of being argued on the face of the statement of case then it should be allowed to continue even if it will almost certainly fail—it is not for the court to weigh up the strength of the case or the evidence at this stage. The fact that there may be an ulterior motive for bringing a case, such as an intention of damaging the other side's business, will not of itself be reason to strike out. An interim application cannot be struck out, see *Port v Auger* (1994) 1 WLR 862.

12.144 A case may be struck out if it should be determined in a way other than litigation in court, see *Thorne v University of London* [1966] 2 QB 237.

Requesting further information

Making a request

12.145 Further information may be sought under CPR Part 18 and PD 18 to enable the issues for trial to be narrowed. Under CPR r 18.1 a court may at any time order a party to:

- clarify any matter which is in dispute in the proceedings; or
- give additional information in relation to any such matter, whether or not the matter is contained or referred to in a statement of case.

12.146 This underlines the principle that full information should be available. The principle of not building costs unnecessarily is maintained by the provision that the further information should be sought informally before seeking a court order.

12.147 If a party feels that a statement of case is not sufficiently clear a request for further information can be made. The procedure can be used to clarify any issue in dispute even if it is not specifically referred to, CPR r 18.1, if for example an issue appears to arise from a witness statement. The court can use this procedure of its own initiative. The party seeking the information can be ordered to pay the costs of providing it, but if the need to seek further information was caused by the inadequacy of a statement of case, the party responsible for that inadequacy will normally have to pay the costs.

12.148 The request should normally be made shortly after the relevant statement of case is served. The first step is a written request for the information, and it should:

- be in a letter or more formally in a separate document, the Request for Further Information;
- if possible be prepared in such a way that a response can be given on the same document, with numbered questions on the left and space for responses on the right;
- be concise, and confined to matters which are reasonably necessary and proportionate to enable the party making the request to prepare his case or understand the case he has to meet;
- state a date by which a response is reasonably expected.

12.149 Skill is required in deciding exactly what to ask about, and how, so that it is clear what information is sought and the other party cannot avoid the issue. If the request relates to a specific document then that document and the relevant part of it should be clearly identified. Questions can ask for details of when where and how something was done. Phrases like 'state precisely . . .' or 'give the full facts and matters relied on in support of . . .' can be useful. Each item of further information sought should be set out in a separate paragraph. Ideally questions will build to show weakness in the case pleaded like a cross examination. The further information sought can only relate to an allegation of fact and not a matter of evidence or argument, or a point of law.

Outline for an application for further information: **12.150**

IN THE HIGH COURT OF JUSTICE   Claim No 2005 HC 1234
QUEEN'S BENCH DIVISION

BETWEEN

A.B.   Claimant

and

C.D.   Defendant

REQUEST FOR FURTHER INFORMATION
UNDER CPR PART 18

This request is made on (date) by the Defendants of the Claimants for further information and clarification of their Particulars of Claim. The Defendants expect a response by (date).

In relation to paragraph 2 of the Particulars of Claim

Of (refer to specific allegation)
1. (Set out questions)

In relation to paragraph 2 of the Particulars of Claim

Of (refer to specific allegation)
2. (Set out questions)

In relation to paragraph 2 of the Particulars of Claim

3. (If question relates to whole paragraph just set out question)
4. (If question is general just set out the question)

Signed: (by lawyer)

For an example see 18.126.

Responding to a request

The response should: **12.151**

- be headed with the name of the court and the title and number of the claim;
- be identified in the heading as the response to the request;

- repeat the text of each paragraph of request, and set out the response underneath;
- refer to and have attached to it a copy of any document not already in the possession of the other party that forms part of the response;
- have a statement of truth.

12.152 Care must be taken in answering the request as the answers will be binding. The response to the application for further information is a formal document that will form part of the statements of case in the action. The response can be drafted in a very narrow way. It is only necessary to provide facts and details of facts, not evidence or argument, though an answer can be provided at greater length if that may strengthen the case.

12.153 The party from whom information is requested can object to answering the request or to the time allowed, if for example the request is disproportionate, infringes privilege, or otherwise infringes the overriding objective. Information about an allegation can be easily sought, but the time taken to find and analyse relevant information to provide an answer may be massive. Any objection must be made in writing within the time given for reply.

12.154 If there is no sufficient response to a request the party seeking information can apply to the court for an order requiring a response. This application does not need to be on notice if at least 14 days have passed since the request was sent, PD18 para 5.5.

12.155 The decision to seek further information on a statement of case should be taken carefully—there may be tactical considerations. There is little merit in seeking further information simply because a statement of case has been poorly drafted or because the other side may know something that you do not—there should be a positive and strategic objective in strengthening your own case or weakening theirs.

12.156 Further information may usefully be sought:

- to enable a party to prepare a case properly—without knowing as precisely as possible the case being made it is difficult to know what law to research and what evidence to seek;
- to clarify the issues so as to save time and costs;
- to remove doubts about how a case will be argued, to assist in the preparation of advocacy;
- to force the other side to narrow down their allegations;
- to cause the other side to see weaknesses in their case—this may persuade them to make admissions or to seek a settlement;
- for the tactical merit of pointing out that the other side are not preparing the case well.

12.157 On the other hand requests for information can:

- encourage the other side to prepare their case more fully;
- build costs and take time;
- lead to a deterioration in the relationship between the parties—it is a tactical consideration whether to ask for further information if it might be helpful even if it is unlikely the court would order it, or if there is little point in seeking information that the court will not order as the other side does not have to reply;
- easily achieve rather less than anticipated where the other side is not obliged to provide the information sought.

Seeking admissions

Where a statement of case makes allegations that are not admitted by the other side, those **12.158** matters are in issue and will need to be proved with evidence at trial. Significant time and costs can be saved if admissions are made. If admissions are not volunteered in the statements of case, they can be sought by the other side. See generally CPR Part 14 Admissions and PD 14 Admissions.

The potential advantages of seeking an admission are that: **12.159**

- the issues remaining in dispute for trial or settlement will be narrowed down;
- costs and time will be saved as evidence on the matter admitted will no longer be required;
- it may be easier to prepare arguments and advocacy as the issues are more limited;
- the time taken at trial and the complexity of the case may be limited.

The areas in dispute can be limited by an admission made: **12.160**

- in a statement of case;
- otherwise in writing, for example in an open letter;
- at a case management conference or other directions hearing;
- in response to a notice to admit under CPR Part 14.

It is therefore not essential to use the formal procedure available under CPR Part 14, but it **12.161** may be useful to use that procedure to ensure that an important admission is formally recorded, or to get the assistance of the court if a case management or other directions hearing is not imminent.

To seek a formal admission, a party may serve on another party a notice to admit facts or part **12.162** of his case as specified in the notice, CPR r 32.18. Such a notice must be served at least 21 days before the trial. An admission in response can only be used in the same proceedings and by the party who served the notice. The court can allow an admission to be withdrawn or amended on such terms as it thinks just. If an admission is not made but should have been made, that can be taken into account in awarding costs. Following a formal admission, the point then is no longer in issue, so no evidence can be given on it at trial. However, it is possible to withdraw an admission that has been made with the leave of the court.

Admissions should be sought for individual allegations that are not really at issue, or where **12.163** new evidence shows that an admission should have been made. There is little point in seeking an admission relating to facts and issues at the centre of the case as it is very unlikely that such matters will be admitted. An admission may be made for tactical reasons if there is merit in making an admission so that the other side do not use evidence that they might otherwise use to prove an allegation.

Short of a formal admission, an informal admission (for example something heard by a **12.164** witness) is ordinary evidence that can be denied at trail. The admission would normally be hearsay but can be admitted under the Civil Evidence Act 1995, s 1. If the statement is made by a party it is admissible provided it is at least partly adverse, is made in the same legal capacity, and is admitted in its entirety. Servants or agents may make admissions for a party. If the party wishes to withdraw the admission the court will weight the balance of prejudice, *Gale v Superdrug Stores plc* (1996) 1 WLR 1089 CA.

KEY DOCUMENTS

Sources of precedents for statements of case

Atkin's Encyclopaedia of Court Forms in Civil Procedure (2nd edn) Butterworths. Updated by reissued volumes and loose leaf noter-up.

The Encyclopaedia of Forms and Precedents (5th edn) Butterworths. Updated by reissued volumes and loose leaf noter-up (also available on Butterworths Services).

Bullen & Leake & Jacob's Precedents of Pleadings (14th edn 2002) Sweet & Maxwell (also on Westlaw).

Butterworths Civil Court Precedents, Butterworths. Loose leaf.

Practical Civil Court Precedents. Sweet & Maxwell. Loose leaf.

W Rose, Pleadings without Tears (6th Edn 2002) Oxford University Press.

Inns of Court School of Law, Drafting Manual (annual) Oxford University Press.

Forms

N1 Claim Form

N1A Notes for Claimant

N1C Notes for Defendant

N9 Defence Response Pack

N9A Admission (specified amount)

N9B Defence and Counterclaim (specified amount)

N9C Admission (unspecified amount and non money claim)

N9D Defence and Counterclaim (unspecified amount and non money claim)

N11 Defence Form

N 266 Notice to admit facts

Court guides

Queen's Bench Guide

Chancery Guide

Admiralty and Commercial Courts Guide

Mercantile Courts Guide

Patents Court Guide

Technology and Construction Court Guide

13

DECIDING WHO SHOULD SUE WHOM

A INTRODUCTION 13.01
The role of insurance. 13.05

B SELECTING THE CLAIMANT(S) 13.09

C SELECTING THE DEFENDANT(S). 13.15
Principles for selecting defendants 13.15
Is the defendant worth suing. 13.23

D AGENCY AND VICARIOUS LIABILITY. 13.25
Agency. 13.25
Vicarious liability. 13.28

E A BUSINESS AS A PARTY. 13.30
The sole trader 13.33
A partnership 13.35
A company 13.39
A limited liability partnership 13.46
A corporation 13.47
An unincorporated association 13.48

F OTHER RULES FOR PARTIES 13.49
Children 13.49
Death. 13.50
People with a disability. 13.51
Trusts 13.52
Charities 13.53
The Crown 13.54
Bankruptcy 13.56
Bodies recognised by foreign law 13.57

G OTHER TYPES OF INVOLVEMENT IN A CASE. 13.58
Involvement in the case 13.59
Substitution of parties. 13.62

H PART 20 CLAIMS 13.63
Counterclaims 13.67
Claims for an indemnity or a contribution 13.70
Claims for some other remedy 13.75

Practical illustrations. 13.76

I   PART 20 PROCEDURE 13.78
General procedure. 13.78
Other matters for the court 13.81

J   DRAFTING THE PART 20 CLAIM. 13.82

KEY DOCUMENTS

A   INTRODUCTION

13.01   The civil litigation model in England and Wales is adversarial. This means that many of the rules and practices in litigation are based on the model of having a claimant and a defendant. The rules allow for the addition of other parties, but only with reference to this basic model. There is no general concept of involving people in the action simply because they may have some involvement in the facts or the remedies sought, save to the extent that a non-party can be called as a witness.

13.02   This historically based model has strengths in giving the parties a strong degree of control over who is involved in an action and in facilitating the identification of issues between them. It can also have drawbacks, in that, for example, only people who are parties will be bound by the outcome of the case.

13.03   The selection of parties is key to success in litigation for both legal and practical reasons.

- There must be a clear cause of action by the party named as claimant against the party named as defendant or the action will fail.
- Loss and damage must be shown to have been caused to the named claimant by the named defendant or damages will not be recoverable.
- If a named defendant is not financially able to meet a claim for damages or costs then success in the action is likely to be hollow.
- It must be possible to trace a named defendant in order to be able to serve the claim form and progress the action.
- There may be reasons for naming more than one claimant and/or more than one defendant.

13.04   It is also important to identify legal personality and legal involvement in a cause of action correctly. Agency or vicarious liability must be identified and spelled out. A business can be carried on in various ways, and it is important to identify the type of business involved in an action correctly.

The role of insurance

13.05   The role of insurance in litigation must be properly understood. There are a number of situations where insurance is common. Many professional people and many businesses carry insurance to cover possible claims by clients, customers, or employees. Occupiers of premises may carry insurance as regards injury to anyone visiting the site. Many householders carry insurance that can include certain types of legal claim.

The fact that a claimant is insured does not mean that the claimant can simply claim on the **13.06** insurance and does not then need to bring a legal action. If injury, loss, or damage has been caused then the insurer will normally want the person responsible to pay so that the claimant's insurer is not out of pocket, and will therefore wish the claimant to sue a potential defendant if there is a cause of action with a reasonable chance of success. Also the terms of an insurance policy will not necessarily cover all the damages that might be recovered by a legal action. However an insurance company may agree to pay a potential claimant rather than risk a legal action that has limited chance of success.

If a defendant is insured, the action is still primarily against the defendant. The action is not **13.07** normally against the insurer, who is not at fault, it is simply that the defendant's insurer will meet the damages at the end of the day. The extent of this liability will depend on the terms of the insurance, and meeting damages ordered is a matter between the defendant and the insurer and not between the claimant and the insurer.

All drivers on the road must carry insurance. If a road accident is caused by a hit-and-run **13.08** driver or a driver who is not insured then the claim will normally be met by the Motor Insurers Bureau which is run by the motor insurance industry to provide a safety net. As an exception to normal principles a motor insurer can now be named as a defendant under the European Communities (Rights against Insurers) Regulations 2002, provided an accident involves a motor vehicle on a road. If a claimant or a defendant is insured then the insurer should be made aware of the potential claim as early as possible.

B SELECTING THE CLAIMANT(S)

There is rarely a problem in deciding who should act as claimant in a case. Normally there is **13.09** one person or body that has suffered a loss and wishes to bring an action. It is those with direct legal rights who should be made parties. It would be possible for each to sue separately, but this would not normally be desirable as it would increase costs and potentially leave the defendant open to numerous actions. A person cannot be forced to be a claimant, but only a claimant in an action can seek remedies and benefit from judgment given. People should not be co-claimants if there is a possible conflict of interest.

Two or more people/bodies can be joined as claimants where there is some common question **13.10** of law or fact that might otherwise be raised in separate actions, or where all the rights to relief claimed arise out of the same transaction or series of transactions, or with the leave of the court. There may need to be more than one claimant if more than one person has a legal claim or wishes to obtain a remedy from what has happened. The possible reasons for advising that there be more than one claimant include the following.

- Where more than one person has a claim on the same or similar facts, for example if more than one person jointly contracted with the defendant.
- Where the claimants have joint rights to property that is the subject of the cause of

action (in which case a co-owner who is not prepared to be a claimant in the action will need to be joined as a defendant, CPR r 19.3).

- Where more than one person has suffered loss arising from the same breach of contract or the same negligence.

13.11   Careful selections as to who is the appropriate claimant may need to be made where:

- one person has contracted as agent for another, in which case the principal rather than the agent should normally be the claimant;
- if more than one person has been injured in an accident, in which case the facts should be considered to see if it is appropriate for both to act as claimants in the same action, or whether the claimants are significantly different and/or there is any conflict of interest so that separate claims should be brought.

13.12   It is normally only a party who can derive benefit from a contract, but one person may of course derive benefits from a contract made by another under the Contract (Rights of Third Parties) Act, where this is the wording or the intention of the contract.

13.13   Where a number of people may have a similar claim there are various possibilities.

- A representative action—if more than one person has the same interest in a claim then the claim may be begun, or the court may order that it continue, by one or more of them as representatives of any other person who has the same interests, CPR r 19.6. This is only appropriate if there is a genuinely common interest and the case may benefit all. Any judgment or order will be binding on all people represented.
- A group litigation order—if a number of claims give rise to common or related issues of law or fact the court can make a group litigation order, CPR rr 19.10 and 19.11. This may be appropriate where a number of people have similar claims, for example against the manufacturer of a defective product. The consent of a senior judge is required, and the order will say which claims are covered by it and give directions for the management of the case. A claimant not within a group action may be able to pursue a separate action, but the court will use its case management powers carefully, *Taylor v Nugent Care Society* The Times, 28 January 2004. See generally CPR Part 19 Parties and group litigation and PD 19B Group litigation.
- The court can also consolidate the hearing of actions if appropriate, whether or not the claimants in the actions can properly be co-claimants, CPR r 3.1.

13.14   A defendant cannot force the claimant to join anyone else as a co-claimant—the defendant will have to join any potential defendant that the claimant has chosen not to sue through a Part 20 claim, see 13.63–13.87.

C   SELECTING THE DEFENDANT(S)

Principles for selecting defendants

13.15   In principle there is no limit on the number of people a claimant can make defendants to an action, so long as there is a cause of action against each and the actions can properly be heard together. It is not possible to join someone as a defendant simply to get a remedy ordered against them if there is not a cause of action against them.

Sometimes there is no choice as to defendant. There may simply be one individual or body **13.16** that can be properly alleged to be responsible, so it is a matter of naming that individual or body correctly as defendant.

It is important to consider whether more than one person may be liable for what has **13.17** happened. Two or more people can be joined as defendants where there is some common question of law or fact that might otherwise be raised in separate actions, or where all the rights to relief claimed arise out of the same transaction or series of transactions, or with the leave of the court. The possible reasons for there being more than one potential defendant include where:

- there is a claim against more than one person on the same or similar facts, for example where one person can be argued to be vicariously liable for another (for example if a lorry driver runs the claimant over while in the course of business both the van driver and his or her employer can be sued);
- there is more than one claim against more than one person on the same or similar facts (for example an employer and a site owner may each be liable for an accident at work);
- more than one person may have separately contributed to an accident;
- more than one person may be responsible for something in different ways, for example, one making a defective item (liable in negligence) and another selling it to the claimant (liable in contract).

If there is more than one potential defendant then the claimant can decide who to sue, **13.18** perhaps selecting the one against whom the evidence is strongest. There are a number of tactical and practical considerations in making a choice. Suing more defendants will almost certainly increase costs as each may have his or her own lawyer, but if there is any doubt as to liability it is better to sue two potential defendants rather than sue one, lose, and then have to start from scratch against another.

If the potential defendants will all be liable for the same cause of action in the same way then **13.19** they should probably normally all be joined on the basis that damages can be recovered from the one most likely to be able to pay. The possible advantages of suing more than one defendant are:

- increasing the possibility of succeeding with a cause of action where there is any doubt on the facts as to who is responsible, or where one potential defendant may have a defence;
- increasing the possibilities for being awarded damages where different damage and loss may have been caused by different defendants;
- increasing the possibility of recovering damages where more than one person can properly be sued and one may not be able to pay all or part of the total damages claimed;
- where a variety of remedies are sought against a range of people;
- to save the cost of separate actions where the causes of action are significantly linked;
- to ensure that coherent judgments are given, where separate cases might result in judgments that are not fully coherent;
- if a limitation period is about to expire then there may be merit in joining a possible defendant anyway and then discontinuing that part of the action if it proves to be weak.

13.20   The potential drawbacks of suing more than one defendant are:

- increasing costs unnecessarily if there is a strong cause of action against one defendant that should cover all loss and damage, so that there is little purpose to be served in suing an additional defendant;
- increasing the complexity of the statements of case if too many defendants and causes of action have to be dealt with together—it may be preferable to have separate actions;
- adding complexity to the case to no effect in that damages can only be recovered once over and there can be no double recovery even if the action(s) succeed against more than one defendant;
- there is probably little point in suing two defendants if the evidence against one is strong and the evidence against the other is weak, unless the latter is joined for other reasons such as ability to pay damages.

13.21   The consent of the court will be needed to add a defendant once the defence is served.

13.22   There may be tactical considerations. If there is a range of potential defendants the claimant can sue one defendant and then leave it to that defendant to decide whether to try to pass on liability by joining someone else under Part 20 proceedings (see 3.55–3.60). However this must be done with care—the defendant may or may not choose to join other possible parties.

Is the defendant worth suing?

13.23   Sometimes it will be fairly obvious that the potential defendant has sufficient assets to meet the damages claimed. An individual or business may well be fairly obviously of good standing and able to meet the claim. A public body like a council or a hospital will need to budget to meet pending claims.

13.24   However a person or body can have the appearance of wealth without actually possessing wealth, for example because substantial debt balances assets, or because assets are leased rather than owned. It is not easy to investigate the wealth of a potential defendant, though this can be done. For example the annual audited accounts of companies have to be filed at Companies House.

D   AGENCY AND VICARIOUS LIABILITY

Agency

13.25   Parties normally contract personally, but a contract may be entered into by an agent. Sometimes this is purely for practical purposes. Sometimes it is a function of legal personality, as a partnership or company will normally have to be represented by individuals. An agency is normally disclosed—that is everyone is aware that a particular agent is acting for a particular principal. The result is that it will be the principals who are bound by the contract and any ensuing action will be between the principals. Sometimes the agency may not be disclosed—one party is acting as an agent but this is not known to the other party. In such a case any ensuing action will be between the disclosed principal and the agent, though it will be possible for the agent to sue the undisclosed principal if appropriate.

The extent of the actual authority of an agent should be agreed between the principal and **13.26** the agent. This may be express authority (explicitly agreed), or implied authority (implied to give practical effect to the authority). In a particular trade or profession usual authority can arise from what normally happens.

The level of authority of an agent should ideally be clear to the person that the agent is **13.27** negotiating with. However in practice this is often not spelled out, and a contract will be binding if it falls within the agent's apparent or ostensible authority. If the actual authority of an agent is less than the apparent authority then an action between agent and principal may result.

Vicarious liability

In a tort action it is not uncommon for an accident to be caused by someone in their capacity **13.28** as an employee. For example someone employed as a driver may injure someone else in a road accident, or one employee may be injured by the actions of another. Where an employee commits a tort in the course of his or her employment then the principle of vicarious liability will apply, and the employer should normally be made the defendant in an action alleging a tort in the course of duty on the part of the employee.

A sole trader, a partnership, or a company can all be vicariously liable for the actions of an **13.29** employee. If one partner causes loss or damage in the course of business, the other partners will normally share liability, Partnership Act 1890, ss 10–11.

E   A BUSINESS AS A PARTY

Where a business is a party to an action, it is important that the correct legal personality be **13.30** used. A business may be run by a sole trader, who may or may not use a trading name, by a partnership, by a company, or by a public limited partnership (plp). The correct legal personality must be used for the proper service of documents, for success in the action, and for enforcement of judgment. An action involving a business will often be based on a contract, in which case the question is who the contract was with. If it is a tort action it will be a question of which body owes a duty.

The legal personality of a business may be closely related to the range of potential defend- **13.31** ants, and whether the defendant is worth suing. For a high value claim careful consideration may be given to the organisations that may be added as defendants and the sort of cause of action that may be used. Equally businesses that are likely to be sued seek to defend their position. There has for example been a growth in actions against accountants and solicitors for professional negligence. The introduction of professional negligence insurance means that successful claims will be met, which makes actions more likely, which in turn leads to an increase in insurance premiums. That may lead to a review of the form in which the business is conducted to try to restrict liability.

The following summary is only intended to provide a basic guide as a starting point. The **13.32** legal practitioner will need to develop a more thorough knowledge and research details. Any business can employ other individuals to work for it. See 12.78 for how different types of business should be named in an action.

The sole trader

13.33 An individual can set up a business without any formalities, save for the need to keep separate accounts for the business and for private purposes. Liability to bring or defend a legal action remains personal, and the sole trader may sue or be sued in her or his name. It is possible that the sole trader will use a business name, and if this is the case the person can be sued using a trading name. If a business name is used then the Business Names Act 1985 requires that the legal name of the person running the business be clear on correspondence etc.

13.34 A judgment obtained against a sole trader can be enforced against personal and business assets. A sole trader with a small business may not have many assets, but may carry insurance to cover business activities. A sole trader can stop a business at any time, but will remain responsible for contracts made and torts committed while the business was running.

A partnership

13.35 No specific formalities are required to set up a partnership. The formation of a partnership is a matter of fact, where people carry on business in common with a view to making a profit and have not incorporated the business. Many professions, such as solicitors and accountants, are normally run in a partnership. Businesses such as building or plumbing are also quite commonly run through a partnership. The Partnership Act 1890 provides a general code for partnerships.

13.36 The assumption is that partners have equal rights and responsibilities, and that their potential liability is joint and several. However there can be different types of partners, especially in a large partnership, or where some partners play a much more active part in a business than others. The rights of partners should be set out in a partnership agreement, though certain terms are implied into such an agreement, Partnership Act 1890, s 24.

13.37 In general terms partners are jointly and severally liable for partnership activities. Each partner generally has ostensible authority to bind the partnership to a contract. All partners can be liable for a tort committed by one partner in the course of a partnership. Any two or more persons claiming as or alleged to be liable as partners carrying on business within the jurisdiction can sue or be sued in the name of the firm as regards a cause of action arising within the jurisdiction, CPR Sch 1. It is possible to get a list of the names of partners in a firm, and because liability is joint and several it is also possible to sue the partners in their own names. Partners must acknowledge service in their own names, even if acting on behalf of the partnership.

13.38 Separate accounts must be kept for the partnership. Any judgment can be enforced against partnership assets or the partners personally. A partnership may well carry insurance to cover business risks. There are legal provisions for the actual members of a partnership to change while the partnership itself continues, otherwise a partnership will continue until it is dissolved.

A company

Unlike a sole trader or a partnership, a company has a separate legal identity. A company **13.39** must be registered under the Companies Act 1985, and must comply with quite complex formalities. A company's activities are governed by a memorandum, which sets out the purposes of a company, and articles of association, which set out how the company is to be run. Each company must be registered with the Registrar of Companies at Companies House and must register annual accounts. Information about companies is open to public inspection. Large trading companies are public companies and their name must end with 'Public Limited Company' or 'PLC'. Other companies and companies limited by guarantee are private companies and their name should end with 'Limited' or 'Ltd'.

Normally a company is owned by its shareholders (who contribute and benefit to the extent **13.40** of their shareholding), or alternatively through a company limited by guarantee (where members guarantee the company to a fixed limited amount—appropriate for a company run for non-trading or charitable purposes). Shares may be traded publicly in a large company, or held by a few individuals in a small family company.

Decisions on running a company have to be taken by individuals. Key decisions can be taken **13.41** by shareholders in general meetings or extraordinary meetings, and provisions for this should be set out in the articles of association. There are complex rules about the holding of meetings to regulate this process. However day to day activity is delegated to directors. Directors can be executive or non-executive.

It will normally be the directors who have the capacity to make contracts on behalf of a **13.42** company. A senior officer or an employee may make agreements that bind the company so long as that individual is acting within his or her ostensible authority. A company can only legally make contracts within the objects section of its memorandum. Any contract outside the stated activities is *ultra vires* and void. In practice this is rarely a problem as Objects clauses are drafted very wide and can easily be varied. There are also forms of protection for an innocent party. A company can be vicariously liable for torts committed by its employees.

A legal action by or against a company should use the name of the company, *Foss v Harbottle* **13.43** (1935) 2 KB 113. A company can be served at its registered office. A director or other official can represent a company at a hearing, provided he or she has authorisation to act (for example from a board resolution) and that is recorded in writing.

A judgment can only be enforced against assets of the company and not against the assets of **13.44** an individual shareholder or director, save for a rare case where that person is also personally liable. Companies may well carry insurance to cover business risks. Companies have substantial obligations as regards drawing up, auditing, and filing accounts. Information about companies including annual accounts is publicly available from Companies House.

Many companies are part of a group of companies, normally through one company holding **13.45** a controlling interest in the shares of another, or through companies holding shares in each other. Such links may be reflected in the people who act as directors in the companies. There may be complex inter-relations between groups of companies, including international or multinational links, where separate companies are formed under the law of individual countries but are run through a holding company or other links. Generally each company in a group remains separate for legal and many financial purposes. A company can be wound up by its members or by the court.

A limited liability partnership

13.46 There can be advantages in sharing management through a partnership, but drawbacks in terms of unlimited liability. A company can have advantages in terms of limiting business liability to business assets, but possible drawbacks in terms of separating ownership (through shareholders) from managers (the directors). Since April 2001 it has been possible to form a hybrid called a limited liability partnership under the Limited Liability Partnership Act 2000. There are formalities similar to those for forming and lodging documents for a company, with the result that an LLP is more like a company than a partnership and should use the name of the partnership with the addition of LLP.

A corporation

13.47 A company as described above is the most common kind of corporation. In more general terms, a corporation may be set up by a Royal Charter or by statute and it has a distinct legal personality. Public bodies such as local authorities are corporations. The charter or statute sets out how the corporation is run, for example with a board of governors or a mayor and corporation.

An unincorporated association

13.48 An unincorporated association has no separate legal personality. Unincorporated associations include bodies such as trade unions, trade associations, and clubs. In fact the association may have some degree of personality so as to be able to make contracts—for example operating at least partly through a company or through a sole trader. Alternatively if members of the association have similar interests it may be possible to use a representative action, CPR r 19.6, or to sue an individual member. An unincorporated association may also be involved in an action, the normal method being to join an officer of the body, such as the Treasurer or Secretary, to represent it.

F   OTHER RULES FOR PARTIES

Children

13.49 A child under 18 must bring or defend an action through a litigation friend, CPR r 21.2. This must be a competent person who is close to the child, such as a parent, but it must be someone with whom there is no possible conflict of interest in the case. On becoming an adult the child can take over the action. Any settlement of an action to which a child is a party must have court approval, CPR r 21.10. It is not necessary to have any court order for this, but appropriate documents must be lodged with the court. See generally CPR Part 21 Children and patients and PD 21 Children and patients.

Death

Following a death, all rights and obligations will vest in the executors or administrators. A   **13.50**
death will only end a personal action such as defamation. Other actions can be brought or
defended by the executors or administrators. To indicate this the words 'executors of the will
of ZZ deceased' or as appropriate should be used.

People with a disability

A person with a mental disorder within the meaning of the Mental Health Act 1983 must act   **13.51**
with a litigation friend. The test is whether a person is capable of understanding the issues on
which his or her consent or decision is likely to be needed in the course of legal proceedings,
with the assistance of legal representatives. A medical report is likely to be required. The
burden of proving that a person has a mental disorder rests if relevant on the person alleging
this, *Masterman-Lister v Brutton & Co* (2003) 3 All ER 162. See generally CPR Part 21 Children
and patients and PD 21 Children and patients.

Trusts

Trust actions are beyond the scope of this book. The legal role, obligations, and rights of the   **13.52**
settlor, trustees, and beneficiaries must be distinguished. It will normally be the trustees who
are parties to an action involving trust property rather than the beneficiaries. Claims relating
to trust property can be brought by or against the trustees without needing to join the
beneficiaries.

Charities

Charities may be run in a variety of ways including through companies. A charity should sue   **13.53**
or be sued in the manner appropriate for the type of body through which it is being run.

The Crown

Claims brought by or against the Crown are governed by the Crown Proceedings Act 1947.   **13.54**
There is a list of authorised government departments and the solicitor for service for each.
Other parts of government must sue and be sued through the Attorney General. Organisations that are related to but not formally part of government functions have at least some
legal personality, see *Broadmoor Special Hospital Authority v R* (2000) QB 775. Some have
formal legal personality, for example hospitals are run through hospital trusts.

A government department, local authority, or health authority can sue or be sued as such.   **13.55**

Bankruptcy

Where a person or body with legal personality becomes insolvent—unable to meet all   **13.56**
debts—then creditors may institute bankruptcy proceedings. If this is done all assets, including legal actions, vest in the trustee in bankruptcy (for an individual) or the liquidator (for a
company), who have duties as regards dealing with the assets and distributing them to

creditors under the Insolvency Act 1986. If an action has already started the trustee in bankruptcy will need a court order to continue the action, CPR r 19.2. If the defendant becomes bankrupt the claim may be stayed or allowed to continue on terms, Insolvency Act 1986, s 285.

There can be tactical considerations as to whether it is better to start bankruptcy or liquidation proceedings or leave a business to recover and then pay later. There are legal provisions restricting people from running a company when they know that it cannot meet its debts.

Bodies recognised by foreign law

13.57   A body recognised by foreign law, such as an Indian temple can be accepted as a party, *Bumper Development Corporation v Commissioner of Police* [1991] 4 All ER 638.

G   OTHER TYPES OF INVOLVEMENT IN A CASE

13.58   Both the claimant and the defendant will want to ensure that appropriate people become involved in an action. People need to be involved as parties if they are to be bound by the outcome of the case, if linked disputes are to be settled as far as possible, and to get the best potential range of people against whom damages and other remedies can be ordered. People may need to be involved as witnesses to get full information about the case.

Involvement in the case

13.59   The basic model for litigation involves a claimant and a defendant. The choice of claimants and defendants is dealt with above. Sometimes it will be necessary to have more people playing a part in an action so that the court can consider all matters relating to a set of facts at the same time, to save costs, and to ensure that everyone will be bound by the outcome.

13.60   There are various ways in which others can play a part in an action.

- The defendant can add additional parties under Part 20 proceedings (see 13.63–13.88).
- In a complex case a claimant can if necessary add additional parties under Part 20 proceedings, if it is appropriate that they become parties in the case but is not appropriate to join them as defendants in the original action (for example if the defendant brings a counterclaim and the claimant wishes to add extra parties in responding to that).
- If there is a claim for a declaration of incompatibility under the Human Rights Act 1998, s 4 then 21 days notice must be given to the crown, CPR r 19.4A and a relevant minister may be made a party.
- Someone who is not a party to the action can be added by intervening if the presence of the intervener is desirable to ensure the court can settle all matters in dispute, or if it is desirable to determine any issue relating to relief claimed between the intervener and a party to the action at the same time as deciding the action, CPR r 19.2. For example an individual may ask to intervene in a representative action to settle a question about who should represent what group. The Attorney General may intervene if there is a question of public policy.

- A person who holds property that is subject to rival claims may issue interpleader proceedings to get the case decided between those claiming the property to avoid being sued.

An alternative to adding people to an action is to start a separate action, and to ask the court that they be heard together if appropriate. **13.61**

Substitution of parties

In rare circumstances a new party can be substituted for an existing party. The consent of the court will be needed after a claim form has been issued. It is not easy to substitute one defendant for another unless there has been a clear mistake, *International Distillers and Vintners v JF Hillebrand (UK) Ltd* The Times, 25 January 2000. It will in particular be difficult to substitute one party for another after the limitation period has expired. An alternative before the expiry of the limitation period is to start a new action with the correct parties. See PD 19 Addition and substitution of parties. **13.62**

H PART 20 CLAIMS

This is one of the few parts of the Civil Procedure Rules 1998 that remains unsatisfactory. It is not easy to propose a simpler procedure, not least because of the number of circumstances in which people can become involved to a greater or lesser extent in the facts of a case. Problems stem from the claimant and defendant model of litigation which does not have an easy logic for joining parties beyond co-claimants and co-defendants. **13.63**

The basic purpose behind Part 20 procedure is to allow others beyond claimants and defendants to the original action to be joined to allow a just overall decision to be made. However it covers such a wide range of possibilities that confusion is almost inevitable. **13.64**

Even in a simple and small case there can be significant questions about who should be joined by whom. If A has a claim against B and B has a linked claim against C, A can only sue B. Unless the facts show a cause of action by A against C, A cannot sue C, and cannot force B to sue C. This could apply on the simple facts that A has been injured by a faulty television, B sold it to A, and C made it and sold it to B. The following section works through some basic scenarios of this type. The same principles would apply where one large company is suing another. **13.65**

A Part 20 claim is any claim other than a claim made by a claimant against a defendant, CPR Part 20.2. All parties save for claimants and defendants in the main action are joined using Part 20 procedure. The three types of claim that come within Part 20 are as follows. It is important to distinguish them as they have different bases and results, and the claim made must be specified on the Part 20 claim form. **13.66**

Counterclaims

If a defendant wishes to bring a claim against the claimant, this is called a counterclaim, and it is technically a Part 20 claim. Technically the defendant is the Part 20 claimant and the **13.67** claimant is the Part 20 defendant. See generally CPR Part 20 Counterclaims and other additional claims, and PD 20 Counterclaims and other additional claims. See also 17.85–17.91.

13.68   The defendant may bring the counterclaim against the claimant and others, creating additional Part 20 defendants to that claim. This model can be set out as C1 sues D, then D counterclaims against C1 adding C2 as a defendant to the counterclaim.

13.69   If a defendant counterclaims then the claimant can add extra parties to defend the counterclaim, which can be set out as C1 sues D, D counterclaims against C1, and C1 adds D as a co-defendant to the counterclaim.

Claims for an indemnity or a contribution

13.70   A claim for an indemnity is a claim that someone else is obliged to provide a reimbursement for money paid or for a loss. It must be based on a specific obligation, such as a contract, a statute, or a principal and agent relationship.

13.71   A contribution is a partial indemnity where that is justified by the nature of the obligation or the facts of the case. A contribution can also arise in tort, contract, or breach of trust under the Civil Liability (Contribution) Act 1978, which provides that if two people are held jointly liable to the same claimant for the same damage then each may claim a contribution from the other. It is a factual test whether the parties are both liable, and whether the parties are liable for the same damage. The operation of the principles is well illustrated in *Royal Brompton Hospital NHS Trust v Hammond* (2002) 1 WLR 1397, HL. The mere fact that it may generally be arguable on the facts that a third party is responsible by no means results in a contribution being payable, *Birse Construction Ltd v Haiste Ltd* [1996] 2 All ER 1.

13.72   To illustrate the contribution, the defendant may wish to allege that other people are liable with him or her for the claim made by the claimant. The defendant may allege that an accident was caused partly by someone other than himself and claim a contribution to any damages found payable, or caused wholly by someone other than himself but who has not been sued by the claimant, in which case the defendant would seek an indemnity. In this model C sues D1. D1 then joins D2 on the basis that on the facts he or she is wholly or partly liable for C's claim.

13.73   Alternatively the defendant may allege that he or she has a separate cause of action that is factually linked to the claimant's claim and therefore ought to be tried together. For example a claimant may bring an action for breach of contract for defects in goods sold. The defendant may then wish to sue in contract the person from whom he or she bought the goods. That person may also have a cause of action against someone else, perhaps the manufacturer of the goods. In this model C sues D, D sues E, and if appropriate E sues F.

13.74   A defendant who wishes to claim a contribution or indemnity from someone who is already a defendant can do so by filing and serving a contribution notice containing a statement of the nature and grounds of the claim, CPR r 20.6. Unless this is filed with the defence it needs the permission of the court. In practice a formal contribution notice is not always served if the parties who will contribute are already all parties to the action, as the judge simply has to apportion damages at the end of the trial. However a formal contribution notice should be served if there is a need to establish the basis for the contribution because it is not under the statute, or if it would be useful to have formal steps such as disclosure to get more information on the contribution.

Claims for some other remedy

The defendant may have a distinct claim against someone being joined as an additional **13.75** party. For example if two cars collide a passenger in one car, C, may sue the driver of the other car, D1, for injuries suffered. D1 may then seek a contribution or indemnity from the driver of the car C was travelling in, D2, and D1 might also claim damages for D1's own injuries as another remedy.

Practical illustrations

If John's house suffers extensive damage from flooding due to a defective jacuzzi, manu- **13.76** factured by Edward, and sues Peter who installed it, Peter might give his lawyer any of the following alternative scenarios:

(a) Peter might say that he has not been paid for the installation of the jacuzzi, or for a lot of other work he has done for John. The lawyer might therefore advise Peter to counter-claim for the money due.

(b) Peter might say that John bought the jacuzzi from Edward, and Peter was simply employed to install it. The problem was caused by a sealed component that Peter could not inspect and had no reason to think was defective. The lawyer might therefore advise Peter that he should claim an indemnity from Edward.

(c) Peter might say that although he contracted with John to do the installation, he actually sub-contracted this job to George and he does not know what happened when the jacuzzi was installed. The lawyer might therefore advise that Peter claim an indemnity from George.

(d) Peter might say that he bought the jacuzzi from Edward and that instructions for installation were supplied. Peter admits that he failed to follow the instructions and is partly responsible, but that the company has changed the instructions it now sends with the jacuzzi having accepted that a page of the original instructions was wrong and potentially dangerous. The lawyer might therefore advise that Peter seeks an indemnity or contribution from Edward for the damages he is likely to have to pay.

(e) John might sue Peter and Edward as co-defendants for all the damage he has suffered, in which case on the facts in (d) Peter's lawyer might advise him to issue a contribution notice against Edward.

In most of the above cases Peter would have the option of starting a separate action. Alter- **13.77** natively he might seek an order that the non-party be added to the claim under CPR r 19.2. However all the above cases are also suitable for Part 20 proceedings (formerly known as third party proceedings).

▌ PART 20 PROCEDURE

General procedure

13.78 The Part 20 claim must be initiated by a Part 20 claim form. This is in many ways like a normal claim form in that it must have particulars of claim on it or as a separate document. The limitation period for any new claim runs to the date the Part 20 claim form is issued. The form must be served within 14 days with a response pack with forms broadly similar to the defence pack. The new party must be served with copies of existing statements of case and other parties must get copies of the Part 20 claim form. This claim form can be issued without permission if that is done before or at the same time as the filing of the defence, CPR r 20.7(3).

13.79 After the filing of the defence permission will be needed to start Part 20 proceedings. This is sought with an application that sets out all the facts of the stage the case has reached and why the additional person be joined, and a draft statement of case to include the party. The court will consider matters such as the reasons for any delay in joining the additional party. If the order is made the court will give directions for how the case proceeds. In tactical terms it will clearly normally be best to add any additional parties before filing the defence.

13.80 The action against the third party can proceed in many ways like the original claim. Essentially the CPR rules apply, with the service of a defence by the defendant to the Part 20 proceedings, and the possibility of directions and interim applications, though the court will try to manage the main claim and the Part 20 claim together, CPR r 20.13. The court will decide procedure at trial. If the main claim is discontinued the Part 20 claim can continue, save that a contribution notice depends on the success of the main claim.

Other matters for the court

13.81 Where there is a multiplicity of parties the court will need to take special care with a number of issues.

- Orders will need to be drawn up carefully to ensure that references to parties are accurate and correct.
- Interim orders such as summary judgment may be sought and awarded against some defendants but not others. If more than one party is found liable to pay damages for a single event the court will need to apportion liability. This will be decided on the facts but it may not be a simple matter. For example if a claimant and two defendants are all held to be equally liable for an accident, is each one third liable, or are the two defendants liable to pay 25 per cent of the damages each? See *Fitzgerald v Lane* [1988] 2 All ER 961.
- It may not be a simple matter to decide what orders should properly be made as to costs, though normal principles will apply.

J DRAFTING THE PART 20 CLAIM

The Part 20 claim form is like a normal claim form in that it must have particulars of claim **13.82** on it or as a separate document, and it must be verified by a statement of truth. The essential rules for and ingredients of drafting a Part 20 claim are similar to those for drafting a claim, save that it can be challenging to include all the necessary elements in a way that is clear and logical and that fits coherently with other statements of case. All facts that it is alleged give a right to the remedy claimed must be included.

The precise ingredients will vary with the claim made and the facts, but normal **13.83** ingredients are:

- setting out clearly who the additional party is;
- setting out in a couple of paragraphs enough of the existing claim to provide a succinct and relevant background to how the claim being made fits in. This would normally include the parties, the claim made, and relevant remedies sought. It is also likely to include a summary of the defence raised. It is not necessary to include details of the other statements of case as copies must be served with the Part 20 claim, CPR r 20,12;
- it may be necessary to summarise and distinguish other Part 20 claims made in the same action;
- setting out the Part 20 claim against the additional party;
- specifying clearly whether an indemnity, a contribution, or some other remedy is sought.

Great care with accurate wording may be needed if, for example, it is argued that the add- **13.84** itional party will only be liable to the defendant if and so far as the defendant is held liable to the claimant. If the defendant has a claim for damages or some other remedy against the additional party this must be set out in full as in a claim.

Claims for a contribution, an indemnity, and damages can overlap, in which case each **13.85** should be properly and clearly pleaded.

In the past a 'Third Party Notice' was drafted in a rather different way, with a general sum- **13.86** mary at the start of the document, no prayer, and references to the third party as 'you'. Precedents and practice that may be out of date should be treated with care, as the draft should now more closely resemble a normal particulars of case.

The rules provide that the full combined description of each party should be set out in the **13.87** heading, PD 20 para 7. This can lead to complex headings, though the parties can be referred to by name in the body of the statement of case.

IN THE HIGH COURT OF JUSTICE   Claim No 2005 HC 1234
QUEEN'S BENCH DIVISION
BETWEEN

AA	Claimant/
	Part 20 Defendant
and	
BB	Defendant/
	Part 20 Claimant

13.88   Or

<u>IN THE HIGH COURT OF JUSTICE</u>   Claim No 2005 HC 1234
<u>QUEEN'S BENCH DIVISION</u>
BETWEEN

	AA	<u>Claimant</u>
	and	
	BB	<u>Defendant/</u>
		<u>Part 20 Claimant (First Claim)</u>
	and	
	CC	<u>Part 20 Defendant (First Claim)</u>
		<u>Part 20 Claimant (Second Claim)</u>
	and	
	DD	<u>Part 20 Defendant (Second Claim)</u>

For examples see 18.128 and 19.144.

KEY DOCUMENTS

Forms

N1C Notes for Defendant
N9 Defence Response Pack
N9A Admission (specified amount)
N9B Defence and Counterclaim (specified amount)
N9C Admission (unspecified amount and non-money claim)
N9D Defence and Counterclaim (unspecified amount and non-money claim)
N11 Defence Form
N211 Part 20 Claim Form
N213 Part 20 Acknowledgement of service
N 266 Notice to admit facts

Court guides

Queen's Bench Guide
Chancery Guide
Admiralty and Commercial Courts Guide
Mercantile Courts Guide
Patents Court Guide
Technology and Construction Court Guide

These are easily available in hard copy and electronic form, see Chapter 24.

14

PURSUING APPROPRIATE REMEDIES AND RELIEF

A THE IMPORTANCE OF IDENTIFYING POTENTIAL REMEDIES AND
RELIEF. 14.01

B REMEDIES A COURT CAN ORDER 14.08
Financial remedies. 14.11
Other remedies. 14.15
Equitable remedies 14.18
Claiming a remedy 14.25

C REMEDIES A COURT CANNOT ORDER. 14.26

D CLAIMS FOR DAMAGES 14.30
General principles 14.30
Categories of damages. 14.34
Legal concepts relevant to damages 14.37

E QUANTIFICATION OF DAMAGES 14.50
Special damages 14.51
General damages 14.52
Economic loss. 14.53
Non-economic loss 14.59
Exemplary damages. 14.62

F A PROACTIVE APPROACH TO DAMAGES 14.63
Providing systematic advice. 14.63
Constructing arguments. 14.66

G CLAIMS FOR INTEREST 14.68
When interest can be claimed 14.70
Rates of interest 14.76
The period for which interest is payable 14.77

H DOING THE ARITHMETIC 14.78

A THE IMPORTANCE OF IDENTIFYING POTENTIAL REMEDIES AND RELIEF

14.01 The litigation process can all too easily focus on winning the action. This is quite justi-fiable—if the case is not won the party may get nothing from it. It tends to be the cases that are most strongly contested that proceed far into the litigation process. Much can turn on winning, such as costs decisions, and sometimes the simple fact of winning is in itself a key objective for the client.

14.02 However, winning a case can be a hollow victory if proper attention has not been paid to the remedies sought. The main purpose of most litigation is to achieve appropriate remedies for the client, and this has fundamental implications for the way in which litigation is conducted.

- From the earliest stages of contact with a client it is important to ascertain what the client wants to achieve in the action.
- Part of analysing a case is the analysis of what remedies may be available.
- Detailed evidence of loss and damage must be collected as carefully as evidence in support of a cause of action.
- Advice on remedies is as important as advising on the cause of action. Sometimes a meeting or an opinion may relate solely to remedies, for example focussing on the quan-tification of damages.
- Statements of case must include allegations relevant to remedies, including allegations relating to causation, foreseeability, or mitigation.
- The choice of parties in a case may include consideration of who needs to be joined to achieve desirable remedies, provided there is a cause of action against each.
- Remedies do not only fall to be considered at trial. Orders to achieve or support desired remedies can be sought at an interim stage, for example through an interim injunction.
- An order must be drafted carefully to ensure it achieves the desired remedies and is enforceable.

14.03 There may be an obvious remedy, such as damages, but the obvious should not be accepted without further thought.

- There may be additional or alternative remedies.
- It may be necessary to seek orders to support the remedies sought, for example an account to determine what money is due and then an order that what is due be paid.
- It may be necessary to seek orders at an interim stage to support a remedy sought, for example ensuring that property one seeks to recover is preserved.
- There may not be a remedy that precisely meets what the claimant hopes to achieve, in which case an imaginative approach may be required.

14.04 For effective litigation there is merit in thinking quite widely as regards the types of remedies sought, the detail of each remedy, and the sort of evidence that might support an appli-cation for a remedy. The fact that there is not direct evidence of existing loss is not necessarily a problem—for example actuarial evidence may be used to argue for future loss in a serious personal injury case.

14.05 Many of the legal concepts used in relation to remedies are actually quite flexible, for example causation and foreseeability, and this flexibility should be used in building arguments. Courts have shown themselves to be open to developing new concepts in providing fair remedies and assessing damages, for example developing wasted expenditure as an alternative to loss of profit in a contract case, and more recently (supported by statute) the development of structured settlements. For sources of law on damages and remedies see 24.18.

A remedy is a positive order, for example that damages be paid. Relief is an order relieving a party of an obligation, for example by rescinding a contract. **14.06**

For the requirements for pleading a remedy in a statement of case see 12.99–12.111. Note the importance of including the chain of factual allegations that give rise to the remedy in addition to asking for the remedy itself. **14.07**

B REMEDIES A COURT CAN ORDER

A court can only make an order that it has power to make by common law or by statute. It is important to select remedies that the court can order, to build statements of case on the basis of what the court can order, and to explain to the client the limitations on what a court can order, if that is relevant to the case. **14.08**

It may be possible to achieve something the client wants through a full consideration of the powers of the court. Equitable remedies and injunctions can be used quite flexibly, or a client may be able to spend damages in a way that achieves a particular end. If it is really not possible for a court to order something that a client wants then negotiation rather than litigation should be considered, as a settlement or consent order can achieve by agreement things a court cannot order. **14.09**

The available remedies may need research in a particular case and this book can provide no more than an overview. The main general types of remedies that a court can order are as follows. **14.10**

- A declaration as to legal rights. This normally relates to the interpretation of a legal document, but can also include an interpretation of facts.
- An enforcement of rights. This may force someone to do something such as return property, or can force someone not to do something, for example through a prohibitory injunction.
- Compensation. This is perhaps the most common remedy sought, and takes the form of financial damages. Additional exemplary damages can be awarded in a few limited circumstances.
- Ancillary orders. Other orders may be needed to give a remedy effect.

Financial remedies

Damages

Financial compensation is the main form of redress for many actions, even if it is not easy to attach a financial figure to what has been lost. This topic is dealt with further below. **14.11**

Payment of money due

14.12   If a specified sum is due, for example the consideration for a contract, then payment of the sum due can be ordered.

An account

14.13   If it is difficult to ascertain a sum due then the court can order an account. This is a detailed written list of the sums due between the parties. Once the account is taken, the money found due can be ordered to be paid.

Interest

14.14   Where a claimant has been kept out of money for some time, interest may need to be added to provide fair compensation. This topic is dealt with further below.

Other remedies

A declaration

14.15   This is a statement by the court of a legal right or position. This may be appropriate where there is some doubt or dispute about a legal right or position. Some other order may be needed in addition to the declaration to enforce the right. The wording of the declaration sought should be as specific as possible, and should be set out in the statement of case. A court may grant a declaration even if it is not specifically sought, *Harrison-Broadley v Smith* [1964] 1 WLR 456.

Restitution

14.16   It may be important to seek the return of a specific asset. If a chattel has been improperly detained, there may be an order for the delivery up of the chattel. It may be important to ensure that the asset is retained prior to the trial. Alternatively, if the claimant shows that he or she is entitled to possession of land, delivery up of possession of the land may be sought.

Specific delivery of goods

14.17   This may be available where property has been improperly detained, and see the Tort (Interference with Goods) Act 1977, s 3.

Equitable remedies

14.18   Where common law remedies are inadequate the court has a discretion to grant equitable remedies. An equitable remedy is discretionary and may be refused if:

- there is delay in applying;
- the claimant does not come with 'clean hands';
- there are reasons of fairness such as lack of mutuality or that an order might cause hardship;
- equity would act in vain and nothing would really be achieved.

An injunction

14.19   An injunction is a flexible and practical option to prevent something being done, or occasionally to require something to be done.

- A final or perpetual injunction may be granted at trial (meaning that it is a final outcome rather than that it will necessarily last forever).
- An interim injunction may be granted before trial, see 16.109–16.139.
- A prohibitory injunction can be granted to prevent a breach of contract or the commission of a tort.
- It is difficult to get a mandatory injunction without a very clear case, see *Redland Bricks Ltd v Morris* (1970) AC 652.

Specific performance

In a contractual action the claimant may primarily want the contract to be honoured, and **14.20** an order for specific performance may be sought to ensure that the terms of the contract are put into effect. Under sale of goods legislation a buyer who is a consumer has the right to require a seller to repair or replace goods where there is a breach of contract, Sale of Goods Act 1979, ss 48A–F.

Recission

In a contractual action the claimant may wish to be returned to the position he or she was **14.21** in before the contract was made. Again there are various circumstances in which specific performance may not be available or may not be possible.

Rectification

A contract may be rectified in limited circumstances, if for example there is an error in **14.22** recording what was agreed

Trust remedies

Numerous other equitable remedies relating to trusts are beyond the scope of this book. **14.23** However there are circumstances in which equitable remedies for trust actions may be used by analogy in developing and arguing for appropriate remedies in other civil cases. For example there are many circumstances in which a constructive trust can arise where someone can be argued to be in a fiduciary capacity, and this was touched on by Lord Denning in *Hussey v Palmer* (1972) 1 WLR 1286. For other recent authorities see *Carl Zeiss Stiftung v Herbert Smith & Co (No 2)* (1969) 2 Ch 276 and *James v Williams* (2000) Ch 1 (CA). For example a court may make orders with regard to the tracing of property and money, including tracing into mixed funds. Also it is possible to recover benefits conferred through mistake, duress, or undue influence. See for example *Kleinwort Benson Ltd v Lincoln City Council (No 2)* (1998) 3 WLR 1095 (HL) and *Nurdin and Peacock plc v DB Ramsden & Co Ltd* (1999) 1 All ER 941.

Although there is perhaps a tendency to see damages as the most usual remedy, this is not **14.24** necessarily the case. If for example a breach of duty is causing anxiety and trauma a declaration or injunction may be the prime remedy, with damages a second choice, *Anufrijeva v Southwark London Borough Council* (2004) 2 WLR 603.

Claiming a remedy

The claimant must: **14.25**

- set out the remedies claimed in a case in the particulars of claim;

- allege and if necessary prove that the facts exist which give rise to the remedy or relief claimed;
- allege and prove anything relevant to the details of the remedy, such as how damages should be quantified;
- establish if necessary that the remedy or relief is available in terms of law in the circumstances of the case.

This is dealt with at 12.99–12.111.

C   REMEDIES A COURT CANNOT ORDER

14.26   The main remedies that can be granted by a court have accumulated over centuries. They are largely the result of common law and of equity, with some remedies provided or modified by statute. There is a significant amount of case law in which judges have developed principles for what remedy is appropriate in particular circumstances.

14.27   The availability of a remedy depends primarily on the cause of action used, and on the facts of the case. It is not possible for a judge to order a particular remedy simply because a claimant has won a case and would like a particular remedy or relief on the general basis that it is argued to be fair. For example in a contract case it may be particularly important to the client to maintain an ongoing commercial relationship, but the court will have no powers in this regard. In a tort case a client may want an apology that a court does not have power to order.

14.28   If a client seeks a particular outcome for a case that a court cannot order then the options are:

- to consider fully and imaginatively the remedies that the court can order to see if court powers can be used;
- to try to negotiate a settlement without starting an action as any terms the parties want can be agreed;
- if it is necessary to start an action, to try to negotiate a settlement before the case goes to trial so as to be able to end the case with settlement or a consent order;
- if the case goes to trial, to ask the judge for permission to draft the terms of the order, if necessary adding a schedule of terms that the court cannot directly order.

14.29   There are also some remedies that the court cannot order as a matter of law. For example, damages for injury to feelings and disappointment are generally only recoverable in a contract case if the contract includes an express or implied term that the contract involves enjoyment, such as a contract for a holiday.

D   CLAIMS FOR DAMAGES

General principles

14.30   Full advice on damages may need to be given at a meeting with a client, see 7.18–7.41, or in an opinion, see 11.58–11.87. The allegations that give rise to the claim for damages need to be set out fully in a statement of case, see 12.99–12.111.

In many cases the most important remedy that the client will seek will be damages. The **14.31** lawyer will need to:

- collect evidence with regard to the quantification of damages, or in the case of a barrister advise on the collection of evidence;
- advise on what heads of damage may be recoverable—the client will sometimes have concerns about specific heads;
- advise on the overall quantification of damages;
- give advice that is as precise as possible on the amount to be recovered under each head and overall—only with precise advice can the client take informed decisions about the conduct of the case; quite precise assessments of damages may be relevant for some purposes, for example with regard to Part 36 offers and payments, see 20.51–20.64.

In a particularly complex case, for example a personal injury case with high loss of earnings, **14.32** nursing costs etc, the opinion of a barrister may be sought dealing wholly or largely with the quantification of damages.

The assessment of general damages is a matter for the discretion of the judge to be decided at **14.33** the end of the trial.

Categories of damages

There are some important distinctions to be made. **14.34**

Liquidated and unliquidated damages

- A liquidated claim is a claim for a specific sum and nothing else, where the sum is already **14.35** known or can already be ascertained exactly. Where there is a claim only for a liquidated sum the exact figure should be specifically claimed. There may be tactical rules for claiming a liquidated sum as procedural rules allow for such a sum to be dealt with quickly.
- The claim is for unliquidated damages where no exact figure can be given, and the amount due has to be left for the judge to decide, as in personal injuries cases and many contractual actions. In an unliquidated claim more detail will normally need to be pleaded to enable the judge to calculate the sum due.
- Damages are said to be liquidated when the claimant puts a precise figure on the amount claimed, either because the claim relates to a precise figure, or because the claimant chooses to claim a set figure to make it easier and quicker to get judgment. Damages are unliquidated when the precise figure claimed is not specified.

Special and general damages

- Special damages are those for which the loss can be calculated at the date of trial. This **14.36** includes one-off losses such as a car written off in an accident, or a recurring loss that is calculable such as loss of wages at £250 per week multiplied by the number of weeks of loss. The only figures that need to appear in a pleading are those for special damage.
- General damage remains at large, and total figures need not be given, though it may still be useful to provide some basic figures from which the loss can be computed.

- Special damages are those where a loss has already been suffered, and for which a figure can already be given (for example the cost or repairing or replacing a damaged item) or for which a specific figure can be calculated at any time (for example loss of earnings from the date of an accident to the date of a trial or settlement).
- General damages include the wider categories of loss that remain at large until quantified by the trial judge or agreed by the parties. This will include future loss and pain, suffering, and loss of amenity (PSLA).

Legal concepts relevant to damages

Causation

14.37   It is for the claimant to prove that loss and damage have been caused by the act or omission that gave rise to the cause of action. A factual chain of events leading from breach or negligence to a head of loss must be adequately indicated in a statement of case and then proved.

14.38   Sometimes causation is obvious and will not be disputed. If a defendant fails to repair a defect in a car's brake properly, and as a result the claimant's car runs into a wall and is badly damaged after the claimant parked it then it is likely to be accepted that the cause of the damage to the car is the faulty repair to the brake. But even in this case there may be some points of dispute—did the claimant properly inform the defendant of the defect that needed to be repaired? Did the claimant fail to apply the brake properly when leaving the car?

14.39   One potential problem in showing causation is that a single event can have more than one cause. Another potential problem is that it may be necessary to show a string of causation where one event led to another.

Reasonable contemplation of the parties

14.40   In a contract case it may also be necessary for a claimant to prove that a particular type of loss was within the reasonable contemplation of the parties at the time the contract was made. If a person enters into an agreement it is reasonable that they be liable for foreseeable loss if they break that agreement, but not that they be liable for a loss they knew nothing about.

14.41   As an example, a decorator may agree to decorate a house within four weeks. If the work is not finished in time the decorator will be in breach, and he or she should reasonably contemplate that the claimant will be put to some inconvenience. It may be that the claimant needed the work finished in time as he had agreed to let the property for a high rent from the day after the decoration was due to be finished, but the decorator will only be liable for loss of letting income if he had sufficient knowledge of this agreement.

Reasonable forseeability

14.42   In a tort case the claimant should be able to recover for any loss and damage which is a reasonably foreseeable result of the tort. If a workman digs a hole in a pavement and fails to put a barrier and warning signs round it then it is reasonably foreseeable that someone will fall into the hole. There can clearly be problems in that one person might reasonably foresee many more potential problems arising in a situation than another.

Remoteness

To be recoverable, damages in tort should not be too remote from the actionable event. **14.43**

Mitigation

A claimant is likely to claim the full amount of loss suffered, but a defendant can claim that **14.44** the claimant's loss would have been lower if the claimant had taken reasonable steps to mitigate the loss suffered. In such a case the claimant will not be able to recover for the loss that could have been mitigated.

There are various ways in which loss can be mitigated. If an item of property can be reason- **14.45** ably repaired at a lower cost rather than replaced then the claimant will normally be expected to mitigate the loss by having the item repaired.

Contributory negligence

This is strictly speaking an issue relevant to liability, but its main effect is on the damages **14.46** payable in a case. When an action is brought in negligence it may be arguable that the claimant was also partly responsible. For example driver A may be negligent in driving into driver B's car, but driver B may also have been negligent in not keeping a proper look out.

If contributory negligence is established—if on the facts both the claimant and the defen- **14.47** dant were partly responsible for the accident—then the judge will have to decide on the facts what the relative responsibility of each was. Contributory negligence is traditionally assessed as a percentage, so there may be a finding of 25 per cent contributory negligence where the accident was one quarter due to the fault of the claimant and three quarters due to the fault of the defendant.

Double recovery

Causes of action and heads of damage may overlap. Each will be recoverable cumulatively so **14.48** long as there is no element of double recovery.

Apportionment

If more than one defendant is liable for loss or damage then the court may be asked to **14.49** apportion responsibility between them. Again a decision will be based on the facts.

E   QUANTIFICATION OF DAMAGES

Different types of damage need to be quantified in different ways. **14.50**

Special damages

The quantification of special damages is relatively straightforward. **14.51**

- List all items of special damage. The client should be asked to list every item of special damage, including everything lost, damaged, or destroyed. The lawyer may be able to suggest possible items.

- Get a figure for each item of special damage. This should be provided on the valuation of what was lost.
- Be ready to provide proof for each item. If necessary there will need to be estimates of value, receipts for replacements etc, but in practice reasonable claims will normally be accepted.

General damages

14.52   The quantification of general damages can be quite complex. In very broad terms the stages are:

- List all heads of general damage. Heads may include loss of profit, loss of earnings, personal injuries etc.
- Propose a basis for assessing damages under each head, see 18.78–18.105 and 19.59–19.117.
- Decide on period of loss for each head. Each head may be finally assessable, or may be assessed up to trial and on an ongoing basis.
- Be ready to provide proof for each item. Proof may be required for the larger items of general damages that are based on financial loss.

Economic loss

14.53   On the face of it, it should not be that difficult to quantify economic loss. If a dress has been damaged beyond repair then damages should cover the value of the dress. But even in a simple example like this many questions arise. Is the claimant entitled to the value of a new dress, or simply to the value of a second-hand dress? What if the dress is irreplaceable? If the dress can be repaired, is the claimant only entitled to the cost of repair?

14.54   If a business has lost profit following a breach of contract it can be a simple matter to ascertain the loss of profit on a particular transaction. However if the loss of business is more theoretical assessment may involve complex calculations and the consideration of accounts.

14.55   There are two basic measures for economic loss in a contract case, and these are considered further at 18.78–18.105.

- Loss of profit. This is essentially the loss of the profit that would have been made if the agreement had been fulfilled. It is for the claimant to argue how this should be assessed on the facts of the case.
- Wasted expenditure. Sometimes the loss of profit may be very speculative or uncertain, but the claimant may have spent money in reliance on the agreement. In such a case the claimant can claim the wasted expenditure as an alternative to the loss of profit.

14.56   If a claimant has lost his or her job because of personal injury then the claimant is entitled to loss of earnings. Again on the face of it this is relatively easy because the amount of wages can be easily ascertained, and if the claimant gets another job on recovery then the wages have been lost for a finite time, so a figure can be produced by multiplying monthly salary by the number of months off work. But again this simple example can easily become more complex. What if the claimant is off work for some time and misses promotion? Should the claimant be expected to take a job with lower earnings that he or she can perform despite the injury? Can the expenses of getting to work be deducted from the damages as they will be saved?

It can be particularly difficult to quantify loss for future events that have not happened, and **14.57** that as a result of a breach or accident will not happen. There is an element of crystal ball gazing, and success is likely to be based on putting together a convincing case for what was most likely to have happened, with whatever evidence and analogies are available. Loss of future profit can be based on figures for existing profits and comparison with a similar business, *Sun Valley Poultry Ltd v Micro-Biologicals Ltd* The Times, 14 May 1990.

It is possible to claim damages in a currency other than sterling if this is appropriate, for **14.58** example, if a foreign law is the proper law of the contract and the price in the contract is specified to be payable in a foreign currency, *Miliangos v George Frank (Textiles)* [1975] 3 All ER 801. It is also possible to get damages in a foreign currency in a tort case if that is necessary to compensate the claimant fairly, if for example negligence causes damage to a foreign ship which is repaired abroad, *The Despina R* [1979] AC 685. If a claimant wishes to have damages awarded in a foreign currency he should specifically plead this, specifying the currency requested and why it is appropriate, *Federal Commerce v Tradax Export SA* [1977] QB 324.

Non-economic loss

It can be very difficult to put a figure on a non-economic loss. There is no obvious way to **14.59** translate the loss of a leg or the grief of bereavement into financial terms. The courts have approved a conventional approach to assessing damages for personal injury (normally referred to as pain, suffering, and loss of amenity or PSLA) and this is covered at 19.59–19.117. It may be necessary to explain this carefully to a client, who may or may not accept the approach taken by the courts and the resulting figures very easily.

There can be particular difficulties in recovering damages for non-economic loss in a con- **14.60** tract case, as the contractual agreement is seen as primarily being a matter of economic relationship. Damages for injury to feelings or disappointment can be recovered in a con- tract case, but generally only where the contract can be seen as being one intended to provide for enjoyment, for example a contract for a holiday. Damages for loss of goodwill for a business can be quantified objectively looking at the size and type of the business etc. Someone with specialist accountancy knowledge will probably be needed for this purpose.

Again there can be particular problems in assessing future loss and damage. Damages for any **14.61** future loss to a business will be a capitalized figure to cover ongoing loss after the figure for damages is determined. In an injury case future financial loss may need to be quantified where a claimant will have an ongoing loss of earnings, possibly including a loss of promo- tion. The appropriate approach to be taken here is outlined at 19.94–19.99. The appropriate sum is based on a medical prognosis for the claimant's condition. If it is difficult to say whether the claimant may or may not suffer a future deterioration in his or her condition then an award of provisional damages may be appropriate, see 19.104–19.105.

Exemplary damages

It may be possible to claim exemplary damages in addition to compensatory damages, but **14.62** this is only where there is alleged to be oppressive, arbitrary, or unconstitutional conduct by a servant of the government, or the defendant's conduct is calculated to produce a profit for him in excess of any damages he may have to pay, *Rookes v Barnard* [1964] AC 1129.

F A PROACTIVE APPROACH TO DAMAGES

Providing systematic advice

14.63 To advise on damages in a systematic way, the following broad stages are involved, and they are likely to be conducted in this general order:

- All the heads of damage that the client has suffered as a result of the alleged wrong need to be specifically identified and listed. This may include encouraging the client to think widely about every way in which she or he is out of pocket.
- It will be necessary to identify whether all the heads of loss suffered by the client will be recoverable. To be recoverable, a head of loss must be factually caused by the alleged breach of duty. In a contract case a head may not be recoverable if it is thought that a particular type of loss was not reasonably foreseeable, or the terms of the contract may limit the heads of damage that can be recovered. In a tort case, damages may not be recoverable if a particular type of damage is thought to be too remote.
- The basis on which damages will be assessed in relation to the cause of action being used must be identified. In a contract case, damages are intended to put the claimant in the position he or she would have been in if the contract had been fulfilled. In a tort case, damages are intended to put the claimant in the position he or she would have been in had the tort not been committed. If there may be more than one way of assessing damages, for example, if it may be possible to sue in tort or contract on the same facts, the relative merits of each possibility should be examined.
- It will be necessary to identify what factual information and evidence needs to be gathered to enable figures to be calculated, and a significant amount of arithmetic may need to be done to assess the sum to be claimed for each head of loss. Where there is loss to a business, the financial manager or accountant of the business may be able to assist.
- It will be necessary to identify what evidence will be required to prove the causation and amount of loss etc if such matters may be disputed.
- An appropriate figure for damages for pain and suffering may need to be identified through research by a lawyer, see 19.90–19.93.
- Appropriate claims for all heads of damage suffered and claimed will need to be made in the statements of case. A schedule of loss listing damages claimed will need to be prepared to accompany a statement of case in a negligence case.
- A defendant may make various allegations that propose a reduction in the figure of damages. If in a tort case the defendant successfully claims contributory negligence, then damages will be reduced by the proportion identified by the judge. Alternatively a defendant may successfully allege that a claimant should have mitigated his or her loss under a particular head, so that damages are reduced or not recoverable.
- Interest may be awarded on all or part of the damages so as to increase the figure payable, see 14.68–14.77.
- Various factors may affect the money actually received by a claimant. Where a claimant has been in receipt of certain state benefits, for example while being incapacitated

following an accident, part of the damages payable by the defendant will be payable directly by the defendant to the government in recompense. This figure will be part of the damages awarded, but it will not be payable to the claimant, see Chapter 19.

To provide an example, if a car has been damaged in an accident then it will be necessary to show:　　**14.64**

- that the damage resulted from the accident, and was a reasonably forseeable consequence of the breach of duty that caused the accident, using an accident report or a garage report (foreseeability);
- how much the damage cost to repair, using a bill for the work done (the amount of damages claimed);
- if challenged, that the cost of repair was reasonable (mitigation).

As another example, if a trader has lost business because of a breach of contract then it will be necessary to show:　　**14.65**

- that the loss of business was caused by the breach of contract, for example with a letter from the person with whom business was lost as a result of the breach (causation);
- that the defendant was aware that the business might be lost if the contract was breached (reasonable contemplation of the parties);
- the value of the business lost (by showing specifically what business has been lost, or by analogy to the profit that would normally be expected from such business);
- if challenged, that reasonable efforts have been made to find replacement business (mitigation).

Constructing arguments

The judge has a great deal of discretion in the assessment of damages, and many of the concepts used in the assessment of damages are very general or flexible. There is a significant opportunity for an effective lawyer to construct arguments both as to the heads of damage that should be claimable, and as to the amount of damages to be awarded under each head.　　**14.66**

To give some ideas of the sort of arguments that may be mounted:　　**14.67**

- Some causes of action can provide a more generous measure of damages than others. For example depending on the facts of the case, misrepresentation damages may or may not be more generous than contract damages.
- Alternative measures for damages may apply in the same case. For example, if there is a total failure of consideration of contract the claimant may choose to claim loss of profit or wasted expenditure, *CCC Films (London) Ltd v Impact Quadrant Films* [1984] 3 All ER 298. In *Dominion Mosaics & Tile Co Ltd v Trafalgar Trucking Co Ltd* [1990] 2 All ER 246 the claimant's premises were burned down and the alternatives were damages for diminution in the value of the site or the cost of alternative premises. It was held that the latter was appropriate as this would mitigate the loss of profits. In *Paula Lee Ltd v Robert Zehil* [1983] 2 All ER 390 it was held that if there were alternative ways of assessing loss on a set of facts, the alternative that was least unfavourable to the defendant should be adopted if that was reasonable.
- It is possible to get damages for the loss of a chance of getting something. In *Chaplin v*

Hicks [1911] 2 KB 786, damages were awarded for loss of a chance to win a prize. To assess the correct figure it is necessary to consider the amount of the prize and how likely it is that the claimant would have won it, thus damages might appropriately be 25 per cent of the value of the prize. Damages for loss of opportunity in the job market can be awarded in a *Smith v Manchester* (1974) 17 KIR 1 award.

- Arguments may be made as regards heads of loss in a case. For example, in *Watson v Willmott* [1991] 1 All ER 473 a child's mother was killed in a car accident and his father then committed suicide. The child was adopted but it was held that damages were recoverable on the basis that he would get less from his adoptive father than he would have got from his natural father. But not every inventive argument will impress the judge. In *Pritchard v JH Cobden Ltd* [1987] 2 FLR 30 it was held that damages were not recoverable in respect of a divorce that it was alleged resulted from injuries suffered in an accident.

G   CLAIMS FOR INTEREST

14.68   Where there is a claim for the payment of a sum of money or damages, the claimant may wish to claim interest in addition. In times of relatively high rates of interest and inflation this can be important. A claim for interest should be pleaded, proved (except for the 'ordinary' interest rate), and specifically referred to in a judgment. It is necessary to identify the basis on which interest is claimed, the rate at which interest is due, and the period over which it is due, and to look at each individual element of damages separately.

14.69   Essentially an award of interest is at the discretion of the judge. A High Court judge can award interest in any action for the recovery of a debt or damages, at such rate as he or she thinks fit or the rules of court provide, on all or any part of the debt or damages, for all or any part of the period between the date the cause of action arose and the date of payment or of judgment in the case. If interest is claimed it should be pleaded, and although there are slightly different requirements depending on the interest claimed, the essential rule is that the claim should be pleaded in full, with all the details of rates, dates and so on that are relevant in assessing the amount of interest to award. These details should be pleaded in the body of the draft, and not just in the prayer, though there seem still to be some variations in practice as to how this is done.

When interest can be claimed

14.70   There are various circumstances in which interest can be awarded. The details to be pleaded will be slightly different for each, but the principle of the need to plead all the appropriate details for assessing the interest to be awarded applies to all.

Interest may be awarded as an inherent part of damages

14.71   For example in a contract case the contract may specify that a rate of interest will be payable in specified circumstances. The term itself gives rise to the right to interest, and should be pleaded with details of the agreed rate and period, and the amount of interest due when the writ was issued, see *Bushwall Properties v Vortex Properties* [1975] 2 All ER 214 and *Fansa v American Express International Banking Corporation* The Times, 26 June 1985.

Interest on a debt

Even if a contract does not specify that interest will be payable, interest on a debt can **14.72** normally be claimed if it is not paid and an action is commenced. However, if there is no agreement, interest is not payable prior to the commencement of the action, *President of India v La Pintada Cia Navegacion SA* [1984] 2 All ER 773. Interest is payable on a dishonoured cheque, Bills of Exchange Act 1882, s 57. There is also an implied term for payment of interest on debts relating to contracts for the supply of goods and services where both parties are acting in the course of business, Late Payment of Commercial Debts (Interest) Act 1998.

Interest may be a foreseeable part of the damages on the facts

If, for example, work is not completed when it should have been, and as a result it is foresee- **14.73** able that the claimant will have to borrow money to find alternative accommodation, then the interest that the claimant has had to pay on borrowed money may be recoverable as part of his damages, see *Wadsworth v Lydell* [1981] 2 All ER 401. This may also happen in a tort action, as in *Tate & Lyle Foods and Distribution v Greater London Council* [1981] 3 All ER 716 where the claimant was deprived of the use of a jetty by the defendant's negligence which caused the river to silt up, and it was held that since the claimant had been deprived of profit he was entitled to recover theoretical interest on the money he was deprived of at a commercial rate.

Interest may be justifiable as a matter of fairness

The court may in its discretion use a higher rate where there has been fraud or breach of a **14.74** fiduciary duty. The court has a general equitable discretion to award interest in a suitable case. In *Wallersteiner v Moir (No 2)* [1975] 1 QB 373 it was held that a court could award interest where the defendant had improperly benefited from a fiduciary position. Similarly, it may be appropriate for the court to award interest, possibly at a high rate, where a trustee has acted in breach of trust, *Bartlett v Barclays Bank* [1980] Ch 515. In *BP Exploration Co (Libya) v Hunt* [1983] 2 AC 352 it was held that it might also be appropriate for the court to award interest to the extent that seemed just where a contract had been frustrated.

Interest as part of compensation

It may be fair that a party is paid interest as compensation for having to wait some time for **14.75** the payment of damages—for example where damages are paid for loss of income that should have accrued much earlier. Interest may in a general sense compensate for the time it has taken for judgment to be reached. The High Court has a discretion to award interest under the Supreme Court Act 1981, s 35A, and the County Court has a general discretion to award interest under the County Courts Act 1984, s 69. The court also has an equitable jurisdiction to grant interest when awarding an equitable remedy such as specific perfor- mance. Interest will automatically be ordered if a defendant admits a claim, CPR r 14.14.

Rates of interest

There are various rates of interest used in different circumstances. The appropriate rate must **14.76** be checked as rates are changed from time to time.

- Contract rate. The rate of interest may be set by a contract, in which case that will be the rate to which the claimant is entitled.

- A rate that is appropriate on the facts of the case. This might be a commercial rate of interest where the claimant has had to borrow money at the commercial rate, see *Tate and Lyle Food and Distribution Ltd v GLC* [1982] 1 WLR 149. It might be the rate of interest that a claimant might have got from investing money where on the facts the claimant has been deprived of the possibility of earning money. A foreign rate of interest may be awarded where that is appropriate for a particular case, see *Miliangos v George Frank (Textiles) Ltd (No 2)* [1977] QB 489.
- There are special rules for interest in claims for personal injuries and death, see 19.73.
- There are special provisions for the rate payable under the Late Payment of Commercial Debts (interest) Act 1998. The rate is 8 per cent above the Bank of England base rate in force on the last 30 June or 31 December before interest starts to run. There is also a fixed compensation payment between £50 and £100.
- Where interest is at the discretion of the court there are two possibilities. The one most commonly used is the rate applied to judgment debts under the Judgments Act 1838. The alternative is the Special Investment Account rate, which is taken from the interest yield on index-linked securities.

The period for which interest is payable

14.77 The period for which interest is payable will also have to be decided to allow the amount of interest payable to be calculated.

- Contractual interest will be payable for the period specified in the contract.
- Interest under the Late Payment of Commercial Debts (Interest) Act 1998 will be payable from the date agreed for payment, from 30 days after the goods or services were supplied, or from the date on which the purchaser had notice of the amount of the debt.
- Interest on other debts will run from the date payment was overdue.
- Interest on other economic loss will run from the date the cause of action accrued, or from the date the loss was suffered if later.
- For non-economic loss interest will normally be payable from the time the claim form is issued.

H DOING THE ARITHMETIC

14.78 At the end of the day all the principles and arguments relevant to damages have to be turned into arithmetic. Some lawyers are not entirely comfortable with figures, and in some cases the assessment of damages will require expert evidence and the help of an accountant, but the lawyer will need to be able to deal with sufficient arithmetic to provide practical advice for a client who wants to know what a claim is worth.

14.79 The most important aspects of damages where arithmetic is important are as follows.

- List heads of loss and attach a figure to each head of loss with assistance from the client and other sources.
- If it is difficult to attach a figure to a head of damage, try to develop an argument for what figure should be attached to it and why.

- Assess the chances of recovering each head of loss and damage, taking into account whether there is sufficient evidence to show causation/foreseeability, how fiercely the item is argued etc.
- Assess the chances of the figure attached to any head of loss or damage being reduced, for example due to contributory negligence or failure to mitigate.
- Add interest as appropriate to each head of damage.
- Consider any other financial factors that may be relevant eg, taxation.
- Reach an overall figure for damages that is as accurate as possible.
- Consider the costs position. What are the likely costs of an action compared to the figure recoverable?

15

THE VITAL ROLE OF EVIDENCE

A THE IMPORTANCE OF EVIDENCE 15.01

B IDENTIFYING WHAT NEEDS TO BE PROVED 15.07
  Identifying the factual elements of a claim 15.08
  Identifying facts that are agreed or admitted 15.11
  Identifying facts that can be proved by the client 15.12
  Identifying facts that can be proved to be material held
    by another party 15.13
  The facts that remain in dispute 15.14

C TYPES OF EVIDENCE 15.16
  Witnesses 15.17
  Statements of case 15.23
  Documents 15.24
  Real evidence 15.30
  Photographs, videos, tape recordings, computer records,
    sketch plans, and models 15.32
  Electronic evidence 15.35
  Admissions 15.36
  Expert witnesses 15.39
  Judicial notice and matters of general knowledge 15.41
  Presumptions 15.44
  Statutes, cases, and legal text books 15.45

D COLLECTING EVIDENCE 15.48
  Being imaginative about potential sources of evidence 15.48
  The stages in collecting evidence 15.55

E THE KEY RULES OF ADMISSIBILITY 15.58
  Judicial control of admissibility 15.58
  Relevance 15.62
  Oral evidence 15.63
  Opinion evidence 15.67
  Hearsay 15.68
  Previous consistent and inconsistent statements 15.82
  Previous court findings 15.83
  Public policy exclusion 15.86
  General points 15.89

F   WHO HAS TO PROVE WHAT 15.92
        Who has to prove an allegation 15.93
        How much evidence is required? 15.95

G   FORMAL REQUIREMENTS FOR WRITTEN EVIDENCE 15.101

H   DRAFTING A WITNESS STATEMENT......................... 15.109
        General guidelines....................................... 15.109
        Preparing to draft a witness statement...................... 15.113
        The evidential content of a witness statement............... 15.118
        The elements of the witness statement 15.123
        Professional principles 15.133
        Pro forma for a witness statement 15.135

I   DRAFTING AN AFFIDAVIT................................. 15.136

J   EXPERT EVIDENCE....................................... 15.140
        The need for an expert 15.143
        Selecting and briefing an expert 15.149
        The format for an expert report........................... 15.160
        Reviewing the report..................................... 15.166
        Formal rules for expert evidence.......................... 15.170

K   DISCLOSURE OF EVIDENCE 15.179
        The principle of disclosure................................ 15.179
        Disclosure of documents 15.184
        Inspection of documents 15.192
        Special orders 15.194
        The use of documents.................................... 15.198

L   EXCHANGE OF WITNESS STATEMENTS....................... 15.201

M   REVIEWING AND ADVISING ON EVIDENCE 15.206

        KEY DOCUMENTS

> It is a truth very certain that when it is not in our power to determine what is true we ought to follow what is most probable.
>
> Descartes, *Discourse on Method*

A   THE IMPORTANCE OF EVIDENCE

15.01   The process for collecting information was considered in Chapter 8, and the process for defining the issues in a case was outlined in Chapter 10. When the issues in the case have been defined from an analysis of the law and the facts, the next stage will be to prove the case on the issues from the party's point of view.

The importance of evidence in civil litigation is sometimes underestimated.   **15.02**

- There has not been a wholesale review of the rules of civil evidence as there has been of the rules of procedure, and the old case law and phraseology of some rules of evidence, such as hearsay, can make the rules appear dated.
- It is possible to hold the view that in civil cases almost any evidence will be admissible by one route or another, and that more complex rules apply primarily in civil cases, because of the need for fairness to the accused and the need to control information available to a jury.
- The majority of civil cases settle, and a case will not have to be proved if it does not go to trial.

However, a good working knowledge of how to use evidence can be as important in a case as   **15.03**
good advocacy.

- Many cases only go to trial because of a dispute of fact, and disputes of fact are decided on the evidence available.
- However key a fact is, it is only of use if it can be proved by admissible evidence.
- A thorough analysis of what can be proved is very important in assessing the real strength of a case.
- It is important to know how to ensure that evidence is admissible at trial, and to be able to challenge evidence submitted by the other side.
- Even if a case is negotiated rather than going to trial, points about what can be proved and the strength of evidence may be very useful in the negotiation.
- The lawyer cannot give evidence in a case—all factual material has to be given to the court through admissible evidence.

Although the rules of evidence have a long history and may sometimes appear complex, the   **15.04**
bases for the rules are relatively practical, and the rules of admissibility in a civil case are
relatively straightforward. Dealing with evidence in practice is less dramatic than in fiction,
but it is likely to be a vital part of effective litigation where facts are in dispute. For sources of
evidence law see 24.16.

The importance of evidence in a case can be misunderstood. Detective novels can give   **15.05**
the impression that cases turn on finding unexpected evidence that suddenly makes other
evidence fit into place. In fact most cases turn on methodically accumulating evidence that
supports the case that is anticipated. American rules and television series can give the
impression that dealing with evidence in court is a matter of standing up and saying 'I object
your Honour' quite frequently, whereas in fact most issues about admissibility are resolved
well before a case reaches court.

A practical approach to evidence is important. The complexity of some rules may make it   **15.06**
appear that evidence can be difficult to get. In fact much evidence is available relatively
easily. Rights quite outside the civil litigation process can be used, for example the Data
Protection Act 1998, see 8.08–8.10. For the possible contents of an advice on evidence
see 11.50–11.51.

B   IDENTIFYING WHAT NEEDS TO BE PROVED

15.07   What needs to be proved in a case should be systematically identified. Many factual matters that arise when a lawyer and client discuss a case will not form part of the case at the end of the day. Many of the facts that do need to be proved can be proved quite simply.

Identifying the factual elements of the claim

15.08   The analytical approach proposed in 10.19–10.27 should identify the issues in the case—the factual allegations that will show all the elements of a legal cause of action. These are the allegations that will be set out in a statement of case as outlined at 12.95–12.98. Each of these factual allegations will need to be proved.

15.09   For example in a contract case it may be necessary to prove:

- that a contract was made;
- what the relevant terms of the contract were;
- that those terms were breached in specific ways;
- that those breaches caused loss;
- what loss was suffered.

Each of these allegations may include a number of details, in that for example in proving that a contract was made it may be necessary to prove who made it, when and where, and whether it was oral or written.

15.10   In a negligence case it may be necessary to prove:

- that a duty of care was owed by the defendant;
- that it was owed to the claimant;
- that the duty of care was breached;
- how it was breached;
- that the breach led to foreseeable injury;
- what those injuries were;
- that the breach led to foreseeable financial loss;
- what the amount of financial loss was.

Identifying facts that are agreed or admitted

15.11   Having identified the facts that need to be proved to show the elements of a legal case, the next stage is to identify facts that are agreed or that the other side will admit. In many cases a significant number of facts will be agreed or admitted and therefore will not require further proof. For example it may be admitted that a contract was made and that it was breached, so that the only live issues are the resulting losses. It may be admitted that an accident happened and that the claimant suffered certain injuries and financial loss, and the only live issue may be whether the accident was caused by the defendant.

Identifying facts that can be proved by the client

In many cases the client's version of events and documents or other evidence held by or **15.12** easily accessible to the client will be able to provide evidence of many of the matters in the case, narrowing still further the remaining evidence that needs to be sought.

Identifying facts that can be proved to be material held by another party

In a number of cases material held by the other party may be able to assist in proving a case. **15.13** For example where an accident happens at work, the employer will hold a record in an accident book, and may well have held an internal enquiry into what happened. Such material will normally be available through disclosure and inspection.

The facts that remain in dispute

The cumulative result may be that relatively few facts remain to be proved by further sources **15.14** of evidence. Having said this, there is often merit in having further evidence to support key points in a case. Also the facts that remain in dispute may be important ones and some cases will go to trial because both sides have difficulties in proving particular key points.

In taking a systematic approach to accumulating evidence there is great merit in using a **15.15** written table or a spreadsheet to cover what elements need to be proved, how each will be proved, and any additional evidence that helps to support each point.

C   TYPES OF EVIDENCE

> An oral contract isn't worth the paper it's written on.
>
> Louis B Mayer

Underestimating the importance of evidence in a case, or restricting the types of evidence **15.16** used can seriously undermine the preparation of a case. A case must be constructed on evidence rather than theory, and a case must be proved by evidence and not by a speech from a lawyer. Many types of evidence are available, and most relevant evidence is admissible in a civil case with limited formalities. Those new to legal practice can see written documents as the best evidence, but there is a wide range of potentially reliable and helpful evidence. See generally CPR Part 32 Evidence, and CPR Part 33 Miscellaneous rules about evidence.

Witnesses

The preferred source of evidence on facts is a witness. This is an historical premise of civil **15.17** litigation and it remains the case, save only that evidence in chief is now provided through a witness statement unless the court orders otherwise, CPR r 32.5. Many rules of evidence stem from the premise that evidence will be given by witnesses—for example real evidence or documents normally need to be proved in court by a witness. See generally CPR Part 34 Witnesses, depositions and evidence for foreign courts, and PD 34 Depositions and court attendance by witnesses.

15.18   Any person is competent to be a witness, unless the court decides that the person cannot give useful evidence due to their inability to understand. If a person under 18 does not understand the nature of the oath then the child's evidence may be heard by the court if the court is of the opinion that the child understands the duty to speak the truth and has sufficient understanding to justify the evidence being heard, Children Act 1989, s 96. In broad terms children over about 14 will generally be thought capable of giving sworn evidence, and younger children will give unsworn evidence. The position for people of limited mental capacity is not clear. If they cannot understand the oath then they probably cannot give evidence, as there is no provision for unsworn evidence.

15.19   Any person who is competent to be a witness will normally be compellable in a civil case, save for heads of state, diplomats, and the judiciary. In a civil case there is general freedom as to the witnesses chosen by each party, save that the court has overall control under CPR r 32.1. There is no property in a witness, so in principle any person can be called as a witness by either side. In practice many potential witnesses are likely to favour one side or the other, and are likely to be used as a witness by the party they are most useful to. A person who is likely to be used as a witness by one side is unlikely to voluntarily provide information to the other party—the evidence they will give will be revealed with the exchange of witness statements. One party might wish to stop a witness giving evidence for the other side but this cannot be done. If for example an expert has given a report that does not favour one side the other side may become aware of that and wish to call the witness, and this cannot be prevented, *Harmony Shipping Co SA v Saudi Europe Line Ltd* (1979) 1 WLR 1380 CA.

15.20   A witness can normally only give evidence about facts and not about opinion or impressions. However a statement of opinion is admissible as evidence of what a witness perceived if it is made as a way of conveying relevant facts personally perceived by the witness, Civil Evidence Act 1972, s 3. This might for example include an impression of the speed of a car or the weather.

15.21   In civil cases the sworn statement of a witness will normally stand as their evidence in chief. The witness statement should include only matters the witness could give oral evidence of, and it will end with a sworn statement of truth. If a witness statement is served and the party intends to rely on that witness, the witness must be called to give oral evidence unless the court orders otherwise, so that the witness can be cross examined, CPR r 32.5.

15.22   A witness is not open to being sued for the evidence he or she gives, *Evans v London Hospital Medical College* [1981] 1 WLR 184, except perhaps an expert witness, *Palmer v Durnford Ford* [1992] 2 All ER 122.

Statements of case

15.23   Each statement of case includes a signed statement of truth, and it therefore provides evidence of the factual allegations made in it. The same principle will apply to further information provided in respect of a statement of case provided that has a signed statement of truth. See 10.56–10.61, and see generally CPR Part 22 Statements of truth, and PD 22 Statements of truth.

Documents

Documentary evidence will be important in a number of cases, especially if there is a written **15.24** contract or other written agreement. Often both sides will have copies of key documents. Key documents should be obtained as early as possible in a case. The origin and relevance of a document must be proved by a witness either through the witness producing the document in court, or through exhibiting the document to a witness statement or affidavit. See generally PD 32 Written evidence.

It was a rule of common law that the original document should be produced wherever **15.25** possible, to ensure its authenticity. In practice a number of exceptions built up allowing a copy to be used or oral evidence provided, for example where the original had been lost. This rule appears no longer to be followed, but it remains the case that the authenticity and reliability of a document needs to be established through agreement or through the evidence of a witness.

In addition to key documents, other documents may provide important supporting **15.26** evidence. For example an accident report may help to prove the cause of an accident, or a contract of employment might be used to prove lost wages. If documents are not to hand it may be possible to get copies—for example banks can provide copies of bank statements.

Business and local authority records can be admitted without further proof, provided a **15.27** certificate signed by an officer of the business or authority is produced in court, Civil Evidence Act 1995, s 9. The absence of an entry in such records can be dealt with by an affidavit of an officer of the relevant body. If the record includes hearsay a notice should be served.

Relevant documents held by another party should be revealed on disclosure and inspection. **15.28** Documents held by someone who is not a party can be obtained by serving a witness summons requiring the specified documents to be produced. A refusal to produce a document can only be justified on the grounds of privilege, otherwise the court may impose a penalty.

There are special rules for special types of documents such as bankers' books. Actuarial tables **15.29** are admissible in personal injury cases, Civil Evidence Act 1995, s 10.

Real evidence

Any physical object which is directly relevant to a case is called real evidence. This can **15.30** include objects that are damaged or are alleged to be defective. Each object needs to be produced in court by a witness who says on oath what the object is, that it is authentic, and how it is relevant to the case. An item cannot simply be produced without a witness to prove it, *Ventouris v Moutain (No 2)* (1992) 1 WLR 817.

Many items that are in a sense physical evidence are actually dealt with in court in some **15.31** other way. For example the location of an accident is often dealt with by a plan and photographs. These need to be prepared by a suitable witness who, as far as possible, is able to deal with any changes at the location between the time of the accident and the time the photographs are taken. Personal injuries are dealt with primarily through a medical report because of the need for the expert view of a doctor.

Photographs, videos, tape recordings, computer records, sketch plans, and models

15.32 All these forms of evidence (sometimes called 'demonstrative evidence' as they illustrate or demonstrate something) may assist in the understanding of a case, and all are admissible if they are produced by a witness who establishes the authenticity of the item. In a sense these items are real evidence. If the item is produced by human intervention it is arguably hearsay and may therefore need a notice.

15.33 Evidence on video may be valuable in a personal injury action, *Ash v Buxted Poultry Ltd* The Times, 29 November 1989. If a video is taken in secrecy and through trespass in breach of Article 8 of the European Convention on Human Rights then the evidence may be excluded, though this will not necessarily be the case if experts for both sides have seen the video and commented on it, *Jones v University of Warwick* (2003) 1 WLR 954.

15.34 The use of evidence of this kind should normally be agreed in advance of trial, for example at a case management conference. There should be agreement as to who should produce the photographs, plan etc to be used at trial, and the other side should have the opportunity to inspect the items.

Electronic evidence

15.35 It is of course increasingly common for contracts to be concluded electronically, or for information relevant to contracts to be sent electronically. If there is a dispute about an e-mail then not only the e-mail itself will be disclosable, but also linked discs and hard discs, backups, and possibly even the server.

Admissions

15.36 Many elements of a case will normally be admitted and will need no further proof. The civil procedure rules encourage admissions, not least as they meet the requirements of the overriding objective in helping to define the issues between the parties and thus save time and costs.

15.37 Some admissions will be made in statements of case. A defence will normally admit a number of the allegations made in the particulars of claim.

15.38 As evidence accumulates it is likely to become obvious that further matters should be admitted. Where the evidence shows that an allegation will not succeed at trial, or is very unlikely to succeed the party making the allegation should consider making an admission to save the cost of the point having to be proved at trial, see 12.158–12.164. Also one party can ask the other to make admissions. A pre-trial review will consider whether any further admissions should be made to save time at trial.

Expert witnesses

15.39 If particular expertise is required to explain or interpret some of the facts and allegations in a case an expert witness should be used. Non-expert witnesses cannot be called upon to theorise about expert matters. A lawyer may acquire some expertise in an area from personal experience or preparing the case, but a lawyer cannot give evidence in the case—the personal expertise of the lawyer can only be of assistance in preparing a case.

There should be a decision at a relatively early stage whether an expert is likely to be **15.40** required, and an appropriate expert should be identified and instructed as outlined below. There may need to be a conference between the lawyer and the expert to ensure that the report of the expert is fully understood. The assistance of the expert may be useful in planning questions to be put to witnesses. As regards briefing an expert witness see 15.140–15.178.

Judicial notice and matters of general knowledge

A fact that is commonly agreed by people in general can be accepted without specific **15.41** evidence if the judge is prepared to take judicial notice of it. In *Dennis v AJ White & Co* (1916) 1 KB 1, judicial notice was taken of the fact that the streets of London are full of traffic. A judge cannot normally take purely personal knowledge into account, *Palmer v Crone* (1927) 1 KB 804, though this is not an easy line to draw.

If the judge is not prepared to take judicial notice of a relatively well known fact it will often **15.42** be fairly easy to demonstrate it by an appropriate witness making reference to an atlas or an encyclopaedia, though this may need to be linked to expert evidence if the reference work does not entirely cover the point, *McQuaker v Goddard* (1940) 1 KB 687.

Matters known to a group of people, such as matters of professional practice like account- **15.43** ancy practice, may be proved by an appropriately qualified person, such as accountancy practices, *Heather v P-E Consulting Group Ltd* (1973) Ch 189.

Presumptions

Some facts are difficult to presume in themselves, but the court may be prepared to assume **15.44** a fact provided relevant supporting facts can be proved. There are various categories of presumption—some are of law and some are of fact, some are rebuttable and some are irrebutable. To provide some examples:

- In a defamation case, proof that a person has been convicted of a criminal offence is conclusive evidence that that person committed that offence, Civil Evidence Act 1968, s 13.
- If someone acts in a judicial, official, or public capacity there is a rebuttable presumption of regularity—it is presumed an act carried out by that person in that capacity has com- plied with necessary formalities, *R v Cresswell* (1873) 1 QBD 446 CCR, but limits on this presumption were noted in *R v Dillon* (1982) AC 484 PC.
- There is also a rebuttable presumption of mechanical regularity in that if a mechanical device is normally in working order it will be presumed to be working properly in a particular instance, *Tingle Jacobs and Co v Kennedy* (1964) 1 WLR 638.
- There are rebuttable presumptions of marriage, legitimacy, and death in defined circumstances.

Statutes, cases, and legal text books

Principles of law can be quite easily presented in court without further proof. Acts of Parlia- **15.45** ment are accepted by a court without further proof, Interpretation Act 1978, ss 3 and 22. Same for European Community Treaties etc, European Communities Act 1972, s 3. It is important to identify and use the precise text of relevant sections, and to refer to a definitions section if necessary.

15.46   Cases are accepted without further proof, though official law reports are preferred. The relevant sections of judgments should be carefully identified. A general reference to a case may be of little assistance to a judge, and time may be wasted trying to identify relevant material in a judgment.

15.47   Where there is a legal issue in a case the court may be prepared to accept argument about the intention of legislation by material from Hansard on parliamentary debates. The court may also be prepared to accept material from a well respected text book, see 9.28–9.30.

D   COLLECTING EVIDENCE

Being imaginative about potential sources of evidence

15.48   Effective litigation is likely to be founded on thinking widely about the range of evidence that is likely to be available to support a case, and being systematic about collecting and evaluating the evidence that is most likely to be useful. The more particular elements of a case are disputed, the more important it is to put effort into collecting evidence. Where a particular point is hotly contested, evidence supporting evidence that is already available may be valuable.

15.49   Some of the evidence that needs to be collected may be relatively routine. Evidence needs to make a full situation comprehensible to a court. In a contractual claim this may involve a systematic collection of documents. Where there has been an accident there may be a need for plans and photographs. Quite a lot of financial information may be required to support a claim for damages.

15.50   Some imagination may be required in identifying potential sources of evidence. What potential witnesses might there be who know something relevant? What documents might have relevance to the situation? Is there relevant physical evidence? Very open or lateral thinking may help. If an accident happens in a public place, might CCTV footage be available?

15.51   However, the desire to gather sufficient evidence always needs to be balanced with the likely cost of collecting evidence. Sometimes it will be proportionately too expensive to collect some evidence that might be available given the amount that is in dispute. Careful decisions may have to be made. If there are several potential witnesses, can one or two of them cover the necessary points? Might it be possible to get an admission so that evidence is not required?

15.52   It may not be possible to find strong evidence on every element in a case. If there is no evidence at all on a key element, the case should probably not be brought as it is likely to fail. However in most cases there will be some gaps, where some evidence is available but it is not very convincing, or where direct evidence is not available and logical and persuasive arguments may need to be used to bridge the gap. This is dealt with at 8.60–8.69.

15.53   Even where there are not gaps there may be weaknesses in the case because some things are particularly difficult to prove. A person's state of mind or intention can often only be proved indirectly, by implication from things they say or do. It can also be particularly difficult to prove a negative.

In addition to proving a case, it is important to consider what evidence the other side has or **15.54** may have, as it may be necessary to collect evidence to contradict it.

The stages in collecting evidence

The collecting of evidence is a progressive process, with various stages of sifting: **15.55**

- In the early stages of the case it will be necessary to collect sufficient evidence about the case to make general judgments about the type of case involved and the strength of the case. The cost of gathering evidence, and the fact that only some parts of the evidence available will be needed at trial, mean that careful decisions should be taken about what is really needed at this stage. Summaries of evidence of the client and key witnesses, key documents, and if relevant expert reports, and a basic understanding about a central matter such as the location of an accident are likely to be sufficient for a relatively straightforward case.
- Once this evidence has been analysed and basic decisions have been taken about bringing an action, it may be possible to move to drafting a statement of case. Before the statement of case is finalised further evidence relating to remedies may be required, for example as regards financial loss or the effects of personal injuries. No case should be settled until sufficient information is available to allow damages to be properly assessed.
- In a larger or more complex case significant further evidence is likely to be required before the formal start of the action to ensure that the decisions about how the case should be framed are sound. It is best to avoid having to amend the statement of case, and once the claim form is filed and served the timetable for exchange of evidence will become relevant, so most gathering of evidence should have been completed in advance. Pre-action protocols or voluntary exchange of information before the claim form is filed will often assist in this process.
- Only once the particulars of claim and the defence are available will it be possible to form a detailed view of what matters are in dispute, and therefore what evidence will be needed at trial. The statements of case should reveal areas of agreement where there should be few problems about evidence, and areas of dispute where more evidence may be required. Each side will need to take decisions about the evidence they will actually use at trial. The evidence of the witnesses to be called at trial will at this stage be put into formal witness statements as outlined below. The evaluation of evidence at this stage is dealt with in greater detail at the end of this chapter. A significant amount of the general factual information that has been collected will not go on to be used in evidence at trial.
- Once both sides have taken decisions about the evidence they will use, lists of documents will be exchanged and they can be inspected, and copies of witness statements will be exchanged.
- Any further issues about the content, forma, and admissibility of evidence will be dealt with by agreement or at case management conferences or pre-trial reviews. The evidence to be used at trial will be put into trial bundles. These matters are dealt with further in Chapter 17.

15.56   In terms of collecting evidence from witnesses, the main witness will often be the client. The first outline of facts provided by a client will need to be supplemented with further facts at a meeting with the lawyer. Areas that are still vague will need to be clarified. The client may need to be pressed for detail where an allegation is contested. The client will need to be pressed for detail on areas on which he or she is likely to be cross examined at trial, so that the strength of the client as a witness can be assessed.

15.57   Witnesses who may support elements of the client's case will often need to be found and interviewed. The solicitor should interview each potential witness, seeing each on their own without the client present. Everything said by the witness should be recorded to produce a written proof of evidence, which the witness should be asked to check. It is only as and when it is decided that the evidence of a particular witness will be used at trial that the evidence of the witness will be put into the form of a witness statement.

E   THE KEY RULES OF ADMISSIBILITY

> A witness cannot give evidence of his age unless he can remember being born.
>
> Judge Blagden

Judicial control of admissibility

15.58   The court has general control over what is admissible in court. All evidence likely to be used in the case must be checked to see whether it is admissible, and if so on what terms. The court will wish to have as much evidence as possible to assist it in taking a decision, and in a civil case almost all relevant evidence will be admissible. There is less risk of evidence being prejudicial in a civil case than in a criminal case, and as most civil trials are by judge alone, the judge can take appropriate decisions as to the reliance to be placed on each piece of evidence.

15.59   In a civil case evidence will rarely be controlled through one lawyer jumping up and shouting 'I object!' Most questions as to the admissibility of evidence will be decided before trial, and there will normally only be further queries and objections if new evidence is raised at a late stage, or if evidence is presented in an unacceptable way. Most decisions about admissibility will be taken at a case conference or a pre-trial review, and much of the evidence to be used will have been exchanged well before trial.

15.60   A court has a power to exclude evidence that is otherwise admissible if, for example, it feels it would be unduly prejudicial, CPR r 32.1. However if evidence is inadmissible there is no general discretion to let it in, *Myers v DPP* (1965) AC 1001.

15.61   For most civil cases, the key rules of admissibility are fairly straightforward, and they are designed to:

- ensure that only relevant evidence is heard by the court;
- ensure that the best source of evidence is used for each piece of information;
- focus on relevance, weight, probative effect;
- ensure that a wary approach is taken where evidence is less reliable, for example because it is second hand because it comes from an indirect source rather than an eye witness;

- try to rule out evidence that can be improperly manufactured, for example by a party simply repeating something that party has said before and trying to pretend that is evidence that what was said was true;
- allow in circumstantial evidence, which may be of value where direct evidence is lacking. Evidence which makes a particular conclusion more likely can be useful, as can several facts that can be combined to make reasonable inferences.

The rules tend to focus on what is inadmissible, leaving most evidence as admissible.

Relevance

The key question is whether evidence is relevant, and that means whether it is related to one of **15.62** the elements of the case as set out in the statements of case. General relevance is not enough— in *Hollingham v Head* (1858) 27 LJCP 241 it was held that a party could not adduce evidence of the terms of contracts with other parties to show what terms of a specific contract were likely to be. At the end of the day it is for the court to decide whether evidence is relevant, but the parties make it relevant by the way they frame their cases in the statements of case.

Oral evidence

A witness can normally only give evidence of something that he or she has seen or heard **15.63** or knows personally. A witness can also deal with a matter he or she believes to be true, provided he or she reveals the source of the information and why he or she believes it. Where a witness only knows facts from some other source, that other source should normally be used to provide first hand evidence.

The weight given to the evidence of a witness depends on how reliable the witness is. The **15.64** reliability of a witness can be undermined because a witness could not see or hear properly, could not see or hear properly in the circumstances at the time, was preoccupied, or had a motive to give biased evidence or to lie. All of these can be raised in cross examination of a witness. However there is a rule of finality—if a witness denies being preoccupied etc that answer must normally be accepted and evidence that goes only to credibility is not generally admissible. Evidence of good or bad character is admissible if it is a fact in issue in the case or directly relevant to the facts in issue. Evidence of a party or witness may also be relevant to credit. Otherwise it is not admissible even if generally relevant.

A lie or silence is treated like any other kind of evidence. It is admissible if it is relevant, and **15.65** the weight to be attached to it is a matter for the tribunal. A failure to reply to an allegation in a letter is not evidence that the allegation is true as there may be many reasons not to reply, *Wiedmann v Walpole* (1891) 2 QB 534. However silence in the face of a direct confrontation over a promise to marry has been held to be admissible as a denial was to be expected if the allegation was untrue, *Bessela v Stern* (1877) 2 CPD 265.

A witness can be asked to deal with any matter that is not inadmissible or privileged. The fact **15.66** that information has a degree of confidentiality does not prevent it being revealed in court— for example documents used to determine promotion applications for employees will not be protected from disclosure for public policy reasons, *Science Research Council v Nasse* (1980) AC 1028.

Opinion evidence

15.67 Evidence of a witness's opinion is generally not admissible. It is not for the witness to form an opinion on facts but for the court. However there is a distinction between expressing an opinion which is essentially a way of summarising a number of facts and expressing an opinion which is beyond the knowledge and/or competence of the individual. As regards the former, where a person is called as a witness in any civil proceedings a statement of opinion by that person on any relevant matter on which that person is not qualified to give expert evidence is admissible as evidence of what the witness perceived if it is made as a way of conveying relevant facts personally perceived, Civil Evidence Act 1972, s 3. Therefore, for example, a witness can give a general indication of speed of a car, but should not give an opinion on whether a particular driver caused an accident.

Hearsay

Defining hearsay

15.68 The basic principles applying to hearsay evidence are simple and entirely justifiable. The area may sometimes be seen as complex because the term 'hearsay' is not plain English, because there is some quite complex Victorian case law, and because some of the detailed rules relating to the use of hearsay in criminal cases are not entirely straightforward because of the particular risk of prejudice. It may be helpful to think simply of the court having a natural and proper preference for first hand rather than second hand evidence, especially where the meaning and reliability of that second hand evidence may be difficult to judge.

15.69 As a simple example, if Anne tells Beth 'Clare told me that she had made an agreement to sell her car to Debra for £3,000' then:

- The court will want the evidence about the agreement between Clare and Debra to be given by Clare because Clare was present when that agreement was made and can give best evidence about it.
- Anne's evidence about the agreement is second hand and is hearsay. Anne cannot reliably prove that there was an agreement between Clare and Debra because she was not present when it was made. There may be all sorts of reasons why Clare made the statement to Anne which may make it difficult for the court to assess its reliability.
- However Anne's evidence may reliably show that Clare thought that there was an agreement, or that Clare wanted Anne to think there was an agreement—for example because Clare wanted Anne to think she was about to get £3,000.
- The point is not that Anne's evidence about the agreement between Clare and Debra is of no use, but rather that it may be unreliable. In a civil case it might be used, especially if Clare was not available to give evidence, because the judge could weigh up how much credibility the evidence had in the context of other evidence.

15.70 The definition of hearsay evidence is provided by the Civil Evidence Act 1995, s 1. At common law a witness could not repeat in court any assertion made by another person whether oral, written, or by conduct to prove that the assertion was true. An assertion can be made by words, gestures, notes, or implication. Confessions and previous statements are covered by the same rules. A statement is not hearsay if it is made in court, but if it is an assertion made outside court that is repeated in court. A reading from a machine is real evidence not hearsay, *Castle v Cross* (1984) 1 WLR 1372 DC.

Hearsay is indirect evidence that may or may not be reliable for all sorts of reasons. The **15.71** assertion has been made outside court, not under oath and in circumstances that are not fully known. The demeanour of the person making the assertion cannot be assessed, and that person may not be available for cross examination in court. There are many opportunities for mistake or misinterpreting what was said.

The relevance of identifying hearsay

Although hearsay evidence is now generally admissible in civil cases, the approach that it **15.72** does not matter whether evidence is hearsay or not is not justified.

- For the purposes of effective litigation it is best to use first hand evidence rather than hearsay evidence if at all possible. This will put the case at its strongest and no difficulties will arise.
- Evidence, especially key evidence on disputed points, should be analysed to identify hearsay evidence. If the evidence is not hearsay it can be used normally.
- If the evidence is potentially hearsay it may be admissible anyway if the purpose is to prove the statement was made, rather than that it is true (for example to show consistency or inconsistency, or to show what the maker of the statement knew or believed). Small points of hearsay are often accepted without challenge, especially if they do not go to facts that are contested. Hearsay evidence can also be admitted where the truth of the content is proved by other evidence, as in *Thomas v Connell* (1838) 4 M&W 267, where a person's statement that they thought they were bankrupt was allowed as evidence where the fact of bankruptcy was proved in another way.
- It may be desirable to use hearsay evidence, if for example first hand evidence is not available or is weak. In such a case appropriate formalities must be followed, as outlined.

The admissibility of hearsay evidence

Hearsay evidence has been made admissible in civil cases, Civil Evidence Act 1995, s 1, **15.73** provided proper rules are followed, s 2. It is necessary to give notice of an intention to use a hearsay statement as evidence.

If the hearsay statement will be proved by the oral evidence of a witness, then service of the **15.74** witness statement is sufficient notice, CPR r 33. This will be the case even though the witness statement is likely to stand as the evidence in chief of the witness, CPR r 33.2. This means that evidence about what the witness was told and the circumstances must be set out clearly in the witness statement for the hearsay to be admissible.

In any other circumstance, for example where the hearsay statement is in a document rather **15.75** than a witness statement, then a separate notice should be served on other parties, CPR r 33.2. If a witness cannot be called, the reason for not calling the witness must be identified when the witness statement is served, and the party seeking to rely on the hearsay evidence must also serve a notice which identifies the hearsay evidence and that it is intended to rely on it, to be served no later than the latest date for serving the witness statements. The notice can cover more than one witness. The need for notice can be waived by agreement of the parties.

15.76 If at trial a party wishes to call hearsay evidence without calling the maker of the statement, another party may call the maker of the statement for cross examination, Civil Evidence Act 1995, s 3. This is done by an application made within 14 days of getting the notice of hearsay evidence to the judge, CPR r 33.4.

15.77 If the maker of a hearsay statement is called to give evidence at trial, then the evidence given on oath at trial will take precedence over the earlier witness statement, Civil Evidence Act 1995, s 6. In such a case reference can only be made to the earlier witness statement with the leave of the court, for example to rebut a suggestion that the evidence has been fabricated, or to refresh memory with the permission of the court, *Morris v Stratford-on-Avon Rural District Council* (1973) 1 WLR 1059. The court may also permit reference to the previous statement in the case of a hostile witness, see Chapter 19. If the witness does not attend for cross examination, evidence can be called to undermine the credibility of the maker and evidence of previous inconsistent statements can be proved, Civil Evidence Act 1995, s 5, subject to the approval of the court, CPR r 33.5.

15.78 Various factors are set out as being relevant to the weight to be given to the evidence, Civil Evidence Act 1995, s 4, and these can be used in advocacy—whether the statement was contemporaneous, why the statement was made, whether it is double hearsay, any motive the maker might have for misrepresentation and whether the statement has been made in a way that could prevent testing. In assessing the reliability of hearsay evidence the court can consider all the circumstances, and some specific factors.

15.79 If there has not been proper notice the hearsay is not necessarily inadmissible, but the court will decide whether the evidence can be used, and the other side can argue about the weight to be attached to it, and there may be questions as to the payment of any costs incurred due to the failure to give notice.

15.80 There have always been limited exceptions to exclusion of hearsay evidence, because such evidence can often be very helpful if properly considered. There is for example an exception in the case of public documents. Such common law exceptions are preserved, Civil Evidence Act 1995, s 7.

15.81 Notice does not have to be given where hearsay evidence is submitted for a hearing other than a trial, CPR r 33.3.

Previous consistent and inconsistent statements

15.82 There can be problems with the admissibility of previous consistent statements (for example because a party may try to manufacture evidence) with previous inconsistent statements (for example because of the potential prejudice to a party). These concerns are primarily of concern in a criminal case because of potential detriment to the defendant. In civil cases that are almost always tried by a professional judge the risk of prejudice is relatively low, so the key question for admissibility will be relevance. The parties can then argue about the proper meaning and use of the evidence. The rules for hearsay will apply where the previous statement was hearsay.

Previous court findings

If there have been previous court proceedings in relation to a set of facts, time and money **15.83** may be saved by relying on the findings in those proceedings rather than requiring that facts be proved again. In a civil case this can be done under the Civil Evidence Act 1968, s 11.

A conviction for an offence by any court in the United Kingdom is admissible as evidence to **15.84** prove that a person committed an offence where this is relevant to an issue in any proceedings, whether or not the person convicted is a party to the proceedings. However the conviction is not conclusive evidence and further evidence may be brought to rebut it. Documents admissible at the hearing at which the conviction took place will generally be admissible to show the facts on which the conviction was based. It will be necessary to show that the person in question did not commit the offence, or that no offence was in fact committed. This is inevitably difficult to do, and there may need to be significant fresh evidence, see *Brinks Ltd v Abu Saleh (No 1)* (1995) 4 All ER 65 and *J v Oyston* (1999) 1 WLR 694. A reliance on s 11 should be clearly pleaded in the statement of case. This provision cannot be used by a convicted person to reopen a question of guilt through libel proceedings, Civil Evidence Act 1968, s 13. It seems that an acquittal cannot be used to prove that someone did not commit an offence.

A civil judgment cannot normally be used as evidence of the facts on which it was based, **15.85** Civil Evidence Act 1968, s 12.

Public policy exclusion

There are a few circumstances in which evidence that is otherwise admissible may be **15.86** inadmissible for general interests of justice—a public policy exclusion. The relevant procedure is in CPR r 31.19. There may be different public interests favouring and against disclosure, and normally a balance between these two needs to be struck, *Conway v Rimmer* (1968) AC 910. The court can raise the issue and take action itself, *Duncan v Cammell Laird & Co Ltd* (1942) AC 1090. The fact that a government department states that the evidence should not be disclosed is not conclusive, *R v Ward* (1993) 1 WLR 619, and whole classes of documents should not normally be restricted.

A claim for exemption for national security, affairs of state, and foreign policy reasons will **15.87** carry weight. The first in particular will often lead to an exclusion. For example a government request that a bank should be able to refuse to produce confidential records on dealings with banks and other businesses was upheld in *Burmah Oil Company v Bank of England* (1980) AC 1090. Information relating to a company's dealings with a foreign state did not have to be revealed in the interests of international relations where there was a border dispute, *Buttes Gas & Oil Company v Hammer (No 3)* (1981) 1 QB 223.

If evidence is excluded for public policy reasons, no party can waive this. It is the informa- **15.88** tion rather than a particular document that is excluded, so it cannot be proved by another route.

General points

Documents and witness statements may not be admissible or inadmissible as a whole. The **15.89** document as a whole may be admissible, but individual allegations may be hearsay or subject to a public policy exclusion. This is not necessarily fatal to the whole document—the inadmissible evidence may be removed or blanked out as appropriate. A similar approach may be taken where only part of a document is relevant to a case and other parts of the document are confidential.

15.90   The court will normally require to know the source of the evidence so that it's reliability can be assessed, as in the case of *British Steel Corporation v Granada Television* [1981] 1 All ER 417. However journalists have protection against having to reveal their sources under the Contempt of Court Act 1981, s 10, which says that no court may require a person to disclose the source of information contained in a publication for which he is responsible, unless it is established to the satisfaction of the court that disclosure is necessary in the interest of justice or national security, or for the prevention of disorder or crime. Equally a journalist will not be in contempt of court for refusing to make such a disclosure. The interests of justice at stake have been interpreted in cases such as *X Ltd v Morgan-Grampian (Publishers) Ltd* (1991) 1 AC 1. Matters like the importance of the evidence and the possibility of getting it from another source will be taken into account. It has been held that the section relates to crime in general rather than to a specific crime.

15.91   Although the rules for the admission of evidence are wide in civil cases, this does not mean that anything will be admissible. In *ITC Film Distributors v Video Exchange* [1982] 2 All ER 246 the defendant picked up documents left accidentally by the plaintiff after a hearing and an injunction was granted for the return of the documents to the plaintiff and to prevent their use.

F   WHO HAS TO PROVE WHAT

15.92   Once all the evidence has been given it is for the court to assess questions of weight and reliability. The court will not only weigh up all available evidence. The outcome of a number of cases will turn on which side has to prove what, and how much evidence has to be offered to prove a particular allegation.

Who has to prove an allegation

15.93   The question of who has to prove what is normally referred to as the burden of proof. If a party makes an allegation, there is a basic evidential burden to show enough evidence to put a fact in issue. A mere allegation with no supporting evidence will fail. Once a fact is in issue, the legal burden of proving an allegation to the satisfaction of the court lies with the party who makes the allegation, though there are a few statutory exceptions, for example in consumer credit cases.

15.94   This essentially means that a claimant will need to prove each allegation in a claim, and a defendant will have to prove each positive allegation in a defence. There may be difficulties in deciding who has made an allegation and has to prove it, if for example in a contract case each side argues for a different interpretation of the contract, see *The Glandarroch* (1894) P 226, and *Hurst v Evans* (1917) 1 KB 352. It is normally the party who makes or who should have made an allegation in a statement of case who will need to prove it, and the court may look behind the actual wording of a document to establish this. This has implications for the wording of a statement of case. If there is doubt the court will consider which party is in the better position to prove a point, *Joseph Constantine Steamship Line Ltd v Imperial Smelting Corp Ltd* (1942) AC 154. Reminding the court of where a burden of proof lies can be important as part of an advocacy submission.

How much evidence is required?

The question of how much evidence is required is normally referred to as the standard of **15.95** proof. The test for most civil cases is that the court will look at the evidence presented and decide on 'the balance of probabilities' whether a case is established or not. The only exceptions to this test are where the allegation made is quasi criminal, for example where the allegation is of deceit or contempt of court, or where a different standard of proof is required by statute. There are also different tests for interim hearings which are dealt with at 16.21–16.25.

It is quite easy to dismiss this test as being simple and well known, but for the effective **15.96** litigator the meaning of this test is of crucial importance. A case is won or lost on whether it has been proved on the balance of probabilities. If you take part in a race the location of the winning post is crucial.

So what does 'on the balance of probabilities' mean? Lord Denning was a great authority **15.97** and he said that it means more probable than not, *Miller v Minister of Pensions* (1947) 2 All ER 372, which would seem to be the natural meaning of the words. There are various ways in which this might be expressed. If a case is evenly balanced, or can be said to be 50:50, the claimant will not win. With the risks of not winning including having to pay the defend-ant's costs in addition to the claimant's own this threshold is very important. On the other hand, the claimant should win on showing that his or her case is more likely than not to be justified. Showing 51 per cent justification is theoretically enough for the claimant. This balance is very important in advising a party, and can be utilised by a good advocate in a submission.

Meeting the standard of proof is in fact more complex for a variety of reasons. **15.98**

- The balance is not a simple one that looks only at how much evidence each party has.
- The balance involves many aspects, including the amount of evidence, the reliability of evidence etc.
- There is more than one balance involved, as the judge will have to decide whether the standard of proof is met as regards each of the key allegations in the case.

While it must be accepted that giving judgment in a case is a complex process that cannot be **15.99** reduced to simple formulae, litigation might be made more efficient if there were research into how judges decide whether the standard of proof has been met in a case.

The matter of having to prove allegations made to the appropriate standard is key to **15.100** winning a case, see 22.34–22.40. This makes full and systematic analysis of evidence particularly important, see 15.206–15.212.

G FORMAL REQUIREMENTS FOR WRITTEN EVIDENCE

15.101   There are a significant number of formal details for the presentation of witness statements and affidavits, set out in PD 32. The main points are as follows, but there are further details in PD 32.

- There should be a full case heading, including the court, claim number, and parties.
- The top right hand corner and the backsheet of the statement must be marked with the party on whose behalf it is made, the initials and surname of the witness, the number of the statement in relation to the witness, the identifying initials and number of any exhibits, and the date it was sworn.
- The witness statement should be expressed in the first person and should as far as practicable be in the witness's own words.
- The first paragraph should give the name and address of the witness, which should be a home address unless the evidence is given in a business capacity. It should also give the capacity if, for example, the evidence is given as a company representative, and the occupation of the witness. It is also normal to state why the statement is made, for example 'in support of my application for an injunction'.
- The text must clearly distinguish which information is known personally to the witness and what is only known indirectly from other sources (and is therefore hearsay). Where a point is based on information or belief, the source and grounds for belief must be stated, for example 'I have been told by my wife and believe that . . .'.
- An affidavit needs to have words swearing truth such as 'state on oath', or 'solemnly and sincerely affirm' for an affirmation. The statement of truth is at the end of a witness statement.
- The material should be divided into numbered paragraphs. Each paragraph should deal with a separate matter and be in a logical order, normally chronological.
- Figures rather than words must be used for numbers and dates.
- A reference to a document should be given in the margin or in bold text.
- All exhibits must be specifically introduced in the text and given a reference number comprising the initials of the witness and a sequential number.
- Each exhibit must be numbered and attached to the witness statement. If an exhibit consists of more than one document, for example a set of letters, the documents should be in chronological order and the front page of the exhibit should list the documents in it.
- The statement or affidavit must only use one side of paper and 3.5 cm margins must be left.
- The statement or affidavit must be securely bound (traditionally with green ribbon, but not with anything that will make it more bulky).

15.102   The affidavit may refer to other documents or objects, and if appropriate and available they should be exhibited to the affidavit. This can include letters, formal documents, diagrams, plans, or reports that are relevant. Something that would not normally be admissible or used as evidence by the court should not normally be exhibited, such as articles from legal periodicals, *Gleeson v J Whippell & Co* [1977] 1 WLR 510. Mere background material cannot be transformed into admissible evidence by being exhibited.

Each exhibit must be specifically referred to in the body of the affidavit, and must there be **15.103** given an identification number, which consists of the initials of the maker of the affidavit, and a consecutive number relating to the number of exhibits that there are. For example, in the affidavit by S. Shylock the numbers would be 'S.S.1', 'S.S.2', and so on. In a second affidavit by the same person in one case the numbers continue rather than start again. The exhibit must be clearly marked in the same way. More than one document, such as a set of letters or e-mails, can be bundled as a single exhibit but should be paginated, with earliest on top and a list of items included. Care should be taken that copies of documents are legible. The exhibits should not be bound up with the statement or affidavit, but should be presented with it. Any exhibit other than a document should be securely marked as an exhibit.

If there is a defect in the wording of a witness statement or affidavit, then words can be **15.104** altered, erased, or added at any stage, but the person who swore the affidavit should initial the alteration and rewrite in the margin any words or figures written on the erased part. If there is a defect in an affidavit or witness statement it may require the leave of the court to use it.

Although a witness statement or affidavit is sworn evidence, it can normally only be used in **15.105** the proceedings in which it is filed and not in any other case, as in *Medway v Doublelock* [1978] 1 All ER 1261.

The role of the lawyer in drafting evidence for a case can be a complex one in terms of **15.106** professional duties and ethics. On the one hand the lawyer will want the evidence to be as strong as possible, but on the other the lawyer is only putting the evidence of the witness into an appropriate form. Rule 704 of the Code of Conduct for the Bar states that a barrister must not devise facts which will assist in advancing the lay client's case, and must not draft any witness statement or affidavit containing any statement of fact other than the evidence which in substance according to his instructions the barrister reasonably believes the witness would give if the evidence contained in the affidavit or witness statement were being given in oral evidence. It is provided that a barrister can prepare a draft including factual statements that are subject to confirmation by the witness. Rule 302 provides that it is Counsel's overriding duty to assist the court in the administration of justice and not deceive or knowingly or recklessly mislead the court.

There is professional guidance on this, for example in 'Guidance on Preparation of Witness **15.107** Statements—Preparing Witness Statements for Use in Civil Proceedings—Dealing with Witnesses—Guidance for Members of the Bar', which is published by the Bar Council. Key points from this document include:

- It is important to remember that the statement will stand as the evidence in chief of the witness and should be prepared as such.
- The witness will have to swear or affirm that contents of the statement are the truth the whole truth and nothing but the truth. The statement should be so drafted that this is possible.
- It is important for the lawyer to make clear to the client that the statement is that of the client, and that the client should check that it is true before signing it.
- It is not the barrister's duty to ensure that the evidence is truthful—this is the duty of the client—but the lawyer may bring to the witness's attention points where the statement may be challenged, for example because other evidence appears to contradict it.

15.108   If after a witness statement has been served a witness seeks to change their evidence careful consideration may be required. The other side should not be misled, so the statement may need to be corrected. This is done by issuing and serving a further statement. If a client substantially changes what he or she says but refuses to sign a further statement the lawyer may need to withdraw from the case as the lawyer cannot mislead the court.

H   DRAFTING A WITNESS STATEMENT

General guidelines

15.109   The initial general outline of facts provided by a witness is unlikely to be appropriate for use in court. It will almost certainly contain irrelevancies, the witness may have forgotten some relevant details, part of what is said by the witness may not be admissible and so on. The key factors are that factual information that is relevant and which is admissible is presented in a clear and logical way.

15.110   For the purposes of effective litigation, the evidence of each witness must be tailored to a form that is appropriate for use in court. This is normally done by turning the material that has been produced into a formal witness statement. Witness statements are normally drafted by lawyers and then read and signed by witnesses to ensure that the evidence is in a useful form, and that rules for witness statements are met. Clearly there are potential advantages for the lawyer in being able to influence how evidence is presented through drafting witness statements, though the statement must still be the authentic statement of the witness and principles of professional conduct must be followed. The Bar Council provides Guidance on the Preparation of Witness Statements.

15.111   Now that it is the norm for evidence to be produced in written form, and that evidence in proceedings other than trial should generally be given in the form of witness statements (CPR r 32.6) skills in drafting witness statements are a key to effective litigation. There are many general principles that apply for producing a good and effective witness statement. The witness statement needs to:

- reflect the purpose for which the witness statement is being prepared;
- cover all the elements required for the purpose for which the witness statement will be used—a witness statement to support an interim application may need to cover very specific areas;
- have a clear structure that is easy to follow;
- comply with the rules of evidence;
- contain only those matters in respect of which the witness can properly sign a statement of truth;
- coherently support the case in general and/or any specific application being made, fitting as well as possible with the statements of case and with other evidence;
- be broadly useful in supporting advocacy in the case, though it will not be appropriate for the statement to contain points of law that the witness would not have personal knowledge of;
- comply with formal presentation requirements that are set out below.

A barrister can meet a witness to investigate or collect evidence, but the barrister should **15.112** consider whether and to what extent contact is appropriate. It may be relevant for a barrister to see a witness whose evidence is key to a case, especially if it is necessary to understand the detail of the evidence or to assess the credibility of the witness. It is normally preferable for the barrister to get a written proof of evidence first and for a solicitor to be present. It is appropriate for a barrister to settle a witness statement and to talk to the witness, but not normally for the barrister to take the full statement from a witness and then act as advocate in the case. Witnesses should normally be seen separately, *Smith New Court Securities Ltd v Scrimgeour Vickers (Asset Management) Ltd* (1994) 1 WLR 1271. The barrister must not place a witness under any pressure to provide anything other than a truthful account, or rehearse or coach a witness, Code of Conduct para 607. The barrister can explain court procedure and seek to put the witness at ease.

Preparing to draft a witness statement

It is not necessary to draft a witness statement with regard to every individual who has any **15.113** knowledge about a case. The lawyer will need to make careful choices as to which witnesses can provide the fullest and most convincing evidence in support of the case, keeping costs in mind. In a straightforward case, witness statements would normally be prepared for the claimant, and for any other witnesses who could support a key element in the case that the client cannot support from personal knowledge. Where a claimant or applicant is not an individual, a suitable person with suitable knowledge of the case should be used, such as one of the senior officers of a claimant company.

The purpose of the witness statement needs to be clear in the mind of the lawyer drafting it. **15.114** A witness statement to be signed by a client to support his or her case may need to be long and complex, whereas a witness statement dealing with a small issue should be focussed on that point and brief. It must be remembered that the statement will stand as the evidence in chief, and that the witness will have to swear or affirm that the evidence is the truth, the whole truth, and nothing but the truth. This must be made clear to the witness.

An effective witness statement will be based on sound preparation. The lawyer drafting the **15.115** witness statement should have to hand all the information that the witness can provide so that a careful selection of content for the witness statement can be made. Any gaps or ambiguities in that information should be clarified with the witness—the lawyer should not make assumptions. It may be necessary for the lawyer to meet a key witness to clarify evidence before drafting a witness statement. All the elements of the legal action on which the witness can usefully comment should be identified, especially where the witness can assist with areas in dispute.

Once all the relevant information that the witness can provide is available, it should be sifted **15.116** and arranged before beginning the draft to ensure that the finished result will be clear and well structured. The initial information provided by a witness will inevitably contain material that is not relevant to the case at all, or that is not relevant to the matters that the witness statement needs to cover, and such material should be weeded out.

In drafting a witness statement the role of the lawyer is to understand the evidence the **15.117** witness can give and to assist the witness in giving it in a coherent and comprehensive way.

It is not the function of the lawyer to try to interpret the evidence, to take decisions about the truth of the evidence, or to prune evidence so that what is left does not give a fair picture.

The evidential content of a witness statement

15.118   A witness statement is a written document that contains the evidence which a witness could properly give orally at trial, CPR r 32.4. A witness statement can only contain those matters on which the witness signing the statement could give oral evidence in court, and decisions about content should therefore be taken with the same care as preparing for an examination in chief. A witness statement should not normally contain any or any significant hearsay evidence unless there is no better way to get this evidence before the court. If it is thought necessary to include material that is not within the personal knowledge of the witness then the source of the material should be given, together with any particular reasons why the witness believes it to be true, for example 'I have been informed by John Jones and I believe that . . .'.

15.119   Because a witness statement is a form of evidence it should not contain any matter which is scandalous, irrelevant, or otherwise oppressive, and the court may order that any material which is not properly included should be removed, see *Savings and Investment Bank Ltd v Gasco Investments* [1984] 1 WLR 271. The witness statement should not contain allegations which are needlessly offensive or unfounded, or any matter which is not really relevant to the purpose of the witness statement.

Style and language

15.120   A witness statement must be written in the first person, and must be drafted as if written by the witness who will sign the statement of truth.

15.121   The witness statement should be drafted in accurate, clear, plain English. It should be as concise as is reasonably possible in the light of the information the witness provides. It should as far as possible use the actual words of the witness, and be written in the ordinary English that the witness would use. If appropriate the precise words used by a witness should be used in the statement. It will often not be appropriate for a witness statement to contain legal terminology. A witness statement provided by an expert may need to include technical language, but this should be presented in as transparent a way as possible. Numbers and dates should be in figures.

15.122   Having stated these principles, the witness statement does not have to be a purely objective summary of facts. The witness statement will be signed as true by the witness, and should adequately express the views of that witness where relevant to the case. If a client has strong views on a particular issue that can appropriately be expressed there is no reason why these should not be in the witness statement. If the views are so strong that they are inappropriate this may need to be discussed with the client.

The elements of the witness statement

Introduction

15.123   The first paragraph should state whether the witness is a party or has some relationship to a party (such as being a spouse or an employee), and the witness's occupation and place of residence. If the witness is giving evidence in a professional, business, or other occupational capacity, the statement should state the address at which he or she works, the position held, and the name of his firm or employer, if any. It may also be relevant to state the purpose of the witness statement if, for example, it is to support a particular application. For example:

I am Julius Caesar, the claimant in this action, a self-employed writer, of 3, The Landing, Dover.

Content

The contents of a witness statement require as much care as planning an examination **15.124** in chief. All relevant, admissible, and supportive information of which the particular witness is aware should be included. Anything which is not relevant should be left out. Anything which does not support the case can be left out, save for in the case of a witness statement that is prepared to support some types of interim application, for which see below. Information that is not relevant to the issues in the case should be left out.

The content of a witness statement will be basically factual. The facts known to the witness **15.125** that are relevant to the allegations in the case should be set out, quoting exact words if appropriate. The opinions of a witness are not appropriate where the opinion is a conclusion that should be drawn by an expert or a judge. It will not normally be appropriate to include argument in a witness statement where this is more appropriately a matter for advocacy at trial.

The witness statement should not normally contain legal argument but should lay a clear, **15.126** factual basis for all the arguments that the lawyer will wish to make. If it is relevant for a witness to refer to their legal position this can be done with an expression such as 'I have been informed by my solicitor and believe that . . .'.

It may sometimes be appropriate to include something that is not strictly a relevant factual **15.127** statement tied to an issue. For example it may be relevant to include statements by a client about his or her reaction to events to show how serious the case is for the client.

It is not for the lawyer to vet the witness's evidence, but there is a professional duty not to **15.128** put in anything the lawyer does not believe to be true, or not justified by the evidence available. All the content should be admissible, and nothing irrelevant should be included.

Structure

Clarity and structure are important because witness statements are normally read by the **15.129** judge and by the other side before a trial. It is therefore important that they are clear and easy to read to convey the key points of the evidence. It is also important to be able to find relevant evidence in a witness statement quickly during a hearing.

It is common for the overall structure of a witness statement to be chronological. The state- **15.130** ment should be divided into numbered paragraphs, and each paragraph should deal with a different topic. Other logical structures are acceptable, for example dealing with the case issue by issue rather than chronologically. Witness statements have tended to get longer as all material to be given as evidence in chief is included. It can be expensive to prepare full witness statements at an early stage if the case settles, but they will need to be prepared for exchange of witness statements.

The statement of truth

15.131 There must be a signed statement that the witness believes the contents of the statement to be true. The witness must be given a proper opportunity to read the draft statement before signing, and the statement may need to be amended in the light of any comments made by the witness. The witness should be made aware that any failure to tell the truth can be punished as contempt of court. The statement should be signed by the witness unless there is a good reason. If a solicitor signs it should be with the client's authority. Deliberately signing a false statement of truth is contempt of court, *Malgar Ltd v RE Leach (Engineering) Ltd* The Times, 17 February 2000, and/or can lead to a penalty in costs, *Molloy v Shell UK Ltd* (2001) All ER (D) 79.

Exhibits

15.132 It is quite a simple process to exhibit a document to a witness statement, and consideration should always be given to what documents might usefully be exhibited. A number of documents will already be in the court file, such as statements of case, or may be submitted as real evidence. Any document which is referred to in a witness statement but which is not otherwise before the court should normally be exhibited to a witness statement. Exhibiting a document that a witness can swear to the truth of can be a useful way of getting letters or a sketch plan in evidence.

Professional principles

15.133 A careful drafting of witness statements can be of significant assistance in putting a case before a court effectively. However a lawyer must take an appropriate professional approach. The facts in a witness statement must come from the witness, and from the information and instructions that the lawyer has been given. The lawyer must not invent information when drafting a witness statement, even if the invention seems to be a reasonable conjecture to fill up a gap in the information available. The witness must be able to personally swear to the truth of everything in the witness statement. If a detail of information is not available the lawyer must check it with the client, leaving a gap in the draft until the information is available. A barrister must not devise facts for a witness statement, and should put in what is in the instructions and what the barrister reasonably believes the witness would say in evidence in court, Code of Conduct Rule 606.

15.134 If a witness wishes to provide additional information, or changes what he or she says after a witness statement has been served (for example in response to the witness statements served by the other side) then a further witness statement should be served, or the other side alerted if the trial is imminent.

Pro forma for a witness statement

15.135

> Made on behalf of the (party)
> Witness: (name)
> 1st statement of witness
> Exhibits: AB1–AB2
> Made: (Date)

IN THE HIGH COURT OF JUSTICE   Claim No 2005 HC 1234
QUEEN'S BENCH DIVISION

BETWEEN

A.B.   Claimant

and

C.D.   Defendant

WITNESS STATEMENT OF (name)

1.
2.
3. There is now shown to me marked AB1 a copy of the contract dated 20 June 2004.
4.
5. There is now shown to me marked AB2 a bundle of correspondence between AB and CD relating to the implementation of the contract
6.
7.

Statement of truth

I believe that the facts stated in this witness statement are true.

Signed: AB

Dated:

I DRAFTING AN AFFIDAVIT

An affidavit is a particular type of formal witness statement that has been in use for some **15.136** time, and that is still required in support of particular types of application. The requirements for an affidavit are very similar to those for a witness statement, save that the affidavit must be formally sworn (which incurs a fee) rather than have the more simple signed statement of truth. The cost of administering the oath makes the affidavit more expensive but there is no other essential difference.

Affidavits tend to be required where the court is particularly concerned to act on accurate **15.137** information, especially where one party is making an application against another party who is not present at the hearing, such as applications for search orders, freezing injunctions, judgment in default where there has been service out of jurisdiction without the need for permission, or a claim of contempt of court.

Affidavits will commonly be drafted by a lawyer following the same principles as for a **15.138** witness statement, save that the introductory paragraph may be more formal, and there must be a jurat in which the witness swears to the truth of the information given. The jurat will consist of the names and signatures of the witness and of the person before whom it is sworn, together with the date and place where the affidavit was sworn. For the affidavit to be valid it must be signed in the presence of an authorised person, a Commissioner for Oaths, or a proper officer of the court. The affidavit should not be sworn before the solicitor of the party on whose behalf the affidavit is to be used, or his or her agent, partner, or clerk.

15.139 An affidavit must be used instead of a witness statement in the following circumstances (PD r 32 para 1). An affidavit can also be used in other circumstances but the costs are not recoverable.

- Where a statute, statutory instrument, rule, order, or practice direction so provides.
- In support of an application for a search order.
- In support of an application for a freezing order.
- In an application for an order alleging someone is in contempt of court.

J   EXPERT EVIDENCE

15.140 An expert must provide genuine help in clarifying issues and taking matters forward, and not simply tell the court what it already knows, in language that is difficult to understand, and at significant expense. Reconstruction experts for an accident are now not commonly allowed.

15.141 Expert evidence can be pivotal to a case, but it is important to identify when expert evidence is really needed, to select an appropriate expert, to get an expert report that is drawn up properly, and to check details. The potential problems of expert evidence have been illustrated by the discrediting of Sir Roy Meadow as a medical expert in cases of injuries to children.

15.142 See generally CPR Part 35 Experts and assessors, and PD 35 Experts and assessors. The Code of Guidance on Expert Evidence from the Expert Witness Institute is also useful, see www.ewi.org.uk. The Academy of Experts produces a similar guide, see www.academy-experts.org.

The need for an expert

15.143 A legal case can arise in any context—a breach of contract case may involve the use of concrete in a building, or a negligence case may involve an accident in a glass factory. The lawyers and the court may have little or no knowledge of the locations and systems involved, and any personal knowledge that they do have will be of limited use as a lawyer cannot give evidence in advocating a case and there are very limited circumstances in which a judge can properly take personal knowledge into account.

15.144 The client may well have better knowledge of the context, but may not have a high level of knowledge or be able to explain the situation very clearly. The court may also be reluctant to rely on the evidence of a party because it may lack objectivity, and because it may be difficult to tell how much expertise the client has. For this reason a witness can normally only give evidence of facts within his or her personal knowledge, and not on matters of opinion. If a point is a matter for an expert opinion the view of a non-expert cannot safely be accepted, though there are grey areas between matters of normal experience and matters requiring expert evidence.

It is therefore inevitable that expert evidence will often be required so that: **15.145**

- the lawyer has expert assistance in understanding the circumstances of the case;
- the lawyer has expert assistance in identifying the issues in the case;
- the lawyer has expert assistance in identifying weaknesses in the case for the other side;
- the court has objective expert assistance in assessing the merits of the case.

Examples of where appropriate expert evidence might be needed include: **15.146**

- medical evidence on the severity of and prognosis for personal injuries;
- guidance on the most likely cause of an accident;
- evidence on how a particular machine normally functions or how a mechanical process is normally carried out;
- guidance on complex accounting or financial procedures;
- assistance on the likelihood that a document has been altered or forged, or on the handwriting on a particular document, for example *Lockheed-Arabia Corp v Owen* (1993) QB 806;
- guidance on foreign law, where that is relevant to a case, for example Nigerian banking law, *Ajami v Comptroller of Customs* (1954) 1 WLR 1405.

Formal requirements for expert evidence to be required for a case and accepted by a judge are **15.147** as follows.

- The subject matter must call for expertise—it must be a matter of science or art outside the experience and knowledge of the tribunal of fact. For example an accident reconstruction expert can help with how an accident may have happened from detailed study of the site of the accident. If the expert only has witness reports available to the court it is less likely that expert evidence will be admissible, *Liddell v Middleton* (1996) PIQR P326 CA.
- That evidence must be helpful to the court in reaching a conclusion, *Midland Bank Trust Ltd v Hett, Stubbs and Kemp* (1979) 1 Ch 379. A judge should prefer the evidence of an expert to that of a non-expert, *Re B (a minor)* (2000) 1 WLR 790, unless there is good reason, see *Fuller v Strum* (2002) 1 WLR 1097. If there is a dispute between experts the judge should resolve the dispute.
- There must be a body of expertise in the area in question.
- The expert witness must be a suitably qualified person in that particular field of knowledge. It is not absolutely essential that the witness be professionally qualified, but they should normally be professionally qualified, and a leading figure amongst those practising in the area. It is for the judge to decide whether an individual is appropriately qualified to provide expert evidence on a particular area. How prominent an expert is used may be partly a matter of keeping the costs of the case reasonable. An expert can only give evidence within their personal expertise.

Having said this, a lawyer may have to make some headway with a case before expert evi- **15.148** dence is available. A lawyer in specialist practice will build up knowledge, and there may be reading material that can provide some general background. A medical dictionary is a useful investment for a personal injury lawyer. Many lawyers will also need to build a working knowledge of areas such as accounts, so as to be able to make sense of accounts in a case and be able to hold a reasonably intelligent conversation with an accountant about any queries.

Selecting and briefing an expert

15.149　There are some bodies that can help, including professional associations, and general bodies such as the Expert Witness Institute, www.ewi.org.uk, and the Academy of Experts, www.academy-experts.org. It has been said that experts now provide a litigation support industry. It is acceptable and indeed now quite common for expert witnesses to have training in writing reports and giving evidence.

15.150　Some professions provide support to members who work as professional experts, for example the Institute of Chartered Accountants offers a programme of accreditation for those who wish to be recognised as experts. It is, for example, necessary that experts know what sort of structure and content an expert report should have, and that the main duty of the expert is to the court rather than to a client. In a high value or important case an expert will be very carefully chosen—they will have to face cross examination by a leading barrister.

15.151　There may be problems with medical experts. There are not clear professional standards or professional overview, and as expert work is competitive there is limited consensus or peer review. There may be a choice as to whom to choose—a GP, an emergency consultant, or a specialist in a particular type of injury, each working within very distinct professional groups, and they provide reports in a private rather than a public market. The British Medical Association provides templates for reports but does not have overall control. The Registration Council of Medical Experts tries to provide standards, but only within its own membership.

15.152　If expert evidence is likely to be required on an issue in a case, it is normally for the parties to select experts and then to persuade the court that a particular expert is appropriate. In the past it was common practice for each party to select their own expert, but this increased costs, not least as each party would select an expert favouring their version of events which could make it difficult for decisions to be reached. Modern practice is, wherever possible, to agree on the use of a single expert who will provide an objective report for the use of both sides. In any event, an expert's duty to the court overrides any obligation to a party giving instructions or paying, CPR r 35.3.

15.153　Once the need for expert evidence has been identified, appropriate individuals to act as experts will need to be found. This may be done by approaching an appropriate professional body. Various guides to experts are available. Solicitors who regularly practice in a particular area of law will build up knowledge of appropriate individuals. A number of people in relevant professions regularly act as expert witnesses, and may be trained in acting as such. The court will need to be persuaded that the individual has appropriate expertise before accepting the evidence. If there is a professional relationship between the party and the expert that may prevent the expert from being called as an independent expert, *Liverpool Roman Catholic Archdiocese Trustees Inc v Goldberg (No 2)* (2201) 1 WLR 2337, but the line is not very clear, *Admiral Management Services Ltd v Para-Protect Europe Ltd* (2003) 2 All ER 1017.

15.154　A list of the qualifications and expertise of a proposed expert will need to be obtained, and a check should be made that the expertise of the individual does include the circumstances in dispute. The logistics of actually selecting an expert may not be easy in the early stages of potential litigation. Ideally a single expert should be selected by both parties, but if a potential claimant needs expert evidence to evaluate a case and does not wish to involve the potential defendant at this stage, this may not be entirely realistic. In general terms, if the case is a large one where the cost of the expert report will not be a matter of great concern, and especially if the report of the expert is central to evaluating the strength of the case, the litigant can simply proceed with selecting and briefing an expert. In a lower value case, or where the matter requiring expertise is less central to the case, a single expert should be used. This can be achieved by one party sending a list of potential experts to the other and the latter accepting a name from that list. Alternatively the parties may agree a list of potential experts and ask the court to make a selection, or the court may give directions as to how the expert be selected.

A distinction must be made between the selection of an expert and the instruction of an **15.155** expert. Selection involves choosing the individual to use. Instruction involves sending the individual the relevant information about the case and setting the questions that the expert is asked to help to answer. A jointly selected expert will not necessarily be jointly instructed, though joint selection will often be followed by joint instruction, especially in a fast track case. When using a single expert in a case, clear decisions must be made about selection, instruction, and payment.

A single expert will rarely be agreed in a serious personal injury case or a high value com- **15.156** mercial case. There are difficulties in using a joint expert in that the lawyers may well need to talk to the expert privately to understand the case, and this would be severely restricted with a joint expert. If there is only one expert, that person may have too great a role in deciding the outcome of the case. If there is a single expert then both sides may in fact also privately seek advice from a separate expert so as to understand the case and know what questions to ask—there may therefore in practice be three experts.

The process of instructing and briefing the expert is important. The party or parties provide **15.157** relevant background information, provide information on the possible nature of the case, and set out the issues on which expert advice is requested. The quality of the report the expert provides may depend on this being done well. The facts should be presented to the expert objectively, and there should be no pressure for the expert to reach a particular conclusion. A careful selection of material to be provided to the expert must be made.

It may be necessary to make arrangements for the expert to visit a site or inspect or test **15.158** something. Orders to allow the expert access for inspection are normally made at the allocation stage. It is not possible to force a person to undergo a medical examination, but proceedings may be stayed if the claimant refuses and in all the circumstances the case cannot therefore be fairly conducted, *Edmeades v Thames Board Mills Ltd* (1969) 2 QB 67 CA and *Starr v National Coal Board* (1977) 1 WLR 63 CA, or the case may be struck out if the lack of an examination makes it impossible for the case to be properly decided. If a medical examination may be unpleasant or intrusive the court will balance the reasonableness of the request with the reasonableness of the refusal, *Prescott v Bulldog Tools Ltd* (1981) 3 All ER 869. It is reasonable to ask for a doctor of the same sex as the claimant, but otherwise there can only be objection to a particular doctor for good reason, such as a significant concern about the doctor's competency or ability to produce a full report. There may be conditions relating to a medical examination, for example that the defendant pay the claimant's travel costs and any loss of earnings, that the doctor will not discuss the case save as is relevant to the medical examination, and that the claimant have a friend or legal representative present during the examination. The claimant will only be able to insist on having their own doctor present if there is a strong reason for this, unless it has been agreed that there be a joint medical examination by doctors for both sides, *Hall v Avon Area Health Authority (Teaching)* (1980) 1 WLR 481 CA.

15.159   Sometimes a general question can be asked of an expert, such as how an accident was caused or whether a machine was defective or not, but often points of detail will arise, for example in that the lawyer may well wish to base particulars of negligence on what the expert says. The allegations and evidence in a case should be coherently related to the expert evidence if possible.

The format for an expert report

15.160   The format for expert reports is fairly closely regulated by CPR r 35.10 and PD 35. The main provisions are as follows, and if they are not followed the report may not be admissible, *Stevens v Gullis* (2000) 1 All ER 527 CA.

- Details of the expert's qualifications must be given (and any limits in expertise as regards the ambit of the report).
- Details of any literature or materials the expert has relied on must be given.
- A statement must summarise the facts and instructions given to the expert as regards the report.
- It must be clear which facts stated in the report are within the expert's own knowledge, and where the expert is relying on something said by someone else.
- It must be clear who carried out any test or experiment used in the report—if the test or experiment was not done by the expert the qualifications of the person who did it must be given, and whether the expert supervised it.
- If there is a range of opinion on an issue, the report should summarise the range and give the expert's own view.
- The report must contain a summary of the conclusions, with any qualifications to those conclusions.
- The report must include a statement that the expert understands his or her duty to the court and has complied with it, and a signed statement of truth.

15.161   In drawing up a report the expert must consider all material facts, including those that might not support the view of the party or of the expert, PD 35 para 1. If some facts are not available, the expert will need to make it clear that the report is provisional. The expert should seek to provide an objective report that does not advocate the case of one party. The expert should not go too far in drawing conclusions and should not seek to usurp the function of the judge.

15.162   An expert can also rely on the expertise of colleagues and on published and unpublished material in reaching conclusions. Such documents can be referred to in giving evidence, and can be admitted as part of the evidence, though articles cannot be put in as evidence if they are not part of an expert report. An expert witness can give opinion evidence, though ultimate decisions of fact will still be for the court rather than the expert, Evidence Act 1972, s 3. The expert may prepare and present diagrams, models, or photographs to assist in presenting the expert opinion clearly.

An expert report should include consideration of factors that detract from as well as support **15.163** the expert's view. The expert should not mislead by omission. It is not the role of an expert to be an advocate for the client. The report should not cover matters not in the statement of case. This may need to be reviewed if the nature of the case changes.

An expert should make it clear if a question falls outside his or her expertise, or where an **15.164** opinion is provisional because not all facts are available. If an expert changes his or her mind after the exchange of reports, that change of view should be communicated to the parties.

An expert report prepared for one party will normally be subject to professional privilege and **15.165** will not be automatically disclosable to the other side, *Megarity v DJ Ryan and Sons Ltd* (1980) 1 WLR 1237 CA. The party might wish to ask the expert to cover further issues or to clarify certain points, or could decide not to use the report at all and to consult a different expert. The report will need to be disclosed before trial if the party wishes to rely on it, or it will only be possible to use the evidence of the expert at trial with the leave of the judge, CPR r 35.13. The court will not order that a report be disclosed if it is not to be used at trial.

Reviewing the report

The expert report should be written by the expert. The lawyer does not have the same role as **15.166** in drafting a witness statement, see *Whitehouse v Jordan* (1981) 1 WLR 246.The lawyer can comment on the areas and issues to be covered, but must tread a careful line. The report should focus on the issues in the case.

Once the expert has produced a report it should be sent to the party or parties who have **15.167** requested the report, but not at that stage to the court. A lawyer may wish to see an expert in conference to clarify some matters in the expert report.

If anything is left out of the report or is not clear it should be clarified if possible to avoid **15.168** difficulty in court. Where one party has selected and instructed an expert there is the possibility of rigorous cross examination at trial, so it may be useful to ask the expert if there are any alternative conclusions possible or any questions or doubts in his or her mind to see what might come up at trial and to prepare to deal with it as far as possible. The expert's duty in court will be to give objective evidence rather than to defend the case of the party.

A party is not forced to use an expert report. If there are good grounds for one party **15.169** challenging the report of a joint expert the court may allow each side to instruct their own experts, *Daniels v Walker* (2000) 1 WLR 1382. If the expert is instructed by one party and the report is very unfavourable the case may be dropped, the party may see if the expert is prepared to modify his or her conclusions, or a report may be sought from a different expert.

Formal rules for expert evidence

Expert evidence cannot be used without the permission of the court, CPR r 35.4. Directions **15.170** on the use of expert evidence will usually be made at track allocation, save that expert evidence is not normally allowed in small claims cases.

The court will try to restrict the use of expert evidence to that which is reasonably required to **15.171** resolve the proceedings, CPR r 35.1. The purpose of expert evidence is to provide objective information for the court and the tendency is towards the appointment of a single expert, CPR r 35.7, and this is the norm in fast track cases. There may be separate experts for each side in a multi-track case, and indeed if the court wishes to direct that a single expert be instructed in such a case, a case management conference should be called unless the parties agree, PD 29.

15.172   The court can at any stage direct a discussion between experts to try to identify and if possible agree issues. Normally such an order will require the experts to set out in writing the issues they agree on and the issues they disagree on, with reasons.

15.173   If the expert is jointly instructed then a lawyer should only see the expert to clarify some matters in the expert report with the agreement of the other, *Peet v Mid-Kent Healthcare Trust* (2002) 1 WLR 210. Further questions may arise—questions for a jointly instructed expert should normally be put in writing and the answers will be considered part of the expert's report, CPR r 35.6. Such questions should normally be put at one time, and as soon as possible after the receipt of the report. The possibility of posing written questions could be used more to assist understanding and define issues.

15.174   In a fast track case questions should be put within 28 days of the receipt of the report, and should normally only seek clarification, unless the other side agrees or the court gives approval, see *Mutch v Allen* (2001) CPLR 200 CA. If in such a case the expert does not answer the court may order that the party who instructed the expert cannot rely on the report, and/or that the costs of the report will not be allowed.

15.175   If each party has their own expert the court will normally direct mutual disclosure of expert reports. It is important to decide which expert will be used before disclosure. If a party does not disclose an expert's report, that party cannot use the report or call the expert at trial without the permission of the court, CPR r 35.13. If an expert report is disclosed then privilege is lost, CPR r 35.11. If the party who obtained the expert report chooses not to use it after disclosure then the other side may choose to call the witness as there is no property in a witness. Alternatively the other party could commission a separate report from the expert, *Harmony Shipping Co SA v Saudi Europe Line Ltd* (1979) 1 WLR 1380 CA.

15.176   The use of expert evidence may be reviewed at a case management conference. The use of reports can be considered, the remaining issues to which expert reports are relevant, and whether any experts should be called to give oral evidence at trial.

15.177   Normally the written report will stand as evidence at the trial, especially if the expert has been jointly instructed. If the report is fully prepared then no purpose is to be served by further questioning or cross examination, though the court can permit further questioning if matters relating to the expert report remain in issue. If the report is not well written there may be a tendency to rely on the conclusions rather than the detail.

15.178   The issues covered by the report will remain matters of fact for the court to decide. The court should accept undisputed expert evidence, *Fairchild v Glenhaven Funeral Services Ltd* (2002) 3 All ER 305 HL. If the experts disagree the judge should give reasons for preferring one expert to another, *English v Emery Reimbold and Strick Ltd* (2002) 3 All ER 385. The fact that recent cases where paediatricians appear to have given misleading expert evidence on the likely cause of death in some babies have shown that experts are not infallible could leave the judge in a difficult position.

K   DISCLOSURE OF EVIDENCE

The principle of disclosure

The adversarial system means that each side will collect their own evidence to support their **15.179** case. Despite judicial case management, a judge has no independent power to obtain evidence. However there is significant emphasis on the disclosure of information, from pre-action protocols right up to trial. See generally CPR Part 31 Disclosure and inspection of documents, and PD 31 Disclosure and inspection. For tactics relating to gathering and using information see 16.144–16.169.

In tactical terms, a party might be keen to make early disclose of some evidence because it **15.180** strongly supports their case, but might prefer to save other evidence for trial so as to take other parties by surprise. This could make it difficult or impossible for the other side to prepare, and might lead to the need for a trial to be adjourned. To meet the needs of the overriding objective, evidence which is relevant to the issues in a case must be disclosed to the other side sufficiently in advance of the trial to enable proper preparation to take place.

From the procedural rules, disclosure of evidence might appear to be a mechanical process, **15.181** and indeed it can be in a case where both sides already have the original or a copy of most of the relevant documents, or where significant information has been exchanged under a pre-action protocol. But in some cases reading documents not previously seen can provide new insights into the case. Failure to carry out the disclosure process properly can result in penalties. The duty to disclose relevant documents continues right up to trial, and the court may not allow evidence to be used if it has not been disclosed.

Clients may not be supportive of the disclosure process. They may feel that documents are **15.182** confidential, or realise that disclosing a document may weaken their case. Despite their duty to clients, lawyers have a professional duty to support the disclosure process. Solicitors have an active duty to warn clients at an early stage of the scope of the disclosure process, and should ensure as far as possible that relevant documents are retained and made available for disclosure. A lawyer may have to cease to represent a client who refuses to comply with disclosure. The nature of disclosure as a staged process may need to be explained, see 8.46–8.48 and 15.55.

The line between the duty of disclosure and inspection and the protection of client privilege **15.183** is not always easy to draw. The existence of all relevant documents must be disclosed, but privilege from allowing inspection can be claimed wherever relevant, see 3.61–3.76. The line has perhaps become more difficult to draw rather than clearer with the modem approach of putting cards on the table rather than keeping information secret for tactical reasons, and with cases where the court has reviewed what documents are covered by legal privilege.

Disclosure of documents

Disclosure applies to all documents relevant to the issues in the case which are or have been in **15.184** the control of a party. It covers not only documents that support the case of the party, but also documents that adversely affect their case, or support another party's case, CPR r 31.6. The only exception is small track cases where only documents to be relied on need to be disclosed.

15.185   The term 'document' includes anything on which information or evidence is recorded, CPR r 31.4, thus including computer records, tapes, and videos. All the retrievable information on a computer hard disk or a whole system is thus disclosable. Documents outside the jurisdiction are disclosable if they are in the party's control.

15.186   In a number of cases significant disclosure of information occurs under a pre-action protocol The court should be told of this in the allocation questionnaire. Directions for disclosure will normally be given at the allocation stage or at a case management conference. The court will set a time period for disclosure, and it will often take place within a couple of months of the filing of the defence, save for a more complex multi-track case. Disclosure will normally be made by both parties at the same time.

15.187   The first stage of the disclosure process involves exchanging lists of documents. The documents must be listed as concisely as possible and in a suitable order. Documents that are claimed to be subject to legal privilege should be on the list but the claim for privilege should be indicated. It should also be indicated if relevant documents are no longer available, and if so what has happened to them. The list should include a disclosure statement unless this is dispensed with by the court or by agreement. A disclosure statement should set out the extent of the search that has been made for relevant documents, and certify that the party understands the nature of the duty to disclose, and that to the best of the disclosing party's knowledge that has been carried out. If it is asserted that it is not reasonable to search for a class of document that should be set out. Making a false disclosure statement can be punished as contempt of court, CPR r 31.23.

15.188   Standard disclosure applies unless the court directs otherwise, CPR r 31.5. The court can dispense with or limit standard disclosure. A party must make a reasonable search for disclosable documents, but what is reasonable will take into account the significance of the document and the expense of finding it, CPR r 31.7.

15.189   The sort of documents that might be disclosable include:

- Communications (letters, e-mails etc)
- Records
- Maintenance records
- Reports
- Plans
- Notes
- Accounts and accountants' reports.

15.190   It appears that it may be possible to effect disclosure by mention of a document in a witness statement or report without actually including it in a list, *Smith Kline Beecham plc v Generics* (2004) 1 WLR 1479.

15.191   A party served with a list of documents is deemed to admit the authenticity of them unless he serves notice that he wishes the document to be proved at trial, CPR r 32.19. Such a notice on Form N268 must be served by the latest date for serving witness statements or within seven days of the disclosure of the document, whichever is the later. A document would be thus challenged if it was thought to be a forgery or to have been altered in some way.

Inspection of documents

The second stage is for the party in receipt of the list to inspect and take copies of documents. **15.192** Having served a list of documents, a party must allow other parties to inspect the documents referred to in the list (save those claimed to be privileged). A party wishing to inspect must send a written notice to that effect, and the other side must give permission within seven days, CPR r 31.15. Alternatively the party can ask for copies of documents to be supplied on paying reasonable copying costs. The court may direct that inspection be done by electronic means. Normally documents should be made available fully, but it may be possible to blank out irrelevant passages, *GE Capital Corporate Finance Group Ltd v Bankers Trust Co* (1995) 1 WLR 172 CA.

It is important to ensure that everything is inspected and copies taken as necessary. Consider **15.193** whether everything that was expected to be made available on discovery has been, and seek special orders if not. Problems with disclosure can be dealt with in a variety of ways. If a party fails to comply with a disclosure direction, the party seeking disclosure should write to the party in default warning that an order will be sought if the direction is not complied with. Then an application can be made for an order compelling compliance. The court may make an 'unless' order specifying a date for compliance—in an extreme case the claim or defence may be struck out for lack of compliance with an order for disclosure.

Special orders

An application for specific disclosure may be made if, for example, it is alleged that the list of **15.194** documents is incomplete. Such an application can be made at any stage in the action. For example a claim for specific disclosure may be sought by a defendant to assist in drafting a defence properly, or may be made at trial if the existence of undisclosed evidence comes to light then.

An order for specific disclosure can provide for the disclosure of specific documents or classes **15.195** of documents, for the carrying out of a search as specified in the order, and/or for the disclosure of documents located in that search. Such an order will usually be made if it seems that standard disclosure has not been made. An application for such an order must specify the order sought and be supported by evidence stating a belief that the other party has or had specific documents that relate to a relevant issue and that are disclosable.

An application can also be made for an order for disclosure of any document referred to in a **15.196** statement of case, a witness statement, an affidavit, or an expert report, CPR r 31.14. The reference does not need to be specific. It may not be possible to get everything referred to in an expert report, PD 31 para 7.

If there is any difficulty getting inspection of documents referred to in the list of documents **15.197** or any document referred to an application can be made for an order for specific inspection, CPR r 31.12.

The use of documents

The wide duty to disclose and allow inspection is balanced by limitations on the use **15.198** that can be made of documents disclosed. Essentially the documents can be used only for purposes connected with the proper conduct of the action, subject to any agreement by the parties, CPR r 31.22. Any misuse of documents could be restrained by injunction, or punished by contempt of court, or striking out any action based on disclosed material.

15.199 However, court hearings are normally in public. Therefore documents read or referred to in court can be referred to outside court, and this can include documents exhibited to witness statements and affidavits. However the court may make an order restricting the use of documents read or referred to in court, see *Lilly Icos Ltd v Pfizer Ltd* (2002) 1 WLR 2253.

15.200 There are very limited exceptions to the process of disclosure and inspection.

- Documents that are privileged must be disclosed by being put on the list of documents (with a brief statement of the basis on which privilege is claimed), but do not have to be made available for inspection. The basis for legal privilege is considered in Chapter 3, and the basis for privilege for without prejudice communications is dealt with in Chapter 20.
- There is no general provision for confidentiality, whatever the nature of the document or the circumstances in which it came into the hands of the parties, though the court may exercise some control about use of a document in an appropriate case.
- There is a privilege against self-incrimination, which can apply where the contents of a document might expose a party to criminal proceedings or to a penalty, see *Memory Corporation plc v Sidhu (No 2)* (2000) 1 WLR 1443. This does not apply where the criminal penalty would only arise in another jurisdiction, or where the penalty is regulatory rather than a criminal sanction. Privilege in this area has been withdrawn where the disclosure is in a case relating to the infringement of intellectual property rights, Supreme Court Act 1981, s 72.
- Disclosure may be withheld where revealing it would be injurious to the public interest. The fact that this can be used for government and defence papers inevitably makes it a somewhat controversial area. The mere fact that the document is on official paper does not suffice, it is for the judge to balance the public interest in concealing the document with the damage to the public interest should justice fail to be done, see *Burmah Oil Co Ltd v Governor of the Bank of England* (1980) AC 1090. A person can apply without notice for an order that disclosure of a document would damage the public interest, CPR r 31.19. If an order is granted it does not have to be served and is not open for inspection. There are queries as to how closely this procedure fits with the European Convention on Human Rights, Article 6(1), on which see *Rowe and Davis v United Kingdom* The Times, 1 March 2000.

L EXCHANGE OF WITNESS STATEMENTS

15.201 The exchange of witness statements is an important part of preparing for a trial. The court will order each party to serve on the other parties witness statements for all the witnesses the party intends to rely on at the trial in relation to issues of fact, CPR r 32.4. The date for exchange will be set at track allocation or at a case management conference.

15.202 Normally mutual exchange of witness statements will take place a few weeks after disclosure of and inspection of documents (so that the witnesses can comment on anything in the documents), save in small track cases where documents are not normally served in advance. If it is not possible to get a signed statement from a witness in time for exchange the court may give permission to exchange a witness summary instead. This will only happen if good reason is shown why a proper signed witness statement could not be obtained in time. A witness may provide a further witness statement after exchange, but only if it is in proper form and disclosed to the other side.

If a witness statement is not served in advance as specified by the court, the witness can only **15.203** be called at trial with the court's permission, CPR r 32.10. If a party does not exchange witness statements when specified by the court, the court will have to take a careful decision if excluding the evidence would make it very difficult for the party to argue his or her case.

It is not necessary to exchange a statement of a witness the party has decided not to rely on, **15.204** and indeed it will be subject to legal privilege. If the witness statement is exchanged then it will cease to be privileged even if the party decides not to use it at trial, *Re Rex Williams Leisure plc* (1994) Ch 350 CA. Once the statement is exchanged the other party may use it at trial, but only with the permission of the court and only as hearsay, CPR r32.5, and see *McPhilemy v Times Newspapers Ltd (No 2)* (2000) 1 WLR 1732.

Once witness statements have been exchanged they may be used only for the current pro- **15.205** ceedings unless the court grants permission, the witness gives permission, or the statement is used in evidence at a public hearing, CPR r 32.12.

M   REVIEWING AND ADVISING ON EVIDENCE

> When you have eliminated the impossible, what ever remains, however improbable, must be the truth.
>
> Sir Arthur Conan Doyle, *The Sign of Four*

It is important to review the evidence available both for and against a case at regular stages in **15.206** the preparation of a case:

* before advising a client on a cause of action;
* after any pre-action exchange of information;
* before starting an action with the issues of a claim form;
* after disclosure and inspection;
* after exchange of witness statements;
* when preparing for trial.

In addition to collecting evidence to support the client's case, it is important to make full use **15.207** of the opportunities for getting evidence from the other side, both pre-action and at the interim stage. Ways of getting evidence and information from the other side include:

* under the terms of a relevant pre-action protocol, see 4.18–4.32;
* through statements of case;
* through disclosure and inspection, see 15.179–15.200;
* through exchange of witness statements, see 15.201–15.205;
* through seeking further information or an admission, see 14.146–12.165;
* through interim orders, see 16.144–16.169;

- informally through letters and telephone conversations (though such evidence may not be admissible if, for example, it is in a without prejudice letter, see 20.44–20.50).

15.208   When reviewing or advising on evidence it may be useful to:

- list separately each issue of each cause of action that will have to be proved;
- under each issue, set out the document or witness that will be used to prove the point (or note that the other side admit the point so it will not need to be proved);
- check that each piece of evidence to be used is admissible (noting any formalities that need to be completed to ensure that the piece of evidence is admissible);
- if there is not sufficient evidence on a point, note whether further evidence might be sought, and if so what.

15.209   The techniques for factual analysis outlined at 10.19–10.26 can be modified for use in analysing evidence. It is important to take a systematic approach and to engage with detail, and a chart similar to that suggested in 10.26 might be used as appropriate. A chart would probably need to be devised for the individual case as there would be different allegations in each case, but a chart would be based on the allegations that need to be made to win the case (defined in the statements of case) and the evidence relating to each allegation. As a basic outline for a possible analysis of evidence a breach of contract case:

Allegation	Full or part admission	Admissible evidence to prove	Evidence undermining the case	How any problem to be addressed
Oral term 1				
Oral term 2				
Variation of contract				
Breach of term 1				
Breach of term 2				
Causation of a head of loss				
Amount of a head of loss				

15.210   In a complex case there is merit in carrying out separate analyses of the evidence for each side so as to be able to identify weaknesses in an opponent's case. Such an analysis can assist in getting a case in order for trial, but also in preparing notes for the examination and cross-examination of witnesses in court.

15.211   In a complex case a barrister may be briefed to provide an advice on evidence, normally before an action is commenced or shortly before the case comes to trial. The purpose of such an advice is to concentrate the minds of the lawyers on what will be most important in court—the precise issues in the case, how each issue will be proved, and, if there are problems, whether the case should be settled. For guidance on writing such an opinion see 11.50–11.51.

A review of evidence might lead to important proposals for developing the case to be **15.212** presented to the client in an opinion or in a conference, for example:

- suggestions for seeking further evidence;
- suggestions for the presentation of evidence;
- consideration of possible amendments to the statements of case.

KEY DOCUMENTS

Forms

N 265 List of documents for standard disclosure
N 266 Notice to admit facts
N 268 Notice to prove documents at trial
N 285 General form of Affidavit
PF 52 Order for Case Management Directions (CPR Part 29)
N170 Listing questionnaire (pre-trial checklist)
N20 Witness Summons

Pre-action Protocols

(These give guidance on the use of expert evidence in the early stages of a case)

Pre-action Protocol for Personal Injury Claims
Pre-action Protocol for the Resolution of Clinical Disputes
Pre-action Protocol for Construction and Engineering Disputes
Pre-action Protocol for Defamation
Professional Negligence Pre-action Protocol
Pre-action Protocol for Judicial Review
Pre-action Protocol for Disease and Illness Claims
Pre-action Protocol for Housing Disrepair Cases

These are all easily available in hard copy and electronically, see Chapter 24.

Expert Witness Institute   Code of Guidance on Expert Evidence   See www.ewi.org.uk.

16

PROCEDURAL RULES AS PRACTICAL TOOLS

A USING PROCEDURAL RULES AS TOOLS 16.01

B THE BASIC PROCEDURE FOR APPLICATIONS 16.15
Making the application 16.17
Giving notice 16.19
The order sought 16.20
Evidence in support 16.21
The hearing 16.27
Hearings without notice to the other side 16.32
Costs 16.37
Enforcement or discharge 16.39
Appeals 16.40
General consideration regarding interim orders 16.42

C THE SCALES OF JUSTICE 16.45

D FAILURE TO ABIDE BY THE RULES 16.50
General provisions 16.50
Applications for sanctions 16.54
The sanctions that may be imposed 16.58

E MAKING APPLICATIONS BEFORE A CASE STARTS 16.63
Injunctions 16.66
Pre-action identification of parties 16.68
Pre-action disclosure 16.71
Pre-action inspection 16.76

F TIME STRATEGIES—CUTTING AN ACTION SHORT 16.79
The options available 16.79
Objecting to jurisdiction 16.83
Default judgment 16.84
Summary judgment 16.95
Dismissal for want of prosecution 16.103

G TIME STRATEGIES—GETTING SOME ISSUES DECIDED
QUICKLY 16.107
Procedural options 16.108

Interim injunctions. 16.109
The types of injunction available 16.110
Tests for getting an injunction 16.113
Procedure for getting an injunction. 16.122
The form of the injunction order 16.126
Obtaining an interim injunction in an emergency or
      without notice 16.134

H   PEOPLE STRATEGIES. 16.140
Involving people as parties 16.141
Involving people as witnesses 16.143

I   INFORMATION STRATEGIES. 16.144
Requests for further information 16.146
Search orders 16.148
The requirements for getting a search order 16.151
The procedure for getting a search order. 16.153
The form of a search order 16.154
Following the grant of a search order. 16.160
Production of documents by non-parties 16.164
Inspection of property 16.167

J   MONEY STRATEGIES. 16.170
Security for costs 16.172
Freezing orders. 16.175
The requirements for a freezing order 16.176
The procedure for getting a freezing order 16.177
Interim payments 16.183

K   COSTS ORDERS FOR INTERIM APPLICATIONS 16.190

KEY DOCUMENTS

A   USING PROCEDURAL RULES AS TOOLS

16.01   For litigation lawyers, interim applications will be much more numerous than full trials. There may be several interim hearings for each case before trial, and many cases will have some interim hearings to deal with specific issues and then proceed to settle without trial. It is very important to understand how interim applications are made and used.

16.02   The most effective way to make use of procedural rules is to be very familiar with them, and to follow the rules properly. Following the comprehensive review by Lord Woolf, the Rules are written clearly, and the natural meaning should be taken in considering what they mean and how they apply. To make best use of the rules it is important to look at the text of the rule, and it is for this reason that appropriate rules and practice directions are cited for appropriate parts of this text. For sources for the rules see 24.04–24.14.

16.03   Having said this, there will be times when it is necessary to interpret what a rule means. The factors in interpreting the Civil Procedure Rules are:

- the overriding objective, though this does not mean that a general concept of justice can overrule what a specific rule says;
- cases decided prior to 1999 should not normally be used in interpreting the revised rules;
- the Human Rights Act 1998, s 3(1) provides that 'so far as it is possible to do so, primary legislation and subordinate legislation must be read and given effect in a way which is compatible with the Convention rights', see *Goode v Martin* (2002) 1 WLR 1828.

Chapter 4 outlines the whole procedure for a case. This chapter focuses on the tactical use of rules before and during a case. The applications that can appropriately be made to court vary with each case, but careful choice of what applications to make at what stage in a case can make a significant difference in how well a case is prepared, and what is in the court file before trial. For further sources on civil procedure rules see 24.16. **16.04**

With the fully revised Civil Procedure Rules, the overriding objective, and the approach of both parties working to clarify issues and to put their cards on the table, there might be a question as to how far former tactics in litigating a case have survived. It is undoubtedly the case that some tactics used in the past are no longer appropriate—endlessly delaying a case because one is likely to lose it, failing to clarify issues in the hope of misleading an opponent, or springing evidence on an opponent at a late stage to try to put them at a disadvantage would now be unlikely to be successful. The court would intervene even if the other party did not. **16.05**

This does not mean that there are not still many practical tactics and strategies that can make a significant difference in the outcome of a case. There are many optional steps and applications that can be used in preparing a case for trial, sometimes even before a case is formally started, and selective use of applications for each case is very important in effective litigation. The majority of cases do not come to trial, and this is often because one party has been able to use the interim stages in litigation to show the strengths of their case, and weaknesses in the opponent's case. **16.06**

The 'interim' stage is interim in being the stage between the issue of the claim form and trial. There are many types of applications that may be made at this stage to progress the action. Some are quite well known and commonly used, such as the interim injunction; others only apply in specific circumstances, like security for costs; and others are only appropriate to particular types of action, such as interim payments. There are of necessity different requirements and tests for different applications, and this can seem complex and confusing to those preparing for legal practice, but many of the details are in fact practical and sensible for the type of application involved. The lawyer primarily needs to be aware of the range of applications that can be made, and then to check the detailed requirements for an application that seems appropriate. **16.07**

For the effective lawyer procedural rules should be seen as providing a useful tool box rather than a set of hurdles. Some applications can achieve a significant advantage in a case and are therefore valuable even if they have quite tight tests. In other applications a judge may have quite a wide discretion, and the lawyer who puts together a good case, perhaps involving principles from the overriding objective, can obtain something worthwhile for the client. The real use that constructive and inventive lawyers can make of interim applications is shown in two clear examples. What is now known as a search order emerged from case law in **16.08** which lawyers persuaded judges to grant a new type of order to allow information that would otherwise be unavailable to be obtained, see *Anton Piller KG v Manufacturing Processes* [1976] Ch 55 CA. Equally what is now known as a freezing order came from case law created by lawyers and judges to address practical problems where justice might be defeated by assets being moved from the jurisdiction, see *Mareva Compania Naviera SA v International Bulk Carriers SA* [1980] 1 All ER 213.

16.09 The questions for each lawyer to consider are:

- Which interim orders might be useful to us in this case (whether for practical or tactical reasons)?
- What is the overall strategy in the case? Is it justifiable to go for a full range of all possible orders in this case? Might it be better to seek a couple of strategic orders and see if that triggers a settlement? Are there key problems in a particular area such as getting information?
- Should an order that is potentially available actually be sought? Is the cost justified?
- Can the end be achieved without actually having to go to court?
- What are our chances of getting the specific order sought? What are the precise requirements for applying? What is the test for success?
- When should the order be sought? Different orders are appropriate at different stages in preparing a case. Ideally an order is sought at a case management conference rather than requiring a separate hearing.
- Should more than one order be sought?

16.10 The full extent of the powers of the court at the interim stage should be kept in mind. The court has some residual authority beyond the specific orders that can be sought, and also general powers, for example to extend or shorten times for compliance with rules or orders, or to adjourn or bring forward hearing dates. A party can ask the court to use these powers where appropriate.

16.11 In considering the many possibilities offered in making interim applications, lawyers need to take a responsible view. Applications should be made to a purpose, and not if they have little chance of success so that the effect will be to delay progress and build up costs. The overriding objective can be used to achieve fairness, but should not be called in aid inappropriately. Points under the Human Rights Act 1998 should not normally be taken with regard to case management decisions, unless there is thought to be very good reason.

16.12 Although the terms claimant and defendant are used for a case, for each application to court there will be an applicant and a respondent. In many cases an application might be made by the claimant or the defendant, so the terms applicant and respondent are used in this chapter to avoid confusion.

16.13 The other side of the coin is that courts now have limited tolerance where the Civil Procedure Rules are not followed in preparing a case, particularly where the result is to waste time or build up costs unnecessarily without good reason. Sanctions may be imposed in appropriate cases, and a penalty can be imposed through the summary assessment of costs. For the sake of the lawyer and the clients this should be avoided if possible.

16.14 It should be noted that the court can itself use case management powers to initiate consideration of procedural matters even if the parties do not.

B   THE BASIC PROCEDURE FOR APPLICATIONS

In broad terms, there is a common procedure for making applications to court before trial of   **16.15**
the action. The elements of this procedure are set out here for convenience so that they do
not have to be repeated with regard to each potential order. However, it cannot be stressed
too strongly that this summary is only an overall guide. The details for each order sought
must be checked with the Civil Procedure Rules. All the following points normally apply
as appropriate to all the orders outlined in this chapter. See generally PD 23 Applications,
CPR Part 23 general rules about applications for court orders, and CPR Part 25 Interim
remedies and security for costs.

There is a general obligation to make an application early in a case rather than later, and   **16.16**
appropriate applications would often be made shortly after the filing of the defence. An
application should be made when there is a court hearing if possible rather than seeking a
separate hearing, but this should not lead to a delay in making the application that might
prejudice the client.

Making the application

Interim orders or directions should normally be sought by issuing a notice on Form N244,   **16.17**
and paying the court fee, CPR 23.4. The notice should state the order sought and the reasons
for seeking it, CPR rr 23.3 and 23.6. The nature of evidence in support should be identified. It
should be clear whether a hearing is sought—sometimes an order can be made without a
hearing, if for example the parties agree to it. If an application is to be made at a hearing that
has already been fixed, proper written notice should still be given (PD 23 para 2.10). The
consideration of orders can be initiated by the court as well as by one of the parties.

The application should normally be made at least a set number of days before the hearing.   **16.18**
This period varies from 3 days to 14 days depending on the type of application made. This
period is to allow time for the court to make preparations and for notice to be given to the
other side.

Giving notice

It is normally only right that a copy of the notice of application and any supporting papers   **16.19**
be served on the other side so that they can attend the hearing and put their point of view.
There are some exceptions where an application can be made without notice to the other
side. This may be the case if giving notice might defeat the purpose of the application.
Alternatively it might be because the application is so urgent that there is not time to
give notice, in which case the court can dispense with the need for an application notice,
CPR r 23.3, though informal notice should still be given if possible, PD 23, para 4.2. Sometimes
an application has to be made urgently and/or without notice. There are special requirements
for evidence in such a case, see 16.35.

The order sought

16.20   The applicant sometimes has to file a copy of a draft for the order sought. Even if this is not a requirement, it is a matter of good practice if the order sought is anything other than short and straightforward. If the order is long or complex it should be provided on disk as well as hard copy, PD 23 para 12. On the importance of drafting an order for an interim hearing carefully see *Memory Corporation plc v Sidhu (No 2)* (2000) 1 WLR 1443.

Evidence in support

16.21   Normally written evidence in support of an application has to be filed at court and served on other parties at least three clear days (and sometimes seven days) before the hearing, CPR r 25.3. Unless the application is properly made without notice the evidence should also be served on other parties. Even if there is no specific requirement for evidence in support in a rule, some evidence may in practice be needed to support the argument being put to the court.

16.22   Further evidence may not be required if all the necessary information is already on the court file. Depending on the stage that the case has reached, the documents on the court file or that should be served in support may include:

- information in statements of case that include signed statements of truth;
- factual information on the notice of application, provided it has a signed statement of truth;
- witness statements with a statement of truth that are served with the application;
- a formal sworn affidavit is required to support an application for a search order, a freezing injunction, or certain other applications.

16.23   The rules for preparation are the same as for a witness statement or affidavit for trial. However written evidence prepared for trial must cover the whole case, whereas written evidence prepared for an interim hearing may focus on specific points, and why a specific interim order should be made. There is some flexibility to allow for the fact that evidence has to be prepared quickly, if for example there is not time to identify or trace an original source that can be stated, *Deutsche Ruckversicherung AG v Wallbrook Insurance Co Ltd* (1995) 1 WLR 1017.

16.24   The quality of the written evidence in support may be very important, especially if the test for success in the application sought is a high one, and/or if the application is contested. There are various requirements for evidence:

- A witness statement, or in certain circumstances an affidavit, is often required as evidence to support an interim application.
- Every aspect of the test for the granting of the order should be covered in the written evidence in support. The court has a power to hear witnesses but this will rarely be done, CPR r 32.2.
- If an application is made without notice then there is a duty on the applicant to disclose any information that does not support their case.
- In the case of some orders there is specific provision for the respondent to file evidence in reply to the evidence supporting the application.

In such a case the contents will be determined by the nature of the application, as different **16.25** information may be required. As appropriate this may include:

- facts giving rise to the claim against the defendant in the proceedings (if those facts are relevant and are not otherwise covered in material available to the court);
- the facts giving rise to the claim for interim relief;
- information that satisfies any particular test that applies to the order sought (for example where an interlocutory injunction is sought);
- the reasons why the relief is sought;
- the precise relief sought.

Witness statements and affidavits used to support interlocutory applications may contain **16.26** hearsay evidence and matters of information or belief, provided the sources and grounds for the belief are given, using a phrase like, 'I have been informed by Ignatius Iago and believe that . . .'. This is justified because it can be much more difficult to provide full and admissible evidence at this stage.

The hearing

On receipt of the application notice the court will notify the parties of the time and date of **16.27** hearing, or that the application will be considered without a hearing, PD 23 para 2.4. Normally the court will serve the notice and documents on the other parties by first class post (so the applicant must file enough copies), but the applicant may notify the court that he will effect service, which must still be done at least three clear days in advance and in compliance with the normal rules for service. Most interim applications are dealt with by a Master (in London) or a District Judge (in a District Registry).

The application can be a dealt with without a hearing, to comply with the overriding objec- **16.28** tive in avoiding the time and costs of a court hearing if it is not really necessary. This can happen if the parties agree there be no hearing, or if the court does not consider that a hearing would be appropriate, CPR r 23.8. The respondent may provide a letter confirming consent. If a party is dissatisfied with an order or direction made without a hearing he can apply within seven days to have it set aside or varied, CPR r 3.3.

A hearing may be conducted by telephone conference call, CPR r 3.1. Such a hearing may **16.29** take place if the parties agree and if they are all legally represented, or are at least assisted by a responsible person.

If there is a hearing it should normally be in public, CPR r 39.2, unless publicity might defeat **16.30** the purpose of the order or there is an issue of national security. If there is a hearing the court may review other aspects of the progress of the case and the parties should be prepared for this, PD 23 para 2.9. The judge will keep a note of the hearing and the decision taken, PD 23 para 8.

The hearing will normally be with notice to the other side and both sides will be present. The **16.31** normal order of events will be for the applicant to make the application for the order sought, referring to the written evidence filed. The respondent will then respond resisting the order. The applicant will then make any points in reply to points raised by the respondent. The hearing will be relatively informal and flexible.

Hearings without notice to the other side

16.32 An application may be heard without notice to the other side if:

- there is real urgency;
- there is no other party to be given notice (for example seeking permission to serve out of the jurisdiction);
- only one party is affected;
- secrecy is essential for the application to be effective.

16.33 In the first case, efforts should be made to contact the respondent even if proper notice cannot be given. The judge should be informed of the efforts made, and of any response. In this case the respondent may appear at the hearing and the judge may listen to the respondent even though formal notice has not been given.

16.34 To ensure fairness there are special duties where an application is not on notice. Evidence in support must say why notice was not given, CPR r 25.3. The party seeking the order has a duty to make full and frank disclosure of all material facts, including those which do not favour the application. If this is not followed the order may be set aside. Where serious issues are involved there is also a duty to make reasonable enquiries. If in doubt, it is better for the applicant to disclose information known. The duty is continuing, so there may be a duty to tell the court if further facts come to light.

16.35 Where an application has been made without notice the written evidence should also cover:

- the facts relied on as justifying an application made urgently and/or without notice;
- details of any notice given to the defendant, or the reasons for giving none, and any answer asserted by the defendant;
- any facts known to the applicant which might lead the court not to grant relief without notice, and this duty of disclosure is particularly strict where freezing and search orders are sought, and any failure to give complete disclosure may well result in the order being refused, or in its being revoked with costs.

16.36 If the evidence has to be prepared very quickly, it may be difficult to get all the relevant information together, though there must still be enough information before the court to justify the making of an order. If necessary the evidence can be hand written and does not need to meet the formal presentation requirements, though the court will expect an undertaking that the evidence will be filed in proper form.

Costs

16.37 If the interim application is dealt with in less than a day, which will normally be the case, the court can make a summary assessment of costs at the end of the hearing, PD Costs para 13.2. To assist, the parties must file and serve at least 24 hours before the hearing a statement of their costs for the hearing. This summary assessment is important—an applicant who has properly obtained an order may get the costs of it immediately. Even if costs will not be paid until the outcome of the case is decided, it is important to get the costs order that most favours the client. For further detail see Chapter 5.

An order requiring costs to be paid before an action can proceed can impede a claimant's **16.38** access to the courts, and must be made with care, *Ford v Labrador* The Times, 5 June 2003.

Enforcement or discharge

Any order made will need to be served on the other parties. In the case of an urgent applica- **16.39** tion made without notice the applicant will need to undertake to serve the papers in the case, and the order made will normally only last for a few days, up to a hearing with both parties present. If an order has been made before the start of a case, there will normally need to be undertakings to issue the claim form etc.

Appeals

It is possible to appeal against interim orders, though this should not be done where costs **16.40** will be wasted as the hearing of the case is imminent. There is reluctance to grant appeals against orders that are case management decisions.

The normal rules for appeal apply to case management decisions, and see PD 52 para 4.4. **16.41** Where there is an application for permission to appeal from a case management decision the court will take into account whether the issue is of sufficient significance to justify the cost of an appeal, whether the possible consequences of the appeal (such as losing a trial date) outweigh the significance of the case management decision, and whether it would be more convenient to determine the matter at trial. If an interim order is set aside, the defendant may be ordered to pay costs thrown away.

General considerations regarding interim orders

In addition to the parties seeking orders, the court can exercise its case management powers **16.42** of its own initiative. This is not intended as a widely creative power, but to further the overriding objective. Orders made in this way must include a statement that a party affected can apply within seven days to have the order varied, set aside, or stayed, CPR r 3.3. If the court intends to make orders of its own initiative it should give the parties an opportunity to make representations.

It is important to note that it is possible to apply for more than one order at a time, **16.43** indeed this is to be encouraged if it will save costs at the end of the day. In tactical terms it may be sensible to apply for orders in the alternative in appropriate circumstances so that if one is not granted another might be, for example seeking summary judgment, or orders regarding the future of the case if that is not granted. Combining orders may also be appropriate in serious cases where commercial interests are threatened, for example in cases of business piracy a freezing order, a search order, and an injunction may be sought at the same time.

If one party seeks an interim order, the other party should consider whether there is any **16.44** purpose in making a cross application for an order to be heard at the same time. This may be a response to the order sought, or an order that is not connected but which can usefully be heard at the same time.

C THE SCALES OF JUSTICE

16.45 The purpose of interim applications is to help the parties to prepare for trial and to meet the interests of justice. In broad terms, when making decisions in applications before trial, the court will apply the overriding objective. At a civil trial decisions will normally be taken on the balance of probabilities, but for the various decisions that may need to be taken at the interim stage, a variety of different tests apply to maintain fairness between the parties on different issues.

16.46 It is not easy to take decisions at an interim stage, when only limited material is before the court, so the court will not wish to pre-judge or prejudice the final outcome of the case. Also the court will wish to serve justice but to avoid wasting court time and costs. In taking some decisions the court will need to balance the interests of the parties, the interests of justice, and the reality of the situation quite carefully. Points about how the court might weigh up all the relevant points from the overriding objective—weighing the scales of justice as it were—will often need to be made in advocacy when making an interim application.

16.47 For some types of application special tests are set, generally because of the risk of prejudicing one of the parties if the wrong decision is taken. There is in broad terms a scale of how tight the tests are that must be satisfied for success with an interim application. The lawyer must specifically identify the correct test to be met for the granting of the order, must identify the elements of the test, and show how they are met in the current case in advising a client on the chances of success and in advocacy.

16.48 The scale of tests can be illustrated as follows:

- An extremely strong *prima facie* case on the merits—this is the very strict test for a search order (which needs strong justification because of the potential effect on a respondent whose premises are searched and whose records etc may be removed).
- The court is satisfied the defendant would be held liable, at a high standard of balance of probabilities—the fairly strict test for an interim payment (which should only be made where the claimant is likely to win or the money will have to be repaid to the defendant).
- The court is satisfied that the defendant would be held liable if the claim went to trial, on the balance of probabilities but a high standard within that range—this is the test for interim payments.
- There is a serious issue to be tried—this is the lower test for an interim injunction (there are other parts of a test to be satisfied, the injunction will only last for a limited period, and damages can be ordered as compensation if it was wrongly granted).
- The respondent has no real prospect of success—a test for summary judgment.

16.49 There is also a scale of how much control the lawyer has over the order granted. Sometimes there is only one form of order, as for example if a statement of case is struck out. Sometimes there is very significant control over the wording of an order, for example in the case of interim injunctions. Where there is control over the detail of the order it is in tactical terms important to think through the details of the order that will best suit the client's needs. In such a case there is normally a requirement that a draft order be filed with the notice of application.

D   FAILURE TO ABIDE BY THE RULES

General provisions

If a case is being conducted in a tactical way, the question might sometimes arise whether   **16.50**
there is any benefit in failing to follow a procedural rule. It may occur to a client that abiding
by a rule might prejudice the chances of success of a case, and the question as to what would
happen if the rule were not followed might arise. Might it not be tactical to avoid a rule
rather than to seek to use it?

One answer is that the lawyer must act within the rules and the spirit of professional   **16.51**
conduct, so the lawyer might need to advise the client that the lawyer could not act in a way
that might mislead the court or abuse court processes. A further point is that the parties have
a duty to cooperate with the court management powers, and that any failure to cooperate
can be met with a range of sanctions.

At one end of the scale, a failure to abide by procedural rules may be insignificant. Quite   **16.52**
unintentionally a party may fail to take a step or make an error that does not prejudice the
other side or mislead anyone. In such a case the court would normally overlook the error or
allow it to be corrected. A pure error, such as using a wrong form, will not automatically
invalidate a step purportedly taken unless the court so orders, CPR r 3.10. The court has a
general power under this rule to make an order to remedy any error in procedure, see *Fawdry
& Co v Murfitt* (2003) QB 104.

At a potentially more serious level, a problem in meeting a time limit may be dealt with by   **16.53**
agreement, so long as key dates in the case management process relating to the court process
are still met. Unless such a variation is barred by the rules, the time for doing something
provided by rules or court can be varied by written agreement of parties, CPR r 2.11. Therefore the first step if there is a problem in meeting a date is to seek to agree a revised timetable
with the other side. If there will be a problem in meeting a key date in the court process
(affecting a case management conference, a pre-trial review, the filing of the listing questionnaire, or the trial date), there will need to be an application to court. The court has a
general power to extend or abridge time limits, CPR r 3.1. It is best to apply for a revised date
before the time limit has expired if at all possible. In considering the application the court
will consider relevant matters such as prejudice to the other side.

Applications for sanctions

At a potentially more serious level, any apparent failure to comply with the court rules   **16.54**
should not go unnoted. If one party appears to have breached a procedural rule, the innocent party should write to the defaulting party giving warning of an intention to apply for
an order if the default is not rectified within a reasonable period, normally seven to ten days,
PD 28 para 5 (fast track), PD 29 para 7 (multi-track).

If the default is not rectified, the innocent party can apply for an order to enforce compli-   **16.55**
ance and/or impose a sanction. Such an application should then be made without delay, or
the delay of the innocent party can be taken into account when the court deals with the

order or sanction. An order against a defaulting party can include directions and/or a sanction, even in response to a first default.

16.56   If a court order contains directions and a party does not appeal or seek to vary it within 14 days of service then it will be presumed the party is content with the order in the circumstances at that time, PD 29 para 6.2. Any breach of such directions can therefore also be dealt with by the court.

16.57   The approach of a court is set out in PD 28. The court will not allow a failure to comply with directions to lead to the postponement of the trial unless the circumstances are exceptional. If it is practicable to do so the court will exercise its powers to enable the trial to come on at the date or within the period set.

The sanctions that may be imposed

16.58   The court will maintain control of the conduct of a case through the imposition of sanctions if it needs to. Some sanctions can be applied at the general discretion of the court and others are linked to specific orders or practice directions. An order imposing a sanction should specify the time within which a specified step should be taken, CPR r 2.9, and it may set out what sanction will be imposed automatically if the specified step is not taken by the specified time. The order may be an 'unless' order, saying that unless a specified step is taken by a set date, the other party can apply for judgment and costs, CPR r 3.5.

16.59   The sanctions that may be imposed by the court include the following, as appropriate.

- An order for the payment of costs relating to a specific matter forthwith.
- An order relating to costs to be taken into account when costs are generally considered at a later stage.
- An order that costs be paid on an indemnity basis (the more generous basis for assessment).
- An order that interest should not be payable, or should be payable at a rate lower than might otherwise apply.
- An order prohibiting the use of certain evidence. For example failure to disclose an expert report at the right time might result in an order it only be used with the permission of the court, CPR r 35.13, or filing a witness statement or exhibit that does not comply with the rules court might result in an order it may not be used in evidence.
- An order for a payment into court, if appropriate to protect a claimant where a defendant is not preparing for trial properly.
- The striking out all or part of the statement of case, CPR r 3.4, where there are very serious or repeated breaches or procedural rules or directions, see *UCB Corporate Services Ltd v Halifax (SW) Ltd* (1999) CPLR 691, or for non-payment of court fees, CPR r 3.7. Such a serious sanction may not be appropriate if the courts have powers to manage the matter, *Biguzzi v Rank Leisure plc* (1999) 1 WLR 1926.

16.60   In deciding whether to impose a sanction, the reason for the failure to comply will be relevant, as will any prejudice to an innocent party resulting from the failure. The party in default should clearly try to remedy the default before sanctions are considered by the court so as to appear in a better light. It may be necessary to weigh up the possible sanctions and to decide which is most appropriate.

If an order containing a sanction is not complied with, the sanction will take effect unless **16.61** the defaulting party applies for and obtains relief, CPR r 3.8. This is done by an application notice supported by evidence. Under CPR r 3.9 the court will consider all the circumstances including nine factors, which will normally all be considered and balanced, *Woodhouse v Consignia plc* (2002) 2 All ER 737:

- the interests of the administration of justice;
- whether the application for relief has been made promptly;
- whether the failure to comply was intentional;
- whether there is a good explanation for the failure;
- the extent to which the party in default has complied with other rules, practice directions, court orders, and any relevant pre-action protocol;
- whether the failure to comply was caused by the party or his legal representative;
- whether the trail date can still be met if relief is granted;
- the effect which any failure to comply had on each party;
- the effect which the granting of relief would have on each party.

If a claim is struck out for breach within the limitation period, a further claim would **16.62** normally be struck out as an abuse of process, *Janov v Morris* (1981) 1 WLR 1389, CA.

E MAKING APPLICATIONS BEFORE A CASE STARTS

A potential claimant may wish to make applications before a case starts. This may be because **16.63** crucial information is required to decide whether the case is worth bringing or not, or it may be to try to maintain the current position until decisions can be taken at trial.

Normally applications can only be made after a claim form has been issued and the court **16.64** record of the case opened. However if an application is sufficiently urgent, or it is otherwise in the interests of justice, a court has the power to hear an application before the main proceedings have been commenced, CPR r 25.2. In such a case the court will normally give directions that the claim form be issued as soon as is reasonably possible after granting an application.

The court will be slow to use powers before an action without good reason. A clear case will **16.65** need to be made that it is in the interests of justice that an application be granted at this stage so as to protect the position of the applicant, or so as to put the applicant in a position to be able to launch the action. Only specific types of application are granted at this stage. The court may give directions for commencing the action and filing and serving documents, unless the outcome of the order may be that no action is commenced.

Injunctions

Sometimes it is necessary to act immediately to prevent something from being done to **16.66** protect the position of the claimant or to prevent the substance of the intended action from being removed—for example stopping a tree from being cut down before a tree preservation order can be sought. In such cases a pre-action injunction can be sought.

16.67 The process and the relevant tests are essentially the same as an application for an interim injunction as outlined at 16.109–16.139. It is particularly likely that an application made before a case starts will be made as a matter of urgency, and made without notice. It is therefore particularly likely that there will be limited time to prepare paperwork, but the lawyer should still take care to get as far as possible in preparing an application notice, evidence in support, and a draft of the order sought to strengthen the chances of obtaining the order.

Pre-action identification of parties

16.68 On occasion it may be difficult to identify the person the claimant should sue, but there may be a link through someone who has become involved in the factual situation, albeit innocently, and who may be able to assist in identifying the wrongdoer. In such a case a Norwich Pharmacal order may help, named after *Norwich Pharmacal Co v Customs and Excise Commissioners* (1974) AC 133 HL. This procedure cannot be used against someone who is merely a witness—other procedures are available to involve a witness in a case—but against someone who is involved in the situation. The procedure cannot be used against someone purely because they might be aware of the identity of a potential defendant, *Ricci v Chow* (1987) 1 WLR 1658 CA. The remedy is discretionary and may not be granted if some other way of achieving a remedy is available. It will not be available if the applicant already has a cause of action in regard to whom the order is sought, *X Ltd v Morgan-Grampian (Publishers) Ltd* (1991) 1 AC 1 HL.

16.69 The process is to start an action against the person who has become factually involved, but solely for the purpose of finding the identity of the person who can be sued. To get an order there must be a real and unsatisfied claim against the alleged wrongdoer which can only be brought if the wrongdoer's identity is revealed. The claimant issues a claim form with evidence in support. This may be done without notice in appropriate circumstances, *Loose v Williamson* (1978) 1 WLR 639. Once the identity of the wrongdoer is revealed the proceedings will be terminated. The claimant will normally have to pay the costs of the person against whom the order is sought, but may be able to claim these as a part of damages at the end of the main case.

16.70 The order can be used for any type of case, *British Steel Corporation v Granada Television Ltd* (1981) AC 1096 HL, save for where a journalist has a statutory defence against disclosure of sources under the Contempt of Court Act 1981, s 10. An order can be sought even if it is not clear that a cause of action has arisen, *P v T Ltd* (1997) 4 All ER 200, if some redress short of a legal action is sought, *Ashworth Hospital Authority v MGN Ltd* (2002) 1 WLR 2033, for a beneficiary to get information relevant to the distribution of trust funds, *Murphy v Murphy* (1999) 1 WLR 282, or to get information relevant to the enforcement of an order, *Merchantile Group (Europe) AG v Aiyela* (1994) QB 366 CA.

Pre-action disclosure

16.71 It may be vital to see a particular document to decide whether there is a case that justifies action. Clearly costs may be saved if an action is avoided or an early settlement is achieved by such a document being made available before a formal action is begun. The point is not to allow general evidence to be seen early, but to focus on documents central to whether there may be a case. This might be relevant where, for example, an action for medical negligence is contemplated, but it is necessary to see medical records to take a decision.

There are various ways in which it may be possible to obtain documents without any **16.72** application to court.

- Individuals have the right to access to their own medical records, Access to Medical Records Act 1988.
- Where personal data is stored, an individual has the right to see it together with information about its source, Data Protection Act 1998, s 7, on making a written request and paying a reasonable fee. This covers computer-based and written filed records, and may be useful in a potential case relating to health, education, or other public records. In certain cases statutory instruments provide further details, for example providing that information about physical or mental health need not be released if disclosure could lead to serious harm to the physical or mental health of anyone. If a data controller does not reply promptly to a written request for information, a court order can be sought to compel compliance.
- Pre-action protocols often provide for pre-action disclosure of crucial information, for example in personal injury cases.
- A pre-action letter may ask for information to be provided voluntarily, see 11.31.

If none of the above is appropriate or effective, an order for pre-action disclosure can be **16.73** sought under the Supreme Court Act 1981, s 33 (or County Courts Act 1984, s 52). An application should relate to a specific document and not a general fishing trip for information, *Shaw v Vauxhall Motors Ltd* (1974) 1 WLR 1035 CA. The requirements are as follows.

- The applicant appears likely to be a party to subsequent proceedings. The applicant needs to show a reasonable basis for an intended action, *Burns v Shuttlehurst* (1999) 1 WLR 1449, but does not have to show that proceedings will be issued, *Black v Sumitomo Corporation* (2002) 1 WLR 1569 (as the document may show that the action is not sustainable).
- The defendant also appears likely to be a party.
- The defendant appears likely to have or have had relevant documents in his or her possession, custody, or power. These must be documents that would be within standard disclosure for an action, CPR r 31.16, which means that the likely issues in the proceedings must be reasonably clear.
- Advance disclosure is desirable to dispose of the anticipated proceedings fairly, or to prevent the need to commence proceedings, or to save costs. The court will balance out factors to decide what is 'desirable' including the strength of the case, the relevance of the documents, and the expense of disclosing them.

An application is made with an application notice in the anticipated proceedings but before **16.74** the issue of any claim form, with evidence in support and notice given. The court has a discretion whether to make an order, and whether to order documents to be disclosed to a claimant or to his or her legal or medical advisers. The order will specify the documents to be disclosed, and may require the respondent to say what documents are no longer in his control and where they have gone, CPR r 31.16. The court does not have to give directions about the commencement of the action, as on seeing the records the applicant may decide not to bring an action. The applicant will normally have to pay the costs unless the respondent acts unreasonably, see *Bermuda International Securities Ltd v KPMG* (2001) CPLR 252.

16.75 There should be good reason for disclosure before the normal time, *Parker v CS Structured Credit Fund Ltd* (2003) 1 WLR 1680. At this stage the court should be very hesitant about determining any substantive issue, *Rose v Lynx Express Ltd* The Times, 22 April 2004.

Pre-action inspection

16.76 To decide whether to bring an action it may be important to have property examined or tested, to have it photographed, or to have tests carried out, for example to decide how an accident was caused or whether equipment is defective.

16.77 If property may become the subject of subsequent proceedings, or a question relating to it may arise in such proceedings, an order can be sought under the Supreme Court Act 1981, s 33. The order can make provision for the inspection, photographing, preservation, custody, or detention of property, or can order the taking of samples or the carrying out of an experiment on or with the property.

16.78 The order is sought by issuing an application notice in the anticipated proceedings, supported by written evidence, and the person against whom the order is sought must be served, CPR r 25.5. The evidence must show, preferably with reference to the statement of case, how the property is relevant to the case.

F   TIME STRATEGIES—CUTTING AN ACTION SHORT

The options available

16.79 To save time and money, and for tactical reasons, both sides may wish to end the proceedings at an early stage.

- The claimant will wish to get judgment as quickly as possible, especially if his or her case is very strong, and/or if the defendant is not prepared to get involved in the litigation process.
- The defendant may wish the action to be brought to a close quickly if the court does not have jurisdiction to hear the case, if the case being brought is very unclear or weak, or if the case is misconceived or improperly brought.

16.80 There is a variety of ways of cutting short an action.

- Objecting to the jurisdiction of the court to try the case.
- Seeking a judgment in default where a statement of case is not filed.
- Seeking an order to strike out a statement of case.
- Seeking summary judgment.
- Seeking an order for dismissal for want of prosecution.

16.81 These can be sought cumulatively, for example seeking to strike out a defence, and seeking summary judgment in the alternative should that application fail, see *Three Rivers District*

Council v Bank of England (No 3) (2001) 2 All ER 513 HL. If the first, second, or fourth of the applications is successful then the action will proceed no further and the court will simply need to make decisions about costs. If either of the other two applications is successful then the applicant will have won the case and the judge will make appropriate orders. If damages remain to be decided the court may list the matter for a disposal hearing, or give directions which could include allocation to a case management track, CPR r 12.7.

Decisions relating to cutting an action short have significant importance in ending an action **16.82** without a full trial, so a court may give direction for the conduct of a case rather than the order sought. Alternatively the action may be stayed if settlement is a possibility.

Objecting to jurisdiction

A defendant may argue that the court has no jurisdiction to hear the case, for example on the **16.83** basis that an action is already proceeding in another jurisdiction, CPR Part 11. The defendant must acknowledge service of the claim form and then make such an application within 14 days, supported by evidence. The court may need to consider the jurisdictional rules outlined in Chapter 4.

Default judgment

A claimant can bring a case to an early conclusion if the defendant fails to defend the case. **16.84** See generally CPR Part 12 Default judgment, PD 12 Default judgment, and CPR Part 13 Setting aside or varying default judgment.

The requirements for such a default judgement under CPR r 12.3 are: **16.85**

- that the claim form and the particulars of claim have been properly issued and served;
- that 14 days have elapsed since the service of the particulars of claim;
- that the defendant has not filed an acknowledgement of service or a defence, or if an acknowledgement of service has been filed, no defence has been filed within 28 days of the service of the particulars of claim.

In a claim seeking to recover money or the delivery of goods, a default judgment is available **16.86** as an administrative matter by completing a form sent by the court when the claim form is issued and returning it to court, where a judgment is entered. If the particulars of claim were issued by the claimant a certificate of service is required.

For other claims there will need to be an application to court for a default judgment, as the **16.87** court needs to exercise a discretion. There will also need to be an application to court in certain types of money and goods cases, CPR r 12:

- where there has been service outside the jurisdiction without the need for permission (as the court will need to be satisfied that local rules for service have been complied with);
- if goods are sought without an alternative of money damages;
- in a tort claim brought by one spouse against the other;
- where the claim includes costs other than fixed costs;
- if the defendant is a child or patient.

16.88   The application is by notice supported by written evidence. The notice must be sent to the defendant, but the evidence in support only if he acknowledged service.

16.89   Final judgment may be given for a set amount of money to be paid, normally within 14 days, CPR r 12.5. This is a good outcome for the claimant, but is only available where the claim is for a specified or liquidated sum of money, so there is merit in specifying a figure in the particulars of claim if possible.

16.90   Alternatively judgment may be given for damages to be decided by the court, which means that liability is no longer in issue but questions of damages or value remain to be decided. This may be an inevitable outcome, for example in a personal injuries claim. If damages remain to be decided the court may list the matter for a disposal hearing. Evidence may be required at the hearing, and if so it should be served on the defendant at least three days in advance. At the hearing the defendant can raise any point that is not inconsistent with the judgment given, *Pugh v Cantor Fitzgerald International* (2001) CPLR 271. Alternatively the court may give directions which could include allocation to a case management track, CPR r 12.7 (relevant to the giving of directions and costs).

16.91   A default judgment is not available if a defendant has applied for the statement of case to be struck out or for summary judgment, or if the defendant has satisfied the claim, or admitted the claim and asked for time to pay, CPR r 12.3. Some types of proceedings are excluded from this procedure and are summarised under PD 12, for example arbitration proceedings and claims for provisional damages.

16.92   As a judgment in default is obtained without a full consideration of the case, it can be set aside in a wide variety of circumstances, either on the court's own initiative or on an application from the defendant (which would often exhibit the defence that the defendant wishes to raise), CPR part 13. The judgment will be set aside as of right if essential procedural conditions have not been met, or if the defendant has in fact satisfied the claim or asked for time to pay. If a proper method of service has been used but the defendant did not in fact receive the particulars of claim then the court has a discretion to set aside the judgment rather than this being as of right, *Godwin v Swindon Borough Council* (2002) 1 WLR 997.

16.93   Alternatively the defendant will need to show the court that he has real prospects of successfully defending the claim, or there is some other good reason that he be allowed to defend, CPR r 13.3. Delay by the defendant and possible prejudice to the claimant are relevant, *Thorn plc v MacDonald* (1999) CPLR 660.

16.94   A claimant may need to seek to have the judgment set aside if it becomes clear it was not properly obtained because the particulars of claim were not properly served and the judgment therefore cannot be enforced, CPR r 13.5. If the judgment is set aside, there may be conditions such as the payment of money into court, and the defendant will normally need to pay costs thrown away.

Summary judgment

16.95   An application for summary judgment can be made to attack a weak case, see generally CPR Part 24 PD 24. Essentially the allegation is that the case is so weak on its facts that it has no real prospect of success, CPR r 24.2. A claimant may seek summary judgment on the basis that a defence is likely to fail, or a defendant may seek summary judgment on the basis that a claim is unlikely to succeed. Summary judgment can be given for part of a case, such as one cause of action where more than one is raised, as well as for the whole case. Summary judgment cannot be sought against the Crown, in residential possession proceedings, in libel actions where there is a significant issue of fact, or where there are allegations of dishonest or unlawful conduct.

The application can only be made once the defendant has served an acknowledgement of **16.96** service or a defence, unless the court gives its permission, CPR r 24.4. The application should normally be made promptly before costs in the action build up. It should normally be made before or when the applicant fills in the allocation questionnaire, PD 26 para 5.3. The notice period is 14 days rather than the normal three, CPR r 24.4. The respondent must file and serve any evidence in reply at least seven clear days before the hearing, CPR r 24.5, with any response from the applicant being served at least three clear days before the hearing. All parties must file evidence seven days in advance if the issue is considered on the initiative of the court. If the application is made after acknowledgment of service but before defence, it is not necessary for the defence to be served before the hearing, CPR r 24.4. If the claim is made before track allocation, the court will not allocate the claim before the hearing, PD 26 para 5.3. If a defendant applies for summary judgment against a claimant, the claimant will not be able to get default judgment until the summary judgment application has been dealt with, CPR r 12.3.

Evidence in support will have to state a belief that there is no defence with a reasonable **16.97** prospect of success, but it is probably best to set out why with references. The test for giving summary judgment is whether the case has a real prospect of success, having regard to the need to treat the case justly. This means realistic rather than fanciful, but not substantial, *Swain v Hillman* (2001) 1 All ER 91.

Summary judgment is unlikely to be granted if: **16.98**

- there are significant disputes about facts and/or evidence that need to be considered in full at trial;
- evidence is still being sought and considered;
- if there is a difficult question of law that requires serious argument, see *Home and Overseas Insurance Co Ltd v Mentor Insurance Co (UK) Ltd* (1990) 1 WLR 153, CA;
- the case in question is a personal injury case, *McCauley v Vine* (1999) 1 WLR 1977 CA, though it is not impossible, *Putty v Hopkinson* [1990] 1 All ER 1057;
- weaknesses in the case can be remedied by amending a statement of case, *Stewart v Engel* (2000) 1 WLR 2268.

Summary judgment may be granted if: **16.99**

- the defendant's evidence is not credible, is unreliable, inconsistent, or irrelevant, see *National Westminster Bank plc v Daniel* (1993) I WLR 1 CA;
- there is no real prospect of success, and if there is no other compelling reason for a case or issue to go to trial, CPR r 24.2.

The hearing will not be a trial, or even a mini trial, of the case itself. If the case needs full and **16.100** detailed argument then that of itself indicates that summary judgment is not appropriate.

The court will not generally go behind the evidence as presented—if there is a serious dispute the case will need to go for trial. If the respondent fails to attend the hearing a summary judgment order will almost certainly be made, though such a judgment might be set aside or varied if the respondent later gave good reason. If the respondent attends the hearing without having filed evidence there will probably be an adjournment with the respondent paying the costs.

16.101   The court can make a variety of orders. It may grant summary judgment on the claim as requested, it may dismiss the application, or it may make a conditional order. If it is possible but improbable that the claim will succeed a conditional order may be made, PD 24 paras 4 and 5.2, which might require a payment into court, or require a specified step in default of which the claim will be dismissed. If there is a set-off the claim will be dismissed up to that amount. An action for specific performance for payment of a cheque will normally be granted without a set-off as a cheque is regarded as the equivalent of cash, and the same applies to similar forms of payment such as a direct debit, *Esso Petroleum Co Ltd v Milton* (1997) 1 WLR 938 CA.

16.102   There are faster procedures for obtaining summary judgment for some claims arising out of mortgage and tenancy agreements, PD 24 para 7. There is also a special procedure for getting summary possession of land against trespassers, CPR r 55.

Dismissal for want of prosecution

16.103   The modern rules for case management mean that if a case is not being pursued properly, it is likely to be struck out as a result of a sanction following a failure to meet a time limit, to comply with some other order of the court. There are two bases on which a case may be dismissed because it is not being pursued properly.

Inordinate and inexcusable delay

16.104   The elements are that the delay must:

- be inordinate (materially longer than is normally professionally acceptable);
- be inexcusable (fault on the part of a lawyer is not a good excuse);
- lead to a substantial risk that it is not possible to have a fair trial, or have caused or be likely to cause serious prejudice to the defendant, *Birkett v James* (1978) AC 297 HL and *Department of Transport v Chris Smaller (Transport) Ltd* (1989) 1 ALL ER 897 HL.

16.105   The court is likely to impose a timetable of steps to be taken, and only dismiss the action if that is not complied with. A case will not generally be dismissed due to delay before the limitation period has expired, *Wright v Morris* (1997) FSR 218 CA, but it is possible, *Thorpe v Alexander Fork Lift Trucks Ltd* [1975] 1 WLR 1459. If the action is dismissed and the case cannot be pursued it may be possible for the party to sue his or her solicitor for negligence. The conduct of the defendant in causing the claimant to think the case is continuing will be relevant, *Roebuck v Mungovin* (1994) 2 AC 224.

Abuse of process

16.106   This might arise if, for example, a claimant continues a case with no intention of bringing it to trial, *Grovit v Doctor* (1997) 1 WLR 640 HL, if there is a wholesale disregard for the rules of court, or if there is a serious disregard such as destroying evidence, *Arbuthnot Latham Bank Ltd v Trafalgar Holdings Ltd* (1998) 1 WLR 1426.

G TIME STRATEGIES—GETTING SOME ISSUES DECIDED QUICKLY

Because of the time it can take for a case to come to trial, it may be very desirable to get some   **16.107**
of the issues in the case decided before the case comes to trial. Both the claimant and the
defendant may have concerns about specific issues that cannot easily wait until the final
determination of the trial. The court will be reluctant to decide some issues before the trial
because of the difficulty of separating out the evidence and argument on a single issue, and
because of the risk of prejudicing the other issues in the case. However, the court is prepared
to make orders to protect the position of the parties until the case is decided, and this is most
commonly done through interim injunctions.

Procedural options

In theory it is quite possible for the court to order the separate determination of an issue in a   **16.108**
case, but normally this power is only used to decide that one issue be decided at the start of a
case if that issue is of particular importance. Normally the court will prefer to support moving to an early trial of the action rather than deciding an issue early. In addition the court
will seek to protect the position of the parties pending trial. If the claimant has a significant
financial difficulty the court may be prepared to act on the probable outcome of the trial and
order an interim payment (see below). Where it is not possible to get a decision on an issue
before trial the remaining option is to negotiate with the other side to attempt to settle
the issue.

Interim injunctions

One of the most commonly used strategic tools is the injunction, see generally PD 25   **16.109**
Interim injunctions. In advising a client and taking instructions the lawyer may need to take
care to explain the potential advantages of an interim injunction but also matters like the
possible effect of an undertaking as to damages. The client will need to understand that if an
interim injunction is not found to have been justified at trial and the respondent has
suffered loss as a result of the injunction being granted, significant damages may be payable.

The types of injunction available

Various types of injunctions may be sought for various reasons, and it is important to   **16.110**
distinguish the types as the tests for getting them and their effects vary.

- An interim injunction may be sought in the course of litigation to prevent damage
  occurring before or continuing up to the hearing of the action. An interim injunction
  may be prohibitory, *quia timet*, or mandatory in nature.
- A perpetual injunction is a permanent injunction that may be granted at trial. It may be
  prohibitory or mandatory in nature.

- A prohibitory injunction is designed to stop the performance of specific acts. In broad terms it is not too difficult to get an injunction that prevents one party breaking another party's legal rights, though tests require a proper balance of the interests of the parties.
- A *quia timet* injunction is designed to prevent an anticipated wrong that has not yet occurred. Because the events have not yet happened, clear proof of the right that will be breached and the basis of the fear will be required. But a *quia timet* injunction can be sought if the applicant can show a well founded fear that he will suffer severe damage, the standard of proof being high. In *Redland Bricks v Morris* [1970] AC 652, excavations by the defendant led to a landslip and the plaintiff sought an injunction to prevent further excavation and to have his land shored up, but this was refused by the House of Lords because the proposed terms were too wide and the cost of complying would be high.
- A mandatory injunction essentially requires a specific thing to be done. It is more diffi-cult to get such an injunction as there are limited circumstances in which one party will have the right to force another party to do something. It is generally possible to achieve what is required by drafting the order as a prohibitory injunction.

16.111 It is crucial to realise that an injunction is a remedy—it is not a cause of action in itself, and it must be based on a cause of action, *Siskina v Distos Compania Naviera SA* (1979) AC 210 and *Mercedes-Benz AG v Leiduck* (1996) 1 AC 284. An injunction may be based on a public right as well as a private one, *Morris v Murjani* (1996) 2 All ER 384.

16.112 The High Court has a general discretion to make such orders where it appears to the court just and convenient to do so, and the orders may have such terms and conditions as the court thinks just, Supreme Court Act 1981, s 37. The County Court has similar powers, save with regard to search orders and freezing injunctions.

Tests for getting an injunction

16.113 To try to ensure success in seeking an injunction the lawyer should:

- identify the tests for the grant of the type of injunction sought;
- ensure that the evidence submitted in support of the application addresses those tests;
- ensure that the order sought is carefully drafted, so that it covers the situation causing concern and is likely to be accepted by the judge.

16.114 A leading case that laid down guidelines is *American Cyanamid Co v Ethicon Ltd* (1975) AC 396. The facts of the case illustrate how important and hotly fought an injunction application can be, with a dispute between two large companies about rights to make and market surgical sutures, and an application by the claimant to restrain the defendant's sales. In preparing arguments as to why an interlocutory injunction should be granted, the tests developed in Cyanamid case are as follows.

Is there a serious issue to be tried?

16.115 At an interim stage the court cannot start to consider evidence in detail and weigh up which party is likely to win on the balance of probabilities. The test is rather that the applicant has to show a serious issue to be tried, by showing that there is a cause of action to be tried, supported by at least some potentially credible evidence, *Dalgety Spillers Foods Ltd v Food Brokers Ltd* (1994) FSR 504. If there is a serious issue to be tried the court considers the next test. It seems that the overall strength of the case may be relevant if a case is clearly strong, *Series 5 Software Ltd v Clarke* (1996) 1 All ER 853.

Would damages be an adequate remedy for the applicant?

Essentially this is a practical point—if the applicant does not get an interim injunction but **16.116** were to win at trial, could money damages adequately compensate the claimant for loss up to trial? If the answer is yes then the court will leave the matter to the assessment of damages at trial. If the answer is no it suggests that the injunction should be granted. Damages will not be adequate if the damage being done is not of a financial nature, if quantum would be very difficult to assess, or if the respondent is unlikely to be able to pay.

Would damages be an adequate remedy for the respondent?

This is the opposite point—if the applicant gets an interim injunction but the respondent **16.117** succeeds in showing at that he is entitled to do what the injuncted activity, will damages be an adequate remedy for the loss the respondent has suffered in the meantime? If damages would be an adequate remedy for the parties there is no need to go further.

Does the balance of convenience favour granting the injunction?

If damages would not be an adequate remedy the court must consider the balance of **16.118** convenience, which can involve a wide variety of factors. For example:

- an injunction may not be granted if it could result in a serious loss of business and possible closure of factories for one side, but only hold up a new product for the other side, *American Cyanamid Co v Ethicon Ltd* (1975) AC 396;
- an injunction may be granted if the picketing of an office is destroying business whereas the other side could make their point in another way, *Hubbard v Pitt* (1976) QB 142 CA.

The status quo

If all other factors are equal, the court will tend to preserve the status quo. The status quo **16.119** is the situation that existed immediately before the issue of the claim form, though it may be the time just before the issue of the application for the injunction if there has been significant delay.

There are some exceptions to the use of the American Cyanamid test. **16.120**

- If there is a negative covenant an injunction to enforce it should normally be granted as of right, *A-G v Barker* (1990) 3 All ER 257 CA. This will apply to covenants in restraint of trade, provided they are reasonable and enforceable, *Faccenda Chicken v Fowler* (1986) 1 All ER 617.
- The facts of a case may involve an injunction finally deciding the case, because relevant events are due to take place soon. In such a case the court should only award an injunction if the applicant's case is very strong, see *Cayne v Global Natural Resources plc* (1984) 1 All ER 225 CA.
- Because of the right to freedom of speech, an injunction will not easily be granted to stop publication in a defamation case if the defendant intends to plead justification, *Bestobell Paints Ltd v Bigg* (1975) FSR 421. This approach is strengthened by the right to freedom of expression in Article 10 of the European Convention on Human Rights, and the court

will only restrain publication where the claimant is likely to succeed, *Cream Holdings Ltd v Banerjee* (2003) 2 All ER 318.

- Cases of breach of confidentiality and privacy require careful consideration, *Douglas v Hello! Ltd* (2001) QB 967 and *A v B plc* (2002) 3 WLR 542.
- There are special considerations in industrial disputes, *NWL Ltd v Woods* (1979) 1 WLR 1294 HL.

16.121 The court may not grant an interim injunction in certain circumstances.

- If there has been a delay in applying.
- If there has been an acceptance of the situation of which an injunction is now sought.
- If the injunction may not in practical terms be enforceable, as the court will not wish to act in vain.
- If the scope of the injunction sought is wide, see for example *Lansing Linde Ltd v Kerr* [1991] 1 All ER 418.

Procedure for getting an injunction

16.122 For an application in the County Court Form N16A should be used with evidence in support supplied. The documents required for a High Court application are:

- the claim form and existing statements of case;
- the application notice, on Form N244;
- a draft for the order being sought, in hard copy with a copy on disk for convenience in amending, see 18.130;
- copies of the supporting evidence—this will normally be given in a witness statement, but can come from the statement of case or the application notice where these contain a statement of truth;
- a skeleton argument will also normally be required unless the case is very straightforward.

16.123 If the application is without notice the same documents are required, but they will normally not have been served on the other party. If the application is urgent the claim form and application notice can be filed later.

16.124 The coverage of the evidence in support is important. It will need to cover:

- the facts giving rise to the cause of action (normally in the statements of case);
- what sort of injunction is sought;
- facts showing the basis for the injunction (if for example there is a negative covenant);
- why it is sought;
- facts relevant to the balance of convenience, the adequacy of damages, and the status quo;
- why the application is so urgent it is made without notice and efforts made to contact the respondent and any responses from the respondent (if relevant);
- any facts known which do not favour the applicant's case (if the respondent is not present).

16.125 The hearing of an application for an interim injunction may be relatively short, but advocacy may need to be quite sophisticated to take the court through the relevant tests and how they apply to the case.

The form of the injunction order

There are five prescribed forms for injunctions for use in the High Court by Practice Direction **16.126** (1996) 1 WLR 1551. The prescribed form for the County Court is N16, or form N117 for an undertaking. There are not yet standard prescribed forms under the CPR, but the five forms provided by the Practice Direction are: Order for Injunction; Order for an Injunction before the issue of a Claim Form; Order Containing Undertaking instead of an Injunction; Adjournment of Application for an Injunction; and Application for an Injunction Treated as Trial of the Action. It is the first of these that will normally be used.

The draft of the order being sought should be prepared with care. **16.127**

- It is important to ensure that it is wide enough and specific enough to meet the client's needs as closely as possible, though it cannot go beyond the applicant's legal rights.
- It must be clear what the respondent should or should not do (which can be checked by reading it from the respondent's point of view).
- It is necessary to include undertakings as to damages that must be given.
- It may be necessary to undertake to serve and if necessary to file documents where this has not yet happened.
- It should contain appropriate provision for costs.
- If necessary, notice of the respondent's right to apply to set the order aside.

The judge will not necessarily make the order in the terms drafted, but it will form a basis for **16.128** discussion at court

The order will normally contain undertakings as to damages. If an injunction is granted at an **16.129** interim stage but found not to have been justified at trial, the party that got the injunction will normally be ordered to compensate the party against whom the injunction was awarded. If appropriate, security for the undertaking may be required. However, in the interests of justice, a poor applicant will not be refused an injunction purely because an undertaking as to damages could not be met, *Allen v Jambo Holdings Ltd* (1980) 1 WLR 1252 CA. The need to give an undertaking as to damages can be a serious drawback and may discourage an applicant from seeking an injunction, which may in turn cause complaints from a party not able to benefit from an undertaking as to damages, *Blue Town Investments Ltd v Higgs & Hill plc* [1990] 2 All ER 89 and *Oxy Electric Ltd v Zainuddin* (1991) 1 WLR 115.

An order requiring a positive action must set out clearly what is to be done, the date by **16.130** which it must be done, and the consequences of failure to comply, PD 40B para 8.

As an alternative to an injunction being granted, a respondent may agree to give an under- **16.131** taking in similar terms to the applicant. This can often arise in negotiations outside court, and it saves the time and cost of a hearing. It can also avoid the need for undertakings as to damages if it is vital to record such an undertaking in an enforceable way—normally by having the undertaking given to the judge so that any breach can be dealt with as contempt of court. Alternatively an undertaking may be part of a consent order made by a judge. Undertakings that are only recorded in writing may be unenforceable or only enforceable through a breach of contract action.

An injunction may be discharged for a variety of reasons, such as material non-disclosure of **16.132** facts, a material change in circumstances, interference with the rights of third parties, or an oppressive effect of the order.

16.133   Breach of an injunction is contempt of court and can be punished as such, with imprisonment for up to two years or sequestration of assets. The injunction must be clearly worded and there must be a penal notice to make this clear, PD 40B para 9. A person giving an undertaking in lieu of an injunction must be required to sign a statement to the effect that he or she understands the terms of the undertaking and the consequences of failure to comply, PD 40B para 9.

Obtaining an interim injunction in an emergency or without notice

16.134   The procedure outlined at 16.109–16.133 should be followed if possible. However there are circumstances in which it may be desirable to depart from the normal procedure.

16.135   Firstly there may be a need to get an injunction quickly. In such a case it is possible to apply immediately, if necessary even before it has been possible to prepare and file the relevant documents. If documents are in draft any order made will contain undertakings that the claim form be issued, that the application notice be filed and served, and that the evidence in support be filed and served, as appropriate. The evidence in support should show why the urgency is such that the normal procedure cannot be followed.

16.136   Arrangements are in place for where an application needs to be made urgently. During the working day a court may clear time for an emergency hearing, for example immediately after lunch or at the end of the day. The solicitor should telephone the court staff so that arrangements can be made for this. During the hours when courts are not sitting an application for an injunction may be made by telephone, but only if the applicant is acting by solicitors or counsel, PD 25 para 4.2. If possible the first contact should still be with the court, PD 25 para 4.5. There are arrangements for contacting an appropriate judge through the High Court or the urgent court business officer of a circuit. A copy of the draft order sought should be faxed through if possible.

16.137   Secondly an application can be made without notice. Normally this will be because the application is urgent so that there is not time to give notice, though it may be because the purpose of the injunction will be undermined if proper notice is given, because for example there is a real risk that the defendant will dispose of or destroy an asset, or otherwise prejudice the position of the applicant if he has notice. Applications should only be made without notice where it is truly impossible to give notice, and informal notice is better than none at all, *Bates v Lord Hailsham of St Marylebone* (1972) 1 WLR 137.

16.138   Again the evidence in support will need to show justification for not giving notice, and any order granted will require copies of the relevant papers to be served on the respondent. An injunction granted without notice will normally only last a few days, until there can be a hearing with both parties present to decide whether the injunction should be continued. The injunction may also give the respondent leave to apply to have the injunction set aside before that hearing.

16.139   If the need for quick action and the failure to give notice are not found to be justified then the application will fail and the applicant will be likely to have to pay the costs of the failed application.

H   PEOPLE STRATEGIES

Both the claimant and the defendant will want to ensure that appropriate people become   **16.140**
involved in the action. People need to be involved as parties if they are to be bound by the
outcome of the case, if linked disputes are to be settled as far as possible, and to get the best
potential range of people against whom damages and other remedies can be ordered. People
may need to be involved as witnesses to get full information about the case.

Involving people as parties

The basic model for litigation involves a claimant and a defendant. The selection of claim-   **16.141**
ants and defendants is dealt with at 13.09–13.57. Sometimes it will be necessary to have
more parties to the action so that the court can consider all matters relating to a set of facts at
the same time to save costs and to ensure that everyone will be bound by the outcome. The
joining of further parties through Part 20 proceedings is dealt with at 13.63–13.87.

In adding additional parties it is necessary to balance the convenience and costs savings   **16.142**
involved in deciding cases together with the potential complexity and the problems
involved in defining issues if too many people are parties to the same action. An alternative may be to start a second action and to ask the court that they be heard together. There
may be tactical considerations in deciding who should be added as a party to an action,
perhaps relating to their ability to pay damages. Parties should not be joined for collateral
purposes such as seeking evidence from them if there is not a proper cause of action
against them.

Involving people as witnesses

It may be important to involve someone in a case because of their knowledge of events or   **16.143**
their expertise. If the person is not a party it may be possible to call them as a witness, which
is covered at 15.17–15.22, 15.109–15.139, and 21.49–21.54. Alternatively it may be possible
to make an application simply designed to get the required information. This is dealt with in
the next section.

I   INFORMATION STRATEGIES

Both parties will wish to get the fullest possible range of information to support their own   **16.144**
case and to undermine their opponent's case. Each party will collect their own information
and evidence as outlined at 8.39–8.45 and 15.48–15.67.

Information held by the other side will normally be made available: **16.145**

- voluntarily;
- under a pre-action protocol, see 4.25–4.27;
- documents will be made available through the disclosure and inspection process, see
  15.179–15.200;

- copies of witness statements will be exchanged as part of the case management process, see 15.201–15.204.

Where information is required but is not revealed through these processes, various applications may be made. It is important to get full information about a case to weigh its strength, even if the case may be settled rather than going to court.

Requests for further information

16.146   Witness statements and other documents may give rise to some questions that are best settled before trial. This can be dealt with under CPR r 18.1, as the procedure for seeking further information can be used to seek clarification of any matter in dispute, or to seek information about such a matter, whether or not it is contained in or referred to in a statement of case.

16.147   The first stage is for the applicant to make a written request setting out what clarification or information is requested, and the date by which a response is reasonably expected. The request should be clear and concise, proportionate, and should enable the applicant to understand the case to be met or to prepare his own case. This request may be by letter or by a formal document. If there is not a response there can be an application to court for an order. Requests must be relevant rather than 'fishing' and must not be oppressive. They must go to issues rather than the credibility of witnesses. The questions should be necessary for disposing fairly of the claim, and should be related to saving costs. Further information may be sought from a body or company in the same way as an individual, and the person answering should make all reasonable inquiries within the company to answer the questions, and should put a statement in the affidavit that this has been done, *Stanfield Properties v National Westminster Bank* [1983] 2 All ER 244.

Search orders

16.148   In an exceptional case the normal exchange of information, even if supplemented by court orders may not be sufficient. If a defendant may simply remove or destroy relevant information then quite radical steps may be needed. In the case of *Anton Piller KG v Manufacturing Processes* [1976] Ch 55 CA, the claimants received information from two employees of the defendants, who were their UK agents, that the defendants were secretly negotiating to supply confidential information to a competitor that could severely undermine the claimants' market. In these circumstances it was likely that the defendants would remove or destroy incriminating evidence if they became aware of the claim, so an application was made without notice for a search order. It was held that in such a case there could be an order for the claimant to enter the defendant's premises to inspect and copy documents. The situation is now covered by the Civil Procedure Act 1997, s 7. Essentially an order can provide for the defendant to allow access to his premises to search for, inspect, photograph, or photocopy listed documents and items.

16.149   Search orders have especially been used in cases of breach of copyright or the 'pirating' of music or video films. For example, in *Universal City Studios Inc v Mukhtar & Sons* [1976] 2 All ER 330 the claimant had the copyright for merchandise connected with the 'Jaws' film, but the defendant produced unlicensed 'Jaws' T-shirts. The order granted required the defendants to hand over all the T-shirts they had, including some that did not belong to them, though the rights of the other owners were protected. The order may also be used to protect evidence that may be destroyed, *Yousif v Salama* [1980] 3 All ER 405.

A search order cannot be used by the claimant as a 'fishing trip' to see what can be found— **16.150** the application and the order made must be specific.

The requirements for getting a search order

The requirements for the grant of an order are: **16.151**

- the applicant must show an extremely strong *prima facie* case on the merits;
- the defendant's activities must cause very serious actual or potential harm to the claimant's interests;
- there must be clear evidence that incriminating documents or things are in the defendant's possession;
- there must be a real possibility that the incriminating material may be destroyed before an application on notice can be made.

These will be applied strictly because of the potentially serious effect on the respondent's **16.152** business if an order is made, and the general implication that the respondent is dishonest, *Columbia Picture Industries v Robinson* [1986] FSR 367. Orders will not be made if the strict tests are not met, *Lock International plc v Bewick* (1989) 1 WLR 1268.

The procedure for getting a search order

A search order should be sought in the High Court before a judge. Application is by appli- **16.153** cation notice, though without notice, often once the claim form has been issued but not served. There must be a potential cause of action to found the claim. A draft order and a skeleton argument should be provided if there is time. Evidence in support should be by affidavit. As the application is without notice there is a duty of disclosure, which is particularly strong with such a draconian order. The claimant's lawyers must be sure of their facts, and prepare a strong and clear case.

The form of a search order

The form for the order is set out in PD 25 Interim Injunctions, and it should be followed **16.154** unless the judge considers there is good reason for some amendment.

The order will provide that the defendant must permit the supervising solicitor and the **16.155** claimant's solicitor with a limited number of other persons to enter his premises. Force may not be used to gain entry. The order will order the defendant to facilitate as appropriate, for example printing out documents held on computer and opening locked drawers. There may be ancillary orders if appropriate, for example requiring the defendant to bring documents or articles from other addresses, to swear an affidavit verifying that all relevant documents have been delivered to the claimant, prohibiting the defendant from warning others, or to disclose names and addresses of other people involved. The order must be drawn carefully as the executing team will be bound by it. Execution of the order needs to be planned with care.

The order must be strictly drawn to cover only those documents or articles that might be destroyed or concealed, *Columbia Picture Industries Inc v Robinson* (1987) Ch 38.

16.156 The claimant will have to provide a number of undertakings including:

- issuing and serving processes and evidence;
- serving the order by a solicitor, together with copies of the affidavits and exhibits and notice of a hearing within a few days;
- serving the defendant with a written report on the execution of the order prepared by the solicitor, which will be seen by the court on the return day;
- abiding by an order as to damages;
- not telling any third parties about the order until the return day;
- not using items seized for any purposes other than the claim unless the court gives permission, *Crest Homes plc v Marks* (1987) AC 829 HL;
- insuring items taken;
- the claimant may have to give an undertaking to reimburse the defendant for any loss suffered if the order is made.

16.157 The claimant's solicitors will also have to give undertakings including;

- keeping all items seized in safe custody;
- delivering the originals of documents to the defendant or the defendant's solicitor within two days (save for documents belonging to the applicant).

16.158 The respondent is protected in various ways including the following.

- The order must be served and the search supervised by a solicitor who is not a member of the firm acting for the applicant. This must be a person with appropriate experience of supervising such orders.
- The order can only be served on weekdays in normal working hours (so the respondent has an opportunity to contact a lawyer).
- The effect of the order must be explained by the supervising solicitor in ordinary language, and the defendant must be advised that he can seek legal advice before complying with the order provided this is done at once.
- The order must only be executed in the presence of a responsible representative of the respondent.
- The number of people used must be limited.
- Unless it is impracticable a list of items removed must be prepared on the spot and the defendant allowed to check the list.

16.159 The defendant may be protected by a privilege against self-incrimination, *Tate Access Floors Inc v Boswell* (1991) Ch 512, save that there are exceptions from protection in intellectual property and passing off cases, Supreme Court Act 1981, s 72, and for prosecutions for substantive crimes under the Theft Act 1968, s 31. It may be possible to ensure that material will not be used for a criminal prosecution, *AT and T Istel Ltd v Tulley* (1993) AC 45 HL, or the defendant may choose not to claim privilege, *IBM United Kingdom Ltd v Prima Data International Ltd* (1994) 4 All ER 748.

Following the grant of a search order

The defendant has two hours to get legal advice, but the supervising solicitor must be allowed in during this time, though the search will not start. The order will expressly provide for the defendant to apply for variation or discharge on short notice. **16.160**

The defendant can apply to vary or discharge with evidence in support by affidavit. This may be done if a basic condition of the order is not satisfied or for material non-disclosure. An order can be discharged even if it has been executed if there is good cause. The order may be varied if it is too wide. **16.161**

The defendant may take the course of refusing to comply with the order and may apply to set it aside, but if the period of the resulting delay is used to destroy relevant material, the court will take a very grave view, *WEA Records Ltd v Visions Channel 4 Ltd* [1983] 2 All ER 589. If the defendant fails to comply they can be subject to proceedings for contempt of court. The refusal could also be used as evidence against them at a subsequent trial. **16.162**

If the order is executed in an excessive or oppressive manner the claimant will be liable under the undertaking as to damages, *Columbia Picture Industries Inc v Robinson* (1987) Ch 38. The claimant must press on with the proceedings without delay and not use the search order as an end in itself. **16.163**

Production of documents by non-parties

Someone who is not likely to become a party to the action may have information that is very important in determining the strength of the case. If this were left to be dealt with by a witness summons the document might not be obtained until trial. The court has a power to order a non-party to produce documents before trial under Supreme Court Act 1981, s 34 and under the County Courts Act 1984, s 53. **16.164**

An order can only be made if the following conditions are fulfilled, CPR r 31.17. **16.165**

- The documents for which disclosure is sought must be likely to support the case of the applicant, or adversely affect the case of one of the other parties to the proceedings. This means something directly relevant to the issues in the case rather than simply a document that might be available on normal disclosure, see *Three Rivers District Council v Governor and Company of the Bank of England (No 4)* (2003) 1 WLR 210. The documents sought should be specifically identified, *Re Howglen Ltd* (2001) 1 ALL ER 376.
- Disclosure must be necessary in order to dispose fairly of the case or to save costs.

An application can be made at any time after the claim form has been issued. It is by application notice supported by written evidence, CPR r 31.17. The order must specify the documents to be disclosed, and may require the respondent to say what has happened to documents he no longer has. **16.166**

Inspection of property

Property that is relevant to an action may be in the possession of one party. The other party may need access to inspect it, or for an expert to inspect it to complete a report. Orders for **16.167** the inspection, detention, custody, or preservation of relevant property, or for the taking of samples or the carrying out of experiments can be made under CPR r 25.1. Orders can be made on allocation or at a case management conference, or as a result of a separate application. The rule is focussed on physical objects, but the court probably has an inherent jurisdiction to order that access be allowed to make a video if appropriate.

16.168 If the relevant property is in the possession of a non-party an order can be made under the Supreme Court Act 1981, s 34 and the County Courts Act 1984, s 53. It is sought by issuing an application notice supported by evidence, CPR r 25.5. Copies of the application must be served on the person against whom the order is sought and other parties to the action.

16.169 If there is a risk that property may be disposed of then detention and/or preservation orders may be made under the above powers. Alternatively the court can make an order for the delivery up of goods which are or may become the subject matter of an action for wrongful interference with goods, Torts (Interference with Goods) Act 1977, s 4. There must be some evidence that the defendant acquired the goods wrongfully, clear evidence that he is likely to dispose of them, and the order should not be oppressive to the defendant, *CBS UK Ltd v Lambert* (1983) Ch 37. The court order must be carefully worded as to who should take and then keep the goods. Application is by a normal application notice.

J   MONEY STRATEGIES

16.170 All parties involved in litigation are likely to have concerns about the financial aspects of the case. The claimant may have concerns that the defendant will be able to meet any order for damages and costs, or may have concerns about having to wait until after trial for the recovery of money or another remedy. The defendant may have concerns as to whether the claimant will be able to pay his or her costs if the defendant wins.

16.171 Both parties are likely to have concerns about costs. On the one hand both are likely to be prepared to build up costs to ensure that the case is won, and in the knowledge that if the case is won the other side is likely to be ordered to pay the costs. On the other hand each party will be concerned about costs they may have to bear at the end of the day. This area is covered at 5.45–5.61.

Security for costs

16.172 A claimant may bring a claim which is arguable, but which he has a limited chance of winning. If the case is lost then the claimant will probably be ordered to pay the defendant's costs, but this is of limited value if the claimant may not have sufficient resources to pay the costs bill. In such circumstances the defendant may seek security for costs, which should normally be done at an early stage in the proceedings. If an order is granted the action will be stayed until the claimant provides a fund out of which the costs may be met. Orders can also be granted against defendants where there is a counterclaim or a Part 20 claim. It is also possible for an order to be made against a non-party if that person has assigned a claim to avoid costs or is contributing to the claimant's costs with a view to recovering something in the action. See generally CPR Part 25 Interim remedies and security for costs.

The mere impecuniosity of the claimant is not sufficient or poor people would be unable to   **16.173**
sue. Impeding access to justice could be contrary to Article 6(1) of the European Convention
on Human Rights, see *Nasser v United Bank of Kuwait* (2002) 1 WLR 1868. The conditions on
which security may be granted are set out in CPR r 25.13:

- The claimant is resident outside the jurisdiction and essentially outside the area where
  service without permission is possible.
- The claimant is a company or other body and there is reason to believe that it will be
  unable to pay the defendant's costs if ordered to do so.
- The claimant failed to give his address on the claim form, gave an incorrect address, or
  has changed his address with a view to avoiding the consequences of litigation.
- The claimant is acting as a nominal claimant, and there is reason to believe that he or she
  will be unable to pay costs if ordered to do so.
- The claimant has taken steps with regard to his or her assets that would make it difficult
  to enforce an order for costs.

If, but only if, one of these conditions is met, the court will consider all the consequences of   **16.174**
the case and in particular the overriding objective. In practical terms the most important
factors are likely to be the merits of the claim, the likely problems enforcing a costs order,
and the impact on the claimant of having to give security. The amount of the order is a
matter for the discretion of the court.

Freezing orders

A claimant may have a strong case against a defendant but be concerned that there is a   **16.175**
serious risk that the defendant will dispose of assets before trial, making it difficult or impossible for the claimant to enforce judgment. A freezing order is a form of interlocutory injunction that can prevent justice being undermined in this way by restraining the defendant
from removing assets from the jurisdiction of the High Court or otherwise dealing with
assets within that jurisdiction, Supreme Court Act 1981, s 37. It is not the purpose of the
order to give priority over other creditors or to put on pressure for a settlement.

The requirements for a freezing order

The requirements for the grant of an order come primarily from the case of *Mareva Compania*   **16.176**
Naviera SA v International Bulk Carriers SA [1980] 1 All ER 213 and are as follows.

- A cause of action justiciable in England and Wales, including where the defendant can be
  served here, *Siskina v Distos Compania Naviera SA* (1979) AC 210 HL. The presence, residence or domicile of the defendant is of itself not relevant, see *Prince Abdul Rahman bin
  Turki al Sudairy v Abu-Taha* [1980] 3 All ER 409.
- A good arguable case must be shown on the available evidence, and not a possible future
  case, *Zucker v Tyndall Holdings plc* (1993) 1 All ER 124 CA.
- The defendant has assets within the jurisdiction. This can include any type of asset, but
  the defendant must hold the asset in the same capacity in which he is being sued, *CBS UK
  Ltd v Lambert* (1983) Ch 37. An asset that is jointly owned can be frozen as regards the
  defendant's share, *SCF Finance Co Ltd v Masri* (1985) 1 WLR 876, and the court will look
  beyond technicalities in related companies, *TSB Private Bank International SA v Chabra*

(1992) 1 WLR 231. In an exceptional case where there are insufficient assets within the jurisdiction the court may grant an order covering assets outside the jurisdiction, *Derby v Weldon (No 2)* (1989) 1 All ER 1002 CA.

- There is a real risk that the defendant may dispose of or dissipate those assets before judgment can be enforced. An order cannot be granted merely because there are assets here, or the respondent could be severely prejudiced while the trial was still some way off. This is quite a practical point and a freezing order is less likely if the respondent is well established within the jurisdiction, or there are arrangements for reciprocal enforcement of judgments where the defendant is. The court will be slow to hold up normal business, *Customs & Excise Commissioners v Anchor Foods Ltd* (1999) 1 WLR 1139, and will look at the relative value of assets, *Rasu Maritima SA v Perusahaan Pertambangan Minyak Dan Gas Bumi Negara* (1978) QB 644 CA.

The procedure for getting a freezing order

16.177 Applications for freezing orders are made without notice or their purpose would be defeated, and an application can be made from before the start of proceedings to after judgment. The notice must set out the nature of the order sought, and there should be a draft of the order sought with a disk. There is a standard form for a freezing order, Annex to PD 25, and this should be followed save where the judge considers there is good reason to depart. Clauses cover assets within the jurisdiction and worldwide and inappropriate clauses should be deleted. A skeleton argument should be submitted if there is time.

16.178 Evidence in support must be in the form of an affidavit, and as the application is without notice there is a duty of full and frank disclosure, PD 25 Interim Injunctions para 3.1. Sanctions may be imposed if there is not full and frank disclosure, *Memory Corporation v Sidhu (No 2)* (2000) 1 WLR 1443 CA. Material facts must be in the affidavit and not other evidence.

16.179 An order cannot exceed the amount of the claimant's claim including costs. The order must make provision for the respondent's normal living expenses, *PCW (Underwriting Agencies) Ltd v Dixon* (1983) 2 All ER 697 CA, and normal trading should be allowed to continue, *Iraqi Ministry of Defence v Arcepy Shipping Co SA* (1981) QB 65. Payments that would undermine the purpose of the order do not need to be allowed, *Atlas Maritime Co SA v Avalon Maritime Ltd* [1991] 4 All ER 769. The order will bind third parties who have notice of it and freeze bank accounts. The order granted will last to a return date a few days later at which the defendant can argue for the discharge of the order. The claimant is expected to give undertakings as to damages, to serve the application and supporting evidence, to inform third parties of their rights, and to indemnify them for any expenses (for example a bank's expenses in freezing a bank account). An impecunious claimant can still get an order, *Allen v Jambo Holdings Ltd* (1980) 1 WLR 1252 CA. The order can make provision for disclosure of documents that enable the applicant to ascertain where assets are. The terms of the order can take the interests of a third party into account, *Arab Monetary Fund v Hashim* [1991] 1 All ER 871.

16.180 The respondent can apply to discharge the freezing order on various grounds including:

- that the claimant does not have a good arguable case when further evidence submitted by the respondent is taken into account;
- that the respondent provides alternative security;

- if there is a material non-disclosure. It will be relevant how grave the breach is and whether it is innocent or deliberate, see *Behbehani v Salem* [1989] 2 All ER 143. The court will try to take a balanced view, *Brink's Mat Ltd v Elcombe* (1988) 1 WLR 1350, and will do its best to do justice, possibly granting a more restricted order.

The claimant must press on to trial within a reasonable time or the injunction will be discharged, *Lloyds Bowmaker Ltd v Brittania Arrow Holdings plc* [1988] 3 All ER 178. The freezing order cannot be used to stop the defendant personally leaving the country—there can be no arrest in connection with a civil action. **16.181**

There may be a problem in the enforcement of freezing injunctions in that it seems that a bank may only be bound once it has assumed responsibility for complying with an order, *Customs and Excise Commissioners v Barclays Bank plc* (2004) 1 WLR 2027. **16.182**

Interim payments

Litigation may take a long time. A party who anticipates success may be very concerned about having to wait a long time for damages, especially if that party is in financial difficulties. The court will be slow to anticipate the outcome of the case and order payment of any damages before trial because of the risks of pre-judging the action, and the significant difficulties that will ensue if a party had any damages paid on account and then did not win at trial. In many cases there is therefore no remedy and a party may have to make financial arrangements to cover the difficulty, move to trial as quickly as possible, or negotiate a settlement. **16.183**

However there could be particular unfairness, for example for a personal injury victim, who may be unable to work and who may need expensive special care. It is therefore sometimes possible to seek an interim payment to get part of anticipated damages paid on account, though only in a case where the claimant is likely to win and the defendant is able to pay. See generally PD 25B Interim payments. **16.184**

The conditions for the award of an interim payment are in CPR r 25.7: **16.185**

- the defendant against who it is sought has admitted liability to pay damages or some other sum;
- the claimant has obtained judgment against the defendant for damages or some other sum to be assessed;
- the court is satisfied that if the case went to trial the claimant would obtain judgment for a substantial amount against the defendant (taking into account any defence the defendant has); or
- the claimant is seeking an order for possession of land and the court is satisfied that if the case went to court the defendant would be held liable to pay the claimant a sum of money for occupation and use of the land.

In a personal injury case an interim payment can only be made if the defendant is insured in respect of the claim, or the defendant's liability will be met through motor insurance or the Motor Insurers Bureau (MIB), or the defendant is a public body. If there is more than one defendant, the test must be satisfied for any specific defendant from whom an interim payment is sought. **16.186**

16.187   The application notice must be served at least 14 clear days before the hearing. Evidence in support will need to be reasonably detailed, including the facts that show a claim can be made under CPR r 25.7, the likely amount of damages, the amount sought, and what it will be used for. A PI claim will also need details of special damages and past and future loss (and will need to get a certificate of recoverable benefits under the Social Security (Recovery of Benefits) Act 1997). The respondent can file evidence in reply at least seven clear days before the hearing, and the applicant can file evidence in response at least three days before the hearing.

16.188   The test for making an order is that the court is satisfied that the defendant would be held liable if the claim went to trial. This is decided on the balance of probabilities but a high standard within that range, *Shearson Lehman Bros Inc v Maclaine Watson & Co Ltd* (1987) 1 WLR 480 CA.

16.189   In considering the amount of an order, the court will not want to risk exceeding the damages likely to be awarded at the end of the case or it might be very difficult to recover money from the claimant. The point is simply to allow the claimant some money while awaiting final judgment, so a 'reasonable proportion' will be awarded. Because this needs to relate to the figure that will actually be awarded, contributory negligence, set-offs, and counterclaims will be taken into account, *Shanning International Ltd v George Wimpey International Ltd* (1989) 1 WLR 981, CA. It is not necessary to show that the claimant needs the money, but it is not irrelevant to tell the court what the money will be used for, *Stringman v McArdle* (1994) 1 WLR 1653. The payment will not be disclosed until the end of the trial as it is not relevant to liability.

K   COSTS ORDERS FOR INTERIM APPLICATIONS

16.190   Some preliminary or interim applications are virtually free standing and it may well be fairest to make a decision as to who should pay for the application straight away. This is particularly the case where the fault of one party has necessitated the application, or where it is easier to take a decision while the facts and circumstances of the application are fresh in the mind. It is also best to avoid saving up too many separate orders for costs to be put together after trial, which may be months or even years later. The costs of interim hearings lasting less than a day are therefore likely to be decided by an immediate summary assessment, save where one of the parties is publicly funded or is under a disability.

16.191   To enable this to take place the parties are required to file with the court and to serve statements of their costs not less than 24 hours before the hearing. It is important to ensure that this statement is reasonably accurate or an expense that might be recoverable as costs may not be recoverable. The orders that can be made and the relevant considerations are dealt with in Chapter 5.

KEY DOCUMENTS

The Civil Procedure Rules 1998

Court guides

Queen's Bench Guide
Chancery Guide
Admiralty and Commercial Courts Guide
Mercantile Courts Guide
Patents Court Guide
Technology and Construction Court Guide

Court forms

The following forms are most relevant to interim applications:

N244 Application notice
N16A General form of application for an injunction
N 117 General form of undertaking
N 266 Notice to admit facts
N 268 Notice to prove documents at trial
N 285 General form of Affidavit
Freezing order Annex to PD 25 (combined worldwide and domestic)
Search order Standard form PD 25 Interim Injunctions

All these are easily available in hard copy and electronically, see Chapter 24.

Pro-formas for interim injunction orders Practice Direction (1996) 1 WLR 1551

Order for Injunction
Order for injunction before the issue of a Claim Form
Order containing an undertaking instead of an injunction
Adjournment of application for an injunction
Application for an injunction treated as trial of the action

17

DEFENDING AN ACTION

A INTRODUCTION 17.01

B THE DEFENCE MINDSET 17.06

C DEALING WITH A DIFFICULT CLAIMANT 17.10
The legally represented claimant 17.11
The litigant in person 17.13

D BEFORE A CASE STARTS 17.16
Notification of a potential action 17.16
Steps to be taken 17.18

E WHEN A CASE STARTS 17.25

F STRATEGY AND TACTICS IN PROGRESSING A CASE 17.28
Cutting short the action 17.30
Clarifying the claim being made 17.31
Protecting the financial position of the defendant 17.32
Passing or sharing the blame 17.37
Making a claim against the claimant 17.41
Using procedural rules 17.43

G THE MAIN TYPES OF DEFENCE TO AN ACTION 17.44
Procedural defences 17.45
Defences to a cause of action 17.46
Defences to a claim for damages 17.47

H RULES FOR DRAFTING A DEFENCE 17.48
The rules for drafting the defence 17.48
Separating out allegations 17.50
Admitting an allegation 17.54
Putting the claimant to proof 17.57
Denying an allegation 17.60
Adding information 17.67
The statement of truth 17.69

I PRINCIPLES FOR DRAFTING A DEFENCE 17.70
Options for the structure of a defence 17.72
Dealing with a poorly drafted particulars of claim 17.76

J DRAFTING A DEFENCE 17.78
Preparing to draft a defence 17.78
Detailed drafting 17.81

K MAKING A COUNTERCLAIM 17.86

L CLAIMING A SET-OFF 17.93

M GENERAL FRAMEWORK FOR A DEFENCE AND
COUNTERCLAIM 17.101

KEY DOCUMENTS

> In case of dissention, never dare to judge till you have heard the other side.
>
> Euripides

A   INTRODUCTION

17.01 Over recent years, an increasing number of books and articles have addressed legal skills, but there is still limited material on how defence lawyers can approach litigation in a coherent and strong way.

17.02 This might be justified in that many rules of procedure and evidence apply equally to all parties in litigation, with relatively few rules that apply wholly or primarily to a defendant. Where there are disputes of law or fact, both sides will have responsibilities for developing arguments and collecting evidence, albeit that primary responsibility lies with the claimant to prove the case on the balance of probabilities. It can also be said that where there is a counterclaim in an action, both parties have the roles of claimant and defendant to some extent.

17.03 There is an extent to which the role of a defendant could be said to be more straightforward than that of a claimant—the claimant has to take an active role in framing and initiating the action, whereas the defence can largely play a reactive role, fending off allegations. The burden of proving the case lies with the claimant, and if the claimant does not satisfy that burden the case will be lost.

17.04 While these points have some truth, the position of the defendant in an action can be rather more complex, and in effective litigation the defendant should normally play a proactive role. The role of the defendant can be particularly difficult if the claimant does not prepare his or her case well.

17.05 The Civil Procedure Rules 1998 encourage cooperation between parties, to replace tactics of non-cooperation that were used in the past. Cooperation is probably more widespread than it was some years ago, but research into the extent to which parties do cooperate, and the effect that has on the adversarial process, would be interesting.

B   THE DEFENCE MINDSET

The whole mindset for defending a claim is rather different from that used to pursue a claim. **17.06**
The claimant is normally motivated by quite a strong desire to achieve compensation and/or
right a wrong. There will tend to be a positive motivation in putting the case together and in
seeking remedies. The claimant will decide on the cause(s) of action. A number of decisions
in progressing the case are made by the claimant. A claimant may be open to building up
reasonable costs to achieve justice, not least because on winning the claimant anticipates
that the defendant will be ordered to pay most of the costs.

In contrast the defendant is normally in a predominantly defensive position. **17.07**

- The defendant will normally have the defensive mindset of resisting the claim and the
  remedies sought, either entirely or in part.
- In any event the defendant will want to restrict the remedies claimed as far as possible,
  and may be very worried about the potential effect of having to meet a judgment.
- The defendant has less control over the commencing of the action, though the Civil
  Procedure Rules 1998 provide for a clearer role for the defendant prior to an action where
  there is a pre-action protocol.
- The defendant may have less control over the conduct of litigation, though the Civil
  Procedure Rules 1998 have made the position of the parties more equal, and the 'cards
  on the table' approach should ensure that the defendant has sufficient information to
  prepare a defence.
- The defendant may be particularly resentful or concerned about the accumulation of
  costs.
- A defendant may be resentful or even angry that a case has been brought at all.
- A defendant may feel defensive in providing information, possibly being somewhat
  economical with the truth or even motivated to lie to the lawyer to avoid the claim.

The overall approach taken by the defendant to the case might be anywhere on a wide **17.08**
scale:

- The defendant may deny any involvement at all in a case. For example there may be an
  allegation that the defendant caused a car accident, and the defendant may respond that
  the accident was nothing to do with him.
- The defendant may accept some limited involvement in the facts giving rise to the case,
  but may deny liability for the accident.
- The defendant may allege an entirely different scenario from the claimant. For example
  the claimant may allege an accident was caused entirely because of directions given
  by the defendant, whereas the defendant may claim that accident was caused by the
  claimant ignoring instructions. In a contract case, there may be one oral agreement
  alleged by the claimant and a totally different one alleged by the defendant.
- The defendant may accept many of the allegations made by the claimant, but may allege
  that they should be seen in a very different way, for example arguing that contributory
  negligence played a significant part in the case, or that liability is avoided by an exclusion
  clause.
- The defendant may accept much of the case in its entirety, but deny a particular part of

the case. This may be an important part of the case, for example denying the causation of the alleged losses.

Each of these has different implications for drafting a statement of claim, for the issues in the case, and for the evidence required and the procedural steps to be taken.

17.09　A case initiated by a claimant may take a very different course depending on the basic reaction of the defendant. It is possible that the whole outcome of the case may depend on the approach taken by the defendant as much as on the basic facts of the case.

C　DEALING WITH A DIFFICULT CLAIMANT

17.10　It is of the essence of the litigation process that it be conducted in a reasonable way. It is entirely acceptable that full use be made of procedural options, and that tactics and strategy be used by both parties, but the litigation process is undermined and cannot work effectively if one side behaves in a wholly unreasonable fashion.

The legally represented claimant

17.11　There should not be fundamental problems where both sides are legally represented, due to the professional duties of the lawyers and their duty to the court. The lawyers should fully understand the litigation process and make proper use of it.

17.12　A difficulty with the way in which a legally represented claimant is conducting a case can be addressed through the use of applications to court, see Chapter 16, through sanctions, see 16.50–16.62, or is necessary through a wasted costs order, see 5.80–5.88.

The litigant in person

17.13　The litigant in person can provide a variety of difficulties. A claimant may choose to conduct litigation personally for reasons of cost. There is a right for a litigant to conduct litigation personally, and the court and the lawyer representing the other side should seek to make appropriate allowances and provide reasonable support. There are nonetheless likely to be problems because the litigant will not fully understand the litigation process.

17.14　Where a claimant seriously misuses the litigation process he or she may be classified as a 'vexatious litigant' under Supreme Court Act 1981, s 42. The test is that the applicant has habitually and persistently and without reasonable cause instituted vexatious proceedings or applications. The court can make a civil proceedings order which prevents the person from continuing or commencing a civil claim without the permission of the High Court. An application for such an order must be made by the Attorney-General. All such orders are listed on the Court Service's website at www.courtservice.gov.uk. Such orders do not breach Article 6.

17.15　In addition the court has an inherent power to order a party to proceedings not to make any further applications in those proceedings, *Grepe v Loam* (1887) 37 ChD 168. As regards modern authorities on such orders see *R v Lord Chancellor ex p Witham* (1998) QB 575 and *B v*

B (Unmeritorious Applications) (1998) 3 FCR 650. From October 2004 Practice Direction 3C provides a framework for the making of civil restraint orders, which can restrain a party from:

- making further applications in current proceedings (a limited civil restraint order);
- issuing certain claims or making certain applications to specified courts (an extended civil restraint order);
- issuing any claim or making any application in specified courts (a general civil restraint order).

D BEFORE A CASE STARTS

Notification of a potential action

Often the potential defendant will be aware that a legal action may be possible the moment that an accident occurs or a contract is allegedly breached. Otherwise the defendant will get notice of the potential litigation through a letter before action or under an appropriate pre-action protocol, see 4.18–4.27. **17.16**

The rules of court and the pre-action protocols strongly support the sending of letters before action, and the supply of some relevant information even before the start of a legal action. Attempts to settle an action before the issue of a claim form are encouraged, not least to save time and costs. To the extent that a claimant has a good case, it is in the defendant's interests to settle at this stage, to avoid costs accumulating that the defendant is likely to be ordered to pay at the end of the day. **17.17**

Steps to be taken

At this stage the important things for the lawyer and the client are as discussed below. **17.18**

To ascertain the defendant's version of events

A full factual statement should be obtained from the defendant. This is likely to need to be reviewed and extended as the nature of the claimant's case emerges. **17.19**

To ascertain as clearly as possible what the claimant is alleging

There are no procedural steps open to a potential defendant before action, but significant information may be available under a pre-action protocol. Where a pre-action protocol applies full use should be made of it by the defence. In any event the claimant may be prepared to respond to informal requests for information. **17.20**

To ascertain the defendant's broad response to those allegations

At the pre-action stage the response of the defendant may not be fully developed. There may be a broad denial of the claimant's allegations, taking quite a strong line of resistance at the start even if this may be modified at a later stage. There may be some acceptance of the claimant's allegations, but great care should be taken over making concessions at an early stage before the case is fully known. **17.21**

To try to prevent a formal action being commenced if possible

17.22 If the defendant completely denies the case being made then a strong stand may be justified to try to persuade the claimant not to bring a formal action. A claimant whose case is not strong may not wish to risk the time and expense of bringing a formal action. Indeed letters threatening action may be sent to see if they will produce any outcome without a strong intention of bringing an action if those letters fail.

To consider whether a pre-action settlement is possible

17.23 Few defendants will wish to receive a claim form in a formal action. Many actions will settle before the claim form is issued, and options should be considered. However, care should be taken not to make admissions that may weaken the defence should a formal action be launched.

To make constructive use of pre-action time

17.24 Once the action is formally commenced, timetables and court management will come into play putting pressure on the parties. The pre-action period should be used constructively to collect information and to make broad plans for the conduct of the case.

E   WHEN A CASE STARTS

17.25 With the potential benefits of pre-action activity it will be rare for a claim form to come as a surprise to a defendant, though this may happen if it has been difficult for the claimant to locate the defendant, or in a relatively small case where the expense of pre-action activity may not be justified. Therefore in the majority of cases the defendant should be prepared to respond to the claim form, though there will be some cases where the defendant will only seek the advice of a lawyer on receipt of a claim form, having dealt with the matter personally till then.

17.26 On the service of a claim form a defendant is entitled to await the service of the particulars of claim, to have more detail of the case alleged. Once the particulars of claim have been served the defendant should respond within 14 days, and the basic options available are set out in the Response Pack that is sent with the documents.

- The first option is to file an admission (Form N9A or N9C). An admission of liability will mean that the defendant is only liable for certain fixed costs. The defendant will have to pay the amount due within 14 days or offer to pay by instalments. There may be a partial admission, in which case a defence must be drafted to cover the rest of the case.
- The second option is to defend the claim. This must be done by setting out the basis on which the action is being defended, which can be done on Form N9B or N9D, though in a complex case a separate defence will be drafted. The parties may agree to extend the time for filing a defence by 28 days, but if they do so the court must be notified in writing, CPR r 15.5.
- A third choice is to acknowledge service. This course is appropriate if the defendant wishes to dispute the court's jurisdiction, or to allow an extra 14 days for the defence to be filed.

In any event the essential reaction of the defendant to the case will need to be ascertained **17.27**
and expressed in a limited time.

- The receipt of formal court documentation might focus the defendant's mind, and the defendant may file an admission rather than take the case further. This will save costs and time.
- In other cases the defendant will wish to file a defence at this stage even if the defendant might prefer not to take the case to trial. The drafting of a defence is dealt with below. If additional time is needed to collect information and draft a defence the claimant should be told.

F   STRATEGY AND TACTICS IN PROGRESSING A CASE

The defendant who proceeds to defend an action may be tempted to adopt a strategy of **17.28**
non-cooperation. Indeed in the past a defendant might also be tempted to prevarication, procrastination, and obfuscation, in the hope that the claimant would cease to pursue the claim. The modern approach of case management by the court makes such an approach much more difficult because the court will set timetables and is likely to impose sanctions on a non-cooperative defendant.

A range of strategies and tactics are open to a defendant. Many of these are outlined in **17.29**
Chapter 16, but are considered here from the defendant's point of view. The actual choice of approach will depend on the circumstances of the case.

Cutting short the action

The defendant may be strongly motivated to bring the action to an end as quickly as **17.30**
possible, especially if the claim is weak and/or poorly expressed.

- The defendant may wish to argue that the court has no jurisdiction to hear the case, if for example it is more properly heard in another jurisdiction. Such a point should be raised soon after receipt of the claim form (see 16.83). Arguments about jurisdiction are increasingly common because it is more common for there to be a choice, and where there is a choice it is quite possible that the different rules will mean that one party prefers one jurisdiction and one prefers another.
- If the claim being made by the claimant is weak then the defendant may seek an order to strike out a statement of case (see Chapter 12) or an order for summary judgment (see 16.95–16.102).
- If the claimant does not pursue the case properly there are various steps that the defendant can take, for example seeking judgment in default if a statement of case is not filed (see 16.84–16.94), or seeking sanctions, including dismissal of the case if necessary (see 16.50–16.62) or dismissal for want of prosecution (see 16.103–16.106).

Clarifying the claim being made

The defendant may need to clarify the claim being made so as to be able to respond to it, to **17.31**
prepare for trial, or consider making an offer in settlement. It is important to review the

information that the defendant has for each of these steps, especially where some information is effectively known only to the claimant. If the claimant has not chosen to provide very full or clear information this may be because there are weaknesses in the claimant's case. If limited information is accepted without question a possible line of defence may not be spotted.

- Information should be contained in the particulars of claim, but if it is not further information can be sought as set out at 12.145–12.157.
- The evidence in support of the claim should come with disclosure of evidence (see 15.179–15.200) and exchange of witness statements (see 15.201–15.205). If it does not then further details can be sought, see 16.144–16.169.
- The defence is the main instrument for setting out whether the defendant denies the whole claim, denies only part of the claim etc, see 17.08.

Protecting the financial position of the defendant

17.32 The financial position of a defendant is subject to many potential risks during litigation. The situation may need to be carefully managed so that the defendant does not end up paying significantly more than is really necessary.

17.33 The defendant is at risk of having to pay damages if the case is lost. The position here is best defended by arguing:

- that a cause of action should not succeed;
- that a head of damage is not recoverable (due to lack or causation, lack of foreseeability, etc);
- that the amount that is recoverable under the head should be as low as possible (simply on the facts of what the claim is worth or due to a failure to mitigate).

17.34 If the defence to the whole claim does not have a reasonable chance of success then the defendant should be advised about making a Part 36 offer, see 20.51–20.68.

17.35 The defendant's position as regards costs also needs consideration. If there is a strong defence such that the claimant is likely to lose and be ordered to pay the defendant's costs then the position is reasonably secure. If success is not likely for the defendant then he or she is at risk of having to pay the claimant's costs as well as his or her own costs. In such a case costs should not be built up unnecessarily, and again a Part 36 offer should be considered.

17.36 A claimant may bring a claim that has limited chance of success, but where the defendant is at risk of being out of pocket because the claimant may not be able to pay the defendant's costs if the claimant loses. In such a case seeking security for costs should be considered, see 16.172–16.174.

Passing or sharing the blame

17.37 A common reaction for a defendant may be to accept that, in a broad sense, the claimant has some sort of claim, but to deny that the defendant is the right person to meet that claim.

17.38 An argument that liability be passed to or shared with someone else must have a proper foundation in law and/or in the facts of the case. Liability for an accident may be passed or shared on the basis of the factual situation of how the accident happened. Liability in a contractual claim may pass because of a contractual term. Legal liability may pass from one person to another because of agency or vicarious liability. There will need to be a full factual and legal analysis to identify which option is appropriate on the facts.

The first possibility is that the defendant may argue that someone else is wholly to blame. If **17.39** that person has already been added as a co-defendant then this can probably be dealt with by setting it out in the defence. If that person has not yet been made a party to the action then the defendant will need to join that person through Part 20 proceedings, see 13.63–13.88. If someone else is said to be wholly to blame then the defendant is likely to be claiming an indemnity from that person. The defendant cannot force the claimant to sue someone else.

As an alternative to seeking an indemnity a defendant may seek a contribution. Again Part **17.40** 20 proceedings will be needed unless the person from whom the contribution is claimed is already a co-defendant. The limitation period for claiming a contribution or an indemnity is two years from the date on which liability in respect of which a contribution is sought was fixed, Limitation Act 1980, s 10.

Making a claim against the claimant

Many cases are not one-sided. Some cases arise from a general dispute in which either side **17.41** might start a formal action as claimant. Alternatively, the facts may show a possible legal claim by the defendant against the claimant, whether or not it is closely linked to the facts in dispute.

Again careful legal and factual analysis of the situation is important. There cannot be general **17.42** allegations about the role of the claimant. Where there are mutual allegations of fault the options are:

- the allegations are simply disputes of fact and do not amount to a claim against the claimant—this would be the case where, for example, there is a dispute about whether the terms of a contract are as alleged by the claimant; material disputes of fact should be set out in the defence;
- that the allegations against the claimant amount to a defence and should be included in the defence as such—this would be the case where contributory negligence is alleged;
- the defendant may have a separate cause of action against a claimant, and this can be brought as a counterclaim—this must be an independent cause of action, and it can continue in its own right if the main action is decided or compromised;
- the defendant may be able to claim a set-off—If the set-off amounts to a full counterclaim it should be claimed as such, and then raised in the defence as a set-off. If it is simply relevant to the calculation of damages it should simply appear in the defence as a set-off. The result will be that the set-off can be set against the claim made by the claimant and judgment will only be given for the difference.

Using procedural rules

17.43   A number of procedural rules may be of as much use to the defendant as to the claimant. As one example, a defendant may want an interim injunction to protect the position in the case up to trial, see 16.107–16.139.

G   THE MAIN TYPES OF DEFENCE TO AN ACTION

17.44   The main types of defence to a contractual action are considered more fully at 18.108–18.119, and the main types of defence to a tort action are considered more fully at 19.129–19.149.

Procedural defences

17.45   The possible procedural defences include:

- a general defence that the court does not have the jurisdiction to try the case;
- a general defence that the action has been brought outside the limitation period. If the claimant has not issued the claim form within the limitation period then the defendant can plead that as a defence. Should the defence be made out the action will be struck out, see 4.33–4.41.

Defences to a cause of action

17.46   The main lines of defence to a cause of action are, as appropriate:

- that the particulars of claim does not set out all the elements required for the cause of action claimed (though it may be possible for this to be remedied by amendment);
- that the admissible evidence does not on the balance of probabilities prove all the elements of the cause of action claimed;
- that a positive defence absolves the defendant from liability, such as the defence of volenti in a personal accident claim.

Defences to a claim for damages

17.47   The main types of defence to a damages claim are, as appropriate:

- that the particulars of claim does not set out all the elements required for the remedies claimed (though it may be possible for this to be remedied by amendment);
- that the admissible evidence does not on the balance of probabilities prove all the elements of the remedies claimed;
- causation—that on the facts the alleged loss was not caused by the breach of contract and is therefore not recoverable;
- forseeability—that on the facts the alleged loss was not a foreseeable consequence of the alleged breach of duty and is therefore not recoverable;
- mitigation—that on the facts the claimant has failed to mitigate his or her loss;

- in a negligence case, that the claimant was also negligent and contributed to the loss and damage—this needs to be set out in the defence and proved.

H   RULES FOR DRAFTING A DEFENCE

The rules for drafting the defence

There are now relatively few rules for drafting a defence. CPR r 16.5 provides: **17.48**

In his defence the defendant must state—

(1) (a) which of the allegations in the particulars of claim he denies
    (b) which of the allegations he is unable to admit or deny, but which he requires the claimant to prove; and
    (c) which allegations he admits.
(2) Where the defendant denies an allegation—
    (a) he must state his reasons for doing so; and
    (b) if he intends to put forward a different version of events from that given by the claimant, he must state his own version.
(3) A defendant who—
    (a) fails to deal with an allegation; but
    (b) has set out in his defence the nature of his case in relation to the issue to which that allegation is relevant, shall be taken to require that allegation to be proved.
(4) Where the claim includes a money claim, a defendant shall be taken to require that any allegation relating to the amount of money claimed be proved unless he expressly admits the allegation.
(5) Subject to paragraph (3) and (4), a defendant who fails to deal with an allegation shall be taken to admit that allegation.

The proper drafting of a defence requires a very careful analysis of the law and fact to   **17.49**
establish quite what the claimant is alleging and quite how the defendant responds.

Separating out allegations

The importance of separating out each individual allegation and dealing with each separ-   **17.50**
ately cannot be over-emphasised. To succeed in the action the claimant must prove every essential element of the claim. The defendant will therefore wish to challenge individual elements with a view to showing that at least one is not made out. For example, if a claimant alleges that he slipped on a sheet of ice in the defendant's premises, this consists of a number of separate allegations—that the defendant owns premises/ that the claimant was in them/ that there was ice/ that there was a sheet of ice/ that the claimant slipped/ that the claimant slipped on ice. Each separate allegation needs to be dealt with specifically if issues are to be properly clarified. Any general denial would leave in doubt what was actually in dispute.

The same level of analysis should be carried out to separate the allegation as to each element   **17.51**
of each cause of action, and as to each head of damage. An allegation of damage includes an allegation that the damage happened, an allegation that it was caused by the cause of action, and an allegation as to the value of the damage.

17.52 It may be difficult to decide which response to each allegation is right. There may be no entirely right answer and it may be a question of choosing which is most appropriate. It is not strictly necessary to deal specifically with each item in particulars of an allegation if the allegation itself is addressed, but detail should be given insofar as it helps to clarify the issues.

17.53 If an allegation is not addressed it will be taken to be in issue, so that the claimant will have to prove it, if the general nature of the defence on that issue appears from what is said in the defence. Otherwise it will be deemed to be admitted, CPR r 16.5. This means that it is important to deal with each individual allegation or it may be taken to be admitted. However the claimant will always be required to prove an allegation of loss or damage unless that is expressly admitted.

Admitting an allegation

17.54 An allegation should be admitted:

- where the instructions from the client are that the allegation is true;
- where the evidence shows that the allegation is true and there is no evidence to show that it is not true;
- where there is no purpose to be served in making an issue of the allegation;
- where an admission can save time and costs.

17.55 Further admissions may be sought as the case progresses to limit the issues at trial. If a party refuses to admit something which he should admit, he may end up paying the costs of proving it.

17.56 However, an allegation should only be admitted if it is agreed that every part of it is true, because every admission made will be binding at trial. If an allegation as contained in a statement of case is ambiguous, inaccurate, or incomplete then the response should clarify exactly what is being admitted.

Putting the claimant to proof

17.57 The opponent should be put to proof where the allegation may be true, but the client is not in a position to know whether the allegation is true, and there is not other credible evidence as to whether the allegation is true or not.

17.58 In the past this type of response was sometimes expressed as 'does not admit'. This was seen as having a tactical purpose in forcing the opponent to prove the point. With the change in the Civil Procedure Rules this is probably no longer good practice, as such a response can escalate costs without purpose. However it is still used.

17.59 The lawyer can be put into a difficult position if the client wishes the other side to be put to proof, even though there is evidence on which a response could be given. The Professional Standards Committee of the General Council of the Bar has given guidance that it may be unethical to require a claimant to prove something that it is possible to admit or deny. The implication of putting the other side to proof is that one does not have evidence oneself and this may unnecessarily increase costs.

Denying an allegation

An allegation should be denied if there is evidence which can be produced if necessary **17.60** which shows that the allegation is not true. The evidence does not have to be conclusive but it should be admissible and credible.

Ensure that a denial is precisely aimed at what is denied. It may be necessary to add further **17.61** information to explain a denial, and the Court Guidelines suggest that a denial should be followed by these reasons.

Some things should not be denied, for example, one should not normally deny an allegation **17.62** that is of little importance but which will be expensive to prove. An allegation of law should not be denied, unless the law as stated is wrong, rather than the factual allegation made. An allegation should not be denied simply because it causes a difficulty for the client. A defence is the result of analysis of the case, it is not a written argument.

The amount of a money claim is deemed to be denied unless admitted. If the value is **17.63** disputed, the defendant should say why and give his own estimate if possible.

It is important to take care in denying a negative allegation, because the result will be that **17.64** the double negative makes a positive. If part of a paragraph in a statement of claim alleges that the defendant did not do something and the defendant denies the whole paragraph, then the effect is to allege that he did do the thing specified.

In the past it was quite common to use a general denial, though there were differing views as **17.65** to whether this was good pleading. Because allegations which are not contested may be seen to be admitted, there was thought to be merit in adding a general paragraph to deny everything that had not been dealt with specifically. This is now clearly not good pleading as it does not assist in clarifying the issues. It is now mandatory under CPR r 16.5 to give reasons, if relevant putting forward a different version of events.

If an allegation is not addressed it will be taken to be in issue, so that the claimant will have **17.66** to prove it, if the general nature of the defence on that issue appears from what is said in the defence. Otherwise it will be deemed to be admitted, CPR r 16.5.

Adding information

In addition to responding to the allegations made, it may be necessary to add information to **17.67** explain or clarify issues. This may be done to raise a line of defence, such as contributory negligence, or simply to put facts in a different light in a 'Yes, but . . .' way. One might admit driving into the claimant, but add that she walked out when the pedestrian light was against her and without looking.

Those things which should be positively pleaded include anything which makes any claim **17.68** or defence of the opposite party not maintainable, any matter which might take the opposite party by surprise at trial if not specifically pleaded, and any matter which, although it does not arise from an existing allegation, puts a different complexion on the allegations made. The defence must include details of the expiry of any relevant limitation period, PD 16 para 13. Other things which should be positively pleaded include performance, release, contributory negligence, lack of jurisdiction, estoppel, any fact showing illegality, a lien, a release, an agreement ending the right of action, or a tender of the amount alleged to be owing. Matters that need to be specifically covered in a personal injury claim are dealt with at 19.123–19.128.

The statement of truth

17.69   The defence must have a statement of truth, see 10.55–10.60.

I   PRINCIPLES FOR DRAFTING A DEFENCE

17.70   The defence is the main statement of the defence case. The basic principles for drafting a defence are broadly similar to those for a particulars of claim. The defence will often be a shorter document than the particulars of claim, but it is by no means a simpler document.

17.71   It is more difficult to draft a defence in a coherent way because of the need to respond to allegations as well as setting out a case. It is nonetheless important:

- to tell a clear and logical story;
- to respond to each allegation of the case as conceived by the claimant;
- to set out the defendant's version of events.

Options for the structure of a defence

17.72   There are two basic options for structure:

- Following the claimant's structure, but not necessarily paragraph by paragraph. Extra facts, such as extra clauses of a contract can be added where relevant in dealing with the plaintiff's allegations, or at the end.
- To use a structure that sets out the defendant's story clearly, if for example the particulars of claim are badly structured or if the defendant's version of events is very different from the claimant's. This can be clearer, but great care must be taken to ensure that a response has been given to each individual allegation.

17.73   It is quite possible to plead more than one line of defence either cumulatively or in the alternative, but this should be done with care. A coherent story should be pleaded save where the defendant does not know what happened. Alternative defences may leave options open, but they can also weaken the case to the extent that the impression is given that the defendant does not have detailed evidence and may not be able to present a clear and consistent case ('Alternatively . . .' 'If which is denied').

17.74   The numbers of the paragraphs of the defence do not need to coincide with the numbers of the paragraphs of the particulars of claim. However there should be a reference to the number of the paragraph being responded to. The defence does not have to respond to anything in the statement of claim which should not be there—if, for example, there is a passage of evidence it is only necessary to respond to the basic allegation made, so long as issues are clarified. Although it is not strictly necessary to plead law, basic legal points such as that the action has been brought outside the limitation period should be included.

Pleading should be as precise as possible, but wide phrases may serve a purpose, for example, **17.75**
'The defendant denies that there was ice in the part of his premises alleged, or any other part', 'The defendant denies that the plaintiff was injured as alleged or at all'.

Dealing with a poorly drafted particulars of claim

If the particulars of claim are poorly drafted then the defendant is at a disadvantage. **17.76**

- If the drafting is so poor that it does not disclose a proper cause of action then an application may be made to strike it out, see 12.138–12.144.
- If there is too little information of the claim being made then further information can be sought, see 12.145–12.157, though this option may alert the opponent to the weakness in the draft causing the opponent to amend it.

If the defects are not serious enough for such action the alternative is to leave the particulars **17.77**
of claim as they are—the defects should be clear to a judge at trial. However there can be problems in pleading a defence where the particulars of claim are vague, superficial, or poorly structured. The defendant should not be pulled into drafting in an equally weak way, but should consider carefully what approach to take.

- If the particulars of claim is vague or superficial then the best option is probably to reply to the paragraphs as they stand, but to plead in a much more specific and detailed way. It is important to ensure that all allegations are addressed.
- If the particulars of claim are poorly structured then the defendant should probably not follow the structure of the particulars but choose a structure that allows for the clearest presentation of the defence case. In doing this it is particularly important to ensure that all allegations are identified and answered.

J DRAFTING A DEFENCE

Preparing to draft a defence

On receiving the particulars of claim in a case, the lawyer should consider the document in **17.78**
some detail with the defendant client.

The defence will take its heading, including the number, parties etc, from the particulars of **17.79**
claim, unless an extra party is added. For sample defences in contract see 18.122, 18.127, 18.131, and 18.133. For sample defences in tort see 19.140, 19.143, and 19.149.

The stages in drafting a defence are normally as follows. **17.80**

- To identify what each paragraph of the particulars of claim relates to, for example the contract, the terms of contract, the breach.
- To separate each paragraph of the particulars of claim into all the separate allegations made (there are likely to be several allegations in each paragraph).
- To identify with the client and from the evidence the basic response to each allegation (admit, deny etc).
- To identify any further information that is required before the defence can be drafted.

- To decide whether a counterclaim will be brought, and whether any further parties should be added to the action.
- To decide whether any positive defences should be used as regards the cause(s) of action or the remedies.
- To decide on an overall logical structure for the defence, and on what should be covered in each paragraph. This will normally follow the claimant's structure in dealing with the contract, the terms etc.

Detailed drafting

17.81   The above process should produce a skeleton defence that identifies the appropriate content for the defence.

- The allocation of responses to the allegations in the particulars of claim and of additional information to the proposed paragraphs for the defence should be checked. The defence will normally have less paragraphs than the particulars of claim unless there is significant information to be added.
- As in the particulars of claim, each paragraph in the defence should deal with a different topic. Several paragraphs from the particulars of claim can be dealt with together, for example, 'Paragraphs 1 to 3 of the particulars of claim are admitted'.
- As regards each individual paragraph, decide what the major reaction is, for example whether most allegations are being admitted or denied. This then allows for general phraseology such as 'The defendant denies each and every allegation in paragraph 2 of the particulars of claim' or 'The defendant denies each and every allegation in paragraph 2, save in that . . .', or 'It is admitted that . . . otherwise paragraph x is denied'.

17.82   In drafting each individual paragraph in the defence the precise wording of the response to each allegation needs care. The point is to be as accurate as possible in terms of the instructions and evidence available. While there is some scope for wording in a way that favours the case, every response must be justifiable.

17.83   The response to an individual allegation may be:

> This is admitted.
> This is admitted, but the following should be added . . .
> This is admitted, but it is not important because . . .
> This is denied.
> This is denied because . . .
> That the opponent is put to proof because the pleader can neither admit nor deny the allegation.

17.84   A defence of contributory negligence must be positively pleaded, see *Fookes v Slaytor* [1979] 1 All ER 137.

17.85   The draft defence should be reread to check:

- that all allegations have been addressed;
- that no admission has been made as regards anything that is in issue;
- that nothing has been denied if there is not evidence to justify the denial if necessary;
- that the points that are in issue are clearly defined for the other side and for the court.

K   MAKING A COUNTERCLAIM

Until the nineteenth century each action had to be brought to court separately, so that if a **17.86**
defendant had a claim against a claimant he or she had to go to the expense and trouble of
bringing a separate action. It is now possible to save time and costs by hearing the actions
together, and this is the purpose of the counterclaim.

If the defendant has a cause of action against the claimant this can be raised in separate **17.87**
proceedings or in the defence. Anything that can be a separate cause of action may be raised
as a counterclaim. A counterclaim can exceed the amount of the claim, and can proceed even
if the claim is dropped. There does not need to be any legal or factual connection between the
claim and the counterclaim. If the counterclaim is not made at the same time as the defence
then court permission may be required, CPR 20.4. If people other than the claimant are made
defendants to the action then court permission will be needed, CPR r 20.5. See generally PD
20 Counterclaims and other additional claims. For sample counterclaims see 18.122, 18.131,
and 19.149.

The counterclaim can be raised on the form in the response pack. The defence and the **17.88**
counterclaim should normally be in the same document, PD 20 para 6. This means that
no separate claim form or Part 20 claim form will be required, though the parties to the
counterclaim should be referred to as the 'Part 20 Claimant' and 'Part 20 Defendant'.

The counterclaim should be drafted in exactly the same way as a particulars of claim. If there **17.89**
is little or no factual connection then the counterclaim can appear just like a particulars of
claim. If there is a factual connection between the claim and the counterclaim then the usual
approach is to refer back to those allegations in the particulars of claim and in the defence
that are relevant to the counterclaim. This can be done for example by referring back to
allegations that a contract has been made and the admission that the contract was made, but
pleading an additional term and breach as a counterclaim.

The principle that the counterclaim is a claim in its own right runs right through all **17.90**
procedural requirements. The claimant should file a defence to counterclaim, and either
party can make appropriate interim applications. The counterclaim continues as an action
in its own right, and the defendant may get judgment even if the claimant's action is stayed,
discontinued, or dismissed. The court may give separate judgments with separate orders for
costs on the statement of claim and the counterclaim, though if both claims are for damages
and a set-off is claimed the court will give judgment for the balance, using its discretion as to
what order to make for costs. In *Hanak v Green* [1958] 2 QB 9 there was an action for breach of
a building contract, but the builder counterclaimed for *quantum meruit* for the work he
had done, and for trespass to his tools by the claimant, the result being that the court
gave judgment for the builder for £10, the difference between the values of the claims of the
two parties.

If the defendant wishes to make positive allegations against the claimant and/or to obtain **17.91**
remedies this must be done as part of the defence and counterclaim—the matters cannot be
brought up informally later. The only option then will be to bring a separate action. In *Impex
Transport Aktielskabet v AG Thames Holding* [1982] 1 All ER 897 the claimant sought summary

judgment for freight owed, but the defendant swore an affidavit which included facts amounting to a counterclaim. It was held that this was insufficient, and as the matter had not been formally pleaded as a counterclaim it could not proceed.

17.92   It is probably not possible to exclude the right to bring a counterclaim or to raise a set-off in a contractual term, *Quadrant Visual Communications Ltd v Hutchinson Telephone (UK) Ltd* The Times, 4 December 1991, but see *Hong Kong and Shanghai Banking Corporation v Kloeckner & Co AG* [1989] 3 All ER 513.

L   CLAIMING A SET-OFF

17.93   A counterclaim may also be a set-off, if it is a money claim to be set against a money claim. If the claimant claims money from the defendant and the defendant also has a justifiable financial claim against the claimant it is only logical that it be possible to set one off against the other.

17.94   If a defendant contends that he is entitled to money from the claimant and relies on that as a defence to the whole or part of his claim the contention can be included in the defence and set-off against the claim whether or not there is also a counterclaim, CPR r 16.6. A set-off can be total (so as to extinguish the claimant's claim), or partial (so as to reduce it). A set-off has no independent life, so if the claim is brought to an end the set-off cannot proceed unless it is also a counterclaim.

17.95   There must be a proper basis for the set-off. The possibility of a set-off should be explored with the defendant client. Most set-offs arise from the same circumstances as a claim. A set-off can only relate to a sum of money. Only money which is already legally due to be paid by the claimant to the defendant can be a set-off, see *Business Computers v Anglo African Leasing* [1977] 2 All ER 741. The position is not entirely clear where the amount due cannot be easily ascertained, *Axel Johnson Petroleum AB v MG Mineral Group* [1992] 2 All ER 163.

17.96   Examples of set-offs include:

- A contractual duty to pay money. For example setting an unpaid consideration for a contract against a claim for damages.
- An equitable set-off. For example a claim for a contract price can be answered with a claim for a reasonable price for work done. This can only happen if the facts of the claim and counterclaim are interlinked.
- Under the Sale of Goods Act 1979, s 53 if a seller sues for the price of goods sold and delivered, the buyer can claim a set-off of damages for breach of implied terms of satisfactory quality, fitness for purpose, or correspondence with description.
- On a claim for the price of service (wages), damages for poor workmanship can be set off.

17.97   The set-off should be pleaded at the end of the defence. Sufficient detail of the basis for and amount of the claim must be given. If it is also a counterclaim then it should be pleaded as a counter claim with a cross reference at the end of the defence. For an example see 18.131.

17.98   The defendant will need to prove the set-off. If the judge accepts the set-off then judgment will only be given for the difference between the set-off and the claim.

Although the position should normally be clear, the facts of a case may make it difficult to **17.99** distinguish between a set-off, a counterclaim, and a matter of mitigation of damage. Cases that illustrate the distinctions include the following.

- In *Nadreph v Willmett & Co* [1978] 1 All ER 746 a firm of solicitors were sued for negligence for failing to renegotiate a lease for a client and the solicitors sought to set off financial advantages that could accrue to the claimant because there had been no renegotiation. It was held that this might be a set-off but on the facts was really a matter of mitigation of damage.
- In *British Anzani (Felixstowe) v International Maritime Management (UK)* [1980] QB 137 the claimant agreed to build a warehouse for the defendant to lease. There were claims for rent arrears by the claimant and for defects in the building by the defendant. It was held that the defendant's claim on the defects might be a set-off, but here the defendant should have argued a counterclaim rather than a set-off.

An action for specific performance for payment of a cheque will normally be granted without **17.100** a set-off, as a cheque is regarded as the equivalent of cash, and the same applies to similar forms of payment such as a direct debit, *Esso Petroleum Co Ltd v Milton* (1997) 1 WLR 938 CA. There are some exceptions, for example where fraud, illegality, duress, or total failure of consideration is alleged. However misrepresentation as regards matter underlying a contract action will not provide an exception, *Sol Industries UK Ltd v Canara Bank* (2001) 1 WLR 1800.

M   GENERAL FRAMEWORK FOR A DEFENCE AND COUNTERCLAIM

17.101

IN THE HIGH COURT OF JUSTICE   2005.B.No.

DIVISION

BETWEEN   A.B. (Name in capitals)   Claimant

                                 and

                                 C.D. (Name in capitals)   Defendant

                                 ───────────────
                                     DEFENCE
                                 ───────────────

(Plead to all the allegations in the particulars of claim in separate numbered paragraphs. The following are examples of possible paragraphs that may be adapted for use.)

1. The Defendant admits paragraph   of the particulars of claim.
2. The Defendant denies paragraph   of the particulars of claim, save in that . . . .
3. The Defendant denies . . . . as alleged in the particulars of claim or at all.
4. The Defendant requires the Claimant to prove that she has sustained loss and damage as alleged in the particulars of claim.
5. The Defendant denies that the alleged loss and damage were caused by the Defendant as alleged in the particulars of claim.

6. The Defendant claims to be entitled to set off against the claimant's claim the sum of £   in that . . . . (set out the facts on which set-off is based).

COUNTERCLAIM

7. (Plead the facts giving rise to the counterclaim in separate numbered paragraphs as if pleading a particulars of claim.)
8.
9.

AND the Defendant counterclaims:

1. (Set out in numbered paragraphs the remedies and relief sought due to the counterclaim.)
2.

Served the   day of   etc.

(Signed)

KEY DOCUMENTS

Forms

N1C Notes for Defendant
N9 Defence Response Pack
N9A Admission (specified amount)
N9B Defence and Counterclaim (specified amount)
N9C Admission (unspecified amount and non money claim)
N9D Defence and Counterclaim (unspecified amount and non money claim)
N11 Defence Form
N211 Part 20 Claim Form
N213 Part 20 Acknowledgement of service
N 266 Notice to admit facts

These are easily available in hard copy and electronic form, see Chapter 24.

18

THE CONTRACT MODEL

A INTRODUCTION 18.01

B POTENTIAL CAUSES OF ACTION IN A CONTRACT CASE 18.04
Breach of contract 18.04
Misrepresentation 18.05
Other options 18.06

C THE ELEMENTS OF A CONTRACTUAL CASE 18.07
Matters preceding the making of a contract 18.08
Matters relating to the making of the contract 18.09
Matters relating to the terms 18.10
Matters relating to performance 18.11
Matters relating to remedies 18.12

D CONTEXTUAL CONSIDERATIONS 18.13
Commercial realities 18.13
Business structures 18.15
Financial processes 18.16
The international element 18.17

E ANALYSING CONTRACTUAL OBLIGATIONS 18.21
Is the contract oral or written? 18.22
When and where was the contract made? 18.24
Who are the parties to the contract? 18.26
What is the consideration for the contract? 18.27
What are the express terms of the contract? 18.28
What are the implied terms of the contract? 18.29
Are there terms which exclude or restrict liability? 18.32

F ANALYSING A CONTRACTUAL ACTION 18.33
Problems with the contract itself 18.33
Breach of contract 18.38
Misrepresentation 18.41
Other possible causes of action 18.53

G SELECTING A CAUSE OF ACTION 18.54
Making choices where there is more than one breach 18.55
Making choices where there is more than one cause of action . . 18.56
The overlap between contract and tort 18.59

H   SELECTING REMEDIES. 18.61

Damages and other money payments 18.62
An injunction. 18.67
Other equitable remedies 18.70

I   PRINCIPLES FOR ASSESSING DAMAGES 18.78

Measures of damages. 18.78
Stages in assessing damages 18.93
Problems with recoverability. 18.101

J   DRAFTING A CONTRACT CLAIM 18.106

K   ADVISING A DEFENDANT. 18.108

The contract and its terms 18.109
The cause of action 18.110
The remedies 18.111
Terms limiting liability. 18.113
A counterclaim or set-off 18.118
Drafting the defence 18.119

L   SAMPLE DRAFTS FOR A CONTRACT CASE 18.120

Example 1. Particulars of claim—sale of goods—specific
        performance. 18.121
Example 2. Defence to particulars of claim in example
        1—counterclaim for money due 18.122
Example 3. Particulars of claim—sale of goods—total
        failure of consideration—return of contract price 18.123
Example 4. Particulars of claim—sale of goods and
        services—breach of terms implied by statute 18.124
Example 5. Particulars of claim—sale of goods—breach
        of express terms—damages for loss of profit 18.125
Example 6. Request for further information related to
        example 4 . . . . 18.126
Example 7. Defence to particulars of claim in example
        5—reliance on an exclusion clause—counterclaim/set-off. . . 18.127
Example 8. Part 20 claim linked to examples 5 and 7. . . . . 18.128
Example 9. Particulars of claim—supply of
        services—breach of contract—application for an
        injunction—claim for wasted expenditure 18.129
Example 10. Application for an interim injunction linked
        to examples 8 and 9. . . . . 18.130
Example 11. Defence to particulars of claim in example
        10—repudiation—partial set-off 18.131
Example 12. Particulars of claim—misrepresentation—
        recission 18.132
Example 13. Defence to particulars of claim in example 11 . . . 18.133

A   INTRODUCTION

A large amount of litigation is founded on problems with the fulfillment of an agreement.   **18.01**
Two parties agree terms, but then a term is breached, or something turns out to be wrong
with the basis upon which the agreement was reached in the first place. The basic contractual model underlies many commercial and business situations, and provides many
principles that apply in cases involving property or sale of goods.

It is crucial for a lawyer to be able to take a strategic overview of the situation to identify what   **18.02**
a case is really about. Is the real problem related to terms or to representations? Might a term
be implied to provide assistance? Has the contract been varied? Have alleged losses really
been caused by a breach of contract or is there some separate cause? Does the contract
continue after a breach or is it over? Whether in a business or domestic situation, everyday
life can make the terms and implementation of an agreement somewhat confused. The
lawyer needs to be able to analyse the basic contract ingredients of a situation with clarity to
take a case forward.

This chapter provides a basic guide to some of the elements to bear in mind when conduct-   **18.03**
ing contractual litigation. Detailed law will need to be researched where necessary, but this
chapter tries to provide a practical framework that should assist in identifying the main
points in a case—what causes of action may arise and what remedies can be sought.
Appropriate practitioner works for further research include:

H Beale, *Chitty on Contracts* (29th edn 2004 and supplements) Sweet & Maxwell
G H Trieitel, *Treitel on the Law of Contract* (11th edn 2003) Sweet & Maxwell
J Beatson, *Anson's Law of Contract* (28th edn 2002) Oxford University Press
R Lawson, *Exclusion Clauses and Unfair Contract Terms* (2003) Sweet & Maxwell
E Macdonald, *Exemption Clauses and Unfair Terms* (2004) Lexis Nexis UK
McGregor, *Damages* (16th edn 1999 and supplements) Sweet & Maxwell
Goff & Jones, *Law of Restitution* (6th edn 2002 and supplements) Sweet & Maxwell
Bowstead & Reynolds, *Law of Agency* (17th edn 2001) Sweet & Maxwell
Gore-Browne on Companies (44th edn) Jordans. Looseleaf
Lindley & Banks, *Lindley on Partnership* (18th edn 2002 and supplements) Sweet &
   Maxwell

B   POTENTIAL CAUSES OF ACTION IN A CONTRACT CASE

Breach of contract

Probably the most common cause of action in a contractual case is breach of contract—a   **18.04**
simple allegation that a term was agreed but that it was not carried out. This is a flexible
cause of action because of the possibilities for implying terms, in addition to the power the
parties have to agree their own terms. Having said this there can be many issues about
the meaning of terms, and what loss actually results from a breach.

Misrepresentation

18.05   Many things may be said with the intention of bringing about a contract. Misrepresentation arises where something is said with the intention of inducing a contract and does induce a contract. The precise elements of a misrepresentation action are important, as is the need to consider which type of misrepresentation to allege, see 18.41–18.52.

Other options

18.06   It is difficult to single out another contractual cause of action as being of general common use in practice. Other options worthy of note include:

- in smaller actions where one party is dealing as a consumer, sale of goods and services legislation is important, especially as regards implied terms;
- in commercial work generally, intellectual property has become quite important, and procedural steps such as search orders may be used;
- a number of other contractual concepts, such as collateral contract or mistake, can assist in analysing a case although they are not commonly used as causes of action.

C   THE ELEMENTS OF A CONTRACTUAL CASE

18.07   Although the legal and factual details of an individual case may be complex, the essential elements of the majority of contract cases are relatively straightforward.

Matters preceding the making of a contract

18.08

- Previous business dealing may give rise to implied terms of contract.
- Representations made that lead to the making of the contract may turn out to be untrue, giving rise to a possible misrepresentation action.

Matters relating to the making of the contract

18.09

- The key elements of two parties, agreement, intention to create legal relations, and consideration must be present. If there are ongoing negotiations it can be difficult to identify precisely when agreement is reached.
- It is important to identify precisely who is contracting for whom. There may for example be questions of agency.
- Certain characteristics of a party may be important. For example it may be relevant to statutory rights or implied terms that a party is dealing in the course of business or as a consumer.
- If the contract was oral there may be particular problems in proving exactly what was agreed.

Matters relating to the terms

- Express terms of a written contract can be easily proved. Issues may relate to what the terms mean. Each side may seek to rely on different terms—if one side sues for breach of contract the other may seek payment or seek to rely on an exclusion clause.
- Proving express terms of an oral contract may turn on proving precisely what was said.
- Implied terms can be very useful in founding an action, provided that the court can be persuaded that there is a sound basis on which to imply a term, and the wording of the term to be implied is carefully considered.

Matters relating to performance

- Is it possible that a variation of contract has been agreed?
- Do some obligations under the contract fall to be performed before others?
- Breach of contract is a common cause of action. It is important to identify as closely as possible which obligation is alleged to have been breached, how, and when.
- If there is a range of potential breaches careful choices should be made as to which to pursue.
- It is crucial to identify what loss and damage flows from which breach to be able to establish causation of loss.
- It is necessary to consider whether a breach is repudiatory or a fundamental breach and a contract is over, or whether the breach leads to a claim for damages and the contract is otherwise treated as continuing.

Matters relating to remedies

- All heads of loss and damage need to be identified.
- To be recoverable, each item of loss or damage must be causally linked to the event giving rise to a cause of action, and to be reasonably foreseeable.
- The overall measure of damage must be considered, especially if there is a choice of measure, for example between loss of profit and wasted expenditure.
- There may be a fundamental decision to take as to whether damages should be sought on the basis of the contract, or whether recission (if available) should be claimed to undo the contract.

D   CONTEXTUAL CONSIDERATIONS

Commercial realities

The general importance of commercial awareness was considered at 3.12–3.15. In many **18.13** contractual actions one or both sides run a business. Awareness of this context is necessary in order to perform an effective service for a client, for example:

- Litigation may have importance for cash flow and the general financial health of a business that will not necessarily be obvious from the facts of the case.
- There may be an ongoing commercial relationship between the parties to a contractual dispute, and it may be important to protect this.
- Commercial reality is that negotiations may go on over some time, much is done by telephone or in meetings, and agreements are often varied. This can present problems for deciding when a contract is finalized and what the terms are.

18.14 It is often said that those entering legal practice tend to lack adequate commercial awareness. It is not easy for someone with limited experience of the commercial world to have such an awareness, but at least an appreciation of the need to try to consider the more general commercial implications of a case can assist.

Business structures

18.15 It is important to be aware of the different ways in which a business can be carried on. This can have implications for identifying the potential defendant accurately, and for seeing whether there are any arguments about who had authority to enter a contract on behalf of a business. The main options are set out at 13.30–13.48.

Financial processes

18.16 Commercial awareness in contractual litigation should extend to the financial realities of how businesses are run. Just to mention a few potentially relevant matters:

- Property. Many businesses lease rather than own buildings, vehicles etc. This can have implications for what assets are actually owned by a business and what a business is worth.
- Loans. Many businesses take out loans to finance development etc. This can have implications for the value and profitability of a business.
- Accounts. All businesses will need to keep annual accounts, though the contents and complexity of such accounts may vary. The lawyer should be able to read a set of accounts so as to be able to gather information about the income, profitability, and capital assets of a business. Accounts must be drawn up for each financial year, and accounts for a business of any size will need to be externally audited. Audited accounts are the most reliable but it may be some time after the end of the year before these are available, so draft accounts may provide more up to date information. A single set of accounts may be unrepresentative and it may be necessary to look at accounts for three years to build a clearer picture of a business.
- Tax and VAT. All businesses are liable to pay tax, whether as income tax (for a sole trader or partnership) or corporation tax (for a company). If a business has an income above a certain level it has to charge VAT and will be liable to pay it. Both VAT and tax may need to be taken into account in calculating loss to a business. There is no easy guide to the principles involved, save to say that:
  — whether figures do or do not include VAT or are or are not net of tax may need to be clarified;
  — damages may as appropriate be calculated as a net loss of profit (after tax etc has been

deducted), which may be appropriate where only net profit has really been lost and the damages will not be liable to tax on receipt;

— damages may as appropriate be calculated using a gross loss (ignoring tax), which may be appropriate where what has been lost would have been taxable, and where the damages will be liable to tax as business income on receipt.

• Goodwill. An established business will have goodwill—essentially a good reputation and a body of regular customers. The goodwill of a business can be valued and loss of goodwill can be recoverable in damages.

The international element

It is increasingly possible that a contract case will have international dimensions as business **18.17** increasingly works on an international basis. In fact the risks of this happening are not as great as one might think, as on analysis many cases with an international fact pattern will only be subject to one legal system.

• Many international corporations and businesses are in fact run through a network of companies or partnerships fully established in separate jurisdictions, so one would only in fact sue the relevant national part of the company.

• If there is an international dimension it is possible, and indeed desirable, to provide for that in the terms of the contract. Many contracts make agreed provision for the law that will govern any breach of contract, or provide for arbitration.

• Areas where trade is common such as the EU tend to have agreements relating to court jurisdiction (note the need to sue where the defendant is domiciled, with the alternative of suing where the contractual obligation was to be performed).

• Disputes about real property, employment law etc tend to be governed by local law.

In any event, as set out at 4.144–4.164, it is possible to start an action here and serve overseas **18.18** with permission where:

• the claim is for a breach of contract within the jurisdiction;

• the claim is in respect of a contract made in the jurisdiction, subject to English law or where it is agreed it be subject to English law (or where this would be the case if the contract were valid);

• there is already a real claim and it is necessary or proper to join the person outside the jurisdiction as a party.

Having said this, there can be significant problems, if for example it is argued that there **18.19** never was a contract because it was void *ab initio, Kleinwort Benson Ltd v Glasgow City Council* (1999) 1 AC 153 HL, or if an action relates to misrepresentations rather than to terms, *Agnew v Lansforsakringsbolagens AB* (2001) 1 AC 223 HL, or because a number of contractual obligations are in dispute, *Union Transport Group plc v Continental Lines SA* (1992) 1 WLR 15 HL.

Within the EU there are special rules for special types of contract, for example consumers **18.20** and those with insurance policies can bring actions in their own country, to assist individuals in litigation against companies.

E   ANALYSING CONTRACTUAL OBLIGATIONS

18.21   The first step in any contractual litigation is to analyse basic matters relating to the making of the contract and its key terms.

Is the contract oral or written?

18.22   If the contract is written or evidenced in writing then the lawyer will wish to see the relevant documents. It is important to consider the wording of the terms and how it might be interpreted. Once a contract has been put into writing that will normally be conclusive as to its terms, and only rarely will oral evidence be admitted to show that there were further terms that were not written down. There are limited circumstances in which a contract has to be in writing to be enforceable, basically where it relates to the sale of land or the disposal of an existing equitable interest in land.

18.23   If the contract is not in writing, the lawyer will want to have full details of everything that was said when the contract was made, which will probably involve getting a full statement from the client and anyone else who was present when the contract was made and who might be a useful witness. An oral contract is just as valid as a written contract and fully enforceable, save that there may be problems in proving its terms, especially if the evidence amounts to one person's word against another's. As there may be evidential problems, supporting evidence for the terms should be sought if possible.

When and where was the contract made?

18.24   Whether it is written or oral, a specific place and time when the contract was made must be identified. There needs to be a point at which there was clear offer and acceptance, clear terms and an intention to create legal relations. Having said this, it is possible for a contract to arise even if some details remained to be finalised.

18.25   It may be difficult to identify when and where a contract was made if there has been a course of dealing between the parties. Two businessmen may well have a series of discussions about a possible deal, and this may make it difficult to identify when a contract crystalises, especially if some of the discussions have been informal, over a game of golf or in a pub.

Who are the parties to the contract?

18.26   It is necessary to identify precisely who made the contract, as this will identify potential parties to litigation. In many contracts an individual acts on behalf of a business, so matters of agency and of actual or ostensible authority may arise. Query if there is a possible relevant claim under the Contract (Rights of Third Parties) Act.

What is the consideration for the contract?

18.27   A contract is only enforceable if there is consideration. The consideration will normally be a money payment, but it might be, for example, a surrender of rights, or a mutual exchange of goods or services. There will in practice rarely be a problem about consideration, but the consideration needs to be identified and set out in the statement of case.

What are the express terms of the contract?

If the contract is written the express terms will appear on the face of the contract, and   **18.28** questions will relate to the meaning of the terms, and whether the terms are enforceable. If the contract was oral then initial work will focus on identifying the terms as precisely as possible from the evidence available. For a claim based on a breach of an express term see 18.125.

What are the implied terms of the contract?

In addition to express terms, the possibility of implying terms into a contract should be   **18.29** considered. A term can only be implied with clear legal justification, and not simply from a general sense of fairness.

The bases on which a term can be implied are: **18.30**

- the officious bystander test—that an officious bystander would say that it went without saying that a particular term should be part of a contract, that that was obvious from the rest of the contract;
- for business efficacy—that a term is a necessary part of the contract to give it business efficacy, or is normal as a term for this particular type of contract;
- from a previous course of dealings—that a term should be seen as part of the contract because it has been part of previous contracts between the parties;
- by statute—for example under the Sale of Goods Act 1979 and Supply of Goods and Services Act 1982 terms are implied that goods and services be of reasonable quality, where one party deals as a consumer.

If the term is implied by statute then the statute prescribes the wording of the term. In other   **18.31** circumstances it is for the claimant to specify the wording of the term to be implied. There is a skill in providing a wording that is justified by the evidence and best suits the client's purposes. The precise wording of an implied term must be set out in a statement of case. For a claim based on a term implied by statute see 18.124.

Are there terms which exclude or restrict liability?

It is quite common for parties to a commercial contract to try to exclude or restrict   **18.32** liability for certain types of breach. In a contract between two businesses this is a reasonable way to control risk. Where a business deals with a consumer who has little choice about terms, unfair terms may be illegal by statute. A defendant will often seek to rely on terms that exclude or restrict liability, and the potential claimant will need to consider them in assessing the potential strength of a case. For a defence based on an exclusion clause see 18.127.

F   ANALYSING A CONTRACTUAL ACTION

Problems with the contract itself

18.33 Even having established that a contractual relationship apparently exists, there can be many problems relating to the contract itself.

The contract may be unenforceable

18.34 Although such matters are not commonly raised in a contractual action:

- a contract may be void or voidable;
- a contract may be illegal;
- a contract may have been undermined by duress or undue influence, so that the contract is not enforceable;
- a contract may be undermined by mistake, though generally there will have to be a mutual mistake on a material matter to affect the contract;
- it may be possible to argue that the contract has been frustrated. This is most likely to be argued by a defendant seeking to avoid an obligation. The courts will be prepared to look at the factual situation to see if a contract has been frustrated, but the argument of frustration rarely succeeds, see *National Carriers v Panalpina (Northern)* [1981] AC 675 and *BP Exploration Co (Libya) v Hunt* [1983] 2 AC 352. It will be necessary to show that a legal or factual situation has undermined the whole point of the contract, identifying the frustrating event precisely. Because of the difficulties of showing frustration, and the limited remedies available it will often be better to use another cause of action.

18.35 The effect of such possibilities needs to be carefully considered. Does the client want to avoid the entire contractual obligation?

The contract may not contain desired terms

18.36 It may emerge from the analysis of obligations that it is difficult to establish that a contract contained a term that the client would hope or expect was there. In such a case there are a number of possibilities.

- If the written document really does not set out the terms agreed then it may be possible to rectify the contract, but that can only be done in limited circumstances.
- If something is said or represented which leads directly to the making of the contract without becoming part of the contract then it may be possible to argue that a collateral contract has arisen and to take action on the collateral contract.
- If a representation has not become a term of the contract and is untrue then it may be possible to bring a misrepresentation action, see 18.41–18.52.

The contract may have been varied

18.37 It is not easy to show that the terms of a contract have been varied, or a contract might too easily be undermined, but it may be possible to establish a variation if there is clear evidence that the variation has been agreed.

Breach of contract

The most common cause of action in a contractual case will be that the defendant has not **18.38**
fulfilled her or his obligations under the contract. Important factors when contemplating an
action for breach of contract include the following.

- Identify the precise breach or breaches alleged as specifically as possible, including what
  term has been breached, and when, where, how, and by whom it was breached.
- If there is more than one potential breach, it will be necessary to decide whether to allege
  them all, or only the most serious.
- It should be clear that a breach has taken place. There may be an actionable anticipatory
  breach before performance of the contract is due, if for example A contracts to sell goods
  to B in three months' time, but then sells them to C before performance is due. This must
  be distinguished from the case where there is only a threat of a breach, so that it may be
  appropriate to negotiate or to seek an injunction to try to ensure performance rather
  than commence an action.

If there has been a serious breach then there may be an important question as to whether the **18.39**
contract as a whole is over. Relevant considerations here include the following.

- It is only possible to treat a contract as over where there has been a serious breach that
  amounts to a fundamental breach or a total failure of consideration. The type of term
  breached and the seriousness of the breach will be relevant to whether the contract can
  be treated as over or not. The point is whether the breach has gone to the root of the
  contract, see *George Mitchell (Chesterhall) v Finney Lock Seeds* [1983] 2 AC 803. The point is
  not how much of a problem has been created for the claimant, but how the breach relates
  to the term—late delivery of goods is only a fundamental breach if time is of the essence
  of the contract.
- Whether the claimant wants the contract to continue, so that other obligations still have
  to be fulfilled, or whether the innocent party is prepared to see the contract as over and
  to sue for damages.
- If a contract has been repudiated then it is open to the claimant to accept or reject
  the repudiation, and the claimant's choice should be communicated to the defendant. If
  the contract is at an end then nothing more can be done under its terms.

If an action for breach of contract is contemplated, a check should be made as to whether the **18.40**
claimant has fulfilled her or his side of the contract. The claimant may be slow to volunteer
information on this and may need to be asked.

- If the claimant has not fulfilled a term that is a condition precedent then it may be that
  the defendant is not yet obliged to perform his or her part of the contract, and this will
  provide a defence.
- If the claimant is also in breach or intends to breach in retaliation for the defendant's
  breach then there may be a counterclaim.
- Unless there has been a fundamental breach, a total failure of consideration, or a
  repudiation that has been accepted, a claimant should be ready, willing, and able to
  perform his or her obligations under a contract in order to be able to sue on it.

For particulars of claim relying on breach of contract see 18.121, 18.124, 18.125, and 18.129.

Misrepresentation

The meaning of misrepresentation

18.41   The mere fact that something is said that turns out to be misleading, or that a defendant does not do something he or she said would be done does not mean that there has been an actionable misrepresentation. A misrepresentation is only actionable when five key ingredients can be identified.

- That a representation of fact has been made, whether written, oral, by conduct, or by silence (a representation of opinion or intention is not sufficient).
- That the representation was made to the claimant, or to people including the claimant, and the defendant intended the claimant to act on the basis of the representation, or at least realised that this was possible.
- That the claimant was induced by the representation to enter a contract, even if the representation was not the only inducement.
- That that representation can be shown to be false.
- That the claimant has suffered loss and damage as a result of relying on the misrepresentation.

18.42   Any term of contract that seeks to avoid or limit liability for misrepresentation will only be effective if it is reasonable, Unfair Contract Terms Act 1977, s 11.

The types of misrepresentation

18.43   Misrepresentations can be of various kinds.

18.44   Innocent. If the defendant can show that he reasonably believed the misrepresentation to be true than the misrepresentation will be characterised as innocent.

18.45   Negligent. If the claimant proves the misrepresentation and the defendant cannot show he or she reasonably believed it to be true then the misrepresentation is characterised as negligent, or simply as misrepresentation as this is the most common case.

18.46   Fraudulent. If it can be shown that the defendant knew that the representation was false, or was reckless as to whether it was false then the action can be brought in fraud or deceit. However, as this is an allegation that the defendant has acted in a quasi criminal way, there is a high standard of proof, and in professional terms such an allegation should only be made if there is reasonably credible evidence and explicit instructions from the client.

Causes of action for misrepresentation

18.47   The potential causes of action that are available where there has been a misrepresentation are given below.

18.48   An action under the Misrepresentation Act 1967. If the five ingredients listed above are shown then the claimant can seek damages under the Act. The misrepresentation will be taken to be negligent unless the defendant can prove it was innocent. For an example of a claim see 18.132.

18.49   An action for breach of contract. Where it can be shown that the representations became terms of the contract then an action for breach is possible. It will not be easy to show that oral representations or something in a separate document became part of a written contract.

An action for breach of collateral warranty. Because of the problems of incorporating separate   **18.50**
representations into a contract it may be possible to argue that the representations formed a
collateral contract with the consideration of entering the main contract.

Negligent misstatement. A misstatement can be actionable under the principles of *Headley*   **18.51**
Byrne & Co v Heller & Partners Ltd (1964) AC 465, but this only applies in specific circumstances where there is a duty to give reasonably accurate information on a particular matter.
Negligent misstatement tends to be more difficult to show than misrepresentation under
the 1967 Act, though an action can be based on an opinion or advice, which an action under
the Act cannot.

Deceit. An action for fraud or deceit can be brought if the claimant can prove that the   **18.52**
defendant made the representation knowing it was false, not believing it to be true, or
reckless to whether it was true or false, *Derry v Peek* (1889) 14 All Cas 337, and *Thomas Witter*
Ltd v TBP Industries Ltd (1996) 2 All ER 573. It is not easy to prove fraud—because the
allegation is essentially criminal the standard of proof will be higher than the normal balance of probabilities. Since an allegation of fraud that fails could have a negative effect on
the defendant's reputation there may be a costs penalty if an allegation is made and fails. In
professional terms a lawyer should only make an allegation of deceit in a civil case if he or
she feels that there is reasonably credible evidence of fraud, and if the client agrees to the
allegation being made. As it is easier to prove statutory misrepresentation and the measure
of damages is essentially the same, that would normally be the preferred cause of action.
Deceit may be chosen where there is clear evidence of fraud, and where recission is the
preferred remedy.

Other possible causes of action

Other possible causes of action in a contractual situation include the following.   **18.53**

- It may be possible for someone who is not a party to a contract to bring an action under
  the Contract (Rights of Third Parties) Act 1999, if the contract expressly provides for this,
  or a term purports to confer a benefit on the third party (unless it does not appear it was
  intended that the term be enforceable by the third party).
- It may be possible to sue a non-party for the tort of inducing breach of contract, where
  someone else knew of the contract and positively encouraged a party to it to breach it,
  see *Merkur Island Shipping Corporation v Laughton* [1983] AC 570.
- Even if there is a contract, there may be options apart from a contractual action. There
  may be a concurrent tort action, for example in negligence. This possibility is considered
  in Chapter 19.

G   SELECTING A CAUSE OF ACTION

Sometimes there will only be one potential cause of action, so the role of the lawyer will be   **18.54**
to assess its strength and then to proceed as appropriate.

Making choices where there is more than one breach

18.55 Sometimes there may be more than one breach of contract, in which case a choice will need to be made as to whether to pursue all breaches or only some of the more serious ones.

- It may be best to pursue only one or two of the most serious breaches if this will help to make it easier to define issues and to keep costs down.
- It may be best to pursue a range of breaches if all contribute to the overall seriousness of the case and are based on the same set of facts.
- The most important factor is likely to be the causation of damages—damages will only be recoverable insofar as they are caused by an actionable breach.

Making choices where there is more than one cause of action

18.56 If there is more than one contractual cause of action then breach of contract will normally be the option of choice. Another cause of action such as breach of a collateral contract would normally only be used if clearly justified on the facts and it added anything to the remedies sought.

18.57 It is quite possible that there may be actionable misrepresentations in addition to breaches of contract. If it can be argued that the misrepresentations have become terms then breach of contract may again be the cause of action of choice. If the misrepresentations have not become terms or relate to other matters then both actions may be brought together. Fraudulent misrepresentation and negligent misstatement are more difficult to prove, and should only be used if clearly justified on the facts.

18.58 It may be an important consideration that the measure for damages for breach is contractual and the measure of damages for misrepresentation is tortious (note that tortious is often corrected by a spell checker to tortuous—which is not the same thing but not wholly inaccurate!).

The overlap between contract and tort

18.59 There are many circumstances in which facts can give rise to causes of action in both contract and tort. This can happen if a contract has been induced by a misrepresentation and has also been breached. It can also happen where a duty of care overlaps with a contractual duty, if for example a contract is made with a professional person such as an architect, where the level of professional duty in tort will normally overlap or coincide with the express or implied terms of the contract. A contract with a tradesperson will often have an implied term of reasonable care and skill, which may well be the same as the duty owed in tort where a tradesperson makes or repairs something.

18.60 Where there is an overlap there may be merit in bringing actions in both tort and contract at the same time, unless a single cause of action is strong and can achieve all desired remedies. The following factors may be relevant.

- The full range of potential causes of action should be identified and evaluated.
- In evaluating the potential success of a cause of action the legal complexity is relevant— the elements for establishing a misrepresentation are more complex than the basic elements of term and breach.

- Which cause of action is easier to prove, and how expensive and difficult might it be to gather relevant evidence?
- Which cause of action leads most directly to the remedies that the client hopes to achieve?

H   SELECTING REMEDIES

There are some basic considerations relevant to deciding what remedies to pursue in a   **18.61** contract case.

- What remedies does the client most want to achieve?
- Does the nature of the breach and the view of the claimant mean that the contract is over? If not, are the other terms of the contract being fulfilled?
- What remedies and measure of damages are available for each cause of action that may be available?
- Is it desirable to keep any continuing relationship with the defendant?

Damages and other money payments

A common remedy in a contract case is a claim for damages. The principles for the quantifi-   **18.62** cation of damages are set out in 18.78–18.105.

Also common is a claim for the payment of the contract price. The contract price may be due   **18.63** under the terms of the contract, or where there is a sale of goods and property in the goods has passed, Sale of Goods Act 1979, s 49.

There may be a claim for the restitution of money where there is total failure of consider-   **18.64** ation, or where money has been paid under a mistake, *Kleinwort Benson Ltd v Lincoln City Council* (1998) 4 All ER 513 and *Wrotham Park Estate Co Ltd v Parkside Homes Ltd* (1974) 1 WLR 798. It should be noted however that it is only normally and logically possible to reclaim the consideration for a contract when the contract is effectively being undone. If a party is suing for breach of contract then the consideration is the price of the obligation being relied on and it cannot be reclaimed.

A money payment can be claimed where there is an unjust enrichment, *Lipkin Gorman v*   **18.65** *Karpnale* (1991) AC 548, and equity may require a defendant to account for profits in other circumstances. It may also be possible to construct an argument based on equitable principles and the creation of a constructive trust. In appropriate circumstances the court can order a defendant to account for profits he or she has made through a breach of contract, *Attorney-General v Blake* (2000) 4 All ER 385.

A claim for *quantum meruit* can be made to provide reasonable recompense where work has   **18.66** been done or value received without a price being set.

An injunction

An interim injunction might provide an appropriate remedy to support a contractual right,   **18.67** see Chapter 16, or a perpetual injunction might if appropriate be claimed at trial. It will normally be necessary to have an express or implied negative term in the contract on which to base the injunction, though see *Films Rover International Ltd v Cannon Film Sales Ltd* [1986] 3 All ER 772. It may be difficult to get an injunction if the contract is too vague, and it will be necessary to show that damages will not be an adequate remedy, see *Shepherd Homes Ltd v Sandham* (1971) Ch 340.

18.68   If a contract has already been breached it should be relatively easy to get an injunction to prevent further breach. If the contract has not yet been breached there will be a high standard of proof that the defendant will breach the contract, and that loss and damage will ensue. Anticipatory breach (where the defendant breaches before performance is due) should be distinguished from a threat to breach, where a *quia timet* injunction can be sought. For an example of a claim for an injunction see 18.130.

18.69   It is not possible to get an injunction that would in effect provide specific performance by the back door—in such a case the criteria for specific performance will be applied, *Sky Petroleum Ltd v VIP Petroleum Ltd* (1974) 1 WLR 567. A restraint of trade clause may be enforced by injunction, but this can cause problems for a contract for personal services if the effect is that an individual will be unable to work so an injunction may be refused, *Warner Bros Pictures Inc v Nelson* (1937) 1 KB 209 and *Page One Records Ltd v Britton* (1968) 1 WLR 157. It will not be possible to get an injunction to prevent a third party inducing a breach of contract, *Warren v Mendy* (1989) 3 All ER 103.

Other equitable remedies

18.70   In addition to an injunction, other equitable remedies may be appropriate in a contract case. Equitable remedies are discretionary, and are subject to equitable principles such as the need for the claimant to come with clean hands (for example not also be in breach of contract), and for the remedy to be sought without delay.

Recission

18.71   The effect of recission is to undo the contract so that the parties are returned to the position they were in before the contract was made, with the return of any property or money. It is important to explain to a client what recission involves—it undoes the contract rather than awarding damages for problems in performance and this may not be the best choice for a client in a particular case.

18.72   A contract may be rescinded if there is a fundamental problem like total failure of consideration, a fraudulent misrepresentation, or undue influence. Recission may also be granted by the court for statutory misrepresentation, or the court may grant damages in lieu of recission. Recission is not an appropriate remedy for mistake, *Great Peace Shipping Ltd v Tsavliris Salvage (International) Ltd* (2002) 4 All ER 689.

18.73   If a person has a right to rescind a contract and wishes to do so it can be done simply by giving notice to that effect to the other party to the contract. A party can only rescind where there is a right to rescind, otherwise they may be seen to be wrongly repudiating a contract. If a party does not rescind they may be taken to be affirming the contract. It may be necessary to involve a court to implement the recission of a contract if the other side does not cooperate.

If recission is sought from the court, the court has a discretion, and recission will not **18.74**
normally be granted if:

- it is not possible to put the parties back where they were, see *Finelvet AG v Vinava Shipping Co* [1983] 2 All ER 658, and *O'Sullivan v Management Agency and Music Ltd* (1985) QB 428;
- the contract has been affirmed;
- there has been a lapse of time or delay in seeking it, but time will run from the time the claimant knows of the facts giving rise to recission, and the right to it, *Peyman v Lanjani* [1984] 3 All ER 703;
- a third party has acquired rights following the contract.

Specific performance

Specific performance may be ordered to enforce the terms of the contract. The purpose of a **18.75**
contract is that it be performed, so specific performance may be particularly desirable where
a contract has an objective that cannot easily be met in another way. For an example of a
claim for specific performance see 18.121.

Specific performance is a discretionary remedy and may not be granted in some **18.76**
circumstances.

- If damages are an adequate remedy, as common law remedies must be exhausted before equitable ones. Damages will not be adequate where what has been contracted for is unique or special, *Sky Petroleum Ltd v VIP Petroleum Ltd* (1974) 1 WLR 576 and *Sudbrook Trading Estate v Eggleton* [1982] 3 All ER 1, or where the contract relates to something ongoing.
- If enforcement would require court supervision, *Tito v Waddell (No 2)* (1977) Ch 106, *Posner v Scott-Lewis* (1987) Ch 25 and *Co-operative Insurance Society Ltd v Argyll Stores (Holdings) Ltd* (1997) 3 All ER 297.
- If the contract is too vague to be specifically enforceable.
- Where the contract involves personal services, or personal rights might be infringed, but see *Hill v CA Parsons & Co Ltd* (1972) Ch 305. In such a case it may be important to try to negotiate a settlement if the contract is to continue.
- If the claimant has accepted another remedy, *Meng Leong Developments Pte Ltd v Jip Hong Trading Co Pte Ltd* [1985] 1 All ER 120.
- A contract for the sale of land will need to be in writing to be specifically enforceable, *Cohen v Nessdale* [1981] 3 All ER 118.

Rectification

A contract may be rectified in limited circumstances. This remedy cannot be used to change **18.77**
the terms of a contract to what a claimant would have liked to have agreed, but only where
terms can be shown to have been agreed but have not been recorded. This can only be done
if there is an error or mutual mistake, not just because one party was mistaken as to what was
intended.

I PRINCIPLES FOR ASSESSING DAMAGES

Measures of damages

18.78   The normal purpose of contract damages is to put the claimant where he or she would have been if the contract had been fulfilled. This effectively looks to the future, and it can take into account the loss of profit or of opportunity that was intended to flow from the contract. This measure can be described as loss of profit or loss of contractual bargain.

18.79   If there are different ways of assessing loss and damage, the claimant is entitled to the measure of damages that is most favourable, provided it is reasonable and should not have been mitigated, *Paula Lee v Zehil & Co* [1983] 2 All ER 390. If there are different ways of performing a contract, it will be assumed that the defendant will choose the most advantageous.

Loss of profit

18.80   It is for the claimant to put together a claim for damages for loss of profit or loss of bargain based on identifying each alleged breach of contract and each head of loss for each breach.

18.81   It is essential to be able to show the causation of loss—that the breach of contract led to or was the effective or dominant cause of the loss. One way of expressing this is that there would have been no loss had the defendant not breached the contract, *Banque Bruxelles Lambert SA v Eagle Star Insurance Co Ltd* (1995) QB 375.

18.82   Each head of loss should also be within the reasonable contemplation of the parties, *Hadley v Baxendale* (1884) 9 Ex 341. Damage which arises naturally will normally be seen as being within the reasonable contemplation of the parties, as will damage that at the time of the contract the parties should have foreseen as a serious possibility if there were to be a breach of the contract. If the defendant's breach caused the claimant to lose a particularly valuable contract with someone else, the claimant will only be able to recover if the defendant knew of the contract, *Victoria Laundry (Windsor) v Newman Industries* [1949] 2 KB 548.

18.83   Damages are normally assessed at the time of the breach, but while this is logical it might lead to injustice in a fast moving commercial world. It seems that the court will assess damages at some other time if good reason is given, *Johnson v Agnew* (1980) AC 367.

18.84   Damages may be irrecoverable or limited in the following circumstances:

* If the loss is too speculative—the claimant may have had unrealistic views of what the contract would lead to, and the defendant cannot be called on to meet this.
* If the loss has arisen because the claimant made a bad bargain, rather than from the breach of the defendant, *C & P Haulage v Middleton* (1983) 1 WLR 1461.
* Where there would be double recovery if the same loss were claimed for two different breaches or under two different heads.

18.85   As regards putting a value on loss of profit, a way must be found to forecast potential future profits even if this is difficult. This may require expert financial assistance. If a figure is difficult to assess it is especially important to develop arguments as to what the client should properly be awarded. It is the task of the lawyer to argue how damages should be assessed—it is for the judge only to decide between methods of assessment that have been put forward, and not to decide a method of assessment personally. In *Western Web Offset Printers Ltd v Independent Media Ltd* The Times, 10 October 1995, the defendant argued that in a recession when the claimant had spare capacity anyway he should only get a net loss of profit (less all overheads) of £38,245, but the Court of Appeal held that the claimant was entitled to a gross loss of profit of £176,903.

The difference in the figures shows that arguments on how to quantify loss of profit are worth developing. **18.86**

- Where there is a ready market for something, loss of profit can easily be measured by comparison with other transactions, see *Lazenby Garages Ltd v Wright* (1976) 1 WLR 459. This may not be easy to assess, *Shearson Lehmann Hutton Inc v Maclaine Watson & Co Ltd (No 2)* (1990) 3 All ER 723, but it is for the claimant to propose how it should be assessed.
- Loss of future profit can be based on figures for existing profits and comparison with a similar business, *Sun Valley Poultry Ltd v Micro-Biologicals Ltd* The Times, 14 May 1990.
- Damages for loss of a chance are recoverable, and the figure awarded may be substantial rather than limited if the chance lost was substantial rather than speculative, *First Interstate Bank of California v Cohen Arnold & Co* The Times, 11 December 1995.
- It may be necessary to chose between diminution in value (what the claimant has lost) and the cost of cure (what it will cost to put things right following the breach).

Wasted expenditure

Where any expected profit from the contract is nebulous or difficult to assess but the claimant **18.87** has spent substantial sums of money in reliance on the agreed contract, the alternative measure of 'wasted expenditure' may be used to reimburse the claimant for the money spent, *Anglia TV v Reed* [1972] 1 QB 60. It would seem that recovering reliance loss is a direct alternative to loss of profit, and the claimant must choose between them and seek the appropriate heads of damage in the statement of case, *CCC Films (London) v Impact Quadrant Films* [1984] 3 All ER 298. For a claim based on wasted expenditure see 18.129.

Damages for misrepresentation

An alternative measure of damages will apply in a misrepresentation case. A claim under the **18.88** Misrepresentation Act 1967 will attract the tort measure of damages, *Andre et Cie v Ets Michel Blanc et Fils* [1977] 2 Lloyds Rep 166 and indeed the deceit measure of damages, *Royscot Trust Ltd v Rogerson* (1991) 2 QB 297. This measure is essentially tortious, and the intention is to put the claimant where he or she would have been had the misrepresentation not been made—which would probably be that the claimant would not have made the contract. This measure is not likely to include the loss of profit that the claimant might have made had the contract gone ahead, but is likely to include recovering the consideration paid for the contract. It seems that damages can be recovered for a profit the claimant would have made as an alternative to entering the contract subject to misrepresentation, *East v Maurer* (1991) 2 All ER 733, or the extra profit the claimant would have made had money been used in a different way, *Clef Aquitaine v Laporte Materials (Barrow) Ltd* (2000) 3 All ER 493. Note that the reasonable foreseeability test does not apply in deceit damages, *Smith New Court Securities Ltd v Scrimgeour Vickers (Asset Management) Ltd* (1997) 4 All ER 769.

If the misrepresentations can be shown to have become terms of the contract then **18.89** contractual damages will apply. These damages will seek to put the claimant where she or he would have been had the contract been fulfilled (ie had the representations been true), which will include loss of profit, but not recovery of the consideration paid for the contract. On appropriate facts damages for both breach of contract and misrepresentation can be claimed, and the lawyer should assess whether some heads of loss and damage might be recoverable in contract but not in tort or vice versa. Tort damages tend to be more generous on remoteness or causation, but may give less if contributory negligence is involved. Contract damages tend to provide more where the contract was particularly advantageous or there is significant economic loss, especially loss of future profits. If actions in tort and contract succeed on the same facts then all damages recoverable in tort and contract should be awarded, provided there is no double recovery.

18.90 The normal tort measure of damages will apply for negligent misstatement.

18.91 A further complexity arises if contributory negligence is raised in a misrepresentation case, through an allegation that the claimant could reasonably have discovered that the representation was false. If there is concurrent liability in misrepresentation and negligence then damages may be reduced, *Gran Gelato Ltd v Richcliffe (Group) Ltd* (1992) Ch 560. However if there is concurrent liability in contract and misrepresentation, contributory negligence will probably not apply, and it is not a defence in deceit, *Standard Chartered Bank v Pakistan National Shipping Corp* (2003) 1 All ER 173.

Quantum meruit

18.92 A further alternative basis for assessing damages is *quantum meruit*, in a quasi contract action where damages cannot be claimed under a contract because no sum was set for the work to be done, or where contractual work has not been finished through no fault of the claimant. In such cases an equitable figure for the value of the work may be claimed to ensure fairness. The award made will depend on the facts of the case, see *British Steel Corporation v Cleveland Bridge Engineering* [1984] 1 All ER 504.

Stages in assessing damages

Identify the appropriate measure of damages

18.93 Any award of damages must be assessed in accordance with an overall measure of damages. The appropriate measure for each cause of action should be identified.

Identify the heads of damage

18.94 All the separate items of loss or heads of damage need to be identified. The client may be asked to produce a list of what has been lost as a basis for this. All consequential and incidental loss should be included, even if the amount of loss is not easy to assess. It is important to look at the position that the client will be left in practically to see that the damages will not leave ongoing loss, see *Bacon v Cooper Metals* [1982] 1 All ER 397.

Causation

18.95 All heads of loss and damage should be recoverable provided a chain of causation from the cause of action to the loss can be identified. This may require establishing a chain of causation with an argument.

Attaching figures to each head of loss

Having identified the heads of damage it will be necessary to attach a figure to each. **18.96**
Provisional figures should be used as early as is reasonably possible, to assist in decisions in
taking the case forward. Figures will be required for the particulars of claim.

As regards the principles for attaching figures to heads of loss: **18.97**

- For loss of profit see 18.80–18.86.
- Values are normally based on market value, unless it is shown some other value should
  be used. If the claimant has had to borrow money at a high rate of interest to address
  problems caused by a breach of contract this may be recoverable, *Wadsworth v Lydall*
  [1981] 2 All ER 401.
- There may be a question as to the currency in which losses are to be assessed (normally
  the currency in which the loss was suffered), and about exchange rates, see *Miliangos v
  George Frank (Textiles) Ltd* (1976) AC 443.
- While there is merit in presenting an argument as to how damages should be quantified,
  this must be structured within normal principles, *White Arrow Express Ltd v Lamey's
  Distribution Ltd* The Times, 21 July 1995.

Proving loss

Unless loss and damage is admitted, both the causation of loss and the value of loss will have   **18.98**
to be proved.

As regards causation of loss, evidence from which damage can be reasonably inferred may be   **18.99**
enough if that is all that can reasonably be expected. For economic loss and future loss there
should ideally be evidence of what profit was expected from what source.

While evidence of future loss can present a problem because there is an element of guess-   **18.100**
work, evidence of profits from similar transactions, and of profits that were projected,
together with evidence showing why that prediction was reasonable may be appropriate.
There needs to be sufficient evidence to show that there was a substantial chance or
probability of profit—a possibility of profit is not enough.

Problems with recoverability

The damages actually recovered by a claimant in a contract case may be less than the dam-   **18.101**
ages claimed for a variety of reasons. Possible problems will need to be taken into account in
advising on what is recoverable. Clearly damages will be reduced or irrecoverable where it is
found that the loss was not caused by the cause of action, that the loss was not reasonably
foreseeable, or that the full amount of the loss claimed has not been sufficiently proved.

Irrecoverable heads

It is not normally possible to recover damages for injury to feelings in a contract case.   **18.102**
Damages may only be recovered where there is an express or implied term of enjoyment in
the contract. It has been held that damages under this head could be recovered where a flat
did not have a roof terrace as represented, *Saunders v Edwards* [1987] 2 All ER 651, but
not where there was no rear entry to property as represented where the case involved
commercial premises, *Hayes v James Charles Dodd* [1990] 2 All ER 815.

The duty to mitigate

18.103   If a head of damage is recoverable, it may still be argued that the amount claimed is too high because the claimant could have mitigated the loss suffered. All claimants are under a duty to mitigate, which requires the claimant to take reasonable steps to reduce loss, and to avoid taking steps that would increase it. A claimant may not have to mitigate if he or she cannot afford to do so, *Perry v Sidney Phillips and Son* (1982) 1 WLR 1297 and *Alcoa Minerals of Jamaica v Broderick* (2000) 3 WLR 23.

18.104   The lawyer should advise the client about the duty to mitigate at an early stage so that the client takes appropriate steps to avoid incurring a loss that may not be recoverable. Some clients will naturally want to mitigate their loss but some will be angry at what has happened and may not wish to do so, and the legal duty must be made clear to them. It is possible to recover the reasonable costs of mitigation as part of the damages in the action.

Contributory negligence

18.105   Contributory negligence is a concept in tort, and applies primarily in a case of negligence. In principle contributory negligence cannot reduce a contract action where there is no allegation of negligence, *AB Maritrans v Cornet Shipping Co Ltd* [1985] 3 All ER 442, or where there is not concurrent liability in tort and contract, *Lambert v Lewis* (1982) AC 225. However, contributory negligence may reduce damages where claims in contract and in negligence overlap, *Forsickringsaktieselskapet Vesta v Burtcher* (1989) AC 852, unless there is strict liability for the contractual claim, *Barclays Bank plc v Fairclough Building Ltd* (1995) 1 All ER 289.

J   DRAFTING A CONTRACT CLAIM

18.106   In general terms the drafting of statements of case in contract follows the normal rules and approach set out in Chapter 12. There are some special rules for drafting in a contract case. Under PD 16 para 7:

- if the claim is based on a written agreement, a copy of the contract or documents constituting the agreement should be attached or served with the particulars of claim, PD 16 para 7.3;
- if a claim is based on an oral agreement, the particulars of claim should set out the contractual words used and state by whom, to whom, and when they were spoken, PD 16 para 7.4;
- if the claim is based on an agreement by conduct, the particulars of claim should specify the conduct relied on and state by whom, when, and where the acts constituting the conduct occurred (together with the assumed effect of the conduct), PD 16 para 7.5.

18.107   Care should be taken in drafting the following matters:

- The making of a contract should be set out in sufficient detail, identifying precisely who made the contract, when it was made, whether it was oral or written, and what consideration was agreed.
- Any terms of a written contract on which the action relies should be set out or referred to specifically. The wording of any implied terms should be given.

- If there is any obligation or condition precedent to the defendant fulfilling obligations, it is best to plead that such obligations or conditions have been fulfilled.
- Clear particulars should be given of a breach, stating as precisely as possible how and when it is alleged the contract was breached.
- Sufficient facts should be given to show causation of loss and damage, and if necessary how such loss or damage was in the reasonable contemplation of the parties.
- If misrepresentation is alleged then the precise wording or nature of the representations made should be given, together with allegations that the representations were intended and did lead to the making of the contract. There should also be an allegation that the representations were false, setting out how they were false. If it is alleged that the representations were fraudulent this should be specifically stated.

K   ADVISING A DEFENDANT

The general approach to defending an action was outlined in Chapter 17. In a contract **18.108** action the following considerations may be relevant.

The contract and its terms

- There may be arguments about whether a contract was concluded, about when or how **18.109** the contract was finalised, or about who the parties were.
- There may be arguments about the meaning of terms in a written contract.
- The defendant may argue that the terms of the contract were varied, in which case the new terms and the basis for the variation must be specifically identified.
- There may be arguments about the terms of an oral contract. This may relate to the terms the claimant asserts, or the defendant may assert additional terms.
- There may be arguments about what terms should be implied into a contract, unless those terms are implied by statute. The defendant may seek to argue there should be further implied terms.
- The defendant may seek to rely on terms of the contract, such as an exclusion clause. Whether this will protect him will depend on the construction of the words and whether they apply to what has actually happened, *Photo Production v Securicor Transport* [1980] AC 827. For a defence based on an exclusion clause see 18.127.
- The defendant may try to argue that he or she is not bound by a contract, for example because it was frustrated, or because of duress or undue influence. Such arguments do not often succeed.

The cause of action

- In a breach of contract case, the defendant may argue on the facts that he or she was not **18.110** in breach of the contract.

- In a misrepresentation case the defendant may argue that any of the ingredients of the cause of action did not exist—for example that the representation was not made, that it was not intended to be relied on, or that it was true.

The remedies

Damages

18.111 It may be argued:

- that some of the claimed heads of loss or damage are not recoverable;
- that the amount claimed for a head of loss or damage is too high or too speculative;
- that there is no chain of causation linking a head of loss or damage to a cause of action;
- that a head of loss or damage was not within the reasonable contemplation of the parties;
- that the claimant should have mitigated the loss or damage alleged;
- that the damages for a particular event have been quantified in advance in the contract.

Other remedies

18.112 Other options are:

- an equitable remedy can be resisted on the basis of delay, that the claimant does not come with clean hands etc;
- a claim for recission be resisted on the basis that it is not possible to put the parties back to their previous positions.

Terms limiting liability

18.113 Many contracts contain terms that exclude liability in certain circumstances, and/or that limit liability. Such terms may be specially negotiated, may be printed on a pro forma that is generally used (for example a document quoting a cost for work to be done), may be small print on a ticket, or may be incorporated from separate documents or signs.

18.114 A freely negotiated term will rarely present a problem, save for a possible argument as to meaning. Any term that excludes or restricts liability will be construed against the party seeking to rely on it.

18.115 Such terms are often standing terms that are not negotiated for each contract and on which the purchaser has no choice. The Unfair Contract Terms Act 1977 provides protection in such circumstances.

- Where a consumer deals with a business or a contract is in a standard form then any term that seeks to exclude or restrict liability will also be subject to the test of reasonableness.
- Liability for death or personal injury through negligence cannot be excluded by contract.
- If a party tries to rely on an exclusion clause as a defence to negligent performance of a contract then there is a test of reasonableness.

18.116 As regards an attempt to restrict liability through a liquidated damages clause, which provides a maximum to be paid in the event of a particular type of breach, a court will not enforce such a clause if it is found to be a penalty, *Dunlop Pneumatic Tyre Co Ltd v New Garage and Motor Co Ltd* (1915) AC 79. The tests for whether a clause is a penalty include whether there is a genuine pre-estimate of damage, whether the clause is intended to cover a wide range of events (making it less likely there is a genuine pre-estimate), and whether the term is unconscionable. The court will also look to see if the clause actually applies to what has happened, *Export Credit Guarantee Dept v Universal Oil Products Co* [1983] 2 All ER 205.

The Unfair Terms in Consumer Contracts Regulations 1999 (SI 1999/2083) contain more **18.117** detailed provisions for banking, mortgage transactions etc, where it is particularly likely that there may be special terms restricting liability, and particularly likely that a consumer may fail to understand the terms. Terms must be written in plain English and unfair terms will not be binding.

A counterclaim or set-off

The defendant may have a counterclaim against the claimant, and/or may be able to claim a **18.118** set-off. In a contract case, a defendant might want to counterclaim for and set off the contract price if it has not been paid, or may want to counterclaim if the claimant is in breach of a term of the contract.

Drafting the defence

The following elements would commonly be part of planning for and drafting a defence in a **18.119** contract case.

- Deal with the claimant's description of the making of the contract and its terms. Most commonly one would admit that the contract was made and who the parties were.
- Allege any further terms on which the defendant relies, dealing first with express terms and then with implied terms.
- Deny the cause of action (breach, misrepresentation etc).
- Raise any specific defence (eg an exclusion clause).
- Require the claimant to prove damage.
- Deny causation of damage of all or part of the damage.
- Allege failure of the claimant to mitigate loss.

L   SAMPLE DRAFTS FOR A CONTRACT CASE

The following sample statements of case are intended to illustrate the structure and elements **18.120** appropriate for common causes of action and defences in a contract case. They are not intended to provide detailed pro formas as it is important that each statement of case is drafted to meet the needs of the individual case.

Example 1. Particulars of claim—sale of goods—specific performance

18.121

IN THE CAMBRIDGE COUNTY COURT   Claim No CB5/2345

BETWEEN

SAMUEL SHYLOCK <u>Claimant</u>

and

ANTONIO MERCHANT GALLERIES (a firm) <u>Defendants</u>

PARTICULARS OF CLAIM

1.   The Defendants are and were at all material times dealers and specialists in modern prints and paintings carrying on business from their galley at 13 Venice Row Cambridge ('the gallery').

2.   On 1 September 2004 the Claimant visited the gallery. At that time there was a show of paintings by the modern Venetian artist Mercy Qualiti. An agreement was made by the Claimant and Basil Bassanio acting in the course of his employment as an assistant at the gallery under which the Defendants would sell to the Claimant a set of 6 paintings entitled 'Pounds of Flesh' ('the paintings'), for a consideration of £30,000. The agreement is set out in writing in a note of sale signed by the parties on 1 September 2004, a copy of which is attached. The Claimant paid a deposit of £10,000.

3.   It was an express or alternatively implied term of the agreement that the paintings would be delivered to the Claimant shortly after the show of paintings ended on 7 September 2004. It was an express or alternatively implied term of the agreement that the balance of the purchase price would be paid on delivery of the paintings.

4.   The Claimant has made several requests for the delivery of the paintings, both orally and in writing, but in breach of the agreement the Defendants have refused and still refuse to deliver the paintings to the Claimant.

5.   The Claimant remains willing and able to pay to the Defendants the balance of the purchase price, £20,000.

AND the Claimant claims:

(1)   Specific performance of the agreement.

(2)   Further or in the alternative, damages for breach of the agreement.

(3)   Interest on those damages under section 69 of the County Courts Act 1984 to be assessed.

Abe A. Rister

Statement of Truth
The Claimant believes that the facts stated in the Particulars of Claim are true.

Dated etc.

Attachment:

ANTONIO MERCHANT GALLERIES

Record of sale:

The series of paintings entitled 'Pounds of Flesh'   £30,000

Sold to: Samuel Shylock

1 September 2004

Deposit paid £10,000

Signed:

Basil Bassanio   Samuel Shylock

Example 2. Defence to particulars of claim in example 1—counterclaim for money due

IN THE CAMBRIDGE COUNTY COURT   Claim No CB5/2345   **18.122**

BETWEEN

SAMUEL SHYLOCK   Claimant/Part 20 Defendant

and

ANTONIO MERCHANT GALLERIES   Defendants/
(a firm)   Part 20 Claimant

DEFENCE

1. Paragraph 1 of the Particulars of Claim is admitted.

2. It is admitted that an agreement was made between the parties as alleged in Paragraph 2 of the Particulars of Claim. This agreement was oral, and is only partly evidenced by the note of sale. It is admitted that the agreement related to the series of paintings entitled 'Pounds of Flesh', but it is denied that there were 6 paintings in the series. There was no discussion as to which paintings were included in the series. It is admitted that the Claimant paid a deposit of £10,000.

3. There are only 5 paintings in the series 'Pounds of Flesh'. Although a painting 'A Drop of Blood' was hung on the same wall at the show, it was for sale for a separate consideration of £15,000.

4. It is admitted that there was an express or implied term that the paintings be delivered after the end of the show. The Defendants offered to deliver the paintings on 9 September 2004 but the Claimant refused to accept them without 'A Drop of Blood'. The Defendants are now and always have been ready and willing to deliver the 5 paintings in the series 'Pounds of Flesh', but the Claimant continues to refuse to accept delivery without 'A Drop of Blood'.

5. It is denied that there was any term that the balance of the price be payable only on delivery. There was an implied term that the balance was payable within 4 weeks, this term being implied from previous business dealings between the Claimant and the Defendants.

6. It is denied that the Defendants are in breach of contract as alleged or at all. It is admitted that the Claimant has made several requests for the delivery of the paintings, but on each occasion has insisted on the delivery of 'Pounds of Flesh' and 'A Drop of Blood'. The Defendant has made it clear on each occasion that delivery will only be made of the 5 paintings in the 'Pounds of Flesh' series as this is all that the Claimant is entitled to.

7. Paragraph 5 of the Particulars of Claim is denied. The Claimant has consistently refused to pay the balance of the purchase price until after delivery of the pictures.

8.   Paragraphs 1 to 5 of this Defence are repeated.

9.   In breach of the implied term the Claimant has failed to pay the £20,000 balance of the purchase price or any part of it, despite frequent requests from the Defendant.

10.   Further the Defendant claims interest under section 69 of the County Courts Act 1984 on the sum of £20,000 at the rate of 8% per year from 2 January 2005, amounting to £394.20 at 2 April 2005 and continuing until judgment or sooner payment at the rate of £4.38 per day.

AND the Defendant counterclaims:

(1)   £20,000.

(3)   Interest under section 69 of the County Courts Act 1984 amounting to £394.20 at 2 April 2005 and continuing until judgment or sooner payment at the rate of £4.38 per day.

Portia de Belmont

Statement of Truth

The Defendant believes that the facts stated in this Defence are true.

Dated etc.

Example 3. Particulars of claim—sale of goods—total failure of consideration—return of contract price

18.123   IN THE BOSWORTH COUNTY COURT   Claim No BW5/3456

BETWEEN

RICHARD GLOUCESTER   Claimant

and

STANLEY LORD   Defendant

PARTICULARS OF CLAIM

1.   By an oral contract made on or about 1 August 2004 between the Claimant and the Defendant at the Defendant's stables at Kingdom Manor, Bosworth Field, Leicestershire the Claimant agreed to buy from the Defendant a motorised horsebox registration number X666 ONO ('the horsebox') for a price of £8,000. This agreement is evidenced in writing on a printed invoice dated 2 August 2004, a copy of which is attached.

2.   It was an implied condition of the agreement that the Defendant would have the right to sell the horsebox at the time that property was due to pass.

3.   The Claimant paid the Defendant the price of £8,000 on 4 August 2004 and took delivery of the horsebox on 6 August 2004.

4.   In breach of the implied condition, the Defendant was not at any material time the owner of the horsebox, nor at any material time did the Defendant have the right to sell the horsebox.

5.   On 30 August 2004 the Claimant was obliged to return the horsebox to Henry Richmond Finance Limited, who were the lawful owners of the horsebox.

6.   As a result of the matters set out above, the consideration for the payment of the sum of £8,000 has wholly failed. In the alternative the Claimant has suffered loss and damage of £8,000 as a result of the Defendant's breach of the implied condition.

7.   Further the Defendant claims interest under section 69 of the County Courts Act 1984 on the sum of £8,000 at the rate of 8% per year from 1 December 2004, amounting to £208.25 at 1 April 2005 and continuing until judgment or sooner payment at the rate of £1.75 per day.

AND the Claimant claims:

(1)   £8,000.

(2)   Alternatively damages of £8,000

(3)   Interest under section 69 of the County Courts Act 1984 amounting to £208.25 at 1 April 2005 and continuing until judgment or sooner payment at the rate of £1.75 per day.

David Brent

Statement of Truth

Dated etc.

(Copy of printed invoice to be attached)

Example 4. Particulars of claim—sale of goods and services—breach of terms implied by statute

IN THE SIDCUP COUNTY COURT   Claim NoS5/4567   **18.124**

BETWEEN

(1) REGINALD ROSENCRANTZ   Claimants
(2) GILBERT GUILDENSTERN

and

CLAUDIUS REX   Defendant
(trading as Kings Decoration)
_____

PARTICULARS OF CLAIM
_____

1.   The Claimants live at Elsinore, 13, Denmark Hill, London SW33 ('the house'). The Defendant was at all material times in business as an interior decorator and as a trader in materials for interior decoration.

2.   By an oral agreement made on 1 March 2004 at the house the Defendant agreed with the Claimants to decorate the living room of the house for a price of £5,000. The Defendant also agreed to sell to the Claimants for a price of £300, 10 litres of paint which the Claimants could use to decorate the bathroom of the house.

3.   It was an implied term of the agreement that the Defendant would complete the decoration work with reasonable care and skill.

4.   Prior to making the agreement the Claimants made it known to the Defendant that the paint for the bathroom was required to cover a damp wall and provide a non-porous covering. It was therefore an implied term of the agreement that the paint should be:

(a)   reasonably fit for that purpose

(b)   of satisfactory quality.

5.   The Defendant completed the decoration work between 20 March and 27 March 2004 while the Claimants were on holiday.

6.   In breach of the term under paragraph 3 the decoration work was of poor quality in that:

(a)   the paint had be applied in a very uneven way

(b)   there were splashes of paint on the carpet

(c)   the marble fireplace had been cracked by a dropped paint pot.

7.   The Defendant supplied the paint for use on the bathroom on 19 March 2004. The Claimants used it to paint the walls of the bathroom between 4 April and 14 April 2004. On 1 May 2004 the Claimants discovered that the bathroom walls were damp and the paint was running. On 20 May the Claimants found that mould was forming on the bathroom walls.

8.   The Defendant was in breach of the term implied under paragraph 4 in that:

(a)   the paint supplied was not appropriate for use on a damp wall

(b)   the paint did not provide a non-porous covering

(c)   the paint was not appropriate for use in a bathroom.

9.   As a result of the matters set out above the Claimants have suffered distress and inconvenience in that they were unable to use the living room or the bathroom for several weeks. They have also suffered loss and damage.

PARTICULARS OF DAMAGE

Cost of getting another decorator to repaint the living room	£2,000
Cost of a new carpet for the living room	£1,000
Cost of a new marble fireplace	£2,000
Cost of getting the bathroom repainted	£1,500
	£6,500

10.   Further, the Claimants claim interest pursuant to section 69 of the County Courts Act 1984 on any amount found due to the Claimant at such rates and for such time as the court thinks fit.

AND the Claimants claim:

(1)   Damages

(2)   The aforesaid interest pursuant to section 69 of the County Courts Act 1984.

A. Fortinbras

Statement of Truth

Dated etc.

Example 5. Particulars of claim—sale of goods—breach of express terms—damages for loss of profit

IN THE HIGH COURT OF JUSTICE   Claim No 2005 HC 5678   **8.125**

QUEEN'S BENCH DIVISION

BETWEEN

PUCK'S PROMOTIONS (a firm)   <u>Claimants</u>

and

ARIEL ENTERPRISES Limited   <u>Defendants</u>

PARTICULARS OF CLAIM

1.   The Claimants own and run 10 retail shops selling games and toys in southern England. The Defendants are and were at all material times in business as wholesalers and manufacturers of magic tricks.

2.   On 21 June 2004 the Claimants entered into a written contract with the Defendants under which the Defendants were to supply the Claimants with magic tricks for a period of three years. A copy of this contract is attached to this Particulars of Claim.

3.   There were express terms of the contract that

(i)   the Defendants would not supply their products to any retail outlets in southern England other than those owned and run by the Claimant

(ii)   all goods would be delivered within 2 months of order.

4.   It was an implied term of the contract that the magic tricks would be reasonably safe for domestic use and would be of reasonable quality.

5.   On 30 July 2004 the Claimants placed an order with the Defendants for

10,000 Elfin rings ('the rings')	£20,000
1,000 boxes of 'Whispering Magic' tricks ('the tricks')	£30,000
5,000 Disappearing cloaks ('the cloaks')	£50,000
	£100,000

6.   The Defendants were in breach of the express term set out in paragraph 3(i) in that the rings were supplied to other retail shops in southern England.

7.   The Defendants were in breach of the express term set out in paragraph 3(ii) in that the cloaks were not supplied until 6 November 2004, and were therefore not supplied in time for sale for the Halloween market.

8.   The Defendants were in breach of the implied terms in paragraph 4 in that the tricks had sharp parts that caused accidents and damage. The Defendants have had to pay compensation to several customers, and had to withdraw the tricks from sale.

9.   As a result the Claimants have suffered loss and damage.

PARTICULARS OF DAMAGE

Under paragraph 6

Loss of anticipated profit on rings which could only be sold at a significant discount	£10,000

Under paragraph 7
Loss of anticipated profit on cloaks which
had to be discounted in the January sale   £25,000

Under paragraph 8
Loss of anticipated profit on the tricks   £20,000
Compensation payments made to customers   £10,000

                                                                  £65,000

In addition the business of the Claimants has suffered general loss of goodwill.

10. Further, the Claimants claim interest pursuant to section 35A of the Supreme Court
Act 1981 on any amount found due to the Claimants at such rates and for such time as
the Court thinks fit.

AND the Claimants claim:

(1) Damages.
(2) The aforesaid interest pursuant to section 35A of the Supreme Court Act 1981.

                                                                  Peimia Fortune

Statement of Truth

Dated etc.

(Copy of written contract to be attached)

Example 6. Request for further information related to example 4

18.126

<u>IN THE HIGH COURT OF JUSTICE</u>   Claim No 2005 HC 5678
<u>QUEEN'S BENCH DIVISION</u>

BETWEEN

                    PUCK'S PROMOTIONS   <u>Claimants</u>
                        (a firm)

                            and

                    ARIEL ENTERPRISES Limited   <u>Defendants/</u>
                                                           <u>Part 20 Claimants</u>

                            and

                    CALIBAN'S CON-ARTISTS plc   <u>Part 20 Defendants</u>

                ─────────────────────────────
                  REQUEST FOR FURTHER INFORMATION
                       UNDER CPR PART 18
                ─────────────────────────────

This request is made on 1 April 2005 by the defendants of the Claimants for further
information and clarification of their Particulars of Claim. The Defendants expect a
reply by 21 April 2005.

In relation to paragraph 3(i) of the Particulars of Claim

Of 'the Defendants would not supply their products to any retail outlets in southern England other than those owned and run by the Claimant'

1. (a) Please state whether the alleged term was written or oral
    (b) If written, please identify the document where the term is recorded and supply a copy of any such document
    (c) If oral, please state when, where, and by whom the term was agreed, and state as precisely as possible the words used.

In relation to paragraph 8 of the Particulars of Claim

Of 'the tricks had sharp parts that caused accidents and damage'.

2. (a) Please state as precisely as possible the alleged defects in the tricks
    (b) Please set out all accidents allegedly caused by the tricks and the damage alleged to result from each.

Of 'The Defendants have had to pay compensation to several customers'

3. (a) Please state how many customers were compensated
    (b) Please state the amount of compensation paid to each customer, and how such compensation was calculated.

In relation to paragraph 9 of the Particulars of Claim

4. Please provide particulars as to how the loss of profit is calculated.

Mack E A Velly

Example 7. Defence to particulars of claim in example 5—reliance on an exclusion clause—counterclaim/set-off

IN THE HIGH COURT OF JUSTICE	Claim No 2005 HC 5678	**18.127**
QUEEN'S BENCH DIVISION		

BETWEEN

PUCK'S PROMOTIONS	Claimants
(a firm)	
and	
ARIEL ENTERPRISES Limited	Defendants/
	Part 20 Claimants
and	
CALIBAN'S CON-ARTISTS plc	Part 20 Defendants

DEFENCE

1. Paragraphs 1 and 2 of the Particulars of Claim are admitted.

2. It is denied that there was an express term as set out in paragraph 3(i). The Claimant expressed a desire for such a term but it was not agreed as part of the contract, and is not included in the written contract. It is admitted that there was an express term as set out in paragraph 3(ii).

3.   The Defendants had an opportunity to examine samples of all products offered for sale by the Defendants. It was an express term of the contract that the Claimant would not be liable in respect of any defects or complaints relating to the quality of products.

4.   Paragraphs 4 and 5 of the Particulars of Claim are admitted.

5.   It is admitted that the rings were supplied to other outlets as alleged in paragraph 6. It is denied that this constituted a breach of contract.

6.   It is admitted that the cloaks were not supplied until 6 November. The Defendants had no knowledge that the cloaks were intended for the Halloween market and any resulting loss was not within the reasonable contemplation of the parties. The claimants failed to take reasonable steps to mitigate their loss by selling the cloaks for the best available price.

7.   The Claimants are required to prove the matters alleged in paragraph 8 of the Particulars of Claim. If there were any defects in the tricks the Defendants will seek to rely on the express term referred to in paragraph 3 above. Further or in the alternative, any defects in the tricks were caused by the Part 20 Defendants who manufactured the tricks.

8.   The Claimant is required to prove the loss and damage alleged, and the actual value alleged.

Mack E. A. Velly

Statement of Truth

Dated etc.

Example 8. Part 20 claim linked to examples 5 and 7

18.128   IN THE HIGH COURT OF JUSTICE   Claim No 2005 HC 5678
QUEEN'S BENCH DIVISION

BETWEEN

PUCKS PROMOTIONS (a firm)	Claimants
and	
ARIEL ENTERPRISES Limited	Defendants/ Part 20 Claimants
and	
CALIBAN'S CON-ARTISTS plc	Part 20 Defendants

PARTICULARS OF PART 20 CLAIM

1.   This action has been brought by the Claimant against the Defendants/Part 20 Claimants. In it the Claimant claims damages and interest for breach of contract as appears from the Particulars of Claim a copy of which is served with this Part 20 Claim.

2.   The Defendants deny that they are liable to the Claimants on the grounds set out in their Defence, a copy of which is also served with this Part 20 Claim. These Particulars of Part 20 Claim set out the Defendant/Part 20 Claimant's claim against the Part 20 Defendants.

3. The Part 20 Defendants are manufacturers and importers of various goods, including toys and fireworks. On 3 February 2004 the Defendants/Part 20 Claimants agreed to buy from the Part 20 Defendants 2,000 boxes of 'Whispering Magic' tricks for a total price of £20,000. This contract was made in writing and is set out in two facsimile transmissions, copies of which are attached to these Particulars of Part 20 Claim.

(i) Fax from the Defendants/Part 20 Claimants to the Part 20 Defendants on 3 January 2004 at 10.30 am
(ii) Fax from Part 20 Defendants to the Defendants/Part 20 Claimants on 3 January 2004 at 5.15. pm

4. It was an implied term of this agreement that the goods were of reasonable quality and were reasonably safe for domestic use.
5. The goods were delivered to the Defendants/Part 20 Claimants on 3 April 2004. The Defendants/Part 20 Claimants delivered 1,000 boxes to the Claimants on 15 August 2004.
6. In breach of the implied term set out in paragraph 4 the tricks are not of reasonable quality and are not reasonably safe for domestic use.
7. If the Defendants/Part 20 Claimants are found liable to the Claimants they will contend that this liability arose because of the Part 20 Defendants' breach of contract as set out above, as a result of which the Defendants have suffered loss and damage.

PARTICULARS OF LOSS AND DAMAGE

(a) The Defendant's liability (if any) to the Claimants.
(b) Any costs the Defendants might be ordered to pay to the Claimant.
(c) Any costs incurred by the Defendants in defending the Claimant's claim.

AND the Defendants claim damages.

Mack E. A. Velly

Statement of Truth

Dated etc.

(Copies of faxes to be attached)

Example 9. Particulars of claim—supply of services—breach of contract—application for an injunction—claim for wasted expenditure

IN THE HIGH COURT OF JUSTICE   Claim No 2005HC 6789   **18.129**
QUEEN'S BENCH DIVISION
BETWEEN

OTHELLO MOORE   Claimant

and

IAGO VILLANO   Defendant

PARTICULARS OF CLAIM

1. The Claimant is and was at all material times an international football player. The Defendant is a self-employed author.

2. By an oral agreement made on 1 August 2004 the Claimant agreed that the Defendant should act as ghost writer for an autobiography the Claimant intended to publish. As consideration the Defendant was to receive 5% of the royalties for the book provided it was completed within 2 years of the making of the agreement. The agreement was made at The Big Truffle restaurant in London.

3. It was an express term of the contract that the Defendant would treat as totally confidential any knowledge gained relating to the Claimant, save insofar as the Claimant authorised the use of such knowledge in advance.

4. It was an express term of the contract that the Claimant would meet reasonable research expenses incurred by the Defendant. The Defendant knew that this expense would be wasted if the book were not completed.

5. In breach of the express term set out in paragraph 3 the Defendant provided substantial information to a journalist for an article revealing many details of the private life of the Claimant in an article in Star Catcher magazine on 1 December 2004. As a result of this fundamental breach the Claimant was entitled to treat the contract as over. The Claimant terminated the agreement on 2 December 2004 communicating this to the Defendant by electronic mail.

6. As a result of these matters the Claimant has suffered disappointment and has incurred the loss and damage. The following expenses were incurred in relation to the Defendant's research

Buying electronic equipment for the Defendant	£10,000
Travel	£7,000
Hotels and food	£6,000
	£23,000

7. The Defendant threatens and intends to make further disclosures about the private life of the Claimant unless restrained from so doing.

8. Further, the Claimant claims interest pursuant to section 35A of the Supreme Court Act 1981 on the amount found to be due to the Claimant at such rate and for such period as the Court thinks fit.

AND the Claimant claims:

(1) An injunction ordering the Defendant not to disclose or cause to be disclosed to any person any personal information relating to the Claimant.

(2) Damages.

(3) The aforesaid interest pursuant to section 35A of the Supreme Court Act 1981.

Ann O. Nimous

Statement of Truth

Dated etc.

Example 10. Application for an interim injunction linked to examples 8 and 9

There would need to be an application notice in form N244, and a witness statement in support. **18.130**

Draft injunction order.

IN THE HIGH COURT OF JUSTICE   Claim No 2005 HC 6789
QUEEN'S BENCH DIVISION
Mr Justice

BETWEEN

OTHELLO MOORE   Claimant/Applicant

and

IAGO VILLANO   Defendant/Respondent

DRAFT ORDER FOR AN INJUNCTION

IMPORTANT

NOTICE TO THE RESPONDENT etc

An application was made on 2 December 2004 by Counsel for the Applicant to the Judge and was attended by Counsel for the Respondent. The Judge heard the Application and read the Witness Statement listed in Schedule 1 and accepted the undertaking in Schedule 2.

IT IS ORDERED that:

THE INJUNCTION

Until after final judgment in this Claim the Respondent must not:
1.   Disclose to any person or cause to be disclosed to any person any information relating to the Applicant.

COSTS OF THE APPLICATION

2.   The Respondent shall pay the Applicant's costs of this Application.

VARIATION AND DISCHARGE OF THIS ORDER etc

NAME AND ADDRESS OF APPLICANT'S SOLICITORS etc

INTERPRETATION OF THIS ORDER etc

THE EFFECT OF THIS ORDER etc

SCHEDULE 1

Witness Statements

The Judge read the following witness statement before making this Order:

Statement of Othello Moore dated 2 December 2004

SCHEDULE 2

Undertaking given to the Court by the Applicant

If the Court later finds that this Order has caused loss to the Respondent, and decides that the Respondent should be compensated for that loss, the Applicant will comply with any Order that the Court may make.

(If the Application were made without notice to the Defendant there would also need to be undertakings to issue and serve relevant documents, including a Notice for the Return Date for a hearing with both parties and copies of the evidence.)

Example 11. Defence to particulars of claim in example 10—repudiation—partial set-off

18.131   IN THE HIGH COURT OF JUSTICE   Claim No 2005HC 6789
QUEEN'S BENCH DIVISION

BETWEEN

OTHELLO MOORE   Claimant/Part 20 Defendant

and

IAGO VILLANO   Defendant/Part 20 Claimant

DEFENCE

1.   The Defendant admits paragraphs 1, 2 and 3 of the Particulars of Claim.

2.   It was also an express term of the contract that the Defendant was to be paid £2,000 per month by the Claimant during the currency of the agreement, this sum to be deducted from the royalties payable following the publication of the book.

3.   It is denied that there was a term as alleged in paragraph 4. The Claimant voluntarily paid various expenses for the Defendant, having arranged for the Defendant to meet some of the Claimant's friends.

4.   It is denied that the Defendant is in breach of contract, as alleged in Paragraph 5 of the Particulars of Claim or at all. The Defendant did not provide any information relating to the Claimant to any journalist as alleged or at all. The Claimant did send the Defendant a communication by electronic mail on 2 December purporting to end the agreement. This was a repudiation of the contract which the Defendant did not accept. The Defendant remains ready and able to fulfill the contract.

5.   It is denied that the losses alleged in paragraph 6 were caused by the alleged or any breach of contract by the Defendant. The sums were spent voluntarily by the Claimant. The Claimant is put to proof as to the amounts alleged

6.   If contrary to this Defence the Defendant is held liable to the Claimant, he will seek to reduce the Claimant's claim by setting off the sum counterclaimed below.

COUNTERCLAIM

7.   The Claimant repeats paragraph 2 of the Particulars of Claim and paragraph 3 of the Defence.

8.   By reason of the matters aforesaid, the Claimant has suffered loss and damage, namely the loss of the £8,000 payable for 4 months work under the contract.

9.   Further, the Defendant claims interest pursuant to section 35A of the Supreme Court Act 1981 on the sum of £8,000 at the rate of 8% per year from 2 December 2004, amounting to £196 on 1 April 2005 and then continuing until judgment or sooner payment at the rate of £1.75 per day.

AND the Defendant claims:

(1)   Damages.

(2)   Interest under section 35A of the Supreme Court Act 1981, amounting to £196 on 1 April 2005 and then continuing until judgment or sooner payment at the rate of £1.75 per day.

Mae O. Pinion

Statement of Truth

Dated etc.

Example 12. Particulars of claim—misrepresentation—recission

IN THE MIDDLESEX COUNTY COURT   Claim No MX5/7890   **18.132**

BETWEEN

URSULA QUICKLY   <u>Claimant</u>

and

JOHN FALSTAFF   <u>Defendant</u>

PARTICULARS OF CLAIM

1.   The Claimant is and was at all material times the owner and manager of a public house known as The Boar's Head Tavern, Eastcheap, London WC1. The Defendant is a dealer in wines, spirits and beers.

2.   On or about 1 April 2004, in order to induce the Claimant to enter into a contract with him for the purchase of wines and beers, the Defendant orally represented to the Claimant that he could supply 'Falstaff Sack' and 'Falstaff Real Ale', both of which:

(a)   Were in excellent condition for drinking.

(b)   Were already supplied to 50 public houses in the London area.

(c)   Were highly recommended in the publication 'Best Booze in Britain'.

3.   In reliance upon the Defendant's said representations, on 1 April 2004 the Claimant entered into a contract with the Defendant to purchase 50 cases of the said 'Falstaff Sack' and 100 barrels of the said 'Falstaff Real Ale' for a total price of £50,000. The contract was partly oral and partly in writing, the amounts ordered and the price being written on the reverse side of a laundry bill, a copy of which is attached to these Particulars of Claim. The Defendant assured the Claimant that a printed invoice would be supplied, but no invoice has been supplied.

4.   The full quantities of the 'Falstaff Sack' and the 'Falstaff Real Ale' were supplied on 3 April 2004. On delivery the Claimant paid £50,000 to the Defendant.

5.   The Defendant's said representations were false in that the said 'Falstaff Sack' and 'Falstaff Real Ale'

(a)   Were not in excellent condition for drinking.

(b)   Were not supplied to 50 public houses in the London area, only 20 such public houses having been supplied, and the majority of those having returned their supplies to the Defendant.

(c)   Were not highly recommended in 'Best Booze in Britain', being mentioned therein respectively only as 'too little body and too long legs' and 'veritable gnat's piss'.

5.   Having discovered the facts the Claimant telephoned the Defendant on 10 April to rescind the contract. The Claimant asked the Defendant to collect the wine and the beer but he has refused to do so. The Claimant is unable to serve the wine or the beer in her tavern and she is keeping it for collection.

6.   By reason of the matters aforesaid, the Claimant has suffered loss and damage. The value of the wine and beer as delivered was £25,000 rather than £50,000.

7.   Further the Claimant claims interest under the equitable jurisdiction of the Court or alternatively under section 69 of the County Courts Act 1984.

AND the Claimant claims;

(1)   Recission of the contract.

(2)   Repayment of the sum of £50,000

(3)   Interest under the equitable jurisdiction of the Court.

Alternatively

(1)   Damages for misrepresentation.

(2)   Interest pursuant to section 69 of the County Courts Act 1984 to be assessed.

Lorde C. Justiss

Statement of Truth

Dated etc.

(Laundry bill to be attached)

Example 13. Defence to particulars of claim in example 11

18.133   IN THE MIDDLESEX COUNTY COURT   Claim No MX5/7890
BETWEEN

URSULA QUICKLY   Claimant

and

JOHN FALSTAFF   Defendant
———
DEFENCE
———

1.   Paragraph 1 of the Particulars of Claim is admitted.

2.   Except that it is denied that the Defendant made the alleged or any oral representations in order to induce the Claimant to enter any contract, paragraph 2 is admitted. The Defendant provided the Claimant with a price list for what he had available to sell and invited the Claimant to place an order. The Claimant offered the Defendant a glass of wine and there was a general conversation relating to the beer and wine trade, but this did not form a part of the contractual negotiations.

3.   It is admitted that a contract was made as alleged in paragraph 3 of the Particulars of Claim, but the Claimant is required to prove that she relied on or was induced by any representations made by the Defendant. The Defendant sent a printed invoice by post on 2 April 2004.

4.   Paragraph 4 of the Particulars of Claim is admitted.

5.   The Defendant had reasonable grounds to believe and did believe at the time the contract was made that the wines and beers supplied were in excellent condition for drinking, this view having been expressed by a wine correspondent in a national newspaper. It is admitted that the references in 'Best Booze in Britain' are as set out in paragraph 5 of the Particulars of Claim, but the Defendant denies that the references in that publication are true. Save for these points the Claimant is required to prove the matters alleged in paragraph 5.

6.   It is admitted that the Claimant purported to rescind the contract in a telephone conversation with the Defendant on 10 April. The Defendant made it clear that he did not accept the recission of the contract. It is no longer possible for the Claimant to return the beer and wine to the Defendant in the condition in which it was supplied. The Claimant is not entitled to rescind the contract.

7.   The Claimant is required to prove that she has suffered loss and damage as alleged or at all.

Peto Bardolph

Statement of Truth

Dated etc.

19

THE TORT MODEL

A INTRODUCTION 19.01

B POTENTIAL CAUSES OF ACTION IN TORT 19.06
   Negligence 19.07
   Breach of statutory duty 19.08
   Occupier's liability 19.11
   Other tort duties 19.13

C THE ELEMENTS OF A NEGLIGENCE CASE 19.14
   The duty of care 19.14
   The level of the duty 19.19
   Failure to meet the level of duty 19.22
   Injury and/or loss and damage has resulted from the negligence 19.24

D THE PRE-ACTION STAGE 19.27
   Pre-action protocols 19.27
   Limitation 19.29

E ANALYSIS OF A TORT CASE 19.36
   The background to a case 19.36
   Accident reports 19.39
   Areas requiring expertise 19.42
   What needs to be proved 19.48

F SELECTING A CAUSE OF ACTION 19.49
   Analysing the range of causes of action 19.49
   The tort/contract overlap 19.52

G SELECTING REMEDIES 19.55
   Damages 19.55
   Return of goods 19.56
   An injunction 19.57
   A declaration 19.58

H ASSESSING DAMAGES 19.59
   The measure of damages 19.60
   Stages in assessing damages 19.67
   Reductions in damages 19.74
   Insurance 19.79

I ASSESSING PERSONAL INJURY DAMAGES 19.82

The system for assessing damages. 19.82

The schedule of expenses and losses. 19.86

Damages for pain, suffering, and loss of amenity (PSLA) 19.90

Damages for future loss of income 19.94

Deductions and additions 19.100

Provisional damages 19.104

Structured settlements 19.106

Damages for fatal accidents 19.111

J DRAFTING A TORT CLAIM 19.118

Drafting a negligence claim. 19.118

Drafting a personal injury claim. 19.123

K ADVISING A DEFENDANT. 19.129

Arguments as regards the cause of action 19.130

Potential defences 19.131

Defences as regards remedies sought 19.132

Contributory negligence 19.133

Joining other parties 19.134

Drafting a defence 19.135

L SAMPLE DRAFTS FOR A TORT CASE 19.137

Example 1. Particulars of claim—negligence—personal injury 19.138

Schedule of expenses and losses 19.139

Example 2. Defence to particulars of claim in example
    1—contributory negligence—volenti. 19.140

Counter schedule of expenses and losses 19.141

Example 3. Particulars of claim—occupier's liability—
    negligence. 19.142

Example 4. Defence to particulars of claim in
    example 2 (causation). 19.143

Example 5. Part 20 claim linked to examples 3 and 4. . . . . 19.144

Example 6. Particulars of claim—employer's liability—breach
    of statutory duty 19.145

Example 7. Particulars of claim—conversion of goods. 19.146

Example 8. Particulars of claim—nuisance—*Rylands v Fletcher*. 19.147

Example 9. Particulars of claim—professional negligence. 19.148

Example 10. Defence to example 9 and counterclaim/Part 20
    claim 19.149

Example 11. Particulars of claim—Fatal Accidents Act claim . . 19.150

KEY DOCUMENTS

What word describes a lawyer who does not chase ambulances?
Retired.

A   INTRODUCTION

Where litigation is not based on a problem with a contractually agreed relationship, it **19.01** is most likely to be founded on a breach of a duty of care imposed by law. This is the basic model of liability for negligence which underlies many situations, from a road accident to professional negligence.

This chapter looks at the special considerations that may apply in a tort action, but it focuses **19.02** primarily on negligence, which is not only the most common type of tort action, but also illustrates a number of principles.

In many negligence cases the defendant will be insured. This has some implications for the **19.03** conduct of the case and who will pay the damages at the end of the day, but it does not affect the principles of liability, see 13.05–13.08 and 19.79–19.81.

There have been expressions of concern about the possible growth of a compensation **19.04** culture, which might imply that there has been a significant growth in negligence litigation. That this might to some extent be true is illustrated by the fact that the money paid in damages by the NHS for clinical negligence rose from £1 million in 1974–75 to over £400 million in 2001–02. It is also a concern that for some smaller claims the costs of litigation exceed the money paid to the victim. On the other hand insurers have a fairly heavy involvement in the defence of negligence claims, and do not report a massive rise in claim numbers. The rise in the damages paid out seems to be due to the fact that the value of claims that has gone up, because of the larger sums needed to pay for lost future income and for care. It would also seem that the courts have maintained the same standards for the levels of duty of care to be expected, so that it has not become easier to win a negligence claim

This chapter provides a basic guide to some of the elements to bear in mind when conducting **19.05** tort litigation. Detailed law will need to be researched where necessary, but this chapter tries to provide a practical framework that should assist in identifying the main points in a case— what causes of action may arise and how damages are assessed. Appropriate practitioner works for further research include:

C Walton, R A Percy, *Charlesworth & Percy on Negligence* (10th edn 2002 and supplements) Sweet & Maxwell

A M Dugdale, *Clerk and Lindsell on Torts* (18th edn 2001 and supplements) Sweet & Maxwell

J L Powell, R Stewart, *Jackson and Powell on Professional Negligence* (5th edn 2002 and supplements) Sweet & Maxwell

A M Dugdale, K M Stanton, *Professional negligence* (2005) Lexis Nexis UK

J Handy and M Ford, *Redgrave's Health and Safety* (3rd Edn 1999) Butterworths

C J Miller and R S Goldberg, *Product Liability* (2004) Oxford University Press

C Booth and D Squires, *The Negligence Liability of Public Authorities* (2005) Oxford University Press

P Barrie, *Personal Injury Law: Liability, Compensation and Procedure* (2004) Oxford University Press

Butterworths Personal Injury Litigation Service, Looseleaf, LexisNexis (Also PI online)

Personal Injury Toolkit on CD ROM Sweet & Maxwell

The Medico-Legal Practitioner Series, Cavendish

Inns of Court School of Law, *Advanced Civil Litigation Manual* (annual) Oxford University Press

Kemp & Kemp Quantum of Damages in Personal Injury and Fatal Accidents Claims Looseleaf and CD ROM, Sweet & Maxwell

Judicial Studies Board Guidelines for the Assessment of General Damages in Personal Injury Cases, Oxford University Press

H McGregor, *McGregor on Damages* (16th edn 1999 and supplements) Sweet & Maxwell.

D K Allen, R Martyn, J Hartshorne, *Damages in Tort* (2000) Sweet & Maxwell

---

B   POTENTIAL CAUSES OF ACTION IN TORT

19.06   There are many potential causes of action in tort, based on duties of care owed to people and to property. A number of common law duties have been defined or extended by statute.

Negligence

19.07   A negligence action may be brought where one person owes a duty of care to another, that duty is breached, and the person to whom the duty is owed suffers injury and/or loss and damage as a result. The situations where a duty of care exist are fairly well established and they include, for example, the duty owed by a car driver to other road users, the duty owed by someone who makes products to someone who uses them, and duties owed by professionals such as electricians or architects. There are specially defined obligations in some areas, such as an employer's duties to employees, which include providing a safe place of work, a safe system of work, effective supervision, proper plant and materials and competent colleagues. For particulars of claim based on negligence see 19.138, 19.142, 19.145, and 19.150.

Breach of statutory duty

19.08   In certain circumstances the duties that are owed by one person to another are defined in some detail by an Act of Parliament or a statutory instrument. This is done for example as regards the duties that an employer owes to employees, or the duties that someone carrying on a potentially dangerous activity owes to anyone who may be affected by that activity.

19.09   Many statutory duties are very detailed. Some are absolute requirements and others require the taking of reasonable care. To establish breach of statutory duty it is necessary to show:

- that the statute or regulations apply;
- that the duty is imposed on the defendant;
- that the duty is intended to benefit the claimant;
- that a breach of the statute or regulation gives rise to civil liability;
- that the defendant is in breach of the duty;

- that the claimant has suffered damage that the statute was intended to prevent; and
- that the breach of statutory duty caused the damage.

If an action for breach of statutory duty is a possibility it will be necessary to consider **19.10** the relevant regulations in detail. What can reasonably be done in a particular industrial situation may be strongly argued, see for example *Larner v British Steel plc* (1993) 4 All ER 102. There may also be issues where the employee as well as the employer has responsi- bilities, see for example *Ginty v Belmont Building Supplies Ltd* (1959) 1 All ER 414. For a particulars of claim based on breach of statutory duty see 19.145.

Occupier's liability

There is a special statutory definition of the duties owed by someone who occupies land to **19.11** visitors, Occupiers' Liability Act 1957. There is a duty to ensure that a visitor to the land is reasonably safe. There are detailed provisions as regards matters such as warning notices. For a particulars of claim based on occupiers' liability see 19.142.

Liability to non-visitors and trespassers is more limited, Occupiers' Liability Act 1984, and **19.12** liability is not easy to establish, *Tomlinson v Congleton BC* (2002) All ER (D) 213 and *Donoghue v Folkestone Properties Ltd* (2003) All ER (D) 382.

Other tort duties

The basic model in many tort causes of action is that of a defined duty, owed by one person **19.13** to another, that duty being breached, and that this has led to injury, loss, or damage. With- out the space to consider all these potential causes of action in detail, litigation can be informed by the principles explored with regard to negligence in this chapter. This approach may apply for example to:

- nuisance, see 19.147;
- *Rylands v Fletcher* liability, see 19.147;
- interference with goods—A number of rights as regards personal property are now brought together under the Tort (Interference with Goods) Act 1997. This includes conversion of goods, trespass to goods, and other damage to goods, see 19.146.

C   THE ELEMENTS OF A NEGLIGENCE CASE

The duty of care

A claimant will have to establish there was a duty of care. The duty of care may arise from a **19.14** relationship in which it is reasonable to impose a duty, such as a driver's duty to other road users, an employer's duty to employees, or a teacher's duty to a child. The facts giving rise to the duty must be clearly identified and set out in the statement of case. If the duty is imposed or defined by a statute or statutory regulations then the prescribed requirements for the duty must be checked, and all the relevant details for the duty to apply must be established in the facts and pleaded.

19.15 The assumption of responsibility is relevant to whether a duty of care is owed and the scope of that duty, *Henderson v Merrett Syndicates Ltd* (1994) AC 145, *Williams v Natural Health Foods Ltd* (1998) 2 All ER 577, and *Watson v British Board of Boxing Control* (2001) 2 WLR 1256.

19.16 Many of the circumstances in which a duty of care is owed have long been established. Recent cases have related to the duties owed by:

- local authorities, see *X v Bedfordshire County Council* (1995) 3 All ER 353, *Barrett v Enfield LBC* (1999) 3 All ER 193, and *S v Gloucestershire CC* (2000) 3 All ER 346;
- police authorities, see *Costello v Chief Constable of Northumbria Police* (1999) 1 All ER 550, *Leach v Chief Constable of Gloucestershire Constabulary* (1999) 1 All ER 215;
- emergency services, see *Capital and Counties plc v Hampshire CC* (1997) 2 All ER 865, *OLL Ltd v Secretary of State for Transport* (1997) 3 All ER 897, *Kent v Griffiths* (2000) 2 All ER 474.

19.17 A tort case may involve the concept of vicarious liability. If an employee is acting in the course of his or her duty when a tort is committed then the employer will be vicariously liable, *Harrison v Michelin Tyre Co Ltd* (1985) 1 All ER 918. The test for vicarious liability is quite wide, save for where an employee has done something that is wholly outside the scope of his or her duty, *Lister v Helsey Hall Ltd* (2001) 2 All ER 769.

19.18 The claimant will also need to establish that the duty of care was owed by the defendant to the claimant. Again there are sometimes some special requirements in statutes and statutory regulations, for example that a duty is only owed by an employer to an employee, or is only owed in factory premises. All the factors defining to whom a duty is owed must be established and pleaded.

The level of the duty

19.19 A duty owed by the defendant to the claimant is normally the duty to take reasonable care. However if the defendant holds himself out as having a particular type of skill or expertise then he or she will be expected to demonstrate that skill or expertise at a reasonably competent level. A doctor will be expected to show the skill of a reasonably competent doctor, and a surgeon the skill of a reasonably competent surgeon.

19.20 It may be necessary to get expert evidence to ascertain what should be expected of a reasonably competent specialist in an area. A case may turn on what is to be reasonably expected, and it will be a matter of fact for the judge to decide on the evidence available.

19.21 A statute may define the level of duty and how it may be fulfilled in a particular way. If a duty is defined by statutory regulations then the way in which the duty should be fulfilled will normally be defined in substantial detail. In a case involving breach of statutory duty where statutory regulations are involved the lawyer will have to work with the detailed words of the regulations.

Failure to meet the level of duty

19.22 Liability will arise where a defendant has breached his or her duty of care, through an action that should not have been taken, or through a failure to take action that should have been taken. Particulars must be given of how the duty owed has been breached—liability does not arise simply because an accident has happened. There is a need to identify in detail what the defendant did or did not do. An accident may have several causes, with a variety of failures to meet a reasonable level of care—a driver may cause an accident by a mixture of driving too fast, failing to indicate a manoeuvre, and failing to keep a proper lookout. This may result in the need to identify and provide quite long particulars of breach of duty.

Again if a breach of statutory duty is involved it is important to work with the detail of the relevant statute or statutory regulations. **19.23**

Injury and/or loss and damage has resulted from the negligence

The fact that there has been an accident that leads to loss and damage will not normally be disputed. The fact that the claimant has a broken leg or a dented car is normally clear and easily provable. What is important is to show the chain that leads in a reasonably foreseeable way from an actionable breach of duty to specific injury, loss, and damage. It is then important to provide sufficient information about that injury, loss, and damage for losses to be quantified. **19.24**

The test for causation is the 'but for' test—that without the breach of duty, on the balance of probabilities, the claimant would not have suffered the loss or damage. **19.25**

Causation may be broken by a supervening event, whether between the tort and the loss and damage, or once loss and damage has started to accrue, which is a matter of fact, *Reeves v Metropolitan Police Commissioner* (1999) 3 All ER 897. If an additional tort is committed by another tortfeasor then it seems that the second tortfeasor will only be liable for any additional loss, *Murrell v Healy* (2001) 4 All ER 345. **19.26**

D   THE PRE-ACTION STAGE

Pre-action protocols

Specific pre-action protocols apply in the key tort areas of personal injury (for claims up to £15,000), professional negligence, and medical negligence. The spirit of the protocol should be followed where it does not specifically apply, see 4.25–4.27. **19.27**

The key elements of a pre-action protocol are that the following steps be taken. **19.28**

- An informal letter simply informing the potential defendant of a possible action.
- The gathering of sufficient evidence to substantiate a realistic claim.
- Once this is done, letters should be send to the potential defendant and to his insurer (if known, otherwise a spare copy to the defendant). This should include a clear summary of facts, a summary of injuries, and information on financial losses. This letter of claim needs to be sent at least six months before the expiry of the limitation period if the terms of the protocol are to be properly complied with.
- The letter should include a list of the documents that the defendant is asked to disclose (for example documents relating to an accident at work).
- The defendant or the insurer should reply within 21 days, if they do not proceedings may be initiated. Provided there is a reply, the defendant can have three months to investigate.

- If the defendant denies liability, or alleges contributory negligence, relevant documents requested by the potential claimant should be sent.
- The claimant should send a schedule of special damages with supporting documents—this is particularly important if liability is admitted and damages are the remaining issue. If the defendant alleges contributory negligence, the claimant should respond to that. This should be done within about a month.
- Medical evidence must be obtained, from a jointly agreed expert if possible. The claimant sends a list of potential experts.
- The defendant should reply to this proposed list within 14 days.
- The medical report should be obtained and circulated.
- Consideration should be given to the making of offers or mediation.

Limitation

19.29　Limitation is discussed generally at 4.33–4.41. Limitation may be a particular issue in a tort case. It may take some time for a potential claimant to realise the extent of injury or damage, or to realise that a legal action is possible and to contact a solicitor. There may be delays in collecting evidence and evaluating the strength of the claim. There may then be delays while attempting to settle the matter. Essentially the limitation period for a personal injury or fatal accident act claim is three years, and for any other tort claim is six years, Limitation Act 1980, and delays should not prevent an action being commenced in time.

19.30　Time normally runs from the date when an injury is sustained, but it may run from the date of knowledge if that is later. The date of knowledge is the time that the claimant should know:

- that the injury is sufficiently serious to justify instituting proceedings (assuming the defendant will not dispute liability and could satisfy a judgment);
- that the injury is potentially attributable to the alleged default;
- the identity of the defendant (including where relevant someone vicariously liable for the defendant).

19.31　It is often not easy to establish what a claimant knew at a specific time in the past, and this may need to be implied from other evidence. Matters like the available information and the intelligence of the claimant have to be taken into account, *Nash v Eli Lilly and Co* (1993) 1 WLR 782). Information which the claimant might reasonably have been expected to acquire is relevant, *Forbes v Wandsworth Health Authority* (1997) QB 402. Where a claimant knows enough to start to investigate whether there is a case against the defendant, for example by going to see a solicitor, time will start to run, *Spagro v North Essex District Health Authority* (1997) PIQR P235. It is not necessary for all the information required to draft a particulars of claim to be available before time begins to run, *Broadley v Guy Clapham and Co* (1994) 4 All ER CA. Time will start to run where a lawyer could have ascertained the identity of a defendant, for example by seeking a police accident report, *Copeland v Smith* (2000) 1 WLR 1371.

19.32　In a negligence action which involves damage other than personal injury there can be similar problems. For example it can be some years before negligence in constructing a building comes to light. In a tort action involving such latent damage (though not a contractual action) the limitation period is the later of:

- six years from the accrual of the action, that is when all the elements of the cause of action existed—on the restrictive interpretation of this see *Murphy v Brentwood District Council* (1991) 1 AC 398;
- three years from the date when the claimant knew he had a cause of action (similar to above);
- in any event there is an overall limitation period of 15 years.

The limitation rules are primarily intended to protect a defendant from a stale action and **19.33** they may result in unfairness for a claimant. The court has a discretion to disapply the limitation period in personal injuries cases under the Limitation Act 1980, s 33. Essentially the potential prejudice to the claimant and to the defendant of not allowing the action to be brought are weighed up, taking into account all the circumstances of the case. Matters like the reasons for the delay and the cogency of evidence are particularly important, as is a decision whether there can still be a fair trial. Because of the importance of such an application it should be decided by a trial judge rather than as an interim matter. The matter can be raised on an application by the claimant, or as a defence to having the action struck out due to the limitation period having expired, though if appropriate it can be dealt with at trial. If proceedings have been issued within the limitation period, s 33 cannot be used to allow a second action after the limitation period has expired, though s 33 can still be used for a different action, *Shapland v Palmer* (1999) 1 WLR 2068.

The role of lawyers is relevant. A claimant should not be criticised for errors in advice from **19.34** his lawyers, *Das v Ganju* (1999) PIQR P260. If the delay has been caused by the lawyer's negligence then the fact that there may be an alternative claim against the lawyers for negligence will be relevant, *Donovan v Gwentoys Ltd* (1990) 1 WLR 472 HL.

There can be difficulties in deciding whether a claim involves personal injuries, and therefore **19.35** whether a three or six year limitation period applies, and whether s 33 can be used. For example this may happen when allegations relating to sexual abuse suffered as a child are brought by an adult, *Stubbings v Webb* (1993) 2 AC 498.

E   ANALYSIS OF A TORT CASE

The background to a case

Whether or not there has been a real growth of a 'compensation culture', tort litigation is **19.36** sometimes conducted with an emotional background. It is not necessarily easy for someone who has been injured to accept that an accident has occurred, and one person can see as a serious nuisance something that someone else sees as acting reasonably. There can be high feelings in a negligence case if there has been serious injury that significantly affects the life of an individual and his or her family. Such circumstances may need to be managed constructively.

There can be particular problems in proving the facts of a tort case. The problems of **19.37** reconstructing the events in an accident were raised at 8.11–8.16. Accidents happen quickly. Witnesses may be motivated to remember events inaccurately. There may be no witnesses save for the person who suffered the accident, and that person may not be able to remember things clearly, may be angry at what has happened, or may not wish to admit any fault.

19.38 Tort cases often turn on disputes of fact, which makes fact gathering and analysis and the collection of evidence particularly important. A high level of interviewing skills may be required to get a reasonably clear and full account of an accident from a client. A witness may be motivated to lie about his or her involvement in an accident. A witness may invent details rather than admit to not noticing or remembering something. Although a lawyer will want to show empathy where someone has been injured, it may be necessary to challenge or check details if evidence given by a client is not clear or does not appear to fit with other evidence in the case. Evidence will be challenged in court, and the strength of possibly weak evidence may need to be tested informally at a reasonably early stage.

Accident reports

19.39 The first item of evidence is likely to be the informal statement from the client. What the client says should of course be accepted as true, but gaps and weaknesses in what the client says will need to be identified, and any areas where what the client says conflicts with other evidence will need to be taken up with the client.

19.40 There will often be a report on the accident that should provide useful general information. There is normally a police report on a serious road traffic accident. There will normally be an accident report where an accident happens at a place of work, or at a place that the public has access to. Such a report can form the basis for a case, but it may need careful consideration, perhaps with the assistance of an expert. If there is not such a report then the lawyer will effectively need to build a report from the evidence available, and may need to construct arguments for how it is most likely the accident happened. Where the report is prepared by the defendant it should be available under a pre-action protocol or on disclosure.

19.41 Plans and photographs may be particularly important in understanding the causes of an accident.

Areas requiring expertise

19.42 There may be complex technical details for the lawyer to understand in order to be able to deal with witnesses and explain the case to a judge.

- In a road traffic accident (or RTA) there may be technical questions regarding the running of a vehicle and how it was maintained.
- In an industrial accident it may be necessary to master the details of a mechanical process and special terminology.
- When claiming a professional person has been negligent, it may be necessary to call expert evidence as to what would normally be expected of a reasonably competent person in that profession.
- Wherever a tort action involved physical injury it will be necessary to get to grips with medical terminology. An adequate grasp of medical terms is essential to understand a medical report describing the severity of and prognosis for injuries to a claimant, and in researching damages for injuries.

General principles for the use of expert evidence are considered at 15.140–15.178. There may **19.43** well be background evidence providing some expert input from an early stage in the case— an accident report will be prepared by people with some expertise, and if someone has been injured there will usually be information in papers from the hospital where the person was treated and/or from their own doctor. In preparing the case this information may be used, but objective expert evidence taking an overview of the situation is likely to be required to assist the court.

The expert to be used should be agreed if possible to save costs. For example the pre-action **19.44** protocol for personal injury provides for the joint selection of an expert and a failure to do this can be taken into account by the court as regards costs. Selection of an expert should be distinguished from instruction. Once the expert is selected the lawyer should draft instructions to the expert with care, setting out relevant information such as a summary of the accident, the type of report required, and any special questions to be answered. The solicitor should arrange for background information such as the patient's medical records to be made available to the expert.

If the expert has been jointly instructed then the resulting report will be sent to both. If **19.45** the expert has been briefed by one side alone then the report will be sent only to that side. Where an expert has been jointly selected under the pre-action protocol the claimant should disclose the report to the defendant and then wait 21 days for possible settlement before starting proceedings. Where one side has instructed an expert, questions of privilege may arise.

The parties will not necessarily be prepared to use a single expert in a complex case. There **19.46** can be problems with discussing and analysing a case where there is a single expert as the consent of the other side will be required. The parties may prefer to have their own expert to discuss the case with fully.

There can be difficulties with medical evidence. After serious injury it may take some years **19.47** for the condition of the person injured to stabilise. It can be difficult to decide when the condition has stabilised, how serious the condition is, what the best treatment is, and what the prognosis is. These matters may be disputed because of their effect on the damages due. If there is a significant dispute, both sides may wish to have their own expert evidence and the defendant is entitled to ask to have the claimant medically examined by a doctor nominated by the defendant, so as to have evidence on which to dispute the claimant's medical condition. A claimant is not entitled to refuse a medical examination merely because he or she is elderly or nervous, but the court can attach conditions to how the medical examination is carried out, *Hall v Avon Area Health Authority* [1980] 1 All ER 516. However, a claimant can refuse to undergo a long series of tests or tests that are painful, *Prescott v Bulldog Tools* [1981] 3 All ER 869. A claimant cannot be forced to undergo a medical examination as this could be an abuse of human rights, but if a claimant unreasonably refuses to undergo a medical examination the court can make relevant orders such as staying the action. The claimant has no right to see a report prepared for the defendant, unless the defendant decides to use it at trial, *Megarity v DJ Ryan & Sons* [1980] 2 All ER 832.

What needs to be proved

19.48 In a negligence case it will normally be necessary to prove the cause of an accident, to show that there has been a breach of duty, and to show that that breach led to loss and damage. If part of the load falls off a lorry being driven along a road and lands on the car behind injuring the car's driver then it should be possible to prove why the load fell off—because ropes were not properly fastened, that locking devices were not properly closed etc. Some-times it may not be possible to prove how an accident happened but it may nonetheless be obvious that the accident should not have happened. In such a case the doctrine of *res ipsa loquitur* may be used—the thing speaks for itself. If a matter is in someone's control and an accident happens which would not normally happen if care were properly exercised, that amounts to evidence that the accident arose from lack of care, unless the defendant offers a reasonable explanation. This is effectively a rebuttable presumption of fact that the accident arose from negligence, *Lloyde v West Midlands Gas Board* (1971) 2 All ER 1240. A lorry should not shed part of its load unless there has been a failure to secure and check it properly, so if the precise cause of the accident cannot be proved, *res ipsa locquitur* can be argued. However the use of *res ipsa loquitur* does not pass the burden of proof to the defendant, *Ng v Lee* The Times, 25 May 1988. While on the face of it the doctrine may seem an easy way out of evidential problems this is not the case. It is always preferable to plead and prove the cause of an accident rather than rely on this doctrine. The use of the doctrine tends to suggest that the evidence is weak.

F   SELECTING A CAUSE OF ACTION

Analysing the range of causes of action

19.49 All potential causes of action will need to be identified from the facts. There may be a single appropriate cause of action, though causes of action may overlap so that a choice needs to be made. The same set of facts may give rise to actions in negligence, breach of statutory duty, and occupier's liability. As set out in Chapter 10, structured analysis requires the consider-ation of the elements of each potential cause of action to check which can most easily be proved and has least legal difficulty. The elements of negligence are dealt with in 19.14–19.26. The elements for breach of occupier's liability are that there be a defendant occupier/of a specific property/the claimant is a visitor to whom a common duty of care is owed/the claimant is injured in the building. If breach of statutory duty is a possibility, it will be necessary to research the exact wording of the relevant statute or regulation to consider the scope of the duty and how it may be breached.

19.50 The choice of causes of action may overlap significantly with deciding whom to sue. Relevant principles are set out at 13.15–13.24, but tort may provide more options than contract. On one set of facts it might be possible to sue the person who actually causes an accident, an employer vicariously liable for that person, or the person who owns the building where an accident occurs. It may be possible to sue the person who sells or provides a defective item, or the person who manufactured it. All potential defendants may be sued but this will increase costs. Choice will of course be based on the relative strengths of cases, and the relative ability of potential defendants to pay. Costs should be kept down by not suing people unnecessarily, but if there is any real doubt more than one defendant may need to be joined.

If a claimant can show that more than one defendant is responsible for an accident then the **19.51** judge will apportion liability. There may be problems where a claimant can show that one of two defendants caused loss or damage but cannot show which, see *Fairchild v Glenhaven Funeral Services Ltd* (2002) 3 All ER 305.

The tort/contract overlap

A potential action in tort may overlap with a potential cause of action in contract where **19.52** there is some form of contract between the parties as well as a duty of care. This might happen if someone buys a product that then causes an accident, if someone buys a ticket to enter a theme park and then goes on a ride that collapses, or where there is a contract with someone to carry out a professional service. The interrelation between tort and contract within an overall law of obligations has been increasingly explored over recent years. There are many examples where actions have been brought in both contract and tort, as in *Esso Petroleum v Mardon* [1976] QB 801, where the case was for breach of warranty and negligent misrepresentation, or *Howard Marine and Dredging Co v Ogden* [1978] QB 574, where the action was brought under the Misrepresentation Act 1967 and for negligence. Even if there are potential actions in contract and tort, the claimant may choose to rely on one alone, as in *Parsons v Uttley Ingham* [1978] QB 791, where the claimant chose to rely on breach of contract.

If there is an overlap, the duties in contract and tort are likely to be similar so that choice of **19.53** remedy is most likely to depend on the measure of damages. However a duty in tort can be wider than the duty in contract, *Holt v Payne Skillington* The Times, 22 December 1995, or a duty in contract may be wider depending on the terms agreed.

As to the measure of damages, Lord Denning has said that the claimant should get the same **19.54** damages for what has been lost whether the action is brought in tort or contract, *Parsons v Uttley Ingham* (above), but other cases have taken a stricter view, and distinctions may still be made. The purpose and intention of damages in contract and tort are different, and there can be merit in putting emphasis on the measure which most favours a client in a particular case. The purpose of damages in contract is looking forward to put the claimant where he or she would have been if the contract had been fulfilled, whereas tort looks back to put the claimant where he or she was before the tort was committed. There are also differences in what is covered, although the two measures of damage seem to be moving closer together. Contract damages focus more clearly on economic loss and there can be problems recovering heads such as hurt feelings, whereas tort damages focus on injury, and purely economic loss is not always available in tort. Contributory negligence may be relevant in tort but not in contract.

G SELECTING REMEDIES

Damages

The main remedy in tort is damages. If the action takes some time to reach a conclusion, and **19.55** especially if the claimant is out of pocket, then interim damages must be sought. If the prognosis includes a possible later deterioration in the condition of the claimant then provisional damages can be sought. The assessment of damages is dealt with below.

Return of goods

19.56   The claimant may seek an order for the return of a specific chattel where appropriate.

An injunction

19.57   An injunction may be appropriate, for example to stop a nuisance or a trespass, or to prevent interference with intellectual property. If there is clear evidence that a tort is likely to be committed then an injunction may be granted as otherwise the defendant might be seen as having a right to commit a tort. Also damages will usually not be seen to be an adequate alternative as otherwise the court might be seen as putting a price on the right to commit a tort. However there are some cases where damages may be seen as adequate, *Jaggard v Sawyer* (1995) 1 WLR 269, or where an injunction might be oppressive to the defendant, *Kennaway v Thompson* (1981) QB 88.

A declaration

19.58   A declaration as to a legal position or rights may be made.

H   ASSESSING DAMAGES

19.59   The main remedy in most tort cases will be damages, so it will be important to advise the client on how damages will be assessed, and what figure is likely to be recoverable. It can be very difficult to put a figure on personal injury and to try to compensate a claimant properly in the case of serious injury that permanently damages his or her life.

The measure of damages

19.60   The basic test for damages in a tort case is to put the claimant where he or she would have been had the tort not been committed, provided the type of loss is reasonably foreseeable and is not too remote. There is an extent to which this looks back to the position the claimant was in immediately before the tort, and an extent to which it looks forward to where the claimant would be but for the tort.

19.61   It is not necessary that the precise type of damage or its extent be foreseen. It seems that the test for reasonable foreseeability is applied less strictly in tort than in contract, *H Parsons (Livestock) Ltd v Uttley Ingham & Co Ltd* (1978) QB 791.

19.62   Damages should be assessed when the damage occurs, though in practice it may only be possible to assess what damage has occurred at a rather later date, so that damages for areas like personal injury are normally assessed at trial. It may be possible to argue that a different date for assessment be used, see *Dodd Properties (Kent) Ltd v Canterbury City Council* (1980) 1 All ER 928.

Damage to property is valued at the cost of curing the damage or at the diminution of value **19.63** in the property, *Owners of Dredger Liesbosch v Owners of Steamship Edison* (1933) AC 449. It is important to argue which measure is justified on the facts, see *Ruxley Electronics and Construction Ltd v Forsyth* (1996) 1 AC 344 HL, and the date on which the value of property should be assessed. Consequential losses such as having to hire a replacement, or loss of income due to the damage are also recoverable.

Purely economic loss is not generally recoverable in negligence, *Leigh & Sullivan Ltd v* **19.64** *Aliakmon Shipping Co Ltd* (1986) AC 785, save perhaps where it is sufficiently proximate and within the scope of the duty owed by the defendant to the claimant, *Junior Books Ltd v Veitchi & Co Ltd* [1983] AC 520. The definition of what counts as economic loss is relatively wide, *Murphy v Brentwood District Council* (1991) 1 AC 398. Pure economic loss is recoverable for other torts, including misrepresentation and deceit. It seems it is also recoverable in professional negligence cases, and for negligent misstatement under *Headley Byrne v Heller and Partners Ltd* (1964) AC 465, *Henderson v Merrett Syndicates Ltd* (1994) AC 145.

Exemplary damages can be awarded in very limited circumstances, such as where the **19.65** defendant's tort is calculated to make a profit that may exceed the damages payable for it, *Cassell & Co Ltd v Broome* (1972) AC 1027. The principles for assessing exemplary damages are not very clear, but see *Thompson v Commissioner of Police of the Metropolis* (1997) 2 All ER 762.

Damages for loss of a substantial chance should be appropriately assessed, *First Interstate* **19.66** *Bank of California v Cohen Arnold & Co* The Times, 11 December 1995.

Stages in assessing damages

Listing heads of loss

The claimant should be asked to list all items of loss, and to think widely. In what ways have **19.67** loss and damage been suffered? Are there linked expenses? Is there consequent distress or inconvenience? From this list, heads of damage that are recoverable should be identified.

Distinguishing types of loss

Special damages. Special damages are those which can be quantified at a set date without an **19.68** assessment by a judge. This includes specific items such as damage to an asset. It also includes an ongoing loss that can be given a regular figure, such as ongoing loss of earnings that can be assessed as £X per week multiplied by the number of weeks of loss. A figure for special damages should normally be agreed rather than contested in court.

General damages. This term covers non-financial loss such as pain, suffering, and loss of **19.69** amenity (PSLA) that needs to be assessed by a judge. It also includes ongoing loss after the determination of the case such as loss of future earnings or earning capacity. The assessment of this kind of damages is outlined below.

Proof of loss. All heads of loss and damage must be proved to have happened, and to have **19.70** been caused by the defendant's breach of duty. Evidence must also be presented for the value of loss and damage. If a head is recoverable then problems with quantification should not be allowed to defeat it—if there is a loss then a basis for quantifying it should be identified and argued. For example the cost of care given by a relative can be assessed on the basis of the cost of a paid nurse, or on the basis of earnings that the relative has lost if it is reasonable for the relative to give up work to care for the claimant.

19.71   It is important to be practical—the main heads of loss require most attention. In a negligence case where injury has been caused the highest damages are likely to be the damages for the injury itself, and damages for loss of income where that is a head of loss.

19.72   Loss of income will include loss of bonuses and commission, if it can be proved that these would normally have accrued. Loss of fringe benefits such as a company car or health insurance can also be claimed. Loss of earnings is always calculated net of tax as that is the real loss of the claimant. There may also be a claim for loss of pension rights. Travel costs and other expenses associated with work must be deducted. The damages can also include loss of promotion or of moving to a better job, with figures being assessed as a loss of a chance.

19.73   Interest. Appropriate interest should be added to each head of damages. Different rates apply to different elements of the damages. As interest is to compensate the claimant for being kept out of money there is quite logically no interest on damages for future economic loss, *Birkett v Hayes* [1982] 2 All ER 70.

Reductions in damages

Contributory negligence

19.74   If a claimant has suffered damage partly as a result of his or her own fault and partly as the fault of another person the claim can still succeed, but damages will be reduced to the extent that the court thinks just and equitable having regard to the claimant's share of responsibility, Law Reform (Contributory Negligence) Act 1945, s 1. This appears to apply to all torts except for deceit and conversion. For a defence based on contributory negligence see 19.140.

19.75   If the defendant alleges contributory negligence then the defendant will need to show that the accident was partly caused by the negligence of the claimant. This will involve alleging in the statement of claim and then proving how it is said that the claimant was negligent. If the judge finds as a fact that there was contributory negligence then he or she will go on to decide as a matter of fact the relative responsibility of the claimant and the defendant for the accident. The apportionment of liability is normally done as a percentage (though a court will normally ignore a low level of contributory negligence).

19.76   The result of a finding of contributory negligence will be a proportionate reduction in the damages that would otherwise be payable. This can have a severe effect—a finding of 50 per cent contributory negligence will halve the damages payable. The extent of contributory negligence is therefore often strongly contested.

19.77   A new lawyer can find it difficult to estimate contributory negligence, but it is essentially purely a matter of argument on the facts. It is literally a question of looking at the detail of how the accident was caused and deciding the extent to which the claimant and the defendant(s) were responsible for it. Apportionment needs to be carefully considered if there is more than one claimant or more than one defendant, *Fitzgerald v Lane* (1989) AC 328, *Wright v Lodge* (1993) 4 All ER 299.

Mitigation of loss

As with contract, the claimant will be expected to take reasonable steps to mitigate loss. It is **19.78** for the defendant to raise and prove any failure to mitigate. This is done by going through each item of damage claimed and considering whether the amount claimed could have been lower if the claimant had behaved in a different way.

Insurance

The general role of insurance is considered in 13.05–13.08. If a claimant is insured for a risk **19.79** relevant to a tort claim the claimant could seek to claim on the insurance rather than bring an action. However if a significant sum of money is involved the insurer may want the claimant to bring an action against the person who caused the loss and damage so that the insurer is not improperly out of pocket. Any money recovered by a claimant through insurance should not normally lead to any reduction in the damages claimable.

If the defendant in a tort case is insured then the defendant will have a duty to inform his or **19.80** her insurer of the claim being made, and to give details of the insurer to the claimant. In the case of a road accident, drivers are required to be insured under the Road Traffic Act 1988. If a driver is not insured or cannot be traced there are legal agreements under which damages are met by the Motor Insurers Bureau run by the insurance industry.

Even if a party is insured, the case is still between the claimant and the defendant. Their **19.81** names will appear on the claim form, even if it is the lawyers for the insurance company that conduct the litigation. The only exception is under the European Communities (Rights against Insurers) Regulations 2002 (SI 2002/2061) which provide that from January 2003 there is a cause of action directly against the insurer where an accident is caused by an un-insured vehicle in a public place.

I ASSESSING PERSONAL INJURY DAMAGES

The system for assessing damages

The assessment of damages in a personal injury case is complex. In principle compensation **19.82** is assessed by a judge in the same way as other damages, but there are particular complexities in deciding what compensation is appropriately awarded for a physical injury such as a shattered leg, and in a very serious case for the damage done to a claimant's whole life. To try to ensure fairness a convention has grown up for assessing damages for pain, suffering, and loss of amenity, see below.

The system for assessing damages for personal injury seeks to identify and cover all heads **19.83** of injury and loss. There are various issues with regard to the current system, which may need to be explained to a client.

- Damages for injuries depend very heavily on accepted norms for particular injuries, and some claimants may find the conventional figures attached to some injuries lower than they might expect.

- Damages are normally awarded as a single lump sum, which can minimise flexibility in adapting damages to need. It can be very difficult to identify a single right time to assess a single figure for damages. Because it may take time to do this, interim payments are available, and because further deterioration may happen later provisional damages can be sought, see below, but both are rough rather than refined instruments to address problems in finding the right time to assess damages. It is gradually becoming possible to achieve a better fit to the needs of the client, for example through structured settlements, see Chapter 20. It is possible for damages to be paid by installments by agreement, or by a court order made with the agreement of the parties, Damages Act 1996, s 2, and in the future it may be possible for the court to order the payment of damages by instalments.

- The payment of lump sum damages may not be ideal for a claimant with limited know-ledge of how to manage the money. The claimant will probably need financial advice on dealing with what may be a very large sum, the idea being that the money be invested to produce sufficient income to provide for care where the effects of the injuries are ongoing. In practice the client may not fully understand the advice, or may not take it. A claimant is under no obligation to spend the damages in any particular way, and it is possible to use the money as if it were a lottery win. There have been newspaper reports of a case where damages were used to set up an armed gang! Even with financial advice, the income available to support an accident victim in a year may vary with the type of investment used and interest rates. The developments outlined in the previous paragraph may also help to address such problems.

- It is only relatively recently that fuller use is being made of the expertise of actuaries and financial experts in assessing loss and compensation as accurately as possible.

19.84 The costs of arguing about liability and the quantification of damages in an accident case can be high, even exceeding the damages payable, and there are arguments that a system other than litigation should be used to settle accident cases. Some other jurisdictions have systems under which fault does not have to be proved and the care needs of an accident victim are met from a central fund. While this has merit in focussing money on accident victims there are problems such as removing liability from those who cause accidents.

19.85 The process for assessing personal injury damages is largely judge-made and could therefore be varied by case law, though with the strong precedent value of current case law it is perhaps unlikely there will be substantial change without statutory intervention.

The schedule of expenses and losses

19.86 In a personal injury claim the particulars of claim must be accompanied by a schedule of the expenses and losses claimed, CPR PD 16 para 4.2. This must include past and future losses. Wherever relevant a basis should be given for calculating loss over a period, for example £x per month. Examples of the heads of damage that may be recoverable are given in 19.87 and 19.88 below and a sample schedule forms part of example 1 at 19.138 below.

19.87 Typical heads of damage for past losses.

- Incidental damage to property
- Medical treatment expenses (can include private treatment)
- Cost of travel to hospital etc

- Medical expenses (including prescriptions and special equipment)
- Nursing care
- Other care
- Loss of earnings and fringe benefits
- Cost of reasonable care provided by friends and relatives.

Typical heads of damage for future losses (if any): **19.88**

- Ongoing medical expenses
- Ongoing cost of travel to hospital
- Ongoing treatment and medical expenses
- Ongoing nursing and other care
- Ongoing loss of earnings and fringe benefits
- Ongoing cost of reasonable care provided by friends and relatives
- Other future losses eg pension rights, see *Auty v National Coal Board* (1985) 1 All ER 930.

It is not possible to argue that costs for future care might rise by more than inflation, see **19.89** *Cooke v United Bristol Healthcare NHS Trust* The Times, 24 October 2003. The cost of converting a house to meet the needs of an injured claimant can be claimed, or the cost of moving to a new home. However the claimant is not entitled to benefit from any linked rise on the value of the property, so damages will normally be awarded on the basis that capital has had to be tied up in the house, see *Roberts v Johnstone* (1989) QB 878.

Damages for pain, suffering, and loss of amenity (PSLA)

There is no easy way to decide what sum of money can properly compensate a claimant for a **19.90** physical injury. It can be difficult to assess the extent of an injury and the likely prognosis. Injuries affect people in different ways and the views of doctors may vary. Because damages are normally agreed at a single point in time, damages for PSLA should be agreed or decided when the extent of injury and what will happen as a result of the injury in the future is reasonably clear.

There are different approaches to calculating damages for personal injury in different **19.91** jurisdictions. In England and Wales the approach is as follows.

- There is effectively a norm for the sum awarded for each kind of injury which has evolved largely through case law. The figure is based on the injuries suffered as outlined below.
- The figure given also broadly takes into account loss of amenity, which includes loss of experience and enjoyment of life. This covers things like being unable to continue to pursue a hobby.
- Damages for additional costs that result from the injury, such as costs of care are recoverable in addition and should be listed in the schedule.

Essentially the stages in making a PSLA calculation are as follows: **19.92**

- Identifying the injuries. The main injuries should be identified from the medical reports. The precise nature, severity, and prognosis for each main injury should be noted. The evidence of the claimant on the effect of the injuries may also be relevant. If there is a conflict of medical evidence it will be decided by the judge. If there are several injuries, damages will normally be based on the main injury with some addition for the others.

- The general band of figures that might be appropriate for the main injury or each injury should be identified. The bands used by judges are published by the Judicial Studies Board (JSB), and can be found in *Kemp & Kemp* and similar sources. The most up to date JSB guidelines should be used, the 6th edition having been published in 2002. A band for an injury might for example be £30,000–£35,000.

- Cases as close as possible to the current case should be identified using hard copy or electronic sources. It is best to use cases decided since March 2000 if possible to avoid the complexity of the uplift in figures following the case of *Heil v Rankin* (2000) 3 All ER 138 (otherwise any amount awarded above £10,000 will need an uplift). Any case that is not relatively recent may also need an increase to deal with inflation (appropriate inflation factors can be found in *Kemp & Kemp* and other sources).

- It is unlikely a decided case will be absolutely identical. The cases found should be considered to see whether they are more or less serious than the case being researched. The cases found should help to identify whether the current case falls at the lower or higher end of the appropriate band.

- The result is normally expressed to the client as a general figure 'about £52,000', or a range '£50,000–£55,000'.

19.93   The figure may also be adjusted to allow for mental distress etc if this is supported by medical evidence. The figure can also be adjusted to allow for loss of physical capacity, such as the ability to carry out housework (provided this was done before the accident and the loss of capacity is supported by medical evidence). There can also be damages for loss of marriage prospects, and possibly for the breakdown of a marriage if it results from the accident, *Pritchard v JH Cobden Ltd* (1988) Fam 22.

Damages for future loss of income

19.94   Loss of income up to the time that damages are assessed or agreed will be determined on the basis of the figures in the schedule. If there is ongoing loss of earnings then it may be possible to make a reasonably simple calculation if, for example, it is likely that the claimant will make a full recovery within a further two years.

19.95   A more complicated calculation will be needed if the injured claimant will not be able to work again, or will only ever be able to earn a much lower income than was previously the case. A conventional approach has been evolved by the courts, but it can only take general account of contingencies such as the possibility that the claimant might have retired early or died before retirement age.

19.96   The general process for assessing damages for loss of future earnings is:

- Establish the net annual figure earned by the claimant (net of tax etc).
- Deduct the expenses of earning that income, which will no longer need to be spent.
- The resulting figure of net annual loss is called the multiplicand.
- The multiplicand is multiplied by a multiplier, which is a theoretical number of years for which the income will be lost. Deciding on an appropriate multiplier can be complex because of uncertainties over when the claimant would have stopped earning etc. Rather

than guessing, the courts now use an approach supported by actuarial expertise, using the 'Ogden Tables'. These tables have been in existence since 1983 and are admissible in court even though the Civil Evidence Act 1995, s19, which provides for this to happen, has not yet been brought into force.

- As the claimant gets a lump sum immediately rather then earning it over years it can be invested so as to earn additional money. The lump sum is reduced so that over time the lump sum and the interest will provide the figure the claimant is awarded. The Damages Act 1996, s 1 provides for the Lord Chancellor to prescribe a rate of return to be used for this calculation, and the normal rate of 2.5 per cent was prescribed in 2001. For background on this area see *Wells v Wells* (1997) 1 All ER 673 and *Warriner v Warriner* (2002) All ER (D) 202.
- Inflation and changes in tax rates are not taken into account, *Lim Poh Choo v Camden and Islington Area Health Authority* (1980) AC 174 and *Van Oudenhoven v Griffin Inns Ltd* (2000) 1 WLR 1413.

In making an assessment for loss of earnings: **19.97**

- Likely pay increases etc should be taken into account. If it is likely that the claimant would have gone on working for many years and income would have increased significantly the court can either use an overall average for likely earnings over the period, or can divide the award into two different periods with two different multiplicands.
- For a female claimant it seems that possible loss of earnings due to leaving work to bring up children and possible loss of support from marriage will cancel each other out, but this is not finally decided, *Hughes v McKeown* (1985) I WLR 963.
- For the position of children see *Joyce v Yeomans* (1981) 1 WLR 549 and *Croke v Wiseman* (1981) 3 All ER 852.
- If the claimant is likely to die younger because of the accident, damages can be recovered for the full original period of life expectancy, but with a reduction for the living expenses that will be saved in the years for which the claimant is unlikely to survive.
- Damages for loss of 'moonlighting' earnings probably cannot be claimed, see *Hunter v Butler* The Times, 28 December 1995.

Where it is difficult to measure loss of earnings a single lump sum may be awarded for loss of **19.98** earning capacity, *Smith v Manchester Corporation* (1974)17 KIR 1.This can apply where the claimant is handicapped on the work market or may have to retire early. The method for deciding the amount of the lump sum is open to argument.

Damages for future expenses are calculated in a similar way, with a payment for capital costs **19.99** and a multiplier and multiplicand used for nursing care etc, though each item may need to be calculated separately.

Deductions and additions

Interest

In an action seeking damages for personal injury or death, the court should normally **19.100** award interest unless there are special reasons to the contrary, but interest will be calculated differently for different parts of the damages, *Jefford v Gee* [1970] 2 QB 130.

- Interest is added to special damages at half the appropriate rate from accident to trial (or the date the loss ceases if earlier). If there are any special circumstances which may justify departing from this rule, they must be specifically pleaded, *Dexter v Courtaulds Ltd* [1984] 1 All ER 70.

- Interest on PSLA damages is added from the service of the claim form to trial, though the claimant may get no interest if he is slow in pursuing his action, *Birkett v Hayes* [1982] 2 All ER 70 and *Spittle v Bunney* [1988] 3 All ER 1031.

- There will be no interest on damages for loss of future earnings or future earning capacity, as those damages do not relate to money that has been withheld from the claimant, see *Joyce v Yeomans* [1981] 2 All ER 21.

Sums that are not deducted

19.101 Sums coming from independent sources, such as a personal insurance policy, are not deducted from damages. Money coming from a pension is also not deducted, *Smoker v London Fire and Civil Defence Authority* (1991) 2 AC 502, save possibly as regards a lump sum, *Longden v British Coal Corp* (1998) 1 All ER 289. Redundancy payments will also not be deductible unless linked to the injury, *Colledge v Bass Mitchells and Butlers Ltd* (1988) 1 All ER 536. Money coming from a charitable source is not deducted.

Sums that are deducted

19.102 Damages will be proportionately reduced if there has been a finding of contributory negligence.

19.103 In many cases of personal injury the claimant will have been in receipt of various state benefits due to illness or unemployment. If the benefits were ignored then the claimant would be overcompensated in getting state benefits on top of full damages. If they were taken into account simply to decrease the claimant's loss, the effect would be to reduce the damages the defendant had to pay at the expense of the state and the taxpayer. A practical result is provided by the Social Security (Recovery of Benefits) Act 1997, which provides that when a person makes a compensation payment in respect of any accident or injury, the amount of recoverable benefits must be paid to the Secretary of State, with the net damages payable to the claimant. The defendant should seek a certificate of recoverable benefits from the Compensation Recovery Unit. The provisions apply whether damages are ordered by the court or agreed. The benefits that are thus recoverable are listed in the statute, being primarily benefits paid to compensate for disability and being out of work.

Provisional damages

19.104 Receiving damages as a single lump sum could be a disadvantage to a claimant whose physical condition could deteriorate. One approach is to delay trial or settlement until the claimant's condition is reasonably settled, but this could keep the litigation process open for far too long. The alternative is that damages can be awarded on a provisional basis. This applies where it is proved or admitted that there is a chance that at some definite or indefinite time in the future the claimant will develop some serious disease or suffer some serious deterioration in his or her physical or mental condition, Supreme Court Act 1981, s 32A. Medical evidence should state a specific and quantifiable risk of a specified deterioration. The greater that risk, the more likely it is that provisional damages will be awarded. The immediate award of damages will be assessed on the basis that the further deterioration will not happen, but the court can order that the claimant be entitled to further damages if the deterioration takes place. The anticipated later event must be serious rather than normal deterioration, and should be measurable and distinct, *Willson v Ministry of Defence* (1991) 1 All ER 638.

The particulars of claim must specifically seek provisional damages as a remedy. If provisional **19.105** damages are awarded or agreed then the order must be carefully drawn up, and papers lodged to be considered should the case come back to court, PD 41. The order should specify the type of deterioration covered and the period within which the claimant may return to court—detailed argument at a later stage should be avoided as far as possible. See generally CPR Part 41 Provisional damages, and PD 41 Provisional damages.

Structured settlements

A structured settlement may be of particular value in a personal injury case where the **19.106** injuries are so severe that the effects of the accident are ongoing and damages will be substantial. Instead of damages being paid as a single lump sum, the structured settlement provides an alternative way of paying damages that can be more closely tailored to meet the claimant's needs, and that may prove attractive to a defendant as payments can be spread over a number of years, and/or the initial cost can be reduced through the purchase of an annuity. It is not attractive for a relatively low value settlement where the costs of setting up and running the settlement will not be justified. The first structured settlement approved by an English court is reported as *Kelly v Dawes* The Times, 27 September 1990.

The making of structured settlements was considerably facilitated by the Damages Act 1996 **19.107** and by the Finance Acts 1995 and 1996. A structured settlement can only be made with the agreement of the parties and not imposed by a court. Normally the form of the settlement is to pay a lump sum for damages to date, and then to purchase an annuity for payments for the future, possibly with further lump sums. Insurers and the Inland Revenue will normally be involved in agreeing terms. The settlement must be in a form approved by the Inland Revenue if it is not to have tax disadvantages. Further lump sums and provision for inflation may be included.

The negotiation of a structured settlement will require practical skill beyond simply spread- **19.108** ing a gross damage figure over a number of years. The size of the annuity, how long it should continue, and whether other payments will be required will require careful consideration. The application for court approval of an agreed settlement will need to be supported by an opinion from Counsel recommending the settlement, a full financial analysis of the case, a draft of the proposed settlement, and confirmation of the approval of the Inland Revenue.

Seeking a structured settlement may well be an objective of negotiation in a suitable case. **19.109** The negotiation can be approached on the basis of deciding damages and then converting it into a structured settlement, or building a settlement to meet the claimant's needs. Both sides should have their own adviser on the terms of the settlement. A number of insurance companies offer expertise in this area.

An award of damages for personal injuries in the form of periodical payments rather than a **19.110** lump sum can be ordered if the parties agree. Where an award is made in respect of future pecuniary loss in a personal injury case the court may order that damages for that future loss be paid in periodical payments without an agreement. The court must be satisfied that continuity of payment is reasonably secure.

Damages for fatal accidents

19.111 Where an accident has resulted in a death there are two areas of loss and damage—that suffered by the deceased (governed by the Law Reform (Miscellaneous Provisions) Act 1934) and that suffered by dependants of the deceased (governed by the Fatal Accidents Act 1976). Both statutes were amended by the Administration of Justice Act 1982. Both actions depend on the deceased having had a cause of action in relation to the death, for example in negligence, and the same cause of action will be used by the estate as regards the deceased and the dependants. For an example of a fatal accident claim see 19.150.

Damages for the deceased

19.112 Any cause of action the deceased had at the time of death can be pursued by the estate. The damages recovered will then pass according to the will of the deceased or as on intestacy. In broad terms damages will be assessed as for personal injuries, including principles of con- tributory negligence, recovery of benefits etc, though there are some differences. Damages will not be awarded for all the injuries as where the claimant had gone on living but only for pain, suffering, and loss of amenity between the accident and death, so if death is instan- taneous nothing will be recovered, *Hicks v Chief Constable of South Yorkshire* (1992) 1 All ER 690. Damages will not be recoverable of loss of income etc after death, or there would be double recovery as the claim would overlap with that for the dependants. Damages are also not recoverable for any loss that happened because of the death, save for funeral expenses. Where death follows the accident quite quickly the loss will be low.

Damages for the dependants

19.113 As regards the dependants, the measure of damage is what they have lost as a result of the death. This includes the money that the deceased would have continued to pay for their support and any additional expense that they have been put to due to the death. The dependants can also recover for losses they have suffered prior to trial as a result of the injuries and death of the deceased. The amount of the dependency must be proved, and this may include difficulties such as arguing how much the deceased spent on his or her family, and what other benefits the deceased provided in areas such as childcare and home and garden maintenance. In broad terms all money spent on or value provided for a partner, children, and other close relatives for all purposes will be recoverable, including fringe bene- fits from the work of the deceased and money provided from benefits received by the deceased, *Cox v Hockenhull* (1999) 3 All ER 577. Calculations usually relate to annual income as existing capital will not be lost and will pass separately on death.

19.114 The method for calculating the dependency should be put forward by the lawyer with appropriate assistance from financial advisers. No single approach is mandatory, though the broad approach is to calculate an annual dependency and then apply an appropriate multiplier for the years for which the dependency would have continued. The most appropriate of the following options should be selected.

- A frequently used option is to calculate what proportion of the annual earnings of the deceased was spent on dependants. In such a case the dependency of a spouse and children might be taken at 75 per cent and of a former spouse at 67 per cent.
- Alternatively the dependency is calculated by taking the salary of the deceased and deducting the money that he or she spent on himself or herself, the rest being seen as being spent on the dependents.
- If appropriate, items of expenditure regularly provided to the dependant should be added up.

There can be particular problems in assessing a dependency, for example in the case of the   **19.115**
death of a main carer for a home and children. If the other parent gives up work to care for
the home and children then the measure may be the lost earnings of that parent, *Mehmet v Perry* (1977) 2 All ER 529. Otherwise the value of all the housekeeping and childcare services
performed may be evaluated and added together, *Regan v Williamson* (1976) 1 WLR 305, but
see also *Cresswell v Eaton* (1991) 1 All ER 484 and *Stanley v Saddique* (1992) QB 1.

Loss of dependency to trial will be assessed, then the annual loss of dependency at the date   **19.116**
of trial will be multiplied by a multiplier depending on the age of the deceased and the
number of years he or she might have gone on working to assess future loss. The use of the
actuarial approach and the Ogden tables is not as strongly established as it is for personal
injury cases, though the tables offer relevant information and a similar approach is justified.
Contingencies relating to dependency such as prospects of divorce or remarriage may
be relevant. There may also be damages for bereavement. A deduction for contributory
negligence may be appropriate to fatal accident claims. Interest should be added as
appropriate. No deductions are made for widow's pensions, charitable payments etc, and
there is no recovery of benefits in a fatal accident case.

Perhaps surprisingly the claims of all dependants are assessed as one sum, even though the   **19.117**
actual dependency of different individuals will be very different. The logic is that the
dependency all came from the income of the deceased. At the end of the day the court will
apportion the sum payable as damages between the individual dependants.

J   DRAFTING A TORT CLAIM

Drafting a negligence claim

The accident

The way in which it is said an accident happened should be set out as briefly and objectively   **19.118**
as possible so it is likely to be admitted. In most cases it will be accepted that an accident
happened. It is the cause of the accident and resulting loss and damage that are likely to be
disputed.

Particulars of negligence or breach

Particulars of negligence or breach of statutory duty must be pleaded clearly and with care.   **19.119**
The particulars must be carefully based on the evidence, and focussed on the key things that
it is argued led to the accident, *Brickfield Properties v Newton* [1971] 1 WLR 862. In the case of

breach of statutory duty the wording of the statute or statutory regulation should be picked up if possible. It is important to balance being as precise as possible about how the accident is most likely to have happened with sufficient generality to provide flexibility should the evidence come out a little differently in court. These principles are illustrated in *Waghorn v George Wimpey & Co* [1969] 1 WLR 1764, where the claimant sued his employers alleging that he fell while crossing a bank at the site where he worked. It came out in evidence at trial that he had in fact fallen some distance from the bank, and his action failed as this was thought to be too radical a departure from his statement of case. For examples of particulars see 19.138, 19.140, 19.142, 19.145, 19.148, and 19.150.

19.120   If there is more than one cause of action, such as negligence and breach of statutory duty, the particulars should be set out separately unless there is a very strong overlap.

19.121   If the claimant is arguing *res ipsa loquitur* that should be specified in the statement of case, though it was held in one case that if a claim for negligence involved all the facts from which *res ipsa loquitur* could be implied, that would be sufficient, *Bennett v Chemical Construction (GB)* [1971] 1 WLR 1571. It is not entirely logical to give particulars of negligence and argue *res ipsa liquitur* (as this principle applies when it is not possible to prove how an accident happened) but in practice they are combined.

Loss and damage

19.122   The facts giving rise to each main head of loss and damage, and showing that it resulted from the breach that constitutes the cause of action must be given in the particulars of claim. The ownership of all property damaged or destroyed must be pleaded to show loss. Figures can be included in the body of the statement of case, or set out in a schedule if that would be clearer. A schedule should list each item of loss and give as precise a figure as possible.

Drafting a personal injury claim

Special rules

19.123   A claim for personal injuries must be brought in the County Court unless the claimant reasonably expects to recover more than £50,000, High Court and County Courts Jurisdiction Order 1991, SI 1991/724, see Chapter 4. In practice even cases well above that figure are likely to be brought in the County Court for convenience and to keep costs down.

19.124   There are some special rules for drafting a personal injury claim (which includes a fatal accident, CPR r 2.3) in PD 16 para 4, see 19.138, 19.142, and 19.150.

- The particulars of claim must include the claimant's date of birth.
- The particulars of claim must include brief details of the claimant's personal injuries.
- The particulars of claim must be accompanied by a schedule of details of any past and future expenses and losses.
- The particulars of claim must be accompanied by a medical report about the claimant's injuries.
- If the claimant is seeking provisional damages, the particulars of claim must make a statement to that effect and the grounds for that claim. This must include a chance that at some future time the claimant will develop a serious disease or suffer a serious

deterioration in his or her physical or mental condition, specifying the type of deterioration anticipated (which must be supported by the medical evidence).

- For a fatal accident there must be a statement that the claim is made under the Fatal Accidents Act 1976 and the dependants on whose behalf the claim is made must be named, including their date of birth and the nature of their dependency.

In a fatal accident case there are various particulars of the dependants and the deceased that **19.125** must be pleaded by statute, see 19.150.

Injury and loss

In a personal injury case the particulars of claim must be accompanied by a schedule of **19.126** details of past and future expenses and losses, PD 16 para 4.2 (see 19.86–19.89).

In addition the particulars of claim must be accompanied by a medical report dealing with **19.127** the details of the claimant's injuries, PD 16 para 4.3. A brief and clear summary of the main injuries, the treatment given, the current state of the claimant, and the prognosis should be included in the body of the particulars of claim. These particulars are normally taken from the medical report. Specialist doctors will often have expertise in providing medical reports for litigation, but this can be covered in briefing the doctor.

Any problems with performing household tasks or pursuing hobbies should be included **19.128** where these are alleged to be heads of damage, and should be supported by the medical evidence.

K   ADVISING A DEFENDANT

There are various basic courses open to a defendant in a tort action, in addition to the **19.129** general lines of defence raised in 17.43–17.46.

Arguments as regards the cause of action

The defendant may argue there is no cause of action—that there is no nuisance or negligence **19.130** etc. The lack of a cause of action may be argued as a matter of law—that even if the facts are true there is no negligence because the events complained of do not legally constitute negligence; or as a matter of fact—that the defendant's version of how the accident happened is different from the claimant's. The defendant may deny that he or she owed a duty of care to the claimant, and/or that he or she was in breach of that duty. Only in a minority of negligence cases will a defendant argue there was no accident. Witness statements and expert reports are as important to the defendant as to the claimant, although the burden of proof lies with the claimant. If the defendant is arguing that the accident had a different cause from that alleged by the claimant then it is helpful for the defendant to show some evidence of his or her version of events.

Potential defences

Secondly, possibly in addition to arguing that there is no cause of action, the defendant may **19.131** argue a positive defence. This may be a technical defence, such as the expiry of the limitation period, or a specific defence provided by the statute or regulations that frame the statutory liability. Other positive defences depend on the facts, such as *volenti non fit injuria*, where the argument is that the claimant voluntarily accepted known risks in a situation, *Morris v Murray* (1991) 2 QB 6. *Volenti* is not easy to establish, *Reeves v Metropolitan Police Commissioner* (1999) 3 All ER 897. Other possible lines of defence in tort, albeit not commonly used, are necessity, or self-defence.

Defences as regards remedies sought

19.132   Defences may relate to the remedies sought as well as to the cause of action, for example:

- The defendant may argue that loss and damage that has been claimed is not a foreseeable result of the negligence or other cause of action claimed.
- Further or alternatively the defendant may argue that the loss or damage was not caused by the defendant but by something else, see 19.143. There is the possibility of *novus actus interveniens*, where some new event rather than the act of the defendant is said to be responsible for the injury or loss suffered by the claimant.
- It is also possible to argue about the severity and valuation of the damage and injury claimed.

Contributory negligence

19.133   It is common in a negligence action for the defendant to argue that the claimant was partly responsible for what happened, and that therefore there is contributory negligence. This should be distinguished from the defence that the claimant was wholly responsible for the accident and that therefore the defendant is not liable at all. If the facts show that the defendant was negligent but that the claimant was also partly responsible for the accident then the court will determine the proportions in which the defendant and the claimant were responsible for the accident. If on the facts the court finds that the claimant was 25 per cent responsible for the accident then the damages will be reduced by 25 per cent. An allegation of contributory negligence must be set out in the defence, which must say how it is alleged the claimant was partly responsible for the accident in the light of the available facts and evidence. It is often not easy to use evidence to construct arguments to show relative responsibility for an accident, but it is important for the defendant and his or her lawyer to consider potential arguments—if damages in a case are potentially £100,000 then the difference between 20 per cent and 30 per cent contributory negligence is £10,000. For defences of contributory negligence see 19.140.

Joining other parties

19.134   In a tort case it is quite common for a defendant to argue that someone else is wholly or partly responsible for the accident. This person may or may not already be a co-defendant. Normally Part 20 proceedings for damages, a contribution, or an indemnity will be required, see 13.63–13.87, and see 19.144 and 19.149.

Drafting a defence

The basic elements of drafting a defence are likely to be: **19.135**

- Deal with any matters relating to duty of care or the location of the accident.
- Deal with the accident—it might be possible to admit it, or it may be necessary to respond to something in the claimant's description of how the accident happened.
- Deal with the cause of action, if appropriate denying negligence as alleged or at all.
- Give any additional facts as to how the accident happened, generally setting out the defendant's version of how it happened.
- Perhaps allege contributory negligence.
- Require the claimant to prove alleged injury, loss, and damage.
- Allege remoteness and/or failure to mitigate.

In drafting a defence in a personal injury action, the defendant must state in his defence **19.136** whether he agrees, disputes, or neither agrees nor disputes but has no knowledge of the matters contained in the claimant's medical report, PD 16 para 12. Where he disputes any part of the medical report he must give his reasons for doing so, and attach his own medical report if he has one. The defendant must also include in or attach to his defence a counter-schedule of expenses and losses, stating which of the claimant's items he agrees, disputes, or neither agrees nor disputes but has no knowledge of, PD 16 para 12. If he disputes an item he must supply alternative figures. The pre-action protocol requires the provision of particulars of loss prior to the claim form, so the defendant should be in a position to admit or deny in the defence.

L   SAMPLE DRAFTS FOR A TORT CASE

The following sample statements of case are intended to illustrate the structure and elements **19.137** appropriate for common causes of action and defences in a contract case. They are not intended to provide detailed pro formas as it is important that each statement of case is drafted to meet the needs of the individual case.

Example 1. Particulars of claim—negligence—personal injury

IN THE HIGH COURT OF JUSTICE   Claim No 2005 HC 9876   **19.138**
QUEEN'S BENCH DIVISION
BETWEEN

PERCY PROSPERO   <u>Claimant</u>

and

ANTONIO ALONSO'S FLYING FUNFAIR plc   <u>Defendants</u>

PARTICULARS OF CLAIM

---

1.   The Defendants own and operate Antonio Alonso's Flying Funfair ('the funfair'). The funfair consists of various mechanical rides and various sideshows, and is located at Sycorax Pleasure Island, Margate, Kent.

2.　One of the mechanical rides at the funfair is called 'Tempest Tossed' ('the ride'). On the ride each visitor is invited to sit in a model boat, each boat providing seating space for two people. When the ride is activated, the boats are mechanically propelled in varying directions at heights up to twenty feet above the ground.

3.　On 13 August 2003 the Claimant attended the funfair as a lawful visitor. He took a seat alone in one of the boats on the ride. An employee or agent of the Defendants fastened a safety bar across the front of the seat in which the Claimant sat.

4.　The ride was activated. The Claimant was propelled by the machinery in an upward direction with such force that he was ejected from his seat and fell to the ground from a height of approximately twenty feet.

5.　The said accident was caused by the negligence of the Defendants, their servants or agents.

<u>PARTICULARS OF NEGLIGENCE</u>

The Defendants, their servants or agents were negligent in that:

(i)　they failed to operate the said ride with any or any sufficient care as to the safety of those who might ride in it

(ii)　they failed to ensure that that those who rode on the ride were safe

(iii)　they failed to provide any or any proper supervision of members of the public using the said ride

(iv)　they failed to give any or any adequate warning as to the possible dangers of the said ride.

6.　As a result of the said negligence the Claimant suffered pain and injury, and has sustained loss and damage.

<u>PARTICULARS OF INJURIES</u>

The Claimant, who was born on 3 March 1963 and was aged 40 at the date of the accident, suffered the following injuries:

(i)　Concussion.

(ii)　Shock.

(iii)　Compound fracture of the right leg.

(iv)　Cuts and abrasions to the right arm and the right side of the face.

The Claimant was taken by ambulance to the Accident and Emergency Department of Margate Hospital. He was admitted to the hospital for treatment. His fractured leg was manipulated under general anesthetic and set in plaster. His head was scanned and he was kept under observation. The Claimant was able to leave hospital on 14 September 2004 with his leg still in plaster. He returned to hospital for the removal of the plaster on 20 October 2004. The fracture has healed but the Claimant suffers from significant residual stiffness in the right leg, and there is a 10% chance that he will develop arthritis within 10 years. He has suffered severe migraines since the accident, and has had psychiatric treatment for post traumatic stress disorder. The migraine headaches are likely to continue for the foreseeable future, and although their seriousness is likely to decrease they may continue in some form for the rest of the Claimant's life. The migraines can be alleviated but not prevented by medication.

The Claimant lives alone, and it is no longer possible for him to perform household tasks such as cleaning. The Claimant can no longer run every day as was his previous practice. The migraine headaches have made it impossible for the Claimant to continue his previous employment as an office manager. He resigned from that post on 30 October 2004.

Further particulars of the Claimant's injuries are set out in the medical report of Doctor Cleo Scylla served with these Particulars of Claim.

PARTICULARS OF SPECIAL DAMAGE

The special damages claimed by the Claimant are set out in the Schedule of Past and Future Expenses and Losses served with these Particulars of Claim

7.   The Claimant will ask the Court to award him provisional damages under section 32A of the Supreme Court Act 1981 assessed on the assumption that the Claimant will not develop arthritis, and to permit him to make a further application for damages if arthritis develops.

8.   Further, the Claimant claims interest pursuant to section 35A of the Supreme Court Act 1981 on the amount found to be due to the Claimant at such rate and for such period as the Court thinks fit.

9.   The value of this claim exceeds £50,000.

AND the Claimant claims:

(1)   Provisional damages; alternatively damages
(2)   Interest pursuant to section 35A of the Supreme Court Act 1981.

Ali Gee

Statement of Truth

Dated etc.

Schedule of expenses and losses

IN THE HIGH COURT OF JUSTICE   Claim No 2005 HC 9876   **19.139**
QUEEN'S BENCH DIVISION
BETWEEN

PERCY PROSPERO   Claimant

and

ANTONIO ALONSO'S FLYING FUNFAIR plc   Defendants

SCHEDULE OF PAST AND FUTURE EXPENSES AND LOSSES

Special damages

1.	Damage to clothing	£150.00
2.	Broken glasses	£200.00
3.	Loss of Ipod music player and discs	£340.00
4.	Costs of travel to outpatient appointments	£180.50

5.	Cost of medication	£120.60
6.	Cost of psychiatric treatment	£2,000.00
7.	Cost of employing a housekeeper to assist with household tasks the Claimant cannot perform from 14 September 2004 to 1 April 2005 at £40 per week.	£1,040.00
8.	Cost of employing a painter to paint the outside of the Claimant's house, which the Claimant had planned to do personally in September 2004 but could not do.	£3,000.00
9.	Net loss of earnings from 30 October 2004 to 1 April 2005 at £24,000 per annum.	£10,000.00
		£17,031.10

Future loss

1.	Continuing loss of earnings from 2 April 2005; multiplier	£
2.	Continuing cost of employing a housekeeper from 2 April 2005	£
		£

(A medical report should also be attached)

Example 2. Defence to particulars of claim in example 1—contributory negligence—volenti

19.140   IN THE HIGH COURT OF JUSTICE   Claim No 2005 HC 9876
QUEEN'S BENCH DIVISION

BETWEEN

PERCY PROSPERO   Claimant

and

ANTONIO ALONSO'S FLYING FUNFAIR plc   Defendant

DEFENCE

1.   Paragraphs 1, 2 and 3 of the Particulars of Claim are admitted, save that it is denied that an employee of the Defendant fastened a safety bar after the Claimant got into the ride. An employee of the Defendant told the Claimant to fasten the safety bar and thought that the Claimant had done so.

2.   Save in that it is admitted that the Claimant fell from the ride to the ground, paragraph 4 of the Statement of Claim is denied.

3.   It is denied that the Defendants, their servants or agents were negligent as alleged in the Statement of Claim or at all. It is also denied that the accident was cause by any negligence on the part of the Defendants. Safety bars were fitted to the ride, and the ride was supervised by a trained employee. A notice attached to the entrance of the ride said 'Safety bars must be fastened before the ride starts'.

4.   Further or in the alternative, the accident was caused wholly or in part by the negligence of the Claimant:

PARTICULARS OF NEGLIGENCE

(i)   On taking his seat on the ride, the Claimant was wearing a personal music player, and was thus unable to hear any of the instructions given to him by the employee of the Defendant operating the ride.

(ii) The Claimant failed to listen to or to obey the instructions of the employee of the Defendant who was supervising the ride.

(iii) The Claimant failed to ensure that the safety bar over his seat was fastened properly or at all.

(iv) The Claimant failed to read and/or to obey the notice placed at the entrance to the ride.

(v)   In the circumstances, the Claimant failed to take any or any reasonable care for his own safety.

5.   Further or in the alternative, the Claimant knew or ought to have known that it was dangerous to ride on the ride without fastening the safety bar. In these circumstances the Claimant impliedly consented to run the risk of any injury arising from his actions.

6.   Except as is set out in paragraph 7 below, and in the counter schedule of loss and expense served with this Defence, the Claimant is required to prove the extent of his injuries and of loss and damage claimed.

7.   (Address matters set out in the Claimant's medical report, stating which are agreed, which are disputed, and which the Defendant has no knowledge of.)

E. Bye-Gumm

Statement of Truth

Dated etc.

Counter schedule of expenses and losses

IN THE HIGH COURT OF JUSTICE   Claim No 2005 HC 9876   **19.141**
QUEEN'S BENCH DIVISION

BETWEEN

PERCY PROSPERO   <u>Claimant</u>

and

ANTONIO ALONSO'S FLYING FUNFAIR plc   <u>Defendant</u>

DEFENDANT'S COUNTER SCHEDULE OF
PAST AND FUTURE EXPENSES AND LOSSES

<u>Special damages</u>

Items 1, 2, 3, 4, 5 and 6 are agreed, subject to the Claimant proving the amounts claimed.

Item 7: the Claimant is required to prove the need for the housekeeper and the amount claimed.

Item 8 is disputed. The repainting of the outside of the house could have been delayed.

Item 9 is agreed as regards both loss and amount.

Future loss

Item 1 is disputed. The loss and the multiplier should be lower.
Item 2: the Claimant is required to prove the ongoing need for the housekeeper and the amount claimed.

Example 3. Particulars of claim—occupier's liability—negligence

19.142   IN THE READING COUNTY COURT   Claim NoRG5/8765

BETWEEN

SCOTT DUNCAN   Claimant

and

(1)   MACDONALD MACBETH
(2)   FLORA MACBETH   Defendants

PARTICULARS OF CLAIM

1.   The Defendants are and were at all material times the joint owners and occupiers of premises known as 'The Thane of Cawdor Hotel', Dunsinane Hill, Birnham Beeches, Berkshire ('the hotel').
2.   On the 31 October 2004 the Claimant entered the hotel as a lawful visitor and guest.
3.   While the Claimant was sitting on a couch in the lounge of the hotel, two ceremonial daggers which were part of the decoration of the lobby ('the daggers') fell from their fitting on the wall and hit the Claimant, causing him injury.
4.   The matters complained of were caused by the negligence and/or the breach of statutory duty under section 2 of the Occupiers' Liability Act 1957 of the Defendants, their servants or agents:

PARTICULARS OF NEGLIGENCE AND/OR BREACH OF STATUTORY DUTY

The Defendants, their servants or agents were negligent and/or in breach of statutory duty in that they:

(i)   failed to attach the daggers to the wall in an adequate manner
(ii)   failed to give any or any sufficient consideration to the best manner of attaching the daggers to the wall, and/or failed to take adequate account of the weight of the daggers
(iii) failed to check whether the daggers remained adequately attached to the wall
(iv)   failed to consider adequately or at all whether the said daggers were a safe form of decoration in the place where they were attached
(v)   failed to take any or any reasonable care to ensure that the Claimant was reasonably safe in using the said premises as a visitor.

5.   As a result of the negligence and/or breach of statutory duty the Claimant has suffered pain and injury, and sustained loss and damage.

PARTICULARS OF INJURIES

The Claimant, who was born on 11 March 1943 and was aged 60 at the date of the accident, suffered the following injuries:

(i)   Two stab wounds to the chest, one of which punctured his left lung.
(ii) Cuts and bruising to his chest and his upper right arm.
(iii) Shock.

The Claimant was taken by ambulance to the Accident and Emergency Department of Reading Hospital and was admitted to the hospital for treatment. He underwent emergency surgery under general anesthetic as his left lung had collapsed and he was bleeding profusely. The Claimant stayed in hospital for two weeks. He has made a full recovery, save that he has difficulty breathing after exercise. This makes it difficult for him to carry out tasks such as decorating and gardening that he has performed in the past.

Further particulars of the Claimant's injuries are set out in the medical report of Doctor Ben Banquo served with these Particulars of Claim.

PARTICULARS OF SPECIAL DAMAGE

The special damages claimed by the Claimant are set out in the Schedule of Past and Future Expenses and Losses served with these Particulars of Claim.

6.   Further, the Claimant claims interest pursuant to section 69 of the County Courts Act 1984 on any amount found due to the Claimant at such rates and for such time as the court thinks fit.

AND the Claimant claims;

(1) Damages.
(2) Interest pursuant to section 69 of the County Courts Act 1984.

H. Rumpole

Statement of Truth

Dated etc.

(A Schedule of Past and Future Loss and Damage and a medical report to be attached)

Example 4. Defence to particulars of claim in example 2 (causation)

IN THE READING COUNTY COURT   Claim NoRG5/8765   **19.143**

BETWEEN

SCOTT DUNCAN   Claimant

and

(1)   MACDONALD MACBETH
(2)   FLORA MACBETH   Defendants
                                            Part 20 Claimants

and

HECATE'S HANDYWOMEN (a firm)   Part 20 Defendants

DEFENCE

1.   The Defendants admit paragraphs 1, 2, and 3 of the Particulars of Claim.

2.   The Defendants deny that the accident was caused by negligence or breach of statutory duty on the part of the Defendants as alleged in paragraph 4 of the Particulars of Claim or at all.

3.   The alleged accident was caused by the negligence of the Part 20 Defendants their servants or agents, who were independent contractors employed to attach the daggers to the wall in the course of redecorating the hotel during October 2004.

4.   The Defendants admit that the Claimant was injured in the accident. The Defendants deny that the Claimant has any significant continuing problem with breathing after exercise, or any continuing problem that is attributable to the accident. The Defendants will contend that the Claimant is as capable of performing decorating and gardening activities as he was before the accident. The Defendants otherwise agree with the matters set out in the medical report of Ben Banquo, but the Claimant is required to prove the extent of his injuries and the consequences of those injuries, and to prove loss and damage. The Defendants will rely on the medical report of Doctor Nan Weatherwax a copy of which is attached. A counter-schedule of loss and expense is also attached.

Norm de Plume

Statement of Truth

Dated etc.

(Counter-schedule of loss and expense and medial report to be attached)

Example 5. Part 20 claim linked to examples 3 and 4

19.144   IN THE READING COUNTY COURT   Claim NoRG5/8765
            BETWEEN

SCOTT DUNCAN   Claimant

and

(1)   MACDONALD MACBETH
(2)   FLORA MACBETH   Defendants
                                                    Part 20 Claimant

and

HECATE'S HANDYWOMEN (a firm)   Part 20
                                                    Defendants

PARTICULARS OF PART 20 CLAIM

1.   This Claim has been brought by the Claimant ('Mr Duncan') against the Defendants/ Part 20 Claimants ('Mr and Mrs Macbeth'). In it Mr Duncan claims damages for personal injury and interest arising out of an accident that occurred on 31 October 2004 at The Thane of Cawdor Hotel ('the hotel') which is owned and run by Mr and Mrs Macbeth. Mr Duncan alleges the accident was caused by the negligence or breach of statutory duty of Mr and Mrs Macbeth as appears from the Particulars of Claim, a copy of which is served with this Part 20 Claim.

2.   Mr and Mrs Macbeth deny that they are liable to Mr Duncan on the grounds set out in their Defence, a copy of which is also served with this Part 20 Claim. These Particulars of Claim set out the claim of Mr and Mrs Macbeth against the Part 20 Defendants ('Hecate's Handywomen').

3.   By a written contract dated 11 March 2003 between Mr and Mrs Macbeth and Hecate's Handywomen it was agreed that Hecate's Handywomen would carry out the restyling and redecoration of the restaurant and lounge of the hotel for a total cost of £66,666 to include all work and furnishings. A copy of this contract is attached to these Particulars of Claim.

4.   It was an implied term of the contract that Hecate's Handywomen would work with reasonable care and skill. Further or in the alternative Hecate's Handywomen had a duty to work with reasonable care and skill.

5.   The work at the hotel was completed in August 2003. The decision to use the daggers and all work in fixing the daggers to the wall was carried out by Hecate's Handywomen.

6.   Hecate's Handywomen were in breach of the implied term referred to in paragraph 4 and/or were negligent in that:

PARTICULARS OF NEGLIGENCE/BREACH OF CONTRACT

(i)   they failed to consider adequately or at all whether daggers were a suitable form of decoration for the hotel

(ii)   they failed to consider adequately or at all the need to maintain a safe environment for those using the hotel when deciding to use the said daggers as decoration, and when deciding to position them above a couch

(iii)   they failed to use an adequate adhesive and/or fixing for the said daggers

(iv)   they failed to take account of the weight of the daggers when fixing them to the wall

(v)   they failed to provide long-term secure fixings for the daggers.

7.   As a result of the matters set out above Mr and Mrs Macbeth have suffered loss and damage.

PARTICULARS OF SPECIAL DAMAGE

Damage to antique daggers	£500
Cost of redecoration	£3,000
Cost of new sofa damaged by blood	£1,500
	£5,000

8.   Further, Mr and Mrs Macbeth claim interest pursuant to section 69 of the County Courts Act 1984 on any amount found due to the Claimant at such rates and for such time as the court thinks fit.

AND Mr and Mrs Macbeth claim:

1.   An indemnity or contribution in respect of:

(a)   the Claimant's claim

(b)   any costs which the Defendants may be ordered to pay to the Claimants

(c)   any costs incurred by the Defendants in defending the Claimants claim.

2.   Damages

3. Interest

Norm de Plume

Statement of Truth

Dated etc.

(Copy of the written contract to be attached)

Example 6. Particulars of claim—employer's liability—breach of statutory duty

19.145 IN THE SOHO COUNTY COURT   Claim No S5/7654

BETWEEN

NICHOLAS BOTTOM   Claimant

and

THE MIDSUMMER-NIGHT'S DREAMY   Defendants
UNDERWEAR COMPANY LIMITED

PARTICULARS OF CLAIM

1. At all material times the Claimant was employed as a weaver by the Defendants at their premises at Athens Court, Greek Street, London ('the factory'). The factory was a factory within the meaning of the Factories Act 1961.

2. Amongst other machinery in the factory there were power-operated spin weaving machines, each fitted with two sharp-edged flying spindles ('the machine'). The machine was a dangerous machine and contained dangerous parts, namely the flying spindles.

3. On 24 June 2004 at about 2.30, in the course of his employment, the Claimant was operating the machine to weave cloth when a flying spindle became entangled in his hair when he bent forward, causing his head to be pulled into the machine.

4. The accident was caused by a breach of statutory duty under section 14 and section 16 of the Factories Act 1961 by the Defendants, their servants or agents.

PARTICULARS OF BREACH OF STATUTORY DUTY

(i)   Failing to fence securely the said flying shuttles, which were dangerous parts of the machine, as required by section 14(1) of the Factories Act 1961, or at all.

(ii) Failing constantly to maintain and keep in position any fencing or guard over the said flying shuttles while they were in motion or use, as required by section 16 of the Factories Act 1961, or at all.

5. Further or in the alternative, the accident was caused by the negligence of the Defendants, their servants or agents.

PARTICULARS OF NEGLIGENCE

(i)   Failing to take any or any adequate precautions for the safety of the Claimant while he was engaged in the said work.

(ii) Exposing the Claimant to the risk of damage or injury of which they knew or ought to have known.

(iii) Providing for use by the Claimant a machine that was defective or unsafe.

(iv) Failing to provide an adequate system of maintenance for the said machine.

(v) Failing to provide and maintain a safe system of work in the said factory.

6. As a result of the breach of statutory duty and/or the negligence, the Claimant sustained injury and has suffered loss and damage.

PARTICULARS OF INJURY

The Claimant, who was born on 1 June 1984, and was aged 20 at the time of the accident was treated by a paramedic and later attended the Accident and Emergency Department of Saint Bartholemew's Hospital. The Claimant suffered severe damage to his scalp and lost a significant amount of hair. He also suffered lacerations to his face and ears. The Claimant visited the hospital on 6 occasions for treatment as an out-patient. He has made a full recovery, save that both his ears remain scarred and elongated.

PARTICULARS OF SPECIAL DAMAGE

The special damages claimed by the Claimant are set out in the Schedule of Past and Future Expenses and Losses served with these Particulars of Claim.

7. Further, the Claimant claims interest pursuant to section 69 of the County Courts Act 1984 on the amount found to be due to the Claimant at such rate and for such period as the court thinks fit.

AND the Claimant claims:

(1) Damages.

(2) The aforesaid interest pursuant to section 69 of the County Courts Act 1984 to be assessed.

J. Austen

Statement of Truth

Dated etc.

(A medical report and a Schedule of loss and damage to be attached)

Example 7. Particulars of claim—conversion of goods

IN THE LEICESTER COUNTY COURT   Claim No LC/6543   **19.146**

BETWEEN

LEAR KING   Claimant

and

(1) GONERIL ALBANY

(2) REGAN CORNWALL

(trading as Regan's Traditional Pawnshop)   Defendants

PARTICULARS OF CLAIM
---

1.   The Claimant is and was at all material times the owner of an antique silver tea set ('the tea set').

2.   The Defendant was employed as a housekeeper by the Claimant from 1 February 1990 to 1 July 2004.

3.   On or about 3 June 2004 the Claimant permitted the Defendant to have custody of the tea set for the purposes of cleaning it and having it valued.

4.   On or about 22 June 2004 the Defendant wrongfully pledged and delivered the tea set to the Second Defendant.

5.   The Claimant has demanded the return of the tea set on frequent occasions but the Second Defendant has not returned the tea set and has wrongfully refused to return it to the Claimant.

6.   As a result of these matters the Claimant has been deprived of the use of the tea set and has suffered loss and damage.

PARTICULARS OF DAMAGE

Value of the tea set   £5,000

7.   Further the Claimant claims interest under section 69 of the County Courts Act 1984 on the amount of damages found to be due to the Claimant at such rate and for such period as the Court thinks fit.

AND the Claimant claims:

1.   Against the First Defendant, damages for conversion.
2.   Against the Second Defendant, an order for the delivery up of the tea set or of its value, namely £5,000; alternatively damages.
3.   Against both Defendants, interest under section 69 of the County Courts Act 1984 to be assessed.

Cordelia Regina

Statement of Truth

Dated etc

Example 8. Particulars of claim—nuisance—*Rylands v Fletcher*

19.147   IN THE ILKLEY COUNTY COURT   Claim No I5/5432

BETWEEN

BASIL BANQUO   Claimant

and

THE THREE WITCHES SOUP   Defendant
COMPANY LIMITED

PARTICULARS OF CLAIM

1.   The Claimant is and was at all material times the owner and occupier of a dwelling house at 1 The Heath, Ilkley Moor, Yorkshire ('the house'). The Defendants are and were at all material times the owners and occupiers of land and premises at 2 The Heath, Ilkley Moor, Yorkshire adjoining the Claimant's premises ('the premises'). At all material times the Defendants have carried on the business of manufacturing soup in the factory for sale in their chain of health food shops.

2.   Since about March 2003 the Defendants have wrongfully caused to issue from the premises noxious and offensive smells, smoke, soot, and other dirty matter. On many occasions these have spread over the Claimant's land and house, thus constituting a nuisance to the Claimant.

3.   The smells, smoke, and soot have caused much annoyance and discomfort to the Claimant and his family and have made the house unpleasant to live in. The Claimant has suffered loss and damage.

PARTICULARS OF SPECIAL DAMAGE

(a)	Damage to paintwork of house	£1,000
(b)	Damage to plants and trees	£1,000
(c)	Loss in value of Claimant's house	£10,000
		£12,000

4.   Further or in the alternative, the matters complained of in paragraph 2 constituted a non-natural user of the premises, and the Defendants wrongly failed to prevent the escape of the said smells, smoke, soot, and other dirty matter onto the Claimant's land.

5.   The Defendant threatens and intends unless restrained by the Court to continue to issue offensive smells, smoke, soot, and other dirty matter from the premises onto the Claimant's land, thus committing a nuisance and causing loss and damage to the Claimant.

6.   Further, the Claimant claims interest pursuant to section 69 of the County Courts Act 1984 on the amount found to be due to the Claimant at such rate and for such period as the court thinks fit.

AND the Claimant claims:

(1)   An injunction to forbid the Defendants, whether by their employees, agents or others, from carrying on their business or permitting their business to be carried on in such a way that offensive smells and vapours, soot and other dirty matter are discharged onto the Claimant's land.

(2)   Damages.

(3)   The aforesaid interest pursuant to section 69 of the County Courts Act 1984, to be assessed.

Sue-Anne B. D'Amned

Statement of Truth

Dated etc.

Example 9. Particulars of claim—professional negligence

19.148   IN THE HIGH COURT OF JUSTICE   Claim No 2005 HC 4321
QUEEN'S BENCH DIVISION
BETWEEN

HAL FIFTH   <u>Claimant</u>

and

(1)   HENRY FORTH-TWO
(2)   ENGLISH ARCHITECTS (a firm)   <u>Defendants</u>

PARTICULARS OF CLAIM

1.   The Defendant is an architect. He is a partner in the Second Defendants who are a firm of architects and carry on business from offices at Palace Yard, Westminster, London SW1. At all material times the Defendants held themselves out to be experienced, competent, and skilled architects. The Claimant has at all material times been the owner of land at England Field, Buckingham, Buckinghamshire ('the land').

2.   The Claimant wished to construct a new house on the land ('the house'). On 1 April 2002 he visited the offices of the Defendants and orally instructed the first Defendant to design a house for him for a fee. The First Defendant agreed to do this on his own behalf or on behalf of the second Defendants.

3.   The First Defendant knew at the time of the agreement that the Claimant would rely on the experience and skill of the First Defendant to design a house that was of sound structure and suitable for construction on the land. The Claimant and the First Defendant visited the land on 20 April 2002.

4.   It was an implied term of the said contract that the First Defendant would exercise all the reasonable care and skill to be expected of a competent architect in producing the design for the house. Further or alternatively the Defendants owed the Claimant a duty to exercise such care and skill.

5.   On 5 October 2002 the First Defendant produced architectural designs for a house to be built on the land ('the designs'). In reliance on the designs the Claimant employed a builder to build the house following the designs. The house was completed on 30 October 2003, and the Claimant moved into the house the following week.

6.   It soon became clear that there were serious flaws in the designs for the house. The house was structurally unsound and was defective in the ways set out in the Schedule attached to this Particulars of Claim. The Claimant had to move out of the house on 1 July 2004 as the structure is unsafe.

7.   In drawing up the designs the Defendants were in breach of the implied term of the agreement and/or the First Defendant was negligent in that:

PARTICULARS OF BREACH/NEGLIGENCE

(i)   the designs were inherently structurally unsound
(ii)   the designs were not firmly based on accepted architectural practice
(iii) the designs failed to take any or any proper account of the nature of the soil and the rocks underlying the land.

8.   As a result of these matters the Claimant has suffered loss and damage.

PARTICULARS OF DAMAGE

(i)	Cost of structural repairs to the house	£ 60,000
(ii)	Cost of renting alternative accommodation since 1 July 2004 £ 2,000 per month	£10,000
		£ 70,000

9.   Further, the Claimant claims interest pursuant to section 35A of the Supreme Court Act 1981 on the amount found to be due to the Claimant at such rate and for such period as the Court thinks fit.

AND the Claimant claims:

(1)   Damages.

(2)   Interest pursuant to section 35A of the Supreme Court Act 1981.

Pom Pusgitte

Statement of Truth

Dated etc.

(Schedule of defects to be added)

Example 10. Defence to example 9 and counterclaim/Part 20 claim

IN THE HIGH COURT OF JUSTICE   Claim No 2005 HC 4321   **19.149**
QUEEN'S BENCH DIVISION

BETWEEN

HAL FIFTH   Claimant/Part20 Defendant

and

(1)	HENRY FORTH-TWO	First Defendant
(2)	ENGLISH ARCHITECTS (a firm)	Second Defendants/ Part 20 Claimants

DEFENCE

1.   Paragraphs 1, 2, 3, and 4 of the Particulars of Claim are admitted. The First Defendant was at all material times acting on behalf of the Second Defendants. It was expressly agreed between the First Defendant and the Claimant on 1 April 2002 that the consideration for the drawing up of the designs would be based on normal charging rates used by the Second Defendants, a copy of which was provided to the Claimant at the time of the making of the agreement.

2.   The First Defendant provided designs for the house to the Claimant on 6 October 2004, but the Claimant is required to prove all other allegations made in paragraph 5 of the Particulars of Claim.

3.   It is denied that the designs for the house were defective as alleged in paragraph 6 of the Particulars of Claim or at all. If there were any defects in the house as built these were solely caused by and the responsibility of the builder used by the Claimant.

4.   It is denied that the Defendants were in breach of the agreement or that the First Defendant was negligent as alleged in paragraph 7 of the Particulars of Claim or at all.

5.   The Claimant is required to prove the alleged loss and damage, and in particular to prove the value of the damage alleged.

6.   Further or in the alternative, if contrary to this Defence the Second Defendants are held liable to the Claimant they will seek to reduce the Claimant's claim by setting off the sum counterclaimed below.

COUNTERCLAIM

7.   Paragraphs 1 and 2 of the Defence are repeated. It was an express term of the agreement that the fee for drawing up the designs be paid within four weeks of the issue of the invoice. It was a further express term of the contract that interest be payable at a rate of 10% per annum on unpaid fees.

8.   On 6 October 2004 the Second Defendants send the Claimant an invoice seeking payment of £7,500, being the fee due for the designs under their normal charging rates.

9.   Despite several requests the Claimant has not paid the fee or any part of it to the Second Defendants, and they are therefore in breach of the express term of contract.

10.   Further the Second Defendants claim interest at the rate provided by the agreement on the sum of £7,500 from 6 November 2003 amounting to £1,125 at 6 April 2007 and then continuing until judgment or sooner payment at the rate of £ 2.05 per day.

AND the Second Defendants counterclaim:

(1)   Damages.
(2)   Interest.

Ivor Beefe

Statement of Truth

Dated etc.

Example 11. Particulars of claim—Fatal Accidents Act claim

19.150   IN THE HIGH COURT OF JUSTICE   Claim No 2005 HC 3210
QUEEN'S BENCH DIVISION

BETWEEN

LAERTES POLONIUS   Claimant
(Son and Executor of the estate of Herbert Polonius deceased)

and

HAMLET PRINCE   Defendant

STATEMENT OF CLAIM

1. The Claimant is the son and executor of the estate of Herbert Polonius deceased (hereinafter called 'the deceased') who died on 13 November 2003, probate of the will of the deceased having been granted to him on 1 January 2004 from the Elsinore District Registry. He brings this action on behalf of the estate of the deceased under the provisions of the Law Reform (Miscellaneous Provisions) Act 1934, and on behalf of the dependants of the deceased under the provisions of the Fatal Accidents Act 1976.

2. On 13 November 2003 the deceased was walking home from the station along Arras Lane, Queen's Common, Essex. The Defendant drove his Sword sportscar registration number EGO 111 in a southerly direction down Arras Lane. The car ran into the deceased, knocking him to the ground.

3. The accident was caused by the negligence of the Defendant.

PARTICULARS OF NEGLIGENCE

The Defendant was negligent in that he:

(i)   Drove at a speed that was excessive on a narrow and winding lane.

(ii)   Failed to keep any or any proper look out for pedestrians.

(iii)   Caused or permitted the said car to proceed on the wrong side of the road.

(iv)   Failed to brake and/or swerve adequately or at all so as to avoid the deceased.

4. Further, in reliance on section 11 of the Civil Evidence Act 1968, the Claimant will adduce evidence at trial that the Defendant was on 13 March 2004 convicted at the Elsinore Crown Court of careless driving contrary to section 3 of the Road Traffic Act 1972 on the occasion when the accident was caused, as evidence of the negligence alleged in paragraph 3.

5. By reason of the matters aforesaid, the deceased, who was aged 60 at the date of the accident, sustained severe injuries from which he died on the same day.

PARTICULARS OF INJURY

The Deceased suffered a fracture to his skull, causing severe concussion, and also fractures to several of his ribs, and to his right arm and leg. He suffered severe loss of blood and substantial internal bleeding.

The Deceased was taken by ambulance to Essex General Hospital, where he died three weeks later without regaining consciousness. Further particulars are provided in the medical report of Dr Osric, a copy of which is attached.

6. By reason of the matters aforesaid, the estate of the deceased and his dependants have suffered loss and damage.

PARTICULARS OF DEPENDENCY

The claim herein under the Fatal Accidents Act 1976 is brought on behalf of the following dependants:

(i)   The Claimant, who was born on 10 November 1984, son of the deceased.

(ii)   Ophelia Polonius, who was born on 7 March 1987, daughter of the deceased.

The Deceased was born on 1 December 1948. He was the sole supporter of the said children. He was employed as a Senior Civil Servant at an annual salary of £150,000 a year, and a substantial part of his income was spent for the benefit of his dependants. This would have continued had he not died.

PARTICULARS OF SPECIAL DAMAGE

Damage to suit	£500
Destroyed brief case	£400
Destroyed personal computer	£2,000
Destroyed mobile telephone	£200
Funeral expenses	£15,000

Full particulars are set out in the attached schedule of expenses and losses.

7.   Further, the Claimant claims interest pursuant to section 35A of the Supreme Court Act 1981 on the amount found to be due to the Claimant at such rates and for such period as the court thinks fit.

AND the Claimant claims:

(1)   Damages on behalf of the estate of the deceased under the Law Reform (Miscellaneous Provisions) Act 1934.
(2)   Damages on behalf of the dependants under the Fatal Accidents Act 1976.
(3)   Damages for bereavement under section 1A of the Fatal Accidents Act 1976.
(4)   Interest under section 35A of the Supreme Court Act 1981 to be assessed.

Peimia Fortune

Statement of Truth

Dated etc.

(Schedule of expenses and losses and medical report to be attached)

KEY DOCUMENTS

Pre-action Protocols

Pre-action Protocol for Personal Injury Claims
Pre-action Protocol for the Resolution of Clinical Disputes
Pre-action Protocol for Construction and Engineering Disputes
Pre-action Protocol for Defamation
Professional Negligence Pre-action Protocol
Pre-action Protocol for Judicial Review
Pre-action Protocol for Disease and Illness Claims
Pre-action Protocol for Housing Disrepair Cases

These are easily available in hard copy and electronically, see Chapter 24.

20

SETTLING A CASE

A THE IMPORTANCE OF NEGOTIATION AND ALTERNATIVE DISPUTE
RESOLUTION 20.01

B TYPES OF NEGOTIATION AND ALTERNATIVE DISPUTE
RESOLUTION 20.07
   Arbitration 20.09
   Mediation or conciliation 20.10
   Negotiation. 20.11
   Expert determination 20.12

C DECIDING TO SETTLE AN ACTION 20.13

D ACTING WITHIN INSTRUCTIONS 20.16

E TIMING ATTEMPTS TO SETTLE 20.23
   The stages when settlement is possible 20.26
   Deciding on the right time to settle 20.32

F STRATEGIES AND TACTICS 20.36
   Strategies 20.36
   Tactics 20.41

G OFFERS TO SETTLE. 20.43
   'Without prejudice' 20.44
   Part 36 payments 20.51
   Part 36 offers. 20.58
   Provisions for all payments and offers 20.61

H REACTING TO AN OFFER TO SETTLE 20.65
   Assessing the offer 20.66
   Responding to the offer 20.68

I CONDUCTING A NEGOTIATION 20.69
   Deciding to hold a negotiation 20.70
   Preparation for a negotiation. 20.75
   Conducting a negotiation 20.77
   Reaching an agreement 20.78
   Points relating to strategy and tactics. 20.79
   Concluding a negotiation 20.80

J   DRAWING UP TERMS OF SETTLEMENT 20.84

Deciding on how to enforce the agreement 20.84

Agreement by exchange of letters 20.88

Terms endorsed on briefs 20.89

Contract or deed 20.90

An order that the action be stayed or adjourned on terms 20.92

A consent order 20.94

A structured settlement 20.101

Outline for a contract recording a settlement 20.102

K   AFTER A SETTLEMENT 20.103

Enforcing a settlement 20.105

Challenging a settlement 20.106

KEY DOCUMENTS

To fight and conquer in all your battles is not supreme excellence; supreme excellence consists of breaking an opponent's resistance without fighting

Sun Tzu, *The Art of War*

A   THE IMPORTANCE OF NEGOTIATION AND ALTERNATIVE DISPUTE RESOLUTION

20.01   It is arguable that the most effective litigation is that in which one does not actually resort to litigation at all. Despite significant reforms in the procedural rules, the litigation system has significant potential drawbacks.

- It can be very time consuming, and the delay in reaching resolution may of itself be a significant problem. It can be very expensive, and even though the winner is awarded costs, the award might not cover all outgoings. In general terms the costs of a trial, with lawyers, experts, and other witnesses are likely to more than double the costs built up before trial.
- There is always some element of risk in leaving a case to the decision of the court.
- The options open to the court in giving a judgment without the agreement of the parties can be limited. A court can decide who wins an action and what damages should be payable, but can generally only make more detailed orders with the agreement of the parties. Anything can be covered in terms reached by agreement.
- The parties lose some degree of control over the outcome of a case if they leave it to a court rather than agreeing it themselves.

20.02   Factors of this kind have led to a significant growth in the use of negotiation, mediation, and other forms of alternative dispute resolution (ADR). This is particularly so for commercial law cases, accident cases where insurers are involved, and family law cases. For books on skills relevant to negotiation and alternative dispute resolution see 24.23.

The Civil Procedure Rules 1998 give specific support for the use of alternative methods of dispute resolution.   **20.03**

- Cooperation and seeking settlement of a case if possible are built into the overriding objective.
- The pre-action protocols focus on the exchange of information and the making of attempts to settle before the issue of a claim form, see 4.25–4.27.
- A party can be penalised in costs if an offer of ADR is rejected without good reason, *Dunnett v Railtrack plc* (2002) 2 All ER 850, but this will depend on the circumstances of the case, see *Halsey v Milton Keynes General NHS Trust* [2004] EWCA (civ) 576.
- At a case review conference an action may be stayed to allow negotiation to take place if an action might be settled.

The vast majority of actions that are begun do not proceed to trial, and many potential actions are settled even before a claim form is issued. The litigation lawyer needs skills in negotiating a settlement to a case that are equal to those required for taking a case to trial. Having said this, negotiation often takes place within the context of litigation, or with litigation as a fallback. There are therefore many similarities in the skills required.   **20.04**

- The depth and width of analysis required for a negotiation is similar to that required for litigation. Negotiation is not a simple way out of a case, it is an alternative way to address the issues.
- Remedies need to be considered in just as much detail for a negotiation as they do for a trial. Significant work is required to assess an appropriate Part 36 payment or offer.
- Many procedural steps can be used as tactics to encourage the other side to negotiate.
- The rules of procedure and evidence can be used tactically in a negotiation, for example 'You may say that, but have you got admissible evidence to prove it?'
- Many of the skills used in advocacy can be equally used in presenting a case to an opponent.
- The likely outcome if the case went to trial needs to be predicted so as to compare it with what is on offer for settlement. There are also negotiation tactics here, for example 'You may say you are not giving way on that, but if I go to court I am sure the judge will order it'.

There are also some issues and problems with ADR. Unless the agreement is made enforceable through a court order there is a lack of coherent judicial or other objective oversight of agreements reached by negotiation. The agreement will only reach court if necessary for enforcement purposes or in an action for breach of the agreement. This may lead to concerns for example about parties being pressurised into agreements.   **20.05**

A party with a strong case does not have to accept ADR rather than go to court, *Halsey v Milton Keynes* The Times, 27 May 2004. Also under Article 6 of the Human Rights convention a party cannot be deprived of the right to a hearing.   **20.06**

B   TYPES OF NEGOTIATION AND ALTERNATIVE DISPUTE RESOLUTION

> Where there are too many soldiers there can be no peace.
> Where there are too many lawyers there can be no justice.
>
> Lin Yutang

20.07   There are many different types of negotiation and ADR, which have different uses in different types of cases. The use of arbitration and mediation are beyond the scope of this book. As both involve an additional party in the decision-taking, preparation is very broadly akin to preparing for a trial, albeit without the same procedural and evidential rules. The rest of this chapter deals with offers to settle and negotiation with which the lawyer may be involved as part of a normal litigation process.

20.08   The choice of a form of ADR may be pre-determined by a clause in a contract. Otherwise it will depend on the needs of the situation—if, for example, expert knowledge is relevant much time can be saved by having an expert as an arbitrator, or as part of a mediation panel. Many groups and bodies offer dispute resolution services, including Centre for Effective Dispute Resolution, www.cedr.co.uk; the City Disputes Panel, www.citydisputespanel.org; and Mediation UK, www.mediationuk.org.uk..

Arbitration

20.09   In an arbitration a decision on a case is taken by an arbitrator rather than by a judge in court. Both parties present their cases to the arbitrator under whatever rules apply in the arbitration scheme being used, or have been agreed by the parties. Arbitration is a dispute resolution method of choice in a number of commercial situations. The terms of a contract may provide for arbitration as a method of resolving any disputes that may arise. See the website of the Institute of Arbitrators, www.arbitrators.org.

Mediation or conciliation

20.10   Mediation can take many different forms. Essentially the dispute is solved with the help of a mediator who will often have had some training in the performance of the role. Rather than having powers to take a decision, the mediator will normally facilitate the making of an agreement between the parties. Mediation may be a dispute resolution method of choice where there will be an ongoing relationship between the parties, and the terms for this are best agreed rather than dictated, for example disputes as to access to children or between neighbours. There are six court-based mediation schemes (for fast and multi-track cases in London and Birmingham, and for small claims, fast and multi-track in Manchester, Exeter, and Leeds) and more initiatives come into being all the time, such as the recently launched pilot at the Central London Civil Justice Centre, see PD 26B Pilot Mediation Scheme at the Central London Civil Justice Centre. The Court of Appeal and the Commercial Court have mediation schemes.

Negotiation

Negotiation takes place face to face between lawyers without an additional party to take a decision or to mediate. The rest of this chapter deals primarily with this form of ADR. **20.11**

Expert determination

Where expert knowledge is required to understand a case or an issue, it can be agreed that a mutually acceptable expert should decide the dispute. This is quite different from using an expert as a witness as the expert will be able to decide the case. It can be agreed that an expert should decide an issue in a case being negotiated between lawyers **20.12**

C   DECIDING TO SETTLE AN ACTION

Settling an action might be seen as in some ways as easier than litigation, not least in that many formal rules of procedure and evidence can be side-stepped, and the process of preparing for a court action can be at least partly avoided. In fact the process for preparing for ADR, negotiating a settlement, and drawing up the terms of settlement are very demanding— there are various ways in which settling an action can actually be more demanding than taking it to court. **20.13**

* Settling the case without sufficient information about its strengths and weaknesses could result in a settlement unfavourable to the client that left the lawyer open to an action for professional negligence.
* Without the familiar formal rules for procedure, preparing the case fully and methodically can be more difficult.
* Depending on the stage at which a settlement is negotiated, the potential benefits of disclosure and making interim applications might not be available.
* A good settlement should anticipate potential changes in circumstances and cover them.
* Negotiating face to face can be more difficult that the relatively controlled structure of a court hearing.
* It is vital to draw up the settlement with great care, as anything that is omitted, unclear, or unenforceable might again leave the individual open to an action for professional negligence.
* The purpose of a settlement is to end the action, and a settlement with bad terms can leave the client in a bad situation from which there may be no escape—it will often be impossible to appeal or bring a new action—so it is vital to get it right first time!

There have been a number of cases, especially in the area of family law, where the courts have criticised badly drawn up settlements. The challenges involved in negotiation and the skills required to negotiate effectively should not be underestimated. **20.14**

Effective skills in negotiation will evolve with practice, and through reflecting on what does and does not work in different situations. Areas of skill that are of particular importance in negotiation include: **20.15**

- an ability to analyse the legal and factual strengths of a case very clearly;
- an ability to judge how much information about a case needs to be collected and analysed before it is possible to decide with adequate accuracy what a reasonable outcome should be;
- the ability to adequately predict the probable weaknesses and strengths of the case for the other side;
- the ability to identify a reasonably clear and comprehensive list of issues to be negotiated;
- the ability to sustain a focus on the client's objectives;
- the ability to structure a negotiation so as to ensure all issues are covered in an appropriate order;
- an adequate ability to use strategy and tactics outside the more formal setting of the courtroom;
- an ability to identify what terms a client should reasonably accept, and to advise the client appropriately on those terms;
- the ability to record a negotiated settlement in a way that is comprehensive and enforceable.

D   ACTING WITHIN INSTRUCTIONS

20.16   While the lawyer should advise on the possibility of settling a case, it is for the client to give instructions in relation to any attempt to settle the case, and in particular as regards terms for settlement, see 3.46. While it seems that a lawyer may have an implied authority to negotiate on behalf of a client, a case should not be settled without the express instructions of the client, not least to avoid any complaints about the lawyer's conduct and any misunderstandings regarding terms of settlement, see, for example, *Marsden v Marsden* [1972] Fam 280.

20.17   In advising a client about a settlement the lawyer should probably:

- state as clearly as possible about how all the client's objectives might be best met in a negotiation rather than litigation;
- advise the client about options for settlement rather than litigation, setting out pros and cons so that the client can take an informed choice;
- discuss what might be agreed with the client before negotiating starts, and if possible agree parameters for what might be acceptable;
- leave a negotiation to consult the client if necessary;
- always tell the client of an offer to settle the case, even if the lawyer would strongly recommend that the offer should not be accepted;
- recommend to a client terms of settlement that appear favourable within the range of what the client might get if the case went to court.

20.18   A matter of professional duty, the lawyer should not accept an offer on the client's behalf without the authority of the client, even if the lawyer thinks the offer is reasonable, and the lawyer should not put undue pressure on a client to accept an offer if the client does not wish to accept it. The lawyer can only set out the options open to the client in clear terms.

If the client does not give express consent to the terms of a settlement, he may object to the **20.19** terms later. The potential problems are illustrated by *Dutfield v Gilbert H Stephens & Sons* (1988) 18 Fam Law 473, where a wife seeking a divorce instructed her solicitors to reach a quick financial settlement. A consent order was agreed, but the wife later sued her solicitors for negligence for not fully investigating her husband's resources prior to agreeing the settlement. In fact her action failed as she had chosen to take a substantial role in negotiation herself, and it was held that the solicitors had only a duty to advise her and not to force her into any particular course, but the potential problems for the lawyer are clear.

The terms and possible effects of a settlement must be clearly explained to the client before **20.20** the client decides whether to accept. The lawyer should try to check that the client understands the terms of the settlement, and the implications of settling. Once the case is settled the action will be over, and if the client has agreed to the settlement then an appeal or a further application are likely to prove impossible. If the solicitor goes so far as to misrepresent the legal position to the client, the settlement might be set aside, *Re Roberts* [1905] 1 Ch 704. The lawyer might also be liable in negligence if he advises the client to accept too little, *McNamara v Martin Motors & Co* (1983) 127 SJ 69.

It is worth checking, as far as is reasonably possible, that the lawyer on the other side is also **20.21** working within the terms of instructions given by the client, see *Waugh v MB Clifford & Sons* [1982] 1 All ER 1095.

There are ethical considerations in deciding on a negotiation strategy. The lawyer needs to **20.22** remain self-controlled and objective to keep control of the case, even if expressing a point in strong terms. It is contrary to professional conduct to make threats in a negotiation, or to lie to an opponent. There are inevitably some grey areas surrounding the application of these principles. In conducting a negotiation there is no obligation to provide information that the opponent is not entitled to at that stage in the case.

E   TIMING ATTEMPTS TO SETTLE

The timing of making an attempt to settle an action should be considered with care. There **20.23** may be quite strong motives to settle, not only to save time and costs, but also to reduce stress for both parties. Sometimes there may be a temptation to try to settle because of possible weaknesses in the case—money in the hand may appear more attractive than taking the risk of complex legal arguments or problems with evidence. From the defendant's point of view, a settlement may be attractive if the sum payable is less than it would probably be at trial, and if the costs of trial were the defendant to lose will be saved.

None of these should result in a settlement being reached before the case has been fully **20.24** analysed. The lawyer that settles a case for less favourable terms than might have been achieved may be open to an action for professional negligence.

Sometimes an opportunity to negotiate arises naturally, for example meeting outside court **20.25** prior to an interim hearing, and such an opportunity should be used where this is potentially in the client's interests.

The stages when settlement is possible

Before commencing an action

20.26   Attempts to settle a potential action will often be made before the issue of a claim form. This is encouraged by the approach of the pre-action protocols, which encourage communication and disclosure of information prior to trial, see 4.25–4.27.

20.27   The advantages of a settlement at this stage are that the potential time and costs of the action are kept to a minimum. Court procedures will not come into play (save for any applications that can be made before action, see 16.63–16.78), and the parties retain control. A Part 36 offer can be made before an action is commenced, see 20.58–20.60.

20.28   The potential disadvantage of a settlement at this stage is that it may be difficult to assess the strength and the value of the action accurately without, for example, the advantage of disclosure of evidence and exchange of witness statements. A settlement must never be seen as a quick and easy way out of a problem—before a settlement is contemplated the lawyer must be sure that he has a sufficiently thorough knowledge of the case. There should be no significant risk of new facts coming to light later that should have been explored before the settlement was agreed or the lawyer may be open to an action for negligence.

After an action has been commenced

20.29   There are tactical issues in balancing attempts at settlement with taking the litigation forward. A claim form may be issued in the hope of persuading the other side to settle rather than risk a trial, or attempts to settle may be dragged out to slow down the progress of the action.

20.30   Once the action has been commenced, the overriding objective encourages settlement, and various procedural steps specifically encourage the possibility of settlement. In particular, each party should consider protecting their position through a Part 36 offer or payment in.

Before trial

20.31   Preparation for trial concentrates the minds of both parties. The potential time and cost of a trial also becomes more real—it is quite possible that a trial will double the costs incurred before trial.

Deciding on the right time to settle

20.32   At any stage in the case, an offer to settle should be based not simply on a general desire not to proceed to trial but on having gathered factual information and on having analysed it sufficiently to be reasonably confident about the strengths and weaknesses of the case, and on a fairly coolheaded calculation of what the case is worth. This analysis should be based on:

- a complete and prioritised list of all the objectives the client wishes to achieve;
- a complete list of all the matters that are at issue in the case, with the main legal and evidential strengths and weaknesses noted against each;
- a list of the remedies sought, and what is the most and least the client can realistically hope for on each matter;
- an analysis of the pros and cons of continuing further in the case.

It will normally be appropriate to go through this list with the client, checking that the list is **20.33** complete, that the client understands the position on each issue, and taking instructions.

The importance of having a clear and justifiable view of the strengths and weaknesses of **20.34** the case cannot be overemphasised—if the strengths and value of the case are overestimated then it may be a waste of time trying to settle, whereas if the case is sufficiently underestimated, the client may not do as well as he or she should. Just to take one example, damages for personal injuries can only be negotiated once the extent of the injuries, the prognosis for the case, and other losses are clear, even if the client is keen to settle quickly.

This is not to say that a settlement can only be negotiated at a late stage in a case. It is quite **20.35** possible for a lawyer to advise at an early stage that a case is probably a suitable one for settlement, but no actual attempts at settlement should be made until a clear view of the case has emerged. Premature attempts to settle may show weakness and unnecessary concessions may be made. The effective lawyer will wish to have sufficient information about the potential strengths and weaknesses of the case for the other side as well as the client's case before framing an offer for settlement or preparing for a negotiation. The information provided under a pre-action protocol should be sufficient to allow an assessment of the case, but may or may not be sufficient to negotiate a settlement.

F STRATEGIES AND TACTICS

> Strategy without tactics is a slow route to victory. Tactics without strategy is noise before defeat.
>
> Sun Tzu, *The Art of War*

Strategies

A strategy is an overall plan for how a negotiation will be conducted. It involves being clear **20.36** about what you want to achieve and how you think you are most likely to achieve it. Just 'seeing how things go' in a negotiation is a potential recipe for disaster in a negotiation if an opponent has a good strategy ready to implement.

Strategy is an overview of the case that relates to: **20.37**

- having clear objectives;
- having plans for structure;
- having a clear grasp of strengths and weaknesses and how they are best used;
- deciding on an overall manner of approach.

Various strategies may be adopted as regards the possibilities of settling a case. Both sides **20.38** may adopt similar strategies, or they may adopt different strategies.

- One strategy is to be completely open to the possibility of settling the case from the start, providing information to allow both sides to assess their case, being cooperative about progressing the case, and making an offer to settle the case as soon as it is reasonably possible to assess the case properly. Such an approach is encouraged by the pre-action protocols, and is most likely to achieve a reasonably speedy settlement without building up costs. If both lawyers adopt this strategy they can effectively take a problem-solving approach to the case. The potential drawbacks of such a strategy are that a lawyer may be tempted to consider an offer before the case is properly evaluated, which could disadvantage the client, or that if only one side adopts this strategy the other side could exploit the cooperation without reciprocating.

- An alternative strategy is to be very assertive, being slow to make offers to settle, emphasising the strengths of the case, and only providing information when necessary. While over-use of a competitive strategy can build up costs, and may add more stress to the conduct of the case, it can be linked with seeking a settlement of the action once the strengths of the case have been made clear, and this can result in a favourable outcome for the client.

- A strategy or tactic that can be of particular use where there will be a continuing relationship between the parties is to think widely about the case and to try to introduce positive and inventive proposals. If there is an ongoing personal or business relationship there may be merit in taking the focus away from the current dispute and setting it in the fuller context of an ongoing relationship. It may be possible to find shared interests that can be taken forward in the agreed settlement. For example, a specific contractual dispute may be resolved as part of renegotiating the terms of an ongoing contract to the benefit of both sides.

20.39 In addition to the strategy adopted for the case, the individual can adopt a personal strategy. The strategy as regards the conduct of the case can be competitive or even aggressive while the individual lawyer can have a very reasonable manner. The overall conduct can be one that focusses on settlement, but the individual lawyer can be quite assertive in presenting the case. Different combinations may suit different cases and different individuals. An aggressive negotiator may appear stronger, and may therefore win a point that someone else might have lost, but being too aggressive may lead to tension and bad feeling. The reasonable negotiator may find the other side much more likely to accept his or her terms, but may make unnecessary concessions.

20.40 Useful work on the effectiveness of different types of negotiator has been done in the United States at the Harvard Negotiation Project. The book *Getting to Yes* by Roger Fisher and William Ury (Random House Business Books) sets out principles that are likely to provide some insights for all negotiators, including a focus on some particular elements of negotiation strategy.

- The need to separate people from the problem rather than argue in personal terms.
- The need to focus on the interests of people rather than take up positions.
- The importance of looking for as many options as possible.
- The value of using objectives.

Their approach is constructive and realistic, and the suggestions for dealing with people who will not behave reasonably in seeking to negotiate a settlement, and avoiding being caught by people who are prepared to use tricks in negotiation should assist any lawyer in becoming a more effective negotiator.

Tactics

Tactics are ways of addressing particular points in a negotiation. Tactics may be used to build **20.41** a strategy, or may be independent points that do not necessarily contribute to overall strategy. Mentioning a recent case may be a tactic to make an opponent worry about whether his or her knowledge of the law is up to date, but it will not necessarily be part of the strategy in the case.

As examples of tactics that may be used: **20.42**

- Produce evidence that you do not have to produce at this stage in the litigation process to convince your opponent of the strength of your case.
- Use surprise, if you have new information not yet revealed to the other side that can usefully be revealed. This is a consideration prior to disclosure of evidence.
- Ask questions to get information that may be useful whether or not the case settles.
- Point out that if an issue went to court the other side would bear the burden of proof.
- Focus on legal and evidential weaknesses in the case for the other side to make them defensive rather than demanding.
- Draw up a schedule of figures and do a copy for your opponent. This can help you to get control of the way in which figures are discussed and which figures are used.
- Make a point of writing down anything provisionally agreed to get control over producing notes of the meeting.
- Suggest options that a court cannot order to make an offer look practical and attractive.

G OFFERS TO SETTLE

> I consider it a mark of great prudence in a man to abstain from threats and contemptuous remarks, for neither of these weaken an opponent. Threats make him more cautious and contemptuous remarks lead to dislike and a desire for revenge.
>
> Niccolo Machiavelli

Any party who embarks on the litigation process should make offers to settle. Whether or **20.43** not the other side is prepared to engage in face to face negotiation, an offer to settle is potentially a very good move in terms of tactics, and protecting the position of the party as regards costs. The offer needs to be carefully calculated to be as effective as possible.

'Without prejudice'

It is important to consider the form in which an offer to settle is made. The correspondence **20.44** between the parties is not privileged and is admissible as evidence in court. An open offer can be used as evidence of an admission, as evidence of weakness, or to suggest what might be appropriate damages if the case goes to court. The use of the words 'without prejudice' has no automatic effect, *Buckinghamshire County Council v Moran* (1990) Ch 623, or the words could be used to hide communications that should be open. The use of the words 'without prejudice' will not protect a statement if the phrase is clearly abused, if for example a party says one thing about an important issue in a 'without prejudice' letter and something opposite at a hearing, *Unilever plc v Procter and Gamble Co* (2000) 1 WLR 2436. On letter writing see 11.26–11.32.

20.45   On the other hand, it can be very useful to be able to show that a party has made reasonable attempts to settle a case at an early stage when a judge is considering what order to make as to costs at the end of the action. If it can be argued that the other side built up costs by not accepting a reasonable offer it is a good reason for getting those costs paid.

20.46   A 'without prejudice' letter can be used for this purpose, but the precise use of this phrase should be understood. The words 'without prejudice save as to costs' should be written at the top of a letter, and the terms offered should then be set out clearly. At the end of the letter the party should expressly reserve the right to refer to the letter as regards costs—otherwise it may not be possible to refer to the letter when costs are discussed, *Reed Executive plc v Reed Business Information Ltd* (2004) EWCA Civ 887. If the letter consists of a genuine offer to settle a case, then that letter will be privileged from production at a trial, see *Rush v Tompkins Ltd v Greater London Council* (1989) AC 1280. Whether a letter is really 'without prejudice' will depend on the contents of the letter and the stage in the action, and whether the letter is part of genuine negotiations aimed at settlement, *South Shropshire District Council v Amos* (1986) 1 WLR 1271.

20.47   The meaning is without prejudice save as to costs. A without prejudice letter should not be put into a trial bundle, and anything said in the letter cannot be referred to at the trial, save that the party writing the letter can bring the offer in the letter to the attention of the judge when the matter of costs is considered, *Guiness Peat Properties v Fitzroy Robinson Partnership* (1987) 2 All ER 716. The rule is to encourage offers to be made without the fear that it can be argued any concession or admission has been made.

20.48   A without prejudice letter may be referred to in court after the final decision on the case has been made, in relation to payment of the costs of a case after a final decision, if an argument arises as to whether there was an agreed settlement and what terms were agreed, *Tomlin v Standard Telephones and Cables Ltd* (1969) 1 WLR 1378, or as regards an action for a contribution to damages, *Gnitrow Ltd v Cape plc* (2000) 1 WLR 2327. The existence of without prejudice negotiations may be relevant to explain delay, *Family Housing Association (Manchester) Ltd v Michael Hyde and Partners* (1993) 1 WLR 354 CA.

20.49   The term 'without prejudice' does not stop what is said in the letter being potentially binding. If the letter sets out terms of a possible agreement then that agreement will be binding if the other side accepts it.

20.50   The 'without prejudice' principle can apply to letters as well as to meetings. If there is a wide ranging without prejudice meeting the court may need to separate out admissions (which are privileged) and non-admissions (which are not), *Unilever plc v Procter & Gamble Co* (1999) 1 WLR 1630. Matters from a without prejudice meeting can be admissible to prove the terms of an agreement reached, where it was sought to set such an agreement aside, for example for fraud, where it is argued there is an estoppel, or when considering costs at the end of a trial.

Part 36 payments

A defendant who seriously wants to settle an action to define his or her liability and to **20.51** prevent costs escalating will normally want to make a formal offer. If that offer actually holds out a sum of money then the other side may be tempted to reach out and take it. Following the spirit of the overriding objective, this approach is encouraged by the provisions of Article 36 of the Civil Procedure Rules, with the money offered being held by the court. The same procedure is open to a claimant seeking to settle a counterclaim. See generally CPR Part 36 Offers to settle and payments into court, PD 36 Offers to settle and payments into court, CPR Part 37 Miscellaneous provisions about payments into court, and PD 37 Miscellaneous provisions about payment into court.

Essentially the offeror assesses a reasonable figure to settle the action and pays that into **20.52** court. Notice of the payment is served on the other side. If the other side accepts the offer the case is effectively over and the proceedings are stayed. The money held by the court carries interest at a prescribed rate which will accrue to the person who paid the money in until such time as the court orders payment out of the money.

There is a great art to assessing the amount to pay into court so that it is enough for the other **20.53** side to take seriously, but not so much that the other side rushes to accept and the client ends up paying more than was strictly necessary to settle the action. The details of the offer, such as interest, need to be thought through so that the offer is clear. Further payments in can be made without permission, provided notice is served on the claimant and any other defendants.

The Part 36 payment notice must use a prescribed form. **20.54**

- It must include the amount paid in, whether it relates to all or part of the claim, and whether it takes into account any counterclaim.
- It will be deemed to include interest until the last day on which it could be accepted without permission, unless it sets out that no interest is offered, or sets out the rate and period for which interest is offered, CPR r 36.22.
- In a Personal Injury case the notice should set out the gross amount offered, and how it is divided between the heads of loss. It must also state the amount of benefits payable under the Social Security (Recovery of Benefits) Act 1997, and that the sum paid in is net of that amount (as it will be separately repayable to the Secretary of State). It is the net figure that will be used in seeing whether the claimant recovers more than the offer.

A party who accepts a payment in is entitled to costs up to the date of serving the notice of **20.55** acceptance, CPR r 36.13. Costs if the payment is not accepted are dealt with below.

A Part 36 payment should not be disclosed to the court until all questions of liability and **20.56** damages have been decided, CPR r 36.19, at which stage any party can bring such a matter to the attention of the judge.

Withdrawal or reduction of the money paid in requires the consent of the court. The pay- **20.57** ment out of money will need the permission of the court if, for example, the money was paid in by only some of the defendants, or if either party is a person under a disability, or in some cases under the Fatal Accidents Act 1976. There can be practical problems where new evidence is received shortly after a payment in. In *Flynn v Scourgall* (2004) 3 All ER 609 a medical report received just after payment in caused the claimant to wish to accept the payment and the defendant to seek to withdraw the payment. It appears that in such circumstances the claimant may not have a binding right to accept and the court may review the facts.

Part 36 offers

20.58   Rather than paying the money into court, a formal offer to settle the case may be made. An offer can only be made where it is not possible to make a Part 36 payment. Therefore it may be used:

- by a claimant, to set out the basis on which the claimant would settle the action;
- before an action is commenced (in which case it will need to be replaced by a Part 36 payment within 14 days of the service of the claim form, CPR r 36.10);
- in relation to a non-monetary claim (if the claim is partly for money there will only be costs consequences as regards a Part 36 payment for the money part CPR r 36.4).

20.59   A Part 36 offer:

- must be in writing in the form of a letter headed 'without prejudice save as to costs';
- must be clear what it covers, and in particular whether it relates to the whole of the claim or part or to specific issues, CPR r 36.5;
- if there is a counterclaim it must state whether it takes it into account;
- same as above on interest;
- it should not include costs, which will be payable in addition if it is accepted;
- it must say that the offer is open for acceptance for 21 days (though as this is a contractual offer it can be withdrawn at any time before acceptance, *Scammell v Dicker* (2001) 1 WLR 631).

20.60   The other side will have 21 days to accept the offer, in which case the action will be stayed, CPR r 36.15 and he or she will get the amount offered and costs up to the date of the notice of acceptance, to be on a standard basis if not agreed, CPR r 36.14.

Provisions for all payments and offers

20.61   To place pressure on the offeree to take the offer seriously there are possible further consequences if the offer is not accepted. If the case goes to trial the judge will not be told about the payment or offer as it might influence his or her judgment. However once a decision has been reached the matter of the offer will be relevant.

- If a claimant does not accept a payment in or an offer and goes on to be awarded a greater sum or to get a judgment which is more advantageous at court the offer will be irrelevant. The implication is that the claimant was right not to accept the offer and press for more so the claimant will get his or her costs in the normal way.
- If a claimant does not accept the Part 36 payment but gets less, or does not accept a Part 36 offer but gets a less advantageous judgment, the implication is that the claimant should have accepted the offer rather than let more costs build up. Despite winning the case, the claimant will be ordered to pay costs incurred by the defendant from the latest date the payment or offer could have been accepted, unless it is unjust to do so, CPR r 36.20. If the payment in exactly equals the damages awarded the defendant should get

costs. The rule on costs will normally be followed, *Burgess v British Steel* (2000) PIQR Q240, save for exceptional circumstances such as the effect of late evidence, *Ford v GKR Constructions Ltd* (2000) 1 WLR 1397.

- If a defendant refuses a claimant's Part 36 offer and the claimant gets more at trial then the implication is that the defendant should have settled for the lower figure in the offer, so the court can award interest at 10 per cent above base rate for all or part of the period since the defendant could have accepted the offer, and may order costs on an indemnity basis with interest on the costs at the same high rate, CPR r 36.21. In deciding whether to make these orders the court must look at all the circumstances of the case including the stage at which the offer was made and the information available to the parties at that time, see *McPhilemy v Times Newspapers Ltd (No 2)* (2002) 1 WLR 934.
- If a defendant refuses and is held liable for a lower figure then the defendant will effectively have won and will get his or her costs.

The effect of interest is important in calculating whether an offer has been beaten. The payment in will include interest only up to the last date for accepting it, but in comparing figures interest from that date to trial must be added, see 14.68–14.79. **20.62**

If the offeree is in any doubt about the terms of a Part 36 payment or offer, clarification can be sought in writing, for example to have the sum split between different causes of action. If the requisite clarification is not provided an application for clarification may be made to court, CPR r 36.9 **20.63**

If the offer is not accepted within 21 days, or if it is made less than 21 days before trial, it can be effectively accepted only if the parties can agree costs, or with the permission of the court. **20.64**

H   REACTING TO AN OFFER TO SETTLE

The client will need to be given clear advice about the terms of any offer to settle, and whether it should be accepted. The final decision as to whether to accept must be that of the client, but the client may well need to lean quite heavily on the advice of the lawyer in deciding how good the offer is compared to what might be obtained by continuing the litigation. The possibilities of an action for professional negligence if a lawyer does not handle an offer to settle properly have already been pointed out. **20.65**

Assessing the offer

The barrister should probably advise the client on: **20.66**

- the precise terms of the offer;
- the extent to which each term of the offer is or is not acceptable;
- what might be obtained if the action continues;
- the pros and cons of continuing the action;
- the implications of accepting the offer or continuing the action as regards costs.

It can be very difficult to decide whether an offer should be accepted: **20.67**

- It will be necessary to evaluate the claim fully, including all financial matters such as the effect of interest. It can be very difficult to make a decision if it is not clear what a single figure offer covers, and this may need to be clarified.
- There will often be some complex risk assessment—What are the chances that the case will be won if it goes to trial? What might the finding on contributory negligence be?
- It will be necessary to consider the likely future conduct of the case if the offer is not accepted.
- There may be unknowns regarding the future conduct of the trial, such as whether the judge will or will not admit certain disputed evidence.

Responding to the offer

20.68 There are various options in responding to an offer, though note that a response to a Part 36 payment or offer must be governed by the relevant rules.

- The response to an offer may be an acceptance. Normally an acceptance will form a binding contract, even if a detailed agreement still has to be drawn up. Therefore only provisional acceptance should be communicated until all details are clear.
- Sometimes the response will be a refusal. In terms of tactics one might simply reject the offer to show that it is inadequate, but some indication as to why and how it is inadequate may help to progress the case.
- The response may be that no decision can be made until details are clarified, in which case the further information required should be made clear.
- The response may be to make a counter-offer, in which case the terms of the counter-offer should be clear, including whether it does or does not incorporate any aspects of the original offer.
- The response may be that the offer is not acceptable as it stands, but that a way forward may be found in a face to face meeting.

I   CONDUCTING A NEGOTIATION

20.69 Sometimes the lawyers will try to negotiate a settlement to a case face to face. Effective negotiation requires specific skills, in particular as regards identifying and pursuing objectives for the negotiation, and as regards presenting the case effectively to an opponent. It is beyond the scope of this book to deal with such skills in detail, but the key elements in conducting a negotiation are as follows.

Deciding to hold a negotiation

20.70 The fact that a negotiated settlement may be a good way of concluding a particular case does not mean that a meeting to negotiate a settlement should be set up immediately. The point has already been made that the timing of a negotiation needs careful consideration. Timing a negotiation properly can be a tactic in itself.

20.71 Even when the time is right, it may be that possible terms for a settlement are more cheaply and easily set out in a without prejudice letter rather than in a more expensive face to face meeting, or that the main issues in the case are financial and that a Part 36 payment or offer is appropriate. A face to face negotiation is most likely to be justified where:

- there are several issues that may need to be balanced against each other;
- where persuasive argument may help to put the case strongly;
- where the meeting may be used to gain more information even if a settlement is not reached;
- where there will be an ongoing relationship between the parties that can be fostered in negotiation.

If the timing is right and face to face negotiation is justified, the negotiation needs to be set **20.72** up carefully. There can be more tactical factors in where the negotiation is held and who is present. A letter suggesting negotiation can deal with providing and asking for information relevant to the negotiation. A telephone call to the opponent may help the lawyer to get a feel for an appropriate approach to a particular issue.

As regards who should be present, in a commercial negotiation the client may wish to be **20.73** present with the lawyers. In other negotiations the lawyers may find it more productive to negotiate without the client being present and then to get client approval for the proposed terms.

As to where the negotiation should take place, there may be little choice if the negotiation is **20.74** to be outside court, though possibly trying to arrange for some degree of privacy may be useful. If the negotiation is to be in the office of one of the lawyers there may be practical or tactical considerations of what facilities there are to hand. In any event the lawyer may need to plan to ensure that legal authorities or items of evidence that might be used are to hand.

Preparation for a negotiation

Much of the potential success of a negotiation lies in the effectiveness of the preparation. **20.75** The key elements in preparing for a negotiation are likely to be:

- identifying all issues on which a negotiated settlement might usefully be negotiated, together with what the client wants to achieve on each issue, and what the client might be prepared to accept;
- identifying as far as possible issues on which the other side might wish to reach a negotiated settlement, as this may assist in achieving a good outcome;
- clarifying the legal strengths of the client's case, so that the legal strengths can be used and concessions are not made where there are legal strengths;
- clarifying the factual and evidential strengths of the client's case, so as to be able to use those in argument;
- being aware of the potential legal, factual, and evidential weaknesses in the client's case so as to be able to plan how to minimise the effects of these in the negotiation;
- having thoughts on potential agenda, strategy, and tactics;
- being fully familiar with the case as the negotiation may take an unexpected turn;
- clarifying instructions for the negotiation with the client.

There can be tactical considerations in whether the agenda for the negotiation is set in **20.76** advance, if so the level to which the agenda is agreed, and who should play what role in setting the agenda. Sometimes the agenda will need careful negotiation, setting the scene for the main negotiation! The agenda may be set simply in terms of agreeing the topics to be covered.

Conducting a negotiation

20.77 The conduct of a negotiation will vary massively, depending on the type of case, the stage the case has reached, the type of issues being negotiated, and the strategy taken by the lawyers conducting the negotiation. A long and complex commercial negotiation with many solicitors in an office will be very different from a negotiation between two barristers on an interim injunction in the half an hour before the case is called into court. However some generalisations can be made.

- Most negotiations will follow some sort of agenda to ensure that all issues are covered in a sensible order. Where there are a number of issues it can be useful to agree such an agenda at the start, not least to provide a framework for the negotiation.
- Structure and pace are quite important in an effective negotiation, especially where time is limited. The agenda can provide a structure, enabling the lawyers to move on if they seem to get bogged down on one issue.
- Presentation style is important. On each issue the lawyer should be able to set out clearly and concisely what the client wants to achieve and what key legal, factual, and evidential points support the client's case. The more persuasive the presentation is the more likely it is to succeed.
- Responding to statements and proposals from the other side in a clear and justifiable way is also important.
- Although the negotiation lacks the formality of a court trial, legal authorities and evidence can and should be used where they help to support a case.
- A negotiation can be used to get information as well as to provide it. This is especially the case where a negotiation takes place before there are any statements of case. It may be important to ask questions to probe the case on a particular issue before making an offer.
- It is important to listen carefully to what is being said by the lawyer for the other side. Careful observation may reveal something of the strengths and weaknesses of their case.

Reaching an agreement

20.78 It can be all too easy to get bogged down in a negotiation, or to be too superficial.

- If an offer is made the details may need to be probed before it is accepted.
- If an agreement is reached on an issue, that agreement should be noted down so that there is no later confusion.
- If it proves difficult to settle an issue after both sides have put their point of view then it is normally best to summarise what the parties have said and to move on to another issue. Repeating points made is rarely effective and can make the atmosphere and progress of the negotiation deteriorate.
- It can be helpful to suggest overall settlements on an issue, for example that if one client made one concession then the other side might make a concession too.

- Concessions should rarely be made without good reason, for example because of a weakness in the case or because one concession is linked to another. Concessions and should also normally be staged, making a series of concessions if forced rather than making a large concession straightaway.
- Flexibility is important, especially if something unexpected comes up.
- Reasoned arguments and objective criteria are professionally appropriate and are more likely to be successful than personal complaints, even or perhaps especially where clients feel strongly. A reference to an independent third party may help in some cases.

Points relating to strategy and tactics

It may be difficult to implement a proposed strategy in practice. Only experience will show **20.79** what is and is not most likely to work. Ideally strategy should be planned in fairly simple terms so that it is easily remembered during the negotiation, or should be planned with some flexibility depending on the approach the opponent takes. Even if a strategy is difficult to implement, certain strategic points should be remembered.

- A settlement should not be for terms that are significantly worse than would be obtained in court. Pointing out the likely outcome if the case went to court may be a useful tactic.
- It is important to remember the 'bottom line' or the least that the client will accept. Sometimes it is better not to reveal this, but sometimes making it clear that the client would not accept a particular outcome can be a useful tactic.
- Remember that if the negotiation fails then litigation will continue—it is not necessary to give information that is requested and sometimes it may be tactical to keep information secret until it needs to be revealed. Documents revealed in the course of an arbitration or negotiation may lose the benefit of privilege, *Shearson Lehman Hutton Inc v Maclaine Watson & Co* [1989] 1 All ER 1056, and *Dolling-Baker v Merrett* [1991] 2 All ER 890.
- Don't reach a settlement for the sake of it. There is always the option of walking away. Sometimes reaching a settlement is very important because the client cannot afford ongoing litigation, but sometimes the alternative is simply going into court with a strong case.
- Even if the negotiation fails, some benefits may be derived from it, for example getting factual information from the other side, and also a clearer picture of what is important to them.
- Remember that some things can be agreed even if there is not an overall settlement.

Concluding a negotiation

If a settlement appears to have been reached, then various steps should be taken: **20.80**

- The terms should be noted in writing. It is important to ensure that both parties have the same understanding as to what has been agreed, and that sufficient detail has been agreed. The court will only enforce the compromise if its terms are clear, *Wilson & Whitworth Ltd v Express Newspapers Ltd* [1969] 1 WLR 197.
- There should be a check that the terms are comprehensive including matters such as costs.
- If an action has been started then it will be necessary to agree what will happen to the action.

- If the negotiation has taken place outside court prior to an interim application then it will be necessary to decide what will happen as regards the interim application, and what should be said to the judge. There should also be agreement as to how the agreement is to be made enforceable, the options of this being outlined below.

20.81 If the agreement is clearly within specific client instructions then the agreement may be final at that point. If it is subject to client approval then that must be made clear. If there is any doubt then client approval should be sought. In any event each lawyer may need to explain the terms of the proposed settlement and what it will mean to the client.

20.82 It is important to be clear about the contractual nature of the settlement. Once the settlement is agreed it will normally be binding, unless it is made conditional on something, see *Smallman v Smallman* [1971] 3 All ER 717. The terms agreed may remain enforceable if a subsequent order does not incorporate all of them, *Horizon Technologies International Ltd v Lucky Wealth Consultants Ltd* [1992] 1 All ER 469. If the lawyer has misunderstood the terms offered the compromise may be set aside, but this will not necessarily happen, *Hickman v Berens* [1895] 2 Ch 638.

20.83 If it becomes clear that a settlement will not be reached then:

- this should be acknowledged, rather than wasting time;
- consideration should be given to whether it is possible to reach agreement on any issues;
- consideration should be given to whether there is any purpose in agreeing to meet again to try to settle the matter, and whether anything can be done in the meantime to facilitate settlement (such as seeking further information);
- the next steps to be taken in the litigation process should be considered.

J   DRAWING UP TERMS OF SETTLEMENT

Deciding on how to enforce the agreement

20.84 There are many different ways in which the terms upon which an action has been settled can be recorded and made enforceable. The best option will depend on the stage the case has reached, the form in which the offer to settle was made and accepted, and how complex the terms of settlement are. In any event, the settlement is essentially a contractual agreement.

- The consideration will normally be the giving up of the cause of action in return for the terms agreed.
- Orally agreed terms will be enforceable, save, for example, that a contract relating to land must be in writing.
- Third-party rights cannot be affected, unless the third party is involved and agrees to be bound.
- The settlement will not normally have to be approved, save that it may need the approval of the court if one party is an infant, or under a disability, or if there is a representative action.

20.85 There will be important differences depending on whether a settlement is reached before or after the issue of a claim form. If the settlement is reached before the issue of a claim form:

- the settlement cannot be recorded in a consent order as the court has no jurisdiction over the case;
- court powers to award interest and make orders as to costs will not apply, so such matters must be dealt with specifically, *President of India v La Pintada Cia Navegacion* [1984] 2 All ER 773. If there is no mention of costs, each side will have to bear their own.

If the settlement is reached after the issue of a claim form then the court will have powers to make a consent order and to make orders about costs and interest. If a settlement is reached it will be necessary to decide what should happen to the action. The main options are: **20.86**

- The action may be dismissed. This can be done if the settlement is recorded in a court order and the court orders that the action be dismissed with consent.
- The action may be discontinued. The settlement or order should record that the claimant will discontinue the action. The result will be that the claimant cannot go back to court as regards any matter concerned with the case.
- The action may be adjourned or stayed on terms. This can be done if the settlement is recorded in a court order and the court orders that the action be adjourned or stayed. In such a case it may be possible for the parties to go back to court if there are problems.
- The action may simply reach a natural end if the judge gives judgment after trial in the form of a consent order.

Whether the action is settled in a contract, on terms, or in a consent order it is vital to consider the exact wording with great care. It ends the case, and there will be little, if any, opportunity to remedy any defect, so the wording must be as tightly drawn as possible. **20.87**

- The terms should be absolutely clear, with no vagueness or ambiguity.
- The terms should bear in mind any foreseeable future events that may affect them.
- The terms should be checked carefully for any omission, loophole, or lack of clarity.

Agreement by exchange of letters

If an offer is made in a letter, whether or not a 'without prejudice' letter, then it can be accepted by letter. The exchange of letters will of itself constitute a contract, and nothing else may be needed in a relatively straightforward case that is settled before an action has been started. **20.88**

Terms endorsed on briefs

If counsel has been briefed, then simple terms or an agreement on an interlocutory matter can be endorsed on counsels' briefs and signed by the parties and both counsel. This is only appropriate if there are only a few terms which can be expressed concisely. The endorsement is essentially simply recording the oral contract. The endorsement has no special forms of enforcement, save that if the agreement relates to an interlocutory matter it may be possible to go back to court as regards that matter, or it may be possible to ask that an undertaking be given to the judge as regards carrying out appropriate terms. In *Green v Rozen* [1955] 1 WLR 741 terms were endorsed on counsels' briefs with the words 'By consent all proceedings stayed on terms endorsed on briefs. Liberty to apply', but it was held that these words did not reserve a right to return to court and a new action would be required to enforce the terms. **20.89**

Contract or deed

20.90 If complex terms are agreed before an action is commenced they are most appropriately recorded in a contract or deed, especially if the terms are intended to be a final solution of all matters, or any enforcement difficulties are envisaged. A written contract is a very flexible way in which to record terms. A deed may be required if it is not clear what consideration is passing.

20.91 The terms agreed by contract can be enforced, if necessary, by a contractual action seeking specific performance or damages. Alternatively, if the contract is repudiated or a dispute arises outside the matters covered by the agreement, an action can be started on the original subject matter of the dispute, so long as the limitation period has not expired. An action cannot be brought on any matter within the agreed settlement as the other side could plead estoppel, unless the settlement was repudiated or invalid.

An order that the action be stayed or adjourned on terms

20.92 Once an action has been started, a judge will have the power to order that proceedings be stayed or adjourned on terms. The agreed terms may be set out in a schedule to the order, or the judge may stay or adjourn the action on the basis that the parties have agreed terms, those terms being recorded separately.

20.93 If the action is stayed or adjourned it may be possible to reopen it if difficulties arise, or the judge may be asked to enforce any terms that were part of the order. Otherwise the action is over and it is unlikely to be possible to return to court. If there are more than two parties in the case, the fact that two parties may have reached an agreement to have the action stayed will not prevent the action being continued by another party.

A consent order

20.94 A consent order is an order which is formally made by the court, but which includes terms agreed by the parties. A consent order can only be made once an action has been commenced, and it must include a term that states whether the action in the case is itself discontinued, dismissed, or stayed.

20.95 The parties should agree the terms of the order that they wish the judge to make. The consent order is normally based on the outcome of a negotiated settlement—the settlement is itself enforceable as a contract, but recording the settlement in the form of an order ends the action and aids enforceability.

20.96 A court order can only include those things the court has the power to order in the action, see *Hinde v Hinde* [1953] 1 All ER 171. If the parties wish to agree something that the court does not have direct power to order then the terms can be set out in a schedule to the order.

20.97 In drafting a consent order, the order must be drawn up in the terms agreed, include the words 'By consent' and be signed by the lawyers for each party. It should contain the name of a judge only if it is made by a judge. Appropriate provisions for court orders should still be complied with, such as orders for provisional damages. The order should include a provision for costs or no costs will be payable. For a sample order see 22.139.

20.98 The terms may be recorded in a schedule, known as a Tomlin order. This is based on an order that the action be stayed on the terms set out in the schedule. If this is done matters such as payment out of money paid into court and costs should still be dealt with in the order rather than the schedule, PD 40B para 3. It is useful as part of the order to reserve liberty to apply as regards enforcing the terms of the order. For a sample order see 22.140.

In an appropriate case a consent order can be entered as an administrative act and sealed by a **20.99**
court officer without the need for the approval of a judge, CPR r 40.6. This can be done to order the payment of money, the delivery up of goods, the dismissal of all or part of the proceedings, an order to stay on agreed terms, and some other cases. The order should be drawn up and sent to the court together with letters expressing the consent of the parties, PD 23 para 10. If there are any doubts or concerns then the draft consent order may be referred to a judge for consideration. Consideration of the draft order may be dealt with without a hearing. The judge has a discretion and does not have to accept the terms drafted by the parties if, for example, the terms are thought to be inappropriate or poorly drafted.

After a consent order is perfected there is no power to vary it, *De Lasala v De Lasala* (1980) **20.100**
AC 546. If it is alleged at that stage that there was fraud or mistake it can only be raised through appeal or a fresh action based on the agreement. The situation may be different if it can be argued that there was no real contractual agreement, *Siebe Gorman and Co Ltd v Pneupac Ltd* (1982) 1 All ER 377. The benefit of a consent order is that it can be enforced like any other court order.

A structured settlement

One particular type of settlement that has come into use in the last few years, and which **20.101**
may be advantageous to both the claimant and the defendant in a personal injury action, is the structured settlement. See 19.106–19.110 and PD 40C Structured settlements.

Outline for a contract recording a settlement

AN AGREEMENT made on the (date) between A.B. on the one part and C.D. on the **20.102**
other part.

A.B. and C.D. have been in dispute as to (set out briefly the basis of the action)

NOW IT IS HEREBY AGREED by way of compromise of the said dispute that:

1.

2.

3.

4.   In furtherance of this agreement:

(a)   A.B. will . . .

(b)   C.D. will . . .

5.   It is agreed that each party will bear their own costs, C.D. agreeing to bear such costs as are occasioned by the drawing up of this agreement.

Dated

Signed by   A.B.   Signed by   C.D.
in the presence of   in the presence of

K   AFTER A SETTLEMENT

20.103   The lawyer and the client need to appreciate the finality of reaching a settlement. Once a contract has been agreed or an order made, there are very limited circumstances in which it is possible to reopen the matter or go back to court. Not only may this be difficult, but it will take extra time and money, which is why it is so important to take care in drafting the settlement in the first place.

20.104   It is not the agreement of terms but the carrying out of those terms that will end the case, and enforceability may be a crucial matter. This will especially be the case where there has been bad feeling between the parties which may mean that one or both are not well disposed to carry out the terms agreed. To assist enforceability:

- the terms should be as clear as possible;
- dates for doing things should be built in;
- one term can be linked to another to assist enforceability;
- penalties for not doing something can be built into the agreement;
- try to ensure that the terms are forward looking as far as possible, so that foreseeable changes in circumstances do not undermine the agreement.

Enforcing a settlement

20.105   As regards enforcing a settlement:

- If the settlement is in the form of some type of contract the terms bind the parties as a contract as soon as they are agreed, *Chanel v FW Woolworth* [1981] 1 All ER 745. If there has been some mistake it might be possible to get the agreement rectified, but this is unlikely where it has been drawn up by lawyers. An action may be brought to enforce the contract.
- If the settlement is in the form of a court order then that order ends the case—the only way to go back to court will be to enforce the terms of the order made. It is possible to leave the case open by including the words 'Liberty to apply' in the order, but these words only have limited meaning, and only effectively allow access back to court as regards the meaning of terms or the enforcement of the order.
- If the action has been adjourned or stayed on terms then it may be possible to revive it.
- A new action may be brought to enforce the terms of a settlement, or to deal with matters not covered by the settlement. See 23.04–23.25.

Challenging a settlement

20.106   As regards challenging a settlement

- A settlement can only be set aside in limited circumstances, for example if it was obtained by fraud or misrepresentation (*Detz v Lennig* [1969] 1 AC 170), mutual mistake, unilateral mistake encouraged by the other side (*Huddersfield Banking Co Ltd v Henry Lister & Son Ltd* [1895] 2 Ch 273), or for economic duress or undue influence, see for example, *D & C Builders v Rees* [1966] 2 QB 107.
- It is not normally possible to appeal against a consent order, or to apply to court to vary

its terms, *Peacock v Peacock* [1991] Fam Law 139. It might be possible to get the agreement rectified, but this is unlikely where it has been drawn up by lawyers.

- The court may decline to enforce a compromise if there is equitable reason for not doing so, or if it can be argued that the terms of compromise have been frustrated. One side may not be bound by the terms of a settlement if they can argue that the other side has breached or repudiated it.
- A court may refuse to enforce a consent order for someone who is not abiding by its terms, *Thwaite v Thwaite* [1981] FLR 280.
- A court can overturn a contract for the settlement of an action where the agreement has been based on a mutual mistake of law, *Brennan v Bolt Burden (a firm) and Others* The Times, 7 November 2003.

KEY DOCUMENTS

Forms

N242A Notice of Payment into Court (Part 36)
N242 Notice of Payment into Court (Part 37)
N243A/Form 201 Notice of acceptance (Part 36)

These are easily available in hard copy and electronically, see Chapter 24.

21

PREPARING A CASE FOR TRIAL

A COMPLETING THE PREPARATION STAGES 21.01

B APPROACHING A CASE STRATEGICALLY. 21.06
   Taking a strategic approach 21.06
   Choices of strategy 21.13

C REVIEWING A CASE 21.25
   When to review a case. 21.25
   Matters to review 21.27

D COURT REVIEW OF A CASE 21.31
   The principle of judicial case management. 21.31
   The stages of court review 21.35

E PREPARING A CASE FOR HEARING 21.42
   The roles of lawyers. 21.43
   Preparing the statements of case. 21.45
   Preparing the evidence 21.46
   Procuring the attendance of witnesses. 21.49
   Preparing trial bundles 21.55
   Preparing the law. 21.61

F PREPARING A SKELETON ARGUMENT. 21.66
   The purpose of a skeleton argument. 21.66
   The content of a skeleton argument. 21.72
   Outline for a skeleton argument 21.77

G PREPARING TO GO TO COURT 21.78
   Preparing to deal with your own witnesses 21.78
   Preparing to deal with the witnesses for the other side 21.84
   Working with the client 21.85

KEY DOCUMENTS

Lawyers spend a great deal of time shovelling smoke.

Oliver Wendell Holmes

A   COMPLETING THE PREPARTION STAGES

21.01   Earlier chapters have set out the framework for the early stages of litigation, see Chapter 4.

- The issues in the case are defined through the statements of case, see 10.19–10.43.
- Information and evidence are revealed when documents and witness statements are exchanged, see 15.179–15.205.
- Interim applications can be made to develop the positions of the parties, see Chapter 16.

21.02   Once these stages have been completed it will ideally only be necessary to review the case and prepare it for trial, especially if it is a fast track case. In such circumstances reviewing the case and preparing for trial may not be entirely straightforward, but the more difficult the preparation is the more important it is likely to be.

21.03   In an ideal world, the claimant's lawyer will have a plan in place for progressing the action before it is formally started. Unless the limitation period is about to expire, the claimant has control over the start of the action, and should have collected sufficient evidence, drafted the statement of case, and taken decisions about what interim orders are likely to be required before the claim form is issued.

21.04   In the majority of cases the claimant will have been in touch with the defendant prior to commencing the action, whether under a pre-action protocol, to see if settlement is possible, or as a matter of best practice. Therefore the defendant should be aware that an action is likely to be launched, and should equally have plans in place for the conduct of the case by the time the claim form is served, see 4.18–4.32.

21.05   If both sides have planned their approach to the action before it even starts then the case should proceed reasonably smoothly, at least through its early stages, but this will not always be the case. Problems can arise even if a case has been reasonably well planned.

- The intentions of the overriding objective in saving time and cost may not be fully met—even if the lawyers seek to act within its spirit, clients may not.
- One party may be better prepared than the other, which can lead to delays or additional work as both sides prepare adequately for trial.
- Plans for the development of the case may be thrown off course, for example because significant new information comes to light.
- Large multi-track cases may be inherently complex and difficult to manage very coherently.
- It may be necessary to alternate between trying to settle the case and advancing it to trial.

B   APPROACHING A CASE STRATEGICALLY

Taking a strategic approach

21.06   The importance of taking a strategic approach to negotiation is outlined at 20.36–20.42. It is equally important to take a strategic approach to preparing a case for trial. There is an extent to which preparation has to be simply methodical—working steadily through the stages of the case as outlined in Chapter 4, especially where the case has no particular complexity. However most cases will benefit from an overall strategy. Strategy may affect:

- the content and tone of communications between the parties;
- the nature of the evidence collected and how it is used;
- the extent to which interim applications are made, and the types of application made at the interim stage;
- the extent to which arguments in law are developed and used;
- the extent to which arguments on the facts are developed and used;
- the manner in which possibilities for settling the action are approached.

Some lawyers regard strategy as a matter of great importance, and in a big case there may **21.07** be meetings purely to discuss strategy. Others will adopt a strategy almost as a matter of intuition. Developing a knowledge of strategy is probably best done through observation and practice in real cases.

An appropriate strategy for a case may evolve in many ways. It may emerge from the nature **21.08** of the case, the client objectives, the sort of approach that the individual lawyer finds most effective, or from the approach being taken by the other side. Strategy may be set in the early stages of the case, or may evolve as the elements of the case come together.

Trial strategy is perhaps more overtly an area for study and development in the United States **21.09** than it is in England and Wales. It might be argued that one effect of the Civil Procedure Rules and the 'cards on the table' approach to litigation is that options for strategy have been reduced. However this is not really the case—some tactics designed to make litigation difficult are now discouraged, but it is still quite possible to take a strategic approach to developing a case and making the best possible use of the rules for civil litigation.

This is an area that would merit more academic study and research. Weak cases are rarely **21.10** pursued to trial. The cases that go to trial tend to be those where both sides have some merit and a chance of winning. If a case could be won with one strategic approach but lost with another then identifying why that should be so is of importance to lawyers and their clients. Many lawyers might argue that there is art in how they approach their cases, but scientific analysis might also produce interesting results.

There are inevitable questions of professional conduct and ethics linked to choice of strat- **21.11** egies. At the most basic level a lawyer must not adopt a strategy that involves misleading the court, lying to an opponent about the case, making threats, or acting outside the client's instructions. In terms of more general ethics, the over riding objective provides a framework of principles. For example the court will try to ensure that as far as possible the parties come to justice on an equal footing, even if one party has more resources than the other. For a lawyer's duties to the court see 3.45.

It has been held that there was no duty of care in tort between one litigant and another **21.12** regarding the conduct of an action, *Business Computers International Ltd v Registrar of Companies* [1987] 3 All ER 465.

Choices of strategy

21.13　Various types of strategy for conducting a case can be identified. A strategy may be adopted throughout a case or may be different at different stages in a case. Different types of strategy may be combined.

Building the strongest possible case

21.14　One strategy is to make steady, realistic progress through a case, building it as strongly as possible, brick by brick. All matters of law, fact, and evidence are developed in the strongest possible way to promote the client's case. This may not appear the most exciting approach to litigation, but it is likely to have the merit of convincing the other side and the court that the case is firm, and that there will be no compromises where the case has merit. Possible drawbacks are that costs may build up and that the outcome achieved might be fair rather than the best possible outcome.

Aiming high

21.15　A potentially more dramatic strategy is to clearly and consistently aim for the highest possible justifiable outcome. Some clients may expect this from their lawyers, and it has the potential for achieving high outcomes if the other side is not well prepared and concedes more than might otherwise be the case. Potential drawbacks are that costs may build up as the other side resists high demands, and that if both sides adopt this strategy a reasonable settlement may prove impossible.

Working for joint benefit

21.16　Litigation does not have to be confrontational. In some cases the parties have shared interests (for example because a commercial relationship will continue after a particular contractual dispute has been settled). In such a case litigation may best be conducted on the basis of identifying joint interests rather than emphasising what is in dispute. Benefits of a good future relationship may outweigh a particular outcome in the current dispute.

21.17　This type of strategy might involve focussing on settling a case rather than to take it to litigation. This can be successful for a client in achieving a reasonable outcome that does not take too long or cost too much. On the other hand proposing settlements can be seen by the other side as a display of possible weakness, and unnecessary concessions may be made in an attempt to settle.

Fighting hard

21.18　Although the Civil Procedure Rules emphasise the importance of mediation, some cases have little middle ground. If on the facts an accident was caused either by A or by B so that one side will win and one side will lose then confrontation is to some extent inevitable. The potential advantage of fighting a case hard is that a good outcome can be achieved for the benefit of the client and the lawyer's reputation. The drawback is that if the fight is not well founded the case will be lost and the client will probably have to pay the costs of both sides.

Taking a legal approach

21.19　Some cases turn primarily on a point of law, or a party may choose to rely on a legal point because the law is not entirely clear. Work on the case will turn particularly on researching and interpreting legal authorities. A well founded legal argument point is likely to lead to success, and even if it is not entirely well founded it may cause the other side to consider the strength of their case carefully. However researching a complex legal point can escalate costs, and a legal point that is hotly disputed or not well founded may lead to a loss of the case with costs, and possibly the need to take the point to appeal.

Taking a factual approach

Most cases turn on their facts. In such a case strategy will be built on collecting and analysing **21.20** evidence on facts. It is also likely to turn on careful analysis of the precise allegations in the statements of case, and on procedural steps related to facts such as disclosure. Strategic preparation of arguments on facts may well win a case where facts are disputed, but the collection and analysis of evidence can be expensive.

Different strategies can be adopted as regards collecting and analysing evidence. One strat- **21.21** egy is to gather all possible evidence at the start of the case to get the fullest possible picture, though building up costs. An alternative strategy is to collect key items of evidence to take a broad decision about the strength of the case and then try to settle it, only gathering full evidence if it proves impossible to settle and the case goes to court.

Focussing energy on key points

If the case is relatively straightforward or resources are limited, an appropriate strategy may **21.22** be to focus effort on key points in the evolution of the case. For example most effort might go into drafting statements of case and into reviewing evidence after disclosure, as is appropriate for the individual case. If the key points to focus on are carefully chosen then the outcome may be successful without building up unnecessary costs. Inevitably if the key points are not well chosen the case may not be prepared and presented as strongly as it might be.

Using the court

Different strategies can be adopted as regards applications to court, as outlined in Chapter 16. **21.23** At one end of the scale applications to court may be kept to a minimum. In a fairly straight-forward case it is only necessary to appear in court for the trial as other matters can be dealt with through forms etc. The advantage of such an approach is that costs are kept down, but the possible drawback is that advantages that might have been obtained prior to trial are wasted.

At the other end of the scale it is possible to make numerous interim applications to court. A **21.24** party may choose to make numerous applications to court if this is thought to be necessary because the other side is not cooperating in the preparation of the case, or if it is thought this might appear as a show of strength that might persuade the other party to settle. Such a strategy may reap benefits in terms of getting helpful court orders prior to trial, but is likely to prove expensive.

C   REVIEWING A CASE

When to review a case

21.25   The effective lawyer will try to keep a reasonably clear and systematic overview of each case, regularly reviewing how the case is coming together. A review is likely to need to be carried out at major stages in the progress of the case such as:

- just before the start of the action;
- when a statement of case is received from the other side;
- when the allocation questionnaire has to be returned;
- after disclosure and exchange of witness statements;
- when significant new information or evidence is received from the client;
- when significant new information or evidence is received from the other side;
- when the pre-trial checklist has to be returned;
- shortly before a court review of the case;
- when there is a significant step such as a new party being joined.

21.26   A review might be carried out informally by the lawyer, or might more formally involve a meeting between the lawyer and the client.

Matters to review

21.27   The elements of a review of the case might include:

- what has happened since the last review of the case;
- whether steps agreed have been taken, and what should happen if they have not;
- whether there are any problems in meeting the timetable for the case;
- the impact of new facts and evidence (it can be difficult to deal with facts and evidence coherently because of the way in which information from the client, from the other side, and from experts and witnesses comes in gradually over time);
- considering whether further information/evidence is required to respond to what has been received;
- reviewing how key facts will be proved;
- the possibility of making applications to court;
- whether the costs of an action remain proportionate to what may be won in the action, and to the chances of success.

21.28   Any review will also need to include a review of the strength of the case. The initial evaluation of the potential strength of the case may well not remain valid right up to trial. In particular, an initial evaluation may be made on the basis of the evidence of the client alone, and this must be reviewed as the other side's view of the case is revealed through statements of case and evidence. It is important that the lawyer passes on the re-evaluation of the case to the client so that client expectations remain realistic.

21.29   In addition, the possibility of settling a case will need to be regularly weighed against what may be achieved by continuing the action. The client should be told of any offers for settlement that are received, and possible bases for settlement should be discussed, see 20.13–20.35.

The client should be kept fully informed of the progress of the case, including any problems **21.30** that arise. Even though the lawyer may be well in control of dealing with things, the client has a right to know what is going on in his or her case, and to be involved in decisions.

D   COURT REVIEW OF A CASE

The principle of judicial case management

In the past the trial date tended to be fixed when the stages of preparing the case had been **21.31** completed. In a big and complex case this is still effectively the case, but the intention of the Civil Procedure Rules, especially in a fast track case, is that there should be a focus on keeping preparations on track for the likely trial date right from the allocation stage. The court now has a proactive role in reviewing the conduct of a case to ensure that it is ready for trial when it should be.

Fast track cases normally have a relatively tight timetable that builds towards trial. A period **21.32** within which the trial should take place (a precise date or a three-week window) is likely to be set on allocation to the fast track even if the precise date is not fixed. Multi-track cases may take longer to go through their stages, but progress towards a likely trial date will be positively monitored. Although the court may show flexibility in reviewing preparations for trial, a trial date will only be moved for good reason. The court will try to ensure that a proposed trial date is met, and if progress is falling behind schedule then the court may give directions to get it back on course that the parties may have to meet within a limited time frame.

The approach of a court is set out in PD 28 para 5.4 (fast track), and PD 29 para 7.4 **21.33** (multi-track).

- The court will not allow failure to comply with directions to lead to the postponement of the trial unless the circumstances are exceptional.
- If it is practicable to do so the court will exercise its powers to enable the trial to come on at the date or within the period set.
- The court will assess what steps each party should take to prepare for trial, direct that they happen in the shortest possible time, and impose sanctions in default. Sanctions can involve limiting the issues that can be raised and the evidence that can be used, as relevant to each direction.
- If it appears that some issues can be ready for trial but others cannot, the court may order that the trial of those issues goes ahead, and that the costs of the later part of the trial be not allowed or be paid by the defaulting party.
- If the court has no option but to postpone the trial it will do so for the shortest possible time, and will give directions for taking necessary steps.
- Litigants and lawyers should be in no doubt that the court will regard postponement of the trial as an order of last resort. The court may require a party as well as his lawyers to attend a hearing at which such an order is sought.

In overall terms the court will wish to pursue the overriding objective, seeing if anything can **21.34** be done to save time and/or costs and to facilitate trial.

The stages of court review

21.35   The key stages at which the court is likely to review the progress of a case are as follows. Depending on the nature of the case and the issues arising, these reviews may be conducted on the basis of completed questionnaires, or with the lawyers for the parties present in court. At any review issues can be raised by the court or by either party. To avoid the escalation of costs the number of applications to court and of separate reviews should be kept to a minimum, with as many matters as possible being considered at a single hearing rather than at separate hearings.

Track allocation

21.36   On allocating a case to a track the court will review how far pre-action protocols have been met, and will be informed through allocation questionnaires of the progress made on the case to date. A trial date will be set at this point for a fast track case, see 4.81–4.99.

Case management conference

21.37   A case management conference can be fixed at any time after allocation, Rule 29.3 and PD 29.5. The timing and content of a case management conference will depend on the needs of the case. Normally it will only be in a more complex case, or a case where there are significant difficulties in preparation, that a case management conference is required.

21.38   At a case management conference a court will set a timetable for stages in the case. It will also give directions for the future conduct of the case that might commonly include:

- consideration of the statements of case;
- consideration of the scope of disclosure of documents;
- consideration of the exchange of witness statements;
- whether expert evidence is required, what such evidence should cover, and arrangements for questions to be put to an expert;
- how costs may be saved;
- fixing a date for trial or a trial window, and what sort of judge would appropriately hear the case.

Pre-trial checklists

21.39   Completed pre-trial checklists must be submitted so that the court can review the progress of the parties in preparing for trial. If necessary the court will give directions to keep trial preparations on track. The trial date may be set or moved if this proves to be unavoidable, see Form N170.

Pre-trial review

21.40   In more complex multi-track cases a pre-trial review may be held about eight weeks before the start of the trial. It will normally be held by the trial judge, and should be attended by those who will be the advocates at trial to work to best effect. Both sides should prepare for the hearing and decide in advance what they hope to achieve, including preparing arguments to support their views. Either party or the court may raise issues.

21.41   The pre-trial review is intended to deal with any outstanding matters to prepare the case for trial, and to ensure that both sides are ready. Matters considered might include the following.

- Whether the statements of case of both parties are in order and the issues to be decided are defined as clearly as possible. Orders can be made for amendment or further information if necessary.
- What issues remain to be dealt with at trial. An admission or partial settlement may have disposed of some issues. In some cases, for example, liability may be admitted so that the hearing only needs to deal with damages. A party can if appropriate be asked to admit a point to save costs.
- Whether a key matter should be dealt with as a preliminary issue. If all or much of the case turns on a particular issue of law or fact, time may saved by determining that matter before the main trial. There should only be a trial of a preliminary issue if an important point can be clearly separated, and not if the issue is really interrelated with others so that overall the case will not be made simpler. The judge will specify the matter to be tried as a preliminary issue very carefully, including the basis on which the issue is to be tried, providing for example that the issue be tried on the existing statements of case, or on an agreed statement of facts.
- The use of evidence at trial. There can be agreement or orders relating to what maps, models, and photographs and so on will be used, or whether and on what terms video evidence may be admissible. It may also be decided how a particular point will be proved. The use of medical and expert reports can be considered. Further orders as to disclosure and inspection can be made.
- The trial date will be finalised, together with how long the trial is likely to last. The court may set a detailed timetable for the trial itself to ensure that time is used efficiently, for example dealing with the order in which issues will be addressed and allocating time for dealing with witnesses.
- A trial judge can make an order excluding certain issues from the trial, CPR r1.4, but this is rarely used.

E   PREPARING A CASE FOR HEARING

Subject to the orders made by the court, the main burden of preparing the case for hearing will fall on the lawyers. Preparation prior to the trial has become increasingly important now that all the evidence to be used and skeleton arguments are revealed in advance. Success at trial is now more likely to be achieved by thorough preparation than dramatic last minute inspiration. The final timetable leading up to trial might be: **21.42**

- Review witness statements, expert reports, and other evidence to ensure they are ready and all notices relevant to admissibility have been served.
- Ensure witnesses and Counsel able to attend trial.
- Complete and return a pre-trial checklist eight to ten weeks before trial.
- Pre-trial review if problems are outstanding.
- File bundles three to seven days before trial.

The roles of the lawyers

21.43 The solicitors will normally be primarily liable for liaising with the court and preparing evidence and bundles of documents. Where a barrister is to be briefed to advocate the case in court, a brief must be prepared for and sent to the barrister who is to appear at trial. This must be sent sufficiently far in advance for the barrister to work on the case, but not so long in advance that it may become out of date. In preparing the brief the solicitor must ensure that all information is up to date, checking whether there has been any further financial loss, change in medical condition and so on.

21.44 The barrister will need to work on the brief when it arrives, and is likely to have to prepare a skeleton argument, see below.

Preparing the statements of case

21.45 The statements of case will form the basis of the trial because their purpose is to define the issues. The court may review whether the issues are sufficiently defined, and the lawyers need to check that the statements of case provide a sound basis for all the lines of argument to be raised at trial. Where there has been significant additional evidence or other evolution of the case since the statements of case were first drafted, then the basis of the case may have shifted and it is important to check that they found the way the case is best argued. Amendment may be necessary, though a major amendment may be difficult or expensive at a late stage.

Preparing the evidence

21.46 Evidence to support the client's case will have come in at various stages as the case develops. Some evidence gathered in the early stages of the case may become out of date or may be undermined by later evidence. A review of the information collected will have to have been carried out prior to the disclosure of evidence and exchange of witness statements, but a further review may be needed to decide whether the evidence is in an appropriate state for use at trial. For a standard approach to reviewing evidence see 15.206–15.211.

21.47 As regards the evidence to support the client's case:

- A check should be made to ensure that there is evidence to support each element of the case, especially if there have been significant changes since the case was originally conceptualised. This needs to be done systematically, perhaps with a grid that lists issues and with each item of evidence that relates to each.
- Any gaps, weaknesses, or ambiguities in the evidence should be identified and addressed. A gap on a key element in the case may be fatal. A gap may be filled by getting further evidence, or by argument or inference from other evidence that is available.
- There should be a check that all the evidence to be used is admissible—that it is in a proper form, that it has been disclosed, that notice has to be given if it is hearsay etc.
- Careful choices should have been made as to which witnesses to be used before witness statements were exchanged. If further witness are needed then witness statements must be drawn up and sent to the court and the other side. It may be agreed that some witness statements will be accepted without the need for the witness to attend trial for cross examination.

- The witness statements will normally stand as the evidence in chief of each witness and they should be reviewed with this in mind. The evidence should be presented in the witness statement as strongly as it would be in examination in chief. The statement must also be complete as it will only be possible to adduce further evidence from the witness in court with the leave of the court. If the witness statement is out of date or incomplete and the original witness statement has been disclosed to the other side then a supplementary witness statement may need to be taken and disclosed. In checking that statements are full and up to date, the review should include checking that matters raised by the other side's witnesses are addressed where necessary and where possible, see 15.109–15.135.
- Expert reports must be checked. The lawyer should ensure that he or she understands technical or medical matters sufficiently well to deal with them in submissions and in cross examination. If not a conference with the expert may be necessary. If the report is not complete or up to date or does not address all relevant issues then a supplementary report may need to be obtained and disclosed. If there is a joint expert then further information can only be sought by agreement, see 15.140–15.178.
- There should be consideration of whether any further physical evidence such as plans, photographs, models, etc, will be needed to explain properly the case in court. Ensure that they are prepared by an appropriate person, and agreed with the other side if possible.
- There should be a decision as to whether the case has particular complexities that may be best explained through information on computer screens, or by video. If so steps will have to be taken for this to be prepared and shown, with the consent of the judge and providing the court has appropriate facilities.

As regards the evidence submitted by the other side: **21.48**

- It is important to plan how their documentary evidence will be answered or undermined at trial.
- There should be consideration as to whether any objection can be made to the admissibility of any evidence to be offered by the other side.
- There should be consideration of whether the other side should be asked to admit a particular point prior to trial.
- Ways in which the evidence to be given by witnesses for the other side might be undermined through cross examination should be planned.
- If one party does not call a witness from whom they have obtained a witness statement then the other side can call that witness. This can only be done to prove the truth of what the witness says—the witness cannot be called just to be cross examined.

Procuring the attendance of witnesses

It will be necessary to ensure that relevant witnesses will attend court. A witness does not **21.49** have to attend if the parties agree that their witness statement will be accepted as it stands. A witness will need to attend if the other side wishes to cross examine the witness.

If a witness is willing to attend, it should be sufficient to inform the witness of the date and **21.50** place of the trial and offer to pay reasonable expenses, checking that the witness can attend. If a key witness may have any problems with availability this should be taken into account in fixing the trial date.

21.51 If there is any doubt as to whether a witness is prepared to attend, a witness summons can be issued and served on them, CPR r 34.2. This is a purely administrative matter. Service must be personal and at least seven days before the witness is required to attend court, and the witness must be offered travel expenses and compensation for any loss of income. The witness summons can require the witness to attend and give evidence personally, or to produce clearly described documents in court, *Panayiotou v Sony Music Entertainment (UK) Ltd* (1994) Ch 142. A summons to produce a document should of course not normally be used simply to get disclosure at a late stage—the court can order that witnesses produce documents much earlier under CPR r 34.2, see Chapter 15, and see *Macmillan Inc v Bishopsgate Investment Trust* (1993) 1 WLR 1372 CA. If a witness who has received a witness summons then fails to attend court there can be committal proceedings in the High Court, or a fine of up to £1,000 in the County Court.

21.52 If a witness cannot attend a trial, for example due to serious illness, a statement may be used under the Civil Evidence Act 1995, though this is not an ideal answer as the evidence will be of less probative value because it is not given on oath or subjected to cross examination. If it is known in advance that a witness may not be able to attend due to business or travel their evidence can be taken on oath before the trial in the form of a deposition, CPR rr 34.8–12. The witness's evidence will be taken on oath before a judge or a court-appointed examiner, and cross examination will be allowed. This can happen where necessary, for example in a hospital. What the witness says will be set out in writing and signed by the witness. The party seeking to rely on a deposition should give notice at least 21 days before trial.

21.53 If a witness cannot be present in court, or has reason to be concerned about being present in court, the court may allow the witness to give evidence through a video link or some other appropriate link, CPR r 32.3 and PD 32 Annex 3. An overseas witness may give evidence by television link if so ordered, *Garcin v Amerindo* [1990] 4 All ER 655. This can only be done if the court has appropriate equipment, the judge gives permission, and arrangements are made well in advance of the trial.

21.54 If a witness is overseas the High Court can order the examination of a witness before a British consular authority, CPR r 34.13, or it may issue a letter of request to the judicial authorities in the relevant country to ask that the witness's evidence be taken.

Preparing trial bundles

21.55 At the trial the judge, the parties, and the witnesses will be constantly referring to the evidence. As the wording of written documents or reports may be important and as witness statements will normally stand as evidence in chief, it is vital that the evidence be in an agreed common format to avoid confusion and time wasting. Therefore trial bundles must be prepared.

21.56 The trial bundle should normally include the following, placed in a suitable order, PD 39 para 3.

- The claim form and all the statements of case.
- A case summary and/or a chronology where appropriate.
- Any requests for further information and responses to requests.
- All witness statements to be relied on as evidence.

- Any witness summaries.
- Any notice of intention to rely on hearsay evidence.
- Notice of intention to rely on any evidence which is not contained in a witness state-ment, affidavit, or report, will be given orally at trial or is admissible hearsay (for example plans etc which are not exhibits).
- Any medical reports and responses to them.
- Any expert reports and responses to them.
- Any order giving directions as to the conduct of the trial.
- Any other necessary documents.

Trial bundles are the responsibility of the claimant's lawyers, though they should be agreed if **21.57** possible by both sides. The court may give directions as to the creation of trial bundles. All the documents in the trial bundle will be admissible as evidence of their content at the hearing unless the court orders otherwise or a party gives notice objecting to the admissibility of a document, PD 32 para 27.

The trial bundle should normally be in ring binders or lever arch files, and if there are more **21.58** than 100 pages they should be divided into sections. If a number of files are needed they should be clearly distinguishable, for example by colour. If there is a lot of documentation it may be appropriate to prepare a separate bundle of core documents, with cross references to the main files. For ease of use they must be paginated continuously throughout, and indexed. If there are any problems with legibility there should be a typed version to accompany a document.

The bundle should be filed by the claimant between seven and three days before the start of **21.59** the trial. There must be enough identical sets for the judge, the parties, and one for the use of witnesses.

In the High Court and the Chancery Division, when lodging the bundle, there should at the **21.60** same time be lodged a reading list for the trial judge with an estimated reading time and an estimated length for the hearing, which is signed by all those who will advocate the case for the parties at the hearing, Practice Direction (R.C.J.:Reading Lists and Time Estimates) (2000) 1 WLR 208. The contact details for all the advocates must be included.

Preparing the law

There may be no issues of law in a case at all but if there are proper preparations must be **21.61** made to identify precisely the legal authorities to be used in court. It is also necessary to make the judge and the other side aware what authorities are likely to be referred to, so that they are able to read the authorities in advance, or at least have them available.

In preparing the case, the lawyers should have kept a clear list of relevant statute, cases, and **21.62** other legal authorities. This should be easily identifiable in the client file so that research does not have to be repeated. However it is important to check that there have been no changes since the original research was completed. If the exact wording of a statute or regulation is important to a case there should be a copy on file. If case law is relevant it is important to work on cases that might undermine as well as support the client's case so as to be ready to make distinctions. Indeed it may be a good technique of advocacy to bring up a case against you and explain why it should not be followed before your opponent has a chance to dwell on it! Careful decisions should be taken as to what material will be used at trial—the court will only wish to be referred to those authorities that are directly relevant to the issues to be decided and not to general background material. The need to check relevant authorities was illustrated in *Banton v Banton* The Times, 4 April 1989, where both counsel suggested that the judge did not have the power to fine in a particular case, though in fact there was authority that he did. As a result both counsel felt obliged to appear for no fee on appeal!

21.63 For any hearing, a full list of any authorities to be relied on at trial needs to be given to the court by 5.00 pm on the day before the hearing. It should also be given to the other parties a reasonable time before the hearing. Check that the authorities you intend to rely on are available at court, or take photocopies.

21.64 In the High Court and Chancery Division a reading list needs to be provided earlier, and the skeleton argument should include the main authorities to be relied on. The legal authorities that may be relied on include:

- Acts of Parliament and statutory regulations, with a reference to the precise Act or statutory regulation, together with the relevant section(s) or paragraph(s).
- Case law. References should be to the official law reports if possible, so the Weekly Law Reports and the English Reports should be used in preference to the All England Law Reports, Practice Direction (Citation of Authorities)(2001) 1 WLR 1001. It is important to be clear what proposition each case is used for, with specific references. Weaker precedents, such as those where only one party attended or where it was simply decided that a point was arguable, should not normally be used. Cases from other jurisdictions should only be used with good reason (though EU and human rights cases are within the same jurisdiction). Cases decided on their facts rather than developing a legal point will not normally be useful.
- Text books. References should be to practitioner works, with references to the relevant pages or paragraphs. A judge may be influenced by a practitioner work that carries particular authority, but the judge will not necessarily accept a textbook view, *Kingshott v Associated Kent Newspapers* The Times, 11 June 1990.
- Parliamentary debates. References to Hansard may be used, *Pepper v Hart* (1993) AC 593, but copies together with a brief summary of the argument to be used must be served on the other parties five days before the hearing, Practice Direction (Hansard: Citations) (1995) 1 WLR 192.

21.65 A bundle or list of authorities must contain a certificate signed by the advocate that the requirements of Practice Direction (Citation of Authorities) (2001) 1 WLR 1001 have been complied with.

F   PREPARING A SKELETON ARGUMENT

The purpose of a skeleton argument

21.66 Having completed all the interim stages, reviewed the case, and prepared the evidence, a final stage of preparation is to prepare the details of the arguments to be advanced in court.

In the past it would be common for arguments to be prepared in some secrecy, and producing surprises in court was regarded as a useful tactic that might lead to success in a case, or at least throw the other side off course. However justice is unlikely to be best served by surprises at trial.

Justice is likely to be best served by clarity in the issues and arguments before the court, and it is now common for skeleton arguments to be required. The use of skeleton arguments started informally in the Court of Appeal in the 1980s, and they were found to be so useful that their use spread. They are now compulsory for High Court actions, and for appeals, PD 52 paras 5.9 and 7.6. Case management powers will be used to provide that skeleton arguments be filed by both parties a set number of days before trial or before a major interim hearing. It is increasingly common practice for skeletons to be prepared for opening submissions (or closing submissions where there will be no opening) and for interim applications. **21.67**

The skeleton argument should be distinguished from the written submission—a full written argument for a case that is an alternative to advocacy rather than a support for it. Written submissions are used regularly in some jurisdictions such as the United States but not normally in this jurisdiction. The skeleton argument provides background—it is not a substitute for advocacy. **21.68**

The purpose of a skeleton argument is to set out the main arguments on the key issues in the case in advance. The point is to provide advance reading to help to focus the conduct of the trial—the skeleton is not a substitute for advocacy. The main points that will be argued and the basis on which they will be argued should be identified, the argument should not be set out in full, and it is not necessary to cover every point that might be raised. **21.69**

Preparing a skeleton argument is an excellent discipline. The ability to prepare a good skeleton argument is a hallmark of an effective lawyer because of the skills of analysis and concise and clear expression that need to be shown. **21.70**

Skeletons should be lodged at court and served on the other parties three days before the hearing. It can make a difference whether skeleton arguments are exchanged simultaneously or in turn, depending on the needs of the case, *Brown v Bennett* The Times, 13 June 2000. **21.71**

The content of a skeleton argument

Guidance on drafting skeleton arguments is provided in PD 52 para 5, in the Queen's Bench Guide (para 7.11.12), in the Chancery Guide (Appendix 3) and in the Commercial Court Guide (Appendix 9). The main requirements are: **21.72**

- The skeleton should provide a structured framework for what will be argued at trial.
- The skeleton argument should be as concise as possible.
- It should identify the key issues in dispute.
- It should outline the overall nature of the case and the key facts relevant to the matter to be decided by the court.
- It should summarise the legal arguments to be relied on, with references to relevant authorities (which may be attached).
- It should outline submissions of fact, with references to relevant evidence in key documents.

- It should link the legal arguments and submissions of fact to the relevant issues.
- If there is a test to be met for the order sought, the relevant test should be set out, and how it is argued the test is met.
- It should set out what conclusions the court is being asked to reach and what decisions it is being asked to take.
- The style will not normally be formal, and it can include easily understood abbreviations.
- It should be in numbered paragraphs for ease of reference.
- It should not include lengthy arguments.
- It should include the name and contact details of the lawyer who prepared it.

21.73 Good drafting will bear in mind that the skeletons will be read by the judge and by the other side before the hearing.

21.74 A skeleton argument should be as succinct as possible. The purpose is to state points, not to elaborate them. Most points can be made in one or two sentences or a few bullet points. Where a point of law is involved, the skeleton should normally state the legal principle and how it is relevant to the case, citing the principal authorities with page references to the principles relied on. Where a question of fact is involved, the skeleton should normally state the facts which it is proposed the court should infer, with cross references to the relevant parts of the witness statements and reports.

21.75 In a complex case a skeleton argument might include:

- a list of relevant people;
- a chronology (required in the Court of Appeal and recommended in the Queen's Bench and Chancery divisions);
- a glossary of technical terms.

21.76 The skeleton should be as brief as the case allows. It should not normally exceed 20 pages of double spaced A4 paper, and it should normally be much shorter.

Outline for a skeleton argument

21.77   IN THE HIGH COURT OF JUSTICE   Claim No 2005 HC 1234

QUEEN'S BENCH DIVISION

BETWEEN

AB	Claimant
and	
CD	Defendant

SKELETON ARGUMENT OF THE CLAIMANT

1. Introduction

1.1.

1.2.

1.3.

2. Background

2.1. ˙

2.2.

2.3.

3. The test to be applied by the court

3.1.

3.2

3.3.

4. Matters to be taken into account by the court

4.1.

4.2.

4.3.

Date: Signed by lawyer:

G   PREPARING TO GO TO COURT

Preparing to deal with your own witnesses

In a civil trial the witness statements and affidavits will have been exchanged and they will **21.78** stand as evidence in chief. In terms of presenting evidence there will be relatively little to prepare, save perhaps for some consideration of the order in which evidence should be presented to make it most convincing.

If the witness statement or affidavit is not very strong it may be necessary to consider how to **21.79** support the witness, through other written evidence, other witnesses, and submissions.

It may be necessary to do some work with the witnesses themselves. The witnesses may well **21.80** be nervous, and it is important to prepare them for the trial and put them at their ease as far as possible, explaining to them court procedure and their own involvement so that they will not feel lost or overwhelmed and can give their evidence as convincingly as possible.

In some other jurisdictions, for example in the USA, it is permissible for the support offered **21.81** to witnesses to be at the level of significant coaching prior to their giving evidence. It is not permissible in England and Wales for lawyers to go so far in coaching a witness in a particular case, as it is thought that this might undermine rather than enhance its truthfulness and reliability. However it is permissible for someone to have general training in how to offer evidence as a witness—for example people who are called as expert witnesses can be trained to give evidence as experts.

It will normally be the solicitor rather than the barrister who sees witnesses prior to trial and **21.82** who goes through their evidence with them. A barrister should normally only meet expert witnesses prior to trial (as this is necessary to assist the barrister in understanding the technical aspects of the case) and not other witnesses.

It is permissible for a witness to refresh his or her mind by re-reading a statement made some **21.83** time ago before going into court, so long as the evidence the witness gives in court is the truth as personally remembered rather than simply material from the statement.

Preparing to deal with the witnesses for the other side

21.84 Their witness statements and affidavits will have been exchanged some time before the trial and it will be possible to work on them in detail. It is important to prepare to cross examine the witnesses for the other side. This is dealt with in Chapter 22. It may be appropriate to consider whether any further evidence is required to rebut matters raised by the witnesses for the other side.

Working with the client

21.85 In preparing the case for court it is important to give sufficient attention to preparing the client. The case will be of even greater importance to the client than it is to the lawyer. In addition to keeping the client informed of what is happening, there should be a full explanation of what is likely to happen at the trial.

21.86 If the client has not been to court before, the procedure should be explained. For example a client may not understand the order in which things will be done, or the way in which witness statements stand as evidence in chief. The full range of possible outcomes for the case should also be explained to help to manage client expectations.

21.87 Both barrister and solicitor should find time to talk to the client outside court before and after the trial to ensure that he or she feels properly involved and knows what is likely to happen.

KEY DOCUMENTS

Forms

The following forms may be relevant to preparing a case for court.

PF 52 Order for Case Management Directions (CPR Part 29)
N150 Allocation questionnaire
N265 List of documents for standard disclosure
N 266 Notice to admit facts
N 268 Notice to prove documents at trial
N242A Notice of Payment into Court (Part 36)
N242 Notice of Payment into Court (Part 37)
N243A/Form 201 Notice of acceptance (Part 36)
N170 Pre-trial checklist
N20 Witness Summons
N163 Skeleton argument

Court guides

These may provide guidance on preparing a case for court.

Queen's Bench Guide
Chancery Guide
Admiralty and Commercial Courts Guide
Mercantile Courts Guide
Patents Court Guide
Technology and Construction Court Guide

These are easily available in hard copy and electronically, see Chapter 24.

22

PRESENTING A CASE IN COURT

A HAVING A DAY IN COURT 22.01

B THE FORMALITIES OF A TRIAL 22.04
   Hearings in open court 22.04
   Who hears the case 22.05
   Forms of address 22.07
   Legal representation 22.08
   Attendance at trial 22.11
   Adjournments 22.12

C THE STAGES OF A TRIAL 22.13
   Before the start of the trial 22.17
   The claimant's case 22.18
   The defendant's case 22.22
   Closing speeches 22.25
   Judgment 22.30
   A trial timetable 22.33

D WINNING A CASE AT TRIAL 22.34

E FINAL PREPARATIONS FOR ADVOCACY 22.41
   General preparation 22.42
   Preparation for an opening submission 22.45
   Preparation for examination in chief 22.47
   Preparation for cross examination 22.49
   Preparation for the closing speech 22.53

F ARGUMENT AND PERSUASION 22.55
   Recreating events 22.56
   Developing arguments 22.60

G THE PRESENTATION OF A CASE 22.65

H OPENING A CASE 22.73

I DEALING WITH WITNESSES 22.77
   General principles 22.77
   The stages for dealing with each witness 22.82
   Matters a witness may be asked about 22.92

Problems in dealing with a witness. 22.99

J   CONCLUDING A CASE 22.110

K   THE JUDGMENT. 22.114
    The giving of the judgment 22.114
    Matters that the judgment can relate to 22.117
    Other decisions to be made at the end of a case 22.120

L   THE DRAWING UP OF ORDERS. 22.125
    The drawing up of an order 22.126
    The drafting of an order 22.131
    Special types of order 22.134

M   GENERAL FRAMEWORKS FOR ORDERS. 22.138
    Order after a trial before a judge 22.138
    Consent order 22.139
    Tomlin order 22.140

KEY DOCUMENTS

This case bristles with simplicity. The facts are admitted; the law is plain; and yet it has taken seven days to try—one day longer than God Almighty required to make the world.

                                                                          Bacon VC

A   HAVING A DAY IN COURT

22.01 Popular views of court hearings are often derived from the drama of novels or television. Such sources will inevitably emphasise the dramatic potential of moving speeches, incisive cross examination, jumping up to shout 'I object!', and fresh evidence given at the last moment. Such sources tend to involve criminal trials rather than civil trials, but these are not necessarily clearly differentiated in the public mind. While there can be drama in a civil court room, hard work and attention to detail are much more characteristic.

22.02 The vast majority of cases settle before they reach court. If the litigation process is being conducted effectively this is entirely appropriate. The litigation process defines issues and tests their legal and evidential strength, and as it does so the real merit of each case should emerge. Where a case has weaknesses, settlement may logically evolve as preferable to going to trial, see 20.13–20.15 and 20.23–20.35.

22.03 If a case does go to trial it is likely to be for one of the following reasons. The reason why the case is going to trial is likely to impact on the conduct of the case in court.

- A significant issue of law may be in doubt because it is not clearly governed by statute or precedent, or because the precedents are conflicting. Such a case might turn primarily on legal argument, or the legal point might be decided as a preliminary issue.

- There may be significant conflicts of evidence on key points. This may arise from differences of views between experts or between other key witnesses. Such a case might turn primarily on cross examination of witnesses, on providing evidence to support key witnesses, and skill in making submissions as to which witness should be believed and why.
- There may be limited evidence on a key point, such as how an accident happened. Such a case might turn on skill in making submissions dealing with the implications of the evidence that is available.
- A number of factual and legal issues may be clear or have been resolved, and the case may go to court simply to deal with some issues. For example liability for an accident may be admitted, but there may be significant arguments as to whether particular heads of damage are recoverable.
- A settlement may prove impossible because of the strength of the views of the parties, even if the lawyers explain to their clients the possible weaknesses of the case and options for settlement. In such a case the lawyer should give very clear advice to the client as to the chances of success of the case.
- Although case management by the court has made it less likely, a case may also go to court simply because it is not very well prepared. If the lawyers have not properly analysed the strengths and weaknesses of the law and the evidence then it is possible that a case which should have settled will end up in court.

B   THE FORMALITIES OF A TRIAL

Hearings in open court

A civil trial will normally be held in open court with the public allowed to attend, a common   **22.04** law principle now reflected in the European Convention on Human Rights, Article 6(1). However this does not mean that any special provision will be made for those who might like to attend. The court may direct a hearing in private if it is necessary in the interests of justice, if publicity would defeat the object of the hearing or matters of national security are involved, or if confidential information is involved and damage might result from publicity. See generally CPR Part 39 Miscellaneous provisions relating to hearings, and PD 39 Miscellaneous provisions relating to hearings.

Who hears the case

Most civil trials are by a judge. In the High Court this will normally be a High Court judge. In   **22.05** the County Court, the judge who hears the case will be a circuit or a district judge, depending on the value of the case.

In a civil case a party can apply for trial by jury only in limited cases, effectively where there   **22.06** is a quasi criminal allegation such as a claim for fraud, defamation, malicious prosecution, or false imprisonment, Supreme Court Act 1981, s 69 and County Court Act 1984, s 66. A jury trial must be claimed within 28 days of the service of the defence, CPR r 26.11, and the court retains a discretion if the case cannot conveniently be tried by jury because, for example, the case involves significant study of documents or accounts. The court has a discretion to use jury trial in other cases but it is rarely used. The role of a jury in a civil trial is not identical to that in a criminal trial. If there is a jury the judge will still have questions of law to decide, such as whether a document is capable of being defamatory, *Nevill v Fine Arts and General Insurance Co Ltd* (1987) AC 68, and may still have to decide if there is a case to answer, *Young v Rank* (1950) 2 KB 510.

Forms of address

22.07 The judge should be addressed as follows.

- A judge in the House of Lords, Court of Appeal, or High Court is referred to as 'My Lord' or 'Your Lordship' or as 'My Lady' or 'Your Ladyship'.
- In the County Court a Circuit Judge, Recorder, or Assistant Recorder is referred to as 'Your Honour'.
- A District Judge or a Chairperson in tribunal is referred to as 'Sir' or 'Madam'.
- Others sitting in a tribunal are referred to as 'Your colleagues'.

Legal representation

22.08 Rights of audience in civil cases are primarily governed by the Courts and Legal Services Act 1990, and by the regulations of the relevant professional bodies. Legal representatives have duties to the court, sec 3.45.

- A party has the right to conduct a case personally.
- A barrister with rights of audience (one who has completed at least six months of pupillage) has rights of audience in all cases in the High Court and the County Courts. The barrister must act within the Bar Code of Conduct.
- A solicitor has full rights of audience for a hearing in Chambers in the High Court and County Courts. If the solicitor obtains the qualification for higher rights of audience (through additional training and experience relevant to advocacy) then he or she can also have rights of audience for High Court and appeal hearings in open court.
- Any person can be heard by the court with the express leave of the court, Courts and Legal Services Act 1990, s 27.

22.09 There are special provisions for others to appear in particular types of cases, which are gradually being extended.

- Solicitors' responsible representatives can appear in High Court and County Court proceedings in chambers, Courts and Legal Services Act 1990, s 27.
- Particular categories of people have rights of audiences for specific purposes by statute, for example local authority officers can be heard in various housing cases.
- Legal executives will in due course have rights of audience under the Access to Justice Act 1999, s 40.
- Employed barristers will have increased rights of audience under the Access to Justice Act, ss 37 and 38 (primarily relevant to the Crown Prosecution Service and the Legal Services Commission).

22.10 Questions as to who may be heard in court are a matter for the judge. A litigant in person may have the assistance of an advisor or 'McKenzie friend', but this person should advise rather than speak, see *R v Bow County Court ex p Pelling* (1999) 1 WLR 1870.

Attendance at trial

If both parties fail to attend a hearing the proceedings are likely to be struck out, CPR r 39.3. **22.11** If one party fails to attend the court may proceed in the absence of the party. If the claimant fails to attend their case will normally be struck out. If a defendant fails to attend the claimant will still have to prove his or her case, though the court may strike out a defence, CPR r 39.3. Any judgment given in the absence of one party may be set aside if good reason for the failure to attend can be shown, *Shocked v Goldschmidt* (1998) 1 All ER 372 CA. The court will also consider whether the application has been made promptly, and whether the applicant has a reasonable prospect of success if the trial is reconvened, CPR r 39.3. A party may be fined for failure to appear, Courts and Legal Services Act 1990, s12.

Adjournments

Once the hearing has started, the court has a general power to adjourn, CPR r 3.1, applying **22.12** the overriding objective, though the court will be very slow to adjourn because of the inconvenience and costs that are likely to be incurred. The reason for seeking the adjournment, any fault in bringing about the need for an adjournment, and the effects if no adjournment is allowed may all be relevant. An adjournment may be necessary to enable a crucial witness to attend. If there is a degree of fault an adjournment may only be allowed subject to a costs or even a wasted costs order, see 5.62–5.88.

C THE STAGES OF A TRIAL

The normal stages of the trial will be as set out below, though the trial judge has a discretion **22.13** to alter the stages, for example by dispensing with opening speeches in a simple case because the issues will be clear from the pre-trial preparations. The judge will seek to ensure steady progress through the stages of the case, and in a big case general time limits for each stage may have been set at the pre-trial review.

Decisions about how the case will be conducted, and whether any point be decided as a **22.14** preliminary issue, may be made prior to trial (for example at a pre-trial review) or at the start of the trial.

Normally the claimant will present his or her case first, unless the defendant has the eviden- **22.15** tial burden (to show some sort of case) on all remaining issues in the case. If there are multiple defendants who have different cases, or if Part 20 proceedings have added other parties, an appropriate order for events will need to be decided. The court may be prepared to adjourn a trial for the discussion of a possible settlement, but settlement will need to be a real likelihood to waste court time and inconvenience witnesses.

Witnesses other than the parties and expert witnesses may be asked to leave court at the start **22.16** of the hearing, so that they are not influenced by the evidence given by other witnesses. However they will be allowed to stay in court if there is no objection.

Before the start of the trial

22.17   The lawyer should see it as a professional duty to be available to meet the client at least briefly immediately prior to the start of the trial. There may be little to discuss if the case is fully prepared, but in many cases the time just before the trial starts will be important for:

- filling in any remaining gaps in the facts;
- getting last minute instructions;
- making any last minute attempts at settlement.

The claimant's case

Claimant's opening speech

22.18   This should outline the key facts of the case and the issues from the claimant's point of view, with reference to the statements of case. It should also outline the evidence that will be presented to support the case and the witnesses who will be called, with appropriate references to the agreed bundle of evidence. The opening speech may be dispensed with if the issues are clear from pre-trial preparations.

Claimant's evidence

22.19   The witnesses supporting the claimant's case should be called in a sensible order. For example an expert may be called after other witnesses have given evidence so as to be able to comment on everything that has been said.

22.20   The witness statement of each witness will normally stand as their evidence in chief, though oral evidence in chief may be given with the leave of the judge, if for example a witness statement needs to be updated. Each witness will be called by the claimant, and after basic questions on identity and acknowledgment of the witness statement, the statement will stand as evidence in chief. The witness will then be offered for cross examination by the defendant. At this stage the case for the defendant may not have been fully outlined, save as emerges from the documents available before the start of the trial, so the questions put in cross examination may not form a very coherent whole. The defendant will need to put to each witness all the parts of the defendant's case on which that witness might be able to comment, and may wish to ask further questions to test the reliability of the evidence given.

22.21   There is a possibility that at the end of the claimant's case the defendant may submit that there is no case to answer, on the basis that the claimant has not established his or her case on the balance of probabilities (though weak cases will normally not reach the trial stage). If the submission succeeds then the case will go no further. If the submission fails then the defendant's case will proceed, though the defendant may be put to an election whether to submit no case or call evidence so that time is not wasted.

The defendant's case

Defendant's opening speech

22.22   This should outline the key facts of the case and the issues from the defendant's point of view, with reference to the statements of case. It should also outline the evidence that will be presented to support the case and the witnesses who will be called, with appropriate references to the agreed bundle of evidence. Inevitably this opening speech may be shorter than that for the claimant as the context of the case should by now be clear and repetition should be avoided.

Defendant's evidence

The witness statement of each witness will normally stand as their evidence in chief, though oral evidence in chief may be given with the leave of the judge, if for example a witness statement needs to be updated. Each witness will be called by the defendant and then cross examined by the claimant. The case for the claimant will have been fully presented, and questions put in cross examination to each witness may fit more easily into a coherent framework. The relevant parts of the defendant's case must be put to each witness for comment. **22.23**

If there is more than one defendant then each defendant will open and call evidence in the order in which they appear on the record, unless the court directs some other approach as being appropriate. **22.24**

Closing speeches

Defendant's closing speech

The defendant will summarise his or her case. The submission should relate primarily to how and why it is argued the defendant should win the case, for example because the claimant has not proved a key issue in his or her case, or because the claimant has not proved his or her case on the balance of probabilities. There should be references to the evidence in the trial, setting out where it supports the defendant's case and does not support the claimant's case, including specific references to what was said by witnesses. **22.25**

Claimant's closing speech

The claimant will summarise his or her case. The submission should relate primarily to how and why it is argued the claimant should win the case, setting out all the elements that had to be proved and the evidence that supports each point. Where the evidence is weak or has gaps then persuasive argument may be particularly important. The weaknesses in the defendant's case may also be pointed out. **22.26**

If the defendant is not adducing evidence then the claimant will make a closing speech at the end of the claimant's case, followed by the defendant's statement of his or her case. **22.27**

No further witnesses can be called once speeches or submissions have begun, save for formal purposes simply to correct an omission, *Price v Humphries* (1958) 2 QB 353 DC. **22.28**

If a new point of law is raised in the closing speech the other side should have the opportunity to reply. **22.29**

Judgment

Judgment may be given immediately, or after an adjournment. The judge should give judgment on all outstanding issues including liability, remedies, and costs. Once judgment has been given on liability and remedies, the parties may be asked to make submissions on **22.30** matters such as costs, and should be ready to do so. The lawyers for both sides may also be asked to assist with the drafting of an order.

22.31   If the judge gives a reasoned judgment the advocates should take full and accurate notes. The notes may be needed to assist in drawing up orders following the judgment, or as a basis for advising on appeal.

22.32   Barristers briefed for the court hearing should make a short note of the judgment on the backsheet of the brief before returning it to the solicitor.

A trial timetable

22.33   In the interests of making best use of time, a full timetable may be set for a trial, or some parts of a trial may be time limited. A fast track case should last no more than five hours, effectively a working day, and the timetable might be as follows. A multi-track case would have longer for each section but time might still be divided in similar proportions, depending on the needs of a case.

Opening statement	15 minutes
Cross examination of the claimant's witnesses	60 minutes
Re-examination of the claimant's witnesses	15 minutes
Cross examination of the defendant's witnesses	60 minutes
Re-examination of the defendant's witnesses	15 minutes
Defendant's closing submission	20 minutes
Claimant's closing submission	20 minutes
Judge's consideration and judgment	30 minutes
Assessment of costs and any other orders	30 minutes

D   WINNING A CASE AT TRIAL

22.34   If a case goes to trial then winning is very important. A great deal of work will have gone into preparation, and almost certainly offers of settlement will have been turned down. Each client will be very keen to win, and there may be a lot at stake not only in terms of potential remedies but also because the loser is at risk of having to pay the costs of both sides.

22.35   Everyone goes to court hoping to win—but most cases have a winner and a loser, unless the judge finds on some issues for one side and on some issues for the other side. An adversarial model of litigation is designed to produce a winner and a loser. In general terms there will be as many losers as winners. The importance of assessing the likely chances of success in an individual case is dealt with at 7.42–7.49. For books on advocacy skills see 24.22.

22.36   To be as sure as possible of winning at trial the lawyer has to focus on the basis upon which the judge will make his or her decision. The judge in a civil trial will not simply form a general impression of the case but is carrying out a fairly precise task based on specific principles.

- In a civil trial the burden of proof is on the claimant. If the claimant does prove his or her case then the claimant will lose.

- In a civil trial the claimant can only argue his or her case on the basis on which it is set out in the statements of case. The claimant has to bring evidence to prove each element of his or her cause of action as set out in the statements of case, save where an element is admitted by the defendant.
- In a civil trial the standard of proof is normally the balance of probabilities. Many attempts have been made to define what this means, for example that it is more likely than not that what the claimant alleges is true. The claimant will need to prove each element of his or her case on the balance of probabilities. The only exceptions are quasi criminal allegations such as fraud or contempt of court, for which the criminal standard of proof beyond a reasonable doubt is relevant.
- A judge can only reach a decision based on current law and the evidence that is before the court.

These tests favour the defendant in that if the claimant has framed the case badly, does not bring evidence on a key allegation, or does not have sufficient evidence to meet the standard of balance of probabilities then the defendant will win. **22.37**

The tests favour the claimant in that the standard of proof is not too difficult to meet. If it is 51 per cent likely that the claimant has made out his or her case then the claimant will win. **22.38**

On the face of it the tests are fairly straightforward, but the operation of the tests cannot always be very scientific or certain. Judges may have to interpret facts where the claimant is unable to produce very compelling evidence. The judge is central to the case, and it is important to ensure that the judge understands the points being made. **22.39**

It is arguable that research into how and why judges reach particular decisions could assist lawyers in assessing the chances of success of a case, and therefore assist with the settlement of cases. **22.40**

E   FINAL PREPARATIONS FOR ADVOCACY

> In law, what plea so tainted and corrupt
> But, being seasoned with a gracious voice,
> Obscures the show of evil.
>
> Shakespeare, *The Merchant of Venice*

If a case goes to trial then advocacy will be central to the chances of success. It is the advocate who conducts the case for the party, makes the speeches, deals with the witnesses, and deals with queries from the judge. The preparation of a skeleton argument was dealt with at 21.66–21.77. The skeleton argument should encapsulate the main arguments in the case, but further preparation will be needed to advocate the arguments. **22.41**

General preparation

A firm basis for good advocacy is confidence in the case, and the best basis for confidence is a thorough understanding of the case, based on analysis and preparation. **22.42**

22.43 There is a degree of personal preference in how much work the lawyer does both mentally and on paper in preparing in detail for advocacy in a trial. Much preparation can be done mentally, especially in the case of an experienced lawyer. However in order to have facts and arguments readily available when they are needed significant written preparation is often required, and this might well include:

- a chart analysing the key elements that need to be proved and what evidence proves each;
- notes for the key points to be made in submissions;
- notes for key questions for the cross examination of witnesses.

22.44 These preparations are most useful in a form in which they can most easily be referred to, with bullet points, highlighting etc. Equally the preparation must be flexible so that it can be adapted to the case as it develops during the trial, with changes and additions to speeches and questions where this proves necessary. Preparation should not be in the form of detailed notes that will need constant reference or the advocate will be constantly looking down rather than focussing on the judge or the witnesses.

Preparation for an opening submission

22.45 Key matters to be covered in an opening submission include:

- introducing the key elements of the client's case;
- introducing the main items of evidence and the main witnesses that the client will rely on;
- putting the strengths of the case in the best possible light;
- anticipating the main points that may be made by the other side, and responding to them tactically if that is possible.

22.46 In a non-jury trial it is possible for the judge to make a direction dispensing with opening speeches. With case management, the level of disclosure of trial, the submission of skeleton arguments etc, the judge and the parties may be so familiar with the case that opening speeches would serve no purpose. This possibility underlines the importance of documents such as the skeleton argument.

Preparation for examination in chief

22.47 As witness statements normally stand as evidence in chief, the preparation of evidence in chief will normally consist of drafting the witness statements with care.

22.48 It may be necessary to consider whether the court should be asked to permit examination in chief in court, for example because the witness statement needs to be updated, or there is any particular reason for hearing from the witness personally.

Preparation for cross examination

22.49 It can be daunting preparing for cross examination if it is assumed that cross examination can only be effective if a witness for the other side crumbles. In practice this will rarely happen, and more harm than good can be done by trying to be too clever, by arguing with the witness, or by being too unpleasant to a witness. In a civil case this can make a bad impression on the judge, and it may force the witness to become more trenchant in putting forward his or her version of events. The level of exchange of information prior to trial makes it rare that there will be something totally new to be put to the witness at trial.

The more modest and realistic aims of cross examination are to try to put the client's case in a more favourable light, and to seek to undermine the witness's credibility to some extent. To fulfil these aims: **22.50**

- There is a duty to put the main elements of the client's case to the witnesses for the other side to see their reaction. A list of the key points in the client's case on which each witness may be able to comment should be made, so as to ensure that all these points are put to the witness.
- The strengths of the client's case that a witness may be able to support should be noted so as to be able to reinforce strengths.
- The parts of what each witness says that damage a client's case should be carefully identified, and decisions taken on how to address this. Sometimes an alternative version of events can be put to the witness, or sometimes a witness's credibility might be undermined. If the point is not a very important one it may be best not to bring attention to it.
- Ways in which each witness's credibility may be undermined should be considered, if for example it is possible that the witness was preoccupied at the time, or could not fully appreciate what was going on, for example because of having an obstructed view. Showing a witness is possibly mistaken or unreliable can decrease the impact of his or her evidence.
- The statements of different witnesses should be compared in detail to identify how what one witness says conflicts with what another witness says, as this may be exploited to show that one witness is not very reliable.
- It may be possible to think of some reason why the witness may not be telling the whole truth, and to seek to bring that out. The client may know something to the detriment of the witnesses on the other side which may be used, though it is ethically wrong to make allegations against the other side unless the advocate has reason to feel they are justified, and that they are relevant to the case.
- All plans must be flexible dependent on the answers the witness gives. A potentially useful line of questions may be quickly shown to be misconceived, or answers may suggest a new line of questions.

Observation and experience of the witness at trial are important in making final decisions about cross-examining. Witnesses are probably less likely to lie in a civil case than in a criminal case, but truth may be used economically or embroidered in the hope of winning a case, and this might be brought out by the skilful advocate. **22.51**

The witness statements and affidavits will have been exchanged some time before the trial and it will be possible to work on them in detail. **22.52**

Preparation for the closing speech

There is an extent to which litigation builds up to the closing speech, which should pull together all the legal and factual elements of the case into a coherent whole. Some lawyers almost start to write their closing speech in their head when they first analyse the case. **22.53**

22.54   The lawyer should make some plans for the content and structure of the closing speech, but it may be unwise to prepare in great detail as it will be necessary to take full account of what emerges during the trial, commenting on the evidence that witnesses have given. Persuasion will be important where there are weaknesses in law or fact.

F   ARGUMENT AND PERSUASION

The life of the law has not been logic; it has been reason.

Oliver Wendell Holmes

22.55   To be credible, a case must be presented in a coherent and convincing way. If the parties have gone to trial rather than settled then both sides have confidence that their case is reasonably strong in law and fact, so it may be coherent argument and persuasion that makes the difference at trial.

Recreating events

22.56   The problem that it is often impossible to recreate the whole truth of an event was considered in Chapter 8. A case cannot be brought if there is no evidence on an element of the claim, but some evidence may be weak, or there may be ambiguities as to how something might have happened. It may be too difficult or too expensive to collect certain pieces of evidence. It is an important part of the skill of an advocate to put together the pieces of evidence like pieces of a jigsaw to form a convincing whole.

22.57   When trying to recreate something like an accident or the making of a contract in the mind of a judge, piecing together the evidence can be expressed as trying to 'run the video'. The advocate may not be able to fully recreate each detail of events, but to win a case it is important to bring events to life, and to try to help the judge to visualise exactly what happened minute by minute, or indeed second by second. Where was the accident? What were the key points about the location? Who was there? What was the situation immediately before the accident? How exactly did the accident probably happen? What happened immediately after the accident?

22.58   This kind of picture is normally built from basic ingredients.

- Plans (to show dimensions, distances etc).
- Photographs (both general and of specific important things, such as the detail of a machine, or the viewpoint of a particular witness).
- Eye witnesses.
- Physical evidence, such as scrapes or skid marks.
- A report (made by someone with appropriate expertise as soon as possible after the incident in question).

22.59   However none of these ingredients is necessarily entirely reliable. Plans and photographs may fail to capture the location fully, or they may not be complete because something has been destroyed or moved since the accident and before trial. A person making a report after an accident may only have partial information. There may be no eye witnesses, or an eye witness may not actually have seen or remembered a key point, or eyewitnesses may contradict each other.

Developing arguments

Preparing for advocacy will be closely linked with the preparations of a skeleton argument, **22.60** but there are other things to be done. The skeleton argument is the basic skeleton of issues, with key legal and evidential points. Advocacy needs to flesh out those bones with fully developed arguments, with persuasion, and with presentation of the evidence to best effect.

Identifying where argument is required

The areas where argument is most likely to be needed should be identified.   **22.61**

- There will need to be a coherent line of argument that runs right through the trial and culminates in the closing submission. This might be called the theory of the case.
- If certain tests have to be satisfied to ensure that a particular cause of action succeeds or that a particular remedy is granted then argument may be needed to show how the test is fulfilled.
- Areas where the evidence is weak may need to be supported by persuasive argument.
- Areas where the law is unclear may need to be addressed by persuasive argument.

Constructing an argument

There are many ways of constructing an argument, and this is the sort of skill that will   **22.62** develop with experience:

- Facts from different pieces of evidence can be pulled together. If direct evidence of a fact cannot be found in one piece of evidence then smaller bits of evidence may together prove sufficient, see 8.66–8.70.
- Reasonable presumptions can be suggested. It may be reasonable to presume something even if it cannot be directly proved. If something is probable that may be enough, not least as the standard of proof is on the balance of probabilities.
- Inferences may be drawn from facts that can be proved. If a witness can provide some facts about seeing a car go round a corner fast and hearing a bang it may be reasonable to infer that there was a collision.
- A theory for how an event probably happened may be evolved from a range of evidence, inference and presumption.
- Other disciplines may assist in the preparation and presentation of argument, for example using logic or a mathematical probability theory such as Bayes' theorem.

Persuading

In addition to constructing an argument, it is important to present it in a persuasive way.   **22.63** Many different factors may make an argument persuasive.

- A step by step presentation that leads to the conclusion being suggested.
- Presenting an argument in as realistic and plausible a way as possible.
- Making the very best use of the evidence that is available.

- Suggesting reasons for favouring one version of events over another.
- Using terminology such as probability, uncertainty and reason to try to directly address the thinking process of the judge.

22.64 However good an argument is, at trial it will be challenged.

- The opponent will try to find and point out the weak links in the argument.
- The opponent will also be seeking to construct an argument to support the case for the other side.
- The argument will need to meet the standard of being true on the balance of probabilities.

G   THE PRESENTATION OF A CASE

22.65 The judge has control of all aspects of the case. It is possible for the judge to direct what speeches should be given, and if appropriate how long the speeches should be and what issues should be addressed. The judge will also have broad control of the evidence being given, and will deal with any queries or concerns about the progress of the case. The judge will normally address any comments to the advocate for each side (unless addressing a witness who is giving evidence).

22.66 Having said this, the adversarial nature of proceedings means that the conduct of the case for each party is in the hands of a person with rights of audience, who will decide how the case is presented, what evidence will be called and will make submissions. The judge will normally allow a reasonable degree of freedom to an advocate for this purpose.

22.67 The presentation of a case must inevitably be adapted to the tribunal, not least in the interests of proportionality and costs. One would not address the magistrates in the same way as the Court of Appeal. The length of speeches, the number of witnesses called and so on should be adapted to the needs of the case.

22.68 It is crucial that a judge be taken through the presentation of a case in a coherent way. The point of presenting a case is to ensure that the judge understands it, and to assist the judge in reaching a decision. The judge needs to be able to follow the overall structure of presentation, each section of presentation, and each point being made. This is probably best achieved not by being repetitive or patronising, but by focussing on and if necessary checking whether the judge understands.

22.69 Evidence needs handling logically, which is not necessarily easy if a single document or witness relates to several aspects of the case. In using written evidence the judge should be taken to key points. There is merit in checking whether the judge has read the document to avoid excessive reading out in court.

22.70 In making a legal submission there is merit in being absolutely clear what proposition is being argued and what the key authorities are. A legal submission can be heavily founded in a skeleton argument and should not need to be laboured.

22.71 The key skills of trial advocacy might be said to be:

- selecting the content for each submission or for dealing with each witness carefully;

- structuring each submission or line of questioning with care;
- aiming for clarity and conciseness.

It is important to be sensitive to whether a judge is unsympathetic to a line of argument. If so **22.72**
consideration must be given to moving on, unless there is a way to put the argument more
convincingly, though as a lawyer you must of course press on if your point is a good one. The
judge's annoyance with a lawyer, even if justified, should of course never be allowed to
prejudice a client (*Millington v KSC & Sons* The Times, 22 July 1986). Equally, it is not part of a
barrister's duty to advance a client's view that a judge is corrupt and biased without any
evidence to support the allegations, *Thatcher v Douglas* The Times, 8 January 1996.

H   OPENING A CASE

> The aim of forensic oratory is to teach, to delight, to move.
>
> Cicero

The contents and length of an opening speech will depend on the complexity of a case, **22.73**
and the extent to which it has been set out in evidence and skeleton arguments disclosed
before the start of the case. An opening speech might last for some hours in a very complex
case, or might be short or even be dispensed with in a simple case.

The main ingredients of an opening speech are: **22.74**

- a clear and full summary of the elements of the case that the party is seeking to prove
  with reference to the statements of case;
- an outline of the key facts of the case from the claimant's point of view;
- an outline of the issues;
- an outline of the evidence that will be presented to support the case, including the
  witnesses and other items of evidence, with appropriate references to the agreed bundle
  of evidence.

An opening speech should effectively provide a plan for what is to follow. It needs to take **22.75**
into account that the judge and the other side are likely to be familiar with the statements of
case and the skeleton arguments. The speech should be given objectively. It can set out facts
that are agreed, but where matters are in dispute care must be taken to make it clear what is
the client's version of events, and not to make any assumption as to what the judge is likely
to find.

An opening speech should try to avoid making too much reference to the case for the other **22.76**
side, save for where this is really necessary to explain the case, or it is decided for tactical
reasons to address a weakness in the case before it is raised by the other side. It is for the
advocate for the other side to make their case.

I   DEALING WITH WITNESSES

General principles

22.77   The basic principle is that all witnesses should normally give oral evidence, CPR r 32.2. This is founded on the historical principle that the most reliable witness was the eye witness, and the best way of ascertaining truth was to see each witness give evidence personally. Ensuring the presence of a witness at trial is dealt with at 21.49–21.54.

22.78   As the rules of evidence and procedure have evolved, practice has moved away from this principle. It is now the norm that evidence in chief is given in a witness statement, though a judge can always direct that evidence in chief be given orally if there is good reason. The move to the use of witness statements should not be seen as undermining the importance of oral evidence—the witness statement should be drafted to fill the same purpose as evidence in chief, and oral cross examination remains very important where there is any dispute between witnesses. Where the witness statement has been served the witness should still attend to give oral evidence unless the court orders otherwise or the statement is put in as hearsay evidence, CPR r 32.5. Sworn evidence given in court is taken as the truth where that conflicts with other evidence given by the witness.

22.79   The wording of a question should be designed to be understood by the witness, using vocabulary that the witness will understand. It is best to ask reasonably short questions, and only to ask one question at a time to avoid confusing the witness (unless of course the purpose is to confuse the witness). The advocate should not react to what a witness says, even if an answer is pleasing or disappointing. On questioning techniques see 6.99–6.112.

22.80   While it may not be an easy task, the lawyer should note key points in the evidence given by a witness so as to be able to quote these points in the closing speech. A barrister may ask a solicitor or pupil to take a note for this purpose.

22.81   Once a witness has started to give evidence, the advocate must not communicate directly or indirectly with the witness until the evidence is finished without the permission of the opponent and of the court.

The stages for dealing with each witness

The witness will be sworn or will affirm

22.82   A witness should normally be sworn or give an affirmation or he or she cannot give evidence. A judgment based on unsworn evidence could be set aside, *R v Marsham ex p Lawrence* (1912) 2 KB 362. Unsworn evidence may be accepted in a small claims case if the court does not require evidence on oath, CPR r 27.8. Counsel can give unsworn evidence on the terms of an agreement, *Hickman v Berens* (1895) 2 Ch 638.

Evidence in chief

22.83   The witness will then give evidence in chief for the party for whom the witness is called. The witness statement will stand as evidence in chief unless the court directs otherwise. This means that the witness will simply be asked to take the oath, confirm his or her name, address, and occupation, and be asked to confirm a copy of the witness statement as their witness statement, and to confirm the statement of truth. The witness may amplify his or her witness statement or may give evidence on matters that have arisen since the witness statement was served, but only with the permission of the court, which will only be given if there is good reason why the witness should give evidence on something more than the contents of the statement.

If the witness does give oral evidence in chief then the questions from the advocate should **22.84** take the witness in a structured way through all the areas on which the witness can give relevant evidence. This must be done in a comprehensive way, as if the witness gives oral evidence in chief, a written statement made by the same witness will only be admitted in evidence in limited circumstances. The evidence must be given by the witness without prompting from the advocate—this must be done without using 'leading' questions (that is questions that guide the witness to a particular answer). It is acceptable to ask leading questions where information is not in dispute, but if in any doubt check with the other side in advance that the information is not in dispute. If a question is leading it does not make evidence given in response inadmissible, but it reduces the weight to be attached to it, *Moor v Moor* (1954) 1 WLR 927.

Because the witness statement is effectively evidence given in open court, a member of the **22.85** public may ask for a copy on payment of a set fee, CPR r 32.13, though the court can refuse if for example disclosure would be contrary to the interests of justice. This right probably does not extend to exhibits, *GIO Personal Investment Services Ltd v Liverpool and London Steamship Protection and Indemnity Association Ltd* (1999) 1 WLR 984 CA. There are provisions for getting copies of court documents in CPR r 5.4 and in PD 5 Court Documents.

Cross examination

The witness will then be cross examined on behalf of the defendant(s). Each witness can be **22.86** cross examined on behalf of each of the other parties in the case. The main purpose of cross examination is not normally to attack the witness, to trick the witness, or to show that the witness is lying or prejudiced, but rather:

- to put all parts of the case of the other party on which the witness may be able to give the witness an opportunity to comment on the alternative version of events;
- to try to undermine the strength of the evidence given by the witness by putting other evidence to the witness or suggesting that what the witness says is incorrect;
- to try to undermine the credibility of the witness by showing that the witness was not attending properly at the time, could not see what was happening quickly, or was confused;
- to try to undermine the general credibility of the witness.

The witness can be cross examined on anything in the witness statement (and the further **22.87** oral testimony if any) CPR r 32.11.

In putting a case to a witness, all the disputed facts that a witness is able to deal with should **22.88** be put. The things that other witnesses say that conflict with what the witness says should also normally be put, perhaps putting the precise words used by the other witness. Any matters that might be mentioned in a submission at the end of the case, for example that a witness was forgetful or mistaken should also be put. In terms of the wording to be used 'I put it to you that . . .' can be antagonistic, 'I suggest that . . .' is probably preferable as being clearer and less confrontational.

22.89   It is possible for leading questions to be used in cross examination, and indeed this can be necessary to allow the functions of cross examination to be properly fulfilled. However formulating questions for cross examination is still a great skill—a good question can be difficult for a witness to answer and can raise doubts in the mind of the judge. If the question is not well phrased it can simply allow the witness to side step answering, or to reinforce evidence given in chief. There is also skill in deciding on an order of questions that is most likely to be effective—for example building the trust of a witness before putting a difficult point, or building a funnel of questions in which the witness accepts a number of points and then has little option but to accept a particular conclusion.

22.90   If an advocate does not cross examine a witness on a particular point then the advocate is deemed to accept what the witness said in chief. This might seriously impede what can be said in a closing speech, though if a full case is not put to a witness it may still be possible to argue generally that the witness is not to be believed.

Re-examination

22.91   The witness will then be re-examined for the party for whom the witness was called. The purpose of re-examination is to deal with any fresh matters that have arisen during cross examination, and if necessary to reaffirm the case put forward in chief if it has been damaged in cross examination.

Matters a witness may be asked about

22.92   The function of each witness is to give truthful and accurate evidence on matters within their knowledge and competence to assist the court in reaching a decision. The approach taken to a witness and the questions used should assist this as far as possible. Since witness statements and other evidence are all exchanged well in advance of a civil trial the case of each side should be relatively clear and there should be few surprises. The issues arising will primarily be:

- Does the judge believe a witness is telling the truth?
- If there are conflicting versions of events, which does the judge think is most credible?
- Will cross examination put the evidence of a witness in a different light?

Limitations on questions that criticise a witness

22.93   Leading questions cannot be used during evidence in chief as it must be the witness who supplies the evidence, not the advocate putting the question. They can be used in cross examination, for example to put different possible versions of events to the witness.

22.94   Questions in cross examination may deal generally with the reliability of the witness, and such questions may on occasion become quite challenging or unpleasant. Questions should not be asked if their only purpose is to vilify, insult, or annoy the witness or another person, and people who are not involved in the case should not normally be criticised in open court. A barrister should not criticise a witness he or she has had an opportunity to cross examine, unless the matters in question have been put to the witness in the cross examination, Bar Code of Conduct para 708.

What a witness says in evidence in court can be put in question by other evidence attacking **22.95** or supporting their credibility. However if a witness denies something that is not covered by other evidence in the case and that goes only to credibility, that denial will be treated as final. The answer of a witness on a collateral matter will normally be treated as final and other evidence cannot be called to disprove it. The only exceptions are that evidence can be admitted to prove a criminal conviction if the witness has denied it, to show bias of the witness in favour of the party, or to put a previous inconsistent statement in the circumstances outlined below. The admission of such evidence is with the leave of the trial judge, and for example evidence of a conviction will be let in if justice cannot be done otherwise, Rehabilitation of Offenders Act 1974, s 4.

The privilege against self-incrimination

A witness cannot normally be obliged to reveal a fact if doing so would make it reasonably **22.96** likely that proceedings would be commenced exposing that person to the risk of any criminal charge or sanction. This general privilege against self-incrimination is not just a principle of English law but is also in Article 6(1) of the Convention on Human Rights. The privilege should be claimed when the question is asked. If a witness answers questions without claiming privilege the evidence is admissible.

This privilege does not apply where the risk is of civil liability or liability under a foreign law, **22.97** but it can extend to penalties under EC law, *Rio Tinto Zinc Corporation v Westinghouse Electric Company* (1978) AC 547. The evidence must create the risk, so there is no privilege where there is already strong evidence of guilt. The privilege may not apply if the potential penalty is trivial, *Rank Film Distributors Ltd v Video Information Centre* (1982) AC 380, and will not apply if the penalty will be avoided, for example because the CPS has agreed not to prosecute, *AT&T Istel v Tully* (1993) AC 45 HL. The privilege extends to a possible criminal penalty for a spouse, Civil Evidence Act 1968, s 14, and to an employee potentially incriminating a company, *Triplex Safety Glass Co Ltd v Lancegaye Safety Glass* (1939) 2 KB 395, though not to one employee incriminating another.

There are exceptions to the privilege against self-incrimination. For example in proceedings **22.98** for the recovery or administration of property, the execution of a trust or account of dealings with property, a person is not excused from answering questions that might reveal an offence under the Theft Act 1968, though any statement made will not be admissible in any subsequent prosecution, Theft Act 1968, s 31, and *Rentworth Ltd v Stephansen* (1996) 3 All ER 244. Where there is an insolvency various statements have to be made under the Insolvency Act 1986 that could be incriminating. Such statements can be used as evidence, though there are limitations on their use in criminal proceedings. There are similar provisions for investigations under the Companies Act 1985.

Problems in dealing with a witness

With the extent to which witness statements are exchanged before trial it should be possible **22.99** to prepare fully to deal with each witness, and problems should be relatively rare if the advocate is properly prepared. However problems can arise if the witness statements have not been well prepared, if there are substantial disputes of fact in the case, or if a witness has any motive to try to twist the truth. A barrister will not normally meet witnesses other than the client and expert witnesses before the trial, and will therefore rely particularly on the solicitor to weigh up whether a witness is reliable.

The witness may fail to say something the witness is expected to say

22.100 The stress of the courtroom situation or the length of time since the events in question may cause a witness to forget something. If a witness forgets details the advocate cannot normally offer any assistance—the sworn evidence must come from the witness and not from a previous statement or from the lawyer. This can be a significant problem—it is the evidence that the witness gives under oath at trial that the judge will rely on. If a witness fails to give evidence on a key point then a case may be lost.

22.101 To try to avoid such a problem a witness may be allowed to re-read a copy of any document he or she made closer to the events in question before giving evidence. This may help the witness to refresh his or her memory prior to giving evidence, though the witness cannot normally use such a document while giving evidence. A witness can only use a document to refresh their memory while in the witness box if the document was made or verified at the time of the events in question or so soon thereafter that the facts were still fresh in the witness's memory (for example a note of a car number made soon after an accident). The document used should be the original if possible and the court and other parties should be allowed to see it.

22.102 Another way to avoid such a problem is for the advocate to take the witness through his or her evidence in a very structured way that is easy to follow. For example a witness may more easily remember events if taken through them chronologically than if questions jump from one topic to another.

22.103 A way to address such a difficulty is to be able to call evidence from another witness on the same point. The witness who does not come up to proof is a danger well known to the lawyer, and one should beware of relying too heavily on one witness on a key point if possible.

The witness may say something that witness is not expected to say

22.104 A witness may be impressed with the importance of being in the witness box and start to embellish his or her story with more detail. A witness might feel that he or she ought to have noticed or remembered more detail than is in fact the case and may try to fill gaps by inventing something that he or she did not see. If possible this needs to be controlled by the lawyer who has called the witness, as the lawyer for the other side may be able to exploit it to show that the witness gives inconsistent evidence or is unreliable.

22.105 Such a problem is best avoided by encouraging the witness to reveal everything he or she knows before the witness statement is drafted, and by double checking before the witness statement is signed that it does set out his or her evidence accurately. It is not advisable for the lawyer to overstate what a witness says when drafting the witness statement because of the risk that if the witness says something different at trial this may make the witness's evidence less convincing.

The witness may say something that is significantly different from what the witness has said before

It is not common for a witness to make radical changes in his or her story in the course of a **22.106** civil trial. However it can happen that a witness will try to provide a significantly stronger story once the witness is focussed on the fact that evidence given can make the difference between winning and losing the case. Another possibility is that a witness may suddenly fear a perjury charge, and give a more truthful story than has previously been provided to the lawyers. If this happens it can be a significant problem as it is the evidence given by the witness in court that will prevail, save in limited circumstances.

The best way to avoid such a problem is to consider the comprehensiveness and reliability of **22.107** the evidence given by a witness at the time the witness statement is being drafted. It may alternatively be possible to call another witness to prove the matter in question, though the other side will be able to point out that the evidence given by different witnesses is inconsistent. If a problem with evidence comes as a surprise the court may give permission to call a further witness.

If the witness has previously made a statement about a matter which is inconsistent with the **22.108** evidence being given in court, the previous inconsistent statement may be allowed in with the permission of the judge. If the judge does give permission the witness should be reminded of the previous inconsistent statement, shown it if it was written, and should be asked if he or she made that statement. The witness should then be asked again about the point in dispute. If the witness now answers in line with their previous statement then this will be taken to be their sworn evidence. If the witness continues to give evidence that is different from the previous statement, then the previous inconsistent statement will be admissible as truth of what said under the Civil Evidence Act 1995.

Another possible solution is that the judge may give permission for a witness to be treated as **22.109** hostile. This is not simply a matter of the witness not supporting the case as had been hoped. A hostile witness is one who does not seem to want to tell the truth, and if the judge finds the witness is 'hostile' the rules of evidence will be relaxed to allow the lawyer to cross examine a witness called to provide evidence in chief. The decision will depend on the demeanour of the witness and the evidence given. The judge may prefer an interim step such as allowing the witness to refresh his or her memory before declaring the witness hostile.

J   CONCLUDING A CASE

You know you need a new lawyer when she starts her closing argument with 'As Ally McBeal once said . . .'.

The structure and content of a closing submission need to be carefully judged. There is an **22.110** extent to which the planning of a whole case and of the conduct of a trial should lead up to the closing submission to the judge.

The key elements of a closing submission are likely to be: **22.111**

- A reminder of the key issues that are in dispute and the decisions that the judge is being asked to make. This might be linked back to the opening speech if there was one.
- A summary of the legal points that support the client's case on each issue where law is relevant (and possibly comment on why legal points raised by the other side should not be followed).
- A summary of the evidence that supports the client's case on each issue, together with comment on why that evidence is to be preferred to the evidence given for the other side. This is likely to include references to the evidence given, with quotation of key points.
- Persuasive comment on how the judge should view any possible gaps or weaknesses in the evidence.
- Reference to the burden and standard of proof in the case, and how this is satisfied as regards the client's case.
- Specific reference to the findings that the lawyer is asking the judge to make.

22.112   Some of these points will overlap with the skeleton argument submitted before trial. The speech will also need to refer specifically to what has actually happened during the trial, especially as regards the evidence of witnesses. A strong case can probably rely primarily on clear statements about the law and the evidence. If the case is weaker or there is significant unclear or contradictory evidence then the advocate will need to say rather more about how the judge should interpret the evidence and view the case, constructing persuasive arguments as suggested above.

22.113   The main point of the closing speech is to lead the judge to a particular judgment. It is useful to structure the speech to this end, and to make sure that the judge grasps the key points. It may assist a judge to say 'I have three main points' and then list them, not least as this may encourage a judge to take notes.

K   THE JUDGMENT

The giving of the judgment

22.114   It could be said that the whole focus of litigation is on the judgment given by the judge. It might appear that the lawyer's task is finished once the closing speech has been made, but close attention needs to be paid to the judgment. In particular:

- Does the judgment cover all matters on which the judge should make a decision? If there are several matters to be considered then it may be useful to have a checklist to hand and to remind the judge if something is not covered.
- Does the judge apply the right tests? See 22.34–22.40.
- What are the reasons for the judgment? Might they give rise to a ground for appeal? Even if the client wins, the possibility that the other side might appeal may need consideration.
- It may be necessary to address the judge as regards the wording of the order, or as regards specific issues such as costs. The advocate should prepare in advance where such matters are likely to need to be dealt with.

22.115   Judgment may be given immediately, or after an adjournment if the judge requires time to consider the case. The judge should give a reasoned judgment, and reasons may be given immediately or at a later date.

It is a judge's duty to make a judgment, and not just to say that he or she can't decide, **22.116**
Cooper v Floor Cleaning Machines Ltd The Times, 24 October 2004.

Matters that the judgment can relate to

The judge does not have a general discretion to take whatever decision he or she wishes. **22.117**

- The judgment must take a decision on the basis of the issues as presented by the parties (though case management by the court should help to ensure that those issues are defined to the satisfaction of the court).
- The judge must take a decision that is justified in law, and where the law is unclear must explain how the decision is justified in law.
- The judge must accept evidence offered by an expert. If expert evidence is in conflict then the judge must state why the view of one expert is preferred to that of another.
- The judge must take a decision based on the evidence provided by witnesses in court, explaining if necessary why the evidence of one witness has been preferred to the evidence of another. If a judge does not accept the evidence of a witness as true then the reasons for this should be explained.

Within this framework the judge has significant residual discretion. Although adequate **22.118**
reasons should be given, the art of deciding whether a witness is telling the truth is not
entirely transparent. Research into how and why judges make decisions, and the bases on
which judges determine whether a witness is telling the truth could be of real interest and
value in developing the trial process.

If there is a claim and a counter-claim the court may, as appropriate, give separate judgments **22.119**
on each, or if there is a set-off simply give judgment for the balance, CPR r 40.13. This has
practical implications for the enforcement of the judgment and for possible costs orders.

Other decisions to be made at the end of a case

The judge may need to make various other decisions at the end of the case. These matters **22.120**
may have to be brought to the attention of the judge by the parties, and the judge may wish
to hear submissions as to the appropriate course to be taken.

- There may need to be a decision on the interest to be awarded on damages, see 14.68–14.77.
- If there has been an interim payment a special form of judgment must be used, see PD 25, and further decisions may be required, see 16.183–16.189.
- In a personal injury claim where the claimant has claimed benefits pending the trial, part of the damages may be payable to the state as a reimbursement under the Social Security (Recovery of Benefits) Act 1997, in which case the judgment must set out specifically the amounts awarded for each head of damage and the amount recoverable, PD 40B para 5, see 19.103.
- There may need to be an enquiry as to damages if an interim injunction has been granted but effectively has been found not to be justified at trial, *Hoffmann-La Roche (F) and Co AG v S of S for Trade and Industry* (1975) AC 295, HL, see 16.109–16.139.

22.121   Once the outcome of the case has been decided, the judge will normally also take decisions on who should pay costs and on what basis costs should be assessed. In a fast track case the judge will normally assess costs immediately. In a multi-track case there are likely to be complex issues regarding what should be allowable for costs, and including orders for costs made on interim applications. There may be an agreement as to costs to avoid the length and delay of an assessment, otherwise there will be a detailed assessment of costs that ends in a hearing before a costs officer, see 5.45–5.61.

22.122   A Part 36 payment in or offer can be brought to the attention of the judge by any party, so that it can be taken into account in making a costs order. If the payment in or offer has been revealed by mistake during the trial the judge will have had to decide whether he or she can proceed to hear the rest of the case without injustice. Any other 'without prejudice' offer that has been made may also be brought to the attention of the judge with regard to costs, see 20.44–20.64.

22.123   If the judge gives a reasoned judgment the advocates should take full and accurate notes. Such notes may be needed to assist in drawing up or reviewing the detail of orders made following the judgment. The notes taken by both sides may be compared to check accuracy for the order. The notes may also be needed as a basis for advising the client about the judgment, and possibly as a basis for advising on and drafting an appeal. Even if the court has recording facilities and can produce a transcript, that will take some time. If the court does not have recording facilities then the advocates' notes are likely to be the basis for the note of the judgment that is used on appeal. Barristers briefed for a court hearing should make a short note of the judgment on the backsheet of the brief before returning it to the solicitor.

22.124   A draft judgment can and should be corrected if it is wrong, *Robinson v Bird* The Times, 20 January 2004.

L   THE DRAWING UP OF ORDERS

22.125   A judgment or order will normally take effect immediately, even though it may take a couple of days to seal and serve the order, CPR r 40.7, though the court may specify a later date for the order to take effect.

The drawing up of an order

22.126   Even the giving of the judgment is not the end of the case. It is the judgment or order that is drawn up to record the outcome of the case that is of lasting importance and it is vital for the lawyer to keep his or her eye on the ball until this is completed. It is vital to get the terms and the details right. The wording of the order encapsulates the outcome of the entire litigation process and all of the effort that has gone into it—it merits careful thought, and if necessary argument.

22.127   The main rules relating to final judgments and orders are in CPR Part 40 and PD 40B. All judgments and orders must be drawn up and sealed by the court, CPR rr 40.2 and 40.3. The judge and the court may take responsibility for this, especially in a reasonably straightforward case, but the lawyers may become involved in a variety of ways.

- The court may direct a party to draw up an order, subject to checking by the court before it is sealed.
- A party may ask the court for permission to draft an order for court approval (so as to have more control over the detail).
- The court may direct the parties to file agreed terms before the court draws up the order.
- The court may require the agreement of the parties to the terms of an order being drawn up by the court, which can be done by sending a draft order to the parties, or by the court giving notice of an appointment at court to agree the terms of the order.
- The order may be a consent order that the parties agree and file.
- The court may dispense with the need to draw up an order.

For a number of interim applications it is necessary to provide a draft for the order sought. **22.128** The prayer in a particulars of claim may also set out the order sought in some detail, for example in the case of an injunction being sought.

If one party has responsibility for drafting they will normally have seven days to file the draft **22.129** with copies for all parties, CPR r 40.3. If the party does not do this, any party may draw up the order and file it.

There are standard forms that may be used in certain situations. For example Form 45 is used **22.130** for a judgment after a trial before a judge without a jury, and Form 47 is used for a judgment after a trial before a master or district judge.

The drafting of an order

The clarity of drafting in an order is obviously of particular importance as it must be abso- **22.131** lutely clear what the outcome of the case is and what individuals are and are not required to do. If there are any problems in clarity then enforcement may prove difficult.

- Every judgment or order must bear the date on which it was given and must be sealed by the court. Most judgments or orders should state the name and judicial title of the judge who made the order, CPR r 40.2 (the main exceptions being consent orders and judgments entered as an administrative act).
- If a judgment or order directs any deed or document to be prepared, executed, or signed, the order must state who is to prepare it, and if necessary approve it, PD 40B para 2.
- If a judgment or order requires a party to pay a sum of money, payment will be due within 14 days unless the court or a rule of court specifies a different period, CPR r 40.11.
- If a judgment is for money to be paid by instalments, the order must set out the total amount due, the amount of each instalment, the number of instalments and the date on which each is to be paid, and to whom the instalments should be paid, PD 40B para 12.
- An order requiring a positive action must set out clearly what is to be done, the date by which it must be done, and the consequences of failure to comply, PD 40B para 8.
- If an injunction order is not obeyed, enforcement may be by contempt of court proceedings, including potentially imprisonment. Because of this possibility, the injunction must be clearly worded and there must be a penal notice to make this clear.

- If the court gives judgment for specific sums of money on a claim and on a counterclaim then it may simply order that the balance be paid, but it may still make two separate costs orders, CPR r 40.13.
- The order must, if appropriate, specifically cover costs and interest. If there is no order for costs then no costs are payable, CPR r 44.13.

22.132 A judgment or order may need to set out certain relevant background information in a preamble. This may include for example:

- any matters agreed by the parties in terms of liability, the amount of damages, or a contribution, PD 40B para 14;
- the findings of a judge under each head of damage in a personal injury case;
- appropriate information where benefits will be recovered under the Social Security (Recovery of Benefits) Act 1997, or where there has been an interim payment;
- any order made during the trial regarding the use of any evidence provided for the trial.

22.133 Once the order is drawn up the court will serve sealed copies on the parties and anyone else the court has ordered be served on, CPR r 40.4. An order may be served on a litigant personally as well as on his or her lawyer, CPR r 40.5. Only the order itself will be supplied at this stage, and not a copy of the judgment containing the reasons for the order.

Special types of order

22.134 Where provisional damages have been awarded the order must specify the disease or type of deterioration in respect of which an application(s) may be made at a future date and the period(s) within which such an application can be made, CPR r 41.2, see 19.104–19.105.

22.135 Where an interim payment has been made the preamble should set out the total amount awarded by the judge and the amount and date of interim payments, PD 40B para 6. If the judge has awarded more, then judgment should be given for the difference. If the judge has awarded less, then there should be an appropriate order for repayment, see 16.183–16.189.

22.136 If the damages include heads from which recoverable benefits can be deducted under the Social Security (Recovery of Benefits) Act 1997 and the defendant has paid a sum in respect of such benefits, there should be a preamble which states the amount awarded under each head of damage and the amount by which each has been reduced, and the judgment should then provide for payment of the balance, PD 40B para 5, see 19.103.

22.137 It may be possible to correct an error in a judgment or order if it is an accidental slip or omission, CPR r 40.12. The slip or omission may be that of anyone involved in drawing up the judgment or order, but it must be a superficial error of expression and not a change in what the court intended. Save for the slip rule a judgment or order can only be queried by appeal.

M   GENERAL FRAMEWORKS FOR ORDERS

Order after a trial before a judge

IN THE HIGH COURT OF JUSTICE
QUEEN'S BENCH DIVISION

Claim No 2005 HC 1234   **22.138**

Before the Honourable Mrs Justice X

BETWEEN

AB	<u>Claimants</u>
and	
CD	<u>Defendants</u>

<u>ORDER</u>

This claim having been tried before the Honourable Mrs Justice X without a jury at the Royal Courts of Justice;

And the Judge having ordered on (date) that judgment be entered for the Claimant against the Defendant as set out below:

IT IS ORDERED that:

1. The Defendant be restrained by injunction from. . . . . . .
2. The Defendant pay the Claimant the sum of £Z (being £Y principal sum and £X interest at the rate of V% per year from (date) to the date of this order).
3. The Defendant pay the Claimant's costs to be the subject of detailed assessment.

Dated:

(A judgment in a personal injury case needs a more detailed preamble setting out the different elements of damage in detail, see PD 40B) (For a judgment giving provisional damages see PD 41)

Consent order

IN THE HIGH COURT OF JUSTICE
QUEEN'S BENCH DIVISION

Claim No 2005 HC 1234   **22.139**

BETWEEN

AB	<u>Claimants</u>
and	
CD	<u>Defendants</u>

CONSENT ORDER

The parties having agreed the terms of settlement of this claim;

BY CONSENT IT IS ORDERED that:

1.
2.
3.   Order as to costs, or no order as to costs.
4.   Liberty to apply.

Dated:

Tomlin order

22.140   IN THE WINCHESTER COUNTY COURT   Claim No W5/9753

Before His Honour Judge A

BETWEEN

AB   Claimants

and

CD   Defendants

CONSENT ORDER

The parties having agreed to the terms set out in the schedule below;

BY CONSENT IT IS ORDERED that:

1.   All further proceedings in this claim be stayed, except for the purpose of carrying those terms into effect.
2.   Each party to have liberty to apply as to carrying those terms into effect.
3.   Order as to costs, or no order as to costs.

Dated:

SCHEDULE

1.
2.
3.
4.

KEY DOCUMENTS

Forms

N163 Skeleton argument

N24 General form of judgment or order

Practice Form 45 Judgment after trial by a judge without a jury

Practice Form 109 Order for reference to the European Court

N259 Notice of Appeal

These are available in hard copy and electronically, see Chapter 24.

23

ENFORCING OR CHALLENGING
A JUDGMENT

A THE STEPS TO BE TAKEN AFTER TRIAL 23.01

B ENFORCING A JUDGMENT 23.04
   Enforcing a judgment debt. 23.08
   Charging orders 23.12
   Execution against goods. 23.13
   Attachment of earnings 23.14
   Orders for delivery/possession. 23.15
   Receivership 23.17
   Contempt of court. 23.18
   International enforcement of judgments 23.19

C DECIDING WHETHER TO APPEAL. 23.26
   The general question of appealing 23.26
   Advising on an appeal. 23.29

D GROUNDS FOR APPEAL 23.37
   An appeal on a matter of law. 23.39
   An appeal on a matter of fact. 23.40
   An appeal on the basis of fresh evidence 23.41
   An appeal on a procedural irregularity. 23.43

E JURISDICTION FOR APPEALS 23.45

F PROCEDURE FOR APPEALING 23.47

G POWERS ON APPEAL. 23.52
   Set a judgment or order aside. 23.52
   Vary an order 23.53
   Order a new trial 23.54

H DRAFTING AN APPEAL 23.55
   The notice of appeal 23.55
   Documents to be lodged on appeal 23.64

I THE POSITION OF THE RESPONDENT TO AN APPEAL 23.65

J PREPARING FOR AN APPEAL 23.71
   General preparation 23.71

    Preparing evidence 23.76
    The skeleton arguments 23.80

K   PRESENTING AN APPEAL 23.82

L   THE APPEAL DECISION 23.88

M   COSTS ON APPEAL 23.96

    KEY DOCUMENTS

A   THE STEPS TO BE TAKEN AFTER TRIAL

23.01   Getting a judgment is a very important stage in the litigation process, but it is still not the end of the process. Litigation is not effectively over until judgment has not only been given but has also been satisfied. This will only happen quickly if all parties accept the judgment in full and are willing and able to satisfy the judgment, and if there has been agreement as to costs.

23.02   In practice there may not be closure on the litigation process for months or even years after judgment:

- It may take weeks or months for costs to be agreed or taxed.
- A party against whom an order has been made may not be willing to comply, and may take steps to avoid or evade compliance.
- A party against whom an order has been made may not be able to comply, for example because they do not have sufficient money to pay a damages order.
- One or both parties may wish to appeal.

23.03   There are ways in which such problems can be minimised.

- Settling an action without resorting to litigation, as parties are more likely to comply with something they have agreed to and tension between the parties may be defused rather than aggravated.
- If it has been necessary to resort to litigation, seeking to end the action with a consent order, or an order in which there is a degree of consent if possible.
- Seeking orders designed to ensure that assets are preserved pending the outcome of litigation where this is possible, for example a freezing order.
- Seeking as far as possible to ensure that an action is brought against a body or an individual that will be capable of paying damages, either through assets or insurance cover. It is possible to get some relevant information, for example company accounts have to be filed at Companies House.
- Considering possible problems with enforcement when weighing up the merits of starting an action.
- Ensuring that the wording of the judgment is clear and comprehensive, especially in the case of an injunction, so that it is as easy as possible to enforce.
- Where possible, building enforcement provisions into the order itself.

B ENFORCING A JUDGMENT

Being able to enforce a judgment is normally a major objective in the litigation process. If **23.04** the judgment cannot be enforced then the claimant will not get justice, and may be left seriously out of pocket having to pay for an action that produces nothing. Even if the loser is normally ordered to pay costs to the winner, such an order is also only worth it if it can be enforced. Such considerations will normally be taken into account in deciding whether to bring an action in the first place.

In some cases there will be no difficulty in enforcing a judgment because for example the **23.05** defendant has resources and is prepared to meet the judgment, or the money will be paid by an insurer. Also some judgments are reasonably easy to comply with, for example as they provide for the delivery of specific property.

The majority of judgments are for damages. A judgment for the payment of money should **23.06** be complied with within 14 days unless some other period is ordered or provision is made for payment by instalments, CPR r 40.11. If money is to be paid by instalments details of amounts, dates etc must be included in the order, PD 40B para 12.

The following is just a basic outline of the types of enforcement that may be available. **23.07** See generally CPR Part 40 Judgments, orders, sale of land etc, PD 40 Accounts, enquiries etc, PD 40B Judgments and orders, CPR Part 70 General rules about enforcement of judgments and orders, and PD 70 Enforcement of judgments and rules for the payment of money.

Enforcing a judgment debt

There are various sources for finding information about the resources of a defendant. One **23.08** party may have personal knowledge of the assets of the other, or some assets might be obviously held. It is possible to use various sources of information—for example records of companies are held at Companies House.

It is possible to get more information about the assets of a judgment debtor. There is a form **23.09** for application, and an order will be made requiring the debtor to attend court and provide information, CPR r 71. The order must be served at least 14 days before the hearing. The debtor can ask that expenses of attending court be paid. The applicant must swear an affidavit giving details of this process and saying how much remains unpaid. The hearing is effectively a cross examination about assets and debts.

A third party debt order can be used to take over a debt owed by a third party, such as a bank **23.10** or a building society. A without notice application must be made in the prescribed form, CPR r 72.3. Without a hearing, a judge can make an interim order that the debt not be paid so as to reduce it below the amount specified in the order. The judge will also fix a date for making a final order. The interim order is served on the person owing the debt not less than 21 days before the hearing. A bank or building society must carry out a search to identify accounts held by the debtor and must provide information about them. Any other debtor has seven days to dispute whether there is a debt or the sum owed. The judgment debtor must also be served, within seven days and at least seven days before the hearing and may apply for hardship payments. Evidence must be filed if it is alleged someone else is entitled to the money. At the hearing the court will decide whether to order the payment of the debt to meet the judgment.

23.11   See generally CPR Part 71 Orders to obtain information from judgment debtors, PD 71 Orders to obtain information from judgment debtors, CPR Part 72 Third Party debt orders, and PD 72 Third party debt orders.

Charging orders

23.12   A charging order can be used to impose a charge on specified property of the judgment debtor to secure the payment of the money due, Charging Orders Act 1979. This can include land, shares, and other securities. The order is normally obtained from the court where judgment was obtained. An application notice in prescribed form must be used, CPR r 73. Again the judge can make an interim order without a hearing. The court should specify who should be served with this order, including other creditors. Anyone who objects to the order being made must file and serve evidence. At the hearing the judge will decide whether an order should be made and the terms. The court is required to consider all the circumstances of the case and the position of other creditors. If the order is made there is no immediate money, but the applicant becomes a secure creditor, and could enforce the charge by seeking an order for sale. See generally CPR Part 73 Charging orders, stop orders and stop notices, and PD 73 Charging orders, stop orders and stop notices.

Execution against goods

23.13   Execution can be carried out against goods. A warrant of execution can be used for judgments for up to £5,000 in the County Court, and a writ of *fieri facias* can be used in the High Court (with cases being transferred there for enforcement if that is appropriate). A bailiff or sheriff will carry out the order, seizing goods to meet the judgment, which may be taken away and sold.

Attachment of earnings

23.14   Attachment of earnings may be sought where the judgment debtor has a salary, Attachment of Earnings Act 1971. The effect of the order is that the employer is directed to make regular payments to the collecting officer of the court. These orders can only be made by the County Court (so the case may need to be transferred to a County Court). There must be a failure to make a payment, so relevant where judgment provides for payment by instalments. Application is by use of a prescribed form. The debtor has to complete a form and committal proceedings can be taken if he fails to. There are protected earnings and a normal deduction rate. The order may be suspended to see if proper payments resume.

Orders for delivery/possession

23.15   If there is a judgment for delivery of specific goods it can be enforced by a writ of delivery (High Court) or a warrant of delivery (County Court).

A judgment for possession of land is secured through a High Court writ or a County Court **23.16**
warrant.

Receivership

If it is impossible to use any other legal method for enforcement, a receivership order may be **23.17**
made. The receiver will then be able to receive moneys receivable by the judgment debtor.
The order is sought with an application notice supported by affidavit, CPR r 69. This must
detail why a receiver should be appointed, and give details of a suitable person. Once
appointed the receiver will be paid and will need to provide accounts of dealings with the
property. Once the duties are completed the receiver will be discharged. See generally CPR
Part 69 Court's power to appoint a receiver, and PD 69 Court's power to appoint a receiver.

Contempt of court

Contempt of court proceedings may be used where a party breaches an order or undertaking. **23.18**
Such a breach lays the party open to committal to prison for up to two years, Contempt of
Court Act 1981. As an alternative the court has a power to impose a fine, take a security,
grant an injunction to restrain further contempt, or sometimes a summary award of damages. An application for a committal is by application notice, with specific identification of
the breach and affidavit evidence in support. The judge must be satisfied beyond a reasonable doubt that there has been a breach. A committal order can be immediate or suspended.

International enforcement of judgments

Where there is an international aspect of a case, matters of enforcement are best taken into **23.19**
account as far as possible in deciding where the action should be brought in the first place.

Enforcing a foreign judgment here

A judgment obtained in another jurisdiction can of course be enforced using the courts of **23.20**
the country in which the judgment was obtained.

There are various international agreements under which a foreign judgment can be regis- **23.21**
tered in the courts of this country for enforcement. This applies for example to a judgment of
a superior court of a Commonwealth country under the Administration of Justice Act 1920,
and to judgments of other EU Member States under the Jurisdiction and Judgments Regulation (EC) No 44/2001. See generally CPR Part 74 Enforcement of Judgments in Different
Jurisdictions, and PD 74 Enforcement of Judgments in Different Jurisdictions.

Where there is not an international agreement, a foreign judgment can be enforced in this **23.22**
country by starting an action claiming the amount of the judgment as a debt. Inevitably this
will not necessarily be an easy or successful process.

Enforcing an English judgment in another country

If an action is being brought in England and Wales and problems with enforcement are **23.23**
foreseen then the possibility of applying for a freezing order should be considered to ensure
that assets within the jurisdiction remain within the jurisdiction, see Chapter 16.

23.24 Once the judgment has been obtained it can be enforced in the ways outlined above to the extent that there are assets within the jurisdiction.

23.25 If there are not sufficient assets within the jurisdiction then the international treaties referred to above may be used. If there is not a relevant international agreement, then enforcement will depend on the rules of the jurisdiction where enforcement is sought. Inevitably this may be difficult and expensive.

C   DECIDING WHETHER TO APPEAL

> Old lawyers never die, they just lose their appeal.

The general question of appealing

23.26 Appeals increase the cost and length of litigation. Ideally effective litigation will avoid an appeal, though this is not always possible in a tightly fought case. The procedure for appeal is only covered in outline here. See generally CPR Part 52 Appeals, and PD 52 Appeals (which was significantly amended from 30 June 2004).

23.27 Ideally the need to appeal is avoided. For example it is not possible to save an argument up for use on appeal—a point not raised at trial cannot normally be raised on appeal.

23.28 There are various different routes of appeal from different levels of decision in different types of hearing by different courts and tribunals. This chapter will deal with the principles of advising on an appeal, drafting grounds of appeal, and preparing for the hearing of the appeal where there is an appeal from the High Court to the Court of Appeal, though many of the points that are made have a wider application for other types of appeal.

Advising on an appeal

23.29 If a case proceeds to judgment, at the end of a trial the general result will be that one party wins and the other loses. The loser will almost certainly wish to consider appealing. Indeed clients may ask about appeal prospects even before a case goes to trial if the case is closely fought. There are limits to what can be achieved on appeal, and risks as to costs etc, so a client must be fully advised before deciding whether to appeal or not.

23.30 Obviously one does not appeal merely because a judge's decision is unfavourable. Against appealing, there is the principle that there is no point in throwing good money after bad, and if the appeal fails the client will end up not only losing the case, but probably also paying the costs of both sides for the trial and the appeal, which is something that should be made completely clear to the client. The costs of appeal will not necessarily be very high as all the evidence has already been collected for the trial, but the costs of the lawyers in researching and preparing for an appeal may well build up.

23.31 Equally, one might consider appealing even after winning if the judge did not grant all the things sought by the client. A case may be very important to the client, with a big point of principle or a large amount of money at stake, so that he or she will be prepared to appeal even if the chances of success are not good.

The decision whether to appeal from all or part of a decision involves the balancing of all the appropriate factors to make a realistic and practical decision. The key issues to consider when deciding whether to appeal include:　　**23.32**

- what grounds of appeal might be available, and whether permission to appeal will be required;
- the tight time limits that apply;
- what form the appeal takes, as this may be relevant to what the court will consider;
- what powers are available to the Court of Appeal;
- the potential risks of appealing, including as regards costs;
- the chances of success—probably only about 25 per cent of appeals succeed.

However keen a client is to appeal, objective consideration of these factors might show that it is probably not worth it. It is for the lawyer to provide advice and for the client to decide whether to appeal, though the lawyer might if appropriate make quite a strong recommendation. The possibility of appealing may be discussed immediately after the judge has given his or her decision, or even before if it is clear that the client is likely to lose, not least because of the relatively tight deadlines for appealing. It is probably best to sleep on the matter and perhaps to have a further meeting with the client before taking a decision.　　**23.33**

Sometimes the client feels very strongly and may want to appeal even if the chances of success are negligible, in which case you should of course try to dissuade him. Conversely, a client may be so exhausted and dispirited by the trial itself that they may not wish to bother to appeal (this can happen particularly in matrimonial cases where emotional strain is added to the strain of the trial). If the chances of a successful appeal are good then the lawyers should of course strongly encourage the client to go on.　　**23.34**

Sufficient information will need to be available about the trial. At the stage of advising on appeal this will normally come from notes kept by the lawyer. Any procedural or evidential concerns that arise during the trial should be raised with the judge at once, but may be raised on appeal if the judge's decision is not favourable, so a full note of the problem and the decision would need to be kept. Notes of oral evidence should be taken when the evidence is given as advice on a possible appeal is likely to have to be given without an official transcript. This does not need to be a full note, and need not include basic information which is not in dispute, but it should contain the major questions and answers on examination in chief and cross examination. The lawyer will also need to have kept a note of the judgment that is sufficiently full to identify points for appeal accurately.　　**23.35**

The possibility of an appeal is something for both sides to consider. Even if one side does not wish to appeal, the other side may do so, in which case the respondent to the appeal is not limited to defending the judge's decision. It is possible not only to argue that the decision should be upheld, but that if necessary it should be upheld on grounds other than those given by the judge. The respondent to an appeal may also argue that the decision of the court below should be varied in whole or in part, or may cross-appeal if he or she did not get all he or she wanted from the original hearing. If it is clear that the one side may appeal, the other side should begin to consider its own position immediately.　　**23.36**

D   GROUNDS FOR APPEAL

23.37   The first stage of advising on appeal will be to list all the possible grounds of appeal of all types, on law, fact, or procedure. These points should be divided into those relating to the judge's findings and those relating to the remedies granted, and whether the points relate to the whole or part of the judgment.

23.38   The next stage is to evaluate the chances of success of each possible ground of appeal. This may well involve intuition or guesswork on the part of the lawyer as to the view that the Court of Appeal will take, and it may well be best explained to the client by giving him the odds or the percentage chance of winning, as in giving advice about the potential success of the original action. The main possible grounds for appeal are given below.

An appeal on a matter of law

23.39   This may be a relatively strong ground of appeal, where the lawyer has a clear argument that the judge made a wrong decision on law, supported by authority.

An appeal on a matter of fact

23.40   An appeal on a matter of fact will usually only succeed if a clear misunderstanding or mistake of fact on the part if the trial judge is shown. This is because the Court of Appeal will only have written evidence, whereas the trial judge will have seen the witnesses giving oral evidence, and may have been able to form impressions of them which are not easily transmitted on the written page.

An appeal on the basis of fresh evidence

23.41   An appeal on a matter of fact is more likely to succeed if fresh evidence has come to light which was not available at the time of the trial. There are only limited circumstances in which fresh evidence can be introduced before the Court of Appeal. Evidence may be admitted of facts which could not with reasonable diligence have been obtained for the original hearing, which would probably have had an important influence on the outcome of the case and which are apparently credible, *Ladd v Marshall* (1954) 1 WLR 1489 and *Hertfordshire Investments Ltd v Bubb* (2000) 1 WLR 2318. The evidence will need to be presented in an admissible form, and there will need to be a good reason why it was not presented at trial.

23.42   The Court of Appeal can also take into account changes in the facts since the trial, and this applies to the facts on which the measure of damages is based as well as the facts of the case itself. The Court of Appeal will be slow to change the award of damages made by the trial judge without good reason, but in *McCann v Sheppard* [1973] 1 WLR 540 a 26-year-old man was injured in a car accident. He was awarded £41,252 in damages, but while an appeal was pending he committed suicide, probably due to depression at the injuries he suffered. It was held that this should be taken into account, and the part of the damages for loss of future earnings was substantially reduced.

An appeal on a procedural irregularity

The potential success of an appeal on a procedural defect will depend on the type of defect, **23.43** whether it was likely to have had a real effect on the outcome of the trial, and whether anything could and should have been done about it at the time. If there is any procedural irregularity at the trial the lawyer should normally object at the time, and it is only if this happens and the judge does not accept his submissions or objections made is there a possible ground for appeal. Once the judge is summing up or giving judgment, it will normally be inappropriate for a lawyer to object to anything said, so something said by the judge at that stage may be the basis for an appeal.

The seeds of the appeal often come from the original trial and the preparations for it. The **23.44** purpose of the appeal is to remedy any defect in the original trial, not to give the lawyer a second chance to get it right. Therefore every cause of action and major argument of fact should be properly prepared and presented at the trial, and a new cause of action or an important new argument cannot normally be raised for the first time on appeal. In *Williams v Home Office (No 2)* [1982] 2 All ER 564, the claimant brought an action for false imprisonment, having been kept in a control unit in a prison. The action failed, and he sought leave after the trial to amend his statement of case to add breach of statutory duty. It was held that this could not be done as it should have been pleaded and argued as part of the case at the first trial. In *Lloyde v West Midlands Gas Board* [1971] 1 WLR 749 the claimant was injured by an explosion in an outhouse where he kept his moped, and where the gas meter was. He sued the gas board, pleading *res ipsa loquitur*, but did not argue it at trial. Damages were awarded on the grounds that the meter was defective, but on an appeal the plaintiff sought to argue the *res ipsa loquitur* point as well. As he had pleaded it the court did not prevent this, but held that as the defendant had not expected it to be raised on appeal there should be a new trial to be fair to both sides.

E   JURISDICTION FOR APPEALS

There are various different routes of appeal from different levels of decision in different types **23.45** of hearing by different courts and tribunals.

- An appeal from a High Court Judge lies to the Court of Appeal.
- An appeal from the Court of Appeal lies to the House of Lords.
- In limited circumstances an appeal can go directly from the High Court to the House of Lords, Administration of Justice Act 1969, ss 12–15.

An appeal from an interim decision is more likely to allow for a general review of the deci- **23.46** sion taken than a formal appeal from the High Court to the Court of Appeal. In very broad terms:

- An appeal from a County Court District Judge lies to a County Court Circuit Judge.
- An appeal from a County Court Circuit Judge, High Court Master, or District Judge lies to a High Court Judge, Access to Justice Act 1999 (Destination of Appeals) Order 2000, SI 2000/1071 and PD 52.

- An appeal is direct to the Court of Appeal for a final decision in a multi-track claim (one that decides the entire proceedings), or in specialist proceedings, or the hearing in the lower court was itself an appeal from a County Court District Judge, see *Tanfern Ltd v Cameron-MacDonald* (2000) 1 WLR 1311 and *Clark (Inspector of Taxes) v Perks* (2001) 1 WLR 17.
- An appeal may be transferred to the Court of Appeal if there is an important point of principle or practice involved, CPR r 52.

F   PROCEDURE FOR APPEALING

23.47 An appellant must file an appeal notice in Form N161. This must set out the grounds of appeal, and if necessary request permission to appeal, CPR r 52.4, and/or permission to appeal out of time, CPR r 52.6. A party cannot at hearing rely on anything not contained in the appeal notice without the permission of the court, CPR r 52.11. If for the first time in the case a party seeks to raise a point under the Human Rights Act 1998 at the appeal stage, appropriate information must be included, PD 16 para 16.

23.48 An appeal notice should normally be filed within 14 days of the decision of the lower court. Permission to appeal out of time can only be granted by the appeal court, CPR r 52.6. The court will take into account specific factors in taking a decision, *Sayers v Clarke Walker* (2002) 1 WLR 3095. The court will look for example at the length of delay, the reasons for it, and the chances of success of the appeal.

23.49 With a few minor exceptions such as committal orders, permission is required for an appeal, CPR r 52.3. Permission can be sought by an oral submission to a judge at the end of a hearing. Otherwise permission to appeal can be sought from the court the appeal is to, including an application in the appeal notice itself. An appeal to the Court of Appeal is normally first considered by a single judge, but if refused can go to a full hearing. Second appeals always need permission from the Court of Appeal, which will only be granted if the appeal raises an important point of principle or practice, or there is a compelling reason for the Court of Appeal to hear it, Access to Justice Act 1999, s 55. The test for permission is whether the appeal has a real prospect of success, and the general importance of the issue raised on appeal. If the point is not of general importance and the costs of appealing do not justify the amount at stake, permission will be refused. An order giving permission to appeal may limit the issues to be heard, or may be made subject to conditions.

23.50 To assist with the preparations for an appeal in the Court of Appeal, the appellant will be asked to complete a questionnaire estimating the length of hearing and setting out the state of preparations.

23.51 Any necessary interlocutory applications may be made while the parties are waiting for the case to come on for hearing. Such applications are normally made by motion to a single judge of the Court of Appeal. For example, bringing an appeal will not automatically stop enforcement of the judgment of the court, though a stay can be sought if appropriate, CPR r 52.7. A stay will only be granted to deprive a successful litigant of what he or she has won in special circumstances. The court will balance the position of the parties and consider whether the appeal has some prospect of success, and if there would be very serious financial consequences without a stay, *Linotype-Hell Finance Ltd v Baker* (1993) 1 WLR 321.

G   POWERS ON APPEAL

Set a judgment or order aside

The Court of Appeal can set a judgment or order aside, though it would be rare for this to   **23.52** happen alone.

Vary an order

The Court of Appeal can vary an order and substitute a new order, or grant an additional   **23.53** order. Although the Court of Appeal has all the powers of the High Court as regards remedies and may substitute different remedies for those granted by the judge at first instance, there are limits on what the Court of Appeal will be prepared to do. It will be slow to grant a remedy that is not sought in the notice of appeal or the respondent's notice, and it will be slow to depart from an inference of fact or an exercise of discretion of the judge at first instance. It will also be slow to vary an assessment of damages, unless the judge made an assessment that was wrong in principle or was clearly based on a misunderstanding of the facts, or fresh evidence has come to light which is relevant to the assessment of damages, though there clearly is a power to change an award of damages rather than order a retrial, Courts and Legal Services Act 1990 s 8.

Order a new trial

The Court of Appeal has power to order a new trial, Supreme Court Act 1981, s 17 and   **23.54** CPR 52.10, but this will not be done frequently. Grounds for a new trial might include the following, but the Court of Appeal would need to be satisfied that a substantial wrong resulted, so that there is a real doubt as to whether the correct decision was reached on liability or remedies.

- Improper inclusion or exclusion of evidence.
- Substantial new evidence.
- A misdirection to the jury, or leaving inappropriate matters to the jury in a jury trial.

H   DRAFTING AN APPEAL

The notice of appeal

The appellant must file an appellant's notice in Form N161 with the appeal court within   **23.55** 14 days, unless the lower court has directed some other time limit, CPR r 52.4.

The notice of appeal must set out the grounds of appeal, together with summary reasons   **23.56** why it is said that the decision of the lower court is wrong or unjust, and whether this is through procedural or other regularity, PD 52 para 3. The appeal may relate to the whole or a specified part of the judgment or order of the court below.

23.57   At the hearing of the appeal, the appellant will not be entitled to rely on any grounds of appeal or to apply for any relief which is not specified in the notice of appeal unless the Court of Appeal gives leave. It is therefore vital that the notice be specific and comprehensive, so it is important to work on listing and checking the potential grounds of appeal. This requires clear analysis—an appeal is likely to be a waste of money if it is not clear what is being appealed against, why, and what outcome the appellant hopes for.

23.58   The sections of Form N161 include:

- details of order or part of order against which appealing;
- grounds of appeal;
- arguments in support of grounds—this can double as a skeleton argument, otherwise a skeleton argument must be attached or follow within 14 days;
- what decisions the appeal court is being asked to make (including orders set aside, orders varied, and new orders substituted, new trial, additional orders); if additional orders also give reasons.
- evidence relied on—this can set out with a statement of truth or add witness statements/affidavits;
- time estimate for appeal, unless appealing to Court of Appeal;
- whether there are any issues under the Human Rights Act 1998;
- the signature of the appellant or his or her solicitor.

23.59   The grounds of appeal should be set out in separate numbered points. It is quite possible that there will only be one or two grounds of appeal if those grounds are thought strong enough alone. Alternatively there may be several grounds of appeal that together build a picture of a judgment or order that should be overturned or altered, though there is probably little purpose served by including petty points. The grounds of appeal should be put in some logical order, for example, grouping together grounds of appeal on a particular point.

23.60   Each ground of appeal should be expressed as concisely and clearly as possible, often just in a sentence or two. The basic reasons for each ground of appeal should be given on the notice, but more detail will be in the skeleton argument that forms part of the documentation. Each ground must specify a ground of appeal, not just a general expression of discontent. For example a general allegation that the judge misapplied law is not sufficient; the specific error should be identified.

23.61   Typical grounds of appeal might include:

- that the judge was wrong in law in making a particular decision;
- that the judge wrongly admitted a particular piece of evidence;
- that there was no evidence to support a particular finding made by the judge;
- that a finding made by the judge was wrong in law and against the weight of the evidence;
- that the judge failed to exercise a discretion at all, or failed to exercise it in line with accepted principles, or exercised his discretion in a way no reasonable judge could have done;

- that the judge took into account irrelevant matters;
- that the judge misinterpreted the facts.

The appellant needs to set out the order or orders which he wishes the court to make on   **23.62**
appeal. Normally the court appealed to will have the same powers as the court appealed
from, so the appellate court can make any order that the judge at first instance could have
made. This may be simple if, for example, the appeal simply seeks to have the order made set
aside, but may require detailed consideration and drafting if the appellant seeks a range of
orders.

It is possible for a notice of appeal to be amended with leave if this proves necessary or   **23.63**
desirable.

Documents to be lodged on appeal

The appellant must lodge a set of documents with the appeal notice. If any are not available   **23.64**
at that time the reason must be given and the time when they will be available.

- Copies of the notice for each respondent, which should normally be served on the
  respondents within seven days, CPR r 52.4.
- A copy of the appellant's skeleton argument, using Form N163.
- A copy of the order being appealed against.
- A copy of the judgment being appealed against. This may be an approved transcript if
  the judgment was recorded, or the judge's written judgment signed by the judge, PD 52
  para 5.
- Any order giving or refusing permission to appeal with reasons.
- Any written evidence in support of any interim application.
- A copy of legal aid or Community Legal Service Funding certificate if relevant.
- A paginated bundle of documents in support of the appeal, including the reasons given
  for the judgment being appealed against, the statements of case, any evidence in support
  of the appeal, and relevant evidence and any skeleton argument from the hearing being
  appealed against. If the appeal bundle is more than 750 pages there should be a core
  bundle of no more than 150 pages.

I   THE POSITION OF THE RESPONDENT TO AN APPEAL

Generally the respondent will take no part in an appeal unless and until permission to   **23.65**
appeal has been granted, unless there is any particular point to make about the merits of the
appeal. If permission to appeal is granted then copies of appropriate papers will be served on
the respondent.

The choices open to the respondent to an appeal are: **23.66**

- to maintain that the decision under appeal was correct for the reasons given by the judge;
- to maintain that the decision under appeal was correct, but for different or additional
  reasons, in which case a respondent's notice is required to set out those reasons, PD 52
  para 7;

- to ask the court to vary the judgment given, which will constitute a cross-appeal, so permission to appeal must be sought, and a respondent's notice is required to set out the grounds for the variation.

23.67   A respondent's notice should be filed within 14 days or as directed by the court, CPR r 52.5. A respondent's notice must be served on the appellant and any other respondents. If the respondent is going to put arguments to the court, the respondent must also provide a skeleton argument. The respondent should also respond to the arguments in the appellant's skeleton, the reply to be filed within 21 days of receipt of the appellant's skeleton, PD 52 para 5.

23.68   At one end of the scale, the respondent may be entirely happy with the judgment and orders at trial and the reasons for them, in which case there is very little for the respondent to do save for making this clear. If the appeal lacks merit this is a personally reasonable approach.

23.69   At the other end of the scale, especially where a case has been hotly contested at trial, it may be that a cross-appeal by a respondent is as full as the appeal itself, as effectively both seek to re-run part or all of the trial, in which case the drafting of the respondent's notice may be as important as the drafting of the notice of appeal.

23.70   There are many variations in between these two points. If the appeal may have some merit then the respondent may wish to protect his or her position by ensuring that the court hearing the appeal is aware of all the grounds on which the judgment should be supported. Alternatively the respondent may be basically content with the existing decision but may wish to argue that it should be varied in some way.

J   PREPARING FOR AN APPEAL

General preparation

23.71   Much of the preparation for an appeal is done in preparing for the original trial. Ideally the need to appeal should be avoided. If evidence and arguments are available but not used for the trial they will not normally be admissible on appeal.

23.72   Some preparation for appeal is done at the trial, when the lawyer will note any possible errors by the judge in dealing with procedure and evidence that may be possible grounds for appeal. It will be necessary to keep notes of oral evidence and of the judge's judgment as transcripts will not automatically be available.

23.73   Some preparation for appeal is done at the end of the trial, as the decision whether or not to appeal will have to be taken as soon as possible after judgment, and preparations will need to begin forthwith. Because of the limited time for lodging and preparing for an appeal some work may be done prior to judgment, though this is likely to be limited as costs should not be built up while the need to appeal is uncertain.

23.74   The lawyer should also decide whether any interlocutory applications will be needed for orders pending the hearing of the appeal, for example to prevent the judgment given from being executed, as there will be no automatic stay of execution. A separate Part 36 offer or payment should be made to protect the position pending an appeal.

There is a duty to let the court know if the case has been or is likely to be settled so that   **23.75**
the judges do not waste their time in reading appeal papers, *Yell Ltd v Garton* The Times,
26 July 2004.

Preparing evidence

As regards the preparation of evidence, much of the evidence used on appeal will be that   **23.76**
used at the original hearing, including affidavits, witness statements, and expert reports.
Official transcripts of oral evidence and of the judgment will also normally be required if
they are relevant, and these should be sought as quickly as possible as they may take some
time to prepare. If only part of the oral evidence is required this should be specified in
seeking the transcripts, or the costs may not be allowed. If an official transcript is not available then the judge's note of the judgment should be used, or in default of that, a note
agreed by counsel. In the last case, the appellant's solicitor should arrange for a copy of
counsel's note to be prepared and submitted to the other side and then to the judge as soon
as the notice of appeal is served to ensure it is ready in time.

Evidence of things which have happened since the date of the trial or hearing is admissible   **23.77**
without leave, and the lawyers on both sides should consider whether there is any material
change in the facts that should be brought to the attention of the appeal court, for example,
matters relevant to the quantification of damages. Such evidence should be presented like
any other evidence, normally through witness statements.

There are some circumstances in which the Court of Appeal will be prepared to hear new   **23.78**
evidence relating to events before the trial. There is a power to receive further evidence on
questions of fact by oral examination in court, or as written evidence, but where the appeal
comes after a full trial or hearing on the merits of the case, further evidence will only be
admitted on special grounds. Leave will be needed to admit the evidence, and leave will only
be given if the evidence could not with reasonable diligence have been obtained for the
original trial, if it is such that it would have had an important influence on the outcome of
the case, even though it would not necessarily have been decisive, and if the evidence is
apparently credible.

The preparation of the bundle of written evidence is important as the appeal hearing will be   **23.79**
wholly or largely based on the documents in the bundle and there are likely to be frequent
references to the bundle. Material relevant to the appeal should be carefully selected and
clearly presented. Note that bundles need careful preparation—for example details of a
without prejudice offer or a Part 36 offer or payment discussed after judgment may need to
be removed, see *Garratt v Saxby* (2004) 1 WLR 2152.

The skeleton arguments

The writing of the skeleton argument will be central to the preparation of the appeal.   **23.80**
Although the appeal notice sets out basic reasons for the grounds of appeal, the skeleton
argument will provide more detail and is likely to play a key role in putting the main points
across to the judges before the appeal hearing.

The use of skeleton arguments was originally developed to assist the presentation of cases on   **23.81** appeal. The skeleton is likely to be the most important document at the hearing. As the appeal court has limited ability to overturn findings of fact made by a trial judge who saw the witnesses, points of law and the application of legal tests are likely to be important on appeal and will need to be fully set out in the skeleton, see 21.66–21.77.

K   PRESENTING AN APPEAL

23.82   The presentation of an appeal in court is rather different from the presentation of a case at trial, though there may be some similarity to the making of some interim applications. The hearing will simply focus on key issues and relevant documents. It is the duty of the lawyers to make clear to a client how an appeal hearing will be conducted, and the extent to which the hearing will be based on substantial pre-reading so that the client is not left with the impression that his case has been insufficiently considered.

23.83   The Court of Appeal generally hears appeals from a final decision with a three-judge court, though a two-judge court may be used for appeals from interim orders, County Court orders, and from final orders by masters and High Court District judges, Supreme Court Act 1981, s 54. Other appeals may be heard by a single judge.

23.84   An appeal is limited to a review of the decision of the lower court, unless a practice direction makes specific provision, or the court considers in the circumstances of the individual appeal it would be in the interests of justice to hold a re-hearing, CPR r 52.11. The appeal court may totally reconsider any matter in issue at the original trial, but only on the basis of the matters raised in the appeal notice and any notice from the respondent.

23.85   Judges hearing an appeal will normally have read in advance the notice of appeal, the skeleton argument, and the other documents lodged, and this will have a significant effect on the conduct of the hearing, as the judges will be able to focus on the central issues without prolonged introductions and without having to consider matters that are not raised on appeal.

23.86   Often the judge will start the appeal hearing by stating what documents and authorities referred to in the skeleton argument have been read. It will normally be unnecessary for there to be any opening speeches, but if it is there should be references to the key passages in the documents rather than extensive reading. The appellant will normally be expected to start with arguments on the strongest ground of appeal. The judge may give an indication of which grounds of appeal are thought to have merit, and may also mention points that the judge would like the lawyers to deal with. This means that a lawyer conducting an appeal must be prepared to move quickly from the details of one issue to the details of another to follow the judge's indications.

23.87   The appeal hearing will normally be conducted entirely on the basis of the written evidence and transcripts in the bundle of documents. If leave is given for oral evidence to be given on appeal the evidence will be heard in the normal way.

L THE APPEAL DECISION

There is no specific hurdle to be cleared to succeed on appeal. Tests for liability, burdens, and standards of proof etc will all be the same as they were for trial. The test is to establish that a ground of appeal exists. **23.88**

However, an appeal will not normally involve a full re-hearing of the case, and a judge hearing an appeal will not try to second guess the judge who originally heard the case. The hearing will focus on the matters raised as grounds for appeal, and an appeal will only normally be allowed if the decision of the lower court was wrong, or was unjust because of a serious procedural or other irregularity in the proceedings of the lower court, CPR r 52.11. It is not enough that the decision of the lower court was an imperfect solution or just one option, so long as the judge took a decision within the generous ambit within which reasonable disagreement is possible, *G v G* (1985) 1 WLR 647. It is not normally for the Court of Appeal to make its own original findings, *Designers Guild Ltd v Russell Williams (Textiles) Ltd* (2000) 1 WLR 2416. **23.89**

In particular findings of fact will rarely be changed on appeal. The view of the judge who heard the whole case and saw the witnesses give oral evidence will be preferred. The judge will have seen the witnesses giving evidence, and a judge's decision about the credibility of witnesses can only be overturned on appeal if the judge was plainly wrong, *Powell v Streatham Manor Nursing Home* (1935) AC 243 HL. However the appeal court may draw different inferences from the facts, or may form a different view of the facts where new evidence has been heard. **23.90**

Equally the exercise of a discretion will rarely be overturned on appeal. Many decisions are matters for the discretion of the judge, especially as regards interim applications, and on appeal the court will only substitute its own discretion in limited circumstances such as the grounds of appeal listed above. **23.91**

A decision of a jury in a civil case could only be challenged as one which no properly directed jury could reasonably have found on the evidence, or where the damages awarded are excessive, CPR r 52.10. **23.92**

The Court of Appeal may give its decision at the end of the hearing, or it may reserve judgment. The court has all the powers and duties of the High Court, and can therefore give any judgment or make any order that that court could have given or made. **23.93**

An order of the Court of Appeal will be drawn up by the Court Associate, not by the parties. There is provision for the sending of drafts in the House of Lords. **23.94**

In an exceptional case the Court of Appeal can re-hear an appeal where new facts are discovered after the original appeal, *Taylor v Lawrence* (2002) 2 ALL ER 353. **23.95**

M   COSTS ON APPEAL

23.96   The cost of appealing may not be very high because of the extensive use of existing evidence etc. On the other hand the cost of a hotly defended appeal can be very high.

23.97   Costs will be at the discretion of the court. A successful appellant may get an order for the costs of the appeal and of the original action ('Costs here and below'), and this may be a source of encouragement to someone with a good case. Equally the loser is at risk of having to pay the costs of the original hearing as well as of the appeal. It will be relevant if a party has only been partly successful, or if some aspects of the appeal have wasted court time. A successful appellant may not get costs if the appeal raised a point of general public importance, or if new points are raised that were not raised at the original hearing, see also 5.45–5.61.

KEY DOCUMENTS

Forms

There are many forms relevant to the enforcement of judgments, see PD 4.

N161 Appellant's Notice
N162 Respondent's Notice
N163 Skeleton argument

These forms are easily available in hard copy and electronically, see Chapter 24.

24

YOUR PRACTICE

A INTRODUCTION. 24.01

B CIVIL LITIGATION RULES, FORMS, AND PROCEDURAL GUIDES 24.04
Civil litigation rules and practice 24.04
Procedural guides. 24.14

C LIBRARY AND RESEARCH MATERIAL. 24.15
Procedure and evidence 24.16
Costs and funding litigation 24.17
Damages and remedies 24.18
Human rights 24.19
International issues and conflict of laws 24.20
Professional conduct and ethics 24.21
Litigation skills—advocacy 24.22
Litigation skills—client care and negotiation 24.23
Litigation skills—drafting and legal writing 24.24
Litigation skills—case analysis. 24.25
Litigation skills—general 24.26

D FURTHER PROFESSIONAL TRAINING. 24.27
Continuing professional development 24.27
Specialist practitioner associations 24.29

A INTRODUCTION

Every case that goes through the litigation process will develop in a different way. The facts **24.01** will never be identical, different evidence will be available, different interim applications will be appropriate, clients will take different views as to what they hope to achieve, and opponents will behave in different ways. Litigation involving different areas of law will present different opportunities and potential pitfalls, and may benefit from different strategies and tactics. Each case that the lawyer litigates must be dealt with individually.

The pace of change relevant to the conduct of litigation is now very fast. It is not only the **24.02** substantive law and rules of procedure and evidence that change. There are now many areas that can impinge on litigation, from human rights to data protection. It is increasingly common for lawyers to enter or to develop a specialist practice. This can make it easier to perceive patterns in litigation and to take on board relevant change, but it can still take time to develop expertise, and effort to retain expertise.

24.03 To assist in the development of civil litigation practice this chapter provides some guidance on sources of information that may be of use, and also resources that may assist professional development.

B CIVIL LITIGATION RULES, FORMS, AND PROCEDURAL GUIDES

Civil litigation rules and practice

24.04 It is absolutely vital for each lawyer to become familiar with at least one of the main sources of civil litigation rules, and how that source is kept up to date. Although the basic content of the main sources is broadly similar, there are sometimes reasons for selecting one rather than another.

24.05 All of the following come out annually and are updated by supplements. All are available electronically as well as in hard copy. All contain The Civil Litigation Rules 1998, the Practice Directions, the Pre-action Protocols, and the Court Guides.

Blackstone's Civil Practice (Oxford University Press)

24.06 This comes as one volume and a CD. It is also available on Lawtel. Blackstone's has the advantage of a significant explanatory text that covers all the areas of the Civil Procedure Rules in some detail. It comes in one volume, which may make it more convenient to carry. It includes less legislation than some other sources.

Civil Procedure—The White Book (Sweet & Maxwell)

24.07 This comes in two volumes with loose leaf folder and a CD. It is also available on Westlaw. The first volume contains the Civil Litigation Rules etc, and the second volume is largely devoted to background legislation. The loose leaf folder contains court forms.

The Civil Court Practice—The Green Book (Butterworths)

24.08 This comes in two volumes. It is also available on Civil Procedure Online. The first volume contains the Civil Litigation Rules etc, and the second volume is devoted to background legislation.

Civil Court Service—The Brown Book (Jordan Publishing)

24.09 This comes as one volume and a CD that contains forms and statutes.

Civil litigation forms

24.10 The use of appropriate forms in civil litigation is important, and well over 500 forms are available. Unfortunately it can be difficult to discover whether there is an appropriate form for a particular purpose. There is not a single numbering system for the forms, and forms for specialist proceedings are mixed in with forms for general use. The use of forms was not codified when the Civil Procedure Rules were drawn up, and hopefully this will be addressed before too long. Relevant forms are listed at the end of appropriate chapters in this book.

Most of the forms that are available are listed in PD 4. They can be modified if circumstances **24.11** require provided that all required information is given.

- Those in Table 1 are forms required by CPR parts 1–75.
- Those in Table 2, which were in use in the High Court before 1999 and have been retained.
- Those in Table 3, which were in use in the County Court before 1999 and have been retained.
- Further forms are authorised by Practice Directions.

Once a form has been identified it is relatively easy to locate and use. If electronic sources are **24.12** used the form can normally be completed electronically.

- Court forms are available on line from www.courtservice.gov.uk.
- CD ROMs with forms accompany *Blackstone's Civil Practice* and *The White Book*.
- Forms can be accessed online via the electronic services that accompany the main sources of the Civil Procedure Rules.
- Volume 3 of *The White Book* contains forms in an A4 format that can easily be photocopied.
- Many forms are available free from County Court Offices.

Court forms are for use in communicating with the court. The use of forms should not be **24.13** confused with the use of precedents for drafting documents such as Particulars of Claim.

Procedural guides

All the main sources of civil procedure rules and practice contain some procedural guides **24.14** that are checklists for conducting particular procedural stages or particular types of application. There is a different array of guides in each source. These guides provide helpful checklists, but they should not be seen as a substitute for reading the relevant rules and practice directions and considering the needs of the individual case fully.

C   LIBRARY AND RESEARCH MATERIAL

Chapter 9 provides general guidance on finding and using sources of law such as statutes **24.15** and cases. It also provides suggestions on keeping up to date. Other sources of material on knowledge and skills relevant to the conduct of civil litigation are as follows.

Procedure and evidence

N Andrews, *English Civil Procedure: Fundamentals of the New Civil Justice System* (2003) Oxford **24.16**
   University Press
D Bean, *Injunctions* (8th edn) Sweet & Maxwell
C Tapper (ed), *Cross and Tapper on Evidence* (9th edn 1999) Butterworths
A Keane, *The Modern Law of Evidence* (5th edn 2000) Butterworths

J Peysner, *Civil Litigation Handbook* (2001) Law Society Publishing

S L Phipson, *Phipson on Evidence* (15th edn 1999 and supplements) Sweet & Maxwell

S Sime, *A Practical Approach to Civil Procedure* (6th edn 2004) Oxford University Press

Costs and funding litigation

24.17 F Bawdon and M Napier, *Conditional Fees* (2nd edn 2001) Law Society Publications

K Biggs, *Fees and Fixed Costs in Civil Actions* (2003) Lexis Nexis UK

D Chalk, *Risk Assessment in Litigation: Conditional Fee Agreements Insurance and Funding* (2001) LexisNexisUK

Butterworths, *Costs Service*, Looseleaf

M Cook, *Cook on Costs* (2004) LexisNexis UK

M Harvey, *Guide to Conditional Fee Agreements* The Association of Personal Injury Lawyers

A Hoffman, *Costs Cases—a Civil Guide* (2003) Sweet & Maxwell

P Hurst, *Civil Costs* (2004) Sweet & Maxwell

P Rogers, *Greenslade on Costs* (2000) Sweet & Maxwell

Damages and remedies

24.18 A Burrows and E Peel, *Commercial Remedies* (2003) Oxford University Press

R Goff and G Jones, *Law of Restitution* (6th edn 2002 and supplements) Sweet & Maxwell

Inns of Court School of Law, *Remedies Manual* (2004–5—annual) Oxford University Press

H McGregor, *Damages* (16th Edn 1999 and supplements) Sweet & Maxwell

G Samuel, *Law of Obligations and Legal Remedies* (2nd edn 2001) Cavendish

A Tettenborn, *Law of Restitution in England and Ireland* (3rd edn 2001) Cavendish

Human rights

24.19 R Clayton and H Tomlinson, *The Law of Human Rights* (2nd edn 2005) Oxford University Press

P Leach, *Taking a Case to the European Court of Human Rights* (2nd edn 2005) Oxford University Press

Lord Lester and D Pannick, *Human Rights Law and Practice* (2004) LexisNexis UK

P Plowden and K Kerrigan, *Advocacy and Human Rights—Using the Convention in Courts and Tribunals* (2002) Cavendish

International issues and conflict of laws

A Bell, *Forum Shopping and Venue in Transnational Litigation* (2003) Oxford University Press   **24.20**

Cheshire and North, *Private International Law* (13th edn 1999) Butterworths

A V Dicey and J H C Morris, *Conflict of Laws* (13th edn 1999 and supplements) Sweet & Maxwell

S Geeroms, *Foreign Law in Civil Litigation* (2004) Oxford University Press

J D McClean, *Morris: The Conflict of Laws* (5th edn 2000) Sweet & Maxwell

Professional conduct and ethics

The Code of Conduct of the Bar of England and Wales (7th edn 2000 as amended)   **24.21**
www.barcouncil.org.uk

The Guide to the Professional Conduct of Solicitors (8th edn 1999 as amended)
www.lawsociety.org.uk

R Pattenden, *The Law of Professional-Client Confidentiality* (2003) Oxford University Press

D L Rhode, *Ethics in Practice: Lawyers' Roles, Responsibilities and Regulation* (2003) Oxford University Press

Litigation skills—advocacy

C Aitkin (ed), *Law, Probability and Risk: A Journal of Reasoning and Uncertainty* Oxford   **24.22**
University Press

R J Aldisert, *Winning on Appeal—Better briefs and oral argument* (1999) NITA Practical Guide Series (USA), see www.nita.org

A Boon, *Advocacy* (2nd edn 1999) Cavendish

R Du Cann, *The Art of the Advocate* (1993) Penguin

K Evans, *The Language of Advocacy* (1998) Blackstone Press Ltd

C Foster, C Bourne, P Popat, and J Gilliat, *Civil Advocacy: A Practical Guide* (2nd edn 2001) Cavendish

A Heaton-Armstrong, E Shepherd, and D Wolchover, *Analysing Witness Testimony: Psychological, Investigative and Evidential Perspectives* (1999) Oxford University Press

M Hyam, *Advocacy Skills* (1999) Oxford University Press

Inns of Court School of Law, *Advocacy Manual* (annual) Oxford University Press

J Munkman, *Techniques of Advocacy* (1991) Butterworths

D Napley, *The Technique of Persuasion* (4th edn 1991) Sweet and Maxwell

N Pascoe and S Gold, *Successful Advocacy* (1995) Butterworths

N Shaw, *Effective Advocacy* (1996) Sweet & Maxwell

F L Wellman, *The Art of Cross Examination* (1997) Simon & Schuster

Litigation skills—client care and negotiation

24.23   J Chapman, *Interviewing and Counselling* (2nd edn 2000) Cavendish

R Fischer and W Ury, *Getting to Yes* (1997) Business Books

D Foskett, *Law and Practice of Compromise* (2002) Sweet & Maxwell

A Fowler, *Negotiation Skills and Strategies* (1996) Institute of Personnel Management

Inns of Court School of Law, *Conference Skills* (annual) Oxford University Press

Inns of Court School of Law, *Negotiation Manual* (2004–5—annual) Oxford University Press

B Scott, *The Skills of Negotiating* (1981) Gower Business Skills

A Sherr, *Client Care for Lawyers* (2nd edn 1998) Sweet & Maxwell

A J Stitt, *Mediation—A Practical Guide* (2004) Cavendish

D S J Sutton and J Gill, *Russell on Arbitration* (2002) Sweet and Maxwell

J Tackaberry and A Marriott, *Bernstein's Handbook of Arbitration and Dispute Resolution Practice* (4th edn 2003) Sweet & Maxwell

W Ury, *Getting Past No—Negotiating with Difficult People* (2003) Random House

Litigation skills—drafting and legal writing

24.24   M M Asprey, *Plain language for Lawyers* (2003) The Federation Press

P Bull and R Castle, *Modern Legal Drafting—A guide to using clearer language* (2001) Cambridge University Press

M Constanzo, *Legal Writing* (2000) Cavendish

Inns of Court School of Law, *Drafting Manual* (annual) Oxford University Press

Inns of Court School of Law, *Opinion Writing Manual* (annual) Oxford University Press

S Payne, *Instructing Counsel* (1994) Tolley Publishing Co Ltd

W Rose, *Pleadings without Tears* (6th edn 2002) Oxford University Press

Litigation skills—case analysis

24.25   E de Bono, *Teach Yourself to Think* (1995) Penguin

D A Binder and P Bergman, *Fact Investigation: From Hypothesis to Proof* (1984) Thomson West

M Constanzo, *Problem Solving* (1996) Cavendish

D French, *How to Cite Legal Authorities* (1996) Oxford University Press

D Greenberg, *A Milbrook Stroud's Judicial Dictionary of Words and Phrases* (2000) Sweet & Maxwell

G Holborn, *Butterworths Legal Research Guide* (3rd edn 2003) Butterworths

Inns of Court School of Law, *Case Preparation Manual* (2004–5—annual) Oxford University Press

J Knowles and P A Thomas, *How to use a Law Library* (4th edn 2001) Sweet & Maxwell

G Macpherson, *Blacks Medical Dictionary* (4th edn 2002) A & C Black

M Parsons, *Effective Knowledge Management for Law Firms* (2004) Oxford University Press

D Raistrick, *Index to Legal Citations and Abbreviations* (1993) Bowker

J B Saunders (ed), *Words and Phrases Legally Defined* (3rd edn 1990) Butterworths

J O Sonsteng, R S Haydock and J J Boyd, *The Trial Book—A Total System for the Preparation and Presentation of a Case* (1984) West Publishing Corporation

Litigation skills—general

F Boyle, D Capps, P Plowden, and C Sandford, *A Practical Guide to Lawyering Skills* (2nd edn 2003) Cavendish **24.26**

H Brayne, N Duncan, and R Grimes, *Clinical Legal Education—active learning in your law school* (1998) Blackstone Press Ltd

C Maughan and J Webb, *Lawyering Skills and the Legal Process* (1995) Butterworths

S Nathanson, *What Lawyers Do—A Problem Solving Approach to Legal Practice* (1997) Sweet & Maxwell

J Webb, C Maughan, M Maughan, M Keppel-Palmer, and A Boon, *Lawyers' Skills* (2004–5) Oxford University Press

---

D FURTHER PROFESSIONAL TRAINING

Continuing professional development

Further professional training for those conducting litigation will fall into four areas. **24.27**

- Keeping in touch with changes in the rules of litigation and evidence. This can be achieved through regular use of updated versions of one of the main sources of the Civil Procedure Rules.
- Keeping up to date in the use of practitioner skills and techniques, which will be at least partly achieved through regular practice.
- Keeping up to date with the substantive law in the areas in which the lawyer practices.
- Keeping up to date with legal areas relevant to litigation, such as human rights and data protection.

All of the above can be supported through continuing professional development providers. **24.28**
They can also be usefully supported through seminars and training within a firm or within chambers.

The Bar Council provides an on line database of continuing professional development courses at www.legaleducation.org.uk/CPD/courses.php as well as providing downloadable guides to continued professional development. The Law Society website includes material on authorised providers of continuing professional development courses.

Specialist practitioner associations

Another useful source of support is the specialist associations formed by practitioners. The **24.29**
following list is indicative rather than exhaustive.

24.30 There are links to specialist solicitor associations through www.lawsociety.org.uk. There are different types of organisation including Law Society Groups, Law Society Sections and Practitioners Associations. Some have their own websites, for example:

Commerce and Industry Group www.cigroup.org.uk
Association of PI lawyers www.apil.com

24.31 There are links to specialist Bar Associations through www.barcouncil.org.uk. Many Associations have their own websites, including:

Administrative Law Bar Association www.adminlaw.org.uk
Bar European Group www.bareuropeangroup.com
Chancery Bar Association www.chba.org.uk
Commercial Bar Association (COMBAR) www.combar.com
Employment Law Bar Association www.elba.org.uk
Family Law Bar Association www.flba.co.uk
Personal Injuries Bar Association www.piba.org.uk
Professional Negligence Bar Association www.pnba.co.uk
Property Bar Association www.propertybar.org.uk
Revenue Bar Association www.revenue-bar.org
Technological and Construction Bar Association www.techbar.org.uk

INDEX

abandonment of claim 97
accident reports 468
adjournment 96, 555
admissions
 evidence 324
 seeking 279
adversarial system 76–77, 132, 174
 implications 77, 282
advice
 see also **opinions**
 appeals 586–587
 breaking bad news 167–168
 causes of action 168
 chances of success 165–167, 169
 damages 169, 310–311
 evidence 169, 355–357
 from lawyer 151, 158, 159–169, 206
 oral 159
 parties 168
 procedure 169
 remedies 168–169
 setting out options 163
 setting out strengths and weaknesses
  164
 settling a case 510
 written 159–160, 206
advocacy
 preparations 559–562
affidavits
 drafting 343–344
 formal requirements 336–338
agency
 principle of 286–287
alternative dispute resolution (ADR)
 importance of 506–507
 types of 508–509
appeals
 advising on 586–587
 costs 598
 decision 586–587, 597
 documents to be lodged 593
 drafting 591–593
 evidence 595
 grounds for 588–589
 jurisdiction 589–590
 notice 591–593
 position of respondent 593–594
 powers on 591
 preparation 594–596
 presentation 596
 procedure 367, 590–591
arbitration 508

argument at trial 562–564
 see also **skeleton argument**
assets
 freezing orders 391–393
attachment of earnings 584

bankruptcy
 persons party to action 291–292
Bar Council for England and Wales 34
 Code of Conduct 60, 61–62, 130
 complaints procedures 68
BarDIRECT 37
barristers
 see also **Bar Council for England and Wales**
 BarDIRECT 37
 the brief *see* **brief**
 comparison with solicitors 34, 60
 direct access 37
 effective working relations with solicitors
  36
 fees 28, 38–39, 40, 110
 future of the legal profession 9
 opinions 231–245
 professional conduct 60–63, 130–131
 public direct access 37
 reasons for instructing 35–36
 role in litigation process 35–36
 selection 38
 written instructions to 41–42, 223
brief
 acceptance 39–40
 backsheet 44
 contents 40, 42–44
 documents to include in 42–43
 information missing from 46
 more than one barrister 40
 nature of 38–39
 return of 39–40
 strategic reading of 45–46
 working on a 44–47
burden of proof
 statements of case 218
business
 as party to action 287–290
business of law 30–31

case law
 use of 194–195, 326
case management 77–78, 89, 95–96, 537–539
 skeleton arguments 545
case review 536–537
 by court 537–539

Index

causes of action
  advice on 168
  assessing 214
  contents of opinion 241–243
  contract cases 419–420, 426–431, 439–440
  defence 406, 485
  factual elements of 213–214
  legal elements of 211–213
  selecting 214–215, 470–471
  selection in contractual cases 429–431
  selection in tort cases 470–471
  tort litigation 462–463, 470–471
  using more than one 214–215
Chancery Division 82, 83
charging orders 584
charities
  as party to action 291
children
  as party to action 290
  witness 322
Citizen's Advice Bureaux 115, 116
Civil Procedure Rules 1998 74, 76
  'cards on the table' approach 24
  human rights issues 55
  overriding objective 14–15
  role of the Woolf reforms 15–17
claim
  abandonment 97
  discontinuance 97
claim forms 84–88, 263–265
  acknowledgement of service 88, 402
  completion 85, 263
  issue 85, 265
  list of forms 105–106
  Part 20 claims 296
  problems in serving 87
  service on the defendant 85–86, 402
  timing the issue 84–85
claimant
  claim by defendant 405
  difficult 400–401
  failure to attend trial 555
  selection 283–284
Clementi, David
  Review of Regulatory Framework 8–9, 34, 50–51
client confidentiality 64–67
client money
  ethical responsibilities of lawyers 52
clients
  assessing client as witness 148
  at trial 556–557
  communication with 20, 134–135, 223, 227
  difficult 152–155
  ethical responsibilities of lawyers 51
  false information from 154–155
  first meeting 78, 135–136
  instructions from 20–21, 78, 145, 153, 170–171
  lawyer's professional duties 61, 130–131
  lawyer's relationship with 128–134, 155
  letters to 227
  management of expectations 133, 548
  meeting 136–155
  objectives 145
  preparing to go to court 548
  representing 19–21, 132
  role of 131–132
  source of facts 179–180
closing speech 561–562, 571–572
codes of conduct
  Bar Council 60, 61–62, 130
  Law Society 60, 62, 68, 130
commercial awareness 52–53
Commercial Court 76, 82
communications
  see also **legal writing**
  client 20, 134–135, 223, 227
  legal professional privilege 64–65, 224
Community Legal Service 28, 57, 115, 116
companies
  as party to action 289–290
Companies Court 82
compensation
  personal injury damages 475–483
compensation culture 7, 461
complaints procedures 62–63, 68
computer records as evidence 324, 352
conciliation 508
conditional fee agreements
  issues surrounding 114–115
  rules 113–114
confidentiality
  legal professional privilege 64–67
consent orders 96, 526–527, 577–578
contempt of court 585
contingency fees 113
continuing professional development 9, 605–606
contract case
  advising a defendant 439–441
  analysing contractual action 426–429
  analysing contractual obligations 424–425
  assessing damages 434–438
  breach of contract as cause 419–420, 427
  causes of action 419–420, 426–431, 439–440
  contextual considerations 421–423
  defence 441
  drafting a claim 438–439
  elements 420–421
  international element 423
  limited liability 440–441
  misrepresentation as cause 420, 428–429
  misrepresentation damages 435–436
  overlap with action in tort 471
  sample drafts 441–457
  selecting remedies 431–433
contribution
  claims for 294–295, 405

contributory negligence 438, 474, 486
corporation
    as party to action 290
cost of litigation 7–8, 16, 27–29, 78, 390–394
    see also **financing litigation**
    access for those of limited means 57–58,
        115–116
    appeals 598
    assessment 119–120, 366–367
    barrister's fees 28, 38–39, 40, 110
    costs orders 99, 117–123, 366–367
    defendant's position 404
    disallowance of costs 69
    effective management 110–111
    funding options 112–113
    interim payments 393–394
    main elements 110
    monitoring 29
    procedural 366
    reasons for problems 111–112
    rules and powers relating to 29, 117–118
    security for costs 390–391
    Solicitors' Costs Information and Client Care
        Code 109
    solicitors' fees 109–110
    wasted costs orders 68–69, 123–125
costs orders *see* **orders for costs**
counterclaim 293–294, 405, 413
    by defendant 441
    general framework 415–416
County Court
    claims before 82–83
    procedure 76, 82–83
court
    see also **hearings; trial**
    choice 82–83
    lawyer's professional duties 60–61, 131
    letters to 227–228
    preparing to go to 547–548
    remedies available to 301–304
court cases
    see also **case law; trial**
    adjournment 96
    allocation questionnaire 89–90
    case management 77–78, 89, 95–96,
        537–539
    changes of track 92
    fast track 26–27, 91–92
    multi-track 92
    small claims 90–91
    timetable 25–27, 95
    track allocation 89–92
Courts and Legal Services Act 1990 34
cross examination
    at trial 567–568
    preparation 560–561
Crown
    as party to action 291

damages
    see also **remedies**
    advice on 169, 310–311
    apportionment 307
    arithmetic calculations 314–315
    assessing 434–438, 472–475
    categories 305–306
    causation 306
    claims 268, 304–307
    contract cases 431, 434–438, 440
    contributory negligence 307, 474, 486
    defences to claim for 406–407
    double recovery 307
    economic loss 308–309
    exemplary 309–310
    fatal accidents 482–483
    general 305–306, 308
    legal concepts 306–307
    liquidated 305
    mitigation 307, 475
    non-economic loss 309
    personal injury claims 475–483
    proactive approach 310–312
    quantification 307–310
    quantum meruit 436
    reasonable contemplation of the parties
        306
    reasonable forseeability 306
    recoverability 437–438
    recovery 437–438
    remoteness 307
    special 305–306, 307–308
    tort cases 472–475
    unliquidated 305
data protection 175
database research
    legal information 196–197, 600–601
death
    damages for fatal accidents 482–483
    of party to action 291
declaration 302, 472
default judgment 96, 375–376
defence 89
    as regards remedies sought 486
    before a case starts 401–402
    cause of action 406, 485
    contents of opinion 243
    contract case 441
    damages claim 406–407
    difficult claimant 400–401
    drafting 411–413, 441, 487
    general framework 415–416
    list of forms 298
    principles for drafting 410–411
    procedural 406
    rules for drafting 407–410
    tort action 485–487
    types 406–407
    when a case starts 402–403

defendant
  advice on contract cases 439–441
  advice on tort action 485–487
  at trial 556–557
  claim against claimant 405
  failure to attend trial 555
  mindset 399–400
  passing or sharing blame 404–405
  selection 284–286
  strategy and tactics 403–406
disallowance of costs 69
disciplinary procedures 62–63
disclosure
  documents 351–354
  evidence 94, 351–354
  legal professional privilege 66–67, 351
  pre-action 372–374
  special orders 353
discontinuance 97
documents
  see also **legal writing**
  appeal, lodged with 593
  disclosure 351–354
  evidence 323, 351–352
  fees and costs 125
  included with brief 42–43
  inspection 353–354
  list of defence forms 298
  pre-action disclosure 372–374
  pre-action protocols 105–106
  production by non-parties 389
  reference sources for litigation rules, forms and
    guides 600–601
  source of facts 180
  sources of precedents 280

e-mail
  court communications 8
electronic evidence 324, 352
electronic legal research databases 196–197,
    600–601
enforcement
  international issues 103, 585–586
  judgment 103, 583–586
  judgment debt 583–584
  jurisdiction 103
Environmental Information Regulations 2004
    175
ethics *see* **general ethics; professional ethics**
European Convention on Human Rights 54
European Court of Justice
  law reports 196
  references to 104–105
European Union
  jurisdiction 101–102
  law 196
evidence
  see also **witness; witness statements**

admissibility 328–334
admissions 324
advice on 169, 355–357
appeal, preparation for 595
collecting 326–328
contents of opinion 243–244
defining the state of a case 209
demonstrative 324
disclosure 94, 351–354
documentary 323, 351–352
electronic 324
expert 344–350, 468–469
hearsay 330–332
identifying what needs to be proved 320–321
importance of 318–319
judicial notice 325
opinion 330
opinion advising on 235
oral 329, 556
pre-action stage 78, 80
preparation for trial 540–541, 547–548
presumptions 325
previous consistent and inconsistent statements
    332
previous court findings 333
proof 334–335
public policy exclusion 333
real 323
relevance 329
review 355–357
standard of proof 335
statements of case 322
support for application 364–135
types 321–326
written 336–343
evidence in chief 560, 566–567
examination in chief 560
execution against goods 584
exhibits 342
expert determination 509
experts
  communications with 224
  evidence 344–350, 468–469
  reports 348–349
  selecting and briefing 346–348, 469
  witnesses 324–325, 385, 468–469

facts
  see also **information**
  analysis 183–184
  availability 182–183
  building a framework for a case 187–188
  contents of opinion 243–244
  defining the state of a case 209
  establishing truth 175–179
  importance of 23, 174
  interaction with law 186–187
  management 174–175, 184–185

facts (*cont.*)
   practical problems 176–179
   sources 179–182
   theories, deduction and logic 185–186
Family Division 82
fatal accidents
   damages 482–483
fees
   see also **cost of litigation**
   barristers 28, 38–39, 40, 110
   conditional fee agreements 113–115
   contingency 113
   Solicitors' Costs Information and Client Care
      Code 109
financial information 182
financing litigation 108–125
   see also **cost of litigation**
   conditional fee agreements 113–115
   no win, no fee approach 115
   options for funding 112–113
   orders for costs 117–123
   public funding 115–116
the firm
   knowledge management 192
forms
   list 105–106
forum non conveniens 103
Freedom of Information Act 2000 175
freezing orders 391–393
   application procedures 392–393
   requirements for 391–392

general ethics 63
   see also **professional ethics**
globalisation 53–54, 100–105
governance
   Clementi Review of Regulatory Framework 8–9,
      34, 50–51

hearings 365–367
   see also **court; trial**
   open court 553
   preparing case for 539–544
hearsay evidence 330–332
High Court
   claims before 83
   procedure 76, 82–83
Human Rights Act 1998 54–57
   Article 6 and right to fair trial 55–57

idealism of lawyers 10
immunity from action
   professional negligence 70–71
indemnity
   claims 294–295, 405
information
   see also **facts**
   facts and figures 182

from lawyer 151, 158–159
   requests for further 386
   search orders 386–389
   strategies 385–390
information gathering
   importance 145–146
   problems 147–148
   questioning techniques 148–151
   techniques 146–147
information management 184–185
injunction 302–303
   contract cases 431–432
   form of the order 383–384
   interim 379, 395
   pre-action 371–372
   procedure 382
   tests for getting 380–382
   tort cases 472
   types 379–380
   urgent application 384
   without notice 384
inspection
   documents 353–354
   of property 389–390
   pre-action 374
instructions
   client's 20–21, 78, 145, 153, 170–171
   contents of barrister's 42
   to barrister 41–42, 223
   to experts 224
insurance
   role in litigation 282–283, 475
   tort cases 475
interest
   claims 268–269, 312–314
   personal injury damages 479–480
   rates 313–314
interim hearings
   orders for costs 120–123
interim orders
   application for 94, 367
   cost orders for interim applications
      394
interim payments 393–394
international issues 53–54, 100–105
   contract cases 423
   jurisdiction 54, 100–103
interpreters 226

judge
   case management 77–78, 537–539
   forms of address 554
   relationship between lawyer and 24–25
judgment 99, 557–558, 572–574
   after 100, 582–598
   drawing up of orders 574–578
   enforcement 103, 583–586
   frameworks for orders 577–578

judgment (*cont.*)
   giving 572–573
   international issues 103, 585–586
   jurisdiction 103
   powers on appeal 591
judgment in default 96, 375–376
jurisdiction
   appeals 589–590
   European Union 101–102
   forum non conveniens 103
   international issues 54, 100–103
   objecting to 375

knowledge management 192

law
   preparation of legal authorities for trial
      543–544
law centres 115, 116
law journals 195–196
law reports *see* **case law**
Law Society of England and Wales 34
   Code of Conduct 60, 62, 68, 130
   complaints procedures 68
lawyers
   see also **solicitors**
   changes in training in litigation 6
   changing legal environment 4–5
   choice 135–136
   idealism 10
   knowledge and skills 17–18
   practice of law 190–192
   preparing case for trial 540
   public image 31–32
   relations between academic lawyers and
      practitioners 10
   relationship with clients 128–134, 155
   relevance of litigation 3–4
   as role models 19
   role of 131–132
   training 9
legal aid 28, 115–116
legal executives 34
legal knowledge
   books and journals 195–196, 326, 461–462,
      600–605
   electronic sources 196–197, 600–601
   keeping up to date 198
   law in practice 190–192, 599–606
   management 192
   meaning of words 198
   other lawyers 197–198
   statutes and statutory instruments 193–194,
      325–326
   use of 190–206
legal principles
   memorising 22
   using 21–22

legal profession
   Clementi Review of Regulatory Framework 8–9,
      34, 50–51
   complaints procedures 62–63, 68
   entry into 18–19
   the future 9
   professional conduct 60–63, 130–131
   types of practitioners 34–35
legal professional privilege
   communications 64–65, 224
   confidentiality 64–67
   disclosure 66–67, 351
   limits 66
   waiver 65–66
legal representation 554–555
legal research strategy 199–206
Legal Services Commission 115, 116
Legal Services Ombudsman 68
legal writing 222–245
   clarity of conclusions and advice 245
   content and structure 224
   figures 225–226
   language 225–226
   letters 227–231
   notes 226
   opinions 231–245
   professional 222–223
   purpose and audience 223–224
   terminology 225
letters
   list of pro-forma 245
   sample 228–231
   to client 227
   to the court 227
   to the other side 227
limitation periods
   action procedure 80–81
   tort cases 466–467
   types of action 81
limited liability partnership
   as party to action 290
litigants
   relevance of litigation 4
litigation
   overriding objective 13–17
   practical approach 22–23
   role of the Woolf reforms 15–17
   working with others 23–25

mediation 508
meetings
   see also **information gathering**
   agenda 142–145
   attendance 138
   clients 136–155
   conclusion 151–152
   involving the client 144–145
   location 137

meetings (*cont.*)
  objectives 139–141, 145
  preparation 141–142
  problems 139–141
  questioning techniques 148–151
  start of 143
  telephone 139
  virtual 138
  with witnesses 138
mental disability
  persons party to action 291
Mercantile Courts 76, 82
misrepresentation
  contract cases 420, 428–429, 435–436
  damages 435–436
mitigation
  damages 307, 475
money laundering
  legislation 58–59
  relevance to litigation 59–60

National Crime Intelligence Service (NCIS)
  58–59
National Health Service
  claims against 7
negligence case
  see also **professional negligence; tort litigation**
  accident reports 468
  analysis of a case 467–470
  cause of action in tort 462, 470–471
  drafting a claim 483–484
  duty of care 463–465
  elements of 463–465
  limitation 466–467
  pre-action protocols 465–466
  sample drafts 487–504
negotiation 509
  see also **settlement**
  conducting 520–524
  importance of 506–507
  types of 508–509
no win, no fee approach 115
Norwich Pharmacal order 372
note taking 226

occupier's liability
  cause of action in tort 463
opening submission 560, 565
opinions
  clarity of conclusions and advice 245
  contents 239–245
  defence 243
  evidence 235
  facts and evidence 243–244
  format and structure 237–239
  preparation for writing 236
  procedural matters 244
  public funding 233

  remedies 234, 243
  role of 231–235
  settlement 235
  types 232–235
orders for costs 99, 117–123, 366–367
  appeals 598
  assessment of costs 119–120
  interim applications 394
  interim hearings 120–123
  principles 117
  rules and powers 117–119
other side
  letters to 227

paralegals 34, 38
Part 20 claims 293–298
  counterclaims 293–294, 405
  drafting 297–298
  examples 295
  indemnity or contribution claim 294–295, 405
  procedure 296
Part 36 payments and offers 517–519
particulars of claim 89, 265–266, 402
parties 282–298
  advice on 168
  businesses 287–290
  children 290
  claimants 283–284
  defendants 284–286
  Part 20 claims 293–298
  pre-action identification 372
  various persons as party to action 292–293,
    385
partnerships
  as party to action 288
personal injury
  assessing damages 475–483
  damages for fatal accidents 482–483
  drafting a claim 484–485
  loss of future income claim 478–479
  provisional damages 480–481
  sample draft for a case 487–490
  structured settlements 481–482, 527
persuasion at trial 562–564
photographic evidence 324
plain English 217, 225
popular culture
  views of lawyers 10
precedents
  sources 280
  use in drafting statement of case 252–253
privilege
  see also **legal professional privilege**
  against self-incrimination 569
pro bono **work** 57
problem solving 167
procedure 74–106
  adversarial system 76–77

procedure (*cont.*)
  advice on 169
  appeals 367, 590–591
  application for interim orders 94, 367
  application for orders 363–367
  applications before a case starts 371–374
  background to litigation 75–76
  'cards on the table' approach 24, 94
  case management 77–78, 89, 95–96, 537–539
  claim forms *see* **claim forms**
  contact with potential defendant 78–79
  County Court 76, 82–83
  defending an action 398–416
  defining the state of a case 209
  directions 95
  failure to follow rules 369–371, 589
  final preparations for trial 98, 532–548
  freezing order, application for 392–393
  getting some issues decided quickly 379–384
  hearing 365–367
  High Court 76, 82–83
  information strategies 385–390
  injunctions 382
  international issues 100–105
  interrupting or ending litigation 96–97, 374–379, 403
  limitation periods 80–81, 466–467
  main elements 93–94
  notice of application 363
  opinions 244
  overriding objective 14–15
  Part 20 claims 296
  pre-action disclosure 372–374
  pre-action identification of parties 372
  pre-action protocols 79–80, 105, 465–466
  pre-action stage 78–80
  reference sources 600–605
  search order, application for 387
  statements of case 88–89, 93, 254–255
  steps prior to issuing claim form 80
  tactical use of rules 360–394, 403–406
  trial and judgment 98–99, 552–578
Proceeds of Crime Act 2002 58, 131
professional conduct 60–63, 130–131
  breaches 62–63
  complaints procedures 62–63, 68
professional ethics 50–52
  see also **general ethics**
  codes of conduct 60–63
professional negligence
  examples 71–72
  immunity from action 70–71
  test for 69–70
professional standards 50–51
  breach of 67–69
  codes of conduct 60–63
property
  inspection of 389–390

public funding 115–116
  opinion advising on 233
public image
  lawyers 31–32

Queen's Bench Division 82

receivership order 585
recission 303
  contract cases 432–433
rectification 303
  contract cases 433
relief
  see also **damages; remedies**
  meaning 301
  specifying in statement of case 267–269
remedies
  see also **damages**
  advice on 168–169
  claiming 267–269, 303–304
  claims for interest 268–269, 312–314
  contract cases 431–433, 440
  declaration 302, 472
  defences regards seeking 486
  equitable 302–303, 432–433
  financial 301–302
  identification 300–301
  injunction 302–303, 431, 472
  meaning 301
  not possible for court to order 304
  opinion advising on 234, 243
  powers of the court 301–304
  recission 303, 432–433
  rectification 303, 433
  restitution 302
  specific performance 303, 433
  specifying in statement of case 267–269
  tort cases 471–472
  trust 303
research strategy 199–206
restitution 302
return of goods 472
rights of audience 554–555
risk assessment 164–165

samples
  contract statements of case 441–457
  letters 228–231
  tort action statements of case 487–504
sanctions
  dismissal of case by judge 97, 378–379
  failure to follow procedural rules 369–371
search orders 386–389
  form of 387–88
  procedure for getting 387
  requirements for grant of 387
self-incrimination
  witness privilege against 569

set-off
claiming 414–415, 441
examples 414
settlement 7
acting on client's instructions 21, 510–511
advice on 510
challenging a 528–529
conducting a negotiation 520–524
consent order 526–527
decision on 509–510
drawing up terms 524–527
enforcement 528
offers 515–519
opinion advising on 235
Part 36 offers 518–519
Part 36 payments 517–518
reaction to offer 519–520
strategies 513–514
structured 481–482, 527
tactics 515
timing 511–513
where claim form has been issued 96–97,
   512
'without prejudice' 515–516
wording for contract to record 527
skeleton argument
appeal, preparation for 595–596
content 545–546
preparation 544–547, 595–596
small claims 90–91
sole traders
as party to action 288
solicitors
see also **Law Society of England and Wales;
   lawyers**
comparison with barristers 34, 60
effective working relations with barristers 36
future of the legal profession 9
professional conduct 60–63, 130–131
role in litigation process 35
specific performance 303
contract cases 433
standards *see* **professional standards**
statement of truth 219–220, 322
defence 410
witness statements 342
statements of case
amendment to 271–273
burden of proof 218
challenging 274–279
checking 217
the defence 89
definition of issues 207–220
development 93
drafting 249–279
evidence 322
focussing on issues 209–211
general contents 216–217

headings 261–263
history 249–250
particulars of claim 89, 265–266
preparation for trial 540
reply and defence to counterclaim
   269–271
requesting further information 276–278
role of 215–216, 248
rules for drafting 254–255
samples for contract cases 441–457
samples for tort cases 487–504
seeking admissions 279
specifying remedies and relief 267–269
statement of truth 219–220, 322
striking out 274–276
style 217–218
tactics 218–219
terminology and wording 260–261
types 88–89, 249
use of precedents 252–253, 280
statute law
use of 193–194, 325–326
staying an action 96–97
strategic legal research 199–206
structured settlement 481–482, 527
success fee 113–114
summary judgment 96, 376–378
'supermarket law' 8, 9

tape recordings as evidence 324, 352
technology
role in litigation process 8, 18
telephone meetings 139
terminology
legal writing 225
meaning of words 198
statements of case 260–261
textbooks 195–196, 326, 461–462
third party claims *see* **Part 20 claims**
time factors
see also **limitation periods**
litigation 25–27, 95
Tomlin order 578
tort litigation
advising a defendant 485–487
analysis of a case 467–470
breach of statutory duty as cause 462
causes of action 462–463, 470–471
damages 472–475
defence 485–487
drafting a claim 483–485
limitation 466–467
negligence *see* **negligence case**
occupier's liability as cause 463
overlap with action in contract 471
reference works 461–462
sample drafts 487–504
selecting remedies 471–472

training
continuing professional development 9, 605–606
lawyers 9
litigation 6
trial
see also **court; hearings**
adjournment 555
advocacy 559–562
argument and persuasion 562–564
attendance 555
by judge 553
by jury 553–554
closing speech 561–562, 571–572
concluding a case 571–572
cross examination 560–561, 567–568
examination in chief 560
final preparations 98, 532–548
formalities 553–555
opening submission 560, 565
order for new trial 591
presentation of a case 564–565
procedure 98–99, 552–578
reviewing a case 536–537
stages 555–558
strategic approach 532–535
timetable 558
winning a case 558–559
witnesses at 566–571
trial bundles
preparation 542–543
trusts
equitable remedies 303
persons party to action 291

unincorporated association
as party to action 290

vexatious litigant 400
vicarious liability
principle of 287

videos as evidence 324, 352
virtual meetings 138

warrant of delivery 584–585
wasted costs orders 68–69, 123–125
procedure 123–124
the test 124–125
witness
assessing client as 148
at trial 566–571
children as 322
communications with 224
cross examination 548, 560–561, 567–568
evidence 321–322, 328
expert 324–325, 385, 468–469
meetings with 138
opinion evidence 330
preparing to go to court 547–548
privilege against self-incrimination 569
problems with 569–571
procuring attendance at trial 541–542
summons 542
sworn 566
written evidence 336–343
witness statements
see also **affidavits**
at trial 566–567
content 341
drafting 338–343
exchange of 354–355
exhibits 342
formal requirements 336–338
pro forma 342–343
statement of truth 342
structure 341
style and language 340
Woolf reforms 13–17
Civil Procedure Rules 1998 15–17
writ of delivery 584–585
written submission 545